Nonprofit
MANAGEMENT

Nonprofit MANAGEMENT

Principles and Practice | Second Edition

MICHAEL J. WORTH

The George Washington University

Los Angeles | London | New Delhi
Singapore | Washington DC

Los Angeles | London | New Delhi
Singapore | Washington DC

FOR INFORMATION:

SAGE Publications, Inc.
2455 Teller Road
Thousand Oaks, California 91320
E-mail: order@sagepub.com

SAGE Publications Ltd.
1 Oliver's Yard
55 City Road
London EC1Y 1SP
United Kingdom

SAGE Publications India Pvt. Ltd.
B 1/I 1 Mohan Cooperative Industrial Area
Mathura Road, New Delhi 110 044
India

SAGE Publications Asia-Pacific Pte. Ltd.
33 Pekin Street #02-01
Far East Square
Singapore 048763

Acquisitions Editor: Lisa Cuevas Shaw
Associate Editor: Julie Nemer
Editorial Assistant: Mary Ann Vail
Production Editor: Karen Wiley
Copy Editor: Teresa Herlinger
Permissions Editor: Karen Ehrmann
Typesetter: C&M Digitals (P) Ltd.
Proofreader: Penelope Sippel
Indexer: Jeanne Busemeyer
Cover Designer: Janet Kiesel
Marketing Manager: Helen Salmon

Printed in the United States of America

Library of Congress Cataloging-in-Publication Data

Worth, Michael J.

Nonprofit management : principles and practice/Michael J. Worth. — 2nd ed.

p. cm.
Includes bibliographical references and index.

ISBN 978-1-4129-9445-3 (pbk.)

1. Nonprofit organizations—Management.
I. Title.

HD62.6.W675 2012

658'.048—dc22 2010047961

This book is printed on acid-free paper.

11 12 13 14 15 10 9 8 7 6 5 4 3 2 1

Brief Contents

Detailed Contents

3 Theories of the Nonprofit Sector and Nonprofit Organizations   45

PART II. Governing and Leading Nonprofit Organizations   73

4 Nonprofit Governing Boards   75

5 Executive Leadership   105

PART III. Managing the Nonprofit Organization 131

6 Ensuring Accountability and Measuring Performance 133

7 Strategic Planning and Strategic Management 167

8 Capacity and Collaboration   193

13   Financial Management   323

PART V. Special Topics   349

14   Advocacy and Lobbying   351

15 Governing and Managing International and Global Organizations   369

16 Social Entrepreneurship   385

Acknowledgments

Writing a book is a collective enterprise, even when the book has one author. Any author builds on the work of others, and this text reflects the wisdom of the many scholars and practitioners who are cited throughout it.

I am grateful to my SAGE editor, Lisa Cuevas Shaw, who encouraged me to undertake the first edition of this book and who made the decision to proceed with this second edition. I am grateful as well to the reviewers, whose frank comments on the first edition have added immeasurably to this revision.

I have learned immensely from my students at The George Washington University, from my faculty colleagues, and from the many nonprofit executives who have participated in various classes of mine over the years. I thank them for the education they have provided me and hope that they will find this book to be a useful contribution to the field. Finally, I express my deepest gratitude to my wife for her patience and forbearance over the months of my effort with this project, both in the writing of the first edition and again as I have undertaken the many revisions that are encompassed in this second edition.

Michael J. Worth
Professor of Nonprofit Management
The George Washington University
Washington, D.C.

Preface

The first edition of *Nonprofit Management: Principles and Practice* was published by SAGE in 2009. It is striking how much the landscape has been altered in the short time since the first edition was completed and important to note that the environment may have changed further between the time of this writing and the time that this book reaches you, the reader.

Changes reflected in this second edition of the book include, most obviously, certain data, but also new laws and different economic conditions. The economic recession that began in late 2007 has had a significant impact on nonprofit organizations. Many experienced major reductions in revenue from all sources, and some found it necessary to reduce staff and programs at a time when many also were experiencing an increase in the need for their services. The depth of the recession and its implications for the nonprofit sector were not fully recognized, by anyone, when the first edition of this book was being written. This second edition notes changes wrought by the recession at various points, but that is not its focus. It is impossible to know what the state of the economy will be when this book is being read. Perhaps the recession that began in 2007 will have permanently altered the landscape for nonprofit organizations and their leaders, or perhaps the economy will have recovered, leaving the recession as just a fading bad memory. Some people, from the perspective of 2010, are identifying limited resources as the "new normal." But history makes a persuasive case for long-run optimism. As most investors know, one of the most dangerous ideas is that things are "different this time." Following past periods of economic difficulty, better times ultimately have returned and the nonprofit sector has continued its growth.

The inevitable lag between research and writing and publication often means that readers should be alert to changes that may have occurred during the process. Thus, even this second edition may have some obsolescence by the time it reaches the reader. There are reminders of this reality throughout the book, and it is recommended that students consult referenced websites and other resources on points that seem subject to change.

This second edition retains many of the chapters from the first edition, all of which have been revised to include updated data and reflect relevant events. Some chapters have been reorganized in response to comments from readers of the first edition, in order to achieve a better flow and, in some cases, bring related topics together in a more logical manner. In addition, new chapters and cases have been added to incorporate new developments in the field.

Philosophy of This Book

Students reading this book are likely to have varied backgrounds. Some may be undergraduates who do not yet have substantial work experience and perhaps wish to explore nonprofit management as a possible career direction. Others may be graduate students who have an interest in nonprofit careers but have not previously studied management. Still others might have studied management as undergraduates but may have limited knowledge of the unique values, characteristics, and circumstances of the nonprofit sector or how the management principles they know can be applied in the nonprofit environment. Yet others may be individuals with considerable experience working in nonprofit organizations who are pursuing further study to increase and broaden their understanding and professional skills.

A Balanced Approach

Some students reading this book may be enrolled in a program leading to a master's degree in nonprofit management. Others may be pursuing a master's degree in business, public administration, or public policy, with a concentration in nonprofit management. Still others may be taking only one course in nonprofit management as an elective in their undergraduate or graduate degree program, seeking only a broad and general orientation to the field.

Given this diversity of backgrounds and goals often found among students taking a course in nonprofit management, a textbook that seeks to provide an overview of the field must include both theoretical concepts and practical applications; it must cover some basics as well as intellectually stimulating issues; it must be both rigorous and accessible to students of varied academic backgrounds; and it must provide both a foundation of knowledge that may serve as a springboard to more advanced study and a comprehensive overview for those students whose one experience with the field will consist of a single course.

This book strives to address all these diverse needs and interests, with the author's humble recognition that it may not succeed in meeting all of them for all students. It attempts to provide a comprehensive exposure to topics relevant to the field of nonprofit management, but it obviously must be selective in its discussion of those topics. This intended balance between comprehensiveness in topics and selectivity in their treatment may frustrate some readers. Some may find their appetites whetted but unsatisfied by the quick tour provided in some parts of the book. Others may find that some chapters include ideas they have seen before in other courses.

Students are encouraged to tailor their use of the book to their own interests and backgrounds. Readers who, for example, already have studied some of the organizational and management theories we will discuss are encouraged to read relevant sections as a refresher but to pay closer attention to material that is new to them. Those to whom the theories are new, and who find their discussion in this book to be too brief, are encouraged to explore the additional resources suggested throughout the book. In sum, it is hoped that this book may provide a kind of comprehensive menu, from which students may select the topics or approaches on which they wish to "click" for more information. Both novices and more experienced individuals may find it a foundation on which they can build, seeking appropriate avenues for further information and learning. And, in all likelihood, professors also will elaborate on some topics and skip lightly over others, as they sense the tempo of their individual classes.

Focus on Charitable Nonprofits

As will be discussed in Chapter 2, the nonprofit sector encompasses an amazing array of organizations with different characteristics, structures, and purposes. This book focuses primarily on that category known as charitable nonprofits and, in particular, those that provide services, such as education and research, health care, arts and cultural programs, and social and legal services. The following chapters also will sometimes mention member-serving organizations—for example, trade and professional associations—but primarily as points of contrast with charitable nonprofits. Religious congregations make up a significant component of the overall nonprofit sector, but religion is the subsector that is the least professionalized—that is, it employs relatively few professional managers. Thus, this book does not devote significant discussion to the management of churches, synagogues, and mosques. We will discuss foundations, but primarily as sources of support for service-providing nonprofits; we will not discuss the management of foundations per se. This book does not exclude, but also does not emphasize, those nonprofits that are primarily advocacy organizations, also known as social welfare organizations. While they are nonprofits, they are also different from charitable nonprofits in important ways, as we will discuss further in Chapter 2. Of course, some principles of governance, leadership, and management discussed in this book apply to all nonprofits and will be of relevance to students intending to work in any component of the nonprofit world.

Focus on U.S. Nonprofits

While this book includes a chapter on nonprofits in the international environment and the chapter on social entrepreneurship includes international examples, it primarily addresses the management of nonprofit organizations in the United States. The American nonprofit sector is the largest in the world; it operates under unique cultural, economic, and legal circumstances. It is where most American students of nonprofit management will pursue their careers. In addition, as governments around the world seek to reduce their expenditures and devolve many functions to nonprofit organizations, many also are looking to relevant aspects of the American model in developing their own nonprofit sectors. Thus, even for students primarily interested in working on the international stage, an understanding of nonprofit management in the United States is both relevant and useful.

Overview of the Book

The first three chapters of this book provide an orientation to the nonprofit sector and a theoretical foundation for the more applied topics we will consider later. Chapter 1 provides an introduction to nonprofit management, both as a profession and as an academic field of study, and offers a justification for studying the topic as distinct from management in government or business. Chapter 2 offers a look at the structure, boundaries, and characteristics of the nonprofit sector and establishes some basic definitions. Chapter 3 expands our understanding of the nonprofit sector by reviewing theories that explain its existence and its role in relation to government and business. That chapter also examines selected theories that describe the nature of nonprofit organizations and explain their behavior.

The next two chapters, 4 and 5, consider the roles and responsibilities of governing boards and nonprofit CEOs and the ways in which these two vital actors interact in leading organizations. The nonprofit governing board has functional, moral, and legal responsibilities. Nonprofit chief executives, whether titled "executive director," "president," "CEO," or something else, lead their organizations in a complex and dynamic environment that will be described. The partnership between the CEO and the board is critical to a well-operating and effective organization.

The next five chapters focus on applied aspects of nonprofit management. Chapter 6 reviews the increasing demands for nonprofit accountability and various approaches to measuring the performance of nonprofit organizations. Chapter 7 discusses the development of organizational strategy, and the tools of strategic planning and strategic management now employed by many nonprofits. Strategic planning is often the first step in the larger undertaking of building the organization's capacity or its ability to achieve the goals identified in the plan. Chapter 8 explores capacity-building efforts by nonprofits. In addition, recent years have brought increased incentives for nonprofit collaboration and even mergers of organizations, topics which are also considered in Chapter 8. Chapter 9 discusses both the theory and the practice of human resource management in nonprofit organizations. One of the significant differences between many nonprofits and business or government is the substantial employment of volunteers to provide the organization's core services. Management of an unpaid workforce requires an understanding of human motivation and skill in managing effective relationships between an organization's volunteers and its paid professional staff. Chapter 10 considers the management of programs for communication and marketing, essential for organizations that are highly interactive with and dependent on the world around them.

The next section of the book, encompassing three chapters, is concerned with the acquisition and management of resources. Chapter 11 reviews the principles of raising philanthropic funds from individual, corporate, and foundation donors. Chapter 12 explores the subject of nonprofits' earned income—that is, efforts to generate revenue through activities other than traditional philanthropy. That chapter explores the myriad and growing commercial partnerships between nonprofit organizations and corporations, including cause-related marketing, sponsorships, licensing agreements, joint ventures, and others. It also considers nonprofit business ventures, the development of revenue-generating activities that provide a stream of revenue to support mission programs.

The securing of revenue and the management of financial resources are interrelated activities. Like many of the topics covered in this book, financial management is large, complex, and important. Chapter 13 provides a few basic concepts and directs students to additional sources from which they can obtain the more detailed understanding they may seek.

The final section of the book includes three chapters that expand our perspective with a brief look at some special topics. Chapter 14 looks at the role of nonprofits as advocates for social change and some of the considerations for managers of such activities. Chapter 15 looks beyond the United States to discuss the work of nonprofit organizations internationally. Chapter 16 examines the growing phenomenon of social entrepreneurship, both within the United States and globally. The Conclusion offers some of my final reflections and observations.

Students may observe that the book does not include a chapter on nonprofit law. Nonprofits are subject to a large and growing body of law at the local, state, and federal levels, and additional regulation of the sector is under discussion as this volume is written. However, I decided to discuss aspects of nonprofit law in the various chapters where they are most relevant rather than in a separate chapter. The book provides references to other resources for students who may want to know more. The book also does not include a separate chapter on ethics; rather, ethical issues are addressed at relevant points throughout the text.

Again, all the following chapters draw on the theoretical and academic literature as well as the writing of experienced practitioners and consultants. Where the topic lends itself to examples, key points are illustrated with actual cases, some drawn from the daily headlines. Students are encouraged to include the cases in their reading of each chapter, to consider the Questions for Discussion at the end of each chapter, and to think about the relevance of what they are reading to any nonprofit organizations with which they may have personal experience.

PART I

Understanding Nonprofit Management, the Nonprofit Sector, and Nonprofit Organizations

Chapter Outline

chapter 1

Yale University became home to the first academic center devoted to the study of nonprofits. The Yale Program on Non-Profit Organizations (PONPO) was founded shortly thereafter in 1978.

©iStockphoto.com/Eivind Arntsen

Nonprofit Management as a Profession and a Field of Study

1

This is a book about the management of nonprofit organizations. The topic begs two fundamental questions: Why do nonprofit organizations need to be managed? And, is management of a nonprofit organization really different from management of a business or government agency? In other words, is there really a need for a book like this, or is management a generic activity that could be learned as well from a textbook on business or public management?

Some may hold a perception of nonprofit organizations as primarily collections of well-intentioned people who struggle with minimal resources to meet human needs, without much attention to the bottom line, and with some disdain for management as an unwelcome distraction from the all-important work of delivering vital programs and services. However, there has been a management revolution in the nonprofit sector in recent decades, and this stereotype, if ever true, does not describe all nonprofit organizations today. Indeed, many nonprofits face management challenges no less complex than those faced by major corporations or large government agencies.

For most people, the term *nonprofit* conjures up the image of a small organization, perhaps run by a tiny band of volunteers more focused on delivering services to people in need than on building or managing an organization. Indeed, most nonprofit organizations are small, with perhaps few if any professional staff, but there are also others with activities that span the nation and the globe and that employ thousands of people.

Mention the word *business,* and people will likely think first of a large corporation such as Wal-Mart or Coca-Cola, although, in reality, most businesses are small. But it is large business enterprises that are the focus of most management texts and MBA case studies. That is because, as in the nonprofit sector, the need for management varies with the size and scope of activity. The corner dry cleaner needs few management skills beyond basic accounting and a rudimentary understanding of how to manage a few employees. The young technology entrepreneur starting a new business in his parents' garage is not focused on management but on development and delivery of a product, much as the directors of small nonprofits are often more concerned with delivering programs than with building or managing the organization. As a company grows, requiring outside investment and employing more people, its need for professional management increases. Founding entrepreneurs are often replaced by MBAs who have formal management training. So, too, as a nonprofit organization becomes larger, it faces more complex and interesting management challenges, especially if it comes to operate in more than one location across the United States or internationally. This book includes some examples drawn from small nonprofit organizations, but it is principally about organizations that have at least some full-time paid staff, and it includes examples and cases drawn from some of the nation's largest and best-known nonprofits.

A Revolution in Management

The nonprofit management revolution of recent decades has been driven by several forces. One overarching force has been the introduction of competition resulting from changes in funding patterns, the growth of the sector, and increasing demands for accountability. The years since the 1980s have seen reductions in federal government funding for many social programs, the devolution of funding to state governments, and increased outsourcing of the delivery of social and human services by government agencies to nonprofit organizations. Nonprofits have been forced to compete for contracts, against each other and, in some cases, against for-profit firms. In addition, many government benefits are now being provided through voucher-type payments made directly to individuals, who are thus transformed into customers, free to purchase the services they need in the marketplace. Such customers can thus select the organizations that will provide services based on perceptions of quality and other considerations; this forces nonprofits to compete for their business. Like the competition for contracts, the competition for empowered customers has forced nonprofits to either become better managed or place their survival at risk.

But government has not been the only force driving change. Other funders, including foundations and even individual donors, have shown an increased concern with the results achieved by nonprofits through the programs they offer. This has been especially true of many newly wealthy entrepreneurs who amassed their fortunes during the technology boom of the 1990s and the thriving financial services and real estate industries of the mid-2000s. Many view their philanthropic giving as a type of investment from which they expect to see a measurable return in the form of effective programs and services. The requirement that nonprofits meet these expectations for measurable results also has increased the need for management.

There has been a shift in thinking about nonprofit organizations that focuses much more on the organization itself than merely on the programs and services it delivers—a concern with organizations' capacity and sustainability, ideas we will discuss later in this book. The 1990s brought searing critiques of traditional philanthropy and the management of nonprofits. Among them was a *Harvard Business Review* article by Christine Letts, William Ryan, and Allen Grossman (1999b), titled "Virtuous Capital: What Foundations Can Learn From Venture Capitalists." The article essentially was an indictment of traditional foundations' grant-making practices, arguing that the short-term program grants made by most foundations were not meeting the need for investment in the long-term capacity of nonprofit organizations themselves. Letts et al. advocated an approach to philanthropy that would parallel the approach of venture capitalists to investing in companies, including a more sustained commitment to support along with the requirement that organizations meet performance standards. Bill Shore's book *The Cathedral Within* (1999), published the same year as Letts et al.'s article, echoed some of the criticisms of traditional philanthropy and argued that the emphasis on programs rather than building organizations was in fact preventing many successful programs from "going to scale," that is, growing to a point that they could have significant impact, because the organizations did not have the capacity to expand. Letts and colleagues, Shore and others contributed to a change in thinking about nonprofits, shifting from the programs they offer to the strength and sustainability of the organizations themselves. It was, in the words of Jim Collins and Jerry Porras (1994), a shift of emphasis from "telling time" to "building clocks." This new emphasis on nonprofit organizational development also has been a force in increasing the demand for professional nonprofit management.

Another reality is that the dramatic growth of the nonprofit sector and its assets has simply raised the stakes. Fueled in part by a wave of philanthropy based on the economic gains of the 1990s and mid-2000s, in part by the continued devolution of government programs, and in part by an increased worldwide interest in philanthropy and voluntary action, nonprofits now employ more people and control more resources than ever before. The nonprofit sector has become a consequential part of the American economy that cannot be ignored. Therefore, it has captured the increasing attention of legislators, the media, and others who demand that nonprofits be accountable for the assets entrusted to them and for the results that they achieve with those assets. This reflects an increased concern with accountability throughout American society, affecting businesses as well as nonprofits. Demands for accountability and the need for systems and procedures to comply with greater scrutiny and regulation also have contributed to the need for trained managers.

In sum, if it was ever true that the typical nonprofit organization fit the image of a well-intentioned but unmanaged endeavor, nonprofit organizations today, other than perhaps the smallest, must be managed. To be otherwise is not only to risk failure in meeting society's needs and expectations, but also to place the organization's survival at risk. However, the question remains whether managing a nonprofit organization is different from managing a government agency or a business corporation. Is management generic, or is management in the nonprofit sector a distinguishable endeavor?

A Distinct Profession

Throughout most of the history of management as a recognized discipline, most theorists have advocated a generic approach, arguing that common management principles would apply equally to all organizations, whether businesses, government agencies, or nonprofits. And there remain some who are skeptical that management in the nonprofit sector is unique or that it requires particularly distinctive skills.

At an operational level, surely management in the nonprofit sector requires many of the same skills that are also important in government or business. There may not be a particularly nonprofit way of processing payroll or implementing a new information system, and, indeed, many of the techniques of business management have been adopted by nonprofit organizations as well. But this book is predicated on the view that nonprofit management is different from management in the business or governmental sector in a variety of ways, including the following four.

First, as Herman and Heimovics (2005) explain, nonprofit management uniquely requires the ability to integrate mission, the acquisition of resources, and strategy.

The choice of a mission for an organization depends on the potential for the acquisition of sufficient resources to carry out that mission. Conversely, the acquisition of certain kinds of resources can influence the mission an organization chooses to undertake. Any mission, no matter how great the cause, is likely to fail if the organization lacks necessary and sufficient resources to pursue it. Moreover, decisions about strategies for acquiring resources must be consistent with the mission and ethical values of the organization. Actions in one realm affect the other realms. The leadership challenge is to see that decisions and actions in one realm are not only consistent with those in other realms but also mutually reinforcing. (p. 153)

Managers of government agencies generally have a single source of revenue—for example, the U.S. Congress or a state legislature—and carry out programs mandated by the law. Managers in business receive revenue from the sale of products or services and have the freedom to decide what goods or services they will provide and to which customers. More sales translate into increased revenues, and activities that are not profitable can be discontinued. The same relationships do not always hold true for a nonprofit. Most nonprofits obtain resources from multiple sources and, like businesses, have considerable freedom to determine the activities in which they will engage. However, one important difference is that increased activity may strain resources rather than enhance them. That is because not all of a nonprofit's customers may pay the full cost of producing the good or service, and indeed, some may not pay at all. Judy Vredenburgh, a former executive of Big Brothers Big Sisters and the March of Dimes, describes the dilemma: "Every time we in nonprofits satisfy customers, we drain resources, and every time for-profits satisfy a customer, they get resources. That sounds very simple, but it has huge implications" (quoted in Silverman & Taliento, 2006, p. 41).

Thus, as Herman and Heimovics (2005) suggest, management of a nonprofit organization requires constant trade-offs among the mission, the acquisition of resources, and strategy. That distinguishes nonprofit management from the management function in the business or public sectors. Management in those sectors, while also complex, at least begins with some fixed points of clear goals and positive relationships between activities and revenues. Managing a nonprofit is more like swimming in the air, with everything variable and in constant motion.

Second, the complex relationships among a nonprofit organization's stakeholders require management that is especially skilled in negotiation and compromise, with a high tolerance for ambiguity. In corporations and in government agencies, the flow of authority from the top down is generally clear. But, as Anheier (2005) describes,

nonprofit organizations consist of multiple components and complex, internal federations or coalitions among stakeholders . . . [therefore] the structure of nonprofit organizations may require a multi-faceted, flexible approach to management and not the use of singular, ready-made models carried over from the business world or from public management. (p. 245)

Jim Collins (2005) recounts a meeting between Frances Hesselbein, chief executive officer (CEO) of the Girl Scouts of America at the time, and a *New York Times* columnist, in which the CEO addressed this unique characteristic of nonprofit management:

[The columnist] asked what it felt like to be on top of such a large organization. With patience, like a teacher pausing to impart an important lesson, Hesselbein proceeded to rearrange the lunch table, creating a set of concentric circles radiating outward—plates, cups, saucers—connected by knives, forks, spoons. Hesselbein pointed to a glass in the middle of the table. "I'm here," she said. Hesselbein may have had the title of Chief Executive Officer, but her message was clear: *I'm not on top of anything.* (p. 9)

Nonprofit management is unique because nonprofit organizations are different from businesses and governmental entities—often reliant on the support of donors and the work of volunteers, pursuing missions derived from values and principles about which there may be disagreement, and engendering a sense of ownership and a desire for influence among multiple constituencies both inside and outside the walls of the organization itself. In this environment, a nonprofit CEO must provide leadership as well as management, a distinction we will explore further in Chapter 5. Robert Higgins, who worked as both a nonprofit executive and a venture capitalist and thus was able to observe the differences between the sectors firsthand, explains,

In most for-profit organizations . . . people arrive with common goals. The board of directors may have different viewpoints, but shareholder value as a fundamental goal is something shared by the board, by the CEO, and by senior management. You start off differently in the not-for-profit world, with each board member arriving with a different set of goals and often different agendas. To manage that as a CEO is much more complex. (quoted in Silverman & Taliento, 2006, p. 38)

Third, managers of nonprofit organizations must measure their success by a double bottom line. A nonprofit exists to pursue a social mission, and success must be measured in terms of its ability to achieve that mission. That is one bottom line. But, in today's competitive environment, nonprofit managers also must pay close attention to the *financial* bottom line if their organizations are to survive and succeed. Ask a room of people, "What's the purpose of Microsoft?" and some may quickly reply, "To produce software," or perhaps some will joke, "To control the world!" But both responses miss the point because Microsoft, like all businesses, has one clear purpose: to increase the value of the business and thus the wealth of its owners. Producing software and controlling the world are but means to that end. To be sure, many corporations today are also guided by principles of social responsibility and ethics, but social progress is not their *purpose*. Indeed, social concerns are properly viewed as constraints on the pursuit of the purpose for which every business exists: to maximize profit in order to increase the value of the owners' equity. Managers may have their own personal social goals, but if they make them a central element of the company's purpose, they will not fulfill their principal responsibility to the owners of the firm.

In contrast, a nonprofit *exists* to serve a social purpose. But, as we have discussed, in today's competitive environment, financial results also require the executive's attention—he or she must manage the double bottom line of financial and social return. And the latter may be ambiguous in its definition, even a subject of disagreement and dissension among the organization's many stakeholders, or difficult to measure.

Fourth and finally, many of the problems that nonprofit managers address are exceptionally difficult and intractable. Andreasen and Kotler (2008) offer a strong example:

While the "difficulty" of one's management challenges may be a matter of opinion, very few corporate chieftains would think it easier to increase market share two percent than to reduce the number of AIDS cases in an African country with volunteer workers, an antagonistic government, countervailing religious and cultural norms, rampant customer illiteracy, and crumbling public infrastructure. (p. 5)

To say that managing a nonprofit is inherently more complex than managing a business of comparable size is not to demean the skills of business managers nor to disparage their clear focus on profit. The creativity and problem-solving skills of business leaders have built great organizations and propelled economic progress. Moreover, it is the wealth created by the business sector that sustains nonprofits and makes social advancement possible. But the need to manage the double bottom line, to relate to disparate and competing constituencies, and often to work against the weight of deep-seated historical and cultural barriers adds complexity to the nonprofit CEO's challenge, a challenge that is too often underestimated by some who observe the nonprofit sector from a business perspective. William Novelli, a former businessman who built the public relations firm Porter Novelli and later served as the CEO of the nonprofit AARP, explains the challenge:

> It's harder to succeed in the nonprofit world. . . . It may be hard to compete in the field of consumer packaged goods or electronics or high finance . . . but it's harder to achieve goals in the nonprofit world because these goals tend to be behavioral. If you set out to do something about breast cancer in the country, or about Social Security solvency, it's a . . . lot harder to pull that off. [And] it's also harder to measure. (quoted in Silverman & Taliento, 2006, p. 37)

This book is based on the premise that nonprofit management is a unique endeavor, distinguishable from management in business or government. It is necessary, however, to acknowledge that some see a convergence of management across the sectors in recent years, as both public managers and nonprofit managers are expected to be more businesslike and business managers are expected to demonstrate more responsibility toward the social and human impact of their actions. As Lester Salamon (2002) observes, if

> nonprofits are becoming more "business-like," the business methods they are adopting have themselves undergone fundamental change in recent years, and many of the changes have involved incorporating management approaches long associated with nonprofit work—such as the emphasis on organizational mission, service to clients, and the need to imbue staff with a sense of purpose beyond the maximization of profit. In a sense, these longtime nonprofit management principles have now been fused with business management techniques to produce a blended body of management concepts that is penetrating business and nonprofit management alike. (p. 6)

Nonprofit Management as a Field of Study

Students taking a course in nonprofit management today might reasonably assume that such courses have always existed. But they are a relatively recent addition to the curriculum at most colleges and universities, and scholarly research in the field, while growing, still does not approach the volume of study devoted to public or business management.

Indeed, recognition of *management* as an identifiable function—in any organizational setting—is relatively recent in the scope of history. While management-like functions have been performed throughout civilized history, the beginning of management as a field of study dates approximately to the late 19th century and the development of an industrial economy. Stephen Block (2001) credits an 1886 paper by the engineer Henry R. Towne as the first call for the development of management as an independent field of study with its own literature (p. 106). The nation's first school of management, the Wharton School at the University of Pennsylvania, was established shortly thereafter, in 1898. The first two decades of the 20th century saw the growth of professional management societies, books, and university programs. The first doctoral dissertation in management was written in 1915. According to Block, interest in management was increased by the experience of American manufacturing during WWII, and the decades since have brought explosive growth in business management education and research, including the development of theories we will explore at relevant points in this book (p. 107). But the early study of management was focused on business organizations, with attention to public management developing later. Interest in nonprofit management has emerged primarily within the past three decades.

As mentioned above, until about the 1960s, most management theorists advanced a "generic approach," arguing that their theories applied equally in all types of organizations, whether businesses, government agencies, or nonprofits. As Hal Rainey (2003), a public administration scholar, emphasizes, "With some clear exceptions . . . the theorists repeatedly implied or aggressively asserted that distinctions such as public and private, market and non-market, and governmental and nongovernmental offered little value for developing theory or understanding practice" (p. 48). However, by the 1960s, some authors began to challenge this approach and to call for more research focused specifically on the management of public agencies. This coincided with a period of growth in the federal government and the development of master of public administration (MPA) degree programs in universities, which for the first time emphasized management skills in government and differentiated the study of public management from the discipline of political science. The National Association of Schools of Public Affairs and Administration (NASPAA) was founded in 1970 and began to accredit such programs.

Attention was drawn to the nonprofit sector by an important national study conducted by the Commission on Private Philanthropy and Public Needs during the period 1973 to 1975. That commission, often called the "Filer Commission" in honor of its chair, business leader John H. Filer, issued a report titled *Giving in America* (Commission on Private Philanthropy and Public Needs, 1975), which was the most detailed study of philanthropy in the United States up to that time. The first academic center devoted to the study of nonprofits, the Yale Program on NonProfit Organizations (PONPO), was founded shortly thereafter, in 1978, and social scientists began to turn their attention to understanding the role of nonprofit organizations in economic and political life. The generic approach was beginning to yield to the view that nonprofit organizations might have unique characteristics that distinguish them from organizations in the other two sectors.

As previously discussed, the 1980s marked a turning point in public policy, with government outsourcing more of the delivery and management of social and human services to nonprofits. That development further increased the need for professional management in nonprofit organizations and captured the interest of some students previously aiming for careers in government. Public administration faculty members saw that a growing number of their students were interested in working in nonprofit organizations and responded by developing programs to teach nonprofit-specific skills (Joslyn, 2004). The number of programs grew throughout the 1980s. That decade also saw the establishment of new research centers and programs, including Case Western Reserve University's Mandel Center for Nonprofit Organizations and the Center on Philanthropy at Indiana University.

Beginning in the 1990s, significant attention of management scholars and writers has turned to the nonprofit sector. Writing in 1990, management guru Peter Drucker observed a "management boom" going on in nonprofit organizations, but he also noted the lack of recognition of nonprofit management as worthy of attention. "For most Americans," he wrote, "the word 'management' still means business management" (p. xiv). But as the nonprofit sector continued to grow throughout the 1990s and into the 2000s, a burgeoning literature sought to adapt the theories and skills of business management to the planning, managing, and financing of nonprofits. Courses in the strategic management of nonprofits and on social entrepreneurship began to proliferate in business schools, and new books applied the techniques used by companies and governments to the nonprofit sector (Oster, 1995; Steiss, 2003). The *Harvard Business Review* came to include occasional articles on the management of nonprofit organizations, with some of the classics collected into a book in 1999. The late 1990s brought an economic boom and a boom in the literature of venture philanthropy, social enterprise, entrepreneurial nonprofits, and business techniques applied to nonprofit organizations (Dees, 1998; Dees, Emerson, & Economy, 2001; Kearns, 2000; Letts, Ryan, & Grossman, 1999a; Oster, Massarsky, & Beinhacker, 2004). The Stanford University Graduate School of Business began publishing a journal, the *Stanford Social Innovation Review,* in 2003, and online journals, blogs, and other forums related to nonprofit management, social innovation, social entrepreneurship, and related topics, proliferated through the first decade of the 2000s.

The literature of nonprofit management is drawn from three principal areas: (1) the work of social scientists who study nonprofit organizations as social and economic institutions; (2) organizational theory, theories of organizational behavior, and management theory from the business and public sectors that have particular relevance for nonprofit organizations; and (3) a rich practitioner literature that offers important understandings. This book is based on the view that a balanced and integrated approach requires drawing on all three literatures, and that is reflected in the materials presented in the chapters that follow.

Nonprofit management, both as a profession and as an academic field of study, is still relatively young. There is an increasing body of academic research, including the work of economists, sociologists, historians, and other social scientists who have developed taxonomies to identify and track the major components of the nonprofit sector; theories to explain the existence and behavior of the sector; theories describing its relationship to government and the business sector; examinations of its role and impact in the U.S. economy; and analyses of related public policy issues. The management of nonprofits also has been the focus of more applied studies drawn from the fields of public administration and business management.

However, much of the nonprofit management literature is still written by or for practitioners and has a prescriptive, how-to-do-it approach. Consultants, including professionals working in for-profit consulting firms, also have made important contributions to the literature of nonprofit management.

This book is a textbook, not a manual for nonprofit executives. But neither is its purpose to offer an entirely theoretical examination of the nonprofit sector. It is intended to provide students who are considering or pursuing careers in nonprofit management with a broad foundation, blending theoretical and practical topics relevant to the work they do or will do. This approach incurs the risk that some pragmatic individuals may find it too academic and that some academics may find it insufficiently grounded, but it is appropriate to provide a comprehensive and useful overview of a field that is still emerging.

Concomitant with the increase in literature, educational programs related to nonprofit management grew rapidly in the 1990s and 2000s. In a 2007 report, Mirabella revealed that the number of undergraduate programs related to nonprofit management grew by 30 percent between 1996 and 2002 and by an additional 36 percent between 2002 and 2006. The number of graduate programs grew by 26 percent over the decade between 1996 and 2006. By 2006, Mirabella identified a total of 426 programs in nonprofit management, offered at 238 colleges and universities (p. 13S). Recent years also have seen a virtual explosion in the availability of training for nonprofit managers and professional expertise directed toward the improvement of management practices in nonprofit organizations, including programs offered by educational institutions, regional associations of nonprofits, nonprofit infrastructure organizations, and for-profit consulting firms.

Formalization of the nonprofit management curriculum in universities has progressed, but it is still an evolving field. In 2001, NASPAA issued "Guidelines for Graduate Professional Education in Nonprofit Organizations, Management, and Leadership." The Nonprofit Academic Centers Council (NACC), a membership association of academic centers and programs that focus on non-profit organizations, issued its first "Curricular Guidelines for Graduate Study in Philanthropy, the Nonprofit Sector, and Nonprofit Leadership" in 2004 and a revised version in 2008.

There continues to be debate about whether nonprofit management should be taught in schools of business or management, in schools of public administration and public policy, or in other academic units. In her 2007 study, Mirabella found that 48 percent of nonprofit graduate concentrations were offered within a college of arts and sciences or a school of public affairs and administration. Another 22 percent were offered in a school of business or a school of business and public administration. Other programs were offered in schools of social work, various other academic units, or in interdisciplinary centers supported by more than one school. Mirabella notes an increase in the interdisciplinary approach, which was taken by just one university in 1996 but had expanded to eight institutions by 2006. For example, at the University of Georgia, the Institute for Nonprofit Organizations operates as a component of the graduate school and offers course-work through departments of social work, political science, and management (p. 16S).

As discussed further in a later chapter of this book, some see a blurring of the nonprofit and business sectors and argue that future nonprofit executives should be trained in business skills, that nonprofit management programs would be better located in business schools than in schools of public affairs and administration or in colleges of arts and sciences. But Michael O'Neill (2007), founder and former chair of the Institute for Nonprofit Organization Management at the University of San Francisco, expresses the opposite point of view. He notes that few business schools have developed extensive programs in nonprofit management and argues that "Nonprofits have different values, different financial systems, different laws to abide by, different people (like volunteers) to manage, and very different goals [than business organiza-tions]" (p. 171S). He predicts that the future will see continued experimentation with regard to nonprofit programs but that business schools are unlikely to become the predominant hosts of nonprofit management programs. In addition, he predicts that despite the standards developed by NASPAA and NACC, nonprofit management curriculum is unlikely to become as standard-ized as the MBA curriculum in the next 20 years (p. 172S).

Toward a Balanced Approach

The literature of the field reveals a variety of opinions and perspectives. Authors often disagree on specific points—for example, on the appropriate roles and relationships of the organization's board and CEO; on the appropriate balance between being businesslike and remaining focused on the nonprofit mission; on the standards by which a nonprofit organization's effectiveness or performance should be measured; and, as discussed above, even on the appropriate educational program needed to prepare nonprofit leaders. One goal of this book is to provide a balanced and integrated overview of the field that incorporates various viewpoints.

There are at least two broad approaches or perspectives reflected in the contemporary nonprofit management literature. Generalization can, of course, sometimes lead to oversimplification; differences in perspective or approach are often nuanced. But students will likely observe that authors writing about nonprofit organizations and nonprofit management today reflect one of two perspectives that are distinguishable, at least in tone and emphasis.

Some see nonprofit organizations primarily as social institutions. The services they provide are important, but nonprofits also are essential for creating civil society, pursuing social change, and sustaining the free expression of ideas and opinions in a democratic society—indeed, for preserving our most important values as a society. Process and involvement are valued nearly as much as the end result. From this perspective, nonprofit managers often are portrayed as stewards of their organizations or servants of society. With regard to the education of nonprofit managers, those who hold this perspective usually emphasize the need to develop an appreciation of nonprofit values, an understanding of nonprofits' role in society, and a capacity for ethical decision making. In discussing charity and philanthropy, they tend to focus on their cultural and historical roots of giving and view giving as an expression of moral and religious values. They do not necessarily deny the usefulness of business methods in managing nonprofit organizations, but some do express skepticism about the possibility of measuring organizations' effectiveness against sometimes lofty missions. Some express concern that the application of business methods and business thinking holds the risk of undermining traditional nonprofit values and diminishing nonprofit organizations' unique contributions to society. They are often uncomfortable about nonprofits becoming too engaged in commercial activities or forming close relationships with business, fearing that nonprofit culture will be eroded and that organizations will lose sight of their social purposes in the pursuit of financial success.

From the other common perspective, nonprofit organizations are social enterprises, essentially businesses that have a social purpose. Those who hold this view do not dismiss the importance of nonprofits' social missions, nor do they necessarily deny the unique qualities and contributions of the nonprofit sector. Most give at least lip service to the idea that a business approach may not be appropriate for every nonprofit organization. However, they tend to emphasize the commonalities between nonprofit organizations and business firms and encourage the use of business principles and techniques in managing nonprofits. They admire nonprofit leaders who are social entrepreneurs and discuss the education of nonprofit managers in terms of developing entrepreneurial and business skills. Their discussions often focus on building the capacity of nonprofits and the application of business methods, such as strategic planning, strategic management, and marketing. They often use the vocabulary of business, discussing a nonprofit organization's "competitive advantage" and "sustainability." Some criticize traditional charity and philanthropy and prefer that nonprofits rely more on earned income—that is, on revenue derived from their own businesslike activities rather than on gifts. They emphasize results and the measurement of organizational performance against defined "metrics." Some even support the idea of nonprofit capital markets that would allocate funds rationally to nonprofit organizations that show high performance, much as stock markets allocate investment dollars to the companies that produce the highest financial returns. Indeed, recent years have seen the initiation of "social stock markets," a development we will address at an appropriate point later in this book.

Again, the above characterizations of these two perspectives are oversimplified, and some writers take a moderate stance between the two poles described. But it is usually not difficult to identify a particular book or article as leaning toward one perspective or the other. This text draws on literature from both approaches and strives to present a balanced and integrated understanding. Where disagreements may exist, it attempts to fairly summarize both sides of the argument. That is because this author believes that effective nonprofit management in today's environment indeed requires a balanced and integrated approach that draws upon diverse perspectives, skills, and tools.

That approach leads to the frequent use of the expression "on the one hand, but on the other hand" throughout this book. Some might prefer to know the "right answer" and learn what is the best way to manage a nonprofit organization. The philosophy reflected in this book is that there is often no right answer and that the best way is often pragmatic and eclectic. It includes viewing a problem from multiple perspectives and drawing from various approaches selectively as situations may dictate. Students will find abundant other materials written by authors who come from one particular viewpoint or another that they may find to be especially attractive or persuasive.

Proceeding With Realism and Pride

This book is based on the view that while there is a need to improve the management of nonprofit organizations, it is a misperception to believe, as some do, that they are generically less well managed than businesses. This misperception is based in part on our society's bias toward defining success primarily in financial terms. The results of good business management are evident in bottom-line earnings, while the results of nonprofit management are reflected in progress toward a social mission, which may be less visible or easy to measure. In addition, the misperception is often reinforced when apples are compared with oranges, which may occur, for example, if someone's image of a nonprofit is as a small organization and that person's image of a business is that of a larger corporation. It may be accurate to observe that some small nonprofits are not well managed. But, it is important to note, the same is true of many small businesses, most of which fail in the first 5 years of their existence. It might be difficult to demonstrate that a family-run bed and breakfast is really better managed than the local homeless shelter, which would be more appropriate than comparing the shelter with a Marriott hotel.

When nonprofit organizations and companies are compared fairly, we find poor and excellent management in both. For example, the American Red Cross, one of the nation's largest nonprofits, confronted many management problems during the 2000s, which were widely publicized. In that decade, there were also highly visible scandals concerning executive compensation and expenses at American University and the Smithsonian Institution and allegations of conflict-of-interest problems at the Nature Conservancy, one of the nation's largest environmental nonprofits. However, it is fair to ask, was the Red Cross less well managed than General Motors, or were ethical failures at nonprofits more egregious than those at AIG? We might also ask, are Habitat for Humanity and Doctors Without Borders less innovative organizations than Microsoft or Intel? Is the Mayo Clinic less capable of managing risk than BP? In a sequel to his best-selling book on business management, which focuses on the social (or nonprofit) sector, Jim Collins (2005) argues that the important difference is not between business management and nonprofit management, but between mediocrity and greatness:

> Most businesses—like most of anything else in life—fall somewhere between mediocre and good. Few are great. Mediocre companies rarely display the relentless culture of discipline . . . that we find in truly great companies. [But] a culture of discipline is not a principle of business; it is a principle of greatness. (p. 1)

The author's purpose in making this point is to dispel any misperceptions that students may hold that nonprofit management is somehow second rate, or, as implied by critical articles seen in the popular media, that incompetence and corruption are rampant in nonprofit organizations. Nonprofit managers are in general highly capable and dedicated individuals, worthy of the respect and regard of their counterparts in the other sectors of business and government. They work in organizations that are different from businesses or government, they have different purposes and goals, and they often work with fewer resources available to them, but they are not categorically less able or successful. Students pursuing education in nonprofit management should do so with a pride and confidence equal to that of their classmates who may be preparing for careers in business, government, or other distinguished professions.

At the same time, students should hold no illusions about the challenges of a nonprofit management career. Although salaries are improving, nonprofit managers are unlikely to achieve the wealth of their counterparts in business or the job security of their colleagues who hold civil service positions in the government. The pressures are significant. As Julie Rogers, president of the Eugene and Agnes Meyer Foundation, observes, nonprofit executives face a never-ending stream of advice from their boards, funders, clients, volunteers, and others: "Focus on finding dependable sources of income. Produce measurable results. Evaluate whether you are making a difference. Be strategic, not opportunistic. Build diverse boards. Spend more time on advocacy. Collaborate with other organizations" (Rogers, 2006, pp. 45–46). And, too often, they are advised to do all this with smaller budgets, smaller staffs, less training, and less recognition than is provided to managers in business or government. Indeed, some recent studies suggest that the complexity of the nonprofit manager's job and the multiple pressures he or she must handle frequently lead to frustration and burnout (Rogers, 2006).

However, nonprofit managers also enjoy unique rewards, including the satisfaction of knowing that they are working to advance those aspects of human life that many consider to be the most important—the arts, education, the preservation of culture, and the development of young people. They experience the excitement of tackling some of society's most daunting problems and protecting society's most vulnerable members, making a difference in their lives and in the future of society. And they know the camaraderie and fellowship that comes from working alongside others who share their values, priorities, and commitments. For many who have dedicated their careers to working in nonprofit organizations, the value of such intangible rewards is beyond measure.

There has been a revolution in the management of nonprofit organizations, resulting from changes in government policy, increased demands for accountability, and the growth of the nonprofit sector in recent decades. Nonprofit organizations now face management challenges comparable to those facing managers of companies and government agencies. There has been a shift in thinking about nonprofits that emphasizes building the strength of organizations themselves rather than just the programs they offer, also increasing the need for professional management.

Chapter Summary

Through most of history, management scholars pursued a generic approach, believing that management in companies, government agencies, and nonprofits shared similar principles. But nonprofit management is a distinct profession because of the unique characteristics, missions, and cultures of nonprofits. Since the 1980s, this uniqueness has been recognized in the development of research centers and academic programs focused on the nonprofit sector and nonprofit management. By 2006, there were more than 400 programs in nonprofit management at colleges and universities. There continues to be discussion about whether such programs should be located in business schools, schools of public policy and administration, or in other academic units. Some universities have established interdisciplinary centers that draw on faculty from various disciplines.

People view nonprofits from different perspectives, some considering them to be social institutions and others considering them to be more like business firms with a social purpose. Many writers take a middle position, but most reflect one or the other perspective. This book attempts to blend these perspectives and to provide a balanced overview of the field. This author believes that successful nonprofit management requires an eclectic approach, drawing concepts and tools from the work of scholars, practitioners, consultants, and others, as they are found to be useful in specific situations.

Although some people portray nonprofits as less well-managed than businesses, that perception often is inaccurate. Small nonprofits should be compared to small businesses, which also often reveal mediocre management, and which often fail. Many large companies are innovative and well-managed and so are many nonprofit organizations. Students preparing for careers in nonprofit management should proceed with pride and confidence that their field is as distinguished as management in business or government. A nonprofit career brings challenges but also unique rewards.

KEY TERMS AND CONCEPTS

Double bottom line   *Interdisciplinary field of study*   *Management*

QUESTIONS FOR DISCUSSION

1. Is nonprofit management best taught in business schools; in schools of public affairs; or in some other school, department, or program of the university?

2. If nonprofit management challenges are as complex as those in business, should nonprofit managers be compensated at the same levels as managers at comparably large companies? Why or why not?

3. Should nonprofit organizations be viewed principally as businesses with a social purpose, or are they inherently different from for-profit companies?

SUGGESTIONS FOR FURTHER READING

Books/Journals

Ashcraft, R. F. (Ed.). (2007, December). *Nonprofit and Voluntary Sector Quarterly, 36*(4) [Supplemental Issue: Benchmark 3: The Third Decennial Conference on Nonprofit and Philanthropic Studies].

Drucker, P. F. (2003). *Peter Drucker on the profession of management.* Boston: Harvard Business School Publishing.

Websites

National Association of Schools of Public Affairs and Administration, http://www.naspaa.org

Nonprofit Academic Centers Council, http://www.naccouncil.org

Chapter Outline

chapter 2

Andrew Carnegie. Carnegie's Gospel of Wealth articulated the distinction between charity and philanthropy and influenced America's tradition of giving. Photos.com/Getty Images/Thinkstock.

Overview of the Nonprofit Sector

2

America's nonprofit sector is large, complex, and diverse, including organizations very different from one another in purpose, size, and other characteristics. As J. G. Simon wrote in 1987, "The sprawling and unruly collection of animals that populate the non-profit world—from churches to civil rights groups to garden clubs to the National Council on Philanthropy—makes this field hard to grasp and study all at once" (p. 69). And, as we will soon discover, the nonprofit sector is even more sprawling and unruly today than it was in 1987.

In this chapter, we will look at the nonprofit sector as a whole and establish basic concepts and definitions that will help bring some order to our understanding of its structure, boundaries, and characteristics. Let's start by taking a brief imaginary tour around one American city, starting from my office on the campus of The George Washington University, located near the center of Washington, D.C. As the nation's capital, Washington, D.C., is home to a significant number of nonprofits, but the variety of organizations that we will see on our tour is typical of what we might find in any American city. A walk through this one city helps give us a sense of the complexity to be found in today's nonprofit sector all across the country.

Leaving my office at the university, we might walk past The George Washington University Hospital, then turn down the street and pass Western Presbyterian Church, just a few blocks from the edge of campus. If it were morning, we likely would see men and women waiting to enter the basement of the church to visit Miriam's Kitchen, an organization that serves breakfast and provides other services to homeless people.

Another turn, and we would walk in front of the national headquarters of the American Red Cross and past the headquarters of the National Park Service. Proceeding farther into town, we would see the headquarters of the National Geographic Society. Eventually, we might walk past the Smithsonian Institution, located in several buildings along the National Mall, which extends from the Washington Monument to the Capitol building. If we walk a loop around the Capitol, we would pass the massive buildings of the Library of Congress. On the return trip to the university, we could take a slight detour and come back by way of 14th Street, which is home to numerous nightclubs. Among them we would see HR-57, which offers live jazz performances. We might swing around Dupont Circle, pass the headquarters of the Brookings Institution, then head south past the Phillips Collection, which is an art gallery; the Urban Institute; and Anderson House, home to the Society of the Cincinnati, which promotes interest in the Revolutionary War. Arriving back at The George Washington University, we might think about the various sights we have seen in our day and try to identify which are nonprofits and which are not. But that would not be as easy a task as it may initially seem.

We have indeed encountered a number of nonprofits on our tour, but some seem more nonprofit-like than others. When the word *nonprofit* is used, many people think first of an organization like Miriam's Kitchen. While it is located in Western Presbyterian Church, it is a separate organization from the church. It is small and supported almost entirely by charitable gifts. Its workforce is predominantly volunteers, and it provides its services to people who pay nothing for them. Most people also would probably recognize the American Red Cross as a nonprofit organization, which it is, although it is chartered by the U.S. Congress and has a mandate from government to provide services to the U.S. military and to the general population in times of disaster. Some might not think of Western Presbyterian Church or other religious congregations as nonprofits in the same way as the Red Cross or Miriam's Kitchen, but religious congregations are indeed a part of the nonprofit sector. So are many art galleries, such as the Phillips; research organizations, such as Brookings and the Urban Institute; and many fraternal organizations, such as the Society of the Cincinnati.

Some nonprofits don't look or feel like nonprofits. HR-57 is a nonprofit music cultural center in Washington, D.C., which takes its name from a resolution passed by the U.S. House of Representatives in 1987, designating jazz as "a rare and valuable national American treasure." But it doesn't seem that different from any other jazz club on 14th Street. On the other hand, some organizations may seem like nonprofits, but the reality is more complex. For example, The George Washington University Hospital, which we would have passed early on in our walk, doesn't seem any different from other hospitals that are nonprofit. But it is in fact a for-profit hospital owned jointly by The George Washington University (a nonprofit) and Universal Health Services (a for-profit hospital management corporation). Although it is right down the street from Miriam's Kitchen and provides services to some of Miriam's clients, as an organization it is really more like Microsoft than Miriam's.

Several organizations display combinations of nonprofit missions and business operations. Our imaginary tour of Washington, D.C., touched two of these—the Smithsonian Institution and National Geographic. The National Geographic Society is a nonprofit organization dedicated to geographic exploration and education. But National Geographic Ventures is its wholly owned for-profit subsidiary that produces television programs, computer software, and other products. On cable TV, National Geographic competes with Discovery Communications, operator of the Discovery Channel and a for-profit business corporation.

The Smithsonian Institution is particularly complex, operating in part like a government agency, in part like a nonprofit organization, and in part like an entrepreneurial business. The Smithsonian receives a significant portion of its support from federal appropriations, but it was founded through a charitable bequest from James Smithson, after whom it was named, and it actively solicits philanthropic gifts for its museum exhibits, educational programs, research, and other nonprofit activities. A division called Smithsonian Enterprises was created in 1999 and manages the business activities of the Smithsonian Institution, including theaters, museum restaurants, and museum stores (Trescott & Grimaldi, 2008, p. C07).

If the line between nonprofit organizations and for-profit businesses is sometimes difficult to distinguish, the line between the nonprofit sector and government itself is also increasingly blurry. Almost one third of the revenue of charitable nonprofits (29.4 percent) comes from government grants and payments for services under programs such as Medicare and Medicaid (Independent Sector, 2009a, p. 3). Some organizations exist primarily as government contractors implementing government-funded programs. However, some government agencies also have begun to tap the private sector for support to supplement the funds they receive from tax revenues—including two we would have passed on our journey around Washington, D.C., the

National Park Service and the Library of Congress. Both are agencies of the federal government that are increasing their efforts to raise private funds to supplement government appropriations.

Further confusing the landscape, there are for-profit companies that look, feel, and sometimes sound nonprofit-like in the way they describe their missions, programs, and goals. Some compete directly with nonprofits engaged in similar activities. Consider, for example, the following description of services offered by one organization:

> We match families with the right health care coverage so they can find a doctor in their neighborhood who speaks their language and meets their medical needs.
>
> We help individuals find a path to sustainable employment.
>
> We improve the lives of children and their families by connecting them to vital child support resources.
>
> We protect patients' rights through an independent and objective appeals process for health programs such as Medicare and Medicaid.
>
> We develop education solutions so children with special needs get the services they need to succeed, while helping school districts comply with federal requirements. (MAXIMUS website, http://www.maximus.com/our-philosophy.)

That sounds like the description of a nonprofit organization's programs, but it is indeed drawn from the website of MAXIMUS, a large for-profit corporation that manages government programs and employs 6,000 people in various locations around the world.

Clearly the lines between the for-profit, nonprofit, and public sectors of our society are sometimes difficult to perceive without close examination. The popular image of a nonprofit organization as a small band of volunteers intending to do good, working with minimal resources, serving people in need, and sharply distinct from business and government is far from the reality of many nonprofit organizations today. To understand how we came to where we are and make sense of the "sprawling and unruly collection of animals" that is today's nonprofit sector, we will need some understanding of the history that brought us to this point—and perhaps some road maps to lead us through the "zoo" (J. G. Simon, 1987).

America's Nonprofit Sector: A Historical Overview

The roots of America's nonprofit sector lie in the ancient traditions of *charity, philanthropy,* and *voluntarism.* J. S. Ott (2001) identifies the Greco-Roman emphasis on community, citizenry, and social responsibility and the Judeo-Christian ethic of helping others as "two diverse ideological streams" that influenced these traditions in Western societies (p. 90). Indeed, virtually all cultures and religions include some emphasis on the importance of service to others, which includes giving or voluntary action.

The legal foundations of America's nonprofit sector are drawn from English law, particularly the Statute of Charitable Uses and the Poor Law, both passed in 1601. These laws clarified the relationship between the British government and the Church of England, defined the legitimate activities to be supported by charity, and established a means to make the trustees of charitable institutions accountable (Hammack, 1998, p. 5). The philosophy reflected in these statutes influenced the development of U.S. law regarding nonprofits and is still reflected in American legal traditions.

Despite their ancient roots, it is in the United States that the traditions of charity, philanthropy, and voluntarism have reached their most elaborated expression. As early as 1835, the Frenchman Alexis de Tocqueville observed the unique propensity of Americans to form "voluntary associations" to address social and political objectives, which he reported in his famous book *Democracy in America*. Indeed, in a young nation born in revolution against the authority of the British government, voluntary organizations and institutions provided many of the services, from schools to volunteer fire departments. A certain mistrust of government has been a pervasive and continuing aspect of American culture and has provided philosophical support for private, voluntary initiatives throughout the nation's history. As we saw in our tour of Washington, D.C., there appears to be some blurring of the nonprofit sector and government in today's environment. But it is important to recognize that the blur was even greater in the earliest days of the nation, when government supported churches, and churches sponsored many of the young institutions that served communities.

The beginnings of our modern nonprofit sector lie in the early years of the 20th century. Amidst the rise of great wealth resulting from the Industrial Revolution, charity and philanthropy became organized activities undertaken on a large scale. This was the time of great philanthropists such as John D. Rockefeller and Andrew Carnegie, who endowed universities, libraries, colleges, and other institutions across the nation. Carnegie's essay, "The Gospel of Wealth," published in 1889, remains a classic statement of the philosophy underpinning the American tradition of philanthropy. Carnegie expresses the responsibility of wealthy individuals to give back to the society that has enabled their accumulation of wealth, saying, "The man who dies thus rich dies disgraced" (p. 664). Carnegie's philosophy remains deeply a part of American culture, as evidenced by many contemporary entrepreneurs and investors, such as Bill Gates and Warren Buffet, who have created charitable foundations with similar expressions of obligation.

Carnegie also helped establish a distinction between the concepts of charity and philanthropy. Although the words are often used interchangeably, and philanthropy is sometimes used as the broader, encompassing term, they describe two different types of giving. *Charity* is appropriately defined as giving intended to meet current individual human needs or to alleviate current human suffering—for example, to feed the homeless or aid the victims of a natural disaster. It is emotionally driven and often impulsive, as evidenced by the outpouring of gifts made through the mail, by phone, and via the Internet within days of the terrorist attacks of September 11, 2001; Hurricanes Katrina and Rita in September 2005; and the Haitian earthquake in 2010.

Philanthropy, on the other hand, is a more rational form of long-term investment in the infrastructure of society, seen, for example, in gifts made to construct new hospitals, endow universities, or create new charitable foundations intended to exist in perpetuity. If the goals of philanthropists were ultimately achieved, it is arguable that the need for charity would be eliminated, since there would exist institutions prepared to meet any human needs that might arise. However, in the imperfect world of the present, both types of giving are important and complementary in their impacts.

Some writers differentiate voluntarism (also called "volunteerism") from charity and philanthropy, arguing that "charity and philanthropy may require little, if any, direct involvement with the beneficiaries [of the services provided]," whereas *volunteerism* is a "very active process that requires active involvement with either the beneficiaries directly or an organization or group that serves a specific population" (Ott, 2001, p. 101). Robert Payton (1988), on the other hand, makes *philanthropy* the umbrella term, defining it in the subtitle of his book as "voluntary action for the public good," including both the giving of time and the giving of money.

Despite its ancient roots and long history in the United States, the concept of a definable nonprofit sector, comparable with the for-profit and governmental sectors, is of relatively recent origin, dating to the work of the Commission on Private Philanthropy and Public Needs (the Filer Commission, mentioned in Chapter 1) from 1973 to 1975. The commission's 1975 report, titled "Giving in America," was the first to characterize nonprofits as constituting a recognizable sector of society. The Filer Commission report came at a time when the nonprofit sector was expanding, in part reflecting changes in government policy. The 1960s and early 1970s were a period of increasing government spending on social programs, starting with the Great Society programs of President Lyndon Johnson. In many cases, government funds were channeled to nonprofit organizations, which provided the actual services. "Indeed," Lester Salamon (2002) observes, "much of the modern nonprofit sector as we know it took shape during this period as a direct outcome of expanded government support" (p. 12).

Beginning in the 1980s, under President Ronald Reagan, federal spending for many social programs was sharply reduced. Since the 1980s, there has been a change not only in the level of government support but also in its form, with important implications for the management of nonprofit organizations. The shift has been away from direct grants to nonprofit organizations and toward providing aid to individuals in the form of voucher-type subsidies. This occurred, for example, in health care, where Medicare and Medicaid reshaped the industry. And it also occurred in higher education, where government funds going directly to colleges and universities diminished, while aid directed to individual students and their families increased. This created a new generation of student consumers and transformed higher education institutions into competitive, marketing organizations. The shift also was illustrated in the welfare reform legislation of 1996, which brought competition to many areas of human services. This empowerment of individuals as consumers through direct subsidies to them has forced nonprofits to compete for customer dollars not only with other nonprofits, but also with for-profit companies that have entered fields that were previously the exclusive preserve of the nonprofit sector. For example, MAXIMUS is now among the nation's largest managers of welfare-to-work programs.

These changes in government funding also account in part for the growing commercialization of the nonprofit sector itself, the increased need for professional nonprofit management, and the demands that nonprofits demonstrate greater accountability and results. Nonprofit organizations comprise a vital and growing sector of our economy and society, but questions about their effectiveness and accountability are topics of national discussion and debate. Some are even reassessing the meaning of concepts such as "community benefit" and "charitable purpose," and the justification of tax exemption for at least some portions of the sector (see Salamon, 2002, pp. 28–29).

Searching for a Common Vocabulary

The nonprofit sector is so diverse and its structure is so complex that it can be confusing, and there are various ways in which people understand it. Diverse understandings are reflected in the fact that there are multiple terms by which the sector is identified.

As Thomas Wolf (1999) points out, describing an elephant as a "non-horse" would seem to most people an unsatisfactory definition (p. 19). But the term *nonprofit organization* really refers to *one* thing nonprofit organizations do *not* do, rather than capturing much about what they are or the diverse programs and services they offer to society. One thing nonprofit organizations do *not* do is distribute profits to individual owners in the form of dividends or use those profits to enhance the wealth of owners through the increasing value of the enterprise.

However, it is important to dispel the common misunderstanding that nonprofits cannot earn profits. Defined as simply an excess of revenues over expenses, nonprofits can and do earn profits. But theses profits must be retained within the organization and be used to further its programs rather than enrich individuals personally. This nonprofit distribution requirement, also called the *non-distribution constraint,* is *one* defining characteristic of nonprofit organizations, but it is clearly not *the* defining characteristic. Indeed, by this narrow standard, the Department of Defense and the State of New York might also be called "nonprofits," since they also have no stockholders or owners to whom any profit is distributed.

While the term *nonprofit organization* or just *nonprofit* is the most commonly used term for these organizations in the United States, those nonprofits that work internationally are generally known as *nongovernmental organizations,* although there is no identifiable nongovernmental sector with the same meaning as the term *nonprofit sector* in the United States. The term *nongovernmental* reflects in part the reality that many such organizations are performing government-like functions in the countries they serve, and that most receive a substantial portion of their revenue from government sources. Many are like arms of government operating just outside the public sphere. Like nonprofit, the term nongovernmental defines organizations by what they are *not*—they are not government agencies. But this term seems equally inadequate. It could apply as well to profit-making companies such as Google and Apple, which are also clearly nongovernmental in their ownership and legal control.

Alternatives to "Nonprofit"

While *nonprofit* is the term most commonly used to describe the sector, there is no shortage of proposed alternatives. Each alternative has its own virtues and shortcomings as well. It is worth discussing some of these terms because each belies a certain view and understanding of the sector. The term *independent sector* has some prominence, since it is also the name of the principal organization representing the interests of nonprofits in Washington, D.C.—Independent Sector (www.independentsector.org). But it raises the question of "independent from what?" Nonprofits are financially dependent on resources derived from both government and private donors and are subject to an increasing array of state and federal law, so independence would not seem to capture their essence.

Some prefer the term *third sector,* placing nonprofits in the universe alongside the commercial economy and government. The term is accurate in terms of size—both the business sector and government employ more people, generate larger revenues, and account for a larger share of economic output. But it also seems to imply a rank order of importance, which would not agree with the values of many people, who may consider religion, education, the arts, medical research, and other purposes served by the nonprofit sector to be among the most important of human endeavors. Furthermore, some scholars suggest that American society encompasses not three but four sectors: business, government, the nonprofit sector, and families and communities. In this broader array, it becomes more difficult to rank the sectors, except by size, in which case families and communities would come first and the nonprofit sector would be fourth rather than third.

The term *charitable sector* is sometimes used, but it is contrary to the reality that charitable gifts, while important, are not the largest source of nonprofit revenues. Nor is the term synonymous with *nonprofit sector,* since there are organizations that qualify as nonprofit under the U.S. tax code but that neither seek nor receive any form of charitable support. This is true, for example, of membership organizations that are funded entirely through dues and those nonprofits whose revenues may consist entirely of grants and contracts received from government. Nor does the term seem appropriate to encompass major institutions, such as Harvard University, that are nonprofit but hardly consistent with most people's understanding of a charity.

Some use the term *voluntary sector.* Voluntarism is one of the foundations of the sector, and many organizations do indeed rely on volunteers, both as members of their governing boards and for at least part of their workforce. But the term does not reflect the reality that in many nonprofits, paid staff members far outnumber volunteers. It also may perpetuate an inaccurate image of nonprofits as universally small and amateurish in their operations, when in fact many nonprofits are substantial enterprises, and professional management of nonprofits has been a growing trend.

The phrase *tax-exempt sector,* commonly used by accountants, attorneys, and other tax specialists, is similar to *nonprofit.* It identifies organizations entirely in terms of their status under U.S. tax law. Nonprofits are exempt from paying federal income tax and generally from state and local income taxes as well. But, again, *tax-exempt* speaks to the legal status of such organizations and says nothing about what they actually do. As we will discuss shortly, the sector encompasses a variety of organizations with few apparent similarities aside from their tax-exempt status.[1, 2]

Another term that has been proposed is *civil society sector* (Salamon, 1999, p. 9). There are many different definitions of *civil society,* and while "the nonprofit sector provides the organizational infrastructure of civil society," the concept itself is more abstract, including "the sum of institutions, organizations, and individuals located between the family, the state, and the market, in which people associate voluntarily to advance common interests" (Anheier, 2005, p. 9). And as Salamon (1999) acknowledges, the term *civil society sector* is like *voluntary sector* in that it "emphasizes the citizen base" of these organizations, while most are not membership associations and many engage large paid staffs (p. 9).

In recent decades, nonprofits have come to be increasingly managed like businesses, and as we will discuss later, some undertake entrepreneurial ventures either directly, through for-profit subsidiaries, or with for-profit partners. Some people have adopted the term *social enterprise* to characterize nonprofits that have a social objective but blend traditional nonprofit methods and commercial principles in their generation of revenue (Dees et al., 2001, p. 9). Although the term *social enterprise* is generally associated with those who especially advocate organizations operating like a business and undertaking efforts to increase revenues from commercial activities, it could be argued that the term captures the positive essence of *all* private organizations having a social purpose, perhaps better than *nonprofit.* Like companies, nonprofits bring together people, resources, and purposeful effort in pursuit of a mission, and they increasingly operate with plans, goals, and established criteria for success—they are indeed enterprises, but their missions relate to social purposes rather than to the enrichment of private individuals. Were *social enterprise* to become a general designation for all such organizations, the sector that contains them perhaps then would be called the *social sector* to differentiate it from business and government. Or, as Jon Van Til (2000) suggests, perhaps something like the French term *economie sociale,* or *social economy,* would be appropriate (p. 12). Indeed, *social sector* has become popular among some business authors in referring to the nonprofit sector (Collins, 2005). However, this broader use of the term has not yet gained universal acceptance, and we generally will use the more common designations of *nonprofit organization* and *nonprofit sector* in the remainder of this book.

Noting the increasing number of organizations that operate under both nonprofit and for-profit legal forms, often called *hybrid* organizations, some authors have suggested that there may be an emerging *fourth sector* encompassing organizations that blend the features and methods of both forms (Sabeti, 2009). Such organizations are discussed in this book, but the term *fourth sector* has not yet been widely adopted.

Size of the U.S. Nonprofit Sector

There are more than 1.9 million nonprofit organizations in the United States (Independent Sector, 2009c, n.p.). They serve a wide range of purposes. Some are "public-serving" and others are "member-serving," terms that will be explained further below (Salamon, 2002, p. 22). The largest group are the charitable nonprofits, classified under 501(c)(3) of the Internal Revenue Code, numbering approximately 1.5 million. Those include many of the public-serving organizations that we all know—hospitals, museums, schools, colleges and universities, religious congregations, orchestras, and nonprofits that provide a range of human and social services. Another significant number, about 140,000, include those classified under section 501(c)(4) of the tax code and include many of the organizations we know for their advocacy on issues, for example, the National Association for the Advancement of Colored People (NAACP), the National Rifle Association (NRA), and the Sierra Club (Independent Sector, 2009a, n.p.).

The nonprofit sector is a significant component of the U.S. economy by any measure. In 2005, nonprofits employed 12.9 million people, approximately 9.7 percent of the workforce. For comparison, this is more than the total number of people employed in the financial services industry (Independent Sector, 2009a, n.p.). In that same year, nonprofits accounted for 8.1 percent of all wages paid, and they spent a total of almost $1.1 trillion, accounting for 5 percent of the U.S. Gross Domestic Product (GDP) (Independent Sector, 2009a, n.p.).

The number of nonprofits in the United States increased dramatically throughout the 1990s and 2000s. The years between 1999 and 2003 saw the creation of 35,000 new religious organizations, 30,000 new educational organizations, 28,000 human services groups, and 5,000 new organizations concerned with the welfare of animals (Gose, 2005). Nonprofit wages and employment have been growing at a rate that is 3 times faster than the general economy in recent years (Wing, Pollack, & Blackwood, 2008, p. 20), making America's nonprofit sector an ever more important component of the U.S. economy and an increasing area of career opportunity.

The growth of the nonprofit sector is attributable to a variety of forces. As discussed above, they include the trend that began in the 1980s toward the devolution of federal programs to state and local governments, and outsourcing of the provision of many services to nonprofits by governments at all levels. Also contributing to the growth of nonprofits was the booming economy of the 1990s, which gave rise to an 81 percent increase in the number of foundations created by wealthy individuals and a doubling of foundation assets, making more money available to fund nonprofit programs (Gose, 2005). In addition, some argue, the growth of nonprofits has been fueled by a reawakening of the spirit of public service among the current generation of Americans. Events such as the attacks of September 11, 2001, the 2004 tsunami in South Asia, Hurricane Katrina in 2005, and the Haitian earthquake in 2010 have called the nation's attention to human needs and the role of nonprofit organizations in helping allevi-ate human suffering. The requirement of community service for graduation from high school has exposed a generation of young people to the idea of volunteering. Many companies also organize volunteer activities for their employees, extending the experience to more Americans and making it even more a part of American culture. Public service also has become a priority of the federal government. In 2009, President Barack Obama signed legislation, named for the late Senator Edward M. Kennedy, to provide an additional $5.7 billion for community volunteer service programs and triple the size of AmeriCorps, the government's service program (Voice of America, 2009).

In his influential, though controversial, 1995 article, "Bowling Alone: America's Declining Social Capital," Robert Putnam discussed a decline in civic engagement among Americans, using the metaphor of his title to suggest that Americans were becoming more isolated and more involved in individual pursuits than in collective interests and activities. Yet a decade later, Putnam and his colleague Thomas Sander reported that young Americans who witnessed the events of September 11, 2001, in their adolescent years appeared to be more involved in public affairs and community life than their older siblings. As Sander and Putnam (2005) note, "We'll have to wait some years to see if this budding civic engagement blossoms, but it could prove to be the largest civic shift in the past half-century" (p. A23).

Differentiating the Nonprofit Sector

As we saw from our imaginary walking tour of Washington, D.C., nonprofits are a widely diverse group of organizations and institutions. Fortunately, there are ways of bringing order out of the apparent chaos by placing nonprofits into categories. Let's review some of them and see if we can gain a clearer picture of this complex arena. We will look at two ways of catego-rizing nonprofits according to their purposes and activities (the National Taxonomy of Exempt Organizations and the IRS classifications), one model that categorizes nonprofits according to who benefits from their activities (public-serving and member-serving), and another that places nonprofits along a continuum according to the degree they are commercialized or use business principles and methods.

National Taxonomy of Exempt Entities

One way to delineate the nonprofit sector is to use the National Taxonomy of Exempt Entities (NTEE). Maintained by the National Center for Charitable Statistics (NCCS), a program of the Center on Nonprofits and Philanthropy at the Urban Institute, the NTEE divides the universe of nonprofit organizations into 26 major groups under 10 broad categories. These categories are based on organizations' purposes, activities, and programs and are similar to the industry clas-sification codes used to group for-profit companies. Box 2.1 lists the 10 broad categories in the NTEE. The complete taxonomy, along with explanations of the categories, is available on the website of NCCS (http://nccs.urban.org/classification/index.cfm).

BOX 2.1 NATIONAL TAXONOMY OF EXEMPT ENTITIES (NTEE) MAJOR GROUPS

Arts, Culture, and Humanities	International, Foreign Affairs
Education	Public/Societal Benefit
Environment and Animals	Religion Related
Health	Mutual/Membership Benefit
Human Services	Unknown/Unclassified

Source: National Center for Charitable Statistics website (http://nccs.urban.org/).

Similar ways of classifying nonprofits include the North American Industry Classification System (NAICS), which uses the same breakout as for the for-profit sector. The Bureau of Economic Analysis of the U.S. Department of Commerce bases some of its data on a definition of "nonprofit institutions serving households" (NPISHs), which excludes nonprofits that serve businesses (Wing et al., 2008, p. 5). The fact that different classification systems are used by various agencies that collect data on the nonprofit sector accounts in part for the fact that estimates of the sector's size and impact are often not consistent.

IRS Classifications

One of the reasons that there are different definitions of the nonprofit sector is that classifications of organizations are developed with varied purposes. For the Internal Revenue Service (IRS), what is relevant is the exemption of nonprofit organizations from the corporate income tax, so the IRS places nonprofits into more than 30 categories (or "classifications") that reflect the basis for their tax exemption (Wing et al., 2008, p. 1). As discussed above, the very term *nonprofit* relates to the treatment of organizations under the U.S. tax code, so the IRS classifications are perhaps the most often mentioned. Moreover, from a practical perspective, how an organization is classified under the tax code is also of the greatest significance to those who govern and manage it, since this status dictates many of the rules by which the organization must operate. Nonprofits qualify for tax exemption under various sections of the Internal Revenue Code (IRC), depending on the nature of their principal activities.

The tax code can be complicated, as anyone who has filed his or her own personal tax returns will testify. Figure 2.1 provides a way to visualize the nonprofit sector and how various organizations are classified by the IRS. It first divides society into the three sectors: government, nonprofits, and for-profit business. The nonprofit sector then is divided into four categories: (1) religious congregations, which are automatically tax-exempt under Section 501(c)(3) and are not required to register with the IRS (Box A); (2) organizations that register with the IRS under Section 501(c) (Box B); (3) organizations that register with the IRS under sections of the tax code *other than* Section 501(c)—for example, political parties that register under Section 527 (Box C).

Take a look at Box B, the 501(c)s. They are further broken down into three categories: (1) the 501(c)(4) social welfare organizations (also often called advocacy organizations) (Box D), (2) the 501(c)(3) charitable nonprofits (Box E), and (3) other tax-exempt organizations that qualify under Section 501(c) (Box F), but not under 501(c)(4) or 501(c)(3). The latter includes, for example, some business associations that are under Section 501(c)(6). You will notice that the 501(c)(3) organizations are further divided into two categories—*public charities* (Box G) and *private foundations* (Box H). We will return to this point later.

Let's take a closer look at the 501(c)(3) and 501(c)(4) organizations that are the primary types discussed in this book. Although they include only about 140,000 organizations (Independent Sector, 2009a, p. 1), we will start with the 501(c)(4) organizations, often called *social welfare organizations* or *advocacy organizations*. Then we will discuss in some detail the 501(c)(3) *charitable nonprofits* that are the largest component of the sector.

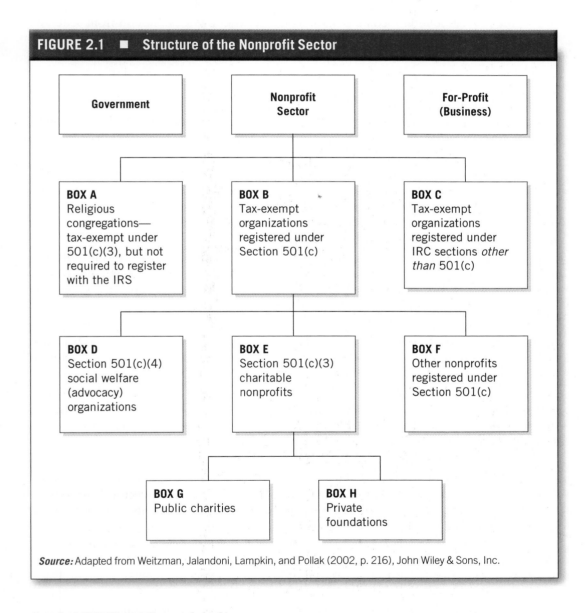

FIGURE 2.1 ■ Structure of the Nonprofit Sector

Source: Adapted from Weitzman, Jalandoni, Lampkin, and Pollak (2002, p. 216), John Wiley & Sons, Inc.

Social Welfare Organizations

There are different types of organizations that are classified under Section 501(c)(4). A small number are HMOs and other medical and dental insurance plans, although they account for the major portion of the revenues in the 501(c)(4) category (Wing, et al., 2008, p. 3). In this book, we generally ignore those organizations and focus of the vast majority of 501(c)(4)s that are considered advocacy organizations, because their purpose is to advance a cause or work for social change.

It is important at this point to distinguish between two concepts: the tax *exemption* of organizations themselves and the tax *deductibility* of gifts made to them. *All* organizations that qualify under Section 501(c) of the IRS code are *tax-exempt;* that is, they are not required to pay federal taxes on their income. (As noted earlier in the chapter, organizations exempt from federal income tax are usually also granted exemption from state and local income taxes.) However, *only* those classified under Section 501(c)(3)—the charitable nonprofits—are both tax-exempt themselves and *also* eligible to receive gifts that are tax deductible for the donors. Thus, the NAACP and the NRA are tax-exempt, but gifts made to them are not tax deductible for the donor because the NAACP and NRA are not classified as charitable organizations.

Advocacy organizations are tax-*exempt*—under Section 501(c)(4)—because they work, in the IRS's (n.d.-b) words, "to further the common good and general welfare of the people of a community (such as bringing about civic betterment and social improvements)." But they cannot receive tax-*deductible* gifts. Why are advocacy organizations different from charitable nonprofits in the eyes of the tax code? One big difference between 501(c)(3) and 501(c)(4) organizations is that the latter do not face the same limitations on political activity that are imposed on the former. They can spend money on lobbying without limitation (IRS, n.d.-a). This is a point we will return to discussing in more detail later in this text.

Because of the different advantages enjoyed and disadvantages experienced by 501(c)(3) and 501(c)(4) organizations, in terms of the tax treatment of gifts and the limitations on lobbying, some organizations have two arms—actually, two separately incorporated but related organizations. One organization is qualified under Section 501(c)(4) and is free to engage in lobbying without restriction. It cannot receive deductible gifts, but it can raise funds through member dues and others types of revenue. The other related organization is qualified under Section 501(c)(3) and is thus eligible to receive tax-deductible gifts. It pursues education, research, and other activities consistent with that classification.

Box 2.2 provides an example in the form of mission statements for the Sierra Club, an internationally known environmental organization based in the United States, and the related Sierra Club Foundation. The Sierra Club itself is a 501(c)(4) social welfare organization that works to preserve the environment, including lobbying for environmental protection legislation. The Sierra Club Foundation is a 501(c)(3) organization that supports certain activities of the Sierra Club. As its description carefully explains, the foundation limits its support to those activities that are consistent with the "charitable, scientific, literary, and educational purposes" allowed for 501(c)(3) organizations. Note the subtle differences in the mission statements of the two organizations. The Sierra Club's mission includes "enlisting" humanity, which suggests the possibility of building political coalitions and encouraging individuals to political action, while the foundation "empowers" the citizenry, something that might be accomplished merely by providing them with information—that is, through education—without any call to political action. These may seem like subtle differences, but facing the possibility of an audit by the IRS and wishing to protect the tax status of both entities, most organizations are precise in monitoring their activities for consistency with tax law.

> ## BOX 2.2 COMPARISON OF CHARITABLE AND
> ## SOCIAL WELFARE (ADVOCACY) ORGANIZATIONS
>
> ### Mission of the Sierra Club, a 501(c)(4) Organization
>
> To explore, enjoy, and protect the wild places of the earth;
>
> To practice and promote the responsible use of the earth's ecosystems and resources;
>
> To educate and enlist humanity to protect and restore the quality of the natural and human environment; and to use all lawful means to carry out these objectives.
>
> *Source:* Sierra Club website (http://www.sierraclub.org/policy).
>
> ### Mission of The Sierra Club Foundation, a 501(c)(3) Organization
>
> The mission of The Sierra Club Foundation is to advance the preservation and protection of the natural environment by empowering the citizenry, especially democratically based grassroots organizations, with charitable resources to further the cause of environmental protection. The Sierra Club is the vehicle through which The Sierra Club Foundation generally fulfills its charitable mission.
>
> ### Description of The Sierra Club Foundation
>
> Working as a funding resource for the environmental community, The Foundation offers its services in receiving, administering, and disbursing funds for tax-exempt charitable, scientific, literary, and educational purposes both to the Sierra Club and to other environmental organizations and projects. Subject to federal tax codes that clearly define the activities with which we can assist, The Foundation is precluded from supporting electoral activities and can expend only a small part of its resources on influencing legislation. While The Foundation is autonomous and is governed by its own Board of Trustees, it works closely with the Sierra Club in pursuing its program and goals.
>
> *Source:* The Sierra Club Foundation website (http://www.sierraclub.org/foundation/inside/background.asp).

Charitable Nonprofits

The tax deductibility of gifts made to charitable nonprofits obviously provides a significant advantage to them in their fund-raising efforts. Consider an individual donor who is in a 25-percent federal tax bracket and who makes a deductible gift of $100 to a charitable nonprofit organization. He or she can deduct that $100 from his or her income before calculating the income tax due. The donor's taxable income is reduced by $100, so the donor's tax bill is reduced by 25 percent of that amount, or $25. This is considered a tax savings because, were it not for the gift, the donor would have paid that amount in additional federal income tax. The out-of-pocket cost of the $100 gift is thus reduced, from $100 to $75 ($100 minus the $25 tax savings). Some view the savings as a form of tax subsidy, or tax expenditure, in the form of foregone federal revenue. And, since many states also permit the deduction of charitable gifts, the donor often has an additional savings on taxes at the state level.

The tax deduction for gifts to charitable organizations is intended to encourage charitable giving and sustain the services provided by charitable organizations. Society has determined that the purposes they serve are to the public benefit and that if the nonprofits did not exist, those services might need to be provided by government. Being eligible to receive deductible gifts makes it easier for charitable nonprofits to raise funds, since the donors are, at least theoretically, able to give more because of the tax saving realized from the deductions.

To be recognized as tax-exempt under Section 501(c)(3), an organization must demonstrate three things; in other words, it must meet three tests. First, it must be *organized and operated* for one or more of eight purposes: charitable, religious, educational, scientific, literary, testing for public safety, fostering national or international amateur sports competitions, and prevention of cruelty to children and animals. (Curiously, the IRC does not specifically mention health care, although it is one of the largest components of the nonprofit sector.) The term *charitable* may seem somewhat imprecise, but the IRS (n.d.-a) defines it to include certain specific activities:

> relief of the poor, the distressed, or the underprivileged; advancement of religion; advancement of education or science; erection or maintenance of public buildings, monuments, or works; lessening the burdens of government; lessening of neighborhood tensions; elimination of prejudice and discrimination; defense of human and civil rights secured by law; and combating community deterioration and juvenile delinquency. (n.p.)

In addition to demonstrating that its primary purposes include one or more of those discussed above, a 501(c)(3) nonprofit must meet two additional requirements. It must meet the non-distribution test, ensuring that its assets are not being used to benefit individual owners and that its managers are not being personally enriched through excessive compensation. And it must limit its political activities. A nonprofit that qualifies under Section 501(c)(3) cannot support candidates for public office and, again, it must limit its expenditures on lobbying—that is, efforts to influence legislation.

Charitable Subsectors

In this section, we will take a brief look at the major subsectors of the charitable nonprofits, excluding religious congregations. Bear in mind that religious congregations are also charitable nonprofits under the tax code and that they are tax-exempt under Section 501(c)(3). However, as we have noted before, religion is a unique component of the nonprofit sector. The U.S. Constitution guarantees the separation of church and state. Gifts to religious congregations are tax deductible, but congregations are not required to register with the IRS, although about half of them do so voluntarily (Wing et al., 2008, p. 139). The principle of separation of church and state prevents government funds from going directly to religious congregations or to organizations that would use them for religious activities. However, congregations are to be distinguished from faith-based organizations that provide social services, which can receive government funds to support their secular programs. Federal legislation passed in 1996, 1998, and 2000 included *charitable choice* provisions to allow faith-based organizations to receive grants under federally funded programs, and proposals to further increase the ability of faith-based nonprofits to obtain such funding generated controversy during the first term of President George W. Bush.[3]

This book does not specifically discuss the management of religious congregations—for example, churches, synagogues, and mosques. Religious organizations are the least professionalized of the subsectors. Although there has been some growth in the number of church managers, the management of most congregations is still done by the clergy and volunteers. In 1998, religious organizations accounted for just 11.6 percent of paid employment in the charitable nonprofit sector (Weitzman et al., 2002, p. xxxvi). As a subsector, religion is also unique in that most of its revenue comes from private gifts (Weitzman et al., 2002, p. xxxvi). Indeed, it is the largest single recipient of gifts, accounting for 35 percent of all giving in the United States in 2008 (Center on Philanthropy at Indiana University, 2009, p. 83).

As discussed below, the charitable subsectors differ significantly in their sources of revenue, the degree of commercialization they reflect, and the extent to which their management has been professionalized—that is, the extent to which they are run by paid staff rather than volunteers.

Arts, Culture, and Humanities. The arts and culture subsector includes museums, performing arts groups, art galleries, folk-life organizations, nonprofit radio and television stations, literary societies, arts education organizations, media and communications organizations, and arts councils and agencies. In 2005, this subsector accounted for almost 12 percent of charitable nonprofits, but only 2.3 percent of the sector's expenses (Wing et al., 2008, p. 166). While this sector counts on earned income from admission fees and other sources, it is also highly dependent on gifts, with support from individuals, corporations, and foundations accounting for almost 41 percent of revenue in 2005 (Wing et al., 2008, p. 166). The management of arts institutions and that of museums are specialty areas within nonprofit management, and professionals often will have attended university programs focused on these fields.

Education. Education is perhaps the subsector best known to students. It includes colleges and universities, preschool, elementary and secondary schools, correspondence schools, libraries, parent–teacher groups, and education support organizations. It will not surprise students to learn that educational institutions receive a significant portion of their revenues from fees for service, including tuition, which accounted for 56 percent of this subsector's income in 2005, making it the second most dependent, after health care, on earned income (Wing et al., 2008, p. 170). Only 15 percent of the revenue of the education subsector comes from gifts, making it one of the least gift-dependent of the charitable subsectors (Wing et al., p. 173).

Higher education, in particular, is a field in which professional management has increased in recent decades. While the senior executives of colleges and universities are still predominantly drawn from the academic ranks, on most campuses there has been a proliferation of mid-level management in areas such as fund-raising, student services, and financial administration. Middle management has grown as colleges and universities have faced increased competitive pressures, greater governmental regulation, and the need to expand revenues through intensified fund-raising programs.

While for-profit education firms—for example, the University of Phoenix—have grown in recent decades, most schools, colleges, and universities remain either nonprofit or government controlled.

Environment and Animals. While the environment and the welfare of animals are important purposes, organizations working in these fields—including environmental preservation organizations, recycling programs, pollution abatement programs, animal protection organizations, wildlife preservation organizations, and zoos—constitute the smallest charitable subsector, representing only 4.3 percent of public charities and 0.9 percent of the nonprofit sector's expenses. It is also a subsector that is highly dependent on charitable gifts, which accounted for 48 percent of its revenue in 2005 (Wing et al., 2008, p. 174). It is important to note that a number of organizations advocating for environmental issues and animal protection are 501(c)(4) organizations, rather than charitable nonprofits under 501(c)(3). The Sierra Club was mentioned above as one example. Such organizations are not included in the totals stated here for this charitable subsector.

Health. The health services subsector is the largest component of the overall nonprofit sector if measured by total revenue, the number of employees, and its share of total wages and salaries. It includes hospitals, home health agencies, outpatient clinics, hospice programs, nursing homes, health maintenance organizations, dialysis centers, community health centers, residential treatment programs for emotionally disturbed youth, blood banks, public health organizations, and disease organizations such as the March of Dimes and American Cancer Society.

The health subsector is huge. While health organizations account for only 13.3 percent of public charities, they represent 61 percent of the nonprofit sector's total expenses and 42 percent of the sector's total assets. The health subsector's revenues in 2005 totaled $672 billion, 88 percent of which came from fees for medical services and goods provided (Wing et al., 2008, 178).

Health services is the most commercialized of the nonprofit subsectors; in other words, many of the organizations are businesslike in deriving most of their revenue from fees charged for services provided. It was one of the first subsectors to become professionalized in its management—that is, to develop large paid professional management staffs rather than depend on volunteers. There are many university programs in health care management and public health, and the salaries of many professional managers in the health subsector, especially in hospitals and large medical centers, are comparable to those in private industry. It is also a field in which nonprofits compete with for-profit firms to a significant extent. In some industries—for example, nursing homes—for-profits have captured the major portion of the market. The health services subsector also has seen the conversion of some nonprofits into for-profit entities, including insurance plans, hospitals, and nursing homes.

Human Service. Human service nonprofits account for almost one third of all public charities, making it the largest subsector if measured by the number of organizations (Wing et al., 2008, p. 142). It includes what many people conventionally think about when the term nonprofit is used—organizations that provide job training, legal aid, housing, youth development, disaster assistance, and food distribution programs (Wing et al., p. 143). But many of these organizations are small; together they represent only 11 percent of the nonprofit sector's total assets and 13 percent of its total expenses (Wing et al., p. 182).

Although many people might consider organizations in these fields as among the most "charitable," they are in fact among the most reliant on government funds, which account for 23 percent of their total revenues (Wing et al., 2008, p. 186). That reflects the devolution and outsourcing of social programs over recent decades, as discussed earlier in this text. This dependence on government funds also makes many human service organizations vulnerable to the social and legal services subsector, the most vulnerable when public policy shifts and government social spending declines. They are also vulnerable, of course, to declines in giving during economic recession, just when the need for their services may be increasing. For this reason, among others, many of the efforts to diversify revenues by developing alternative sources, including business enterprises, have occurred in this subsector. It is also the focus of much of the discussion regarding the need for improved management and accountability in the nonprofit sector as a whole. While there are certainly many volunteers working in human service organizations, there also has been a trend toward more professionalized management of such organizations in recent decades. In many instances, volunteers are managed by staff who have specialized training and skills in the management of volunteer programs.

International and Foreign Affairs. The subsector of international and foreign affairs includes over 5,000 organizations. They encompass those engaged with international exchange programs, international development and relief efforts, international peace and security, and human rights. It is a relatively small subsector, accounting for just 1.9 percent of expenditures by all public charities reporting to the IRS (Wing et al., 2008, p. 188).

Funding Intermediaries. Funding intermediaries are organizations that exist for the sole purpose of directing money to other nonprofits (Salamon, 1999). They are an important category of charitable nonprofits, and they are tax-exempt under Section 501(c)(3). But they are also different from the organizations described in the previous section of this text. With some exceptions, they generally do not themselves operate programs that provide services directly to individuals. Rather, their role is, in a sense, to be like the bankers of the nonprofit sector, channeling private giving to other, service-providing nonprofits. As we will discuss in the next section, some are public charities—for example, United Way, Network for Good, and community foundations. They raise money from the public and then redistribute it to other organizations that serve their local communities. Others are private foundations. These are 501(c)(3) organizations that generally do not operate their own programs but rather make gifts or grants to other nonprofits that do. *Foundations* are created by individuals, companies, and other donors who give money to the foundation, generally earning a tax deduction. The way in which foundations then manage and disburse that money varies, but many retain the original gifts, invest them, and use only the income earned on those investments to make grants to operating nonprofits. However, private foundations differ from other organizations that are tax-exempt under Section 501(c)(3)—they are not *public charities.*

Public Charities and Private Foundations

As we saw in Figure 2.1, there are two different types of nonprofit organizations that are exempt under Section 501(c)(3)—public charities (Box G) and private foundations (Box H). There are technical definitions of these terms established in tax law, but it is sufficient to understand that *public charities,* as the term suggests, are organizations that receive support from a relatively large number of donors or from government, that is, from the public. They include most of the nonprofits discussed in the preceding sections of this chapter. Both public charities that provide direct services, such as hospitals, and funding intermediaries that are public charities, such as United Way, generally spend a significant portion of the gifts they receive each year.

Private foundations, on the other hand, usually have only one or perhaps a few donors—often one person, one company, or the members of a family. For example, the Bill and Melinda Gates Foundation was funded through gifts from Bill and Melinda Gates, and the Ford Foundation was created through gifts from Henry Ford. It is a common misunderstanding to think that the Gates Foundation was created by Microsoft and the Ford Foundation by the Ford Motor Company. In reality, the funds used to establish the Gates Foundation were those belonging to Bill and Melinda Gates personally. Likewise, the Ford Foundation was created by Henry Ford with his personal fortune, not by the Ford Motor Company. There were over 71,000 private foundations in the United States in 2005, an increase of 77 percent from 10 years before (Wing et al., 2008, p. 102). That growth reflects, in part, the economic boom of the late 1990s and mid-2000s, which enabled many wealthy people to create foundations to manage and perpetuate their philanthropy.

Private foundations receive a different tax treatment from that of public charities. One significant difference is that tax deductions allowed to individual donors for gifts to private foundations are more limited than for gifts to public charities. In addition, the investment earnings of private foundations are subject to a tax, and they face a requirement for minimum spending of their investment returns that does not apply to public charities. Indeed, what level of spending should be required of private foundations and what should be included in the definition of that spending have been sources of debate and legislation in recent years. Unlike public charities, private foundations are not permitted to engage in lobbying. Many nonprofit organizations generally prefer to be classified as public charities in order to avoid the limitations and costs that come with being deemed a private foundation. They will take care to assure that their revenues are sufficiently diversified and that their activities are consistent with public charity status, which the IRS may sometimes challenge.

Let's add yet another complication! There are organizations that use the word *foundation* in their name but are in fact public charities. One type, *community foundations,* receives gifts from members of a particular community and makes gifts to support a variety of service-providing nonprofits in that community. Another type of foundation that is a public charity are *institutionally related foundations.* They are the fund-raising arms of their host or parent organizations. They are public charities because they solicit and receive gifts from the public, but, unlike the United Way or community foundations, which make grants to multiple organizations, this type of foundation directs its support to just one organization. Such foundations are commonly associated with public universities. For example, the University of Maryland Foundation raises funds for the state university it serves. Some federal government entities also have affiliated foundations that seek private gifts to supplement the funds that the agency receives through public appropriations. An example of this is the National Park Foundation, a fund-raising entity that supports the National Park Service. And, as in the case of the Sierra Club and The Sierra Club Foundation, there are foundations associated with nonprofit organizations that do not themselves qualify to receive tax-deductible contributions.

To complicate things yet further, there are private foundations that do not make any, or many, grants to other nonprofits and that may not even have the term *foundation* in their names. For example, Colonial Williamsburg, in Virginia, and Longwood Gardens, in Pennsylvania, are legally private foundations, but all their funds are used to support their own programs and operations. They are thus called *operating foundations* and, with some exceptions, are not sources of financial support for other nonprofits. For these organizations, being a private foundation is a matter of status under the tax law and relates to the source of their support, but their operations may be similar to those of nonprofits that are public charities.

We will consider foundations again in Chapter 12 as part of our discussion on fund-raising. Students who are interested in how foundations are managed will find there are many excellent resources including books as well as the websites of the Council on Foundations (www.cof.org), the Forum of Regional Associations of Grantmakers (www.givingforum.org), and Grantmakers for Effective Organizations (www.geofunders.org), among others.

Salamon's Anatomy

We now have discussed two basic ways of differentiating the nonprofit sector: the NTEE and the classifications of organizations under the IRS code. Let's look at a couple of other ways that scholars have divided up the sector. Both the IRS classifications and the NTEE group organizations according to the principal *activities* in which they are engaged. Some people have sought other ways of categorizing nonprofits. A number of scholars have attempted to develop various maps to bring greater clarity to our understanding of the structure of the nonprofit sector along other lines (Gamwell, 1984; Smith, 1991; Sumariwalla, 1983; Van Til, 1988, 2000). Among them is Lester Salamon. In his book *America's Nonprofit Sector* (1999), Salamon divides the universe of U.S. nonprofits into two broad categories, member serving and public serving, and then defines various subcategories on each side of that divide—a design he calls the "anatomy" of the nonprofit sector (p. 22).

As the term implies, *member-serving organizations* exist primarily to secure benefits for the people who belong to them or who support them through dues, membership fees, or other contributions. They include, for example, social and fraternal organizations, business and professional associations, and labor unions. In general, their sources of support and the beneficiaries of their programs are one and the same, although society may benefit indirectly—such as through the improvement of skills among members of a profession that serves the public's needs. These organizations are tax-exempt but not eligible to receive tax-deductible gifts. They are not charitable organizations (although some may have affiliated charitable foundations). Salamon's (1999) examples of *public-serving organizations* include churches, the charitable and social welfare organizations we have discussed, as well as foundations and other funding intermediaries.[4]

Salamon's Anatomy (Salamon, 1999) provides another useful way to think about the nonprofit sector, classifying nonprofit organizations, not by the nature of their activities, like the IRS or the NTEE, but rather by who receives the principal benefit of those activities. However, while it adds clarity in certain respects, it also raises questions. For example, Salamon puts churches in the public-serving category. They surely are tax-exempt and eligible to receive tax-deductible contributions—they are 501(c)(3) organizations, but it seems possible that their activities might more directly serve their own members than the general public. He classifies political parties as member-serving organizations. It is true that they are *not* 501(c)(3) organizations under the tax code. But it isn't clear exactly what benefits their members derive from their affiliation (Anheier, 2005, p. 64). Despite its weaknesses, Salamon's Anatomy has contributed to the vocabulary of the nonprofit field, and it is not unusual to hear people refer to organizations as "member serving" or "public serving."

The Spectrum of Organizations

So far, we have looked at ways of differentiating nonprofit organizations according to their purposes and activities (the IRS classifications and the NTEE), according to who benefits from their activities (Salamon's [1999] member-serving and public-serving categories), and according to their sources of support (public charities and private foundations). Yet another way to differentiate nonprofits is according to the degree to which they are commercialized—that is, the extent to which they operate like businesses.

In their 2001 book, *Enterprising Nonprofits: A Toolkit for Social Entrepreneurs,* Dees et al. (2001) depict a spectrum of nonprofit organizations (which they call "social enterprises"; see Table 2.1). Each endpoint of the spectrum represents an extreme—that is, a pure example of two alternate conditions. The spectrum encompasses every possible point in between. In Dees et al.'s spectrum, the two extremes are organizations that are "purely philanthropic" and those that are "purely commercial," defined by their "general motives, methods, and goals" and their relationships with their key stakeholders (p. 15). In other words, we might think of those at the left endpoint of the spectrum as the most nonprofit-like and those at the right endpoint as the most businesslike. In between, at various points along the spectrum between the two extremes, are most nonprofit organizations today.

Let's walk through Dees et al.'s (2001) spectrum, thinking about three organizations, including two we saw on our hypothetical tour of Washington, D.C.—Miriam's Kitchen and The George Washington University—and a third that is familiar to all of us, Microsoft Corporation. Even Miriam's, which is close to what most people would think of as a purely philanthropic nonprofit and thus somewhere close to the left end of the spectrum, is not entirely pure according to Dees et al.'s criteria because it does employ paid staff. But it is close enough to serve as an example for our discussion. Microsoft, most would agree, is close to a pure example of a commercial organization, at the right end of the spectrum. The George Washington University is somewhere in between—in Dees et al.'s terminology, it is a hybrid that is somewhat nonprofit-like and somewhat like a business. This is true of most private colleges and universities and, in some ways, increasingly true of public universities as well.

TABLE 2.1 ■ The Social Enterprise Spectrum			
	Continuum of Options		
	Purely Philanthropic	**Hybrid**	**Purely Commercial**
General motives, methods, and goals:			
	Appeal to goodwill	Appeal to mixed motives	Appeal to self-interest
	Mission driven	Balance of mission and market	Market driven
	Goal is social value creation	Goal is social and economic value creation	Goal is economic value creation
Key stakeholders:			
Beneficiaries	Pay nothing	Pay subsidized rates and/or a mix of full payers and those who pay nothing	Pay full market rates
Providers of capital	Make gifts and grants	Provide below-market capital and/or a mix of below-market capital, market-rate capital, and gifts	Charge market rates
Workforce	Volunteers	Accept below-market wages and/or a mix of volunteers and paid staff	Receive market-rate compensation
Suppliers	Make in-kind gifts	Provide special discounts and/or a mix of full price, discounts, and in-kind gifts	Charge market prices

Source: Adapted from Dees et al. (2001, p. 15). Used with permission of John Wiley & Sons, Inc.

What characterizes organizations that are purely philanthropic? As Dees et al.'s (2001) chart indicates, such organizations *appeal to goodwill* rather than *self-interest*. People engage with Miriam's Kitchen because they hold compassion and concern for homeless individuals. But few would buy the Windows operating system because Microsoft needs the money! What about universities? They appeal to *mixed motives*. People do feel altruistic about universities; that's why many alumni continue to make gifts long after they have graduated. But, for most students, attendance at a university is also a practical investment. Although some may value learning for its own sake, most are likely motivated to study at least in part by self-interest—that is, an interest in their own financial and career futures.

Philanthropic organizations are *mission driven*. If they are purely philanthropic, then, at least theoretically, they pursue the mission without any regard for the financial bottom line. Although this image may comport with the stereotype that some may hold of nonprofits as organizations run by dedicated volunteers unconcerned with money, an example of that purest form would be somewhat difficult to find in today's nonprofit world, for many of the reasons we already have discussed. On the other hand, Microsoft is unlikely to produce software that nobody wants to buy, regardless of what social value it might serve—it is, like all businesses, *market driven*. What about a university? Again, most are mixed, *balancing commitment to a mission with responsiveness to the market*. A university may continue to offer academic programs or to support research efforts that are not profitable, indeed, that even require a subsidy, because they are important to its educational mission. But most universities also respond to the market, developing new programs and expanding others that are attracting increased student interest.

Philanthropic organizations are concerned with creating *social value*—that is, with improving the lives of individuals and their communities; they are not about making money for its own sake. In contrast, as we have discussed before, the principal goal of a business is to create *economic value*—in other words, to generate profits and increase its owners' wealth. Again, the hybrids that Dees et al. (2001) define pay almost equal attention to both components of the double bottom line, focusing on the creation of *both social and economic value,* or in the words of Bill Shore (1999), they are "doing good by doing well."

Let's look at our three sample organizations' relationships with some of their key stakeholders—their beneficiaries (clients), those who provide them with capital funds; their workforce; and their suppliers. At purely philanthropic organizations, clients *pay nothing* for the services they receive, like the hundreds of homeless men and women who are served by Miriam's Kitchen. On the other end of the spectrum, people generally pay for their Microsoft software at whatever *market price* prevails. And hybrids? Let's consider a typical undergraduate classroom in a private university. Some students will be attending on full scholarships—they pay nothing in the way of tuition. Others, from more affluent families, may be paying the full tuition price listed in the university bulletin, while still others will be paying some portion of the listed tuition with scholarships to cover the rest. This is typical of hybrid nonprofits, including universities and hospitals, which often serve a *mix of full payers and subsidized clients*.

If Miriam's needs capital to expand or meet special organizational needs, it will obtain it through fund-raising for *gifts* or *grants*. Microsoft will issue new stock or borrow money, paying the full *market rate* of interest. Hybrids often mix these methods; for example, a university may have a campaign to raise capital dollars through gifts but may also borrow funds for the construction of new buildings. Nonprofits sometimes can borrow at *less than the market rate of interest,* although some will also borrow at the going market rate.

The purely philanthropic workforce is composed entirely of *volunteers*. As we have discussed, this is the case for some small nonprofits, although many (including Miriam's Kitchen) have paid staff members in addition to a substantial volunteer workforce—they are not, in Dees

nonprofit organizations are behaving as hybrids, this new organizational form creates an entity that is indeed a hybrid under the law. Its emergence may represent the beginning of a fourth sector such as Sabeti (2009) describes, but as of the time of this writing, the L3C is still a new development that cannot be fully evaluated (Williams, 2009).

Commercialization of nonprofits is a source of controversy. Some observers consider the increasing use of business methods in nonprofits and their efforts to develop streams of earned income to be desired, reducing their dependence on government and on gifts and increasing their effectiveness. In his influential 1999 book, *The Cathedral Within,* Bill Shore writes that nonprofits "forfeited the marketplace long ago, simply walked off the field . . . and chose instead to settle for the crumbs instead of the cake" (p. 205). He argues that nonprofits should begin businesses that generate revenue as a way to gain independence from philanthropic giving and government funds. "Redistributing wealth is not going to be enough," Shore says. "Creating new [economic] wealth is the only course for nonprofits and community-based organizations struggling to meet social needs" (p. 208). Shore is the founder of the nonprofit Share Our Strength, an antihunger organization based in Washington, D.C. Consistent with his own advice, he also created Community Wealth Ventures, a for-profit subsidiary of Share Our Strength. Community Wealth Ventures earns revenue by advising nonprofits on how to start revenue-producing businesses and directs its profits to help support Share Our Strength's programs.

However, others express concern that the increasing commercialization of the nonprofit sector may eventually lead some organizations to put profit ahead of their social missions. For example, Burton Weisbrod (2004), an economist who was a pioneer in studying the nonprofit sector, cites the YMCA, which he says has "morphed into a health-and-fitness goliath" (p. 40). Observing the YMCA's increasing presence in upscale neighborhoods, where it competes with for-profit health clubs, Weisbrod questions whether it has strayed from its traditional mission of serving low-income families and asks "whether it has become overly commercialized and whether it [even] deserves tax-exempt status" (p. 43). He advocates policies to limit the commercial activity of nonprofits while creating stronger tax incentives to encourage traditional charitable and philanthropic giving. Thus, the issue of commercialization is more than philosophical; it has implications for the continued tax-exempt status of some nonprofits. We will revisit some of these issues again in Chapter 12, when we discuss nonprofit earned-income strategies, and in Chapter 16, where we will consider social entrepreneurship.

Commercialization and Tax Exemption

A companion to the common misunderstanding that nonprofit organizations cannot earn profits is the idea that nonprofits are *always* exempt from taxation. They are exempt from income taxation on revenues related to *exempt activities,* that is, activities that directly address their social missions. But revenues from activities that are not related to the mission are subject to the *unrelated business income tax* (UBIT). An activity is unrelated and subject to this tax if it meets three requirements: (1) It is a trade or business, as defined by the IRS; (2) it is regularly carried on; and (3) it is not substantially related to the exempt purpose of the organization. The definition of "substantially related" is provided by the IRS (2005a) with characteristic clarity:

> To determine if a business activity is "substantially related" requires examining the relationship between the activities that generate income and the accomplishment of the organization's exempt purpose. Trade or business is related to exempt purposes, in the

statutory sense, only when the conduct of the business activities has causal relationship to achieving exempt purposes (other than through the production of income). The causal relationship must be substantial. The activities that generate the income must contribute importantly to accomplishing the organization's exempt purposes to be substantially related. (n.p.)

Activities carried out by volunteers; a trade or business carried out for what the IRS calls the "convenience" of clients or members; and sales of donated merchandise, for example, in a thrift shop, are specifically excluded from UBIT. So, for example, universities are not taxed on revenue from dining halls or other food operations since these services are provided for the convenience of students (although it may surprise students to learn this). Similarly, a university parking garage used exclusively by students and faculty would not generate unrelated business income—it is there for convenience and is related to the educational mission. But a garage open to the general public might not meet that test in the view of the IRS.

Most business activities undertaken by nonprofits are related to the mission, and the revenues generated are therefore not taxable. For example, a nonprofit that develops a business to employ individuals with disabilities is serving its mission of providing job training and rehabilitation, even though the services it provides may generate substantial revenue and even compete with the services provided by for-profit companies. But the line is not always clear. For example, one area of dispute has been gift shops operated by museums. If an art museum gift shop sells products that include reproductions of paintings in its exhibits, that could be related to its mission of educating and informing the public about art. But sales of products that are not related to the museum's collections might be regarded as unrelated and subject to the UBIT (IRS, 2005b).

One concern is that unrelated business activities could become a substantial part of the organization's activities. If they do—in general, if the amount of the nonprofit's time and resources devoted to the business activity exceeds that devoted to its mission (generally more than 50 percent of activities)—the nonprofit would be in danger of having its tax exemption revoked. The issue of related and unrelated income is far from settled and is often an area of dispute between nonprofits and the IRS. In subsectors where commercialization has advanced the most—for example, health services—the tax exemption of institutions is a topic of continuing political debate. In other words, as a nonprofit becomes more like a commercial enterprise, moving as it were from left to right across Dees et al.'s (2001) spectrum, there could come a point at which it will be deemed to have crossed over the line, ceasing to be a nonprofit at all.

Implications for Nonprofit Managers

What are the implications of increasing commercialization, the blurring of the sectors, the emergence of new legal forms, and related policy debates for the practice of nonprofit management? Today's nonprofit sector requires that managers be somewhat hybrids themselves. They must combine a commitment to their organization's nonprofit mission with business skills, to manage the double bottom line. They must hold an appreciation for the nonprofit sector's unique history and traditions while also understanding how to succeed in a competitive marketplace. They must be able to adapt to the social and political forces affecting their organizations while also preserving the core values and defending the special status of their organizations. In other words, as was said in the introduction to this book, nonprofit management requires a unique blend of skills, distinguishing it from management in government or the for-profit sector. Current trends suggest that the task will not become less challenging in the years ahead.

Chapter Summary

America's nonprofit sector is large and diverse. Its roots lie in the ancient traditions of charity, philanthropy, and voluntarism; voluntary efforts were prominent in the nation's early days. But the sector's modern form is a product of 20th-century history and especially the period since the 1970s. Although *nonprofit organization* and *nonprofit sector* are the terms most commonly used, others have proposed a variety of alternative names for the sector.

The nonprofit sector is growing steadily and includes about 1.9 million organizations. These organizations may be placed in categories according to the tax-exempt classifications used by the IRS or the more elaborated categories of the NTEE, both of which determine categories based on organizations' principal activities. Most organizations registered with the IRS fall into two classifications. "Charitable nonprofits" are both exempt from taxation under Section 501(c)(3) of the IRC and also eligible to receive tax-deductible gifts from individuals and other donors. Social welfare organizations (often called advocacy organizations) are tax-exempt under Section 501(c)(4), but gifts to them are not tax deductible because they are not limited in their expenditures on lobbying activities.

Religious congregations are charitable nonprofits under Section 501(c)(3), but they are unique in being protected by the U.S. Constitution and are not required to register with the IRS. Leaving aside religious congregations, the charitable nonprofits are dominated by the subsectors of arts, culture, and humanities; education; environment and animals; health; human service; and international and foreign affairs. These subsectors show significant differences in their sources of revenue and the extent to which their management has been professionalized. Also important are funding intermediaries, which generally do not operate programs but rather receive gifts that are directed to other nonprofit organizations. They include public charities, such as the United Way, and private foundations. Private foundations are charitable nonprofits, but they are not public charities and thus are subject to different rules under the tax code. There are public charities that use the term *foundation* in their name, but they are not classified as private foundations because they raise money from multiple sources.

In addition to the NTEE and IRS classifications, nonprofits may be defined as member-serving or public-serving. Another way to classify organizations is on a spectrum defining the extent to which they are purely philanthropic or purely commercial.

Many nonprofits today are said to be hybrids. They are not purely philanthropic or purely commercial but fall somewhere between those two extreme cases. This is because they demonstrate a mixture of philanthropic and commercial motives, methods, and goals, and their relationships with their stakeholders demonstrate a mix of philanthropic and business characteristics. Many nonprofits have become more commercial at the same time that some businesses are expressing more concern about social goals. Some see the emergence of hybrid organizations as the beginning of a fourth sector alongside government, business, and traditional nonprofits. The low-profit, limited liability company (L3C) is a legal form of organization created in several states that may mark the beginning of such a fourth sector. Blurring of the sectors pleases some and concerns others, who fear that nonprofits will drift away from their social missions. In this environment, nonprofit management requires a unique combination of commitment, knowledge, and skills.

Notes

1. The terms *nonprofit* and *tax-exempt* are not strictly synonymous, since there are some for-profit entities—for example, certain partnerships—that are also not required to pay income tax, and there are organizations that are required to pay taxes but do not distribute profits to owners (Hopkins, 2005, p. 30).

2. It is a fine but important distinction to understand that the IRS does not "grant" tax exemption to nonprofit organizations. If they meet appropriate criteria, they *are* tax-exempt under the law. The IRS merely "recognizes" that status conferred by the law (Hopkins, 2005).

3. There is a distinction between churches, synagogues, and mosques and nonprofit organizations that are faith-based but provide social services to their communities without regard to religious affiliation.

4. Although we do not focus on member-serving organizations in this book, students who are interested will find a rich array of resources, including those available through the American Society of Association Executives (www.asaenet.org), a professional association comprising trade and professional association managers, based in Washington, D.C.

KEY TERMS AND CONCEPTS

advocacy organizations

charitable choice

charitable nonprofits

charity

civil society

faith-based organizations

hybrid organization

Independent Sector

institutionally related foundations

low-profit, limited liability company (L3C)

member-serving organizations

National Taxonomy of Exempt Entities (NTEE)

nongovernmental organizations

operating foundations

philanthropy

private foundation

public charity

public-serving organizations

social enterprise

social welfare organizations

supporting organization

tax deductible

tax-exempt

unrelated business income tax

voluntarism

QUESTIONS FOR DISCUSSION

1. If you had $25 to give today to any nonprofit organization, which one would it be? Now, imagine that you are 75 years old and have $1,000,000 to give to an organization at the event of your death—that is, through your will. Which one would it be? Do your answers reflect a difference between charity and philanthropy?

2. If you were the president of a private college or university, what things would you consider in making a decision on a possible tuition increase, which might enhance your bottom line but possibly work against your mission of providing educational opportunity?

3. Should gifts made by individuals to a nonprofit organization that receives the largest portion of its revenues from fees for services be fully tax deductible, partially tax deductible, or not deductible at all? Explain your answer.

4. Suppose a nonprofit organization operates a business that is related to its mission, such that revenue is not subject to the UBIT, but it competes directly with a for-profit business nearby

that must pay taxes. (Think of the nonprofit jazz club HR-57, which exists on the same street as for-profit bars and clubs.) Is that unfair competition with the for-profit businesses? And should the nonprofit be taxed just to level the playing field? Why or why not?

SUGGESTIONS FOR FURTHER READING

Books

Hammack, D. C. (1998). *Making the nonprofit sector in the United States.* Bloomington: Indiana University Press.

O'Neill, M. (2002). *Nonprofit nation: A new look at the third America.* San Francisco: Jossey-Bass.

Ott, J. S. (2001). *The nature of the nonprofit sector.* Boulder, CO: Westview Press.

Powell, W. W., & Steinberg, R. (2006). *The nonprofit sector: A research handbook* (2nd ed.). New Haven, CT: Yale University Press.

Salamon, L. M. (1999). *America's nonprofit sector: A primer* (2nd ed.). New York: Foundation Center.

Salamon, L. M. (2002). *The state of nonprofit America.* Washington, DC: Brookings Institution.

Websites

Alliance for Nonprofit Management, http://www.allianceonline.org/

Aspen Institute Program on Philanthropy and Social Innovation, http://www.aspeninstitute.org/policy-work/nonprofit-philanthropy

Council on Foundations, http://www.cof.org/

Independent Sector, http://www.independentsector.org/

Urban Institute Center on Nonprofits and Philanthropy, http://www.urban.org/center/cnp/index.cfm

Chapter Outline

chapter 3

The freedoms of speech, religion, assembly, and petition, enshrined in the First Amendment to the U.S. Constitution, have supported voluntary action by nonprofit organizations on issues such as civil rights, women's rights, and the environment. Nonprofits often have focused public attention and helped create changes in social attitudes that paved the way for eventual legislative action.

© iStockphoto.com /Leif Norman

Theories of the Nonprofit Sector and Nonprofit Organizations

3

I n this chapter, we will discuss some theoretical views of the nonprofit sector and nonprofit organizations, as a foundation for consideration of more applied management topics in later chapters. We will first examine some macro theories advanced by scholars from various disciplines. These theories attempt to explain the nonprofit sector as a whole, addressing questions such as why the nonprofit sector exists at all in the United States; what role it plays in American society; and what relationship it has to the other two sectors, private business and government. In the second section of the chapter, we will consider some micro theories—that is, theories that attempt to explain nonprofit organizations as individual units. These will include concepts drawn from organizational theory that help explain why nonprofit organizations look and behave the way they do, how they make decisions, and how they are different from both public and for-profit organizations.

Explaining the Nonprofit Sector

Theories that seek to explain America's nonprofit sector have been developed by economists, sociologists, historians, political scientists, psychologists, social psychologists, anthropologists, and scholars in other disciplines. As we will discuss, some theories are at odds with others, and each theory has its advocates as well as critics.

Nonprofit Theory Across the Disciplines

Historians explain the existence of America's nonprofit sector as largely a result of historical forces and events. As noted in Chapter 2, the growth of America's nonprofit sector closely parallels the development of the nation itself. The nation was founded in rebellion against the authority of the British monarch, and skepticism toward government is deeply imbedded in

American political attitudes. Moreover, many American towns and cities developed before local governments did, and vital services often were provided by voluntary associations, including volunteer fire departments, libraries, schools, and hospitals. In the small towns of early America, people came together to meet common needs and provide for the poor, their voluntarism often reflecting religious convictions. Religion played an important role in colonial America, and missionary and charitable organizations were often founded by a religious congregation. The freedoms of speech, religion, assembly, and petition, enshrined in the First Amendment to the U.S. Constitution, also have created a hospitable environment for voluntary action throughout the nation's history, especially for organizations seeking social change. For example, the civil rights and women's rights movements focused public attention on injustices and helped create changes in social attitudes that paved the way for legislative action. Nonprofits have taken the lead in raising environmental concerns that are now receiving attention from governments and international agencies around the world.

As the nation grew, movements such as urbanization, industrialization, and immigration increased the need for nonprofit organizations to serve diverse populations. The evolution of U.S. law further supported the growth of the nonprofit sector. The income tax was introduced in 1913, and Congress approved tax deductibility for gifts to certain nonprofits 4 years later (Ott, 2001, p. 144). Changes in public policy, including the expansion of government social programs in the 1960s and 1970s and their reduction and devolvement in the 1980s and 1990s, also have shaped today's nonprofit sector. In sum, historians explain today's nonprofit sector as a consequence of America's unique past, critical historical movements and events, and policies that tended to reinforce the sector's development and growth.

Theories advanced by sociologists, which focus on relationships between and among people in groups, also offer important insights on the nonprofit sector. Sociologists' theories describe how involvement in nonprofits helps socialize individuals, reinforce norms and values, and develop "social capital," creating "interpersonal bonds of trust and cooperation and counteracting loneliness and isolation" (O'Neill, 2002, p. 42). Their theories emphasize "the roles of community networks of individuals, groups, and organizations; niches; and the importance of community elites and influentials for nonprofits" (Ott, 2001, p. 233). Sociologists discuss nonprofits as mediating structures, operating as buffers between individuals and the larger institutions of government and business. Berger and Neuhaus, in their prominent book *To Empower People: The Role of Mediating Structures in Public Policy* (1977), argued that in our complex society, people need organizations like nonprofits to provide such interfaces. Their thinking was cited by some as one justification for the Reagan administration's efforts to devolve social programs to state and local governments and nonprofits during the 1980s.

Political scientists have looked at nonprofit organizations with respect to their role in supporting democratic traditions and in terms of power relationships between citizens and government. They have identified four major functions that nonprofits perform in relation to government:

1. *Accommodate diversity:* Nonprofits give voice to groups with differing values, beliefs, and practices that cannot be fully accommodated within government, with its obligation to treat all citizens equally.

2. *Undertake experimentation:* Nonprofits can undertake research and development (or "R&D") for social programs. In other words, nonprofits can begin new programs on a smaller scale and incur greater risk than government can with public funds. New programs developed by nonprofits that prove to be successful then may provide models and eventually be incorporated into larger government efforts.

3. *Provide freedom from bureaucracy:* Nonprofits may be able to respond more efficiently and quickly to new needs because they do not have the large bureaucracies that characterize government.

4. *Attention to minority needs:* Government's priorities must be consistent with those of the majority of voters. There may not be political support for programs to meet the needs of minority groups that do not possess sufficient political power. Nonprofits fill such gaps created by political realities (Douglas 1983, 1987).

Economists have made significant contributions to theories of the nonprofit sector, but as Ott (2001) notes, "Nonprofit organizations provide an interesting challenge for mainstream economic theory" (p. 181). Economists analyze the working of markets in terms of the variables of supply and demand and based on certain assumptions about human nature that nonprofits, at least on the surface of things, would seem to defy. How can we explain labor markets in which people work without compensation or the seemingly irrational act of giving away one's money?

The Failure Theories

Because some readers may be more familiar with the science of economics than others, let's define a few terms before we discuss economic theories of the nonprofit sector. Some key concepts include *private goods, public goods, externalities,* and *free riders.*

By *goods,* economists mean what we conventionally think of as goods—that is, products that are *things*—but they also include services and intangible benefits, such as our enjoyment of a symphony, the knowledge we acquire through education, and the solace we may gain from participation in religious services.

Working on the principle of supply and demand, the market is an efficient mechanism for regulating the production and distribution of what are called private goods—that is, products or services that we buy and consume as individuals, with no significant impact on others. These would include, for example, the clothing and food that we buy and consume, as well as the services that we personally receive, such as haircuts or personal training sessions at a health club. With a private good, the person who pays also gains the full benefit of the good. Unless you choose to lend your friend your shirt or share your fries, enjoyment of the good is all yours, and society is not significantly affected by your consumption of it. The market works well for private goods, because we as consumers vote with our dollars. In other words, we buy the products we like and allow others to sit on the shelves; ultimately, the latter will disappear from the market. The market thus determines—very efficiently and effectively—what private goods are produced and who consumes them.

But some goods have what economists call *externalities:* Very simply, their consumption affects other people, either negatively or positively. For example, your new barbeque grill may bring great pleasure to you and your cookout guests, but its smoke may annoy your neighbors. The smoke is a negative externality. On the other hand, if you beautify your yard, the shrubs and flowers you purchase and plant may create a positive externality for your neighbors—an improved neighborhood and perhaps enhanced property values.

Some goods create so many positive externalities that it is not possible to confine the benefits to an individual purchaser. For example, if you were to hire a private contractor to pave your street, your neighbors also would benefit from a smoother ride but without paying for it. You would be paying the *full costs* of such improvement, even though your neighbors would benefit as well. In other words, there would be a disconnect between the cost that you would incur and the portion of the benefit you would receive. Your neighbors might say "thanks," but you might perceive the situation as unfair.

In situations like that—the privately funded street paving—those who benefit without paying are known as *free riders*. They benefit from your expenditure at no cost to them—you are paying the fare, and they are just riding along for free! Who would be willing to spend his or her resources under such circumstances? Well, just about nobody, so the market is not a very good mechanism for ensuring that such goods will be produced at all. Therefore, when there is a potential problem with free riders, we as a society may decide that the good should be provided by government; in other words, we treat it as a public good. This is clearly a fairer way to provide public goods than leaving their production to the market. In this way, because everyone (or a large group of people) benefits, everyone is forced to pay for these goods through the tax system.

To sum it up, then, if the purchaser is able to capture all the externalities, it makes sense to have a product provided through the free market—to treat it as a private good. But if the externalities are so great that the good also will benefit many others who do not pay—the free riders—then the market is unlikely to provide it, and it should be provided as a public good.

Market and Government Failure

One problem is that, in some situations, the market does not work effectively or efficiently. Economists call this *market failure* (Hansmann, 1987; Weisbrod, 1975, 1988). There are various reasons why the market may fail. For example, there may be a type of market failure that economists call *contract failure,* essentially a breakdown in the ideal or typical relationship between a buyer and a seller. This may occur when there is *information asymmetry,* meaning a situation in which the seller has more information about the product than does the purchaser, undermining the economic assumption that exchanges occur with complete knowledge on both sides of the deal.

Information asymmetry might be especially likely to occur in the case of complex or intangible products. For example, it is difficult for a person to judge the actual quality of the education or medical care he or she is receiving (Young, 2001a, p. 193). Moreover, in some cases, the purchaser may actually be a different person from the one who is receiving the service—for example, parents who pay the tuition fees for their children's college education or adult children who pay for parents' nursing home care. In these instances, it may be difficult for the purchaser to obtain accurate information, even from the consumer, about the actual quality of the good or service being provided. The market also does not work well for people who are poor or belong to groups that face discrimination, since they may not have the resources with which to purchase what they need or may face other barriers.

In situations where the market does not work, government often steps in to fill the gap. But there also may be *government failure*. This is not meant to imply that government is incompetent, but rather that there are political, structural, and systemic reasons that may prevent the government from filling the gaps left by the private market.

Among those reasons is the fact that government must by its nature respond to the needs and demands of the majority. Weisbrod (1975, 1988), who is credited with introducing the "public goods theory" of nonprofits, discusses the concepts of "demand heterogeneity" and the "median voter." In the simplest terms, *demand heterogeneity* means that in a diverse society such as the United States, there may not be universal agreement about what goods and services government should provide. Various groups may want different kinds or different amounts of some goods. The *median voter,* that is, one of the typical voters who comprise the largest single bloc, may not support some of the governmental activity that other groups may favor.

Government may be unable to provide services that some may desire but that are politically controversial—for example, family planning services for poor women. Or the problem may not yet be recognized as relevant to the majority—as, for example, AIDS in the first years of the pandemic in the early 1980s—and thus not command the attention of government.

Government also might fail to fill the gaps left by the private market because the time horizon of elected officials is often short; they need to focus on issues of current concern to the electorate and on policies that can show progress within their terms in office. They may not be able to find political support for undertaking solutions to problems or issues that require many years to come to fruition. For example, some people do not accept the idea of global warming, and others do not think much about it because its most serious implications seem far in the future. It is not a problem that the market can easily address, and while public awareness of the problem is growing, until quite recently there has not been a political consensus for strong government action and the subject remains controversial.

Finally, government agencies are of necessity often large and bureaucratic; as a result, they may not have complete information, especially on local problems, and their size may make it difficult to undertake quick action. Their perceived bureaucracy also may inhibit individuals from interacting with them, thus limiting government's ability to meet needs and leaving gaps that are unaddressed by either the market or government. Who can fill such gaps?

Nonprofits as Gap Fillers

In the context of the failures theories, nonprofit organizations are essentially gap fillers—they fill the gaps left by market failure and government failure, providing the goods and services that the other two sectors, for whatever reasons, could not.

For example, maybe the market has failed because of information asymmetry: Individuals just do not have complete information or lack the ability to understand or judge the quality of the good they seek to purchase. In such circumstances, they may choose to receive services from a nonprofit. Students may choose to enroll at a nonprofit (or state) university rather than a for-profit school. Adult children may prefer to entrust their aging parents' care to a church-sponsored nursing home rather than one operated by a for-profit company. They may do so because they believe that the non-distribution constraint removes the motive to exploit consumers, because they believe that nonprofit leaders are driven more by altruistic motivations than are for-profit managers, or because they do not trust for-profit providers for some other reason. This thinking, known as the "trust theory" of nonprofits, has been developed over the past three decades by various scholars, including Hansmann (1987), who is often credited for it.

As we have noted, sometimes government is simply too constrained by its size and complexity to respond quickly, especially in situations that may affect only a small group of people or a single community. For example, while the federal or state governments may respond to major disasters, nonprofit relief organizations like the Red Cross or Salvation Army may be more nimble in responding to the needs of victims in smaller, local disasters, such as an individual house fire or local flooding (Salamon, 2001, p. 164).

Nonprofit organizations also provide a buffer between individuals and large government agencies, which people may find difficult to access. For example, organizations that serve immigrants, the mentally ill, and the homeless help them to access government programs that may provide benefits—a task that some would find daunting on their own (Young, 2001b, p. 190).

In essence, the failure theories' explanation of the existence of nonprofits is parallel to the vocabulary issue we discussed in Chapter 2. Just as the term *nonprofit* connotes what such organizations are *not,* the failure theories explain their role by what others *do not do;* that is, nonprofits serve needs that the private market and government, for various reasons, do not meet. Although they enjoy wide support, the failure theories leave unanswered questions: How do we explain industries in which both nonprofits and government provide services (e.g., education)? Or in which nonprofits and for-profits compete side-by-side (e.g., in health care)? Moreover, some critics dismiss the failure theories as missing the unique and positive realities of nonprofit values, motivations, and contributions to society (Ott, 2001, p. 185). For example, Lohmann (1992), whose theory we will soon discuss, mentions activities such as worship, contemplation, help, inquiry, self-expression, and other purposes served by the nonprofit sector, arguing that "any theory of economics that reduces [such] goods to the basic categories of production, consumption, and exchange is reductionist and misleading" (p. 62).

Supply-Side Theories

Before we conclude our discussion of economic theories, it is important to consider other approaches that go beyond the failure theories and explain the existence of the nonprofit sector based on supply-side forces. In economics, a *supply-side* theory explains events based on the motivations of and incentives given to those who produce a good or a service rather than on the motivations of those who have the capability and desire to consume it—which constitute "demand." In other words, supply-side theories look at the *push* side of the market rather than the *pull.*

Supply-side nonprofit theorists observe that many nonprofits are, either currently or historically, outgrowths of religious congregations, motivated by faith rather than primarily economic incentives. Thus, we cannot explain them by market forces alone; rather, we need to consider what is known as the *entrepreneurship* theory of the nonprofit sector. This theory attributes the existence of nonprofit organizations to the vision and initiative of individuals who have created and built them. Such individuals are often motivated by religious zeal or strong secular values of idealism and social justice (James, 1987; Rose-Ackerman, 1996; Young, 1983).

The entrepreneurship theory is implicit in the writing of a number of contemporary authors who gained attention in the 1990s and 2000s. For example, Dees et al. (2001) write that

> social entrepreneurs . . . are the reformers and revolutionaries of society today. They make fundamental changes in the way that things are done in the social sector. Their visions are bold. They seek out opportunities to improve society, and they take action. (p. 5)

The Ashoka Foundation (2005), which provides support for promising social entrepreneurs around the world, also points to the power of such individuals to lead fundamental change:

> Identifying and solving large-scale social problems requires a social entrepreneur because only the entrepreneur has the committed vision and inexhaustible determination to persist until they have transformed an entire system. The scholar comes to rest when he expresses an idea. The professional succeeds when she solves a client's problem. The manager calls it quits when he has enabled his organization to succeed. Social entrepreneurs go beyond the immediate problem to fundamentally change communities, societies, the world. (n.p.)

Supply-side explanations complement the theories of market and government failure by defining nonprofits as more than gap fillers. They suggest that nonprofits exist not just to pick up the pieces left behind by the market and government, but also as organizations different from business and government that are driven by vision and values. We will return to a more detailed discussion of social entrepreneurship in Chapter 16 of this text.

Theories of Altruism and Giving

Some scholars offer theories to explain the nonprofit sector based on the motivations underlying altruism and philanthropic giving. We consider them at this point in the text because their perspective is similar to that of the supply-side economic theorists. That is, they focus not on those who consume the goods and services that nonprofits provide (the demand side), but rather on those who supply the funds to support the work of nonprofits. Theories related to altruistic behavior and giving predate the nonprofit theories of economists and continue to be a focus of scholars. They are drawn from the work of philosophers, theologians, and legal scholars as well as psychologists, social psychologists, and other social scientists.

The following are some of the questions raised by theorists who focus on charitable and philanthropic giving: Do people really make gifts based on altruism, or is philanthropy merely a tool used by the wealthy to exert control over society? And what influence do tax benefits play in the motivation of individuals to make gifts? In other words, is charitable and philanthropic giving always motivated by ideals, or do donors also expect to receive some benefits for themselves?

Kathleen Kelly in her 1998 book, *Effective Fund-Raising Management*, which includes a review of the research literature around these questions (pp. 44–45), joins those who conclude that donors have mixed motives (Jeavons, 1991; Martin, 1994, cited in Kelly, 1998, pp. 44–45; Payton, 1991; Van Til, 1988). These theorists find that altruism plays a role in giving, but so does self-interest. Kelly concludes that "donors hold interests both in self and in a common good" and that giving is a "social exchange," in which donors give money in exchange for positive feelings, influence, recognition, and tax benefits, among other rewards. Regarding the importance of tax incentives, Kelly argues that "the tax deductibility of gifts is vital to sustaining America's philanthropic tradition" (p. 48).

But in a controversial 2001 article, the sociologists Paul Schervish and John Havens deemphasize the importance of financial incentives to giving. They describe a "new physics of philanthropy," arguing that donors are motivated by six "supply-side inclinations": (1) *hyperagency,* or "the enhanced capacity of wealthy individuals to establish or substantially control the conditions under which they and others live"; (2) *identification,* that is, a donor's empathy with the needs of others; (3) *association,* meaning donors' participation in activities that bring them into contact with people in need, leading them to identify with those individuals and their needs; (4) contemplation of their own *death,* guiding them perhaps to a desire to leave some legacy behind; (5) *gratitude* for the benefits they have received and a desire to give back to society; and (6) *tax aversion,* the desire to minimize their taxes through the deductions they earn for their charitable gifts (pp. 225–229).

Schervish and Havens (2001) argue that for these reasons, or some combination of them, individuals are "inclined" to be philanthropic. They do not need to be cajoled or scolded into giving, nor are self-interested motivations paramount. Although these authors acknowledge the desire to avoid taxes as one motivator for making gifts, they argue—and this is a controversial conclusion—that repeal of the estate tax "will not negatively affect charitable giving and may even prove to be a boon for philanthropy" (p. 234). This position is at odds with Kelly's (1998) and with the findings of most economists who have studied the relationship between taxes and giving.

We will consider the question of donor motivations again in Chapter 12 of this volume.

Theory of the Commons: An Interdisciplinary Approach

Roger Lohmann's *The Commons,* published in 1992, presents an interdisciplinary theory of the nonprofit sector that offers a different perspective and introduces some new vocabulary with which to discuss the sector. Lohmann challenges the economists' failure theories directly.

Lohmann (1992) uses the term *commons* in various ways. In some contexts, *commons* refers to nonprofit organizations themselves. But used more abstractly, the commons comprises a "protected space for the collective expression of what people find most important in their lives" (Van Til, 1992, p. xi) or "an economic, political, and social space outside the market, households, and state in which associative communities create and reproduce social worlds" (Lohmann, 1992, p. 59).

Lohmann (1992) argues that common goods are a *third category,* alongside private goods (provided through the market) and public goods (provided by government). Nonprofits are not just making up for the failure of the market and government—they are not just gap fillers. Rather, they produce a distinctive third kind of good—*common goods.* How are common goods different from private and public goods? Unlike private goods, common goods cannot be consumed alone by an individual. But neither are they of interest or benefit to all people, like public goods. As Lohmann explains,

> One of the most powerful criticisms of the application of the public goods orientation to nonprofit or voluntary action is that most commons fail to fit the description of a public good. [For example,] church services, lodge meetings, food pantries, scientific meetings, amateur athletic events, and most other commons are available to some people (members and participants) without being available to all. Thus, they fail to meet the criterion of indivisibility, which is one of two defining characteristics of public goods.
>
> Yet many of the desired or preferred ends or objectives of common action are clearly not private goods either. They cannot be fully alienated and controlled exclusively by particular individuals without ceasing to be what they are. There is an undeniably other-oriented quality to any religious ritual, scientific finding, or artistic expression, for example. (p. 171)

Whereas a private good benefits only the individual who consumes it and a public good benefits all of society, common goods benefit (or are of interest to) all the members of the particular commons but possibly not those beyond. This helps explain how organizations that may hold entirely opposite positions or goals can coexist. The "good" of one common may be viewed as a "bad" by members of another common, but the existence of the commons fosters social and political pluralism. In other words,

> no assumptions need to be made about the universal desirability of common goods. In most instances, it is sufficient that common goods are shared or held jointly by members of a particular commons, even in the face of indifference or hostility from others. (Lohmann, 1992, p. 18)

Lohmann (1992) directly addresses shortcomings of the failure theories. He acknowledges that economic theories are useful in explaining nonprofits that derive a substantial portion of their revenues from earned income—for example, "through ticket sales or fees charged for services, such as orchestras, opera companies, hospitals, nursing homes, and various types of social service agencies" (p. 175). But, he argues, "Contemporary economists have largely ignored large portions of the commons" (p. 175).

Lohmann's work is widely admired. For example, Van Til (1992) calls it "original, robust, and powerful" and "the first definitive large-scale theory of the voluntary and nonprofit sector" (p. xii). But it is not universally accepted, and economists in particular take issue with Lohmann's (1992) assertion that their tools of analysis are unsuited to understanding nonprofit organizations. For example, Dollery and Wallis (2003) write that, "compared to sociological and other non-economic theories of the voluntary sector, economic theorizing represents a rather rare success story in the conceptual analysis of voluntary organizations" (p. 34). Indeed, while Lohmann's theory is persuasive with regard to many nonprofits, his concession that traditional economic theories *do* apply to nonprofits that rely substantially on earned income is a significant one, especially since earned income is the predominant source of revenue for the sector overall and for many of its largest organizations. His examples of commons include many organizations that would fit Salamon's (1999) member-serving category—for example, associations of bird watchers or car collectors and amateur athletic leagues—rather than the commercialized nonprofits that are an increasingly large component of the sector. But, like the supply-side economic theorists and those who identify altruistic motivations of donors, he succeeds in arguing that the failure theories do not provide a complete explanation for the nonprofit sector and in establishing the importance of shared values and purposes among those who participate in the sector's work.

Changing Definitions of Private, Public, and Common

Now that we have established the concepts of private, public, and common goods, how can they be applied to better understand today's nonprofit sector and explain some of the changes that we already have observed—for example, commercialization within the nonprofit sector and the shifting roles of government?

Clearly, if private goods benefit only their consumers, then they should be paid for by the individuals who use them. Public goods benefit everyone, and payment is thus compelled from all through the tax system. And common goods, because they are of interest or benefit only to members of the particular commons, should be funded by members of that particular commons. Most would agree on these simple rules, but there is often disagreement on the details and debate about whether certain goods should be considered private, public, or common. None will likely disagree that military defense is a public good to be provided by government or that a soft drink is a private good that should be paid for by the individual who consumes it. And most would agree that religious worship fits Lohmann's (1992) concept of a common good, that churches, synagogues, and mosques should be sustained by adherents of their respective faiths collectively rather than through appropriated public funds. But for other goods, there may be disagreement, and public attitudes may change over time.

For example, where should we place health care? In many nations, it is considered primarily a public good, to be provided to everyone through government programs. In the United States, health care has the characteristics of private, common, and public goods. Government programs support health care for some members of society, so we regard it at least in part as a public good.

But nonprofit hospitals are supported in part through philanthropic gifts from members of the community they serve, as if they are common goods. Some analysts call for greater privatization of health care, in the belief that giving consumers more control will increase efficiency, reduce unnecessary treatment, and bring down costs. So some regard medical care as primarily a private good, at least in part. These viewpoints were evident in the health care debates in the U.S. Congress during the Clinton administration in the 1990s and again during the administration of Barack Obama in the late 2000s. They will likely continue in one form or another despite passage of the health reform act in 2010.

Historically, K–12 education has been considered a public good in the United States, based on the belief that an educated citizenry is of benefit to all of society because it is essential to a successful democracy and a healthy economy. In early U.S. history, higher education was a private good. But beginning with the founding of the land grant universities in the mid-19th century and until recent decades, higher education was increasingly treated as a public good. State support of public universities, the establishment of community colleges, and federal assistance to colleges and universities and their students sought to make higher education more like K–12, accessible and affordable to anyone with the ability to succeed—like a public good. But in the past three decades, higher education has come to be considered more like a private good, with government support for higher education declining in many states, and students and their families being expected to shoulder an increasing portion of the cost. In other words, the prevailing view has swung to the point that higher education is seen primarily as an investment made by an individual and his or her family, with the benefits accruing mostly to that individual in the form of higher income. "Lawmakers increasingly view higher education as a private good that should be supported by students and donors, rather than as a public good that deserves state support" (Selingo, 2003). But education is also a common good, and educational institutions are supported in part through contributions from individuals who share an interest in them, like religious congregations.

Most people today probably think of highways as a public good, but in the nation's early days, it was not uncommon for roads to be developed by private interests, and there have been recent proposals in some states to privatize certain highways by charging tolls that would go to the private investors in the highway (Guerrero, 2005). And what are we to make of the Blue Ridge Parkway Foundation (www.brpfoundation.org), a "professional fund-raising organization" established to help fund projects to improve a road owned and operated by the National Park Service? Are roads public, private, or common goods? When national parks that were previously free start to charge admission fees, it represents some movement of the good they provide from the public toward the private sphere. And when foundations are created to raise funds for the support of public parks, it begins to give them characteristics more like those of common goods. When a performing arts center that is primarily supported through audience fees and philanthropic gifts receives a government grant, it has moved from somewhere between private and common to a position that is some blend of private, common, and public. Again, we find that boundaries are not always clear, definitions are not always fixed, and thinking can change over time.

Lohmann (1992) suggests that public support for what are in reality common goods is often provided in response to "appeals by various leisure classes for tax-supported patronage of particular common goods valued by those leisure classes" (p. 187). He explains that such appeals are often based on the argument that there is an indirect benefit to society. For example, advocates for greater public support of higher education might argue that there is a benefit to all citizens in having well-educated leaders, although the students who attend universities may et al.'s (2001) terminology, "pure." However, it is likely that no one volunteers at Microsoft. The company pays *market wages* and, indeed, competes in the marketplace for talent. Universities, as any professor will testify, are somewhere in between; professors do not work for free, but neither do they earn the salaries their talents might command in a purely commercial enterprise.

How do nonprofits obtain needed supplies? A purely philanthropic nonprofit would have all its supplies *contributed;* that is, it would receive them through *gifts-in-kind.* Miriam's does receive such gifts, although it also purchases some of the food it needs for its breakfast program. However, it is doubtful that Microsoft ever receives such gifts, and it likely pays the *market price* for its pencils as well as its PCs (although it may negotiate some discounts based on volume rather than the generosity of its suppliers). As a hybrid, a university may receive some gifts-in-kind, pay market price for some products, and receive educational *discounts* on others.

Again, it is important to emphasize that the concept of a spectrum includes various points along the line rather than two or three discrete categories, so organizations may be hybrids to a lesser or greater extent. Indeed, the reality in today's nonprofit sector is that relatively few organizations offer an example of the purely philanthropic as Dees et al.'s (2001) chart defines it. Most are hybrids to some degree, even Miriam's Kitchen. Most private universities are hybrids, commercialized to a considerable degree, and even state universities have moved in that direction, receiving a diminishing portion of their revenues from state funds and an increasing portion from tuition charges and gifts (Selingo, 2003).

Are there examples of purely commercial organizations? Microsoft may come pretty close, but some argue that for-profit businesses are in fact becoming more nonprofit-like. While many nonprofits demonstrate increasing degrees of commercialization—that is, they are moving from left to right across Dees et al.'s (2001) spectrum, many corporations are becoming more attuned to their social responsibilities, tempering their pursuit of profit at least somewhat with a concern for social value. In terms of Dees et al.'s spectrum, they may be moving to the left (no political pun intended!). Because of these movements in both directions across the spectrum, some see a blurring of the nonprofit and for-profit sectors. Some celebrate it, while for others it arouses deep concern.

Emerging New Models

Some who observe the blurring of the sector and the emergence of hybrid organizations call for a new legal framework and a new definition of organizations. In a 2009 report, Sabeti (2009) describes the increasing use of business methods by nonprofits and the growing responsiveness of business to social concerns, and sees "a new class of organizations with the potential for generating immense economic, social, and environmental benefits . . . emerging" (p. 2). Sabeti continues, "A critical mass of organizations within the three sectors [public, for-profit, nonprofit] have been evolving—or converging—toward a fundamentally new organizational landscape that integrates social purposes with business methods" (p. 2). This convergence is creating a new, or "fourth sector" that Sabeti thinks "can be consciously developed and expended through broad recognition and engagement" (p. 1).

Along similar lines, there has been a movement in the United States to create a new category of legal entity that spans the boundary between business corporations and nonprofits. The *low-profit, limited liability company* (or L3C) was first created under Vermont law in 2008 and by 2009, more than 60 companies had registered. By the end of 2009, five other states had passed similar legislation. This new form of legal entity is intended to pursue social purposes, like a nonprofit, but is also able to accept investments from foundations and others. While many be the primary beneficiaries of the education they receive there. Similarly, arts patrons might advocate for public support of the arts because they provide an indirect benefit to society, not just to those who participate as their patrons. Lohmann disputes such arguments, saying that such claims are "demonstrably untrue, simply by virtue of the fact that many people never even attend artistic performances" (p. 186).

As attitudes of the public and its political leaders change over time, goods may come to be viewed as more public, more private, or more common—in varying combinations—and the roles of business, government, and nonprofits will evolve to reflect that new philosophical and political landscape. The debate about the proper nature of certain goods and services has been taking place since the founding of the United States and is likely to continue. It is a central issue in differing political views and affiliations.

Lohmann's (1992) theory provides us with both the vocabulary and the concepts with which to consider some of the most fundamental political and public policy debates and to understand some of the tides of change affecting today's nonprofit sector.

Explaining Nonprofit Organizations

The theories we have been discussing so far in this chapter are macro theories—they attempt to explain why nonprofit organizations exist and what role they play in our society. We now will shift our discussion to micro theories, theories that look inside nonprofit organizations and attempt to explain why they behave the way they do and make the decisions they make—how we can understand them as *organizations*. This discussion will include a look at the characteristics of nonprofit organizations, a review of some concepts from the field of organizational theory, and principles related to the structure and culture of nonprofit organizations. There is a rich literature in the fields of organizational behavior and organizational theory, but historically, much of the theory has been generic, meaning that its originators apply it to all forms of organization, whether business, government, or nonprofit. Recent years have produced "a veritable wave" of theories addressing the distinctive features of nonprofit organizations, but as Ott (2001) says, "there is not, cannot be, and should not be a single theory of nonprofit organizations" (p. 269). Our discussion of theories is thus of necessity selective.[1]

Characteristics of Nonprofit Organizations

As we saw in Chapter 2, the nonprofit sector encompasses an array of organizations and institutions that are very different from one another. Is it possible, then, to identify some characteristics that are associated with what it means to be a "nonprofit"? In his 1999 book, *America's Nonprofit Sector: A Primer* (2nd ed.), Lester Salamon identifies six qualities that characterize nonprofit organizations: They are *organized entities,* they are *private,* they are *non–profit distributing,* they are *self-governing,* they are *voluntary,* and they are of *public benefit* (pp. 10–11). Let's discuss these qualities one at a time.

Organized Entities

There are loose and informal groups of people who undertake voluntary efforts similar to the programs of nonprofits, but the organizations that we will consider in this book are generally chartered as *formal organizations.* Most are incorporated under state law and enjoy the same benefits as business corporations—that is, status as a legal person in and of itself, separate from the individuals who may control it.

Private

Although nonprofit organizations have a commitment to public service, they operate in the *private* sector rather than as agencies of government. Many receive government funds, and indeed, government funds make up the largest source of revenue for some. Some authors use the term *nonprofit agencies,* implying that they are essentially like units of government. However, it is important to be clear that the control of nonprofit organizations lies outside the sphere of government, and they have considerable autonomy to set their own strategies, design their own programs, pursue revenues through multiple means, and select those who will benefit from their services.

A government agency, by contrast, is generally obligated to provide services to anyone who qualifies, or as Thomas Wolf (1999) describes it, they have "a requirement of equity" (p. 20). The requirement may be specifically defined—for example, people making below some level of annual income or people over a certain age—but the agency is required to provide services to anyone who meets those criteria, within the limits of resources appropriated to it. Nonprofit organizations may receive government funding that requires them to provide specific services to qualified individuals as a condition of accepting the funds. However, in general, they have both the liberty and the challenge of defining their own constituencies, deciding the services to be offered, and deciding which funding they will or will not accept. Both government agencies and nonprofits may have missions, but government agencies also face mandates, which most nonprofits do not.

Non–Profit Distributing

As we already have discussed, nonprofits, by definition, do not distribute any excess of revenues over expenditures to benefit individual owners. Any profit that a nonprofit organization generates must be reinvested in the organization itself rather than used to pay dividends to owners or investors. This requirement is indeed one of the primary criteria for being recognized as a nonprofit organization, and any violation of it could be a cause for the IRS revoking recognition of the organization's nonprofit status. It is also required that compensation to employees of the organization be reasonable, so that managers are not being enriched as if they were in fact owners of the enterprise. Indeed, nonprofit executive compensation is an area of potential abuse that has received increasing attention from the Congress and the IRS in recent years. The standard of reasonableness does not mean that nonprofit executives must be paid low salaries; in fact, in some fields, nonprofit salaries are comparable with salaries for similar jobs in the for-profit sector. It does require, however, that nonprofits justify the compensation paid to their executives, to ensure that they are receiving payment in exchange for the services they provide to the organization rather than a share of profits disguised as salary or benefits. We will return to the question of nonprofit compensation again at various points in this book.

Self-Governing

Nonprofits are self-governing, which is another way of saying that they are not controlled either by the government or by individual owners. Control of the nonprofit lies with a board of directors or a board of trustees, a group of individuals who have overall responsibility for ensuring that the organization serves its nonprofit mission and uses funds in accordance with that mission and the law. The board also has responsibility for the overall welfare of the organization itself.

Voluntary

Although many nonprofits employ significant numbers of paid staff, they are rooted in the tradition of voluntarism. Most—though not all—members of nonprofit governing boards are volunteers, who serve without compensation. Moreover, many organizations also engage substantial numbers of service volunteers in delivering their programs. Even nonprofits that employ significant numbers of staff often had an earlier period in their histories when volunteers were the predominant workforce, and the values of inclusion and openness to varying opinions often remain important components of their cultures. Indeed, nonprofits can be somewhat unruly forums of debate about even basic questions of values, mission, and priorities.

Of Public Benefit

Nonprofits are privately controlled entities, but they exist to serve a social purpose that has been deemed to be of public benefit. The public benefit is obvious with regard to some organizations. For example, who would argue with the benefits of feeding the hungry, eliminating drunk driving, or fighting drug addiction? In other instances, however, definition of the greater good will vary between those who advocate the two opposite sides of a controversial issue. For example, there are organizations that hold pro-life or pro-choice positions. Some advocate prayer in public schools, while others emphasize the separation of church and state and oppose school prayer. Some citizens see environmental organizations as accomplishing important public benefits, while others may see them as extremist roadblocks to economic progress. All these organizations may be tax-exempt because they are deemed to be of public benefit. In such cases, the public benefit that all of them advance is the protection and encouragement of free and open debate, a value presumably shared by those on all sides of an issue in a democratic society.

A nonprofit's purpose is stated in broad terms in its charter and is elaborated in its mission statement. The *mission statement* is a guide to every action taken by the organization and is the principal standard against which its performance should be measured. Amending a charter is a complex process, but the mission of an organization is more easily changed. Indeed, consideration of the mission is usually among the first steps undertaken in an organization's planning process.

The mission is so central to all nonprofit organizations that they are said to be "mission driven." The mission is their purpose, and accomplishing it is their overriding goal. This commitment to a mission is a fundamental difference between nonprofits and the for-profit sector, and one of the reasons why nonprofit management is a distinctive professional field.

As noted above, government agencies also have missions, to which the individuals who work in them are often highly dedicated. But government agencies are ultimately controlled by elected officials, who must respond to the wishes of the majority. They can only support programs according to what is politically feasible—that is, those favored by a majority of the voters. This is not to disparage the practice of politics, or to imply that politicians do not have personal convictions, but merely to state the reality that if officials do not meet the expectations of the majority over time, they will be replaced by others whose programs are more reflective of the majority's preferences. Thus, political viability is in a sense an ultimate test as fundamental to the purposes of government as profit is to business (Wolf, 1999, p. 27).

Nonprofits stand somewhere between business and government. They are driven neither by the need to maximize profit nor by the need to meet the expectations or desires of a majority, but rather by achievement of the missions for which they exist. Like businesses, some nonprofits can and do generate profits. But, by definition, the generation of revenue is the *means to the end* of providing the public benefit envisioned in their charters and fulfilling the social purposes expressed in their mission statements.

The characteristics of nonprofit organizations identified by Salamon (1999) help explain *what* they are. Now let's look at some concepts and theories that go to the *why* of how nonprofit organizations look and behave as they do.

Nonprofits as Open Systems

To many people today, the word *bureaucracy* provokes negative images of a slow-moving, complex, unresponsive institution—perhaps a government agency like the motor vehicles department or even a large university. But in the early years of the 20th century, the sociologist and economist Max Weber advanced the idea of a bureaucracy as an ideal model. Characterized by rules and a formal hierarchy of positions, he thought a bureaucracy to be especially capable of efficiency and effectiveness. For decades after Weber's pioneering work, his concept of a bureaucracy remained central in organizational theory, and other scholars expanded on his work, studying issues such as the span of manager control, the roles of managers, and other questions based on his idea of organizations as machine-like entities. Later scholars, such as Barnard, Simon, Cyert and March, Lewin, Maslow, McGregor, Argyris, and others, began to chip away at Weber's principles by placing more emphasis on human needs, motivations, and incentives rather than on formal organizational structures, eventually leading to development of the "human relations school" of management (Rainey, 2003, pp. 32–40). But Weber's concept of a bureaucracy, operating with formal structures, rules, and machine-like precision, probably still comports with many people's image of how an organization works.

Theories based on Weber's concept of bureaucracy usually focus on *internal* dynamics and on the behaviors of individuals within the organization. Beginning in the 1960s and 1970s, however, thinking about organizations began to shift toward viewing them as systems and analyzing their ability to adapt to different circumstances, or contingencies, in the *external* environment facing them. A landmark book by Daniel Katz and Robert Kahn (1966) presented a classic description of organizations as open systems that is still often cited. Widely read books authored by Peter Senge (1990, 1994) describing "learning organizations" also were based on systems theory. This shift in attention from the internal mechanics of an organization's operation to studying the effects of pressures and constraints brought to bear on the organization by the social context in which it exists was a profound change.

The simplest system includes inputs, a transformative process that acts on the inputs—that is, changes or manipulates them in some way—and the outputs resulting from that process. Systems also include feedback loops. *Feedback* enables the system to adapt to changing circumstances—that is, to learn and alter its behavior accordingly. In their ability to learn and adapt, systems are less like machines and more like living organisms. Indeed, some theorists study systems using principles drawn from the study of living organisms. For example, *population ecology* is an approach taken by some sociologists to explain the birth and death of organizations. They analyze organizations in terms of population density—that is, the number of organizations occupying particular niches—and the competition for resources among them. Population ecologists see some organizations as being selected in a Darwinian competition for scarce resources.

They tend to place less emphasis on the ability of organizations to survive by adapting to environmental changes than do some other theories—for example, the resource dependence model we will consider below (Aldrich, 1999).

Systems theorists make a distinction between closed and open systems. A system is closed or open depending on the extent to which it interacts with and is influenced by the environment in which it exists. A totally *closed system* would be one that is entirely self-sufficient and impervious to influences from its environment. It is difficult to conceive of an example of this extreme situation; no organization is insulated against all impact from outside. But some government agencies may be relatively closed. For example, those that provide essential services and have relatively assured appropriations may enjoy a high degree of autonomy in determining their own policies and procedures. A nonprofit that has a large endowment and thus can rely on investment earnings for all its operating support, not requiring revenue from donors, government, or fees for service, also might operate as a relatively closed system. This could describe foundations, for example, and indeed, foundations have been criticized in recent years for being insufficiently responsive to the world outside.

Most nonprofit organizations, however, are *open systems*. They are dependent on and interact frequently with their external environments. This is true because of their dependence on external resources, their social missions, and the involvement of volunteers at various levels of the organization.

As we have discussed, most nonprofit organizations have voluntary cultures. This has important implications for how they work. Individuals *choose* to be associated with a nonprofit. This is obviously true of service volunteers, people who perform the organization's work for no compensation and are free to stay or leave as they see fit. But it is often true that even paid staff of nonprofits have a voluntary *attitude,* meaning that they are motivated as much by the nature of the work and the organization's mission as by the pay, and often see themselves as performing a service. Even organizations that are highly commercialized or that rely primarily on government contracts have a "long history, deep traditions, and cultures steeped in voluntaristic values" (Ott, 2001, p. 289).

Most nonprofit governing boards are composed of volunteers, who may be drawn from constituencies served by the organization or from among its donors and who, in some cases, may have worked their way up through the ranks to join the board after having served as volunteers in delivering the organization's programs. The nonprofit board plays a boundary-spanning role; that is, its members are a part of the organization and represent the organization to the outside world, but they also are representatives of the outside world who bring the views and desires of the organization's stakeholders to bear on the organization and its management. The boundaries between "inside" and "outside" the organization may be fuzzy and permeable. Volunteers often work alongside paid staff, and communication flows back and forth across the formal boundaries of the organization. Volunteers providing the organization's services and also sitting on its governing board bring their own views and values to the board's discussions, and since they are not bound by the constraints of paid employment, they can be forcefully outspoken. Thus, communications both within the organization and between the organization and its external environment often do not follow the paths and patterns of formal authority.

Because nonprofits serve a public purpose, are subsidized through tax exemption and—in the case of charitable nonprofits—the tax deductibility of gifts, and because they often serve as contractors to government in the delivery of public services, they are subject to the scrutiny and opinions of government officials as well as the media, recipients of their services, and the general public. Unlike businesses, which have the relatively simple and clear goal of generating profits, nonprofits often have ambiguous goals, and there is often lack of agreement on how achievement of the goals should be measured. This leaves plenty of room for debate and discussion, which are not easily contained within the organization's walls. In sum, most nonprofits are very open systems, interacting with their external constituencies and needing to adjust to changes in their environment all the time.

Resource Dependency

Expanding on the open systems theory, Pfeffer and Salancik's (1978) *resource dependence theory* explains the behavior of organizations in terms of their dependence on external constituencies—for revenue, information, and other resources. Although the theory has been around for more than 30 years, it is still widely cited and applied in research on nonprofit organizations.

According to this theory, we can understand the choices and behavior of organizations less by studying their internal structures and dynamics than by focusing on their interdependencies with external organizations and individuals who hold power over them by virtue of the resources they provide. For example, if a nonprofit receives most of its funding from government, the government will be able to impose its policies on that organization. An example of this can be seen in higher education, where government support was leveraged to require that colleges and universities make changes in their admissions policies favoring affirmative action and in their allocation of resources to provide equal support for men's and women's athletic programs (Pfeffer, 2003). An organization that is highly dependent on a single foundation or a major individual donor also loses some of its autonomy and must respond to the priorities or demands of those who provide it with needed resources.

Goal Displacement

One significant risk of resource dependency is what is called *goal displacement*—that is, actions taken by the nonprofit to alter its goals and activities to satisfy the contributor of funds. This sometimes occurs not as a result of overt demands by funders, but in more subtle ways, when an organization expands its programs and activities into areas that may be appealing to donors or when it avoids activities that may alienate donors. For example, Karen Froelich (1999) looked at public broadcasting stations to see if their programming decisions were influenced by their need to raise funds from corporate donors. She found that, "although respondents insisted that program content was not influenced by corporate support, they demonstrated the *opposite* via 'self censoring' behavior that continually pressures stations to provide programming more readily salable to corporations" (p. 256, italics added).

Resource Dependency and Performance Measurement

Resource dependency helps explain some recent trends and issues in the nonprofit sector, including efforts to make nonprofits more accountable for performance. Government funders, foundations, and federated funders such as United Way can impose performance standards on nonprofits that receive their support and establish the achievement of certain goals as conditions for future support. The extent to which organizations are constrained by such requirements depends on how important the resources of a particular funder are. For example, United Way has been a leader in advocating the use of outcomes measures as a method for evaluating nonprofit effectiveness (something we will explore further in Chapter 6). To the extent that individuals make unrestricted gifts to United Way, permitting it to allocate those funds to specific organizations, United Way holds considerable influence over those organizations and can require that they follow its approach to measuring effectiveness. However, to the extent that individuals designate their United Way gifts to specific organizations, or bypass United Way and make gifts directly to the organizations themselves, perhaps through online giving portals like Network for Good, United Way loses the ability to influence those organizations. The trend toward designated gifts has made organizations less dependent on United Way and thus has reduced United Way's ability to influence their priorities and policies.

Internal Impact of Resource Dependency

An important insight from resource dependence theory is that *external* resource dependencies also can affect power relationships and structures *within* the organization. As Pffefer (2003) explains, "The people, groups, or departments inside organizations that . . . manage important environmental dependencies, and help the organization obtain resources, [hold] more power as a result of their critical role" (p. xiii). Consider, for example, an organization that depends primarily on charitable gifts for the largest portion of its revenues. The person who raises such money—perhaps the chief executive or a fund-raising professional—will hold power within the organization because he or she delivers so much of the revenue on which it depends. Requests for increases to the fund-raising budget or perhaps a higher salary for the chief fund-raising officer are likely to be favorably received. Alternatively, think about a commercialized nonprofit that derives most of its revenue from fees for services. Gifts may be less important to the organization, and hence its fund-raisers may have less internal clout. For example, they may have a more difficult time gaining approval of increased budgets. Such an organization is more dependent on fee-paying consumers or clients than on donors, and internal power thus may lie more with those who are experts in marketing or customer relations.

How does dependence on government funds affect a nonprofit organization? Froelich (1999) argues that "the most pronounced effects of government funding involve changes in internal processes and ultimately in the structures of nonprofit organizations" (p. 6). For example, she points to studies showing that the government's "dense web" of regulations and required accounting and reporting have altered the internal structure of arts organizations. She calls government "the primary force driving out the technical experts in arts management in favor of professional arts administrators, many of whom know little about the art forms they are managing" (p. 261).

The influence of resource dependency on an organization's internal structure, processes, and culture is so great that over time nonprofits may indeed become more like those very organizations that are their principal sources of revenue. For example, nonprofits that are primarily government contractors may come to "look, think, feel, and act" much like a government agency (Ott, 2001, p. 357). In contrast, those that receive a high percentage of their revenues through fees-for-service and other business activities may come to exhibit the characteristics of entrepreneurial business firms.

Organizations Adapt to Resource Dependency

Organizations use a variety of strategies to try and maintain their autonomy—that is, to resist external pressure on their decision making. They may try to make changes to accommodate to the external demands, perhaps by undertaking internal reforms, or they may try to alter the environment in a way that ameliorates the demands (Pfeffer & Salancik, 1978). For example, when in 2004 the nonprofit sector was threatened with new federal legislation to curb perceived abuses, the organization Independent Sector responded both with proposals and guidelines for self-regulation of the sector and with intensive lobbying efforts aimed at forestalling (or at least influencing) the proposed new federal legislation (Panel on the Nonprofit Sector, 2005, 2007).)

Managing Resource Dependency

A hallmark of resource dependence theory is the idea that "although organizations [are] . . . constrained by their situations and environments, [they have] opportunities to *do things* . . . to obtain, at least temporarily, more autonomy and the ability to pursue organizational interests" (Pfeffer, 2003, p. xii, italics added). In other words, organizations need not be helpless captives of their funding sources. They can make strategic choices that enable them to *manage* resource dependency in a way that maximizes their autonomy.

One way to reduce dependency and thus maintain more autonomy is to diversify the sources of revenue. For example, an organization that is highly dependent on gifts may decide to develop a revenue-producing business to reduce its reliance on donors. Or an organization that relies on the support of one government agency or foundation may focus on broadening its base of individual donors. The goal is to reduce dependence on any one source of revenue in order to achieve the autonomy needed to determine its own mission, programs, and measures of effectiveness.

Isomorphism

Resource dependency suggests that some nonprofits may become more like their primary funders. Other scholars see a tendency for organizations in the same field to become more like *each other* as a result of facing similar influences from their environments. Called *isomorphism,* this concept is drawn from the work of organizational scholars who use institutional theory.

Like resource dependency and population ecology, *institutional theory* represents "a continuation and extension of . . . open systems conceptions" (Scott, 1995, p. xiv). It recognizes the importance of an organization's environment and emphasizes the constraints placed on it by rules, expectations, norms, and values. Institutional theory describes organizations' efforts to gain legitimacy by embracing the norms, values, beliefs, and mores prescribed by the environment in which they exist.

Walter Powell and Paul DiMaggio (1991) describe three types of isomorphism—coercive, mimetic, and normative—and we can find examples of all three at work in the nonprofit sector. *Coercive isomorphism,* as the term implies, is "forced" on organizations. This pressure might come, for example, from laws, government regulations, accrediting bodies, or accounting rules established by the Financial Accounting Standards Board. There also are several standards of nonprofit behavior that have been established by watchdog organizations, such as the Better Business Bureau's Wise Giving Alliance and Independent Sector. Such standards do not have the force of law, but they can nevertheless be coercive, since the media attention given to organizations that do not meet them may have a negative impact on giving and other sources of support. In other words, nonprofit organizations, particularly in the same field, might tend to become more alike over time simply because they are *forced* to play by the same sets of rules.

Mimetic isomorphism refers to the tendency of organizations to mimic each other—that is, to look to the example of similar organizations for models to be adopted. Many nonprofit organizations today engage in benchmarking, a practice we will discuss more fully elsewhere in this book. "In benchmarking, an organization that has defined an opportunity for improved performance identifies another organization . . . that has achieved better results and conducts a systematic study of the other organization's achievements, practices, and processes" (Letts et al., 1999a, p. 86). Through this approach, organizations try to identify the best practices of other organizations they consider to be similar to them, and thus learn ways to improve their own operations. It is not surprising that this leads eventually to different organizations in the same field doing things in much the same way.

Normative isomorphism arises when organizations are influenced by the same standards of professional practice. For example, doctors follow the same ethical codes, so some things will be done the same way in all hospitals; social service organizations will reflect the norms of the social work profession; and university professors' similar understandings about academic freedom will affect the way in which all colleges and universities operate.

Explaining Nonprofit Organizational Structures

Isomorphism creates a tendency for organizations to become more alike, but we can observe that there are also often differences. For example, some organizations are relatively bureaucratic and centralized, with everyone following tightly prescribed policies and procedures sent down from the top. Others are more entrepreneurial and flexible, with decisions being made closer to the action in the field. What explains such differences?

As we already have discussed, some of the explanation lies with resource dependency. Structure is influenced by the organization's principal sources of support. For example, those that are dependent on just a few sources of support may operate with more centralized management, to achieve consistent communication with funding sources and ensure compliance with funders' requirements. Those that have more broad-based public support may be more decentralized, to tap the involvement and support of larger numbers of volunteers and local donors.

But a nonprofit's structure also is influenced by other variables, including the task environment it faces. The *task environment* includes the nature of the goods or services it provides; the type of technology it uses; the degree of uncertainty it faces in its environment; the complexity of its environment; the dynamism or rate of change in its environment; whether its units are tightly or loosely coupled, that is, in what time, proximity, and sequence they must interact as they produce the organization's product or service; and whether the interactions are complex or linear, that is "the extent to which interaction sequences in operations are well known, predictable, unambiguous, and recoverable among operational units" (Anheier, 2005, pp. 152–154). In simplest terms, how an organization is structured may depend in part on whether the work it does is straightforward, follows some clear set of procedures, and is predictable, or whether it often faces complex, unique, and messy situations that cannot be well predicted in advance.

Let's consider an example that illustrates this idea. One of the nation's largest nonprofits, the American Red Cross, engages in two principal activities—blood services and disaster relief. It collects blood, processes and stores it, and provides it to hospitals and other medical facilities as needed. It also responds to natural disasters, providing immediate relief to victims in the form of food, shelter, and other help. Handling the blood supply requires precision, and it needs to be done one way. Disasters are different. Of the more than 70,000 disasters to which the Red Cross responds annually, the majority are local, including incidents such as house fires, hazardous material spills, and transportation accidents (see www.redcross.org). The timing and nature of events are unpredictable—each situation is different and requires a somewhat different, tailored response. Blood services and disasters thus present different task environments, and the Red Cross organizes itself differently for each of these activities.

In local disasters, most services are provided by local chapters, which operate in a relatively decentralized manner with the support of local donors and volunteers. In this area, there is relatively loose coupling between the national office and local chapters. Blood services were once more decentralized, but the Red Cross reorganized its blood services in the 1990s in the face of growing national concern about HIV infection. This reorganization created a more centralized structure and additional bureaucratic policies and procedures (www.redcross.org). In other words, the organizational structure changed when the nature of the task was changed by HIV. Following Hurricane Katrina in 2005, the Red Cross's disaster relief services also were reorganized, to reflect the new task environment presented by the seemingly more frequent incidence of catastrophic disasters affecting large geographic regions as well as the potential for terrorist incidents that have regional or national implications. Because the nature of the task had shifted, the organization needed to develop an organization consistent with the changed reality.

Organizational Culture

Any of us who has experience with organizations—as employees, volunteers, students, or in any other capacity—knows that formal structures and written rules often do not fully account for "the way things work around here." There are unwritten rules of behavior that govern things such as what people wear (suits or jeans), how people address each other (by first name or formal title), whether personal phone calls and e-mails can be received during working hours, whether or not people who work together also socialize outside the office, and many other realities of day-to-day organizational life. These realities often are controlled not by formal policies, but rather by *organizational culture*.

Scholars long have studied the subject of organizational culture, but the "topic [of culture] really came alive in the management literature" following the publication in the 1980s and 1990s of popular business books that emphasized the importance of culture in successful corporations (Rainey, 2003, p. 307). Peters and Waterman's book, *In Search of Excellence,* published in 1982, focused the attention of corporate managers on the idea of corporate culture and inspired additional research.

The lesson of Peters and Waterman (1982) was simple: Great companies that produce excellent results have core values that are widely shared; in other words, they have strong cultures. In their 1994 book, *Built to Last: Successful Habits of Visionary Companies,* James Collins and Jerry Porras identified several characteristics that were associated with successful business corporations. Like Peters and Waterman, they found that culture was important. Successful companies have core values that are widely understood and often codified; they undertake efforts to protect the core values; they have a shared understanding of "purpose" that goes beyond the maximization of profit; and they demonstrate strong, "cult-like" cultures that are often perpetuated through promotion from within.

Culture is a word that is frequently used in everyday conversation, and most people probably have a reasonably accurate understanding of what it means. But organizational scholars offer precise definitions. For example, Edgar Schein (1992) breaks culture down into three categories: (1) *artifacts and creations*—for example, logos, symbols, ceremonies, rituals, and words used in conversations; (2) *basic values*—the less observable understandings of "how things are done around here," for example, who communicates with whom within the organization and in what manner, what external relationships are important, and so forth; and (3) *basic assumptions*—for example, how people see things, their personal theories about human nature, and expectations about whether people in the organization should be entrepreneurial and aggressive or compliant and passive.

It may be an oversimplification to speak of an organization's culture, as if it is coherent and uniform throughout. Most organizations, except perhaps the smallest, will include various subcultures—that is, groups of individuals "who share strong values about basic beliefs with some, but not all, of the other members of the organization" (Clegg, Kornberger, & Pitsis, 2005, p. 277). For example, executives may have different values and beliefs than do rank-and-file staff or volunteers. Staff members may have values derived from their professional cultures; for example, doctors and nurses working in hospitals may be influenced by professional norms not shared by professional hospital managers. University development officers may have more favorable views of business than do their academic colleagues who interact with businesspeople less frequently. The leadership and staff in the national headquarters of a nonprofit organization may see things quite differently from those who work in the local chapters. In hybrid organizations, like those we discussed in Chapter 2, there may be cultural differences between staff who provide mission-related services and those who are engaged in the revenue-producing business ventures of the organization.

Is there something that can be called "the nonprofit culture," some set of values and beliefs that runs commonly and consistently across the nonprofit sector? A number of authors assert that there is. We mentioned earlier in this chapter that many nonprofits, even those that may be largely dependent on earned income and paid staff, have a "long history, deep traditions, and cultures steeped in *voluntaristic values*" (Ott, 2001, p. 289, italics added). Christine Letts and colleagues (1999a) describes a "service culture" in nonprofits, stating that

> organizational issues hold little appeal for the several types of nonprofit employees who populate much of the sector. . . . [M]any nonprofit employees develop a "just do it" attitude that places more value on service than on the analysis and measurement needed to improve organizational performance. (p. 33)

Letts et al. also observe a "cooperative [rather than competitive] nature" in nonprofit workplaces and nonprofit professionals who see their work as "artistry" that is diminished by performance measurement (pp. 33–34). Frumkin and Imber (2004) claim that

> many nonprofit employees, and even some donors and volunteers, are uncomfortable with the language and practices of business and may be skeptical of the values and motives of people trying to introduce business concepts . . . [and that] the sector overall . . . seems to have a bias towards small organizations, local autonomy, and consensus-driven decision making. (p. 70)

In addition, Anheier (2005) states that "the organizational culture of nonprofit organizations encourages conflict avoidance rather than engagement" (p. 253).

The fact that culture exists and is an important aspect of understanding organizations is well supported and resonates with our own experience as individuals. However, as we have discussed, the nonprofit sector is diverse and complex, so it may not be a simple matter to describe a universal nonprofit culture. In addition, the blurring of the for-profit, governmental, and nonprofit sectors may be changing the culture of at least some organizations. The working of isomorphism may not be constrained to organizations within the same sector: Nonprofit hospitals may become more like for-profit hospitals. Nonprofit museums may become more like for-profit entertainment venues. Human services organizations may become more like competitive service businesses. As alluded to in Chapter 2, nonprofits are adopting the methods and vocabulary of the marketplace, becoming more businesslike at the same time that some corporations are emphasizing missions, vision, and values, and implementing more socially responsible policies. In essence, some nonprofits may be developing more corporate-like cultures, while some corporations are becoming more nonprofit-like in theirs. In this changing environment, it may be increasingly unrealistic to describe a distinctive nonprofit culture that is universally characteristic of all organizations across the entire sector.

Chapter Summary

Scholars in various disciplines have developed theories to explain the nonprofit sector as a whole and the behavior of individual nonprofit organizations. Theories drawn from economics surround the concepts of public goods and private goods, externalities, and free riders, and explain nonprofits as gap fillers that compensate for the failures of the market and government. Other theories address the supply side and explain nonprofits in terms of social entrepreneurship; the contributions that nonprofits make to freedom, pluralism, and joint action; and motivations for altruism and giving.

Lohmann's interdisciplinary theory of the commons explains nonprofits as providers of common goods, a third category of goods alongside private and public. The definitions of what is private, public, or common may change over time, reflecting current philosophical and political trends.

Nonprofit organizations exhibit six characteristics: (1) They are organized entities, (2) they are private, (3) they are non–profit distributing, (4) they are self-governing, (5) they are voluntary, and (6) they are of public benefit. These characteristics have implications for how they behave as organizations. Their purposes are stated in their mission statements. The mission is so central to nonprofit organizations that they are said to be mission driven.

Organizational theorists discuss nonprofits as open systems that respond to the pressures and constraints presented by their environments. Their behavior reflects their resource dependency, and nonprofits face the risks of goal displacement and loss of autonomy if they are too dependent on one or a few sources of funding. Most attempt to manage resource dependency by diversifying the sources of support and remaining committed to their missions.

Isomorphism describes the tendency of organizations in the same field to become alike. This may result from external pressures, the inclination of organizations to adopt each other's practices, or the commonalities of professional codes practiced by the organization's staff members. The organizational structure of a nonprofit also may be determined by the task environments it faces.

An organization's culture—the informal rules about "the way things are done around here"—has received increased emphasis in management literature over the past two decades. Some authors describe an identifiable nonprofit culture, but the much-noted blurring of sectors may be reducing the cultural differences, especially between nonprofits and business firms.

Note

1. There is a distinction between the terms organizational behavior and organizational theory, although most books on management blend the two fields and some consider organizational behavior to be the larger, encompassing field. Scholars of organizational behavior generally focus on the behavior of individuals or groups in organizations, often drawing on the disciplines of psychology and social psychology. Their interest is often in questions related to topics such as motivation, work satisfaction, and leadership. Organizational theory, which is usually based on sociology, is more concerned with the organization as a whole, considering topics such as organizational culture, environment, structure, and effectiveness (Rainey, 2003, p. 8).

KEY TERMS AND CONCEPTS

bureaucracy	*institutional theory*	*private goods*
contract failure	*isomorphism*	*public goods*
externalities	*market failure*	*resource dependency*
free riders	*mission driven*	*supply-side theory*
goal displacement	*open systems*	*task environment*
government failure	*organizational culture*	*theory of the commons*
information asymmetry	*population ecology*	

CASE 3.1   The Smithsonian Institution and the Catherine B. Reynolds Foundation

The Smithsonian Institution, an educational and research institution in Washington, D.C., is best known for its 19 museums and 7 research centers. It is an unusual hybrid of federal government agency and nonprofit institution. It was chartered by Congress as a charitable trust in 1846, in response to a bequest from the Englishman James Smithson, who left a gift to the United States of America to establish an institution "for the increase and diffusion of knowledge among men." But the Smithsonian is administered by the federal government, and courts have held that it is legally part of the federal government. More than two thirds of its workforce are employees of the federal government, while others supported by private funds are known as "trust fund employees." Although significant governance reforms were undertaken in 2007, in 2000 the Smithsonian was governed by a 17-member Board of Regents, including officials of the federal government and private citizens. The Secretary of the Smithsonian is the paid chief executive, who is appointed by the Board of Regents.

Throughout most if its history, the Smithsonian relied on ample funding from the U.S. government. But beginning in the 1980s, federal funds failed to keep pace with the Smithsonian's needs. Faced with a change in its environment, the Smithsonian "didn't exactly turn on a dime," and battles over the influence of private donors over the content of exhibits led to subsequent "knock-down, drag-out funding fight[s]," centered in particular on one of the Smithsonian's most prominent components, the National Museum of American History (Thompson, 2002).

(Continued)

(Continued)

By 2000, federal funds were only sufficient to cover the Smithsonian's core budget, including salaries. Private funds needed to be raised for new exhibits, and some standing exhibits had become dated. Deferred maintenance on the Smithsonian's extensive physical facilities had allowed many to deteriorate. Recognizing the need for change, the Board of Regents reached outside the scientific and museum communities for a new secretary—the title of the chief executive officer—someone who could bring business methods and private resources to bear on the Smithsonian's mounting problems. Lawrence Small, appointed by the Board of Regents as the new secretary in 2000, came from a background in banking and finance rather than science or museum management. Small noted the deteriorating condition of the Smithsonian's facilities and the continuing decline in federal funds, and he committed himself to "a vision that involves two M's: modernization and money," with most of the money to come from more aggressive fund-raising in the private sector (Thompson, 2002, p. 22).

Small had met Catherine B. Reynolds, a Washington-area entrepreneur who controlled a large foundation bearing her name. She shared Small's view that the National Museum of American History needed to be updated, and in May of 2001, she announced a gift of $38 million from her foundation to support a project on which she and Small had agreed: a 10,000-square-foot "hall of achievement" exhibit, intended to portray the lives of eminent Americans. Small and Reynolds had agreed that the selection of individuals to be portrayed would be determined by a special advisory committee of 15 people, with 10 being appointed by the Reynolds Foundation. *The Washington Post* reported that the contract between the Reynolds Foundation and the Smithsonian provided that if the committee could not agree, the dispute would be resolved not by the curatorial staff, but by the secretary himself ("Museums and Money," 2001).

The museum's staff erupted in anger, writing directly to the Smithsonian Board of Regents saying that the obligations Small had made to the Reynolds Foundation "breach[ed] established standards of museum practice and professional ethics" (Thompson, 2002, p. 26). The story caught the attention of the news media, resulting in a flurry of stories representing the museum curators' views and a *New York Times* editorial asking "what is the curatorial rationale for a permanent exhibit that seems to open the door for commercial and corporate influence at one of the capital's keystone institutions" ("Museums and Money," 2001). The American Historical Association, including prominent historians among its members, joined the debate in support of the museum staff's views. Museum staff began to post "Dump Small" stickers in elevators, on bulletin boards, and on their own lapels (Sciolino, 2001b). A series of meetings were held between the curators and Ms. Reynolds to try and reach a common understanding, but they did not resolve the differences.

At least two issues were central to the controversy. The first was a difference in philosophy about the meaning of history and the purpose of museums. Historians and museum curators believed that the purpose of museums was to educate and that the study of history should not focus on the personal stories of "great" men and women. Rather, they argued that the teaching of history should focus on broad historical forces and movements, often portrayed in exhibits through their impact on the lives of everyday people. They believed that the purpose of a museum was to encourage people to think critically about history, not to inspire people personally. As one curator expressed it, "We are not a great man/great woman place. . . . This museum is about context, about putting people and events in place within the social fabric" (Thompson, 2002, p. 18). But Ms. Reynolds held a different view of history and the purpose of the museum's exhibits—it should be to inspire young people by portraying the lives of famous Americans and extolling the virtues of entrepreneurship in achieving success. "The foundation was created out of a very entrepreneurial business," Ms. Reynolds said, "and that is the spirit and culture we want to apply to the philanthropic world" (Sciolino, 2001a).

The second, and broader, issue was the question of who should control the content of museum exhibits—professional historians and museum curators, or donors. To what degree should private donors have a say in museum exhibits to be developed with the money they are voluntarily giving? One scholar asked, "Will the Smithsonian Institution actually allow private funders to rent space in a public museum for the expression of private and personal views?" (Thompson, 2002, p. 16). Scholars accused Small of "selling" the museum to wealthy donors, with jeopardizing the "integrity and authority" of professional curators, and with having "[pre-empted] the issue of control" by reaching an agreement with the Reynolds Foundation without adequate consultation with his own staff (Sciolino, 2001a).

Small responded, saying that "government funding cannot do it all" and pointing out that the idea of private donors—who had something to say about how their money would be used—was not exactly new. After all, the Smithsonian Institution had been founded with James Smithson's gift! Small said, "We make no apologies for seeking private support to develop programs or facilities that the public wants and benefits from." He argued, "In all cases, we retain intellectual control while demonstrating to donors that their money can be spent productively and prudently. Does that mean we don't consult them? Of course we do. But the Smithsonian regents and staff control, without limitation or question, the Smithsonian activity (Small, 2001, p. A25).

In February of 2002, Ms. Reynolds cancelled the bulk of her foundation's pledge to the Smithsonian, saying merely that she felt the exhibit would not adequately portray "the power of the individual" (Lewis, 2002). But important questions remained, for the Smithsonian and generally for other organizations. Like the Smithsonian, others have long relied on relatively assured sources of revenues, perhaps the government, a single foundation, or some other generous source. But many find themselves now needing to pursue new and more diversified sources of financial support. The questions that need to be addressed clearly go beyond the specific one raised by the Reynolds Foundation's gift to the Smithsonian, that of how history should be portrayed and who should decide. There are more generic questions: What trade-offs are appropriate, realistic, and necessary for institutions and organizations striving to meet their financial needs and develop new sources of revenue while preserving their traditional missions and values? And how can CEOs meet expectations for their leadership in such a time of change?

Additional Sources: Cash (2002); Sciolino (2001c).

CASE 3.2   The National Trust for Historic Preservation

The National Trust for Historic Preservation is a private, nonprofit membership organization dedicated to saving historic places and revitalizing America's communities. Having been chartered by Congress in 1949, the Trust became known for its ownership and operation of historic properties and its annual list of America's Most Endangered Historic Places. It also provided educational programs, issued grants to support local preservation projects, and joined court cases in support of preservation laws and causes. In 1982, it filed its first case as a plaintiff—against the U.S. Army Corps of Engineers. And, in 1994, it became the leader in the successful effort to prevent development of a Walt Disney theme park near the Manassas National Battlefield Park, which pitted the Trust against powerful business interests (see National Trust website, www.preservationnation.org/about-us).

The Trust had continued to receive an annual unrestricted appropriation from Congress since its founding and, by 1995, government funds accounted for $7 million of its $35 million total budget. The balance came from private sources, including income from a modest endowment of about $33 million (K. Adelman, 2005;

(Continued)

(Continued)

Kennicott, 2009). But the Trust's efforts were often controversial with members of Congress, and the annual appropriation process required the Trust to lobby vigorously on its own behalf to maintain government support. The 1995 budget cycle was especially bruising. While the Trust ultimately received its full appropriation, it was a close call, with one congressional committee voting to cut it in half (K. Adelman, 2005). Richard Moe, who had been appointed president of the Trust in 1993, reached a decision. "We decided [that] persuading Congress is [too] consuming an effort—and chancy," Moe recalls. "Rather than be full-time lobbyists [on our own behalf], we wanted to lobby for others—for the National Park Service, tax credits, preservation policies. We wanted to be in control of our own destiny" (K. Adelman, 2005, n.p.). Congress agreed to guarantee limited support for a 3-year transition, and the Trust committed to going without unrestricted federal appropriations thereafter.

The Trust reduced staff, cut some programs, launched a strategic planning effort, and started a capital campaign—the first of two it would successfully complete in the next 15 years. It developed new revenue streams through partnerships with corporations and entrepreneurial programs, such as Historic Hotels of America, which provides the Trust with a fee from reservations placed through it with over 200 hotels nationwide. It also initiated new donor programs and organized trips to historic landmarks for major individual benefactors. Foundation fund-raising was intensified and grants came to provide 20 percent of total revenue. The Trust's membership grew to 270,000 by 2005 (K. Adelman, 2005). The National Trust built partnerships with local organizations across the country and opened six regional offices of its own. Its budget expanded to over $70 million, and its endowment grew to almost $200 million by 2008 (National Trust for Historic Preservation, 2008).

Freedom from federal support and a more diverse structure of revenue enabled the National Trust to pursue a more expansive agenda and increase its effectiveness as an advocate for historic preservation. Following Hurricane Katrina in 2005, the Trust worked to protect 37,000 historic structures in New Orleans. It opened a New Orleans office, completed demonstration projects, and lobbied Congress for $40 billion in grants to be funded through state preservation officers to help people rehabilitate their homes. And it fought the U.S. government in court to prevent federal funds from being used for demolition of substantial parts of the Mid-City Historic District (Kennicott, 2009; McDill, 2006).

The work of the National Trust for Historic Preservation gradually expanded the understanding of "preservation" from saving buildings to a more holistic approach of protecting entire neighborhoods, town, communities, and the environment. Furthermore, it changed the thinking of the business community. "Preservation is much more widely accepted today than it was fifteen or twenty years ago," Moe said in 2009. "Developers don't look at demolition as the first option as a rule, they look at the possibility of adaptive reuse and renovation" (Kennicott, 2009, p. C12).

Additional Sources: Lubell (2005).

QUESTIONS FOR DISCUSSION

1. How are the concepts of open and closed systems reflected in the case of the Smithsonian Institution and the Catherine B. Reynolds Foundation?

2. How does the theory of resource dependence relate to the case of the Smithsonian Institution and the Catherine B. Reynolds Foundation?

3. What cultures were at play in the case of the Smithsonian Institution and the Catherine B. Reynolds Foundation, and how did the interplay of cultures influence the controversy and the outcome?

4. Should higher education be considered a private good, to be paid for by those who benefit from it? Or should it be considered a public good, available as a right to all citizens (like K–12 education)?

5. How does the case of the National Trust for Historic Preservation reflect the concept of resource dependence discussed in this chapter? How does it reflect the interaction between sources of revenue and priorities?

6. Think back on (or read again) the discussion in Chapter 2 about the functions that nonprofit organizations perform with regard to government. How does the case of the National Trust for Historic Preservation reflect those various roles?

7. If you needed to stay in the hospital, would you prefer to go to a nonprofit hospital or one managed by a for-profit company? Or would it not make any difference to you? Why?

SUGGESTIONS FOR FURTHER READING

Books/Articles

Anheier, H., & Ben-Ner, A. (2003). *The study of the nonprofit enterprise.* New York: Kluwer Academic.

Clegg, S., Kornberger, M., & Pitsis, T. (2005). *Managing and organizations: An introduction to theory and practice.* Thousand Oaks, CA: Sage.

Lohmann, R. A. (1992). *The commons.* San Francisco: Jossey-Bass.

Powell, W. W., & Steinberg, R. (2006). *The non-profit sector: A research handbook* (2nd ed.). New Haven, CT: Yale University Press.

Steinberg, R. (2004). *The economics of nonprofit enterprises.* Northampton, MA: Edward Elgar.

Weisbrod, B. A. (1988). *The nonprofit economy.* Cambridge, MA: Harvard University Press.

PART II

Governing and Leading Nonprofit Organizations

Chapter Outline

chapter 4

Working successfully with the board is critical to an executive's effectiveness. In most cases, the CEO is appointed by and reports to the board; it is also essential to his or her professional survival.

© iStockphoto.com/Picsfive

Nonprofit Governing Boards 4

The governing board of a nonprofit organization holds ultimate responsibility for ensuring that the organization serves its mission and for the overall welfare of the organization itself. In addition, as we discussed in Chapter 3, the board plays a critical boundary-spanning role in the open system of a nonprofit organization, connecting the nonprofit to its community and constituencies, often including important sources of financial support. Understanding the board's responsibilities and role and knowing how to work with the board is an essential skill of effective nonprofit managers, especially chief executive officers (CEOs). This chapter will discuss the nature and responsibilities of governing boards, some characteristics of effective boards, and some challenges faced by nonprofit boards today. It also will consider the important question of the relationship between the board and the organization's CEO. But before we get started, it is important to clarify some terminology.

The boards we are concerned with here are those that have a legal responsibility for governing their organizations—they are *governing boards*. Nonprofit organizations may have various groups that are called "boards" but that do not have such responsibilities—for example, advisory groups that may contribute their expertise to the organization and help raise funds but that do not hold any legal authority for its governance. Such boards often play an important role in the organization, but they are not governing boards and will not be the focus of this chapter.[1]

Nonprofit organizations may use different terms to identify their governing boards. Most nonprofits are chartered as corporations, and members of the governing board are directors of the corporation under the law. Thus, many organizations use the term *board of directors* to identify them. Educational, cultural, and medical institutions often use the term *board of trustees*. Other organizations may use the term *board of governors, governing council,* or something else to describe their governing boards. This book generally uses the generic term, *governing board,* except when discussing the board of a specific organization, in which case it maintains the name that organization uses.

In many cases, the person who heads the board is called the "president" of the organization, and the paid staff person who manages the organization is called the "director" or "executive director." Some nonprofits—for example, universities, hospitals, and major arts and cultural institutions—have adopted corporate terminology, calling the head of the board the "chair" and the paid executive the "president." Others have adopted another corporate term, *chief executive officer,* or just "CEO," to identify the top paid staff person. This chapter refers to the top board officer as the "chair" and the paid executive of the organization as the "CEO."

One more point before we begin our discussion: The previous two chapters have drawn primarily from the academic literature, but this chapter relies much more on the practitioner literature. A substantial literature on boards has been developed by practicing nonprofit managers and consultants who work with boards and CEOs. Most of it *describes* what boards do or *prescribes* practices that boards should follow. Although the body of academic research on nonprofit boards is growing, it is still "limited, exploratory, and diffuse" (Callen, Klein, & Tinkelman, 2003, p. 496). This chapter draws on some of that research where it is especially relevant, but the practitioner literature is the more extensive, and it is the largest source of citations in this discussion.

Types of Governing Boards

Nonprofit governing boards are not all the same. For one thing, they differ in the way their members are selected. This may have important implications for how they operate and what agendas, priorities, and pressures members may bring to their work on the board. Different types of boards also may interact differently with the organization's CEO. For anyone working in a nonprofit organization, especially as a CEO or other senior executive, understanding how individuals come to be sitting at the governing board table is essential to understanding and working successfully with the board. Working successfully with the board is not only critical to the executive's effectiveness, it is also essential to his or her professional survival, since in most cases the CEO is appointed by and reports to the board. Table 4.1 on page 79 summarizes types of boards and some of the advantages and disadvantages of each, which are discussed in the following paragraphs.

Elected Boards

Some boards are *elected* by the membership of the organization. This is common in member-serving and advocacy organizations. The methods used to elect the governing board vary; for example, some elections are conducted by mail, and others are conducted at an annual meeting. Depending on the political and cultural environment within the organization, elections may be contested, and some individuals may, in effect, campaign for seats on the board. In other cases, a nominating committee of the existing board presents recommended candidates, who are often approved in a *pro forma* vote (that is, as a formality) by the membership.

Having an elected board may result in uncertainty about who will govern the organization from one year to the next—the outcome of elections is not always assured, and this may present a challenge to the CEO. What the board expects of the CEO may change; alliances and factions on the board may develop and shift; and the board's values and priorities may be dynamic, as political and philosophical crosscurrents among the membership find their way into the boardroom. The controversy that surrounded the election of the Sierra Club's board in 2004 provides an interesting illustration.

In 2004, anyone could join the Sierra Club with a $25 dues payment, and all members were eligible to vote in the election of the board. (That was an unusually low threshold for voting eligibility. Many organizations limit those eligible to vote to members who have been active for a certain period of time.) The Sierra Club's board included 15 members, and 5 seats were open for election that year. Individuals who were strong advocates for more restrictive U.S. immigration began to organize and encourage people sympathetic to their views to join the Sierra Club. Their goal was to have their sympathizers elect new board members who would change the Club's position on the immigration issue. Within 3 months, 30,000 people became new members of the Sierra Club, compared with only 22,000 the previous year. Some of these new members had been organized by the anti-immigration candidates who were, in effect, running for the board. The election became contentious. Some described the outsiders' efforts as a "hostile takeover" and accused them of pursuing "the greening of hate." Others portrayed their efforts as addressing needed reform in the Club's operation and claimed that their election would increase the Club's effectiveness (Greene, 2004).

The insurgents did not prevail, but the Sierra Club case illustrates the potentially tumultuous environment that may be created when governing boards are elected by an organization's membership. To be the CEO of such an organization requires a high tolerance for discussion, debate, and uncertainty. In addition, the membership terms of an elected board tend to be relatively brief, and turnover on the board may make it difficult to sustain its focus on long-range goals and plans. Doing so requires considerable repetition of presentations and discussions, to maintain consensus among the changing membership of the board. It may be difficult to motivate members of an elected board to make gifts or engage in fund-raising, since the ability and inclination to do so have not been the criteria in their selection. The skills of board members may be uneven, since their personal popularity or their positions on certain issues may have been the considerations in their election. However, elections do help ensure that the board will be representative of the constituency the organization serves and that the organization and its executive will be responsive to members' views and priorities. Elected boards are less likely than the next type, self-perpetuating boards, to become stale, uninvolved, or homogeneous in their membership.

Self-Perpetuating Boards

Most charitable nonprofits have *self-perpetuating boards*. New members of a self-perpetuating board are selected by the existing members of the board, who identify and enlist individuals according to criteria established by the board itself. When a new nonprofit organization receives a charter, it must identify the original, founding members of the governing board. Those individuals then have the authority to develop bylaws, which specify the total number of members of the board. The original board members then may select others to join them, up to the maximum permitted under the bylaws (which, of course, the board retains the authority to change). As individuals leave the board or complete their terms of service, the remaining members select others to take their seats, and this cycle continues as long as the organization exists.

In contrast to a board elected by the membership, a self-perpetuating board creates a relatively stable situation for the organization and its CEO. Although the bylaws of many boards do limit the number of terms that members may serve, self-perpetuating boards tend to have longer terms than elected boards, and the board's membership changes more slowly. Thus, the board's policies and culture may reflect continuity, reinforced by the tendency of its members to select successors who generally share their values and views. Indeed, in some cases, strong or long-serving CEOs may gain significant influence in the selection of board members, in effect choosing their own bosses.

One advantage is that a self-perpetuating board can craft its own membership, selecting individuals specifically to bring needed skills or augment its strength in areas important to its work. Many boards maintain an inventory of the expertise and connections represented among their members and make a systematic effort to identify and recruit new members to fill any identifiable gaps. For example, if someone with financial expertise is needed, the board can seek out such an individual and recruit him or her to join the board in order to add those skills.

A social service organization may try to find someone with professional social work experience who can help the board evaluate program recommendations from its staff. If the organization desires to increase the amount of support it receives from corporations, the board can identify and recruit corporate executives who may be helpful in that regard.

But these advantages of the self-perpetuating board are accompanied by some potential weaknesses as well. One is that the board may come to be unrepresentative of the constituency or community the organization serves. If the existing members of the board do not recognize the importance of diversity, they may continue to select new members who are just like them, drawing on their own business and social circles to fill board openings. Over time, the organization could become out of touch and be unable to adapt sufficiently to changes in its environment. Another risk is that a self-perpetuating board may become too stable in its membership and too complacent. There have been cases in which self-perpetuating boards, without the scrutiny that comes from the broader constituency of the organization, have been too lax in their oversight of their CEOs or even the behavior of their fellow board members, with disastrous results for the organization.

Appointed and Hybrid Boards

A third way in which board members may be selected is through appointment by some authority outside the organization. This is the typical model for public organizations; for example, the boards of state universities are usually appointed by the governor of the state. Few nonprofits have totally appointed boards, but some do have a number of appointed members. This is sometimes the case in nonprofit organizations that are affiliated with a religious congregation, which may have board members appointed by a church authority. Colleges and universities may have board members appointed by an alumni association. Organizations that work closely with government may have some board seats held by individuals who are appointed by a governmental authority. Boards also may have some seats that are held *ex officio*—that is, designated to be held by the individual who holds a certain office or position. For example, the head of the board of trustees of the Catholic University of America is the Archbishop of Baltimore, who serves ex officio. The organization's CEO often holds a seat on the board in an ex officio capacity, which may come with or without a vote.

Other boards are hybrids, with some members being elected, some appointed, some self-perpetuating, and some serving ex officio. Until governance reforms were implemented in the mid-2000s, the Board of Governors of the American Red Cross was an especially complex hybrid including 50 members. Eight were appointed by the president of the United States (an appointed component), 12 were at-large members elected by the governors themselves (a self-perpetuating component), and 30 were elected by delegates representing Red Cross chapters and Blood Services regions across the country (an elected component). The president of the United States served as the honorary chair of the Board of Governors in an ex officio capacity (www.redcross.org).

Hybrid boards may represent the best of both worlds, encompassing an elected component that helps keep the organization responsive to its constituencies; a self-perpetuating component that provides stability, continuity, and perhaps financial support; and an appointed component that ensures the organization's accountability to a parent organization or government. However, hybrid boards also can present challenges. For example, if elected, appointed, and self-perpetuating members hold different views or agendas, stalemate may result. Ex officio members may not always feel a real commitment to the organization and its mission, having just landed on the board by virtue of some other position they hold. If this is the case, they may not fully participate in the work of the board or develop a full understanding of the organization and its work. Indeed, following criticisms of the American Red Cross's response to Hurricane Katrina in 2005, some cited the structure of the board as an area of needed reform. After a long study, the Red Cross announced in October of 2006 that it was undertaking major changes to its board to strengthen the organization's governance. The reforms, initiated in 2007 and planned for completion over a period of years, will include reducing the membership from 50 to 20 and increasing the number of self-perpetuating members. Under the new structure, individuals appointed by the president will serve on an advisory committee rather than as regular members of the governing board (Schwinn, 2006b).

TABLE 4.1 ■ Types of Governing Boards

Type of Board	Advantages	Disadvantages
Elected	Helps ensure that the organization and the CEO will be responsive to members' needs and priorities	Division among the membership may create disagreement on the board. Turnover on the board may make it difficult to sustain focus on long-term goals and plans. Skills of board members may be uneven, since personal popularity or positions on issues may influence election.
Self-perpetuating	Can maintain continuity of culture, priorities, goals. Can craft the board membership to gain needed skills. Can select members who are helpful in fund-raising	May become unrepresentative of the community or constituency. May become too stable to respond to changes in the environment. May become too passive and yield too much authority to the CEO
Hybrid (including appointed, self-perpetuating, ex officio)	May combine the responsiveness of elected boards, the stability of self-perpetuating boards, and accountability to an appointing authority—for example, a sponsoring church	Different interests and loyalties of board members may lead to a stalemate. Ex officio members may not be fully committed to the organization.

The Board's Responsibilities

Now that we understand different types of boards and how their members come to sit at the table, exactly what are their responsibilities? And to whom are they accountable for meeting those responsibilities? The answers are not always simple.

As Bruce Hopkins (2003) describes it, nonprofit governing board members are "fiduciaries of the organization's resources and guardians of its mission" (p. 1). The board is accountable, that is, answerable, "for everything the organization does and how those things are accomplished" (Howe, 2002, p. 30). In the corporate world, it is clear to whom the directors are accountable and for what. Members of the corporate board of directors are the agents of the owners (the principals), and their responsibility is to direct and monitor the activities of management in the interests of the owners. Those interests also are quite clear—the maximization of economic value, consistent with sustainability of the business and the values of the owners. There are, of course, boards in the public sector as well. Most of them also have an identifiable constituency whose interest they serve; for example, a city council is accountable to the citizens of the city who elected them. But with nonprofits in the private sector, it is not always so clear to which owners the governing board is accountable.

Perhaps the owners of a member-serving organization are the members—it is primarily their interests that the organization exists to serve. But suppose the organization is a professional association that also sets standards for practice and certifies members of the profession. It may be primarily a member-serving organization, but doesn't the public—especially individuals served by members of the profession—also have some interest at stake? Who owns a charitable nonprofit, chartered to pursue a mission in the public interest? Are the owners the donors who support the organization through their philanthropy, the clients served by the organization, or perhaps the general public? If it is the general public, how can the board serve its interests when there may not be consensus about what the public interest means? Lacking the simple measure of results that the bottom line provides to business, by what standards should a nonprofit's effectiveness be evaluated, and who should determine those standards? Without clarity or agreement about who owns the organization, it is difficult to answer those questions. This creates an environment in which the board's responsibilities and role may be the subject of discussion and debate.

The Board's Legal Responsibilities

Some governing board responsibilities are unambiguous; they are defined by law. Most laws affecting nonprofit boards are state laws, enforced by state attorneys general and state courts. However, the federal government, and specifically the Internal Revenue Service, has gained increasing power in recent years.

A landmark case in 1974 is often cited as providing the most definitive statement of nonprofit board responsibility. In that case, *Stern v. Lucy Webb Hayes National Training School for Deaconesses and Missionaries* (usually known as just "The Sibley Hospital Case"), parents of children who had been patients at the hospital alleged that members of the board had mismanaged the hospital's assets and had placed hospital funds in accounts at banks in which they had personal financial interests. The parents claimed that hospital charges were unnecessarily high because of actions by the board. Judge Gerhard Gessell found that the Sibley board members had not really benefited financially and that the hospital had not been disadvantaged by the board's practices—in other words, the parents lost, but in the process of stating his decision, Judge Gessell clarified the standards of legal responsibilities of nonprofit boards that are still applied. Those responsibilities are summarized as the duties of *care, loyalty,* and *obedience.*

Care, Loyalty, Obedience

The *duty of "care"* in this context means paying attention and exercising due diligence in monitoring the organization's finances and supervising the actions of its management. Board members who do not attend meetings, who sleep through meetings, who do not read board materials, or who vote without understanding the issues are guilty of a lack of care. Included within the concept of care is the requirement that members of the board act in a prudent manner in managing the organization's finances—for example, by ensuring that any endowment assets are invested in a diversified portfolio to minimize risks. This does not mean that the board will necessarily have violated its responsibilities should it make the wrong investment decisions and the organization's assets decline, but merely that it should exercise common sense and not lose money as a result of recklessness, indifference, or failure to seek appropriate advice.

The *duty of loyalty* means that members of the board put the interests of the organization above their own personal financial interests or that of another organization with which they may also have a formal relationship. Individuals cannot use their position on a nonprofit board to enhance their own businesses or financial position. Closely related to the concept of loyalty is that of *conflict of interest.* A conflict of interest may arise, for example, when the board has to vote on whether to give a business contract to a company that may be wholly or partly owned by a member of the board itself or that perhaps may employ a board member's relative. Or a conflict could exist if the board is voting to enter some kind of partnership with another nonprofit, and one of the voting members serves on both boards. Conflicts of interest are not unusual, especially in smaller communities, where there may not be much choice about which suppliers or contractors the nonprofit can use and where prominent business leaders who own those businesses may serve on multiple nonprofit boards. Conflicts of interest are not illegal per se, but it is important how the board deals with them. Well-managed boards have formal conflict-of-interest policies that describe the procedures to be followed. Such policies usually require that potential conflicts be disclosed and that the board independently determine whether any business transaction that gives rise to the conflict is disadvantageous to the organization.

A legal concept related to conflict of interest is that of *private inurement.* Anyone who is an insider—generally any board member or officer of the organization—cannot unreasonably benefit from the organization's funds. This is related to the non-distribution constraint that was previously discussed. Nonprofits cannot use their profits to benefit owners, nor can they pay unreasonable amounts to board members or executives, which might have the same effect as sharing the profits with them—that is, giving them financial benefits as if they were owners. For example, a board can pay its CEO a salary and other compensation that is reasonable in exchange for his or her services, but anything exceeding a reasonable amount may be illegal private inurement. Likewise, an organization can do business with a company owned by a board member, but only if the payment is appropriate for the goods and services received.

The *duty of obedience* requires that the board make sure that the organization is complying with the law and, in addition, that any decisions or actions taken are consistent with the organization's mission and governing documents, including its charter. Following the law may seem a simple charge, but ensuring that the organization does not drift from its mission may require greater vigilance, especially if that drift may bring with it some unanticipated risks.

Intermediate Sanctions

In general, if a board member carries out his or her duties faithfully and prudently, he or she is unlikely to be found personally liable for any losses that the organization may incur. Just making a mistake, or even a bad decision, is not in itself a violation of the board's responsibilities, provided that one has met the standards of care, loyalty, and obedience in making it. However, the risks to individual board members are somewhat higher today than they were prior to 1996, when federal legislation was passed providing the IRS with the authority to impose *intermediate sanctions*— that is, financial penalties to punish individuals who engage in or permit improper transactions.

Prior to the passage of intermediate sanctions, virtually the only weapon available to the IRS in dealing with a nonprofit board that violated its fiduciary responsibilities was to drop the atom bomb by revoking the organization's tax-exempt status. Facing an all-or-nothing situation and reluctant to take a drastic step that might essentially impose a death sentence on the organization, the IRS had few options. Intermediate sanctions provided a fly swatter alternative to the atom bomb of revoking tax-exempt status by permitting the IRS to impose penalties on *individual* board members or officers who engage in an *excess benefit transaction,* meaning one in which "a person's level or type of compensation is deemed to be in excess of the value of the person's services" (Hopkins, 2005, p. 219). The intermediate sanctions legislation and the regulations that the IRS has issued pursuant to it are complex and beyond the scope of our discussion here, but in summary, the penalties can involve return of the excess benefits received as well as additional penalties. Because it made the possibility of IRS action more than a remote threat, the passage of intermediate sanctions was a wake-up call to nonprofit boards.

One of the first applications of intermediate sanctions involved the board of Hawaii's Bishop Estate, a charitable trust created through the will of Princess Bernice Pauahi Bishop, a descendant of King Kamehameha I, and has as its sole purpose supporting the Kamehameha Schools for children of native Hawaiian descent. It was reported in 1999 that the Bishop Estate was the largest landowner in Hawaii, and its assets were estimated at between $5 billion and $10 billion. According to the princess's will, the trust was to be governed by five trustees, who would be appointed by the justices of Hawaii's Supreme Court (Greene, 1999).

In the 1990s, the IRS began investigating the trust and expressed its concern about the activities of the trustees. Among other issues, the IRS said that the trustees were receiving excessive compensation for their services, reported to be more than $1 million annually to each (Greene, 1999). The IRS threatened to terminate the Bishop Estate's tax exemption, which would have required it to pay millions of dollars each year in federal taxes as well as state and county taxes, thus diminishing the benefit of its assets to the schools and the children. Reacting to the IRS criticism, in 1999, Judge Kevin Chang of the Hawaii probate court removed four of the five trustees and accepted the resignation of the fifth, saying that their "inaction and indifference" was "a breach of duty" (Greene, 1999, p. 30).

The IRS decided to pursue intermediate sanctions against the removed trustees. In 2001, the former trustees announced that they had settled with the IRS but did not disclose the details. The media reported that the State of Hawaii also had brought a case against the trustees. This, too, was settled, but the court records were sealed, so the final result could not be known (Schwinn, 2002).

Sarbanes-Oxley Act

Following corporate governance scandals in the early 2000s, including the demise of Enron and WorldCom, Congress passed the Sarbanes-Oxley Act in 2002. Sarbanes-Oxley placed new requirements on the governance of publicly traded for-profit corporations. Only two provisions of Sarbanes-Oxley apply as well to nonprofit organizations, those regarding the destruction of documents and protection for whistle-blowers. However, Sarbanes-Oxley served as another wake-up call for nonprofit boards, and many nonprofits have voluntarily adopted some or all of its provisions (Williams, 2006). In addition, some state laws—for example, the California Nonprofit Integrity Act of 2004—have incorporated Sarbanes-Oxley-type requirements. Sarbanes-Oxley will be discussed again, in more detail, in Chapter 6 of this book, which discusses nonprofit accountability in a broader framework.

In 2004, the organization Independent Sector created a Panel on the Nonprofit Sector in the wake of several controversies involving nonprofit governance. The panel issued reports in 2005,

2006, and 2007, offering over 150 recommendations and 33 principles for good governance and ethical practice by nonprofits, many of which reflect Sarbanes-Oxley-like practices (Panel on the Nonprofit Sector, 2007; see also Independent Sector, 2007b). The panel's principles address governance and ethical practices of nonprofit *organizations*. They encompass but also go beyond the practices of governing boards. A fuller discussion of these principles can be found in Chapter 6 of this volume.

Form 990

In 2009, the IRS introduced a revised version of Form 990, which nonprofits having at least $25,000 in annual revenues are required to file. The revised 990 included a number of changes, such as a new Part VI (see Figure 4.1), which requires "yes" or "no" answers to questions specifically addressing the practices of nonprofit boards. In effect, what had previously been a financial report was changed into a financial and *governance* report.

To be clear, while all organizations that are required to file Form 990 must complete Part VI, the policies and practices described are generally *not required* by the Internal Revenue Code. That fact is even stated clearly in the heading for Part VI on the 990 form (IRS, 2009). However, the IRS implies that providing the right answers may be well-advised.

> In general, the policies and practices described in Part VI are not required by the Internal Revenue Code. However, organizations are required by the Code to make publicly available some of the items described in Question 18 of Part VI. . . . The IRS will use the information reported in Part VI, along with other information reported on the form, to assess noncompliance and the risk of noncompliance with federal tax law for individual organizations and across the broader exempt sector. (n.p.)

Introduction of the new form captured the keen attention of nonprofit boards and gave rise to many publications, seminars, and other programs to assist board members in properly completing the form. As this chapter was being written in 2010, many boards were continuing to seek guidance on some of the questions, including, for example, any process required to be followed regarding the board's review of the form before it is filed, as addressed in question 10. In a 2008 survey of governing boards, the accounting and consulting firm Grant Thornton found that most organizations were following the practices suggested by Form 990 with regard to governance policies, fiscal oversight, executive compensation, and audits. But only 45 percent had a process in place for the board to review Form 990 before filing, suggesting that introduction of the new form would require the firm's attention in the following years.

The Board's Functional Responsibilities

The law primarily dictates the things nonprofit boards *cannot* do—fail to exercise care, place its own members' individual interests above those of the organization, or lead the organization in directions inconsistent with its mission and the law. But what is it exactly that boards should *do?*

A number of authors have offered lists of a board's functional responsibilities—that is, job descriptions listing the duties that boards should perform (see, e.g., Axelrod, 1994; Ingram, 2003; Nason, 1993). Most lists are similar on the principal activities in which the board should be engaged, although there are often differences among the experts with regard to the division of specific tasks between the board and the organization's CEO. The following responsibilities

FIGURE 4.1 ■ IRS Form 990, Part VI

Part VI Governance, Management, and Disclosure *(Sections A, B, and C request information about policies not required by the Internal Revenue Code)*

Section A. Governing Body and Management

		Yes	No
For each "Yes" response to lines 2–7b below, and for a "No" response to lines 8 or 9b below, describe the circumstances, processes, or changes in Schedule O. See instructions.			
1 a Enter the number of voting members of the governing body	1a		
b Enter the number of voting members that are independent	1b		
2 Did any officer, director, trustee, or key employee have a family relationship or a business relationship with any other officer, director, trustee, or key employee?	2		
3 Did the organization delegate control over management duties customarily performed by or under the direct supervision of officers, directors, or trustees, or key employees to a management company or other person?	3		
4 Did the organization make any significant changes to its organizational documents since the prior Form 990 was files?	4		
5 Did the organization become aware during the year of a material diversion of the organization's assets?	5		
6 Does the organization have members or stockholders?	6		
7 a Does the organization have members, stockholders, or other persons who may elect one or more members of the governing body?	7a		
b Are any decisions of the governing body subject to approval by members, stockholders, or other persons?	7b		
8 Did the organization contemporaneously document the meetings held or written actions undertaken during the year by the following:			
a The governing body?	8a		
b Each committee with authority to act on behalf of the governing body?	8b		
9 a Does the organization have local chapters, branches, or affiliates?	9		
b If "yes," does the organization have written policies and procedures governing the activities of such chapters, affiliates, and branches to ensure their operations are consistent with those of the organization?			
10 Was a copy of the Form 990 provided to the organization's governing body before it was filled? All organizations must describe in Schedule O the process, if any, the organizations uses to review the Form 990	10		
11 Is there any officer, director or trustee, or key employee listed in Part VII, Section A, who cannot be reached at the organization's mailing address? If "Yes," provide the names and addresses in Schedule O	11		

Section B. Policies

		Yes	No
12 a Does the organization have written conflict of interest policy? If "No," go to line 13	12a		
b Are officers, directors or trustees, and key employees required to disclose annually interests that could give rise to conflicts?	12b		
c Does the organization regularly and consistently monitor and enforce compliance with the policy? If "Yes," describe in Schedule O how this is done	12c		
13 Does the organization have a written whistleblower policy?	13		
14 Does the organization have a written document retention and destruction policy?	14		
15 Did the process for determining compensation of the following persons include a review and approval by independent persons include a review and approval by independent persons			
a The organization's CEO, Executive Director, or top management official?	15a		
b Other officers or key employees of the organization	15b		
Describe the process in Schedule O. (see instructions)			
16 a Did the organization invest in, contribute assets to, or participate in a joint venture or similar arrangement with a taxable entity during the year?	16a		
b If "Yes," has the organization adopted a written policy or procedure requiring the organization to evaluate its participation in joint venture arrangements under applicable federal tax law, taken steps to safeguard the organization's exempt status with respect to such arrangements?	16b		

Section C. Disclosure

17 List the states with which a copy of this Form 990 is required to be filled ▶
18 Section 6104 requires an organization to make its Forms 1023 (or 1024 if applicable), 990, and 990-T (501)(c)(3)s only) available for public inspection. Indicate how you make these available. Check all that apply.
   ☐ Own website   ☐ Another's website   ☐ Upon request
19 Describe in Schedule O whether (and if so, how), the organization makes its governing documents, conflict of interest policy, and financial statements available to the public.
20 State the name, physical address, and telephone number of the person who possesses the books and records of the organization: ▶

Source: IRS form 990 (http://www.irs.gov/pub/irs-pdf/f990.pdf).

are common to most board job descriptions, although, as we will see later, some authors express contrary views.

Appoint, Support, and Evaluate the CEO

Although the CEO may serve as an ex officio member of the board, he or she is generally appointed by the board and serves at the pleasure of the board, subject, of course, to any contractual terms that may be negotiated at the time of appointment. However, having appointed the CEO, the board also has a responsibility to support that individual. This includes acting as a sounding board for the CEO to discuss ideas and problems, and also coming to his or her defense when pressures may arise from within or outside the organization. If the board's response to every criticism of the CEO's actions is to challenge him or her or take the side of the critic, the board will quickly undermine the CEO's ability to be effective, and it is unlikely to attract or retain a strong executive. But the board also is responsible for setting expectations for the CEO, monitoring his or her performance against those expectations, and providing the executive with performance evaluations. Of course, if expectations are regularly not met, the board also has the responsibility of dismissing the CEO and beginning a search for his or her successor.

The relationship between the governing board and the CEO is complex, and it is a topic that generates its own considerable literature. The subject is of such importance that we will return to a more thorough discussion of it shortly.

Establish a Clear Institutional Mission and Purpose

Establishing the organization's mission is the responsibility of the board. Although the organization's charter states its purposes in broad terms, the board can and should periodically review its mission; indeed, doing so is often the first step in the process of strategic planning.

Approve the Organization's Programs

Although experts advise boards to avoid becoming involved in the details of management, most think that the board should approve the programs undertaken by the organization, to meet its responsibility for ensuring adherence to the mission and protecting the organization's financial viability. For example, the board of a liberal arts college would need to consider whether establishing a business school would be consistent with its mission, the implications for the college's financial resources, and the ability of the college to maintain its academic standards and reputation in light of such an expansion of its programs. The board of an organization serving dinners to the homeless would need to consider any extension of its activities to provide medical services or transitional housing. Because such decisions relate directly to the mission, which is the responsibility of the board, they cannot be delegated to the CEO or the staff.

Ensure Sound Financial Management and the Organization's Financial Stability

Protecting the organization's assets is, of course, central to the board's legal responsibility as fiduciary. Most boards approve annual budgets and receive regular reports of the organization's financial status. Many boards, especially since the passage of Sarbanes-Oxley, also have separate audit committees that meet with outside auditors of the organization's finances (Williams, 2006).

Some authors say that board members' responsibility to ensure the organization's fiscal soundness implies an obligation to provide their own financial gifts and actively engage in fund-raising. Indeed, except perhaps for the debate about the appropriate relationship between the board and the CEO, no subject commands more ink, or more lung power, than the role of the board in giving and raising philanthropic funds. Of course, not all boards are expected to provide their personal financial support to the organizations they serve. Boards of member-serving organizations often have no significant responsibility for fund-raising, since the largest portion of revenue may come from dues, subscriptions, or meeting fees. Organizations that are primarily or entirely dependent on revenue from government contracts and grants also may not place emphasis on the board's fund-raising role. But in most charitable nonprofits, the board is expected to play a significant role in providing and soliciting philanthropic funds.

There are divergent views on whether board members should be required to give or raise a specific minimum amount, and the question raises some complicated issues. Some boards require a minimum personal gift from each board member. However, if this requirement is substantial, it may make it more difficult to achieve appropriate diversity among the board membership without making exceptions to the policy for those who may bring important skills and qualities but do not possess financial capacity. Then again, making such exceptions may introduce the perception that there are two classes of board members—those who give and those who don't. If that perception exists, those who cannot provide financial support may too readily defer to those who are known to be important sources of support to the organization. On the other hand, if the minimum is set so low that all board members can meet it, it can have the effect of converting an intended floor into a ceiling. In other words, some board members who have the financial ability to give more than the minimum may come to see the minimum as all that is expected of them, foreclosing the possibility of larger gifts. Such a situation may leave the organization with less total revenue than it might otherwise receive (Worth, 2005, p. 73).

Some boards do not set a minimum for personal giving by board members but adopt what is often called a *give-or-get policy,* requiring that each board member either give personally or solicit gifts from others to total the minimum amount. However, this may also establish a standard that some board members may find difficult to meet, especially if they are not involved in business or professional circles that provide access to wealth. Furthermore, it raises the risk that board members may solicit gifts without coordination with the organization's staff, creating a potentially chaotic situation that could alienate donors. An alternative to setting minimums for board giving and getting is to simply establish the expectation that each board member will give and participate in fund-raising proportionate to his or her capacity to do so. If that standard is firmly embedded in the culture of the board, then conscience and the judgment of peers may motivate the board to its peak fund-raising performance without the risks inherent in defining specific minimum amounts. Whatever approach is taken by individual boards, the subject of the board's responsibility for giving and fund-raising is on the agenda for discussion at many nonprofit organizations today (Worth, 2005).

Establish Standards for Organizational Performance and Hold the Organization Accountable

The board should define the standards by which an organization's effectiveness in achieving its mission is to be evaluated. Establishing standards to judge whether the organization is effectively employing the resources entrusted to it in pursuit of its mission is a fundamental aspect of the board's responsibility to those who provide financial support, to the society that grants the organization exemption from taxation, and to those whose needs its programs serve.

Some authors see the role of nonprofit boards as especially important because many nonprofits do not face the same market discipline that business firms do. As John Carver (1997) explains, "Without a market to summarize consumer judgment, [a nonprofit] organization literally does not know what its product is worth. . . . In the absence of a market test, *the board must perform that function*" (p. 7, italics original). Christine Letts and colleagues (1999a) elaborate on this point:

> Compared to their for-profit counterparts, nonprofit boards carry a much bigger burden in demanding and supporting performance. . . . [In the for-profit world,] both boards and management can use market feedback to assess how well they are performing: customers, investors, and creditors all make evaluations that eventually show up in the bottom line. . . . In contrast, the nonprofit board must often substitute for many of the feedback systems available in the marketplace. Nonprofit clients very often do not have a choice of providers, and are therefore unlikely to signal dissatisfaction by "voting with their feet." [Funders of nonprofits] may signal dissatisfaction by withdrawing their support, but are much less likely to play the affirmative role of a shareholder activist or institutional investor. (p. 133)

For these reasons, Letts et al. argue that "nonprofit boards are more vital [than for-profit boards] in ensuring performance and accountability" (p. 132).

How do the activities of actual boards compare with the functional responsibilities identified in the board literature? In 2008, Grant Thornton conducted a survey of nonprofit boards and asked what activity or responsibility was the "most important focus" of the board in the preceding year. Of those responding, 44 percent identified strategic planning, 19 percent fund-raising, 17 percent "ensuring effective programs," 16 percent "management oversight," and 4 percent protecting the organization's "reputation" (p. 3). When asked to evaluate the board's "strength" on each activity, the highest scores (7.1 to 7.9 on a 10-point scale) related to the accountability items, that is, ensuring effectiveness, management oversight, and protecting reputation. Strategic planning rated 6.8 and fund-raising was rated the lowest, at 5.1, suggesting that boards may not see themselves as having relative strength in that area.

The Board and the CEO

The relationship between the governing board and the organization's CEO is the subject of an extensive literature, reflecting divergent views. The questions addressed in this literature go well beyond who does what. They include fundamental assumptions about the nature of nonprofit governance and leadership.

At the heart of the matter is the question of who leads the nonprofit organization. In some organizations, the CEO may be dominant, with the board playing a passive role. The CEO proposes and the board disposes, often with little discussion or debate. As noted earlier, the CEO may even come to influence the selection of board members, in effect choosing his or her own bosses. This situation could arise in any organization, but it is especially common in organizations led by their founders, a special case we will discuss further in Chapter 5.

The realities of many organizations may enable CEOs to gain the upper hand. Boards are composed of "part-time amateurs," while the organization's staff, including the CEO, are "full-time professionals" (Chait, Holland, & Taylor, 1999, p. 3). In other words, the CEO may know more about the organization and its programs than do the lay trustees, especially if its programs involve highly technical services, and board members may be reluctant to show their ignorance by questioning. Large boards pose a special challenge in this regard. Individual board members may be unwilling to risk embarrassment by challenging a CEO's proposals in front of a large number of other board members, or they may assume that others on the board are well-informed and just go along with what appears to be a consensus. The CEO may control access to information about the organization, and indeed, the CEO may be the only one who knows what information actually exists. He or she may determine what information reaches the board and develop the agenda of matters that the board will even get to consider. In sum, it may be possible for a CEO to manipulate the board, orchestrate board meetings, and relegate the board to the role of a rubber stamp for his or her initiatives.

The danger in such a scenario is that the CEO could lead the board and the organization in directions that are inappropriate or risky and that the board may not be able to meet its responsibilities for ensuring adherence to mission, fiscal soundness, and optimum performance. For example, in 2002, the Washington, D.C., community was shocked by allegations that the long-serving executive director of the United Way of the National Capital Area (UWNCA), Oral Suer, had received as much as $1.6 million in improper payments, including nonreimbursed cash advances, encashment of vacation and sick leave that he had in fact taken, and reimbursement for travel and entertainment that were personal rather than related to United Way business. Those improper payments were alleged to have occurred over the period of 27 years that Mr. Suer was employed at the UWNCA (Wolverton, 2003b). The UWNCA's board had 45 members, and some observers attributed the abuses to the board's large size and the fact that the executive director had maintained tight control over communication with the board and among its members. One former employee of the organization told the *Chronicle of Philanthropy,* "This was definitely a 'clapper' board. They listened to staff members tell wonderful stories about how much money we were raising, and they applauded instead of asking tough questions" (Wolverton, 2003b, p. 27). Others cited the organization's internal culture, which made it difficult for the board to meet its fiduciary responsibilities. One board member said that the board met only four times a year, a total of 8 hours, and that the large board discouraged her from speaking. She said that she didn't have the phone numbers of the other board members, so she was unable to follow up with them after meetings. When she tried to obtain the numbers, a secretary at UWNCA told her that the numbers were confidential (Wolverton, 2003b).

But an alternative scenario, in which the board micromanages the organization and usurps the authority of the CEO, is no better. Such a board is likely to find it difficult to attract or retain a strong chief executive and may find itself making decisions about details outside its expertise. What most experts recommend is neither of these extreme scenarios but rather a partnership between the board and the CEO in the leadership of the organization. There are, however, different views on exactly how this partnership should be constructed and should operate.

Various authors have addressed the subject of the board–CEO relationship, and a comprehensive review would be beyond the scope of this chapter. But let's compare the thinking of three authors who are widely cited and whose different approaches highlight the major issues. First, we will look at John Carver's "policy governance model," described in his 1990 book *Boards That Make a Difference* and in subsequent editions published in 1997 and 2006. Carver draws a clear line between the board's responsibility for *policy making* and the executive's responsibility for *implementation* and provides what he calls an "operating system" to ensure that the distinction is maintained. Next, we will review the concept of "governance as leadership," described by Richard Chait, William Ryan, and Barbara Taylor (2005) in their book of that title, which was sponsored by BoardSource, an organization that provides research, education, and assistance to nonprofit organization boards. Chait et al. target Carver (2006), writing that "governing is too complicated to reduce to simple aphorisms, however seductive, like 'boards set policies which administrators implement'" (p. 5). Instead, they advocate a leadership role for the board that blurs the distinction between policy and implementation and focuses the attention of both boards and CEOs on "what matters most." And, finally, we will consider the research of Robert Herman and Dick Heimovics (2005), who argue that the most effective CEOs are those who accept the reality of their "psychological centrality" in the organization and provide "board-centered leadership," working to "develop, promote, and enable their boards' effective functioning" (p. 157).

Carver's Policy Governance Model

According to John Carver (2006), boards should be the leaders of the organization, "not by invading territory best left to management but by controlling the big picture, the long term, and the value laden" (p. 6). But his diagnosis of the prevailing reality is bleak. He observes boards mired in the trivial, largely reactive to staff initiatives, and absorbed in reviewing and rehashing actions the staff has already undertaken (pp. 19–20). Carver argues that board committees are often organized in a way that leads to this condition. Committee responsibilities often coincide with those of senior managers; for example, there may be committees on finance, fund-raising, program evaluation, and other areas of the organization's operation overseen by professional staff. In many cases, the staff prepares materials for meetings of the relevant committee and influences what items the committee considers. This structure pulls the board's attention into the details of each of the management silos. Board members thus become either super managers or just advisors to the professional staff. This prevents them from staying focused on big-picture matters such as mission and goals. As Carver writes, "Our tradition of board work encourages boards to derive their agendas from staff-based divisions of work. This common board practice is tantamount to classifying a manager's functions on the basis of his or her secretary's job areas" (p. 46).

Carver (2006) calls for a clear distinction between the work of the board and that of the management staff, and argues that the board should lead the organization, by focusing its attention on establishing *policies*. But this does not mean the kinds of policies that boards often discuss, such as personnel policies, which really reflect the work of management and are related to implementation rather than leadership of the organization. The board should make policies that reflect the board's values and the interests of the "moral owners" of the organization.

In Carver's (1997) model, boards lead by developing and maintaining policies in four areas:

1. *Ends to be achieved:* Ends policy statements describe what the organization is to achieve and "could be called results, impacts, goals, or outcomes as well as ends, each title having its own connotations" (p. 31). The broadest ends statement would be the organization's mission. More specific ends policies might address more detailed goals—for example, those related to products, consumers, and costs.

2. *Means to the ends:* In Carver's model, means statements are expressed in terms of "executive limitations"—that is, boundaries that the CEO may not cross in pursuing the ends established by the board. For example, the broadest statement of policy in this area might be that the CEO not violate the law. More detailed limitations might address more

specific constraints, perhaps levels of cost and debt that may not be exceeded. Carver argues that by stating executive limitations in negative terms—that is, by prescribing what executives may *not* do—the board preserves maximum flexibility for the CEO. Subject to the constraints that the board has explicitly stipulated, the CEO is free to determine the best methods for achieving the ends that the board has established, without the board's inappropriate involvement in operations.

3. *Board–staff relationship:* Policy statements in this area clearly delineate the responsibilities of the board and the CEO, defining what decisions are delegated to the CEO and which ones are retained by the board. This category of statement also includes specific criteria for monitoring and evaluating the CEO's performance. Carter argues that one benefit of such clarity is that it addresses the common concern about board members communicating directly with other staff within the organization or with other volunteers. "When the roles are clear, it is possible for anyone to talk with or elicit wisdom from anyone with no harmful effects on the 'chain of command'" (p. 118).

4. *Process of governance:* This fourth category of policy addresses the board's own role and operation, clarifying which owners it represents and defining its own "job process and products"—for example, the procedure through which new board members are elected (p. 33).

A board practicing Carver's (1997) model would be driven in its meetings by the need to develop and maintain its policy manual. When issues arise, the first questions to be addressed would be to which category of policy the issue belongs, whose issue it is, and whether it is addressed by an existing policy—if not, a new policy needs to be adopted, eliciting discussion and debate. Carver argues that this approach steers boards away from the mundane, from show-and-tell presentations by staff, and from merely rubber-stamping the staff's recommendations. According to Carver, following the policy governance approach leads the board toward discussions that are focused on the long term and rooted in the board's values and perspectives (p. 181).

Chait, Ryan, and Taylor: Governance as Leadership

Now let's examine a different approach, the governance-as-leadership model proposed by Chait et al. (2005). The authors agree with many of Carver's criticisms of the way boards operate today. Boards are not leading their organizations. They are reactive to staff initiatives. They structure their work in a way that draws them into managerial details and routine technical work. Indeed, these authors argue, things are turned upside down. Boards are so mired in operational details that they are, in effect, *managing* their organizations. Meanwhile, CEOs are articulating missions, beliefs, values, and cultures—in essence *leading* their organizations and engaging in activities that "closely resemble conventional notions of *governing*" (p. 3, italics added). As the authors explain,

> In theory, if not in practice, boards of trustees are supposed to be the ultimate guardians of institutional ethos and organizational values. Boards are charged with setting the organization's agenda and priorities. . . . Boards are empowered to specify the most important problems and opportunities that management should pursue. If this logic holds, as we contend, then many nonprofit executives are not only leading their organizations, but . . . they are actually governing them as well. (p. 3)

With sophisticated leaders at the helm of nonprofits, a substantial portion of the governance portfolio has moved to the executive suite. The residue remains in the boardroom. This surprise twist in the story line suggests that the real threat to nonprofit governance today may not be a board that micro*manages* but a board that micro*governs,* while blind to governance as leadership. (pp. 4–5, italics original)

But while their diagnosis of board problems is similar to Carver's (1997), Chait and his colleagues (2005) offer a quite different prescription. Instead of drawing sharp lines between policy and implementation, clearly dividing the role of the board and that of the CEO, they call for breaking down the barriers and focusing the attention of both the board and the CEO on the critical issues facing the organization. In other words, the question should not be, "Is this an issue of policy or implementation?" Rather, the question should be, "Is the issue at hand important or unimportant, central or peripheral?" (Taylor, Chait, & Holland, 1999, p. 62).

In their book, Chait et al. (2005) define a new model, which they call "governance as leadership," based on three "modes" of governance in which a board may be operating at any given time:

1. *The fiduciary mode:* When the board is operating in this mode, it is concerned with the "bedrock of governance," that is, with matters such as stewardship of tangible assets, faithfulness to mission, performance accountability, and obedience to law—in other words, generally addressing its legal responsibilities.

2. *The strategic mode:* When operating in the strategic mode, boards go beyond their basic fiduciary responsibilities and "create a true strategic partnership with management," addressing matters such as the organization's long-term directions and goals (p. 69).

3. *The generative mode:* A board in generative mode is engaged in generative thinking—that is, the creative, out-of-the-box thinking in which visionary leaders often engage. It relates to values and judgments, encompasses "sense making" (essentially, coming to understand things in new ways), and may result in insights that lead to paradigm shifts. The authors say that generative thinking is a necessary foundation for setting direction and goals and thus an essential activity of leadership.

Chait et al. (2005) observe that most boards work only in the fiduciary and strategic modes and therefore are not participating in leadership of the organization. However, "when trustees work well in *all three* of these modes, the board achieves governance as leadership" (p. 7, italics added). Thus, rather than maintaining a clear distinction between what is the board's territory and what is the CEO's, Chait et al. propose that boards and CEOs focus together on what matters most, moving together among the three modes as appropriate to address the issues at hand. Setting goals, and thus using generative thinking, cannot be a task for the CEO or the board alone but rather must be a *shared* activity.

Because we resolutely regard this [generative thinking] as shared work, we cannot offer what the board-improvement field so often promises trustees and executives: a set of bright lights that neatly divide the board's work (policy, strategy, and governance) from the staff's (administration, implementation, and management). It simply makes no sense to reserve generative work for boards when leaders are vital to the process, or to reserve for leaders work that belongs at the heart of governance. Generative work demands a fusion of thinking, not a division of labor. (p. 95)

Simply stated, Carver (1997) envisions the board and the CEO on opposite sides of the table, one clearly labeled "policy" and the other "implementation." Chait and his coauthors (2005) envision a three-sided table, each representing one of the modes discussed above. The board and the CEO sit together on one side but move around the table to the other sides, depending on the nature of the business to be considered at the time.

Which model is "right"? Does Carver's (1997) policy governance model improve board performance? Does Chait et al.'s (2005) governance-as-leadership approach improve performance? One 2003 study, by Patricia Nobbie and Jeffrey Brudney, compared organizations using the Carver model with others that had received training from BoardSource (sponsors of Chait et al.'s work), and suggested mixed results. There were few differences, and those were generally not significant. The job satisfaction of CEOs working under the Carver model measured somewhat higher than that of the others, but the researchers found the difference to be statistically non-significant. One important conclusion of the study was that boards that had received training tended to perform better than those that had not been trained, regardless of which model had been used. Carver, with characteristic confidence, responds to the Nobbie and Brudney study in the 2006 edition of his book, arguing that his model is superior and that the latter authors' choice of variables reflects an inaccurate understanding of its purpose.

Herman and Heimovics: Psychological Centrality and Board-Centered Leadership

In Carver's (1997) approach, boards lead their organizations. Chait et al. (2005) describe a model for leadership shared by the board and the chief executive. Robert Herman and Dick Heimovics (2005) provide a third perspective. Based on their research concerning effective nonprofit CEOs, they offer a pragmatic approach, concluding that CEOs should lead but that their leadership needs to be *board centered* and designed to support the board in meeting its governing responsibilities.

The *purposive-rational model* of organizations, based on Max Weber's theory of the bureaucracy, conceives of the board as the top of a hierarchy and the CEO as merely its agent. Indeed, Herman and Heimovics's (2005) review of the normative literature on nonprofit boards finds that most research has been based on that model and thus "has advanced a heroic ideal for nonprofit boards" (p. 155). However, they apply the *social-constructionist model* and explain that "official or intended goals, structures, and procedures may exist only on paper. Actual goals, structures, and procedures emerge and change as participants interact and socially construct the meaning of ongoing events" (p. 156). Regardless of what the organizational chart or the conventional view of organizations may suggest, Herman and Heimovics find that the reality in most organizations is that of *executive psychological centrality*. In other words, it is the CEO who is actually *seen as* responsible for the organization's success or failure. They interviewed CEOs, board chairs, and other staff members and found that *all* of them saw the chief executive as "centrally responsible for what happens," including both successful and unsuccessful events (p. 156). This does not imply that the CEO holds more formal authority than the board or that the CEO *is* indeed the central figure in the life of the organization. "Psychological centrality" means that he or she is *perceived as* responsible, even by members of the board.

If this is the reality, then what do Herman and Heimovics (2005) recommend that CEOs should do? They do *not* recommend that CEOs become autocrats or demote their boards to rubber stamps, but rather that they take a leadership role to ensure "that boards fulfill their legal, organizational, and public roles" (p. 156). In exercising board-centered leadership, CEOs take responsibility for "supporting and facilitating the board's work." In doing so, they engage in six behaviors that Herman and Heimovics observed among the effective, board-centered executives they studied (p. 158):

1. Facilitating interaction in board relationships

2. Showing consideration and respect toward board members

3. Envisioning change and innovation for the organization with the board

4. Providing useful and helpful information to the board

5. Initiating and maintaining structure for the board

6. Promoting board accomplishments and productivity

Herman and Heimovics (2005) conclude that not only are the CEOs who have developed these board-centered leadership skills effective in their roles, but they also have hardworking, effective boards. "The board-centered executive is likely to be effective because he or she has grasped that the work of the board is critical in adapting to and affecting the constraints and opportunities in the environment" (p. 159). In a study of "high-impact nonprofits," Crutchfield and Grant (2008) draw a similar conclusion, writing that while "many leaders try to minimize their interactions with their board, or they perpetually fight with them . . . great nonprofit leaders have a positive relationship with the board. They share leadership to advance the larger cause" (p. 178).

Nonprofit Board Effectiveness

"So," students may be wondering at this point in the chapter, "what's the bottom line?" Are most nonprofit boards effective or not? What are the characteristics of effective boards? What is the right way to define the relationship between the board and the nonprofit CEO? What is indeed the best model for governance, and what are the best practices that boards should follow?

Critics of Board Performance

In answer to the question of how nonprofit boards are doing, there is no shortage of negative commentary. For example, Chait et al. (1999) reported that "after 10 years of research and dozens of engagements as consultants to nonprofit boards, we have reached a rather stark conclusion: effective governance by a board of trustees is a relatively rare and unnatural act" (p. 1). Carver (1997) essentially agrees, writing that "the problem is not that a group or an individual *occasionally* slips into poor practice, but that intelligent, caring individuals regularly exhibit procedures of governance that are deeply flawed" (p. 9, italics original).

Writing in the *Stanford Social Innovation Review,* Michael Klausner and Jonathon Small (2005) note little improvement since Chait et al.'s (1999) and Carver's (1997) observations of several years before. Klausner and Small reference a 2004 newspaper story that revealed financial mismanagement at the Beard Foundation and write, "In recent years, news reports like this one increasingly suggest that too many directors of nonprofit organizations are failing to govern"

(p. 42). They cite the opinions of (unnamed) "commentators [who] suggest that each and every director should work harder and more effectively at governance" and conclude, "In our view, the commentators are right on the money" (p. 43).

Such criticisms cannot be ignored, but it may be prudent to question the evidence behind such sweeping statements. Most are based on experience rather than research. Some are reported by consultants who are called on to work with troubled boards and whose samples therefore may be somewhat self-selecting. Others, like Klausner and Small (2005), generalize from single anecdotes. Moreover, some assessments reflect the values and views of the assessor about what nonprofit organizations and their boards should be like. Surely, instances of board corruption or mismanagement are to be deplored. But it is reasonable to question whether individual cases illustrate the systematic failure of nonprofit governance or merely reveal the frailties of particular boards and individuals, which are unfortunately all too often visible in business and government as well. However, it is equally reasonable to believe that the performance of boards and their members can be improved and to continue the search for best practices in nonprofit governance.

The Search for Best Practices

Various researchers have attempted to identify behaviors that are associated with effective nonprofit governing boards—that is, to identify those practices that, if followed, will lead to effective governance. In 2005, BoardSource assembled a panel of experts to address the question. Their consensus produced the following "twelve principles that power exceptional boards":

1. *Constructive partnership:* Exceptional boards govern in constructive partnership with the chief executive, recognizing that the effectiveness of the board and that of the chief executive are interdependent.

2. *Mission driven:* Exceptional boards shape and uphold the mission, articulate a compelling vision, and ensure the congruence between decisions and core values.

3. *Strategic thinking:* Exceptional boards allocate time to what matters most and continuously engage in strategic thinking to hone the organization's direction.

4. *Culture of inquiry:* Exceptional boards institutionalize a culture of inquiry, mutual respect, and constructive debate that leads to sound and shared decision making.

5. *Independent-mindedness:* Exceptional boards are independent-minded. When making decisions, board members put the interests of the organization above all else.

6. *Ethos of transparency:* Exceptional boards promote an ethos of transparency by ensuring that donors, stakeholders, and interested members of the public have access to appropriate and accurate information regarding finances, operations, and results.

7. *Compliance with integrity:* Exceptional boards promote strong ethical values and disciplined compliance by establishing appropriate mechanisms for active oversight.

8. *Sustaining resources:* Exceptional boards link bold visions and ambitious plans to financial support, expertise, and networks of influence.

9. *Results-oriented:* Exceptional boards are results-oriented. They measure the organization's advancement toward its mission and evaluate the performance of major programs and services.

10. *Intentional board practices:* Exceptional boards intentionally structure themselves to fulfill essential governance duties and to support organizational priorities.

11. *Continuous learning:* Exceptional boards embrace the qualities of a continuous learning organization, evaluating their own performance and assessing the value they add to the organization.

12. *Revitalization:* Exceptional boards energize themselves through planned turnover, thoughtful recruitment, and inclusiveness (n.p.).[2]

BoardSource's 12 principles of governance offer an attractive description of an exceptional board and reflect the consensus of a distinguished panel of experts assembled to develop them. But it is nevertheless primarily a compilation of practitioner wisdom rather than science. There remains a relative paucity of research on the subject of nonprofit board performance, and there is no single definition of board effectiveness. This is so in part because there is no single standard for defining the effectiveness of nonprofit organizations. As John Carver (2006) notes, the variables chosen for measurement in some research studies seem to imply

> that effectiveness in governance is to be judged by whether board members are more fulfilled, challenged, or involved; the CEO is happier or the board is less meddlesome; the board raises more funds; grant revenues are increased; committees are more active; or the board chair perceives the CEO to be meeting his or her objectives. (p. 337)

But the link between such variables and the effectiveness of boards—or organizations—remains elusive.

In a 2002 review of the literature on nonprofit effectiveness, Robert Herman and David Renz conclude that "[board] effectiveness is whatever significant stakeholders think it is, and there is no single objective reality." Calling the concept of best practices "somewhat of a holy grail," they advise nonprofit boards and CEOs to take a skeptical view of "one right way" prescriptions:

> Many sources that claim to offer "best practices" for NPO [nonprofit organization] boards or management provide little or no basis for their assertions. *The evidence from our . . . study does not support the claim that particular board and management practices are automatically best or even good (that is, that using them leads to effective boards and organizations).* We prefer to talk in terms of "promising practices" to describe those approaches that warrant consideration.
>
> Not only is there no "silver bullet" (i.e., one practice that ensures board effectiveness)—there is no "silver arsenal." In the context of other research, we support the assertion that boards (perhaps with facilitative leadership from their chief executives) need to identify those processes that are most useful to them. Boards should not use a practice just because other boards, experts, or consultants say it is useful. They should ask some key questions: Does the practice fit this board's circumstances? Does the practice actually help the board reach good decisions? Does the practice contribute to the organization's success? (pp. 6–7, italics original)

Herman and Renz's (2002) caution should not be interpreted as saying that the literature on nonprofit governing boards has nothing to offer and should be disregarded. Rather, their conclusions are consistent with the philosophy expressed in Chapter 1 of this text: There is often no right answer, and the best way is often pragmatic and eclectic. This includes viewing a problem from multiple perspectives and drawing from various approaches selectively as the situation may dictate.

The Challenge of Nonprofit Governance

Serving as a member of a nonprofit board today is an interesting and challenging assignment. Nonprofit boards are buffeted by strong crosscurrents emanating from virtually all their constituencies. The forces of law, media scrutiny, and more demanding funders are pushing them to do a better job of governance. At the same time, the financial pressures facing many nonprofits in light of diminished government support, increased competition for philanthropy, and the rising needs and expectations of their clients are leading to greater emphasis on their responsibilities to serve as the organization's advocates, protectors, and fund-raisers. As the brief review in this chapter reveals, the literature of nonprofit governance includes an abundance of advice, but some of it is inconsistent, even contradictory. Today's boards are being exhorted not only to raise money and promote the organization, but also to be more aggressive in monitoring its performance. They are told to develop independent sources of information about the organization's operations but to stay focused on the big picture and not meddle in operations, to maintain a clear line between themselves and their CEO but not to forfeit their responsibility for leadership.

Nonprofit boards are expected to be Janus-like—that is, like the Roman god of doorways and arches, who was said to have two faces and be able to look outward and inward at the same time. Nonprofit organizations are open systems, with vaguely defined and often porous boundaries. The board is positioned on that boundary, between the organization and its external environment. From that position, the board is expected to look inward, fulfilling its fiduciary responsibilities on behalf of the membership or society. It is a kind of watchdog, responsible for ensuring that the organization is accountable for the resources entrusted to it, that those resources are used effectively in pursuit of its mission and for representing the interests and viewpoints of the owners, whoever they may be.

But board members are also expected to be looking outward in order to meet their responsibilities to the organization itself and advance its interests. This is especially true for boards of charitable nonprofits, which may depend at least in part on philanthropic support. Because they are often leading citizens themselves, board members bring credibility to the organization in the broader community and authenticate its worthiness to receive support. They serve as its ambassadors and advocates, increasing its visibility and reputation within their own social and business circles. They protect the organization against inappropriate intrusions on its autonomy by government, donors, or other external forces. Further, they have a responsibility to ensure the organization's financial strength and sustainability, which many accomplish in part through giving or helping secure financial resources. These dual responsibilities—to society and to the organization itself, looking inward at the same time as looking outward—can sometimes be complex and competing. As Chait et al. (1999) explain,

> Boards constantly wrestle with when to be "product champions" and when to be studied neutrals—whether to stand and cheer like rabid partisans when the President of the

United States delivers the State of the Union address or to remain seated and stone-faced like the Supreme Court justices. (p. 3)

As Table 4.2 suggests, the complex responsibilities of boards may imply somewhat different ideal qualities in the individuals selected to serve, depending on which set of responsibilities is emphasized—a possible trade-off between what is often called "wisdom" (shorthand for the skills and judgment needed to govern well) and "wealth" (meaning the ability to give or obtain funds and other external resources). To fulfill their fiduciary responsibilities, boards must include individuals of integrity, and at least some will need to have specialized knowledge in finance and perhaps in professional fields related to the organization's programs and services. For example, a human services organization might need some board members with a background in social work, and it may be important that the boards of medical institutions include at least some members who understand medical terminology or the economics of health care. To properly represent the needs of the community and clients served by the organization, boards also need diverse memberships reflective of their constituencies, perhaps even including some who have been beneficiaries of the organization's programs—for example, former clients, patients, or students.

But to advance its reputation, protect its interests, and secure funds, a nonprofit also needs board members who are individuals of stature in their communities, perhaps having influence with governmental officials or other regulators, and who have either the wealth to be significant donors or access to other individuals, foundations, or corporations that can provide financial support. John Pocock (1989) notes that "wealth and wisdom are not mutually exclusive [qualities of human beings]" (quoted in Worth, 2005, p. 50). He is, of course, correct in that there may be *individual* candidates for governing board service who are possessed both of wisdom and of wealth—that is, who are equally well suited to meet their responsibilities for governing the organization and for serving as its external advocates and fund-raisers. But not all individuals may be strong in all the requisite qualities. Boards attempting to craft their membership and faced with selecting a new member to fill an open seat may indeed face a dilemma regarding which qualities should be emphasized.

TABLE 4.2 ■ The Board's Sometimes Competing Responsibilities

To society:	To the organization:
Accountability for resources and results	Advocacy and authenticity
Adherence to mission and law	Protection of autonomy
Representation of community needs	Fiscal stability and sustainability
Indicated board member qualities:	**Indicated board member qualities:**
Integrity	Stature
Expertise on programs and finances	Influence
Knowledge of community/clients	Wealth or access to wealth

Likewise, in deciding on which issues to focus its limited time and attention, a board may face either-or choices between the tasks associated with governing and those associated with advancing the organization, its interests, and its resources. Today's environment presents increasing pressures on boards to do all things better—to be better stewards and better fundraisers and to become more engaged with the organization's planning, programs, and effectiveness while also giving and raising more funds to support its work. The proper trade-offs between wealth and wisdom and how to balance the sometimes competing demands are questions prompting discussion—and some anxiety—in many nonprofit boardrooms today.

Chapter Summary

The governing board holds ultimate responsibility for the nonprofit organization. There are various types of boards, including those elected by the organization's membership; self-perpetuating boards; boards appointed by some outside authority; and hybrids, which may include elected, self-perpetuating, appointed, and ex officio members. Each of these types offers advantages but also introduces risks for the organization and the board.

The governing board's fiduciary responsibilities are defined in law and include the duty of care, the duty of loyalty, and the duty of obedience. Since the passage of intermediate sanctions in 1996 and the Sarbanes-Oxley Act in 2002, there has been increased scrutiny of nonprofit boards by the federal and state governments, the media, and other organizations. Under intermediate sanctions, nonprofit board members can face individual penalties for violating their fiduciary responsibilities, and many boards adopted new conflict-of-interest and disclosure policies in response to that legislation. Although Sarbanes-Oxley applies primarily to publicly traded corporations, many nonprofit organizations have voluntarily adopted some or all of its provisions, and some have been encompassed in legislation passed by states. Independent Sector's Panel on the Nonprofit Sector developed 33 principles for good governance in 2005 and 2006, and the implementation by the IRS of a revised Form 990 in 2009 further focused the nation's attention on nonprofit accountability and the responsibilities of boards. The panel's recommendations and the revised Form 900 include Sarbanes-Oxley-like principles, and they will be considered further in Chapter 6 of this book.

Functional responsibilities of boards have been defined in the literature and include appointing, supporting, and evaluating the CEO; establishing a clear institutional mission and purpose; approving the organization's programs to ensure consistency with its mission and financial prudence; ensuring sound management and financial stability; and establishing standards by which the organization's performance will be evaluated. Some people view the board's responsibility to ensure the organization's financial stability and sustainability as implying an obligation on the part of board members to give from their personal resources and actively engage in fund-raising. Some boards have policies requiring that members give or raise a minimum amount, but others rely on a culture that encourages members to participate as appropriate to their capacities. A 2008 survey found that most boards rated themselves as strong on governance responsibilities but relatively weak on fund-raising.

The relationship between the governing board and the CEO is the subject of a substantial literature. In some organizations, especially those managed by a founder, the CEO may be a dominant figure, and the board may be largely reactive to the executive's initiatives. Most experts call for a partnership between the board and the CEO but differ on how that partnership should be designed. Three experts discussed in this chapter include John Carver, whose policy governance model suggests a clear separation of roles, defined in policies established by the board related to ends, means, board–staff relationships, and governance process. Chait and colleagues proposed a model they call "governance-as-leadership," in which the lines between the responsibilities of the board and the CEO are broken down and both work together in focusing on the most critical issues and questions facing the organization. Leadership is shared, particularly when both engage in generative thinking. The research of Robert Herman and Dick Heimovics revealed that in reality both board members and the chief executive see the CEO as primarily responsible for the organization's success or failure, a condition they call "executive psychological centrality." They advise CEOs to accept that reality and practice board-centered leadership, not usurping the responsibilities of the board but rather supporting and facilitating its work.

In today's environment, there is considerable emphasis on the effectiveness of nonprofit governance. There are many criticisms, but there is a paucity of research to substantiate many of them. BoardSource and others have identified best practices of effective boards, but research by Herman and Renz suggests that there may be no one right way that works for every organization.

Nonprofit boards today face conflicting pressures. They are expected to do a more effective job of governing but also become more active in generating financial support for the organizations they serve. The appropriate trade-offs between the wealth and wisdom needed to meet these sometimes competing priorities are a matter of current discussion and debate in many nonprofit boardrooms.

Notes

1. Some experts recommend that advisory groups not be called "boards" at all but rather "councils" or by some other term that does not imply legal responsibility for the organization.

2. Reprinted with permission from Twelve Principles of Governance That Power Exceptional Boards a publication of BoardSource, formerly the National Center for Nonprofit Boards. For more information about BoardSource, call 800-883-6262 or visit www.boardsource.org. BoardSource © 2006.

KEY TERMS AND CONCEPTS

board-centered leadership	executive psychological centrality	intermediate sanctions
board of directors		Panel on the Nonprofit Sector
board of trustees	ex officio	policy governance model
BoardSource	fiduciary mode	private inurement
conflict of interest	Form 990	purposive-rational model
duty of care	generative mode	Sarbanes-Oxley Act
duty of loyalty	give-or-get policy	self-perpetuating
duty of obedience	governance as leadership	social-constructionist model
excess benefit transaction	governing boards	strategic mode

CASE 4.1 The American University

The American University is an independent, coeducational institution of about 10,000 undergraduate, graduate, and professional students, chartered by the U.S. Congress and located in Washington, D.C. In early 2005, Benjamin Ladner had been president for 11 years, during which the university campus had expanded, applications had increased, and the endowment had grown (Jaffe, 2006, p. 78). But then, in March of that year, the board of trustees received an anonymous letter alleging that Ladner had used university funds for extravagant personal expenses.

Ladner's employment contract allowed for the reimbursement of expenses for university-related activities and provided other specific benefits, such as a car and driver. It was reported that the contract had been signed only by Ladner and the chair of the board of trustees and that it was never approved by the full board. Some trustees had expressed concern about the president's high compensation, but the board's audit committee had never examined the president's expenses (Jaffee, 2006). One unhappy trustee said, "It began to feel like the board reported to [the president] rather than the reverse" (p. 118).

When the anonymous letter was received, one trustee suggested going after the whistle-blower, but the board decided to start an investigation of the president's expenses (Jaffee, 2006). The president was placed on leave, and a law firm and auditor were engaged to review his expenses. The president hired his own lawyers and maintained that he had not knowingly misspent university funds (Fain, 2005a). The board split into two camps. One supported the president and said the board was at fault for not having monitored his expenses. Another blamed the president for poor judgment and called for his permanent dismissal (Jaffee, 2006). Statements by the two factions reached the media, and acrimony among trustees became public. Four members of the board, including the chair, resigned (Fain, 2005b).

Upon completion of the audit, in October of 2005, the board voted to dismiss the president, although controversy remained over his severance compensation. Some members of the board maintained that his employment contract was not valid because it had not been presented to the full board (Fain, 2005c). Senator Charles Grassley, then chair of the U.S. Senate Finance Committee, began an investigation, and some people claimed that because the university was chartered by Congress, the Congress should replace the board (Jaffee, 2006). The controversy led, in part, to the IRS's closer examination of the compensation of university presidents and gave impetus to the efforts of Independent Sector to establish clear principles of good governance for the entire nonprofit sector (which are discussed elsewhere in this text).

By June of 2006, the university's board of trustees had developed and adopted recommendations to improve its inclusiveness, accountability, and oversight (Fain, 2006). The reforms included expanding the board such that individuals who had served during President Ladner's administration were no longer a majority. In addition, the bylaws were amended to include a student and two faculty as nonvoting members. Other reforms included performance evaluations of trustees, procedures for greater board oversight of the president's contract and expenses, and provision for town hall meetings between the board and members of the university community (Fain, 2006).

CASE 4.2 Robin Hood Foundation

The Robin Hood Foundation is a nonprofit that funds poverty-fighting organizations in New York City. Its board includes prominent Wall Street hedge fund managers as well as other well-known figures. An article by Donmoyer and Fitzgerald (2007) in *The Washington Post* raised questions about Robin Hood's "rainy-day fund," which had grown to $144.5 million from $20 million in a decade. The article noted that about half the fund was invested in hedge funds, managed by members of the Robin Hood board.

The article stated that there was nothing illegal about the arrangement. Robin Hood's executive director also pointed out that the managers are among the best and that the foundation's investment returns had been excellent. The amount of management fees being paid was standard in the industry. He said that decisions on where to invest were made by a committee of Robin Hood's board and that it was not allowed to invest in funds managed by members of that committee. He also explained that the board members received fees for managing the foundation's funds because their company policies did not allow them to charge different fees to different investors. The director of the Better Business Bureau's (BBB) New York Philanthropic Advisory Service said that Robin Hood met BBB's standards for charity accountability. (The BBB standards are discussed in Chapter 6 of this text.)

But, according to the article, some people raised questions about the role of Robin Hood board members in managing the organization's funds. Senator Charles Grassley, a member of the Senate Finance Committee who is often critical of nonprofit organizations, said, "I don't remember Robin Hood keeping [management fees] as his cut." An official of the Kellogg Foundation described the situation as "flirting with self-dealing" (Donmoyer & Fitzgerald, 2007, p. F7). The national president of the Better Business Bureau's Wise Giving Alliance also raised questions: "You start to wonder what happens in the year that the hedge fund doesn't do well. Does the board have the power to fire the hedge-fund manager?" (p. F7).

CASE 4.3 The Hershey Trust

Milton Hershey was the founder of the Hershey Chocolate Company, which is now known as Hershey Foods, the maker of "Hershey's Milk Chocolate," "Hershey's Kisses," and other products with which all Americans are familiar.

Hershey and his wife, Catherine, did not have children of their own. In 1909, they founded a school to educate poor male orphans, created a charitable trust to support the school, and appointed nine trustees to manage the trust for the school's benefit. In 1918, after his wife's death, Hershey gave his entire personal fortune, consisting mostly of stock in the company, to the Hershey Trust to support the Milton S. Hershey School. The school today enrolls a diverse student body of about 1,200 low-income young men and women on a residential campus in central Pennsylvania. The students do not pay tuition or other fees, since the trust receives $80 million from its interest in the chocolate company each year to support the school's operation (McCracken, 2009).

By 2001, the Hershey Trust had grown to over $5 billion, most of which was stock in Hershey Foods. Indeed, the charitable trust owned a controlling interest in the company, and company stock was 56 percent of the Trust's assets (Gadsden, 2002). As of 2009, as mentioned above, the trust's annual income from the chocolate company provided more than $80 million toward the school's operation. With 6,200 employees, the company was the largest employer in its hometown of Hershey, Pennsylvania (Scully, 2009).

However, in 2002, the trustees of the Hershey Trust were concerned by the lack of diversification in the trust's investments and by the increasing competition from other candy makers. Fearing that the chocolate company's decline could endanger the school's future, they proposed selling the trust's controlling interest. Wrigley, best known for its chewing gum, was prepared to pay $12.5 billion (McCracken, 2009).

The Hershey community strongly objected, fearing the loss of jobs and a negative impact on the local economy. Under Pennsylvania law, the state attorney general oversees charitable trusts. The attorney general at the time, Mike Fisher, sided with the community and petitioned the state court to block the sale,

(Continued)

(Continued)

arguing that it "could have profoundly negative consequences" for the Hershey region. The court agreed, and the sale was stopped. The Pennsylvania legislature later passed a law affirming the court's decision (Larkin, 2002). Some argued that the attorney general and the court had overstepped their authority and had dangerously altered the law regarding the fiduciary responsibilities of charitable trustees. They might now be required to make their decisions not only in light of the interests of the trust's beneficiaries, but also in consideration of local political and economic pressures (Larkin, 2002).

The chocolate company's position continued to decline after 2002. By 2009, Hershey Foods had suffered years of stagnating revenue and a slumping stock price, which reduced the assets of the trust and thus the revenue of the school. In addition, a wave of mergers in the food industry was presenting increased competition from large multinational producers. Meanwhile, Hershey was finding it difficult to grow its business outside of the United States and derived only 10 percent of its revenue from overseas (Wachman, 2009).

Mars merged with Wrigley in 2008 and, in 2009, Kraft made a bid to take over the famous British candy brand, Cadbury (Scully, 2009). The trustees of the Hershey Trust were deeply concerned by this new challenge to Hershey Foods. They knew the law would not permit them to *sell* the company, but they considered making an offer to *buy* Cadbury. Kraft had offered $16.5 billion for Cadbury, and Hershey would need to offer more. Hershey was only half the size of Cadbury and a fraction of Kraft's size. Buying Cadbury would require borrowing massive amounts of money. It was reported that differences arose between the views of the company's board and management, on the one hand, and the board of the charitable trust on the other. The company's board and management were concerned that such borrowing would cause the company's credit ratings and stock price to decline, raise the cost of future borrowing, and hurt profits. The charitable trustees were concerned that failing to buy Cadbury would mean that Hershey would find it even more difficult to compete internationally in the future and that the long-term interests of the trust and the school would be jeopardized (Wachman, 2009).

Throughout January of 2010, there was daily speculation in the financial media about a possible Hershey counteroffer for Cadbury. But, on January 22, Hershey announced that it would not proceed, and Kraft announced that Cadbury had accepted its revised offer of 11.9 billion British pounds ($19.4 billion). Kraft and Cadbury combined would become the largest candy company in the world (Gural, 2010).

QUESTIONS FOR DISCUSSION

1. Should boards of nonprofits be concerned only with the intention of donors and the interests of those who benefit from the nonprofit's assets, or should they also consider the impact of their decisions on local communities, as the court directed in the case of the Hershey Trust?

2. Why might the board of Hershey Foods and the trustees of the Milton S. Hershey Trust have held somewhat different views of the possible bid for Cadbury? To whom and for what are the respective boards accountable?

3. What are the issues in the case of the Robin Hood Foundation? Although they are legal, are the relationships between the board and the managers of the organization's finances appropriate? Why or why not? What safeguards would you introduce to assure the organization's donors that the board is behaving properly?

4. Which of the governing board's legal and functional responsibilities discussed in this chapter are relevant to the controversy at The American University?

5. Do you see any ways in which the recommendations of Carver, Chait et al., and Herman and Heimovics might be relevant to The American University case?

SUGGESTIONS FOR FURTHER READING

Books

BoardSource. (2010). *The handbook of nonprofit governance*. San Francisco: Jossey-Bass.

Carver, J. (2006). *Boards that make a difference: A new design for leadership in nonprofit and public organizations* (3rd ed.). San Francisco: Jossey-Bass.

Chait, R. P., Ryan, W. R., & Taylor, B. E. (2005). *Governance as leadership: Reframing the work of nonprofit boards*. Hoboken, NJ: Wiley.

Eadie, D. (2009). *Extraordinary governing boards* (2nd ed.). Sudbury, MA: Jones & Bartlett Learning.

Worth, M. J. (2005). *Securing the future: A fund-raising guide for boards of independent colleges and universities*. Washington, DC: Association of Governing Boards of Universities and Colleges.

Worth, M. J. (2008). *Sounding boards*. Washington, DC: Association of Governing Boards of Universities and Colleges.

Websites

Association of Governing Boards of Universities and Colleges, http://www.agb.org/

BoardSource, http://www.boardsource.org/

Independent Sector, http://www.independentsector.org/

Chapter Outline

chapter 5

The deep commitment of a leader, as evidenced by his or her willingness to sacrifice and suffer for the cause, confers a charismatic appeal. Martin Luther King Jr. never held public office. But the words "I have a dream" created a vision of a different America that inspired millions and changed the nation more dramatically than most presidents of the United States have ever been able to do.

National Archives, Records of the U.S. Information Agency, Record Group 306 (ARC ID 542014)

Executive Leadership

5

C hapter 1 of this text discussed why nonprofit management is a distinctive undertaking, different in important ways from management in the for-profit sector or in government. Among these differences were the need for nonprofits to integrate mission, the acquisition of resources, and strategy; the complex relationships among a nonprofit organization's stakeholders (including volunteers) that require negotiation and compromise and demand that executives possess a high tolerance for ambiguity; and the need to manage a double bottom line of financial results and social impact.

These differences may not directly affect the work of everyone employed at a nonprofit organization. For example, there is no particular nonprofit way of processing bills or payments, programming computers, or maintaining physical facilities. Many who work in the nonprofit sector are engaged in such technical work, and their skills may be readily transferable across the for-profit, nonprofit, and governmental sectors. Even those who provide the services of a nonprofit organization may not perform their functions in any unique way. For example, a doctor working in a nonprofit, for-profit, or government hospital will follow the same medical protocols; a counselor working with clients recovering from drug or alcohol addiction may use the same treatments whether working in a nonprofit organization or a state-managed entity; and teachers in private and public schools may teach a similar curriculum. Where the unique characteristics of nonprofit management come together with the greatest significance is in the position of the chief executive officer. The CEO is a position requiring unique skills in both management and leadership, which this chapter explores. In this examination, we will draw on the theoretical literature of leadership as well as the practitioner literature produced by consultants, other experts, and nonprofit CEOs themselves.

The CEO's Job

What do nonprofit chief executives actually do? In other words, what is the job description? Of course, because no two organizations are exactly the same, the CEO's job may vary widely from one to another. In some, fund-raising may be an important expectation, while in others it is not. In organizations that have mostly paid professional staff, the skills required of a CEO may be different from those needed to lead an organization that relies on volunteers for a substantial portion of its workforce. Also, as discussed in Chapter 4, the type of governing board with which the chief executive works may greatly influence the types of challenges that he or she may face.

While recognizing these inevitable differences, Richard Moyers identified 10 basic responsibilities of the nonprofit chief executives in a 2006 publication for BoardSource:

1. *Commit to the mission:* The CEO must understand the mission, keep the mission prominently in mind when making decisions, and guard against mission drift.

2. *Lead the staff and manage the organization:* The CEO has direct responsibility for hiring, training, developing, and motivating the staff; developing an organizational structure that suits the organization's work; and ensuring that day-to-day operations and programs are effective and efficient.

3. *Exercise responsible financial stewardship:* While the governing board has overall responsibility for ensuring the organization's financial soundness, it is the chief executive who must manage its assets, revenues, and expenditures on a day-to-day basis and ensure that controls are in place to protect the organization against fraud or waste.

4. *Lead and manage fund-raising:* The CEO's responsibility for fund-raising will vary from one organization to another and is shared with the governing board. In charitable nonprofits, the CEO's direct engagement in fund-raising, planning fund-raising programs, and managing the fund-raising staff may consume a substantial portion of his or her time and energy.

5. *Follow the highest ethical standards, ensure accountability, and comply with the law:* Again, the governing board may set policies (remember Carver's executive limitations discussed in Chapter 4) that establish standards and procedures to ensure legal and ethical behavior. However, it is the chief executive who needs to put these policies into practice in the organization's daily life and set an example through his or her own behavior.

6. *Engage the board in planning and lead implementation:* Planning for the organization's future is a shared responsibility of the board and the CEO, but the reality in many organizations requires that the chief executive take a significant role in initiating the planning effort, providing the resources for planning, and defining issues and questions for the board to deliberate.

7. *Develop future leadership:* In many organizations, the CEO plays a role in developing the leadership of the board, both informally and often as a member of the board's nominating committee. There is also an increasing emphasis on the importance of the CEO's preparing for possible staff departures by developing a bench of qualified successors and, indeed, for preparing the way for a smooth transition when he or she may leave the chief executive's position.

8. *Build external relationships and serve as an advocate:* Some research considered later in this chapter emphasizes that effective chief executives are those who are externally oriented—who are constantly alert to opportunities and threats in the external environment and engaged in building external partnerships for their organization.

9. *Ensure the quality and effectiveness of programs:* The board may set the standards by which the effectiveness of programs is to be evaluated, but the CEO must ensure that the right questions are asked and the right data collected so that a process of evaluation and continuous learning is a part of the organization's ongoing work.

10. *Support the board:* Just as the governing board has a responsibility to support its CEO, the CEO has a reciprocal responsibility to support the board. Moreover, as we discussed in Chapter 4, research suggests that effective CEOs are ones who practice board-centered leadership.[1]

Two realities are evident in Moyer's list of CEO responsibilities. One is the number of areas in which the chief executive shares responsibility with the governing board regarding mission, financial stewardship, fund-raising, accountability, planning, performance standards, and the work of the board itself. This explains why the relationship between the CEO and the board is so complex and why so many experts have focused on delineating the CEO and board responsibilities in each area.

The second observation that emerges from a review of the CEO's responsibilities is that they involve both *managing* and *leading.* The CEO is responsible for ensuring that financial management systems are in place, for the hiring and evaluation of staff, and for monitoring the quality and effectiveness of programs. But chief executives are also expected to be external spokespersons for their organizations, able to articulate the mission and make a persuasive case for financial support; to be capable of motivating both paid staff and volunteers to high performance; and to hold a vision and strategy for the organization's future, which, working together with the board, they translate into a plan for the organization's advancement and growth. These latter tasks require something beyond management: They require that the CEO be a leader.

Management and Leadership

Although people may use the words interchangeably, leadership and management are not the same thing. *Management* is generally concerned with day-to-day operations, with making things work. It emphasizes policies, procedures, rules, and processes. Management is transactional; the manager provides rewards in exchange for the work contributions of others or imposes sanctions (punishments) on those who do not meet the requirements of their assignments. A manager is often concerned primarily with maintaining a smooth operation, that is, keeping the machine running and avoiding breakdowns, rather than with change.

Leadership is more about purpose, vision, and direction—that is, more about the "where" and the "why" rather than the "how." In a widely quoted statement, Bennis and Nanus (1985) suggest a moral element to leadership: "Managers are people who do things right and leaders are people who do the right thing" (p. 21). Leadership is interactive; that is, it is a *process,* and it involves a *relationship* between the leader and the people who are led. There can be no leaders without followers, and both play a part in the process of leadership. Leaders are focused on change, and that change is not directionless; leadership involves moving people toward the achievement of some defined *goals.* Some of the differences between leaders and managers are summarized in Table 5.1.

TABLE 5.1 ■ Managers and Leaders Compared	
Managers	**Leaders**
Concerned with mastering routines	Concerned with vision and judgment
Adopt impersonal or passive attitudes toward goals	Active and visionary about the future
Excel in problem solving and work design	Seek out opportunities and take risks
Work with people in carefully controlled ways	Passionate about their work and likely to cause turbulence
See themselves as conservators or regulators	See themselves as agents of change

Source: Based on Denhardt, Denhardt, and Aristigueta (2009, p. 181).

Sometimes, the roles of leader and manager are performed by different people; indeed, some argue that the two roles require different personal qualities or skills rarely found in the same individual. At other times, one person may have the responsibility both for leading the organization and for managing its affairs—for example, the CEO of a small nonprofit. But the functions of leadership and management are different, and such people need to be able to switch from one role to the other as the needs of the organization and the occasion may dictate. Indeed, there are those who assert that founders of nonprofit organizations often exhibit strong qualities of leadership but may be unable to provide the management the organization needs as it grows, sometimes leading to the problem known as founder syndrome, discussed later in this chapter.

In larger organizations, CEOs often play the leadership role and delegate management responsibilities to subordinates, such as a chief operating officer. It is possible for a CEO to delegate management to others, but only the CEO can provide leadership to the entire organization. Leadership of the organization is not a responsibility that can be delegated.

All organizations need both leadership and management to be successful in the long run. It is conceivable that an organization—whether a for-profit business, a government agency, or a nonprofit organization—can survive for a time with only good management. But to thrive and grow, an organization also needs leaders who define vision, articulate direction, set goals, and influence others to achieve these together.

Nonprofit organizations especially need leadership. The reasons are rooted in their characteristics, which we have discussed in earlier chapters. Corporations and government agencies generally have well-defined missions, straightforward measures of performance, and revenue that is derived from either appropriated funds or quid pro quo transactions with customers. In contrast, nonprofits are *values based* and *mission driven*. There is not always consensus about mission or about appropriate ways of measuring performance against the mission. Financial and other resources are often bestowed *voluntarily*. Leadership is essential to develop consensus about mission and performance and to articulate a vision that gains and holds the commitment of volunteer board members, service volunteers, donors, and others. This book includes the current chapter on executive leadership simply because leadership is so central to the role of a nonprofit CEO. A lack of leadership by the CEO of a nonprofit organization will eventually, and inevitably, lead to drift, decline, and failure.

Overview of Leadership Theories

We have established that leadership is critical in nonprofit organizations. Now let's turn our attention to understanding it by looking at some fundamental questions. Are leaders born or made? If they are made, what specific knowledge or skills do individuals need to acquire in order to be strong leaders? What is it that successful leaders actually do—in other words, are there specific behaviors that are associated with effective leadership? These are questions that long have been asked, and there is a substantial body of research that has sought to provide answers.

It is important to remember two points as we review some of the well-known leadership theories. First, most of the theories are generic; that is, theorists intend them to apply to leadership in all types of organizations, not just nonprofits. And second, as in our earlier discussion of governing, there may be no one right theory of leadership that is applicable in every situation, at all times.

Leadership theory has evolved over the decades. Among the earliest theories were the *trait theories,* which explain leadership in terms of the innate characteristics of individuals who are leaders. They are essentially "great man or woman" theories, which hold the qualities of leadership to be fundamental aspects of an individual's personality. In the past, some have looked to physical characteristics to explain why certain people are leaders; for example, physical height and a resonant speaking voice—essentially male qualities—were once considered intrinsic to leadership, although they would not explain Golda Meir, Indira Gandhi, or Mother Teresa! Other trait theorists have pointed more to elements of personality, character, or psychology. For example, in 1948, Stodgill studied leaders and found them to be better than the average person in terms of intelligence, alertness, insight, responsibility, initiative, persistence, self-confidence, and sociability. Since it is difficult for individuals to change their intelligence or personalities, trait theories imply that leaders are born, not made; that is, leadership is not something that can be taught or learned (Northouse, 2004, p. 16).

The trait theories, however, do not seem to provide the whole answer. Thus, in about the middle of the 20th century, theorists began to take a different approach, developing *skills theories* of leadership. Skills theories hold that it is not the innate qualities of individuals, such as physical appearance or even intelligence, that make them effective leaders. Rather, there are specific skills that effective leaders possess; in other words, effective leadership depends less on what the leaders are and more on what they are able to do. For example, in 1955, Daniel Katz (cited in Northouse, 2004, pp. 37–38) suggested that effective leadership depends on the leader possessing skills in three areas: *technical* (knowledge of the job, profession, or task), *human* (the ability to work with people), and *conceptual* (the ability to understand ideas and principles). A skills theory is the assumption underlying most leadership training or development programs.

Beginning in the 1950s, leadership researchers started to move beyond studying the traits and skills of individual leaders toward looking at what it is that leaders actually *do*—that is, they considered whether it was possible to identify specific *behaviors* associated with effective leadership. Among the most famous of leadership studies that followed this approach were those conducted at Ohio State University. These studies identified two basic types of leader behaviors: *task behaviors* (actions that relate to the work to be done) and *relationship behaviors* (actions that focus on the feelings of subordinates). At about the same time, similar studies conducted at the University of Michigan identified essentially the same categories, which researchers there labeled *production orientation* and *employee orientation*. The ways in which leaders mix task and relationship behaviors can define a leadership style.

Among the theorists who analyzed leadership styles are Blake and Mouton (1985) who developed the well-known *managerial grid*. This grid is based on different combinations of task and relationship behaviors and defines four styles. Organizations that are high on production (task) and low on relationships are said to have *authority-obedience management*. Essentially, they are dictatorships, although they may be productive. Those high on relationships and low on concern for production are described as having *country club management*. They may be great places to work, but they get little or nothing accomplished. Organizations that are low on both concern for people and production exhibit *impoverished management*. These would be dreadful places to work, and most people likely would not stay long in such an uninspiring environment. The ideal type, showing high concern for both people and production, is called *team management* (Rainey, 2003, p. 292). It is likely that most readers can imagine situations, or perhaps have even experienced ones, in which each of these styles is practiced.

It might seem obvious that what may be an effective leadership style in one situation may not be so under different circumstances. But the idea that effective leadership behavior might depend or be *contingent* on the situation was a new insight in leadership theory in the 1960s.[2] In this way of thinking, effective leadership would require matching the leader's style to the situation. Different situations might call for different combinations of task-oriented and relationship-oriented behaviors. But what defines a "situation"? Exactly what differences between situations are relevant to determining the right leadership style (Northouse, 2004)?

One of the best-known *contingency theories* is the one developed by Fiedler in 1967. According to Fiedler, the situation may be favorable or unfavorable to the leader, depending on three variables: *leader–member relations* (e.g., the degree of trust, cooperativeness, and friendliness between the leader and followers), the *task structure* (whether the job to be done is clear and specific or ambiguous and uncertain), and the *position power* of the leader (i.e., the formal position of authority the leader holds.). The most favorable situation is when all three variables are high, and the least favorable is when all three are low, but there can be moderately favorable situations that show some combination of favorable and unfavorable conditions. According to Fiedler's findings, task-oriented leaders do best when conditions are very favorable or very unfavorable, while relationship-oriented leaders do best in the intermediate circumstances (cited in Rainey, 2003, pp. 292–293).

Contingency theories add a level of sophistication beyond the trait, skill, and behavior theories of leadership. They begin to explain why some styles of leadership may be successful in certain circumstances and not in others. Imagine, for example, a situation in which a nonprofit chief executive is facing the need to mobilize staff and volunteers to provide relief to victims of a natural disaster. The urgency of the situation makes everyone inclined to be cooperative. Let's also assume that the executive is trusted and well liked by the staff and volunteers. The task is clear and unambiguous: It is to provide food, clothing, and shelter to the victims as quickly as possible. These circumstances—cooperativeness, trust, a clear task, a leader with formal authority—would be a situation that Fiedler's model would define as favorable to the leader. A task-oriented style likely would be most effective. The important thing would be to get the job done, and there would be little need to concentrate on relationships among people, which are already good. But imagine a different situation, one in which an acting executive director has been on the job for just a few months while a search for a permanent director is proceeding. This person leads an environmental advocacy organization and is trying to mobilize volunteers to support critical environmental legislation by contacting their elected representatives. The task seems clear and specific. However, the person's position power is weak because of the acting status, and he or she may not have been in the role long enough to have gained the trust and friendship of the staff and volunteers. In Fiedler's theory, this situation is intermediate in its favorableness to the leader, who likely would need to devote considerable attention to nurturing his or her relationships with the volunteers and staff to mobilize them to action; in other words, the leader would need to emphasize relationship behaviors more than task behaviors.

Although not a theory per se, one approach to leadership that has gained a following and spawned a number of books is that of *servant leadership,* advanced by Robert Greenleaf (1977). Greenleaf argues that leadership begins with the leader's values and commitments and that moral leaders are more concerned with serving others than with meeting their own self-interest. Servant-leaders exhibit honesty, integrity, character, and spirit. Rather than trying to impose their will on others, they listen, empathize with others, and focus on relationships, approaching the position of leader as a type of stewardship of the organization, with the goal of social improvement (Denhardt et al., 2009, p. 190).

Transformational Leadership

A 1978 book by political scientist James MacGregor Burns, titled simply *Leadership,* had seminal influence on thinking about the topic and offers insights that may be of particular relevance to leadership in the nonprofit sector. First, Burns made a distinction between transactional leadership and transformational leadership. *Transactional leadership* is an exchange process, in which the leader exchanges rewards or punishments for the behaviors of others: If you come to work, you will get paid; if you don't, you won't. If you miss work too often, you will be fired. Thus, transactional leadership is essentially like management. In contrast, *transformational leadership,* as the name implies, is leadership that *changes* people. According to Burns, transformational leadership inspires and enables people to grow, both morally and in terms of their levels of motivation. It empowers individuals to go beyond self-interest and pursue goals that are in the common interest. Transformational leaders accomplish this by developing a relationship with followers and tapping into their personal values in a way that matches them to the values of the organization. They motivate followers not based on rewards and punishments, but by appealing to these shared values and ideals.

Let's consider a simple example that might illustrate transactional and transformational approaches. Tom is the CEO of a nonprofit organization that delivers meals to house-bound older people. He is addressing a meeting of his staff, and he is concerned that some have been showing up late for work, delaying the delivery of meals to clients. One way to approach the issue would be for Tom to say something like,

> I've noticed that I am the first one here in the morning. Some of you don't show up until an hour later. As a result, some meals are being delivered late. If this continues, I will need to consider docking the pay of staff who report late and firing people if it continues. I will expect to see you all here at 6 AM tomorrow morning.

However, taking a different approach, Tom might say something like,

> I am concerned. I know that some of our clients wait for their meals to be delivered and that in fact their contact with our volunteers may be the high point of their days. When I see that we are late in getting the meals out the door in the morning, I cannot help but worry about a lonely older person, perhaps a little hungry, who is left waiting because maybe we had other things to do that morning. I know you share my concern about that. I know our clients appreciate everything you can do to make sure we are meeting their needs—and on time—because they count on us.

Which approach is more likely to result in staff arriving earlier? The first is purely transactional: You do (or do not do) this, and I will do (or not do) that. The transactional approach may be effective in the short run; after all, staff members rely on their paychecks. But the effects of Tom's speech may wear off in a few days unless he repeats it and his threats are backed up. That will require his continuing intervention, possibly undermining his relationships with the staff over time. The second approach has tones of transformational leadership. It appeals to shared values rather than the promise or threat of consequences. It may move staff members to change their behaviors by affecting changes in their own heads and hearts. If accomplished, such change will likely be more lasting and powerful than the tools of a more transactional style.

Burns's book inspired work by other scholars, who adopted, expanded, and refined his ideas. One prominent leadership scholar, Bernard Bass (1985; Bass & Avolio, 1994), developed a more comprehensive model of transformational leadership. He differed slightly with Burns on some points. For one, Bass emphasized that transformational leaders also use transactional techniques in that they do provide goals and rewards for reaching them. This is not a problem as long as they do not overemphasize these techniques, especially those that are negative. Rewards may be more consistent with transformational leadership than are punishments. In other words, there may be times when the hypothetical CEO Tom may find that some staff members do not respond adequately to his values-based approach and will indeed need to be subject to "transactions" (Rainey, 2003, pp. 304–305).

Most of the leadership theories considered in this chapter describe a leader's relationship with *subordinates*. What is significant about the concept of transformational leadership is that it also offers an approach to leading *organizations*—especially those that are values based and mission driven. A nonprofit chief executive must lead more than the members of his or her paid staff. Among others, the CEO must also at times lead donors, volunteers, and even members of the board.

Think back to the earlier example of Tom speaking to members of his staff. The transactional approach, using rewards and punishments to change behavior, might be effective with the staff, at least in the short run. But how could that approach be effective in motivating individuals to give or members of the board to increase their efforts in fund-raising, or in inspiring volunteers to work longer and harder? Would not those goals be better accomplished by identifying how the values of those individuals coincide with those of the organization and appealing to those values in a way that the desired behavior is dictated from within their own hearts?

In a sequel to his best-selling book on companies, *Good to Great*, Jim Collins (2001) observes how nonprofit leadership is unique, and he describes two types (or styles) of leadership that have similarities to Burns's transactional and transformational approaches. *Executive leadership* exists when the leader has the power to simply make decisions. *Legislative leadership* is a style that "relies more upon persuasion, political currency, and shared interests to create the conditions for the right decisions to happen" (Collins, 2005, p. 11). Nonprofit executives often do not have the formal power of corporate CEOs. They generally do not have the financial resources with which to offer significant monetary incentives. Indeed, some of their workforce is not paid at all, and even those who are may be motivated as much by their commitment to the mission as they are by their financial needs. Rather than lead through rewards and punishments, nonprofit executives must use the less raw, but considerable, power of ideas, persuasion, inspiration, and relationships to lead others—and their organizations—in the directions they wish them to pursue.

Charismatic Leadership

The idea of charisma is one that is familiar to most people. When asked to name someone who is a leader, people often will mention the names of political figures, such as Ronald Reagan, Martin Luther King Jr., Barack Obama, or Hillary Rodham Clinton. When asked what makes all these individuals unusual, some inevitably will use the term *charisma*.

The prominence of Burns's concept of transformational leadership has led to an increasing interest in *charismatic leadership,* which remains an active area of research today. Some debate whether transformational and charismatic leadership are the same, different, or overlapping concepts, but fine distinctions need not concern us here. The two types of leadership are, at the least, related.

There is debate about the nature of charisma. Is it based on personal characteristics of the leader—is it some kind of "right stuff" that some people just have and others do not? Or is charisma defined by behaviors that can be learned? Some argue that theories of charismatic leadership really represent a retreat to the earlier trait theories. But Bass and other scholars have identified specific behaviors that may cause followers to *attribute* the characteristics of charisma to the leader. In other words, a leader is someone who behaves in certain ways that cause others to see him or her as charismatic (Bryman, 1992).

What are some of the behaviors that may cause others to see the leader as charismatic? Here are some that researchers have identified (Rainey, 2003, p. 305):

- *The leader advocates a vision that is different from the status quo but still acceptable to followers.* Leadership is about change, but not change so radical as to alienate potential followers. Martin Luther King, Jr., advocated an end to segregation and racial discrimination. This represented not only a change from the status quo in America in the 1960s, but also a change that King's followers, and eventually the nation, came to accept as morally compelling. Rather than call for violent revolution, King advocated nonviolent means, remaining within the boundaries of what his followers and sympathizers could find acceptable.

- *The leader acts in unconventional ways in pursuit of the vision.* King led boycotts and marches. Nelson Mandela spent 27 years in jail in protest against South Africa's inhumane system of apartheid. Neither brought about change merely by giving occasional speeches or by other more conventional means.

- *The leader engages in self-sacrifice and risk taking in pursuit of the vision.* Mandela sacrificed 27 years. Mother Teresa lived a life of poverty among the poor. King ultimately gave his life. The deep commitment of a leader, as evidenced by his or her willingness to sacrifice, even suffer, for the cause compels attention and confers a charismatic appeal. "By showing unswerving dedication to the vision, making personal sacrifices, and engaging in unconventional behavior . . . [charismatic leaders] inspire their followers to transcend their self-interests for the sake of a collective goal" (Choi, 2006).

- *The leader displays confidence in his or her own ideas and proposals.* Perhaps the undoing of Jimmy Carter as president of the United States (he was not reelected to a second term) was a speech he gave to the nation in which he acknowledged his own shortcomings as president and described the nation's mood as discouraged. (This speech is often referred to as Carter's "malaise" speech, although he did not use that word.) In contrast, Ronald Reagan's optimistic vision of "morning in America" was an important factor in his election to the presidency in 1980, although many opinion polls showed that a majority of Americans disagreed with his specific positions on issues. Similarly, it was Barack Obama's optimistic assurance that "yes, we can" that inspired many of his supporters in 2008. Charismatic leaders command our following, partly because they appear so certain that their course is right.

- *The leader uses visioning and persuasive appeals to influence followers, rather than relying mainly on formal authority.* Martin Luther King, Jr., never held public office. But the words "I have a dream" created a vision of a different America that inspired millions and changed the nation more dramatically than most presidents of the United States have ever been able to do.

- *The leader uses the capacity to assess context and locate opportunities for novel strategies.* Charismatic leaders read the moment; that is, they can take the temperature of their times and followers and create opportunities to demonstrate their cause in dramatic and novel ways. In 1987, Ronald Reagan stood yards from the Berlin Wall and addressed himself to the leader of the Soviet Union saying, "Mr. Gorbachev, tear down this wall!" It was a dramatic moment, which Reagan must have known would resonate with people on both sides of the wall at that point in history. Just over 2 years later, the wall was gone, not entirely as a result of Reagan's speech but rather as the culmination of historical forces that were gathering strength. However, Reagan understood the context and used the opportunity of his visit to the wall to dramatize the issue. Many years later, then-presidential candidate Barack Obama spoke to a large and enthusiastic gathering in Berlin, signifying in a visual way that his policy approach to Europe would represent change and improve U.S. international relationships.

To the above list of behaviors of charismatic leaders, James Fisher (1984), who writes about the use of charismatic leadership by college and university presidents, adds the idea of *social distance.* He suggests that to be perceived as charismatic, the leader cannot permit himself or herself to be too familiar. Consistent with the military's long-standing rule that officers are not to fraternize with enlisted personnel, leaders may be friendly, but not too much so. They can be congenial but never silly. They can socialize with subordinates (or board members or donors) but never stay too long or drink too much. If charisma is something attributed to leaders, as psychologists suggest, it seems that we may prefer just a bit of mystery and to believe that they are just a little different from us.

Although they play an important part in contemporary leadership theory and research, the ideas of transformational leadership and charismatic leadership have their critics. Some raise academic issues, saying that charisma is too ill defined to measure or analyze. Others say the idea of charismatic leadership is really just a newer version of the "great man/great woman" theory of leadership. (Remember the issue from our case in Chapter 3 about the Smithsonian's National Museum of American History and the Catherine B. Reynolds Foundation?) Still others raise substantive concerns about the risks of charismatic leadership to organizations: For example, the power of charismatic leadership may be abused, or an organization dependent on a charismatic leader may be vulnerable if that leader leaves, retires, or dies (Northouse, 2004, pp. 185–186).

The Effective Nonprofit CEO

If leadership is so vital to the success of the nonprofit organization, what do we know about what makes an effective nonprofit CEO? We have discussed some major theories of leadership, but what evidence do we have of what actually works best in the nonprofit sector?

As with the topic of governing boards, much of the literature on nonprofit executive leadership is prescriptive. In other words, "It tells more about how to lead and much less about how leaders actually go about their business" (Dym & Hutson, 2005, p. 6). And, as is the case with governing boards, a significant portion of the literature on nonprofit leadership has been written by consultants or reflective practitioners and is practitioner oriented in its approach.

Empirical research focused specifically on nonprofit leadership is growing. But research on effective nonprofit leadership faces challenges. One problem is how to define it; this is bound up with the larger issue of how to define an effective nonprofit organization. As in measuring the effectiveness of the nonprofit board, the idea of CEO effectiveness is also socially constructed, and the definition of what constitutes an effective nonprofit CEO may vary according to the perceptions of the organization's diverse constituencies.

Indeed, a common method that researchers have used for identifying effective nonprofit leaders is based on perceptions. Nonprofit executives or perhaps opinion leaders, such as foundation officers and academics, are asked to identify those CEOs whom they deem to be most successful or effective. The characteristics of these CEOs are then compared with those of another group of CEOs who were not named. But this method is problematic and raises the question of how the nominators are defining "effective." Those identified as effective may simply be the most visible or popular in their fields. Charismatic leaders may be favored over others of different styles because they are often highly visible and magnetic personalities. Or the executives identified by their colleagues as being effective might have been those who had been active as presenters at professional conferences or as authors, perhaps demonstrating their knowledge about nonprofit leadership, but not necessarily bearing any relationship to their performance as leaders of their own organizations. Furthermore, it is not always clear whether survey or interview respondents are describing how things are, how they believe they should be, or how they think they should respond.

Many studies based on surveys of perceptions reflect what seem to be trait or skills theories of leadership. For example, nonprofit CEOs interviewed by Hudson (2005) identified openness and honesty as the most important qualities of effective nonprofit chief executives. In another study, nonprofit sector opinion leaders identified passion and commitment, vision, integrity, trust, and credibility (Light, 2002). Similar traits are also mentioned in the practitioner-oriented literature—integrity and trust (Pidgeon, 2004), vision, initiative, openness, and responsiveness (Howe, 2004).

Some research studies and the practitioner literature have also identified skills associated with effective nonprofit leadership. They commonly identify interpersonal skills, communication skills, delegation skills, staff management skills, the ability to articulate and write a message, and the ability to raise funds (Howe, 2004; Light, 2002; Pidgeon, 2004). Many of the skills identified are, of course, generic and would seem to be useful to leaders in any organization. The skills unique to nonprofits (e.g., fund-raising) are essentially technical, and others mentioned are more related to management than to leadership.

Some authors do describe behaviors of effective nonprofit CEOs, but most of this literature is prescriptive. It tells us what CEOs should *do* to be effective, and it often emphasizes areas on which the chief executive should focus his or her time and attention. Five areas are frequently mentioned, and these are discussed below.

Focus on Mission

The importance of staying focused on the mission is emphasized by almost all authors on the topic of effective nonprofit CEOs. The mission is the nonprofit's reason for existence, and the CEO should use it as a guide for every decision. As Frances Hesselbein, former CEO of the Girl Scouts, expresses it, "Mission is the star we steer by. Everything begins with mission, everything flows from mission" (quoted in Dees et al., 2001, p. 19). Many nonprofit boards include leaders from the business community, who may sometimes find it attractive to direct the organization toward activities that are financially lucrative but that may distract it from its primary mission. Staff may sometimes propose activities that would be "nice to do" but that may not advance the mission directly. The CEO can use the mission as a shield against such pressures from the staff or board, to explain, justify, and give coherence to his or her actions.

Focus on the Board

Many authors emphasize the importance of the CEO's relationship with the board. Chapter 4 discussed the research of Robert Herman and Dick Heimovics (1991, 2005), who identified board-centered leadership as the behavior distinguishing effective CEOs from others. As they report their research findings,

> Analysis showed that executive leadership in relation to staff and in relation to the board are independent and distinct factors. Effective and comparison executives differed little in leadership with their staffs. The most important finding was that the effective executives provided significantly more leadership to their boards. (Herman & Heimovics, 2005, p. 157)

Focus on External Relationships

Effective nonprofit leaders are those who are not excessively focused on internal management. They are not obsessed with policies and procedures and the day-to-day activities of their subordinates. Rather, they "delegate much of the management of internal affairs and focus on the external" (Herman & Heimovics, 2005, p. 159). Practical strategies for enhancing external impact may involve developing an informal information network, including contacts in government, other nonprofits, foundations, and professional associations, to supplement hard data with soft information about emerging trends and practices in the field.

Fund-raising is an important aspect of the external activity of many nonprofit CEOs, and indeed, its importance is growing as government support for many programs has been reduced. While the opinion leaders and nonprofit CEOs interviewed by Light (2002) mentioned fund-raising as an important skill, it is surprising how seldom it is addressed in much of the nonprofit leadership literature.

Share Leadership and Empower Others

In their 2008 study of high-impact nonprofits, Crutchfield and Grant determined that effective nonprofit CEOs share leadership with others. This sometimes includes having two people in top positions, with complementary skills—for example, someone who is good at outside relationships and another who specializes in internal operations. It also includes developing a team of leaders within the organization, that is, having bench strength and empowering members of the leadership team.

Focus on Key Roles and Priorities

In their well-known work on leadership, Nanus and Dobbs (1999) address the question of where the nonprofit CEO needs to direct his or her attention—their answer: almost everywhere. They define four quadrants in which the CEO may focus and operate at any given time—inside the organization, outside the organization, on present operations, and on future possibilities. They identify six roles defined by these four areas and argue that the effective CEO needs to be proficient in *all* of them. When the CEO combines an internal perspective with attention to present operations, he or she is acting in the role of "coach," guiding staff and others who are

performing the organization's work. Looking inward but with a view to the future, the CEO is playing the role of "change agent." When CEOs are focused outside the organization but concerned with present operations, they are performing as "politicians" and as "fund-raisers." And when CEOs are focused externally and looking to the future, they are performing as "visionaries" and "strategists."

Herman and Heimovics (2005) urge nonprofit CEOs to stay focused on key "goals or outcomes [that are] crucial"; that is, they advise nonprofit CEOs to "know your agenda" (p. 160). A well-managed organization may have goals derived from a formal process of strategic planning, but effective executives have their own short list of priorities—a few key things they wish to accomplish. Those priorities may be drawn from the plan or be supplemental to it. Rather than scatter their attention and efforts across a broad list of goals, CEOs will be more successful if they can limit their priorities to a few critical initiatives that will define their leadership of the organization and focus their own attention and that of others on those items. Carlson and Donohoe (2003), both former nonprofit executives and now consultants, agree, advising, "Don't let a list of priorities exceed five items, and three is better" (p. 33).

Remembering that board members, donors, and even staff may not be thinking about organizational goals all the time and that they face innumerable distractions in their own personal and professional lives, it is important for the CEO to keep the short-listed goals constantly in front of them and to ensure that they have the same information and perspective as the CEO, so that they will come to share his or her understanding of what the priorities are and why. For example, one university president regularly sent packages of clippings to his senior staff and the board, articles highlighting trends or issues that he thought might have a bearing on decisions the university would eventually need to face. His purpose was to ensure that when the decisions came before the board, the trustees would have read the same things that he had and thus would understand the context for his recommendations. Leaders also need to simplify the priorities and "lay a bread-crumb trail" to key decisions through communications and small actions that lead the way to larger changes, as a way of preparing the board and others, so that when changes need to be made, they will not seem to come out of the blue. The leaders will have prepared their constituents for change, one step at a time (Herman & Heimovics, 2005, pp. 160–161).

Use the "Political Frame"

In their insightful and practical research on nonprofit executives, Herman and Heimovics (2005) find that effective CEOs are distinguished from others by their use of a "political frame." Indeed, they say this is a finding of their research in which they have particular confidence. The concept of frames was developed by Bolman and Deal (2003). A *frame* is a perspective or a way of seeing and understanding things—like seeing the glass either half empty or half full.

By referring to nonprofit CEOs using a political frame, Herman and Heimovics (2005) do not mean that they see things in terms of partisan or elective politics, but rather that they recognize the inevitable interplay among the organization's important constituencies. The *political frame* is a perspective through which the CEO sees and understands the environment in terms of the pressures brought by various constituencies that compete, bargain, and negotiate over the allocation of resources. Leaders using this frame will be sensitive to external forces that might affect the organization and, therefore, devote their time and effort to maintaining relationships and influencing various competing constituencies.

Right Person, Right Place, Right Time

In a book focused on leadership in the nonprofit sector, but with more generic applications as well, Dym and Hutson (2005) argue that nonprofit executive effectiveness results from having the right person in the right job at the right time; in other words, it is necessary to have a good fit between the leader and the needs of the organization at the time.

They propose an *alignment model* that seeks to integrate the major leadership theories, that is, to provide "an overarching conceptual framework that brings the theories together, or at least describes how the theories relate to one another" (Dym & Hutson, 2005, p. 36). The leader's fit with the organization involves traits as well as skills, leadership style as well as situation. In other words, there is no one right theory, but all have relevance in the context of the right time and place. Invoking many of the major leadership theories in one paragraph to describe their concepts of fit and alignment, they write,

> If one were to align a leader who is determined and communicates well and whose personality and behavior (style) fit well with the organizational culture, who understands how to structure the organization's future and light up the pathway to success, who communicates frequently with direct reports and makes staff followers feel supported and understood, and who holds high standards in a way that is sensitive to both individual and group psychological needs—if someone were to see such alignment, what would be witnessed is effective leadership. (p. 345)

Dym and Hutson (2005) provide an *alignment map* (see Table 5.2), summarizing the components on which they say alignment must be achieved. It encompasses the characteristics of the individual as well as characteristics of the organization and of the community or market that the organization serves. All three must be aligned to produce a perfect fit. Thus, for example, a charismatic leader with an extroverted personality might be a good fit for an advocacy organization that is working to gain public awareness and change public policy, but such an individual might not be a good fit as a director of a museum, university, or think tank, where a more collegial, participative style might be more readily accepted. An executive director who does not speak Spanish and has little understanding of Hispanic/Latino culture would not be a good fit as the executive director of an organization that serves primarily Hispanic/Latino clients. A leader who comes from the business world—or even from a different type of nonprofit organization—might find it difficult to be effective in a nonprofit organization that has an established culture different from that with which he or she is familiar. An organization that encourages self-empowerment among its clients would not be aligned with its mission if its own leadership behaved in autocratic ways. In other words, for a CEO to be effective, his or her traits, styles, skills, and values need to be in sync with the organization and its constituencies. Too much dissonance may diminish the CEO's ability to lead or even, in the case of a bad fit, result in his or her eventual departure.

However, according to Dym and Hutson (2005), alignment is a two-way process. It may involve change by the leader and by the nonprofit itself: "Leaders must . . . align themselves to organizations by adapting themselves to the organization's structure, process, culture, and strategy—and by aligning the organization's to fit their style. Both processes are necessary for effective leadership" (p. 100). But, they advise, alignment should not be perfect and some tension is desirable. "A fit that is too perfect leads to stagnation. . . . Close but imperfect fit combines the smooth functioning we associate with efficiency and effectiveness with the flexible adjustment to change we associate with creativity" (p. 67).

	Leader	Organization	Community/Market
TABLE 5.2 ■ Dym and Hutson's Alignment Map			
Basic nature	Character and style	Organizational type	Patterns and norms
Underlying principles	Personal values	Organizational culture	Larger culture
Means available	Individual skills	Organizational resources	Economy and industry
Purpose and direction	Personal objectives	Mission and strategy	Community needs and market demands

Source: Dym and Hutson (2005, p. 93).

Founder Syndrome

As Dym and Hutson (2005) discuss, one leadership style may be appropriate at one point in an organization's history and another at a different time. The idea that the organization's need for leadership might change over time derives from *life-cycle theories* of nonprofit organization development, which describe specific stages through which organizations naturally evolve.

For example, charismatic leaders are often seen leading an organization in its early stages, where the vision and inspiration of a committed founder drive volunteers and early-generation staff members to exceptional effort. However, as the organization matures, it may require a different kind of leader—one "who feels comfortable in and supported enough by the stable organization to begin to implement long-term growth projects" (Dym & Hutson, 2005, p. 89). In other words, as the organization grows, adds staff, develops systems, and expands its programs, there will be an increased need for professional management, and the charisma of the founder may no longer suffice. (We will discuss organization life cycles in more detail in Chapter 8.)

There are many examples of nonprofit organizations founded by visionary and charismatic individuals who became the first executive directors. The founder attracts and inspires dedicated and loyal volunteers, donors, and staff. The board may consist of individuals recruited by the founder, who generally acquiesce to his or her authority and charisma. But at some point, as the organization grows and its needs for professional management, formal systems, and a more deliberate approach increase, the founder may not possess the required management skills or may be unable to adjust his or her vision of the organization to the new reality. He or she may prefer the entrepreneurial culture of the early organization.

The founder is likely to have a deep dedication to the organization and its cause—it may be the founder's life, and he or she may expect staff to make similar personal sacrifices. Founders often have task-oriented styles and are described as "difficult" and "demanding" by their subordinates. Like a controlling parent, the founder may have become accustomed to making all the decisions and may resist any initiative from the board or staff to be more independent. That style might work in the early days when the staff and board comprise a small number of loyal followers who share the founder's enthusiasm, but it may become less tolerated as the organization comes to require a larger staff of technical specialists and professional managers. Passion may no longer be an adequate substitute for rational decision making.

But the founder's psychological identification with the organization—after all, it's the founder's baby—may make it impossible for him or her to accept a more democratic, team approach. The situation becomes more stressful as staff turnover increases, management errors begin to mount, systems spin out of control, and the board feels increasingly torn between its loyalty to the founder and its responsibility to the organization. The board may begin to add more outsiders, people who are not personally selected by the founder and who bring more professional skills. These outsiders have less loyalty to the founder, and the balance begins to shift, increasing tension between the founder/executive director and the board: The organization is suffering from what is commonly called *founder syndrome.*

The arrival of founder syndrome in the life of the organization poses a challenge, even a crisis. Eventually, some crisis or event may trigger an explosion, resulting in the dismissal of the founder. Board members and staff loyal to the founder may leave amid bitterness, while others scramble to save the organization. Often the founder will be replaced by a professional manager, who then faces the challenge of rebuilding and developing new relationships. Or if the crisis is not resolved, the founder's departure may precipitate the organization's decline into turmoil and eventual death. Dym and Hutson (2005) portray the ugly scene:

> There is a declining certainty about the organization's original purpose. People wonder whether they were naïve to think they could accomplish so much in the first place. They question whether they can survive without being more realistic about their goals, their methods, and the people they trust. As doubt creeps in, people grow more conservative, more cautious. They see problems where before they mainly saw solutions. They begin to invest less of themselves—their hopes and dreams, their willingness to risk, and their time. Or they begin a somewhat frenzied and exhausting alternation of investing more and less. (p. 118)

If the transition from the founder to a professional manager is traumatic and risky for the organization, following the founder also can be a challenging assignment for the new CEO. It may be that the board, perhaps feeling guilty over its dismissal of the founder as executive director, has allowed him or her to remain as a member of the board—an unfortunate decision that may provide a platform for the founder to criticize and undermine the new executive. In other cases, the founder may be retained as a consultant or perhaps in an honorific position to engage in fund-raising and other external tasks. But, under these arrangements, unless the founder has exceptional wisdom and grace and the new executive shows unusual understanding and sensitivity, the situation is likely to remain volatile for some time, continuing to burden the organization and distract it from pursuit of its mission.

Of course, there are enlightened and wise founders, who recognize their own limitations and their organization's changing needs. In this situation, founder syndrome really does not exist, since there are many options for providing both the leadership and management that the organization requires. For example, the founder may take on more of an external role, delegating much of the day-to-day management to others, perhaps an associate director, chief operating officer, or executive vice president. But, in such a scenario, it is also essential for the founder to avoid end runs around the new operating officer by staff who may have been hired by the founder, and to support and reinforce the operating officer's authority and control.

Executive Transitions

Every nonprofit will eventually face the need to replace its CEO. Sometimes the need is first recognized by the board, and the current CEO needs to be persuaded—or forced—to step down. As we have discussed, this can be especially difficult when the chief executive is a charismatic founder of the organization, but the involuntary departure of any CEO is a difficult and potentially wrenching experience for an organization. In other situations, the CEO may initiate the change. This may occur for several reasons. The CEO may receive a better offer from another organization or perhaps just feel burned out and want a change of scene. For some CEOs, there comes a point when they feel that their major goals for the organization have been accomplished and that it is just time to move on to something new. This may occur at the completion of some major effort, for example, a successful fund-raising campaign, or on reaching some milestone, such as 10 years of service (Weisman & Goldbaum, 2004). There is a difference, of course, between an anticipated departure, such as retirement, and one that comes as a surprise, such as when the CEO receives an unanticipated job offer that is just too good to turn down. In the first instance, the board has time to prepare for the transition; in the second, some boards may be caught unprepared to make one of the most critical decisions they will ever face.

In business corporations, it is not unusual for chief executives to come up through the ranks. They are often individuals who have worked in the company for a long time, are steeped in its culture, and are knowledgeable about its products and markets. Indeed, as a corporate executive approaches retirement, it is not unusual for there to be an heir apparent who has been groomed for the top position for years.

Boards work in the same way with regard to their own membership; bylaws often include limits on how long the board chair can serve, and thus, the transition in leadership is predictable and planned. There is often a vice chair of the board or even a chair elect, who is well prepared to take over the job in a smooth transition. But nonprofit CEOs are more often than not recruited from outside the organization. This is frequently because the organization is thinly staffed and tightly budgeted and cannot afford the luxury of a number-two executive with the capability to be the CEO (Wolf, 1999). The lack of an internal candidate for the chief executive position might also exist if the organization is still led by a founder, who may not have provided others with the opportunity to learn and grow sufficiently to be prepared for leadership. Thus, nonprofits may be faced with the need to appoint as CEO an individual who is a virtual stranger—not someone whom they have known or have had the opportunity to get to know in more junior positions before advancing him or her to the top office. In these circumstances, the selection of a new CEO may carry some risk that the wrong person will be selected, with potentially serious consequences for the effectiveness and stability of the organization.

There is a growing literature concerning executive transition planning, and an increasing number of nonprofits are preparing for the eventuality even before the CEO's departure is foreseen or imminent. Internal preparation is a shared responsibility of the board and the CEO. If the organization is large enough to have staff members capable of eventually filling the CEO position, the CEO can intentionally prepare those individuals by including them in important meetings and decisions, providing them with opportunities for additional professional training, giving them assignments with responsibility that can help develop their leadership skills, and exposing them to the board so that they will know the board and the board will know them (Weisman & Goldbaum, 2004). This requires, of course, a confident CEO with a participative style of leadership and a genuine commitment to the organization even beyond his or her own tenure as its leader.

In small organizations, there may be no internal candidate believed capable of rising to the CEO position within any reasonable period of time. But the CEO can still prepare for the possibility of a transition whether planned or unexpected, by developing systems, documenting policies and procedures, and sharing responsibility with others in a way that will make it possible for a successor, or perhaps an interim director, to maintain the organization's activities with minimum disruption. Boards are advised to ensure that such internal planning is occurring and also to remain aware of leaders in other similar organizations whom they might try to recruit should the need arise (Weisman & Goldbaum, 2004).

The need for transition planning goes well below the level of the CEO. Other staff members, for example, program directors or even key volunteers, may need to be replaced and there may not always be advance warning. Again, communication, documentation, and cross-training of staff in the responsibilities of each other's jobs can minimize disruption during the period of transition after someone leaves the organization.

Most nonprofits continue to appoint their chief executives from outside and conduct searches to identify and select their new executive leaders. A full discussion of the search process is beyond the scope of this text, but many excellent resources are available, through BoardSource, CompassPoint (www.compasspoint.org), and other organizations, describing how to conduct an effective search. As competition for management talent has intensified, professional executive search firms also have come to play a larger role.

The search for a new CEO must be rooted in the organization's own understanding of itself—its mission, its values, its vision, and its goals. The process cannot be rushed, and it is often about far more than just finding someone qualified for the job. To define who may be the right person in the right place at the right time, the organization must have a clear understanding of its past, its purpose, its constituencies, and its aspirations.

Leading Change

Leadership often involves change. Indeed, Kee and Newcomer (2008) observe that "some . . . argue that leadership is inherently change-oriented—that the function of management is to protect and nurture the status quo, while the function of leadership is to continually examine better ways of doing things" (p. 23).

There are a number of prominent *change theories* and models. Kee and Newcomer (2008) propose a taxonomy of change models, placing some well-known theories into the categories of *leader-centered, follower-centered,* and *change-centered* leadership, each of which have advantages and disadvantages (p. 23). While arguing for "a model of change leadership that engages other stakeholders in a 'whole systems' approach to the change process," Newcomer and Kee acknowledge that "the dominant advice in the literature on change management is that . . . leaders . . . must overcome resistance to change through a variety of top-down approaches" (p. 32).

Indeed, one of the best-known authors on change, John Kotter (1996), advocates a top-down approach. Kotter's model is based on business corporations, which is why some scholars fund it less than ideal for nonprofit organizations. However, elements of it may be adapted to the nonprofit setting. One hallmark of the model is its emphasis on the importance of organizational culture—the shared values, attitudes, feelings, beliefs, rituals, habits, codes of conduct, and other such characteristics of an organization—invisible rules that may support or hinder an initiative for change.

Kotter (1996) describes eight common mistakes that leaders trying to implement change are prone to make and proposes a parallel eight-step change process to avoid them. According to Kotter, efforts at transformational change in an organization often fail because leaders allow too much *complacency;* that is, they do not engender a sufficient sense of urgency about the need for change. For example, in a mature organization, decline may be gradual, and future threats may not be visible to most people. As long as the operating budget is balanced, there is no negative publicity or scandal, and staff positions seem secure, most people may be content to continue with business as usual and not be receptive to changes that would disrupt their worldviews or routines.

Leaders often fail to develop what Kotter (1996) calls a "powerful guiding coalition" in support of change. In other words, they too often try to drive the change alone without first developing a critical mass of allies—perhaps including key staff members, members of the board, and others—who share their commitment to the need for change. Leaders some-times underestimate the power of *vision.* They try to bring about change through a series of actions—incremental changes, perhaps small modifications to procedures, reorganizations of staff, or modest enhancements to fund-raising or communications programs. These are steps along the way that may appear unconnected to those who do not see or understand the larger vision toward which they are intended to lead. Leaders may try to operate behind the scenes, without adequately painting the picture of what the future will be like. In that case, they are unlikely to build the steam necessary to propel real and lasting change in the organization. The inertia of current culture and practice may be just too strong to overcome with an incremental approach.

Too often, change leaders *undercommunicate* the vision, perhaps relying on routine com-munication vehicles such as newsletters, annual reports, and other publications. They may assume that everyone in the organization carefully reads and considers such publications—or takes them seriously—and is thus sufficiently aware of the plan for change and shares the leader's commitment to it, when in fact this may not be true.

Kotter (1996) says that leaders may fail because they do not create "short-term wins"—that is, set intermediate goals that can be achieved and reassure followers that the ultimate longer-term changes can be successfully reached. Setting some achievable short-term goals and celebrat-ing their attainment can be an essential tactic to retain the commitment of staff and volunteers to a long-term change process and prevent frustration and inertia from bringing it to a halt midstream.

But there is also the risk of *declaring victory too soon.* Change may have occurred on the surface, but leaders err when they do not stay with the program long enough for the changes to "sink down deeply into the [organization's] culture" (Kotter, 1996, p. 13). Only by *anchoring the changes* in the organization's culture can the leader pursuing change ensure that the board and successive generations of management will also adhere to new ways of doing things. As Kotter explains,

> Smart people miss the mark here when they are insensitive to cultural issues. Economically oriented finance people and analytically oriented engineers can find the topic of social norms and values too soft for their tastes. So, they ignore culture—at their peril. (p. 15)

Kotter (1996) offers an eight-step change process that avoids each of the potential mistakes (p. 21). To ensure that the momentum for change is not overwhelmed by the inertia of existing culture and practices and to make certain that the change is real and permanent, the leader should follow the steps sequentially, not moving on to the next until the previous has been solidly accomplished:

1. Establish a sense of urgency

2. Create a guiding coalition

3. Develop a vision and strategy

4. Communicate the change vision

5. Empower broad-based action

6. Generate short-term wins

7. Consolidate gains and produce more change

8. Anchor new approaches in the culture

What is the essential ingredient of successful change? Kotter (1996) argues that it requires 70 to 90% leadership and just 10 to 30% the skills of management. "Leadership defines what the future should look like, aligns people with that vision, and inspires them to make it happen despite the obstacles" (p. 26). But leadership may be in short supply when an organization needs it to drive essential change. Kotter describes a life-cycle theory of business firms that is reminiscent of the nonprofit life cycles we discussed earlier. Companies start as entrepreneurial businesses, then grow and achieve a position of market dominance. As size and dominance increase, control becomes most important, and management predominates over leadership. However, that can produce a bureaucratic, inward orientation that causes managers to become complacent about performance. The situation requires change, but the forces of complacency and inertia make change difficult, requiring "sacrifice, dedication, and creativity." These cannot be engendered through coercion but instead require "leadership, leadership, and more leadership" (p. 31).

Chapter Summary

The position of CEO in a nonprofit organization is different from similar positions in government or the business sector, for reasons that relate to the distinctive nature of nonprofit organizations themselves. While every organization, regardless of sector, requires capable management in order to be effective, nonprofits especially need CEOs who can exercise strong leadership. This is true because they are organizations based on values and driven by their missions, which mobilize commitment and support by appealing to a shared vision.

Theorists have defined leadership in terms of individual qualities, skills that leaders possess, and behaviors that successful leaders exhibit. However, contemporary theories recognize that effective leadership may be contingent or situational; that is, it may depend on the circumstances, including human relationships, the nature of the task, and the formal position of the executive.

James MacGregor Burns offered a definition of transactional leadership that sounds very much like management. The transactional leader rewards or punishes others in exchange for the work that they perform and emphasizes rules, policies, and procedures to ensure that things are done right. Burns introduced the concept of transformational leadership, in which the leader enables individuals to experience their own moral and motivational growth by appealing to values that they share with the organization. This text suggests that transformational leadership may be especially appropriate in organizations that often attract the participation of people motivated by commitment to their values-based missions. The concept of charismatic leadership is frequently observed in the founders of nonprofit organizations. They are individuals who inspire others to extraordinary effort through the model of their own commitment and their articulation of a vision, among other behaviors.

Various scholars and practitioners have tried to define the effective nonprofit CEO. Some reflect trait theories or skills theories of leadership, while others have described the behaviors of effective chief executives. The behaviors most often identified involve the CEO focusing his or her attention on the mission, the board, external relationships, and a few key priorities while understanding the political reality of competition among constituencies for the organization's resources. A framework offered by Dym and Hutson seeks to integrate various leadership theories and describe how effective leadership arises when the individual, the organization, and its community or market are aligned—in other words, when the right person serves in the right place at the right time.

Some organizations will face a significant challenge when a founding CEO leaves the organization, either voluntarily or through a forced transition. Chief executive transitions in general have received greater attention in the recent literature of nonprofit management. Organizations and their boards are encouraged to prepare and plan for changes in executive leadership and to base the search for a new CEO firmly in the organization's mission, values, vision, goals, and aspirations. Leadership often involves change, and some authors argue that it is inherently so. There are various theories of change leadership, including those that are leader-centered, those that are follower-centered, and those that are change-centered. Each has its advantages and disadvantages, and the model selected should be appropriate to the organization. One common principle is the importance of anchoring changes in the organization's culture.

Notes

1. Reprinted with permission from The Nonprofit Chief Executive's Ten Basic Responsibilities, a publication of BoardSource, formerly the National Center for Nonprofit Boards. For more information about BoardSource, call 800-883-6262 or visit www.boardsource.org. BoardSource © 2005.

2. Although somewhat different and often presented separately in other texts, *situational theories* and *contingency theories* of leadership have in common the idea that there is no one right style of leadership that can be successful in all organizations or under all circumstances. This book just uses the term *contingency theory* to encompass that concept.

KEY TERMS AND CONCEPTS

alignment map	*charismatic leadership*	*executive leadership*
behavior and style theories	*change-centered*	*follower-centered*
Blake and Mouton managerial grid	*contingency theories*	*founder syndrome*
	employee orientation	*leader-centered*

leadership	*skills theories*	*transactional leadership*
legislative leadership	*situational theories*	*transformational leadership*
management	*succession planning*	*transition planning*
production orientation	*task behaviors*	
relationship behaviors	*trait theories*	

CASE 5.1   A Change in Leadership at Habitat for Humanity

Habitat for Humanity International is an ecumenical, faith-based nonprofit dedicated to eliminating substandard housing and homelessness. Habitat constructs houses with the assistance of volunteers and partner families, who then purchase the homes with affordable loans. It has built more than 200,000 homes housing more than 1,000,000 people in 3,000 communities around the world (Habitat for Humanity International, 2005). Habitat has been hailed as one of the most successful nonprofits of the past 30 years and "one of the most dramatic examples of social entrepreneurship . . . that blends commercial and social methods to generate much of the cash, labor, and materials needed to construct its programs" (Dees et al., 2001, p. 12).

Habitat was founded in 1976 by Millard Fuller, who led the organization as its CEO for many years. Fuller had acquired wealth before the age of 30 and then dedicated himself to a life of service. While he was the CEO of Habitat, Fuller accepted an annual salary of only $15,000, declined raises, and lived for 23 years in a modest house without air-conditioning (Bixler, 2005). Fuller was widely praised as a visionary, and his commitment attracted volunteers and donors to Habitat, including former President Jimmy Carter, who became one of the organization's most prominent advocates.

But by the early 2000s, issues began to arise between Mr. Fuller and Habitat's board. As Fuller approached the age of 70 in 2004, he sought to extend his service as CEO until 2005, when Habitat would complete its 200,000th house. But the board began to plan for transition and appointed a former board chairman as Managing Director. Although Fuller retained the title of President and Chief Executive Officer, he was said to have complained that the board's decision forced him into a figurehead role (Pierce, 2004).

The board had received a specific complaint about an incident involving Fuller and a Habitat employee and conducted an investigation. Although the board found insufficient proof of wrongdoing, the process brought to the surface other issues that had been developing over a period of years (Jensen, 2005). One board member observed that a gradual change had occurred in the composition of the board, saying, "There was a movement to start engaging board members who had some 'juice'—people who were powerful in different fields and were well connected." The changing board became critical of Fuller for undertaking some projects without its approval (Pierce, 2004), and Fuller became critical of the board, saying, "I've always seen Habitat for Humanity as a movement. . . . There's a certain mentality on the board now that wants to change it into an organizational bureaucracy" (Jensen, 2005).

In January of 2005, the board fired Fuller and his wife, who also had held a position at Habitat, and appointed an interim CEO. The interim CEO explained the situation saying, "The strength of vision and ego that was so important for the beginning and initial growth of Habitat are not what we need today to provide the structure for what has become a large, far-flung operation" (Jewell, 2005, p. 24). Fuller spoke out against the board's action, saying trustees were not committed to the faith-based nature of Habitat and just wanted to replace him with a "high paid bean counter" (Jewell, 2005, p. 24).

Some Habitat for Humanity affiliates, volunteers, and donors spoke out in opposition to the board's action and in support of Fuller. Fuller created a new organization, which he called "Building Habitat," but he later changed its name to the Fuller Center for Housing after Habitat for Humanity filed suit alleging infringement of its trademark (Wilhelm, 2005a). Habitat for Humanity undertook a search for a new CEO and eventually hired Jonathon Reckford, a former businessman with Goldman Sachs and Best Buy. Reckford met with Fuller. Afterward, Fuller said, "I was not prepared to like the guy, but I did" (Wilhelm, 2005a).

Reckford committed the organization to continued growth but said that it needed to "build the platform" for that growth and determine the right organizational structure and ways of maximizing effectiveness (Wilhelm, 2005a). Fuller continued to voice opinions about Habitat's directions.

Reflecting on the controversy that had surrounded the transition in leadership from Habitat's founder, one nonprofit scholar observed, "Habitat for Humanity is much bigger than one man, and that speaks of Mr. Fuller's success" (Minor, 2005). Mr. Fuller passed away in 2009 at age 74.

CASE 5.2   Crisis and Change at N Street Village

N Street Village (NSV) is a nonprofit organization in Washington, D.C., that provides services to homeless and low-income women as they move to stable housing and self-sufficiency. NSV was founded in 1973 by Luther Place Memorial Church and provides food, clothing, showers, transitional and permanent housing, mental and physical health care, and support to women entering the workforce. It serves nearly 800 women each year (NSV, 2010).

Mary Funke was appointed as executive director of NSV in 2004 and immediately faced a financial crisis that previously had not been well understood by the staff or the board. She recognized that urgent action would be needed, but also that the current crisis was deeply rooted in long-term problems, which would require more complex planning and change. They included a lack of accountability and performance standards and a culture that included a "God will provide" approach to finances.

Funke engaged an accountant who produced a report to the senior executive staff and board that pointed to the seriousness of the immediate situation. Funke proposed an immediate response, which included a $200,000 budget reduction, the closing of one program, the elimination of nine staff positions, and intensified fund-raising. She also articulated a longer-term vision that involved creating a nonprofit business model with a commitment to the following:

- Performance, financial, administrative, and program accountability
- Outcomes measures
- Best principles of accounting and finance
- Up-to-date knowledge and information technology infrastructure
- Complete administrative documentation
- Effective staff, board, and volunteer communication systems

As the emergency measures were implemented, Funke took a hands-on approach, meeting personally with the staff whose positions would be cut and communicating regularly with both internal and external stakeholders—remaining staff members, the board and volunteers, clients, donors, and the sponsoring church.

To advance her long-term vision, Funke implemented a planning process. She facilitated a full-day retreat with the staff and conducted a SWOT analysis (an analysis of strengths, weaknesses, opportunities, and threats), giving the entire staff an opportunity to participate in developing a 5-year strategic plan. The biggest challenge was changing the culture from one in which the staff and board had been

(Continued)

(Continued)

content for so long as core services were being provided to clients. To develop a culture of performance, client satisfaction surveys were implemented; strategic goals and objectives were updated yearly based on stakeholder feedback; job descriptions were updated; budgeted funds were provided for staff training; and a performance management system was created, with staff participating in the development of their own performance goals.

By 2006, NSV was meeting its goals and its financial situation had been stabilized. It applied for the Washington Post Award for Excellence in Nonprofit Management. The staff benchmarked other organizations, developed the application as a team, and succeeded in winning the competition. The impact on staff morale was significant. To date, NSV has continued to flourish, with a new culture of performance and a staff that feels a sense of belonging.

Source: Summarized and adapted from Kee, J. E., Newcomer, K. E., *Transforming Public and Nonprofit Organizations: Stewardship for Leading Change* (2008). Vienna, VA: Management Concepts, Inc. (pp. 96–101). Jessica Griffin, a graduate student in the Trachtenberg School of Public Administration and Public Policy at The George Washington University, was the primary author of the original case study. Used with permission.

QUESTIONS FOR DISCUSSION

1. Which theory or theories seem to best describe the career of Millard Fuller at Habitat for Humanity? Of what is the story of his departure an example?

2. Which theory or theories seem to best describe the leadership of Mary Funke at N Street Village?

3. In what ways does the process for change at N Street Village reflect Kotter's model?

4. Are leaders born or made? Can anyone learn to be a leader, or does it require some innate qualities or characteristics of the individual?

5. Could one individual be a great leader in government, a corporation, or a nonprofit? Why or why not?

6. Is leadership necessarily moral? Was Hitler a leader even though he was evil? Why or why not?

7. Who are some contemporary leaders that you would identify as charismatic? How do they exhibit the behaviors of charismatic leaders identified in this chapter?

SUGGESTIONS FOR FURTHER READING

Books

Burns, J. M. (1978). *Leadership.* New York: HarperCollins.

Carlson, M., & Donohoe, M. (2003). *The executive director's survival guide: Thriving as a nonprofit leader.* San Francisco: Jossey-Bass.

Collins, J. (2005). *Good to Great and the social sectors: A monograph to accompany Good to Great.* New York: Harper.

Dym, B., & Hutson, H. (2005). *Leadership in nonprofit organizations.* Thousand Oaks, CA: Sage.

Kee, J. E., & Newcomer, K. E. (2008). *Transforming public and nonprofit organizations: stewardship for leading change.* Vienna, VA: Management Concepts.

Northouse, P. G. (2007). *Leadership: Theory and practice* (4th ed.). Thousand Oaks, CA: Sage.

Weisman, C., & Goldbaum, R. I. (2004). *Losing your executive director without losing your way.* San Francisco: Jossey-Bass.

Websites

Center for Creative Leadership, http://www.ccl.org/leadership/index.aspx

Leader to Leader Institute, http://www.pfdf.org/

PART III

Managing the Nonprofit Organization

Chapter Outline

chapter 6

Accountability requires not only that the resources entrusted to the nonprofit not be misused but also that they be used to maximum benefit in pursuing the organization's mission. However, this component of accountability turns out to be the most complex, since there is not always consensus on how results should be measured.

© iStockphoto.com/Dirk Freder

Ensuring Accountability and Measuring Performance

6

Nonprofit organizations enjoy considerable autonomy in defining their missions, setting their own goals, and crafting their own strategies for achieving those goals. They are private organizations, but they are granted charters to serve purposes that society has deemed to be of public benefit. The organizations are exempt from taxation, and donors are permitted deductions for gifts made to charitable nonprofits to further those purposes. Tax exemption and the tax deductibility of gifts represent foregone government revenue and therefore are regarded by many as a form of tax subsidy; in other words, to some extent, nonprofits are working with the public's money. That gives society an interest in ensuring that they are *accountable* for their use of the resources entrusted to them and that those resources are indeed being directed toward the pursuit of their social missions. But what exactly is society entitled to expect?

The question is a little like asking, "What is a good student?" Does one qualify just by attending all classes, turning in papers on time, and showing up for exams—that is, by not breaking any of the rules of the course? Or is a good student someone who studies hard and seeks help from the professor when something is not clear—in other words, someone who shows exemplary student behavior? Does being a good student require earning good grades? Do grades accurately reflect what a student may have learned in a course, or is it possible that a better measure would be to compare what he or she knew at the beginning of a course with what he or she knew at the end, maybe basing the label of "good student" on some measure of "value added"? As we will see in this chapter, similar questions arise when we consider ideas such as the accountability, effectiveness, and performance of nonprofit organizations.

Defining and Ensuring Accountability

To be *accountable* essentially means being required to answer, to take responsibility, for one's actions. Perhaps the narrowest concept of accountability for a nonprofit would require merely following the law—for example, obeying the non-distribution requirement, avoiding conflicts of interest, treating staff without discrimination, and filing IRS reports as required. But that might seem to be a minimal standard to expect. Perhaps we might look for something more, not just following the law but also going beyond the requirements of law to follow best practices in governing and managing the organization—in other words, doing the right things as well as not doing things that are wrong.

But does even a definition of accountability that expects nonprofits to do the right things really go far enough? For example, the board may meet regularly, the budget may be invariably balanced, the staff may be happy and motivated, and there may be a written strategic plan, but that does not ensure that clients are recovering, the symphony is achieving artistic excellence, or public attitudes on the environment are being changed. Thus, perhaps accountability needs to include more than just avoiding transgressions and exhibiting model behavior. It may need to encompass demonstrated effectiveness in achieving the purposes for which the nonprofit exists. That requires not only that the resources entrusted to the nonprofit not be misused, but also that they be used to maximum benefit in pursuing the organization's mission. As we will see, however, this component of accountability turns out to be the most complex, since there is not always consensus on how results should be measured, or even on how they should be defined.

The question of to whom nonprofits must account has long been asked—to clients, to donors, to the larger community, and/or to other stakeholders? It has gained more precise answers in recent years, as governments have increased their reporting requirements and a variety of other entities have cast the light of transparency on nonprofit behavior.

Concern about the accountability of nonprofit organizations has a long history. As early as 1918, the National Charities Information Bureau was created to educate the public about nonprofit organization behavior in order to reduce the incidence of charity fraud. But concern about accountability became heightened in the 1980s, 1990s, and 2000s. In 1992, the widely publicized misuse of United Way funds by the man who was then president, William Aramony, for which he was convicted and served jail time, shocked the nation. Again after September 11, 2001, accusations that some charity fund-raising appeals were misleading and questions about the use of the funds given to help victims of the terrorist attacks further undermined the public's confidence in the integrity of the sector. Controversies at the Nature Conservancy, American University, and other organizations in the mid-2000s captured the attention of the media as well as the U.S. Congress and further heightened concern about accountability in the nonprofit sector. The sector responded by developing voluntary principles for accountability, but the potential for additional legislation remained. The broader definition of accountability, including the requirement to produce results, also has become more pronounced with the growing impact of donors who view their giving as social investment and demand specific evidence of the impact of their support. For these reasons, the topics of accountability and performance are intrinsically linked today, and both are explored in this chapter.

Mechanisms for Accountability

There are three principal mechanisms by which nonprofits are held accountable: the *rule of law, self-regulation,* and *transparency*—that is, holding nonprofit behavior up in clear view for donors, the media, and others to see. Let's take a look at what is currently in place in these three arenas.

Requirements of Law

Chapters 3 and 4 covered some of the legal requirements facing nonprofits, so we need only review a few key points here. Nonprofits must comply with laws at both state and federal levels.

State governments grant nonprofits their charters, and state attorneys general and state courts have the authority to take action against law-breaking nonprofits. This can include the removal of board members who violate their fiduciary responsibilities and possibly even revoking of the organization's charter. Most states also have laws regulating the behavior of nonprofits in specific areas—for example, requiring that they be registered in order to solicit gifts from the general public.

At the federal level, regulation of nonprofits is carried out primarily by the IRS's Division on Tax-Exempt and Government Entities. The IRS has the authority to impose intermediate sanctions or to revoke an organization's tax exemption, eliminating its ability to raise tax-deductible gifts and subjecting it to the requirement to pay income taxes itself. Nonprofits that receive federal funds above certain amounts are also subject to additional rules with regard to their use of the federal dollars. Organizations with revenues greater than $25,000 (except religious congregations) are required to file an annual Form 990, 990-EZ, or 990-PF with the IRS. As discussed in Chapter 4, beginning in 2009 (with filing of the Form 990 covering 2008), the IRS introduced a revised form that greatly expanded the information required. The revised 990 includes questions related to governance as well as finances and programs. (See Figure 4.1 for the Form 990, Part VI questions related to governance.) Since 2008, even small nonprofits that are not required to file Form 990 are required to electronically file Form 990-N, also known as the *e-Postcard*. It includes minimal information that essentially reflects the organization's existence, without the data encompassed by Form 990.

In 2002, as noted in Chapter 4, Congress passed the Sarbanes-Oxley Act, responding to corporate governance scandals. While Sarbanes-Oxley (or "SOX," as it is commonly called) pertains primarily to publicly traded corporations, two of its provisions—those regarding protection for whistle-blowers and destruction of documents—also apply to nonprofit organizations. Some states, including California, have passed legislation directed at nonprofits that essentially incorporates Sarbanes-Oxley-type requirements (Nonprofit Integrity Act, 2004). Many nonprofits have voluntarily adopted Sarbanes-Oxley provisions as a way to assure their donors that they are operating with high integrity, transparency, and sound governance. In addition, Form 990 implies that nonprofits should comply with some Sarbanes-Oxley practices, even if not required to do so by law.

Principles of good governance and ethical practice established by the Panel on the Nonprofit Sector, which we will discuss soon, also include many points consistent with Sarbanes-Oxley. These developments clearly have pushed the definition of accountability beyond just "do no wrong"; it now includes adherence to best practices in governance and ethical behavior. Using the "good student" we discussed at the beginning of the chapter as a metaphor, nonprofits are now expected to do more than just not be absent from class and miss paper deadlines; they are also expected to demonstrate that they have done their homework, have studied, and have engaged in other activities defined as "good student" behaviors.

The federal Pension Protection Act of 2006, as its title implies, is principally focused on the reform of pensions, but it also contains a variety of provisions that affect the nonprofit sector. They include, among others, changes in the law regarding charitable giving, tighter regulation of certain types of nonprofit organizations, greater communication between the IRS and state authorities regarding action taken against nonprofits, and the requirement that nonprofits with unrelated business income make public their Form 990-T (Johnson, 2006).

This text does not include a complete discussion of laws affecting nonprofit organizations. Moreover, regulations change frequently and the law may change at any time. The suggested readings at the end of this chapter include books that provide detailed discussion of the nonprofit legal framework, and students will find the website of Independent Sector (www.independentsector.org) to be an excellent source of up-to-date information on new or pending legislation.

Self-Regulation: Standards and Accreditation

If the nonprofit sector would prefer not to be burdened by increased government regulation, then the alternative is to develop more effective mechanisms for self-regulation. In 2004, concern about nonprofit accountability prompted the Finance Committee of the U.S. Senate to hold hearings and consider proposals for significantly increased regulation of the nonprofit sector at the national level. At the committee's request, Independent Sector convened a Panel on the Nonprofit Sector to develop recommendations. The panel's report was presented to the Congress in June 2005; it suggested increased enforcement of existing state and federal law, increased reporting by nonprofits, and some additional legislation. But its emphasis was on the importance of maintaining the sector's independence and on its capacity for self-regulation (Independent Sector, 2005).

The Panel on the Nonprofit Sector's recommendations and 33 principles for good governance and ethical conduct were published in 2007 and are summarized in Table 6.1. The principles are organized into four broad areas: legal compliance and public disclosure, effective governance, strong financial oversight, and responsible fund-raising. Students will note that some of the principles are reflective of Sarbanes-Oxley requirements and the questions in Part VI of Form 990, which was discussed in Chapter 4.

There are a number of well-known standards of practice in addition to the Panel on the Nonprofit Sector's principles, some of which are the basis for *accreditation* of nonprofits by various authorities.

There is a long history of accreditation of educational and health care institutions. For example, schools and colleges are accredited through regional associations. Individual institutions engage in self-studies according to a process defined by the accrediting body and are evaluated through intensive visits by teams from peer institutions. Professional schools within universities have separate accrediting mechanisms; for example, law schools are accredited by the American Bar Association and business schools by the Association to Advance Collegiate Schools of Business. Health care organizations, including hospitals, nursing homes, health care networks, and other service providers, are accredited by the Joint Commission on Accreditation of Healthcare Organizations, itself a nonprofit organization.

Although educational accreditation is voluntary, accrediting bodies are recognized by the U.S. Department of Education, and accreditation is required in order to be eligible for certain government funds. Likewise, accreditation of health care organizations is voluntary, but the power of government creates a significant incentive, since status as an accredited health care provider is required in order to be eligible to receive certain government reimbursements, an essential source of revenue for many organizations.

In the broader nonprofit sector, the accreditation of organizations is a relatively recent concept, having its origins in the development of accountability standards and definitions of best practices by state associations of nonprofits and others. As one example, the Maryland Association of Nonprofit Organizations (2010) developed Standards for Excellence in nonprofit management that are well regarded and have become a model for other state associations across the country. The Maryland standards are based on 8 guiding principles and 55 standards related to these principles. The guiding principles are presented under the categories of mission and

TABLE 6.1 ■ Principles for Good Governance and Ethical Practice

Legal Compliance and Public Disclosure

(1) A charitable organization must comply with all applicable federal laws and regulations, as well as applicable laws and regulations of the states and the local jurisdictions in which it is based or operates. If the organization conducts programs outside the United States, it must also abide by applicable international laws, regulations, and conventions that are legally binding on the United States.

(2) A charitable organization should have a formally adopted, written code of ethics with which all of its directors or trustees, staff, and volunteers are familiar and to which they adhere.

(3) A charitable organization should adopt and implement policies and procedures to ensure that all conflicts of interest, or the appearance thereof, within the organization and the board are appropriately managed through disclosure, recusal, or other means.

(4) A charitable organization should establish and implement policies and procedures that enable individuals to come forward with information on illegal practices or violations of organizational policies. This "whistle-blower" policy should specify that the organization will not retaliate against, and will protect the confidentiality of, individuals who make good-faith reports.

(5) A charitable organization should establish and implement policies and procedures to protect and preserve the organization's important documents and business records.

(6) A charitable organization's board should ensure that the organization has adequate plans to protect its assets—its property, financial and human resources, programmatic content and material, and its integrity and reputation—against damage or loss. The board should review regularly the organization's need for general liability and directors' and officers' liability insurance, as well as take other actions necessary to mitigate risks.

(7) A charitable organization should make information about its operations, including its governance, finances, programs, and activities, widely available to the public. Charitable organizations also should consider making information available on the methods they use to evaluate the outcomes of their work and sharing the results of those evaluations.

Effective Governance

(8) A charitable organization must have a governing body that is responsible for reviewing and approving the organization's mission and strategic direction, annual budget and key financial transactions, compensation practices and policies, and fiscal and governance policies.

(9) The board of a charitable organization should meet regularly enough to conduct its business and fulfill its duties.

(10) The board of a charitable organization should establish its own size and structure and review these periodically. The board should have enough members to allow for full deliberation and diversity of thinking on governance and other organizational matters. Except for very small organizations, this generally means that the board should have at least five members.

(11) The board of a charitable organization should include members with the diverse background (including, but not limited to, ethnic, racial, and gender perspectives), experience, and organizational and financial skills necessary to advance the organization's mission.

(12) A substantial majority of the board of a public charity, usually meaning at least two-thirds of the members, should be independent. Independent members should not: (1) be compensated by the organization as employees or independent contractors; (2) have their compensation determined by individuals who are compensated by the organization; (3) receive, directly or indirectly, material financial benefits from the organization except as a member of the

(Continued)

TABLE 6.1 ■ (Continued)

charitable class served by the organization; or (4) be related to anyone described above (as a spouse, sibling, parent, or child), or reside with any person so described.

(13) The board should hire, oversee, and annually evaluate the performance of the chief executive officer of the organization, and should conduct such an evaluation prior to any change in that officer's compensation, unless there is a multi-year contract in force or the change consists solely of routine adjustments for inflation or cost of living.

(14) The board of a charitable organization that has paid staff should ensure that the positions of chief staff officer, board chair, and board treasurer are held by separate individuals. Organizations without paid staff should ensure that the positions of board chair and treasurer are held by separate individuals.

(15) The board should establish an effective, systematic process for educating and communicating with board members to ensure that they are aware of their legal and ethical responsibilities, are knowledgeable about the programs and activities of the organization, and can carry out their oversight functions effectively.

(16) Board members should evaluate their performance as a group and as individuals no less frequently than every three years, and should have clear procedures for removing board members who are unable to fulfill their responsibilities.

(17) The board should establish clear policies and procedures setting the length of terms and the number of consecutive terms a board member may serve.

(18) The board should review organizational and governing instruments no less frequently than every five years.

(19) The board should establish and review regularly the organization's mission and goals and should evaluate, no less frequently than every five years, the organization's programs, goals, and activities to be sure they advance its mission and make prudent use of its resources.

(20) Board members are generally expected to serve without compensation, other than reimbursement for expenses incurred to fulfill their board duties. A charitable organization that provides compensation to its board members should use appropriate comparability data to determine the amount to be paid; document the decision; and provide full disclosure to anyone, upon request, of the amount and rationale for the compensation.

Strong Financial Oversight

(21) A charitable organization must keep complete, current, and accurate financial records. Its board should receive and review timely reports of the organization's financial activities and should have a qualified, independent financial expert audit or review these statements annually in a manner appropriate to the organization's size and scale of operations.

(22) The board of a charitable organization must institute policies and procedures to ensure that the organization (and, if applicable, its subsidiaries) manages and invests its funds responsibly, in accordance with all legal requirements. The full board should review and approve the organization's annual budget and should monitor actual performance against the budget.

(23) A charitable organization should not provide loans (or the equivalent, such as loan guarantees, purchasing or transferring ownership of a residence or office, or relieving a debt or lease obligation) to directors, officers, or trustees.

(24) A charitable organization should spend a significant percentage of its annual budget on programs that pursue its mission. The budget should also provide sufficient resources for

effective administration of the organization, and, if it solicits contributions, for appropriate fund-raising activities.

(25) A charitable organization should establish clear, written policies for paying or reimbursing expenses incurred by anyone conducting business or traveling on behalf of the organization, including the types of expenses that can be paid for or reimbursed and the documentation required. Such policies should require that travel on behalf of the organization is to be undertaken in a cost-effective manner.

(26) A charitable organization should neither pay for nor reimburse travel expenditures for spouses, dependents, or others who are accompanying someone conducting business for the organization unless they, too, are conducting such business.

Responsible Fund-Raising

(27) Solicitation materials and other communications addressed to donors and the public must clearly identify the organization and be accurate and truthful.

(28) Contributions must be used for purposes consistent with the donor's intent, whether as described in the relevant solicitation materials or as specifically directed by the donor.

(29) A charitable organization must provide donors with specific acknowledgments of charitable contributions, in accordance with IRS requirements, as well as information to facilitate the donors' compliance with tax law requirements.

(30) A charitable organization should adopt clear policies, based on its specific exempt purpose, to determine whether accepting a gift would compromise its ethics, financial circumstances, program focus, or other interests.

(31) A charitable organization should provide appropriate training and supervision of the people soliciting funds on its behalf to ensure that they understand their responsibilities and applicable federal, state, and local laws, and do not employ techniques that are coercive, intimidating, or intended to harass potential donors.

(32) A charitable organization should not compensate internal or external fund-raisers based on a commission or a percentage of the amount raised.

(33) A charitable organization should respect the privacy of individual donors and, except where disclosure is required by law, should not sell or otherwise make available the names and contact information of its donors without providing them an opportunity at least once a year to opt out of the use of their names.

Source: Reprinted with special permission of Independent Sector, a nonprofit, nonpartisan coalition of charities, foundations, and corporate philanthropy programs whose mission is to advance the common good by leading, strengthening, and mobilizing the independent sector. www.independentsector.org

program, governing board, conflicts of interest, human resources (including both volunteers and staff), financial and legal accountability, openness (or transparency) and disclosure, fund-raising, and public affairs and public policy (including public education and public policy advocacy). The standards essentially describe recommended best practices—that is, a set of guides for behavior that reflect a consensus about how a well-managed and accountable nonprofit should operate.

Like other state associations, Maryland's offers a voluntary certification program to organizations that wish to demonstrate their adherence to its Standards for Excellence. Similar to the accreditation process in educational and health care institutions, the process requires that the organization complete a lengthy application, pay a fee, and be approved by a team of trained peer reviewers. Organizations that successfully complete the process are entitled to use of a Standards for Excellence Seal, a kind of "Good Housekeeping Seal" of approval, in their solicitations and other materials (Maryland Association of Nonprofit Organizations, 2010).

Charity Watchdogs

Nonprofits may find it in their own best interest to voluntarily comply with some set of standards or codes of behavior and seek accreditation from a recognized organization. But there is an increasingly influential array of charity watchdog organizations that proactively examine nonprofit organizations, applying their own standards. They are not really examples of "self-regulation" because they undertake their evaluations with or without the cooperation of the organizations on which they focus. They are an important force in creating increased transparency, and they have influence because of the visibility they enjoy, but they are also often controversial.

For example, among the best known may be the ratings of colleges and universities and hospitals by popular magazines, notably *U.S. News & World Report,* which have been shown to influence students' choices about where to attend college and patients' decisions about where to receive medical care. Such ratings surely do not have the force of law, but they are powerful. A negative ranking poses a significant potential threat to an organization, since publicity may deter potential customers, chill giving, or even invite scrutiny from government. And yet, many educators and hospital administrators do not agree that the standards by which *U.S. News* determines its rankings are appropriate or indicative of quality.

One well-known charity rater that operates at the national level is the Better Business Bureau (BBB) Wise Giving Alliance. Formed in 2001 through a merger of the National Charities Information Bureau and the Better Business Bureau's Philanthropic Advisory Service, the Wise Giving Alliance (hereafter, the Alliance) focuses its attention on the largest nonprofits in the United States. The BBB undertakes investigations of an organization based on complaints or inquiries from the public (in the long-established tradition of consumers reporting businesses to the BBB). While it does not rate organizations, it does report whether they meet or do not meet its various standards, which are available on its website (www.bbb.org/us/Wise-Giving).

Since the BBB has a long history and an established reputation as a watchdog that acts to protect consumers against unethical business practices, the Alliance standards for nonprofits are among the best known and most widely cited in the news media. For example, the Alliance made news in 2001 when it temporarily dropped the American Red Cross from its list of organizations meeting its standards, in the wake of controversy concerning the organization's post-9/11 fund-raising. (Its approval was subsequently restored.) Beginning in 2003, the Alliance offered charities that meet its standards the use of a "BBB national charity seal" in their promotional and solicitation materials.

The BBB standards are based on best practices; that is, they prescribe what accountable nonprofits should *do* in the areas of governance and oversight, measuring effectiveness, finances, fund-raising, and informational material. They require that organizations have a mechanism for measuring results that involves the governing board, but it is important to note that they do not prescribe the *specific* standards that organizations must apply. The BBB standards require that organizations "have a board policy of assessing, no less than every two years, the organization's performance and effectiveness and of determining future actions required to achieve its mission." And the organization must submit "to [its] governing body, for its approval, a written report that outlines the results of the aforementioned performance and effectiveness assessment and recommendations for future actions" (BBB Wise Giving Alliance, 2010). In other words, the BBB standards emphasize process and accountability, but they are not about setting specific standards of effectiveness or performance, aside from a couple of key financial ratios, which we will discuss below.

Many nonprofit organizations have accepted the idea of best practices, adhere to one or another of the recommended standards, and have sought some type of accreditation or certification. In a 2005 study by Salamon and Geller, 65 percent of organizations surveyed were participating in some type of best practice accreditation program and identified several benefits of doing so, including improved staff and board knowledge, improved accountability and governance, and enhanced staff attention to the organization's mission (pp. 10–11). It may be that in addition to the potential threat of negative publicity, the widespread acceptance of voluntary standards reflects, as Light (2000) suggests, institutional theory at work. Enunciated standards become a part of the conventional wisdom of what constitutes ethical or sound practice and are increasingly adopted by organizations that seek recognition for being consistent with the norms of the subsector or profession within which they operate.

But the questions remain: Does doing the right things ensure that the organization is effective in accomplishing its mission? Or that it can be described as a high-performing organization? Is there some mechanism that automatically leads from best practices in governance and management to a successful nonprofit organization? Light (2000), and others, conclude that the connection is unclear:

> Even if one could develop hard measures of finance, mission, record keeping, and operations, [funders of nonprofits] would be hard pressed to demonstrate a link between any single measure and overall organizational effectiveness. There is no evidence, for example, that having a merit pay system for staff is related to organizational effectiveness, or that holding six board meetings instead of three improves performance, or that adopting a strategic planning process is somehow going to improve outcomes. (p. 52)

Measuring Performance

If doing the right things does not guarantee that the organization is effective in achieving its mission, then we need some standards by which to evaluate results. But how should results be defined, and how should they be measured? Although the subject has been the focus of an intense national conversation in recent years, there is still no consensus answer or even a consistent vocabulary among experts in the field. Some use the terms *organizational effectiveness* and *organizational performance* synonymously. Others define performance as broader than effectiveness, with the latter measuring achievement against mission and the former encompassing "other concepts such as efficiency, productivity, or quality" (Baruch & Ramalho, 2006, p. 41). For example, let's consider a nonprofit that meets the needs of clients. That could define an effective program and an effective organization. But if the organization loses money every year, the staff are miserable, and management is always just skirting the law, it would be hard to say it is high-performing as an organization. Being effective may be necessary to be high-performing, but it is not necessarily sufficient.

It is also important to distinguish between *effectiveness* and *efficiency*. As Kelly (1998) explains it, efficiency is "a measure of the proportion of resources used to produce outputs or attain inputs–cost ratios," whereas effectiveness "is measured by comparing the results achieved with the results sought." As Kelly further observes, "Although efficiency may help an organization be more effective, the two concepts are not interchangeable" (p. 428). Indeed, some argue that an emphasis on efficiency may in fact work against the effectiveness of organizations by discouraging investment in capacity, a topic that will be discussed in greater detail in Chapter 8.

Another important distinction is that between program effectiveness and the effectiveness of an organization. *Program evaluation* is a method that many nonprofits use to determine whether specific programs are effective in achieving their goals and objectives. A program "is a set of resources and activities directed toward one or more common goals, typically under the direction of a single manager or management team." Program evaluation is "the systematic assessment of program results and, to the extent feasible, systematic assessment of the extent to which the program caused those results" (Newcomer, Hatry, & Wholey, 2004, p. xxxiii).

Organizational effectiveness looks at the broader question of whether the organization as a whole is effective in achieving its mission. Of course, for a small nonprofit with a single program, the distinction may not be very meaningful. For larger, more complex organizations with broad missions, however, the difference may be significant. For example, a university might have a very effective basketball team, one that frequently wins championships, but it may not be a very effective university overall.

Financial Ratios as Measures of Performance

In the business world, financial data and ratios are the principal ways to measure a company's performance and strength. A company's earnings, earnings per share, stock price, and the ratio of stock price to earnings (the P:E ratio) are important variables that investors consider. Some have applied a similar approach to nonprofit organizations. The advantages of using financial indicators are that the data are objective, readily available, and easily compared, across either the nonprofit sector or particular subsectors. But critics argue that they fail to account for the realities faced by many organizations, that they may be at best misleading, and that they are potentially destructive.

A 2004 study by the Urban Institute and Harvard's Hauser Institute (Fremont-Smith & Cordes, 2004) looked at 10 monitoring organizations that use financial ratios and found a variety of measures being applied, including variations of the following:

- The ratio of program expenses to contributed income
- The ratio of fund-raising expenditures to private support received—that is, the cost of raising a dollar
- The percentage of total expenditures (or income received from contributions) applied to charitable programs or activities
- The percentage of total expenditures applied to fund-raising and administrative (overhead)
- Accumulated cash and asset reserves in relation to operating budget

Until 2010, one of the prominent charity raters, Charity Navigator, based its ratings exclusively on financial ratios. Its approach is summarized in Table 6.2. In response to widespread commentary on the limitations of such ratios, it was reported in late 2009 that Charity Navigator would review its methodology during 2010, with the intention of decreasing its emphasis on overhead costs and devising new methods of evaluating the results of programs ("Proving That Charity Works," 2009). Any new methodology developed by Charity Navigator in 2010 was adopted too late to be incorporated in this text, so students should consult the organization's website to see what resulted from the review. (www.charitynavigator.org).

Unlike the BBB Wise Giving Alliance, which rates nonprofits according to whether they meet or do not meet its standards, Charity Navigator ranks nonprofits using a system of "stars," like those used by Morningstar to rank mutual fund performance. Under its 2010 approach, at least through mid-2010, Charity Navigator does not establish an absolute standard for program expenditures or fund-raising costs, but for the former, higher is better and for the latter, lower is better; that is, the higher the percentage spent on programs and the lower the percentage spent on fund-raising, the more stars the organization will receive. Charity Navigator evaluates organizations on the basis of "organizational efficiency" and "organizational capacity," both defined in financial terms, using the indicators described in Table 6.2. The seven categories of indicators are combined to calculate an overall numerical rating, which Charity Navigator then compares with the ratings of all the charities it surveys, charities with similar missions, and organizations in the same peer group as the one being rated.

TABLE 6.2 ■ **Charity Navigator Approach to Rating Organizations**

Organizational Efficiency:

We assess four key indicators to determine how efficiently and responsibly a charity functions day to day.

1.	Program Expenses: Percent of total functional expenses spent on programs and services. (higher is better)
2.	Administrative Expenses: Percent of total functional expenses spent on management and general. (lower is better)
3.	Fundraising expenses: Percent of total functional expenses spent on fundraising. (lower is better)
4.	Fundraising efficiency: Amount a charity spends to raise $1. (lower is better)

We combine the scores in these four categories to obtain an overall efficiency score. Based on the score, we assign a rating of between zero and four stars to each charity (four being the highest).

Organizational Capacity:

We assess three key indicators to determine how well a charity is positioned to sustain its programs over time.

5. & 6.	Primary Revenue Growth & Program Expenses Growth: Measures a charity's average annual growth of primary revenue or program expenses over its three to five most recent fiscal years. (higher is better)
7.	Working Capital Ratio: Determines how long a charity could sustain its level of spending using only its net available assets, as reported on its most recently filed Form 990. (higher is better)

We combine the scores in these three categories to obtain an overall capacity score. We then assign a capacity rating of between zero and four stars (four being the highest).

Overall Rating:

We combine all seven categories to obtain an overall score. We use this rating to compare a charity to all charities in our sample, to charities pursuing similar missions, and to a small set of charities in its peer group. Please review Our Ratings Tables for more information on the scales we use to assign ratings and What Do Our Ratings Mean for a description of our star system.

Source: Charity Navigator (2010).

Two of the variables most emphasized by those who use financial ratios to rate charities are the cost of fund-raising and the percentage of expenditures that go for overhead rather than for programs and services. As mentioned above, while the BBB standards do not in general emphasize financial ratios, they require that an organization's spending on fund-raising be no more than 35 percent of the funds raised. However, the BBB also permits an organization to offer a justification for higher ratios, an accommodation to individual realities that some raters do not make. The Maryland standards establish a 3:1 ratio for fund-raising costs (i.e., expenditures should be no more than about 33 percent of gift revenue), and they also permit some flexibility:

> A nonprofit's fundraising costs should be reasonable over time. On average, over a five-year period, a nonprofit should realize revenue from fundraising and other development activities that are at least three times the amount spent on conducting them. Organizations whose fundraising ratio is less than 3:1 should demonstrate that they are making steady progress toward achieving this goal, or should be able to justify why a 3:1 ratio is not appropriate for their organization. (Maryland Association of Nonprofit Organizations, 2010)

The percentage of total expenditures directed toward program-related activities, rather than overhead or fund-raising, is viewed by some as a measure of an organization's efficiency in delivering its services. Too low a percentage may even be seen as a potential red flag, suggesting that management is deriving excessive compensation or other benefits from the organization or that fund-raising has replaced mission as the organization's highest priority. For example, the BBB standards require that at least 65 percent of expenditures be devoted to programs but, again, they allow that organizations not meeting that standard may provide an explanation.

Indeed, organizations that spend too much on overhead or fund-raising may be making inefficient use of donor funds or perhaps may be spending too lavishly on salaries and other overhead costs. Very high fund-raising costs may suggest the possibility of inefficiency, or even unethical or fraudulent behavior. But, critics argue, rating organizations based on their overhead and fund-raising costs may create perverse incentives. For example, this approach may simply encourage organizations to engage in creative accounting to allocate costs to programs rather than administration. Insisting on low fund-raising costs also may place young organizations at a disadvantage. They often need to invest substantial amounts in developing a database of regular donors that will ultimately produce continuing revenue at lower costs. Moreover, low fund-raising costs may not be realistic for an organization that advocates unpopular causes or lacks a constituency of major donors (Fremont-Smith & Cordes, 2004).

Others critics argue that "the fundraising efficiency standard is not a measure of efficiency at all. [Rather,] it documents the sunk costs associated with cultivating donors" (Hager & Flack, 2004, p. 3). In other words, looking at just this year's fund-raising costs ignores the substantial amounts that the organization may have spent in earlier years to develop relationships with donors who now make larger gifts, lowering the per-dollar cost of fund-raising today.

Still others argue that high program-spending ratios are not a measure of organizational effectiveness, and indeed, they may even work against building effective organizations by encouraging them to "value thrift over excellence." Trying to maintain a low ratio may cause an organization to invest too little in "good governance, planning, compliance and risk management, collection of data for service performance evaluations, and staff training" (Hager & Flack, 2004, p. 4).

Financial ratios do provide one perspective on the operations of an organization. However, despite their ease of use, they may not present the complete picture. While this approach has gained visibility among many donors, leading thought in the field appears to be moving away from an emphasis on this method. In the view of some critics, "the undue emphasis on financial ratios diverts attention and resources from the development of more meaningful measures that address performance against mission and program objectives" (Hager & Flack, 2004, p. 4).

Measuring Against Peers

If simple financial measures applied to all nonprofit organizations are potentially misleading, perhaps a more accurate picture may be obtained from comparing data from organizations that are similar in their mission, size, location, and other characteristics. Comparing similar organizations is at the heart of benchmarking.

As Poister (2003) notes, the term *benchmarking* is often misused. Some organizations set goals for future years in their strategic plans and then measure their progress by looking at targets, which they call "benchmarks." But in its proper definition, benchmarking involves comparisons among organizations, either at the macro (whole organization) or at the micro (program or function) level. Benchmarking involves collecting data from multiple organizations "in order to 'peg' the performance of a particular [organization] in relation to [those offering] comparable programs" (p. 238). For example, an organization might look at statistics on client outcomes across a group of organizations providing services to individuals with similar problems or compare its patterns of gift revenues with those of similar organizations. This macro approach, called *statistical benchmarking,* may be a useful technique in strategic planning and may help highlight strengths or weaknesses of the organization that require further analysis.

Another approach to benchmarking, what Poister (2003) calls *corporate benchmarking,* "compares the organization's practices with those of others doing similar things but who are deemed to be the best at doing it" (Murray, 2004, p. 361). A technique adopted from business, this type of benchmarking requires identifying best practices—that is, the most effective or efficient methods of performing specific functions—and seeing how the subject organization compares with the best. It is thus not really a tool for evaluating the whole organization, although some assume that "a thorough program of benchmarking will 'roll up' to provide a good indicator of how well the organization is doing overall" (Murray, 2004, p. 361).

Christine Letts et al. (1999a), advocates of benchmarking, argue that it "bridges the gap between great ideas and great performance" (p. 86) and that the nonprofit culture of openness and sharing may make it a more feasible approach for them than for competitive businesses. However, like the use of financial ratios, benchmarking also has its critics. For one, it requires a larger investment of time and effort than comparing financial ratios, which are readily available from Form 990s. Second, there is no way to really know whether the practice being studied is related to an organization's overall effectiveness. For example, how does the amount of time required to process the payroll relate to whether it is an effective organization? In addition, it is often difficult to identify the specific indicators on which the best practice is to be compared. For example, what number best indicates how many clients have "recovered" from an illness or addiction? It is also often tricky to identify which organizations can really be considered alike. For example, nonprofits in different cities may face very different funding environments and more or less favorable markets for volunteers and staff.

Benchmarking is a useful tool, but perhaps more for examining specific program or administrative functions than for evaluating the effectiveness or performance of an organization. Moreover, since the selection of peer organizations is often complicated by local factors, benchmarking may be better used as a tool for learning than for evaluating. If used (or perceived) as a technique for evaluating the performance of specific departments or staff, it also may come to be manipulated; that is, individuals may try to game the system by selecting peer organizations with which they think they may have the most favorable comparisons.

Measuring Against Mission (Outcomes)

Financial ratios and benchmark data may provide some insights into a nonprofit's performance, but mission is the heart of the matter. It is the very purpose for which a nonprofit exists. Thus, the most important indicators of effectiveness should be related to its success in accomplishing that mission. As Brian Gallagher, president of the United Way of America, expressed it in 2005,

> Financial accountability is just table stakes. You *have* to get that right first. But, ultimately, the American public should hold our sector accountable for delivering on our missions. . . . We should be asked to report concrete results that are tied directly to our missions, not just the level of activity we produce. (n.p., italics original)

The outcomes approach to measuring program effectiveness has gained wide acceptance, in part through the efforts of the United Way of America, which applies it in evaluating its supported organizations. It also has been adopted by many foundations and government agencies for measuring their grantees' effectiveness.

The United Way outcomes model is illustrated in Table 6.3, which highlights the key variables: inputs, activities, outputs, and outcomes. *Inputs* are the resources dedicated to the program, including money, staff, volunteers, facilities, equipment, and supplies, as well as the constraints imposed by the external environment. *Activities* are what the program does—for example, tutoring children, feeding the homeless, or providing job training. *Outputs* are the direct products of the activities and are often relatively easy things to measure—for example, the number of children tutored, the number of homeless fed, and the number of individuals trained in employment skills. But measuring outputs does not make the connection to the program's goals, which are generally to change in some way the individuals it serves and to make a lasting difference in their lives. *Outcomes* are the changes that occur in the individuals as a result of their participation in the program—for example, new knowledge, expanded job skills, or a better position in life.

Outcomes may be measured immediately after the individual completes the program (initial outcomes); after a longer period has elapsed, say a few years (intermediate outcomes); and after an even longer period of time (long-term outcomes). Thus, it may be found that students who participate in an after-school tutoring program improve their grades, but are they still succeeding academically 2 years later? Do they go on to complete college in larger numbers than students who do not participate in the program? Are they more likely to be employed a decade after their participation in the program? Obviously, measuring outcomes over the longer term can require considerable effort and expense, perhaps involving the tracking of former clients and follow-up surveys. That can be difficult for organizations that serve clients who are highly mobile and difficult to reach—for example, homeless people.

But measuring outcomes is not quite the same as evaluating programs. In other words, it is one thing to establish that outcomes have occurred, but evaluating the program requires determining that these outcomes were in fact caused by the program (Kopczynski & Pritchard, 2004). That requires developing a sound and plausible *logic model*—that is, a theoretical explanation

TABLE 6.3 ■ United Way Program Outcome Model			
Inputs	**Activities**	**Outputs**	**Outcomes**
Resources dedicated to or consumed by the program, e.g., money, staff and staff time, volunteers and volunteer time, facilities, equipment, and supplies Constraints on the program, e.g., laws regulations, funders' requirements	What the program does with the inputs to fulfill its mission, e.g., feed and shelter homeless families, provide job training, educate the public about signs of child abuse, counsel pregnant women, create mentoring relationships for youth	The direct products of program activities, e.g., number of classes taught, number of counseling sessions conducted, number of educational materials distributed, number of hours of service delivered, number of participants served	Benefits for participants during and after program activities, e.g., new knowledge, increased skills, changed attitudes or values, modified behavior, improved condition, altered status

Source: United Way of America (1996).

of the links all the way through the process from inputs to outcomes. Figure 6.1 on page 149 depicts the logic model of a program offering tutoring to at-risk teens. It shows how the organization believes the process works. To justify using school graduation rates as an outcome measure for its program, the organization would need to explain how the mentoring experience *causes* students to complete their homework and attend school more regularly and how homework and attendance affect graduation rates. Otherwise, the rate of students' graduation from high school cannot be a useful indicator of the tutoring program's outcome. One obvious problem in developing such logic models is how to identify the external influences that can cause the outcome in addition to the activities associated with the program. This becomes more of an issue the higher up in the model one ascends. For example, students' grades and graduation rates may be positively affected by the tutoring program, but they also could be affected—either positively or negatively—by students' experiences at home or in the community where they live (Poister, 2003).

One obstacle to measuring outcomes is the loftiness and vagueness of many mission statements. For example, the mission of one organization serving the needs of older people is to enable them "to live with dignity and independence." One educational institution includes as a part of its mission "fostering a love of learning." But how are the outcomes of "dignity" or "love of learning" to be defined or measured? And if they are defined and measured and found to exist, how can the organization be sure that its programs are indeed what created them? In other words, what is the organization's *impact* on the measured changes, since there are many factors that influence the lives of older people and students? Sometimes it is necessary to identify more easily obtained intermediate indicators that the logic model suggests may be proxies for the outcomes desired.

An instructive example is provided by the experience of The Nature Conservancy (TNC) in the 1990s. TNC was struggling with the question of how to measure its performance against its ambitious mission, "to preserve the plants, animals, and natural communities that represent the diversity of life on Earth by protecting the lands and waters they need to survive." For 50 years, it had measured its success by looking at two figures that were readily available, the amount of money it raised and the quantity of land this money enabled it to protect—what became known as "bucks and acres." But these two measures really reflected the *means* TNC was using, not the *ends* it was committed to achieving. They were inputs, but not outcomes. If the mission was ultimately to preserve biodiversity on Earth, how could TNC be sure that the means it was employing—the acquisition of money and land—was indeed having an impact on the achievement of that purpose (Sawhill & Williamson, 2001)?

Possibly a better measure of TNC's effectiveness in achieving its mission might have been to count the number of species existing on the planet each year—to measure biodiversity. That would be an outcome. But even if it were practical to take an annual global inventory, the number continues to decline every year, despite TNC's efforts, for reasons way beyond TNC's control. The impact of its programs is small compared with all the other forces affecting the survival of species on Earth. Indeed, using that figure as an indicator of effectiveness in achieving the mission would doom TNC's performance to be assessed as a continual failure because that figure inevitably declines. Moreover, it would be meaningless as a measure of the outcomes of TNC's own efforts.

After considering the problem, TNC adopted a family of measures, including the number of species existing on land it *controls*. Easier to count than all the species on the entire planet, and more reflective of TNC's own efforts, this intermediate number could provide a realistic and feasible proxy for the organization's impact on the Earth's overall biodiversity. This approach thus requires developing

> micro-level goals that, if achieved, would *imply* success on a grander scale; indicators of goal achievement that can be measured with a feasible level of effort, and that arguably are affected by the organization's efforts rather than other extraneous and uncontrollable factors. (Sawhill & Williamson, 2001, p. 23, italics original)

The challenge is greater for some organizations than for others. Let's consider an organization with the simple mission of "providing a hot meal every day to homeless people." It is perhaps hard to improve on a simple count of the number of meals served—and perhaps a measure of the food's temperature—as a way to measure effectiveness in delivering that straightforward and uncomplicated mission. Those are outputs, not outcomes, but they may be all the organization really needs to know. But take a more complicated mission, say that of the American Cancer Society: "Eliminating cancer as a major health problem by preventing cancer, saving lives, and diminishing suffering from cancer, through research, education, advocacy, and service" (www .cancer.org). Unfortunately, many variables affect the incidence of cancer and cancer death rates—individuals' lifestyles, environmental factors, and the availability of medical care, among others. Just measuring the national cancer rates, whether they are found to be increasing or declining, would not tell the American Cancer Society much about the effectiveness or ineffectiveness of its efforts. But research has demonstrated that screening and educational programs are effective in reducing cancer incidence and mortality; thus, the American Cancer Society can make a sound theoretical link between the effectiveness of its screening and educational programs, which can be more easily evaluated, and achievement of its larger mission, the prevention and eventual elimination of cancer (Sawhill & Williamson, 2001). Obviously, however, the validity of any micro-level indicator as a measure of effectiveness toward achievement of a broader mission depends on the soundness of the *logic model* behind it—that is, the chain of theoretical reasoning that explains exactly how the organization's efforts led to the desired larger result.

It must be emphasized, however, that the outcomes model does not necessarily incorporate other important aspects of organizational *performance*. For example, it is possible to conceive of an organization that is delivering effective programs but whose sustainability as an organization over the long run is imperiled by financial imbalances. It could also be possible to achieve positive program outcomes, but at a very high cost; in other words, the organization could be very inefficient. Moreover, measuring program outcomes does not tell us anything about the organization's ability to learn and adapt to change.

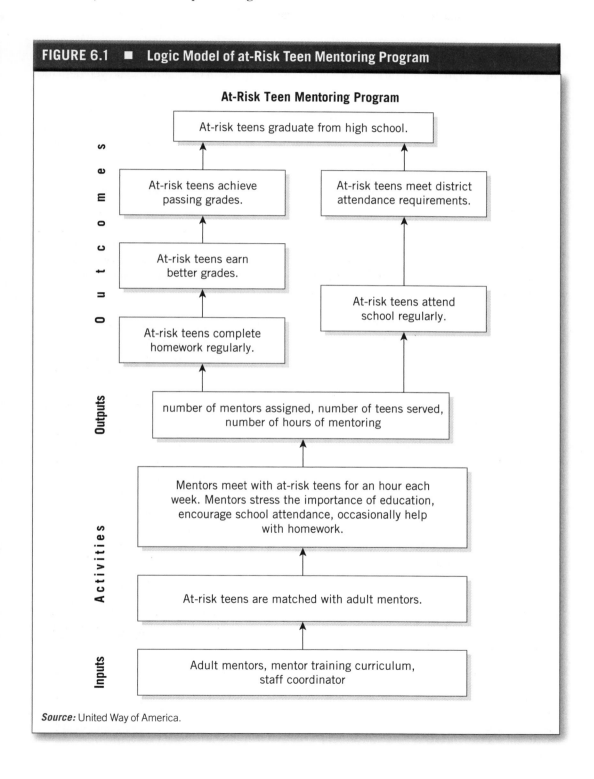

FIGURE 6.1 ■ Logic Model of at-Risk Teen Mentoring Program

At-Risk Teen Mentoring Program

Source: United Way of America.

Common Indicators

As mentioned above, measuring the performance of nonprofit organizations has gained more attention, but the proliferation of approaches has proved frustrating to many. Some have cited the complexity of academic approaches and the demands on staff time and attention to compile and analyze data. Some have questioned to what extent the data compiled are actually used in the operation of many organizations. And some scholars have even concluded that systemically measuring impact in the nonprofit sector is impossible (Lamkin et al., 2006). And yet, demands for performance data are unlikely to abate.

To address this need, in 2004 the Urban Institute and the Center for What Works undertook a project to identify a common set of outcomes and outcomes indicators that nonprofits could use to inform practice and that could be practical to implement. The project's team identified 14 separate program areas regarding their missions, the outcomes they sought, and potential outcomes indicators for tracking progress toward those program areas' missions.

The first step was development of an outcome sequencing chart, essentially a logic model, to explain how outcomes would ultimately lead organizations in each area to fulfill their missions. The chart was then applied to 14 program areas, including adult education and family literacy, advocacy, affordable housing, assisted living, business assistance, community organizing, emergency shelter, employment training, health risk reduction, performing arts, prisoner reentry, transitional housing, youth mentoring, and youth tutoring. In addition, the project's 2006 report included a generic "nonprofit taxonomy of outcomes" as a guide for organizations in program areas in which specific indicators had not yet been developed. As an example, Figure 6.2 includes the outcome sequence chart and common outcome indicators for programs in the field of affordable housing.

The 2006 report issued by the Urban Institute and its partner, the Center for What Works, included several caveats, including acknowledgment that further research would be needed to test and revise the core indicators for the 14 areas, add indicators for additional program areas, and develop a common framework for general guidance. In addition, at that time, the project had not developed specific organization-centered outcome indicators; in other words, the framework did not yet extend to the broader questions of organizational performance ("Building a Common Outcome Framework to Measure Nonprofit Performance," 2006). Students should consult the websites of the Urban Institute and the Center for What Works for updated information on further project work.

Balanced Scorecard

Financial ratios may be an indication of organizational performance, but they do not measure whether the organization's mission has been achieved. Outcomes measure effectiveness against mission, but may not provide insight on broader organizational performance. Benchmarking may be useful as a learning tool, but has shortcomings as a method of evaluating performance, as discussed above. The *balanced scorecard,* and variations on the concept, has been adopted by some nonprofit organizations as a tool for monitoring indicators across various dimensions. Like other models, it has its strengths and weaknesses.

The balanced scorecard is a concept developed by Kaplan and Norton (1992) as a way for businesses to obtain, as the term suggests, a balanced perspective on performance by combining financial data with other considerations. It has since been adopted by many nonprofit organizations and government agencies as a way to combine financial ratios and other data in

FIGURE 6.2 ■ Affordable Housing Program Description

For Community Development Corporations and nonprofit housing organizations, to improve the quality of families and communities, by helping to develop, produce, and manage low-cost affordable housing in safe neighborhoods including rental units and home ownership programs. This program area does not include support services. Organizations providing support services may refer to other applicable program areas, such as employment training, adult education, youth tutoring and youth mentoring, and prisoner reentry.

Outcomes Sequence Chart

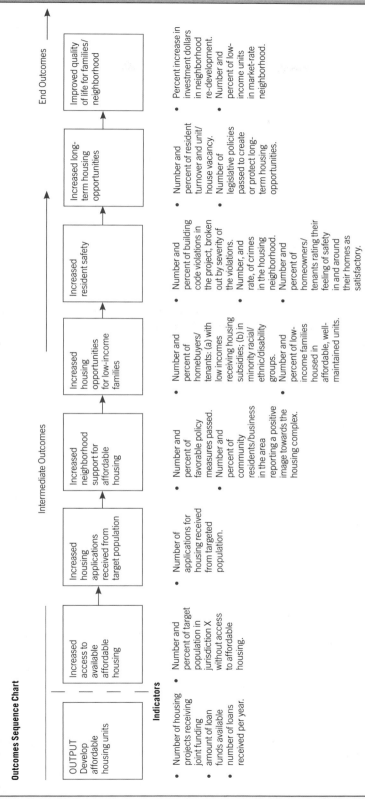

Source: *Candidate Outcome Indicators: Affordable Housing Program.* Urban Institute website (http://www.urban.org/center/met/projects/upload/Affordable_Housing.pdf).

measuring organizational performance. The balanced scorecard looks at an organization from four perspectives:

1. *The financial perspective,* including financial performance indicators
2. *The customer or client perspective,* including measures of customer satisfaction
3. *The internal business perspective,* including measures of operational efficiency and quality
4. *The innovation and learning perspective,* including measures of the organization's ability to adapt to changes in the environment (Murray, 2004, p. 359)

Paton (2003) offers a variation of the balanced scorecard designed specifically for nonprofits, which he calls the *dashboard.* His model seeks to answer two fundamental questions: Does it work? In other words, "do the different activities, services, and programs achieve broadly the results intended?" (pp. 139–140). And is the organization well run? Paton notes that there may be a relationship between how well run an organization is and the effectiveness of the programs it delivers, but that the two are separate matters and both need to be measured in order to obtain a complete picture of the organization's performance:

> A valuable and innovative service may be provided by an organization that is inefficiently administered, or even by one whose funds are being discretely embezzled; and a well-administered organization with excellent morale may be delivering high-quality programs to clients whose needs are slight compared to those of the client group originally envisaged. (p. 140)

Paton's (2003) dashboard thus looks at the organization from five perspectives, encompassing short-term, medium-term, and long-term measures:

1. *Current results:* Monthly checking against key targets—for example, a summary of achievements, a finance report, a marketing report
2. *Underlying performance:* Annual reviews of the appropriateness and cost-effectiveness of programs and support functions—for example, service outcomes, business outcomes, and external comparisons
3. *Risks:* Monitoring of the ways the organization may be put in jeopardy—for example, by a liquidity crisis, legal or procedural noncompliance, or a breakdown in key relationships
4. *Assets and capabilities:* Annual reviews of capacity to deliver future performance—for example, physical and financial assets, external reputation and relationships, expertise and process knowledge
5. *Change projects:* Regular reports on projects intended to bring about improvements in the organization that the board and the CEO are supervising directly (p. 142)

Many nonprofit organizations use a dashboard to provide an overview of performance to executives and the governing board. It often includes key variables and graphics displays on a single page that provides a comprehensive snapshot of the organization at a point in time, change compared to previous periods, and progress toward goals. The dashboard often summarizes key indicators with regard to both program outcomes and financials.

The balanced scorecard also has its critics. For example, Meyer (2002) notes that the balanced scorecard really measures very different things—for example, financial results and customer satisfaction, numbers that must be looked at alongside each other rather than combined. It does not provide a single measure of an organization's performance. He suggests instead the idea of identifying correlations between measures. For example, do good financial results always go along with customer satisfaction? If so, there is no need to measure customer satisfaction directly, since it can be assumed from the financial results. Using this approach, he offers what he calls *activity-based profitability analysis* as a simpler alternative to balanced scorecard approaches.

Social Return on Investment

The concept of the double bottom line has been mentioned earlier in this text. It refers to the need for nonprofit managers to look to both their organization's financial performance as well as the social impact of its programs. In 1996, the Roberts Enterprise Foundation (now known simply as REDF), a venture philanthropy fund based in San Francisco, pioneered the concept of *social return on investment* (SROI) as a way to put a dollar figure on—that is, to monetize—the social value created by nonprofits. The idea was to add social return to financial return in order to generate a single number—in dollars—that could be used as an indicator of the organization's performance and value.

As a venture philanthropy fund, REDF approaches giving as a form of investing in a select group of nonprofits, called its portfolio organizations. And, like other investors, REDF seeks to measure the return on its investments. Financial return is easy to understand: If you invest $100,000 and receive $10,000 in income, that's a return of 10%. But how do we measure the less tangible social benefits created by a nonprofit's programs? SROI provides a method for measuring those social benefits in dollar terms so that they can be compared with expenditures to produce a single number as simple to understand as the rate of return on a philanthropic investment.

REDF's SROI methodology evolved from *cost–benefit analysis,* a technique drawn from applied economics and most often used to evaluate government programs. As Kee (2004) explains it,

> Cost–benefit analysis attempts to assess a program or project by determining whether societal welfare has or will increase (in the aggregate more people are better off) because of the program or project. Cost–benefit analysis can provide information on the full costs of the program and weigh those costs against the *dollar value of the benefits* [italics added]. The analyst can then calculate the net benefits (or costs) of the program or project, examine the . . . ratio of benefits to costs, determine the rate of return on the original investment, and compare the program's benefits and costs with those of other programs or proposed alternatives. (p. 524)

The advantage of this approach is that it produces a ratio that can be used to compare programs against programs. But putting a dollar value on social benefits—that is, monetizing them—can be a challenge. As an example, let's consider a program that offers job training, helping people move from welfare to work. The benefits may include the new income taxes paid by the people who become employed, savings through lower welfare costs, less need for homeless shelters, and perhaps savings in the cost of policing as fewer people are on the streets. These benefits can be given a dollar value and summed to find the SROI in the non-profit's job-training programs. But that does not include, for example, the very real benefits of reduced fear and social tension resulting from the decrease in crime. Though real, they are hard to measure, especially in dollar terms. Moreover, costs are incurred to support the program today, but many of the benefits may not be realized until far into the future. For example, one benefit of an after-school tutoring program that helps young people complete high school may be their higher wages after graduation. That is, at least theoretically, easily stated in dollar terms. But increased education also may lead to healthier and happier lives through their lifetimes, although this is hard to capture and harder to monetize (Kee, 2004).

Although SROI has been adopted by a number of organizations, especially social enterprises that worked with REDF and other venture philanthropy funds, REDF no longer uses SROI exclusively as its measure of an organization's social performance. A 2008 report by Javits acknowledges the shortcomings of the model:

- The SROI analysis process is resource intensive;
- Engaging the practitioner is essential and time-consuming;
- Metrics are important, but metrics aren't everything;
- SROI is a good tool, but SROI isn't everything. (n.p.)

Javits (2008) goes on to say,

> One of the primary flaws was that the model was built on, and had the tendency to focus attention upon, cost savings to society, while it did not adequately incorporate many of the ways that social enterprise employment improved peoples' lives. For example, while social return could and did measure the dollar value of reduced time in prison or jail, we were not able to incorporate factors that we were unable to quantify, such as improved family relationships or mental health status. (n.p.)

REDF has moved to a system it calls Ongoing Assessment of Social Impacts (OASIS), which continuously collects and analyzes data on a range of key indicators of performance. It is, in essence, a balanced scorecard approach. Its website (www.redf.org) is rich with literature and tools related to performance measurement.

Blended Value

The emerging concept of blended value builds on the idea of social return on investment by adding a third component—impact on the environment. With the increasing focus by nonprofits on financial results and the growing corporate concern about social responsibility, many observers note a blurring of the nonprofit and for-profit sectors; in other words, they argue that nonprofits and business firms are becoming more alike and that it should therefore be possible to define some common measures of performance that could be applied to *all* organizations *across the sectors,* including nonprofit, for-profit, and hybrid enterprises. Blended value is advanced as the answer. Simply defined,

> Value is what gets created when investors invest and organizations act to pursue their mission. Traditionally, we have thought of value as being either economic (and created by for-profit companies) or social (and created by nonprofit or non-governmental organizations). What the Blended Value Proposition states is that all organizations, whether for-profit or not, create value that consists of economic, social and environmental value components—and that investors (whether market-rate, charitable or some mix of the two) simultaneously generate all three forms of value through providing capital to organizations.
>
> The outcome of all this activity is value creation and that value is itself non-divisible and, therefore, a blend of these three elements. (Blended Value, 2006, n.p.)

Baruch and Ramalho (2006) analyzed a variety of scholarly articles, some reporting research on nonprofits and others reporting on for-profits. They found some common ground in the measures that those various studies used to measure organizational effectiveness. However, as they observed, "all measures seemed to correspond to broadly diffused concepts" (p. 58). In other words, organizations in different sectors can be compared using similar measurements, but only at a very high level and in very general terms. Corporations and nonprofits do have characteristics in common, since both are organizations, but limiting the study of effectiveness to their common characteristics may require a level of generalization that is simply not informative. For example, both dogs and cats might be evaluated by their effectiveness in winning their owners' hearts, as well as eating, drinking, and sleeping. But none of these qualities would be related to their effectiveness in catching mice or guarding a junkyard, tasks for which cats and dogs are generally superior, respectively.

In the past, corporations have worked to maximize *economic* value, while nonprofits have tried to maximize *social* value—that is, to increase SROI. However, the blended value theorists say, value should be thought about as having three components: economic value, social value, and environmental value (Blended Value, 2006). Both companies and nonprofits should be measured by how much of all three they create—in total. Thus, companies may create considerable economic value, but through socially responsible behavior they may also create some social value. For example, companies earn profits for their owners but also create jobs for the less well-off. Nonprofits may score high as creators of social value and lower than companies in creating economic value, but many now operate revenue-generating enterprises, and they may also earn profits and contribute to the economies of their communities. Both companies and nonprofits may affect the environment, in positive or negative ways. In other words, the blended value advocates call for "breaking down the silos" and developing a single measure to evaluate for-profits and nonprofits in terms of the total benefits, or value, that they create (Blended Value, 2006).

Although the use of blended value to measure organizational performance across the nonprofit and business sectors is intellectually intriguing, there are several challenges to its wider acceptance. For one, there are some critics who challenge the very concept of corporate social responsibility, one of the silos across which blended value measures would be built (Doane, 2005). There are strong incentives for corporations to maximize financial returns, including the ratings of financial analysts and the pressure of shareholders seeking to maximize the financial returns on their investments. And, of course, there remain the inherent difficulties of defining and measuring social impact in both sectors.

However, work continues on innovative concepts similar to blended value and on the idea that social enterprises might be valued and receive investments much like for-profit companies. In 2008, the Rockefeller Foundation awarded a grant of $500,000 to develop a *social stock market* to be based in London. "The market would allow investors to trade shares in projects that seek to preserve the environment, such as clean technology, and that promote health care, aid for the poor, or other social goals" ("Rockefeller Foundation Gives $500,000," 2008).

Performance Measurement: The Continuing Debate

Management inherently involves the strategic allocation of resources to achieve and improve results. A complete disregard for results achieved as a result of resources expended would be not only irresponsible and unacceptable to those who provide those resources, but it would also be, by definition, *nonmanagement.* However, nonprofit managers are confronted with sorting through an array of options and selecting the measures and methods that will meet both their own need for useful management information as well as the expectations of funders, watchdogs, and regulators. There continues to be a debate both about the appropriate methods to be applied and the emphasis that should be given to efforts to measure results.

One concern that some express is the wide array of proposed standards and methods and the lack of a vocabulary or process that is universally accepted or stable. As Baruch and Ramalho (2006) note, this leaves nonprofit practitioners and scholars vulnerable to "fads with doubtful empirical and theoretical foundations presenting themselves as simple recipes" (p. 59). Another concern is the amount of time and effort devoted to measuring effectiveness and whether indeed the effectiveness of organizations with limited capacity may be compromised by the effort required to compile, analyze, and report data. Some argue that nonprofits could eventually reach a condition of analysis paralysis, consumed with measurement to the preclusion of action. A more philosophical concern is expressed by Paton (2003), who sees a risk of developing "disconnected managerialism," a situation "where modern discourse and methods are conspicuous (and may even play well externally), but they do not impact the main work, except as noise and a burden" (p. 161). In other words, if nonprofit managers work to the numbers, there is the risk that the numbers will gain more importance than the vital work their organizations are committed to performing. That is, too much emphasis on measuring performance could create a "Dilbert world," in which the passion and commitment of the professional staff and volunteers are replaced by caution, even skepticism, which might undermine the nonprofit culture and its traditional strengths.

Writing in the *Chronicle of Philanthropy,* Kennard King (2006) raises similar concerns about the risks to nonprofit values in an excessive focus on performance:

> When Americans want to preserve and promote values other than making a buck, they come together in nonprofit organizations. When they want to solve problems they see in society, they come together in nonprofit organizations. When they aspire to make the world a better place, they come together in nonprofit organizations. And that points to the real danger of the overzealous application of outcomes thinking: By undermining the value of our aspirations, we take away the purpose and meaning of the work of nonprofit organizations. (p. 63)

In a 2010 column written for VPP News, the online letter of Venture Philanthropy Partners, VPP founder Mario Morino also expresses concerns. Identifying himself as someone who has been "strident" in advocating the importance of outcomes and assessments in the past, Morino (2010) now is worried that

> the vast majority of funders and nonprofits are achieving, at best, marginal benefit from their efforts to implement outcomes thinking. Granted, there has been some truly meaningful progress. Select hospitals like the Cleveland Clinic and Mayo Clinic have made great strides in assessing their outcomes and being transparent about their performance. And the Edna McConnell Clark Foundation and a few others have keenly focused on the challenge of social outcomes and have dealt with them well. Yet many other efforts may end up misdirecting, even wasting, precious time and financial resources. In some extreme situations, well-intentioned efforts may actually risk producing adverse effects on nonprofits and those they serve. (n.p.)

Morino (2010) does not oppose performance measurement, but he calls for more appreciation of "soft outcomes"—for example, a holistic approach to services and the impact that nonprofits may have on community building. To clarify, he writes,

> The point is this: When public or private funders establish performance metrics and then tie significant rewards or consequences to their achievement, organizations and people will migrate to the behaviors that will allow them to meet their defined targets. If the metrics are appropriate and closely tied to mission, this is a good thing. But if the metrics are overly simplistic and unmoored from mission, then organizations will go racing in the wrong direction. To paraphrase Yogi Berra, they'll get lost, but they'll be making good time. (n.p.)

Failure to measure performance is the antithesis of managing and is unacceptable in the environment in which nonprofit organizations exist today. However, practical good sense is required. It may be, as Paton (2003) suggests, that the appropriate position for nonprofit managers is a middle ground between ignoring the need for measuring effectiveness and making it the purpose of the organization. "In considerable measure they are obligated to support measurement and performance improvement—to object can easily appear self-serving and irrational." On the other hand, "they are fully entitled to have misgivings" (p. 164).

Managers may be tempted, and encouraged by their boards and funders, to embrace the performance jargon and techniques of the day. However, in doing so, they may run the risks we already have identified—distraction from the work of the organization and the potential dissatisfaction of their staffs. But, as Paton (2003) notes,

> the alternative—to be negative and distrusting toward performance measurement [altogether]—would be a betrayal of management's role and responsibilities. Indeed, it can easily become so, slipping into a cynical, overly political attitude, in which the gulf between professional stance and private belief grows steadily wider and more uncomfortable. (p. 165)

The middle position, which Paton (2003) finds to be the "proper one," is to be "realistic about the range of possibilities,"

> to engage constructively with measurement while being very alert to its limitations and misuse, and to approach the performance agenda positively while also being fully aware that every valid and useful method can also become an occasion for goal displacement by being pursued inappropriately or excessively. (p. 165)

Chapter Summary

There is an increasing demand that nonprofit organizations be accountable—that is, responsible for their actions. For some, this has a narrow meaning of following legal and ethical requirements; others include the requirement that nonprofits follow recommended best practices in governance and management. A still broader definition includes the responsibility to demonstrate that the organization is achieving results, that the resources entrusted to it are used not only ethically and legally but also efficiently and effectively.

Accountability is enforced by state and federal laws, but the nonprofit sector also has established methods for self-regulation. These include standards of best practice and programs through which nonprofits can gain accreditation or certification indicating their adherence to such standards. Charity watchdogs and raters, private organizations that evaluate nonprofits according to their own standards, also have influence because of the visibility their ratings command. Transparency, that is, the easy public availability of Form 990 and other sources of data, also has enabled donors to become a force for accountability.

It is necessary to distinguish among program effectiveness, organizational effectiveness, and organizational performance. Effectiveness relates to achieving the mission, but performance is a broader concept that also includes financial results and other variables related to the overall organization. In evaluating effectiveness and performance, some emphasize financial ratios, including the percentage of expenditures devoted to programs rather than overall management and fund-raising. But it is important to distinguish efficiency from effectiveness, with the latter related to accomplishment of the mission rather than merely minimizing costs. Some argue that an undue emphasis on efficiency could undermine effectiveness, by causing organizations not to invest in capacity.

Among other approaches to evaluating performance is benchmarking, which compares organizations with others with similar characteristics, but this may be a technique better suited to learning than to evaluation. An influential approach that is advocated by the United Way and many funders, is outcome measurement. This approach requires developing a logic model that links inputs to activities, to outputs, and to outcomes, the latter representing changes in the people who are served by the program. Outcomes may be measured immediately following completion of the program, over an intermediate term, or over the long term. Long-term measurement may be difficult and costly. The Urban Institute and the Center for What Works have developed common indicators for nonprofits working in specific fields as well as universal core indicators that might apply to all nonprofit organizations. The balanced scorecard seeks to integrate internal, external, and program variables to provide a comprehensive picture of an organization's performance. Many organizations using a balanced scorecard approach prepare a dashboard, a simple and often graphic portrayal of key variables that is used to monitor and communicate performance. Some venture philanthropists and scholars have adopted the tools of cost–benefit analysis and social return of investment (SROI) to measure social impact. Others have developed concepts of blended value, incorporating financial, social, and environmental impacts, which they would apply to both nonprofit and for-profit entities.

All methods of measuring nonprofit performance offer advantages as well as disadvantages. There is a continuing debate about the best methods to use and the appropriate emphasis to give to measurement. Nonprofit managers must be committed to performance measurement but should not become overly focused on it to the detriment of delivering their mission's programs.

KEY TERMS AND CONCEPTS

accountability	*blended value*	*cost–benefit analysis*
accreditation	*charity raters*	*dashboard*
activity-based profitability model	*common indicators*	*effectiveness*
balanced scorecard	*corporate benchmarking*	*efficiency*

e-Postcard

Form 990

inputs

logic model

outcomes

outputs

Pension Protection Act of 2006

performance

Sarbanes-Oxley Act

social return on investment
(SROI)

statistical benchmarking

CASE 6.1 The Nature Conservancy

The Nature Conservancy (TNC) is one of the nation's largest nonprofit organizations. Founded in 1951, by 2004 it controlled more than $3 billion in assets and employed 3,200 staff in 528 offices located in every U.S. state and 30 other nations (Ottaway & Stephens, 2003).

According to its website, TNC's mission is "to preserve the plants, animals, and natural communities that represent the diversity of life on Earth by protecting the lands and waters they need to survive." TNC purchases land itself, which it then preserves, and also operates a Conservation Buyer Program, which enables private individuals to purchase land, subject to conservation easements. By accepting an easement on the property, the buyer agrees to permanent limits on the scale and type of development that will be allowed, thus preserving at least a portion of the property in its natural condition. The program is consistent with TNC's philosophy of "compatible development," that is, the idea that some conservation is better than none and that through this practical approach, TNC can leverage the resources of private individuals and companies to accomplish more conservation than it could working by itself.

Under the Conservation Buyer Program, TNC buys land, then obtains the conservation easements. Because they limit what can be done with the land, the easements reduce its market value. TNC then sells the land to the private buyer at the reduced price, and the buyer makes a gift to TNC for the difference.

In 2003, a series of three articles in *The Washington Post* written by Joe Stephens and David B. Ottaway (2003b, 2003c) leveled serious criticisms against TNC and its practices. The articles raised a number of issues, including TNC's relationship with corporations, the consistency of some of its entrepreneurial activities with its mission, and compensation and loans made to employees. The Conservation Buyer Program received some of the strongest criticism.

The *Post* articles noted that conservation buyers had included individuals who were donors or active volunteer leaders of the organization, who appeared to have had an inside track on purchasing property. Property purchased by conservation buyers included beautiful wooded sites, on which some buyers were able to build homes despite the environmental easements. The authors suggested that while the transactions may have been legal, many of the owners gained valuable land for a discounted price and a deductible gift without really having to alter their plans for the land. As the *Post* authors describe one of the transactions,

On New York's Shelter Island, the Nature Conservancy three years ago bought an undeveloped, 10-acre tract overlooking its Mashomack Preserve, an oasis of hardwoods and tidal pools located just a stone's skip from the exclusive Hamptons. Cost to the charity: $2.1 million.

Seven weeks after, it resold the land, with some development restrictions to [a former chair of the TNC regional chapter] and his wife. Cost to the [buyers]: $500,000. (Stephens & Ottaway, 2003c, p. A01)

(Continued)

(Continued)

Like other conservation buyers, the couple in this transaction then made a $1.6 million gift to TNC, enabling it to recoup what it paid for the land. The donors received a tax deduction for the gift. The *Post* authors cite tax experts who disagree on whether such deductions were legal, with a key issue being whether the donors had received a quid pro quo for the gift (Stephens & Ottaway, 2003c). TNC assured the *Post* authors that the gifts were not tied to the land transactions, but the authors interviewed some donors who said they believed that they were.

TNC's president at the time, Steve McCormick, issued a sharp response to the series of articles within a week of their publication. He claimed that the articles had "painted a distorted picture" with its accusations and, while defending the Conservation Buyer Program, announced that TNC would immediately suspend all new conservation buyer transactions (S. McCormick, 2003; Stephens & Ottaway, 2003d).

Following a yearlong review of its policies and practices, including the assistance of an outside panel, TNC announced in 2005 a wide range of changes, including restructuring of the TNC board, adoption of a number of principles from the Sarbanes-Oxley Act, a strengthened audit function, and new conflict-of-interest policies. With regard to the Conservation Buyer Program, the following new policies were implemented among others (TNC, 2005b):

- Transactions will no longer be undertaken with related parties (generally board members or employees), although such transactions are not prohibited by law.
- Transactions with major donors will be undertaken only following advance review against TNC's strengthened conflict-of-interest policies.
- The land will need to fall within a priority conservation site, established by scientists.
- The land will be offered for sale in a manner that provides an "open and equitable purchase opportunity to all potentially interested parties."
- TNC will obtain independent appraisals to ensure that it receives fair value for the land sold.
- When a gift is solicited in connection with a land sale, TNC "must document that fact and provide the buyer with a statement of the link between the gift and the sale."
- TNC will obtain community input on future use of the land.

The Washington Post series focused attention not only on the Conservation Buyer Program but also on a range of TNC policies and practices. During the following year, while TNC was developing its own strengthened policies, the Finance Committee of the U.S. Senate conducted its own investigation and released a report in 2005 that was critical of a number of TNC's practices, some of which already had been addressed in TNC's own reforms. The Senate Committee's review of TNC coincided with its consideration of broader legislation regulating the nonprofit sector and influenced its thinking about wider reforms (TNC, 2005a).

By 2006, the TNC website featured the Better Business Bureau Wise Giving Alliance seal, certifying full compliance with its standards, and the positive ratings TNC received from Charity Navigator, the American Institute of Philanthropy, and other watchdog organizations.

In an analysis of *The Washington Post* series on TNC, the scholars Max Stephenson Jr. and Elisabeth Chaves (2006) state that the authors used a rhetorical style that "strongly directs the reader toward specific conclusions through inference and implication" (p. 350). Stephenson and Chaves conclude that the series influenced the policies of the organization and the public policy debate on nonprofit accountability. They also provide an interesting perspective on TNC's response to the communication issues presented by the publication of the *Post* articles.

CASE 6.2   Youth Villages

Youth Villages was founded in Memphis in 1986 through the merger of two campuses that provided residential treatment to emotionally and behaviorally troubled young people. In subsequent years, the organization has expanded, eventually opening offices in 11 states and the District of Columbia. As it grew, Youth Villages also expanded its programs beyond residential treatment to include intensive in-home services, treatment foster care, adoption services, community-based services, transitional living services, family-based care for children with developmental disabilities, and specialized crisis services. Over 30,000 children have been served in the past 20 years (Youth Villages, 2010).

The founder of Youth Villages, Patrick Lawler, explains, "In the early years, we thought we were in the business of raising other people's kids. But many kids were not doing well after they left us" (Levine, 2006). That led Lawler and his associates to implement new models, including the multisystemic therapy model (called "MST"), developed by Scott Henggeler of the University of South Carolina. MST is a holistic approach that encompasses the children's families as well as the children themselves. MST is now used in 30 states and 10 countries (Levine, 2006).

By offering a continuum of services, Youth Villages aims to help children overcome their challenges and live at home. If a child must receive help beyond his or her own home, residential treatment is provided in the least restrictive setting for the shortest amount of time possible, with transition to a group home or foster home if necessary before returning home. The adoption program helps to find permanent homes in cases where it is not possible for children to return to their birth families (Youth Villages, 2010).

Youth Villages' model is based on extensive research. The organization established its own research department in 1994, which collects and analyzes data from all youth who have participated in Youth Villages programs for at least 60 days. The youth are tracked at 6, 12, and 24 months post-discharge, and Youth Villages has amassed one of the largest outcome datasets in the country. In addition, the organization has formed research partnerships with 15 colleges and universities to study its data and refine its outcome evaluation process. The findings of research are used to improve Youth Villages' programs and improve outcomes for young people (Youth Villages, 2010).

Youth Villages' results are summarized by the Edna McConnell Clark Foundation, which since 2004 has invested more than $21 million in the organization:

Since 1994, 82% of youth served have remained home successfully two years after discharge. A remarkable 83% have had no trouble with the law, and 82% are either still in school, have graduated, or are getting their GED at 24 months post discharge. Just 13% had been placed at any point in highly restrictive residential treatment centers, psychiatric hospitals, or juvenile facilities. Compared with traditional child-welfare services, Youth Villages' in-home program offers a 38% lower average monthly cost, a 71% shorter average length of stay, and a long-term success rate twice the national average (80% vs. 40%). Furthermore, Washington State Institute for Public Policy estimated that utilizing MST rather than traditional services saves taxpayers from $31,000 to $130,000 per participant. (Edna McConnell Clark Foundation, 2010, n.p.)

In addition to its program successes, Youth Villages has operated with business principles and financial soundness. Beginning in 2007, the Edna McConnell Clark Foundation launched a Growth Capital Aggregation Pilot (GCAP) program with three of its grantee organizations, including Youth Villages, to help them grow, achieve financial sustainability, and serve more children. In 2008, the foundation awarded $39 million to the program, which was matched with $81 million from co-investors (other donors) and members of the organizations' boards. The organizations are permitted to draw down funds for growth capital only if they achieve agreed-upon performance milestones, which include securing reliable, renewable funding (Edna McConnell Clark Foundation, 2010). In 2009, when he announced creation of a $50-million Social Innovation Fund, President Obama cited Youth Villages as an example of a results-oriented nonprofit that the fund is intended to help expand (Lee, 2009). Figure 6.3 shows Youth Villages' dashboard for 2009, which includes both program and financial data.

FIGURE 6.3 ■ Youth Villages Dashboard

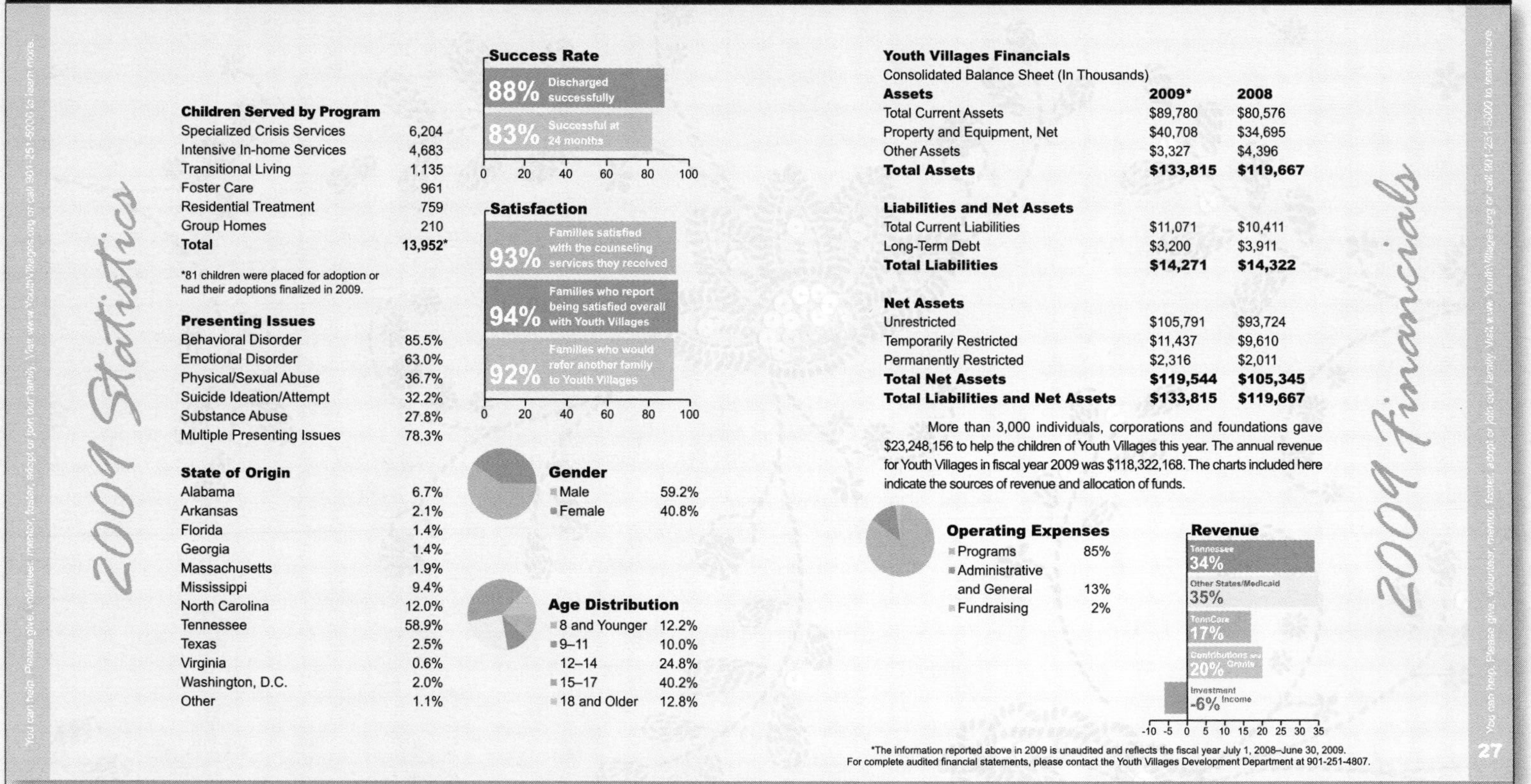

2009 Statistics

You can help. Please give, volunteer, mentor, foster, adopt or join our family. Visit www.YouthVillages.org or call 901-251-5000 to learn more.

Children Served by Program

Specialized Crisis Services	6,204
Intensive In-home Services	4,683
Transitional Living	1,135
Foster Care	961
Residential Treatment	759
Group Homes	210
Total	**13,952***

*81 children were placed for adoption or had their adoptions finalized in 2009.

Presenting Issues

Behavioral Disorder	85.5%
Emotional Disorder	63.0%
Physical/Sexual Abuse	36.7%
Suicide Ideation/Attempt	32.2%
Substance Abuse	27.8%
Multiple Presenting Issues	78.3%

State of Origin

Alabama	6.7%
Arkansas	2.1%
Florida	1.4%
Georgia	1.4%
Massachusetts	1.9%
Mississippi	9.4%
North Carolina	12.0%
Tennessee	58.9%
Texas	2.5%
Virginia	0.6%
Washington, D.C.	2.0%
Other	1.1%

Success Rate

88% Discharged successfully
83% Successful at 24 months
0 20 40 60 80 100

Satisfaction

93% Families satisfied with the counseling services they received
94% Families who report being satisfied overall with Youth Villages
92% Families who would refer another family to Youth Villages
0 20 40 60 80 100

Gender

Male	59.2%
Female	40.8%

Age Distribution

8 and Younger	12.2%
9–11	10.0%
12–14	24.8%
15–17	40.2%
18 and Older	12.8%

Youth Villages Financials

Consolidated Balance Sheet (In Thousands)

Assets	**2009***	**2008**
Total Current Assets	$89,780	$80,576
Property and Equipment, Net	$40,708	$34,695
Other Assets	$3,327	$4,396
Total Assets	**$133,815**	**$119,667**
Liabilities and Net Assets		
Total Current Liabilities	$11,071	$10,411
Long-Term Debt	$3,200	$3,911
Total Liabilities	**$14,271**	**$14,322**
Net Assets		
Unrestricted	$105,791	$93,724
Temporarily Restricted	$11,437	$9,610
Permanently Restricted	$2,316	$2,011
Total Net Assets	**$119,544**	**$105,345**
Total Liabilities and Net Assets	**$133,815**	**$119,667**

More than 3,000 individuals, corporations and foundations gave $23,248,156 to help the children of Youth Villages this year. The annual revenue for Youth Villages in fiscal year 2009 was $118,322,168. The charts included here indicate the sources of revenue and allocation of funds.

Operating Expenses

Programs	85%
Administrative and General	13%
Fundraising	2%

Revenue

Tennessee 34%
Other States/Medicaid 35%
TennCare 17%
Contributions and Grants 20%
Investment Income -6%
-10 -5 0 5 10 15 20 25 30 35

*The information reported above in 2009 is unaudited and reflects the fiscal year July 1, 2008–June 30, 2009. For complete audited financial statements, please contact the Youth Villages Development Department at 901-251-4807.

2009 Financials

You can help. Please give, volunteer, mentor, foster, adopt or join our family. Visit www.YouthVillages.org or call 901-251-5000 to learn more.

27

Source: Success in Black and White: Youth Villages 2009 Program Report (2010). Used with permission by Youth Villages.

QUESTIONS FOR DISCUSSION

1. Are the issues and questions raised in the TNC case related to the concepts of accountability, effectiveness, or organizational performance? To which of those terms is this case most relevant?

2. How does the TNC case relate to the Panel on the Nonprofit Sector's principles?

3. How are the concepts of effectiveness, efficiency, and organizational performance reflected in the Youth Villages case?

4. Which of the approaches to measurement discussed in this chapter are illustrated in the case of Youth Villages?

5. If Youth Villages was to apply the social return on investment (SROI) approach, what would be some of the cost savings to society that might be calculated (i.e., the benefits in dollar terms)?

6. Below are excerpts from the mission statements of three nonprofit organizations in the field of education. Based on these statements, what metrics would you use to measure their effectiveness? Could all three use common indicators, or would the indicators need to be different based on their distinctive missions?

   • The SEED Foundation is a national nonprofit that partners with urban communities to provide innovative educational opportunities that prepare underserved students for success in college and beyond.

   • The District of Columbia College Success Foundation is a nonprofit organization created in 2006 to expand the pipeline of low-income and underrepresented students who complete a baccalaureate degree by providing students the educational and financial incentives, mentoring, and other supports necessary to gain admission to the colleges and universities of their choice.

   • College Summit is a national nonprofit organization that partners with schools and districts to strengthen college-going culture and increase college enrollment rates, so that all students graduate career- and college-ready.

SUGGESTIONS FOR FURTHER READING

Books

Niven, P. R. (2008). *Balanced scorecard: Step-by-step for government and nonprofit agencies.* Hoboken, NJ: Wiley.

Paton, R. (2003). *Managing and measuring social enterprises.* Thousand Oaks, CA: Sage.

Poister, T. H. (2003). *Measuring performance in public and nonprofit organizations.* San Francisco: Jossey-Bass.

Wang, X. (2009). *Performance analysis for public and nonprofit organizations.* Sudbury, MA: Jones & Bartlett Publishers.

Wholey, J. S., Hatry, H. P., & Newcomer, K. E. (Eds.). (2004). *Handbook of practical program evaluation* (2nd ed.). San Francisco: Jossey-Bass.

Websites

Balanced Scorecard Institute, http://www.balancedscorecard.org/

BBB Wise Giving Alliance, http://www.give.org/

Blended Value, http://www.blendedvalue.org/

The Center for What Works, http://www.whatworks.org/

Charity Navigator, http://www.charitynavigator.org/

Guidestar, http://www.guidestar.org/

Maryland Association of Nonprofit Organizations, http://www.marylandnonprofits.org/

REDF, http://www.redf.org/

United Way, http://www.unitedway.org/outcomes/

Urban Institute, http://www.urbaninstitute.org/

Chapter Outline

chapter 7

Strategic planning begins with where the organization is, defines some new place where it wants to be, and develops a plan to get there, all in the context of its mission and values and the realities of the environment in which it operates.

© iStockphoto.com/Creativeye99

Strategic Planning and Strategic Management

7

Nonprofit organizations are driven by their missions, and those who work in them, as staff or volunteers, are often motivated primarily by their passion for the social purpose that the organization serves. But, as discussed in Chapter 6, society increasingly demands that nonprofits be accountable for the use of the resources entrusted to them. While passion for the cause is essential, nonprofit organizations also must apply tools of rational management. This chapter and the following one discuss some such tools for planning, decision making, and organization building. The current chapter discusses the development of strategy, the process of strategic planning, and the broader concept of strategic management.

Understanding Strategy

In 1967, Herb Kelleher, a Texas lawyer, and Rollin King, one of his clients, were sitting in a restaurant. On the back of a napkin, Kelleher drew a triangle, labeling the points Dallas, Houston, and San Antonio. He had an idea. Instead of flying passengers into a major hub airport and then redistributing them back out to smaller cities, like the major airlines did, what if an airline flew directly between the smaller cities? And what if that airline offered no frills, like food service or reserved seats, which would save on costs? Short flights, lower costs, lower fares. Although he had not written a strategic plan, Kelleher had a winning strategy simple enough to be sketched on the back of a napkin—and thus, Southwest Airlines was born (Hartley, 2000)!

In 1989, Robert Egger was managing nightclubs in Washington, D.C. His fiancée persuaded him to join her in a volunteer program that passed out food to the city's homeless from trucks that toured the streets and parks. This gave him an understanding of the prevalence of hunger. He began to think about the tons of food that were wasted every day by restaurants, hotels, and caterers throughout Washington. He put these two realities together, which led him to found DC Central Kitchen. The Kitchen collects surplus food, processes and repackages it, and today provides more than 4,000 meals a day to shelters and other facilities throughout the area, while also providing job training to homeless people who work in the kitchen. Like Kelleher, Egger (2002) didn't start out with a strategic plan, but he had a winning strategy.

Management scholars and consultants have offered many definitions of *strategy,* and there is also no agreement on exactly what it is or how to develop it. It may be articulated in a plan, that is, a written document, or it may be more intangible, perhaps no more than an idea or an approach to reaching a goal. Strategy is focused on the long term, not on the day-to-day, or, as Allison and Kaye (2005) write, "It is concerned with the longer-term course that the ship is steering, not with the waves" (p. 12). La Piana (2008) places the emphasis on action, defining strategy as "an organized pattern of behavior toward an end" (pp. 4–5). Developing strategy does not necessarily require any particular process or result in any written document at all. It does require creativity and a different way of seeing reality. In this chapter, we will look at the process of strategic planning, but it is important to keep in mind that "strategic thinking, acting, and learning are more important than any particular approach to strategic planning" (Bryson, 2005, p. 172).

Kevin Kearns (2000) identifies three approaches to formulating strategy for an organization. The first is the *visioning approach*. This approach begins with the leader's vision and then works backward to determine "what strategies, tactic, actions, and resources are needed to achieve it" (pp. 31, 41). A charismatic leader knows what he or she wants to accomplish and the staff scramble to make it happen. This approach has its advantages and may be the only realistic way to go in a new or young organization or one facing a crisis, situations in which, as we will discuss later, formal strategic planning may not be useful or appropriate. The visioning approach also may create an entrepreneurial "do it now" culture, one that can be very inspirational and motivating, and produces an opportunistic and flexible organization that can move quickly to seize new opportunities that may arise. But it can be risky as well. The leader's vision may not always be 20/20. Relying on the leader's vision may leave the organization open to external threats that the optimistic leader just can't or won't see but that are real. It is an approach to formulating strategy, but it may become increasingly inadequate as the organization grows and becomes more complex—in other words, as it gains more to lose.

Another approach to developing strategy that Kearns (2000) describes is the *incremental approach*. Strategy evolves out of experience as the organization goes along, one decision at a time, buffeted by bargaining and the push-and-pull of its constituencies. This may be a pragmatic accommodation to the complexity of many nonprofits' environments and their diverse constituencies, and it may produce an organization that is flexible and open to new opportunities. But it may also produce an organization that keeps moving to who knows where. It is not strategic planning and, indeed, some would question whether an organization operating this way has a strategy at all (p. 44).

The third approach to developing strategy is what Kearns (2000) calls the *analytical approach,* one in which "you use logic and in-depth analysis to improve the strategic fit between your organization and its environment." This approach is what most people have in mind when they say *strategic planning* (p. 32).

Strategic Planning and Strategic Management

Strategic planning is more than a strategy; it is a *process* that produces a *product*—a strategic plan—that puts meat on the strategy and points the way to implementing it. John Bryson (2004), a widely cited author on strategic planning, defines it as "a disciplined effort to produce fundamental decisions and actions that shape and guide what an organization . . . is, what it does, and why it exists" (p. 6). While Bryson emphasizes the need to achieve clarity about the organization's mission and set priorities, Allison and Kaye (2005) point to the value of the strategic planning *process* in building *consensus* about the priorities that are identified: "Strategic planning is a systematic process through which an organization agrees on—and builds commitment among key stakeholders to—priorities that are essential to its mission and are responsive to the environment" (p. 1).

Strategic planning begins with where the organization is, defines some new place where it wants to be, and develops a plan to get there, all in the context of its mission and values and the realities of the environment in which it operates. It is a practice that began in the corporate world and has been adopted by government and the nonprofit sector. Today, most nonprofit organizations except the newest and smallest engage in some form of strategic planning—both because they find it an effective tool and because many funders, including foundations, regard it as an essential badge of a well-managed organization.

Strategic planning is not to be confused with what is sometimes called *long-range planning,* a term that was more commonly used in the past. Long-range planning really involves projecting trends and data into the future—that is, estimating what is *going to happen* based on certain assumptions. In contrast, strategic planning is goal oriented and action oriented—its purpose is to change the future rather than merely predict it. A strategic plan is likewise not the same as a business plan, which will be discussed in Chapter 12. Most business plans are developed for specific programs, initiatives, or ventures to be undertaken by the organization, rather than the whole organization. Business plans build on the decisions made in strategic planning, but they are more focused on implementation and financial elements, typically including detailed projections for revenue and expenses over at least 3 years. Strategic planning is also not the same as *operational planning,* which, as the term suggests, relates to the actions necessary to implement the strategic plan. Most significantly, to repeat, a strategic plan is not synonymous with strategy. Indeed, Mintzberg (1996) calls the belief that the two equate "the planning school's grand fallacy," observing that "establishing a plan will not ensure the creation of a strategy" (p. 141).

Strategic management is a concept that was developed in the business world and that has been applied to government and the nonprofit sector. As Koteen (1997) acknowledges, the term "does not possess an exact, universally accepted definition" (p. 25), but he offers at least a description:

> Strategic management emphasizes an ongoing process that integrates strategic planning with other management systems . . . [it] seeks to use and merge all necessary approaches and resources to reach strategic goals . . . it embraces the entire set of managerial decisions and actions that determine the long-run performance of an organization. (p. 21)

In other words, strategic management is an integrated approach to managing the organization that is based on the strategic plan and includes the entire cycle of strategy formulation, implementation, and evaluation. The goals of the strategic plan drive decisions on managerial matters such as program design, budgeting, organizational structure, human resources development, and evaluation. The goals provide "guidelines to direct resources and talent into the highest priority activity" (Koteen, 1997, p. 27). Strategic management thus links strategy and implementation.

The Strategic Planning Process

Every doctor defines "infection" in the same way, and every lawyer knows what a "tort" is. But the vocabulary of strategic planning is unsettled. That is to say, various experts use different terms to mean the same thing. For example, some say "purpose" instead of "mission" and use the terms *goal* and *objective* in different ways, sometimes interchangeably. Some say "programs," and others say "activities." There is also no universally accepted planning process, although most models include the same essential concepts. For example, some experts recommend that development of the organization's vision should occur early in the process, while others say the vision should be defined toward the end of planning after more discussion has taken place. Written strategic plans also are organized in various ways. Allison and Kaye (2005) are right to say that "It doesn't really matter what you call certain concepts, as long as everyone in your group uses the same definitions" (p. 20). But the proliferation of terms requires that planners establish clarity about the concepts and not become distracted by differences in terminology.

There are various models for strategic planning, and we only explore a select few in this text. The *Harvard policy model,* developed at the Harvard Business School by various scholars over a period of decades, is the most commonly mentioned and is the inspiration for several well-known variations. In practice, most strategic planning models are a hybrid of the various approaches, which is appropriate because the planning process needs to be tailored to fit each specific situation (Bryson, 2001).

A basic, generic strategic planning model is depicted in Figure 7.1 and includes the steps common to many models.

- Plan to plan—that is, determine the process, the players, and their roles.
- Clarify the organization's mission, values, and vision.
- Assess the situation—that is, scan the external environment and the organization's internal realities.
- Identify the strategic issues or strategic questions that need to be addressed.
- Develop goals, strategies, and objectives.
- Write and communicate the plan.
- Develop operational/implementation plans.
- Execute the plan.
- Evaluate results.

Planning to Plan

It is important to have a plan for planning, that is, to identify what process will be used, who will participate, and what information will be needed to inform the planning. There needs to be agreement among the participants on points such as the purpose of the effort; the steps in the process; the form and timing of reports that will be issued; the role, functions, and membership of any group or committee empowered to oversee the effort; the role, functions, and membership of the strategic planning team; the commitment of the resources necessary for proceeding with the effort; and any important limitations or boundaries for the effort (Bryson, 2004, p. 35).

Some organizations use an outside consultant to guide their strategic planning process; others prefer to manage it themselves. Some plan an off-site retreat at some point in the process—perhaps a day or weekend in which the participants devote extensive time to discussion of strategies without the normal interruptions of daily business. Up-front time devoted to planning for the planning will be well spent if it avoids misunderstandings or wasted motion during the planning process itself.

FIGURE 7.1 ■ **Basic Strategic Planning Model**

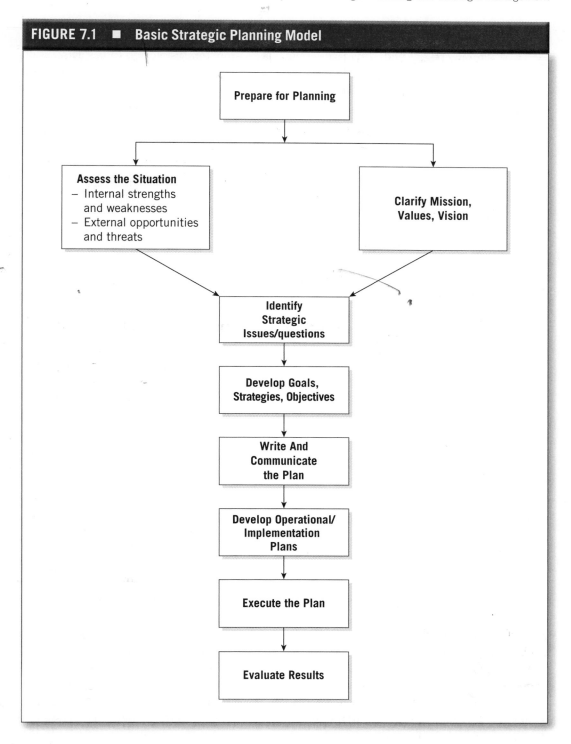

Defining Mission, Values, and Vision

Effective planning begins with consensus about basics—mission, vision, and values. Discussion on these basics often can take considerable time, and some pragmatic individuals, eager to jump into identifying issues and goals, may find the exercise frustrating. But experience has shown that neglecting to create a solid foundation for planning by achieving consensus on the basics of mission, vision, and values will likely lead to a breakdown in planning at some later stage.

Mission

As we have discussed before, mission is everything to a nonprofit organization—it is the reason the organization exists, and it must be the starting point for its planning. James Phills (2005) speaks eloquently to this point:

> Mission is the psychological and emotional logic that drives an organization. It is the reason why people get up in the morning and go to work in a nonprofit. . . . Mission [defines] the social value that the organization creates. The key feature of social value—whether it is spiritual, moral, societal, aesthetic, intellectual, or environmental—is that it transcends economic value. Thus, it is inextricably linked to fundamental human values, which are the basis for intrinsic worth or importance. (p. 22)

It is important to distinguish mission from mandates. *Mandates* are functions that the organization is *required* to perform, perhaps by its charter or law. For example, a college may have a charter that requires it to enroll only women students. The American Red Cross has mandated services that it is required to provide to the government under its congressional charter. If the organization faces mandates, they will need to be clarified at the outset and incorporated in the plan. They are "givens." But, in general, nonprofit organizations have fewer mandates than do public agencies and thus have considerable freedom to design their own futures; this may include redefining their missions.

We might think that an organization's mission should be relatively unchanging. Indeed, a performing arts organization is not likely to one day alter its mission statement to address environmental issues or the welfare of animals. But there are often shifts that require a rethinking, or at least a restatement of the mission. For example, you may recall Miriam's Kitchen, the Washington-based organization serving homeless people, that we passed in our hypothetical walking tour back in Chapter 2. Miriam's began as a breakfast program, and its mission was once simply to provide a healthy meal each day to homeless men and women. But as its programs evolved, it began to offer case management services to its breakfast clients, expanded medical services, and other programs. Over time, the scope of its operations had changed, and it became essential to consider a broader mission statement that enveloped all the organization's activities: "Our mission is to provide individualized services that address the causes and consequences of homelessness in an atmosphere of dignity and respect, both directly and through facilitating connections in Washington, DC" (www.miriamskitchen.org). This broader statement of mission encompassed what Miriam's was actually doing but did not represent a complete departure from its original purposes.

Saying that the mission can change is not to suggest that organizations should simply expand their programs and then change their mission statements to fit. But, inevitably, programs and missions often will evolve as the organization grows and expands its capabilities. Revisiting the mission is really asking the question, "What business are we in?" and getting to the right answer sometimes requires adopting a new perspective. There is always a trade-off between keeping the mission sufficiently broad and keeping it sufficiently focused. There is a risk in going to extremes in either direction. Too narrow a mission statement may be too constraining, making it impossible for the organization to grow or expand. But a statement that is too broad may become meaningless and open the door to *mission creep*—a gradual evolution away from the organization's purposes into ancillary activities that may eventually result in an organization that is very unfocused.

There are different philosophies about mission statements. Some prefer fairly simple statements that are almost like a slogan—they capture the essence of the organization's purpose in a sentence. But most mission statements say not only what the organization does, but also, at least briefly, how it does it. Some organizations develop separate statements of their vision and values, while others include some components of vision and values in their mission statements, either explicitly or implicitly. Box 7.1 provides a sampling of mission statements that reflect various approaches.

BOX 7.1 MISSION STATEMENTS

Boston Symphony Orchestra

Our mission is to foster and maintain an organization dedicated to the making of music consonant with the highest aspirations of the musical art, creating performances and providing educational opportunities at the highest level of excellence. (www.bso.org)

Strathmore

Strathmore Mission: The Strathmore Hall Foundation nurtures art, artists and community through creative and diverse programming of the highest quality.

Guiding Principles: Devoted to Artistic Excellence, Dedicated to Education, Committed to Community. (www.strathmore.org)

American Cancer Society

The American Cancer Society is the nationwide, community-based, voluntary health organization dedicated to eliminating cancer as a major health problem by preventing cancer, saving lives, and diminishing suffering from cancer, through research, education, advocacy, and service. (www.cancer.org)

Environmental Defense Fund

Environmental Defense Fund is dedicated to protecting the environmental rights of all people, including future generations. Among these rights are access to clean air and water, healthy and nourishing food, and flourishing ecosystems.

Guided by science, Environmental Defense Fund evaluates environmental problems and works to create and advocate solutions that win lasting political, economic and social support because they are nonpartisan, cost-efficient and fair.

Environmental Defense Fund believes that a sustainable environment will require economic and social systems that are equitable and just. We affirm our commitment to the environmental rights of the poor and people of color.

(Continued)

(Continued)

As an American organization, Environmental Defense Fund will always pay special attention to American environmental problems and to America's role in both causing and solving global environmental problems. (www.edf.org)

Teach for America

Our mission is to build the movement to eliminate educational inequity by enlisting our nation's most promising future leaders in the effort. (www.teachforamerica.org)

Big Brothers Big Sisters

The Big Brothers Big Sisters mission is to help children reach their potential through professionally supported, one-to-one relationships with mentors that have a measurable impact on youth. (www.bbbs.org)

Values and Vision

Most organizations clarify their values and vision in the first phase of strategic planning. The vision statement is a description of an ideal future. Some vision statements describe the future of the organization itself; these are internal vision statements. For example, Special Olympics envisions a future in which "Special Olympics is an unprecedented global movement which, through quality sports training and competition, improves the lives of people with intellectual disabilities and, in turn, the lives of everyone they touch" (http://northamerica.specialolympics.org). Other vision statements paint a picture of the ideal world that the organization is striving to shape; they are external vision statements. For example, the Arizona Humane Society envisions "a world in which all people regard companion animals as lifelong, valued family members; embrace their responsibility for the welfare of animals; and respect, value and protect the animals with whom we share this earth" (www.azhumane.org).

Some experts suggest that developing a vision statement should come later in the strategic planning process, not at the beginning, believing that planners need to go through other phases of planning before they are able to develop a consensus about their vision of the future either internally or externally (Bryson, 2004). But many models call for developing the vision along with the mission and values as an early step in planning.

Values are those principles that the organization holds most important. For example, an arts organization might value the artistic quality of its work the highest, or the diversity of its audience. As mentioned above, sometimes values are implicit in the mission statement, and other times they are presented separately. Sometimes values are identified as "guiding principles," "fundamental assumptions," or in some other way. For example, compare the mission statement of the Boston Symphony Orchestra in Box 7.1 with the mission and guiding principles of Strathmore, a performing arts center near Washington, D.C. While both organizations are dedicated to artistic excellence and education, commitment to the local community is made explicit in Strathmore's mission statement and its guiding principles (values).

Taken together, statements about mission, vision, and values establish a preamble to the strategic plan and the lens through which everything is viewed in order to develop goals for the organization's future.

Assessing the Situation

As discussed in Chapter 3, nonprofits are open systems; that is, the boundaries between the organization and its environment often blur, and changes or pressures originating in the environment will have a profound impact on what the organization is able to do and how it needs to go about doing it.

Strategic planners need to collect information in two arenas—within the organization and outside it. There are various methods available for analyzing internal and external conditions, but the most commonly used is the SWOT analysis mentioned in Chapter 5—a method that comes from the Harvard policy model noted above. In this approach, the organization itself is surveyed to identify *strengths* (S) and *weaknesses* (W), and the external environment is examined to discern *opportunities* (O) and *threats* (T). The ultimate purpose of the exercise is to develop a comparison between the organization's own strengths and weaknesses and the opportunities and threats facing it in the external environment, in order to identify strategic issues that need to be addressed.

Strengths and weaknesses of the organization may be analyzed in terms of assets or competencies. That is, what resources does it have or lack and what does it do well or poorly? As a result of this analysis, it will identify its *core competencies*—"the organization's strongest abilities, most effective strategies and actions, or best resources (broadly conceived), on which it can draw routinely to perform well" (Bryson, 2004, p. 42). Its weaknesses might also be viewed in terms of resources that are lacking or the organization's ability to perform in certain areas. For example, identified weaknesses might include inadequate facilities, insufficient staff, poor fundraising performance, or a chronic inability to meet performance objectives.

The external scan, to identify opportunities and threats, might encompass things such as demographic trends; trends in philanthropy, grant making, or government funding; a *stakeholder analysis,* to identify the characteristics, values, perceptions, expectations, and concerns of stakeholders, including clients or customers, donors, and relevant government officials; and an analysis of the positions and programs of competitors or partners offering similar services.

It is essential to focus on factors that are relevant to the organization, in other words, to be selective. For example, there may be national trends that are affecting performing arts organizations, but are all of them relevant to an opera company in Chicago? Do national birth rates really provide useful insight for an organization that serves children in a city with a large and growing immigrant population? Not being selective in looking at the environment can cause the process to just bog down and overwhelm the planners with too much information.

Part of the environmental scan requires research on other organizations. Kearns (2000) suggests looking at three categories of organizations—those that offer related programs and services, those that offer similar programs and services, and those that offer substitutable programs and services (pp. 54–55). So, for example, an organization that is involved in addictions counseling would need to be alert to trends affecting hospitals, government agencies that fund addiction counseling programs, and homeless services organizations that may be sources of referrals. Organizations that offer similar programs or services in other markets or locations may be relevant, too. An addictions counseling program in Boston should examine trends affecting similar organizations in Baltimore and Los Angeles, since they may also face similar situations. Other types of nonprofits also need to scan what is happening with regard to their competitors. For example, a YMCA/YWCA needs to be aware of trends in health club memberships and the expansion of for-profit health clubs in its community. Colleges need to know which other institutions recruit students in the same high schools, and theaters need to know what other nearby theaters offer to their audiences. Some may resist the idea of competition among non-profit organizations, but it is a reality that many, if not most, need to address in their planning.

As an example, Table 7.1 shows the hypothetical results of a simple SWOT analysis that might be conducted by the board of an urban theater. The theater has strengths, including a good reputation for quality performances and a capable artistic director. It faces opportunities presented by the gentrification of the downtown area by college-educated people and the city's plans to develop an arts district, offering the potential for larger audiences. But lack of any staff dedicated to marketing is a weakness and possibly an obstacle to capitalizing on that opportunity, as is the small and outdated facility. Threats to the organization include the possibility that its one principal donor might lose interest or perhaps suffer reversals that would make continued support impossible, the possibility that the artistic director or actors may no longer be willing to work in the old and outdated facility, and competition from other theaters that may have better facilities and a stronger base of financial support.

Identifying Strategic Issues

Drawing on the information available from the environmental scan and guided by the organization's own mission, values, and vision, the next step in strategic planning is to identify the key *strategic issues* (sometimes called *strategic questions*) facing the organization. Strategic issues are "the fundamental policy questions or critical challenges facing the organization's mandates, mission and values, product or service level and mix, clients, users or payers, cost, financing, structure, processes, and management" (Bryson, 2004, p. 42). The strategic issues or questions define areas in which the organization needs to take action. This could mean taking defensive action to protect against threats, or it might mean developing new initiatives to grow, expand, or improve in order to seize opportunities presented by the environment. There is a need to set priorities by separating issues into categories. For example, Bryson (2004) classifies strategic issues into four types:

1. Developmental issues that go to the heart of the organization's vision and goals, involving "a fundamental change in products or services, customers or clients, service distribution channels, sources of revenue, identity or image," or some other fundamental change

2. Issues that require no organizational action at present but that must be continuously monitored

TABLE 7.1 ■ SWOT Analysis for an Urban Theater	
The Organization (Internal)	**The Environment (External)**
Strengths: Reputation for quality performances Capable artistic director Good location near downtown	Opportunities: More college-educated people living downtown New restaurants opening nearby City's plan to develop an arts district in our neighborhood
Weaknesses: Facility too small and outdated No staff dedicated to marketing or fund-raising Overdependence on one major donor	Threats: Competition from other organizations Loss of key major donor Artistic director and/or actors may no longer be willing to work in old facility

3. Issues that are on the horizon and likely to require some action in the future and perhaps some action now

4. Issues that require an immediate response and therefore cannot be handled in a routine way (p. 44)

There are various approaches to the identification of strategic issues. Bryson (2004) summarizes seven: the direct approach, the goals approach, the vision-of-success approach, the indirect approach, the oval mapping approach, the issues tension approach, and the systems analysis approach (pp. 161–164). A discussion of each of these approaches is beyond the scope of this text, but students will find other sources that explore them in detail, including Bryson's book, among the suggested readings at the end of this chapter.

Sometimes the identification of strategic issues is complex and controversial. As Bryson (2004) describes it,

> Identifying strategic issues typically is one of the most riveting steps for participants in strategic planning. Virtually every strategic issue involves conflicts over what will be done, when it will be done, where it will be done, who will do it, or who will be advantaged or disadvantaged by it. These conflicts are typically desirable and even necessary because they clarify the issues. (p. 154)

But sometimes the situational assessment readily reveals the strategic issues or questions facing the organization; they just "fall out" of the analysis of strengths, weaknesses, opportunities, and threats. For example, some of the strategic questions the theater shown in Table 7.1 likely would need to consider are rather obvious: How can we prepare for the possible loss of our principal donor? How can we provide the quality of facilities that our artistic director and actors require? How can we improve our marketing and take advantage of the changes in our neighborhood to increase our audiences and meet the competition of other organizations? Strategies and initiatives can later be developed to address each of these issues.

Setting Goals

Goals are directions that the organization will pursue *with respect to the strategic issues* that it has identified. In the context of strategic planning, they are sometimes also called *strategic goals* or *strategic directions.* Koteen (1997) divides goals into three types: those addressed to *program* thrusts, that is, those that go to services that the organization provides; those addressed to *institutional concerns,* matters that need to be addressed to build a more effective organization (i.e., capacity, culture); and *financial goals,* which of course, have to do with resources (p. 126).

Goal statements are stated in broad terms and do not need to be quantifiable. (Keep in mind that some planning models describe these broad statements as "objectives," "strategic objectives," or by some other term.) Goal statements generally use action verbs—words such as increase, improve, enhance, ensure, strengthen, expand, develop, sustain, encourage, or initiate. For example, Table 7.2 summarizes six goals identified by Gettysburg College in its strategic plan. The goal statements articulate broad directions but do not state *how* they will be accomplished; for example, the college will "sustain an environment that attracts and retains outstanding faculty and staff" or "enhance the global focus of the educational experience." Nor do the goal statements include the measures by which success will be defined. That comes later.

TABLE 7.2 ■ Gettysburg College Strategic Plan

GOALS AND STRATEGIES

GOAL #1: Sustain an environment that attracts and retains outstanding faculty and staff, supporting teaching, advising, research, and other creative activity.

Strategies

- Provide appropriate, up-to-date facilities and resources that support our academic program, are suited to contemporary educational needs, and allow us to respond to changing pedagogies.
- Provide compensation and conditions for success for faculty and staff that are competitive with those offered by the nation's preeminent liberal arts colleges.
- Adopt a five-course teaching load for full-time tenure-track and tenured faculty to allow additional time for them to work with and advise students and for research and creative activity.
- Create new endowed faculty positions.
- Support faculty scholarship and professional development by increasing College funding for these activities and by helping faculty attract external grant support.
- Expand programming within the Johnson Center for Creative Teaching to support excellence in teaching and advising skills.

GOAL #2: Enhance support for student research and creative activity.

Strategies

- Establish a coordinating office for student-faculty research.
- Increase support for student summer research and senior projects.
- Expand opportunities for student travel to academic and professional conferences.
- Increase support for field trips, to expand the integration of experiential learning in courses across the curriculum.
- Establish an annual symposium to showcase student research and creative work.

GOAL #3: Enhance the global focus of the educational experience.

Strategies

- Support the continued infusion of global themes throughout the curriculum.
- Promote and enhance opportunities for study abroad.
- Develop programs that help students better integrate their off-campus experiences into their overall educational program.
- Develop new ways for students to share stories and insights from their off-campus experiences with other members of the Gettysburg community.

GOAL #4: Promote leadership, teamwork, civic engagement, and community service as key priorities within the co-curricular program.

Strategies

- Establish attractive and modern residential, social, and dining spaces designed to promote positive interactions among students, staff, and faculty.
- Expand programs that advance the intellectual, civic, and social interests of our students.
- Build on historic and evolving strengths in co-curricular offerings, intercollegiate athletics and recreation, and other programs that contribute to the spirit of the College.
- Enhance leadership training and collaborative experiences involving diverse teams of students.
- Expand support for the Honor Code and promote the ethical development of students.
- Expand opportunities for students to practice self-governance in organizations and living units.
- Increase student access to and participation in community service by expanding programming of the Center for Public Service and enhancing the integration of service learning into the curriculum.

GOAL #5: Expand professional development opportunities for staff.

Strategies

- Increase support for staff travel to professional conferences and workshops.
- Increase support for in-house professional training and leadership development.

GOAL #6: Establish an environmental sustainability program for the campus, to more fully engage students, faculty, and staff with one of society's most pressing challenges.

Strategies

- Expand educational programming for faculty, students, and staff on topics related to environmental awareness and responsibility.
- Develop green-campus protocols that integrate environmentally sustainable practices into on-going College operations.
- Develop design standards for future construction and renovation projects that incorporate forward-thinking green practices with respect to building site selection, water and energy efficiency, materials, and indoor air quality.

Source: Adapted from "Strategic Directions for Gettysburg" (http://www.gettysburg.edu/plan/home/).

Strategies

Once goals have been established, the planners next need to determine *strategies* to achieve them. Developing strategies is, of course, the heart of the strategic planning process. This is when the organization determines what it will do to address the strategic issues that it has identified as a result of its SWOT analysis and to achieve the goals that it now has established.

David La Piana (2008) identifies three levels of strategies: *organizational strategies*—broad directions and those that relate to mission, vision, trends, competitors, partners, and market position; *programmatic strategies*—related to the programs and activities implemented to achieve specific outcomes; and *operational strategies*—those "aimed at enhancing . . . administrative efficiency, preparedness, and execution" (p. 26). His model of planning portrays the three categories as a pyramid, with organizational strategy at the top (to be addressed first), programmatic strategies at the middle level (they come next), and operational strategies at the bottom of the pyramid (to be addressed last). In addition to addressing strategies in the proper sequence, it is essential that planners achieve alignment throughout these levels to assure that programs and operations support the achievement of the mission (p. 25).

Various scholars have developed core or generic organizational strategies that nonprofits might follow. For example, Kearns (2000) identifies four strategies: growth, retrenchment, stability, and collaboration. These would seem to be virtually exhaustive of possible strategies in the broadest sense. But strategic planners need to develop more specific strategies with respect to programs, activities, and the goals that they have identified. For example, Table 7.2 includes strategies that Gettysburg College has developed related to each of its six goals. Strategies may include developing new initiatives, expanding current programs, or decreasing or even eliminating others. One technique for making such decisions is offered by portfolio analysis, which will be considered in a later section of this chapter.

Objectives

Objectives are specific, quantified targets that represent steps toward accomplishing the goals. (Again, remember that in some models, these objectives statements are called "goals.")

Objectives are often stated in the form of "Increase (something) from (some number) to (another number) by (deadline)." The statement could, of course, also use "decrease," "reduce," or some other verb that implies a change in the value used to define the objective. This form is useful in communicating not only what the objective is, but also how ambitious it is—it enables any reader of the plan to see exactly what rate of change is anticipated and the date by which it is to be achieved. For example, in the case of the theater depicted in Table 7.1, an objective might be, "Increase the number of major donors from 1 to 10 within three 3 years." For new activities, objectives need to be stated differently, and in some cases, a numeric objective may not be appropriate—just accomplishing something may constitute achievement of the goal, although a deadline should be included. For example, the theater might establish objectives such as, "Retain an architect by June 1 to begin planning for renovation of our facility," "Appoint a director of development within 6 months," and "Establish promotional partnerships with six neighborhood restaurants by the beginning of the next season." There need not be a one-to-one correspondence between objectives and goals—that is, achievement of an objective might well address more than one goal.

Quantifiable objectives create the bridge from strategy to implementation by setting specific targets to be achieved. Operational plans then can be developed to spell out in detail exactly what will be done, when, and by whom in order to achieve the objectives in the strategic plan.

Writing the Strategic Plan

Strategic plans are, almost by definition, written documents. The written plan records the decisions reached and the goals, strategies, and objectives to be pursued. Usually, it is best if one or two people do the actual writing, but the draft is often used to stimulate wider discussion throughout the organization and its constituencies. Eventually, the governing board should take formal action to adopt the plan as the organization's policy.

The length of the written plan varies. Some plans may be no more than a few pages, summarizing mission, vision, values, and core strategies, and including a list of programs and objectives. Others may run 50 pages or more and include appendices with supporting data. As an alternative to a narrative document, some organizations use a columnar format showing the relationships among strategies, goals, and objectives (Allison & Kaye, 2005). Some plans provide year-to-year objectives for the next 3 to 5 years. But this may assume an unrealistic ability to forecast in detail, and it may be preferable to state objectives to be accomplished over the entire period of the plan, combined with a detailed operating plan for the first year (p. 262).

Once the written plan has been completed, it is important to use it as a tool for communication throughout the organization. One of the benefits of strategic planning is that it helps build wide consensus and common understanding about mission, vision, values, goals, and strategies. That benefit is sacrificed if it remains a document available only to a select few in management.

Developing an Operational Plan

Once the strategic plan is in place, there remains the job of developing a detailed operational plan—that is, a plan for implementation. This will include identifying specific tasks to be completed, establishing a timeline for their completion, assigning responsibility for each task, identifying the resources that will be needed—human and financial—determining the right organizational structure, identifying what information systems will be required, defining measures by which the completion or success will be determined, and other operational details. As we have said, some organizations combine the strategic and operational plans in one document, but developing them requires separate processes, usually with different individuals involved. Whereas board members and representatives of other constituencies may be involved in developing the strategic plan, the detailed work of producing an operational plan generally needs to be done primarily by the staff.

Identifying Strategic Issues and Developing Strategies

As noted above, strategic planning is a tool developed in the business world that many nonprofits have adapted to their environment. There are additional tools that have been adapted from business that can be usefully applied in the two steps that are at the heart of the strategic planning process—the identification of strategic issues and the development of strategies to address them. Because these concepts were developed in the business sector, the vocabulary they use—terms such as "competitive advantage"—may sometimes seem strange in the nonprofit sector. But with appropriate adjustments in our understanding of the terminology, many of the concepts can be useful in nonprofit strategic planning.

Portfolio Analysis

One useful tool is *portfolio analysis,* a technique used by business firms to determine if their various programs, products, and services are in line with their strategies and goals. "Portfolio" in this context does not mean a collection of investments in stocks and bonds, as most people might understand the term, but rather the array of programs and services that an organization offers. Portfolio analysis places various programs into categories—the cells or boxes of a matrix based on some set of variables considered to be most relevant.

Perhaps the best known version of portfolio analysis is the *growth-share matrix* developed by the Boston Consulting Group. It is used to evaluate company products or services based on the rate of growth in a particular market and the share of the total market that their products and services represent (Kearns, 2000). In its original form, this model may not be of great value to many nonprofits, which may be concerned about the growth of markets (i.e., growth in need for services) but are often less concerned with their market share. But others have developed variations that offer a better fit to the nonprofit environment and can be useful tools in the strategic planning process.

Kevin Kearns (2000) provides a portfolio analysis matrix that offers one way for nonprofits to identify strategic issues. Table 7.3, which is based on Kearns's model, portrays the situation of a hypothetical urban medical center. The city and its population are changing, with implications for the demand for various medical services that this institution provides. Moreover, other medical centers, both within the city and its suburbs, have emerged as competitors. Table 7.3 provides a grid that highlights intersections of the medical center's strengths and weaknesses with the opportunities and threats facing it from the environment, in order to illuminate the strategic issues that its planners must consider. In the upper left (northwest) quadrant, opportunities presented by the environment coincide with areas of strength for the organization. The population of this city is growing older, increasing the incidence of cardiovascular disease and the need for related medical services. (Remember that in the vocabulary of SWOT, a growing need for services is an "opportunity" for the organization that provides them, however perverse that may sometimes seem. It may help the organization think about it as an "opportunity to be of service.") The medical center always has had a reputation for excellence in cardiology and cardiac surgery, so an opportunity presented by the environment coincides with one of its strengths. The strategic issue (or question) presented is, "How can we leverage our strong programs in cardiology and cardiac surgery to meet the growing need (seize the opportunity)?" Strategies to be considered might include expanding facilities, recruiting new physicians with a specialty in cardiology or cardiac surgery, or other initiatives.

In the lower left (southwest) quadrant, there is an opportunity presented by the environment, but it is in an area in which the organization is relatively weak. With the city's aging population—the baby boomers are turning 60—there is a growing market for cosmetic surgery. But this medical center has never been a leader in this area—other medical centers in the city have always been stronger in this field. The strategic issues for the center are as follows: Should we invest in our cosmetic surgery program to meet the growing need, in other words, to seize the opportunity of a growing market in this field? Should we seek a partnership to compensate for our weakness in this field, perhaps some type of marketing relationship with one of the health club chains in the area? Or, should we phase out our cosmetic surgery services and concentrate our efforts in areas where we are strong, for example, in cardiology and cardiac surgery?

The upper right (northeast) quadrant of the grid includes a threat that will potentially affect an area in which the organization is strong. The medical center has always been well-known as an excellent place for women to give birth—it's been a great strength for the center over the years. But there are fewer young families living in the city—many are now raising their families in the suburbs. Further, suburban hospitals have built new birthing facilities closer to where young families live, threatening to take much of this business away from the center. The medical center knows it can't abandon this area of care. It's one of its strengths; it already has made

TABLE 7.3 ■ Strategic Issue Grid: Urban Medical Center		
	Opportunities (Growing Need for Services)	**Threats**
Strengths	**Strategic issues**	**Strategic issues**
	How can we leverage our strong programs in cardiology and cardiac surgery to meet the growing need (opportunity)?	How can we mobilize to avert the threat from suburban hospitals to our strong birthing program or at least minimize their negative impact?
Weaknesses	**Strategic issues**	**Strategic issues**
	Should we invest in our cosmetic surgery services to meet the growing need?	How can we minimize the damage to our rehabilitation program from the new specialized hospital across town?
	Should we seek a partner in this area? Should we phase out cosmetic surgery?	Should we phase out our weak rehabilitation program?

Source: Based on Kearns (2000, p. 130).

significant investment in this area, and if it leaves the field, it will be giving up a significant amount of revenue. The strategic issues for the center are as follows: How can we mobilize our strong birthing program to avert the threat or at least to minimize its negative impact? The planners might consider ideas such as developing a new, more modern birthing center or perhaps installing more state-of-the-art technology or offering specialized services that will encourage suburban women to continue coming downtown to have their babies.

The bottom right (southeast) quadrant of the grid portrays a situation in which the organization faces a threat in an area where it is relatively weak. The medical center has never been strong in providing rehabilitation services—and now a new specialized rehabilitation hospital has opened across town, posing a serious threat. The strategic issue for the medical center is this: How can we minimize the damage from this threat? Maybe by cutting our rehabilitation program back to the minimum and reducing costs? Or, should we just close down this weak program altogether and refocus our efforts on areas in which we have greater strength?

Grids such as the one developed by Kearns (2000) thus provide a useful tool for organizations to identify the strategic issues facing their organizations and begin to formulate strategies to address them. Now, let's take a look at another model that introduces some additional complexity—MacMillan's competitive strategies matrix.

MacMillan's Strategies Matrix

A portfolio analysis model development by MacMillan (1983) for application to nonprofits suggests core strategies the organization might pursue. MacMillan's model looks at each of the organization's programs or services according to three criteria:

1. The organization's *competitive position* with regard to the program, which might be *strong* or *weak:* Again, competition may not be a comfortable concept for many nonprofits—it is a concept drawn from the business world. But another way to interpret this is to think about whether the organization can claim superiority over other organizations in its ability to deliver the program. In other words, does the organization have resources, skills, advantages of location, or other advantages that make it the best organization—or potentially the best—to provide this program or service?

2. The *attractiveness* of the program to the organization, which might be *high* or *low:* In other words, to what extent does the organization really want to offer this program or service? This assessment would be based on a variety of criteria, including its fit with the mission, its potential for attracting resources to support the program, and others.

3. The extent of *alternative coverage,* that is, similar services offered by other organizations, which might be *high* or *low:* In the business world, this really means, "Are there many competitors in this market?" But a nonprofit may look at it as the question of whether there are other options available to people who need the service.

Because there are three variables to be considered, each of which may be high or low, a matrix depicting this model is three-dimensional; that is, it has width, length, and height. The space is divided up into eight cells, or eight scenarios, that exist with regard to each program considered. MacMillan (1983) suggests a strategy for each scenario. Table 7.4 summarizes the eight scenarios. It also shows the strategy recommended by MacMillan for each, using terms taken from the business vocabulary, as well as a description of each situation in ordinary language—that is, in the words that a group of nonprofit planners might actually use in their conversations.

MacMillan's (1983) matrix does provide a nonprofit with a way of recognizing patterns that may help clarify thinking about each specific program and also about the relationship of its portfolio to its mission as an organization. As Kearns (2000) observes, if an organization finds that all its programs fall into scenarios 1 to 4, that is, encompassing just those that are highly attractive, that may suggest it is drifting away from addressing the most hard-core social problems in favor of those that are the most lucrative, perhaps in terms of paying customers or the ease of raising gifts. That might cause some concern about its adherence to mission.

On the other hand, if all its programs fall into scenarios 5 to 8—scenarios in which the programs are relatively unattractive, perhaps because they are tangential to the mission or difficult to support in the long term—Kearns (2000) speculates that the organization may just be responding to the availability of short-term funding for some programs, running the risk that it will be stuck with them if the funding evaporates (p. 126). MacMillan (1983) recommends that an organization try to build a balanced portfolio of programs in which it has a strong competitive position, in other words, where it is able to achieve high quality compared with other organizations (scenarios 1, 2, 5, and 6), including some that are attractive and some that are not. In simplest terms, the portfolio may include some moneymakers, which help subsidize other programs that lose money but are at the heart of the organization's mission (the "soul of the agency" programs). Applying MacMillan's thinking, an organization would achieve such an ideal balance of programs by

- Giving up programs to other organizations that can do them better, even if they may be attractive financially and in other ways;
- Encouraging other organizations to abandon programs in which it has a clear advantage and can operate with greater quality and efficiency;
- Making sure that all its programs are consistent with its mission and strategy;
- Considering partnerships or collaborations with other organizations, a subject we will consider in more detail in Chapter 8.

The Strategic Planning Debate

As stated earlier in this chapter, strategic planning in some form is practiced by most nonprofit organizations. However, it is important to recognize that strategic planning has its critics.

One criticism was mentioned briefly earlier in this chapter: Strategic planning is not synonymous with and does not inevitably produce *strategy*. The risk is that traditional strategic planning may produce a list of goals, but not anything bigger (LaPiana, 2008). In their 2005 book, *Governance as Leadership,* Chait et al. (2005) reinforce this point, writing that "disillusionment with strategic planning has escalated." They observe that in too many plans, "dreams trump reality," that is, they include "blue sky" goals without addressing existing barriers to their achievement (p. 57). Too many plans include specific goals but no more than a vague strategy for achieving them. When a strategy is described, it too often fails to acknowledge the implications for change in the status quo of organizational architecture, people, and resources. They call this "planning by wishful thinking" (p. 58).

According to Chait et al. (2005), formal plans often reflect overconfidence in predictions about the future and do not adequately anticipate unforeseen circumstances. Finally, they

TABLE 7.4 ■ MacMillan Scenarios

Scenario	Competitive Position	Program Attractiveness	Alternative Coverage	Suggested Strategy (MacMillan)	The Situation in Ordinary Language
1	Strong	High	High	Aggressive competition	We're the best at this, or we easily can be, and we really want to do it. There are a lot of other organizations offering the same thing, but we're going to compete head-on and try to persuade them to yield this program to us.
2	Strong	High	Low	Aggressive growth	We're the best at this or we easily can be. We really want to do it. And, there is almost nobody else doing it. It's an open road—let's invest in this program and grow it quickly before others start to compete with us.
3	Weak	High	High	Aggressive divestment	We would really like to continue offering this program, but we are just not good at it and probably never will be. There are a lot of others doing it and they are a lot better than we are. Let's just get out and let them have it.
4	Weak	High	Low	Build strength or sell out	We would really like to do this, and there are few others who do it. But let's be realistic, we just aren't very good at it. We either need to invest in this program to make it good or find some other organization that can do it better and is willing to take it on.
5	Strong	Low	High	Build up best competitor	We're the best at doing this, but it is just not attractive to us to do it any longer. We don't want to let people down who rely on this program, but there are other organizations that do the same thing. Let's talk to the next-best organization and help them take this over from us.
6	Strong	Low	Low	Soul of the agency	We are the best and almost the only organization doing this. We're really known for it. It's not that attractive to us in many ways—for one thing, we lose money on it. But a lot of people depend on us and have nowhere else to go. We just have to find a way to keep it going.
7	Weak	Low	High	Orderly divestment	This is just not an attractive program for us, and we're not that good at it either. A lot of other organizations offer the same thing. No rush, but let's gradually direct people elsewhere and phase this program out.
8	Weak	Low	Low	Joint venture	We're not very good at this, and we really don't want to do it. Some people need the program, but not that many. We're stuck with it for now, but let's see if we can find another organization that's willing to partner with us in this area, so we can focus on our higher priorities.

Source: Based on MacMillan (1983).

observe that some strategic plans really reflect the consensus of the CEO and senior executives, which the board is asked to merely ratify.

Others point to the amount of time and effort that is required by the traditional strategic planning model, arguing that it may prove frustrating to the organization's staff and distract them from management of current programs. Indeed, when strategic planning is mentioned, some people will resist, or perhaps groan, based on previous negative experiences—the long meetings spent debating every word in the mission statement, the weekend retreats filled with team-building exercises. The weeks and months go by, and a 200-page report is produced. The report then goes on the shelf and life goes on as before.

Some experts make the case that a process requiring perhaps 6–12 months to complete may put the organization "on hold" for too long, causing it to defer decisions, miss emerging opportunities, and fail to respond to pressing current needs while awaiting the outcome of the planning process (La Piana, 2008). In addition, strategic planning usually occurs on a fixed cycle, perhaps every 3 years, which some find too infrequent for the fast-changing environment that most nonprofits face. Among those who make this argument, La Piana, a consultant to nonprofit organizations, proposes a continuous, "real-time" strategy development model that he characterizes as a "planning-doing cycle" (p. 19).

Some critics of strategic planning suggest that the approach is inherently flawed. Others acknowledge that it may fail only because of mistakes in implementing the process or perhaps because of exaggerated expectations about what it can achieve. Strategic planning is not a panacea for every organization's problems at every point in its existence or under all circumstances. As mentioned earlier, it may not be a useful thing to undertake in a new organization, especially one guided by a charismatic, visionary leader. Likewise, strategic planning may not make sense for an organization that is in a state of crisis. What's the point of taking time to debate the mission or scan the environment when the roof is caving in, the creditors are at the door, or the executive director has just resigned and the staff is scrambling to keep things afloat until a new CEO can be found?

Strategic planning is a useful and important vehicle for many nonprofit organizations. However, strategic planning should not become the purpose of the organization, which is to say, it should not become an all-consuming activity. Properly conducted, strategic planning doesn't need to consume everybody's time. Bryson (2004) suggests that it should take no more than 10 percent of any key decision-maker's time during the year, and even that may be more than most organizations will require (p. 14). But neither is strategic planning a one-shot, over-and-done exercise. Planning cannot just be about putting a report on the shelf. It needs to be a continuous part of the organization's way of operating, and the plan itself needs to be a living document that is revisited and adjusted in light of experience and the changing environment.

Strategic planning is not a substitute for leadership. Unfortunately, some organizations may try to make it so. Perhaps confused and out of ideas, board members or managers may say, "What we need is a strategic plan." They hire a consultant, go through a series of meetings and retreats, and end up with a document that is as lifeless and unimaginative as the paper it is printed on. Planning may provide a roadmap for implementing a vision, but it is not the vision, and it can only succeed if it is used as a tool of leadership.

Despite its critics and its limitations, strategic planning offers many benefits. It forces the organization to think about its mission and to confront basic questions about where it stands, what it does, and where it wants to go. It requires that the organization look beyond itself to the environment around it and see itself in the context of broader trends and forces, including the society, economy, and other organizations. It provides a basis for rational decision making, rather than relying on guesswork or intuition. It may help to build consensus and understanding about mission, vision, values, and goals throughout the organization. And, when properly executed, it may produce strategies that can help guide a nonprofit toward achievement of its mission.

Chapter Summary

Strategy is an abstract concept that may simply mean a direction or a new, innovative approach to getting from one place to another. It may arise from a leader's vision, incrementally from smaller decisions the organization makes one at a time, or from a formal analytical approach such as strategic planning.

Strategic planning is a process that many nonprofit organizations have adopted from the business world. It is a useful tool for organizations in designing their futures, but may not be appropriate in every situation. Strategic management is a broader concept that links the goals of the strategic plan to decisions on managerial matters such as program design, budgeting, organizational structure, human resources development, and evaluation.

There are many different models for strategic planning, and most organizations practice a hybrid of different approaches. One well-known version is the Harvard policy model, on which many alternative models are based. Most start with clarification of the organization's mandates, mission, vision, and values. The opportunities and threats presented by the external environment are compared with the organization's internal strengths and weaknesses (the SWOT analysis) in order to identify strategic issues or questions on which the planners need to focus. Broad goals are then established and strategies, programs, and objectives are developed to achieve them. Operational plans are written to set specific timetables and accountability for the achievement of the objectives according to the plan.

With appropriate modifications in vocabulary, tools that businesses use to analyze their competitive environment may be adapted to help nonprofits identify strategic issues. Portfolio analysis models developed by Kearns, MacMillan, and others suggest generic strategies under various scenarios defined by the organization's strengths or competitive position, the desirability of the program, and the extent to which other organizations are providing coverage.

Some critics of strategic planning say that it is an inherently flawed process. They argue that it may lead to setting goals but not strategy, that it is time-consuming and may distract the organization from current opportunities and problems, and that its periodic nature does not permit an organization to be responsive and flexible in real time in a fast-changing environment. Strategic planning is not a panacea for all problems. It may not be appropriate for some organizations at some points in their history, and it cannot substitute for vision or leadership. But, properly executed, strategic planning can bring many benefits.

KEY TERMS AND CONCEPTS

core competencies	*goals*	*internal vision statement*
external vision statement	*Harvard policy model*	*mission*

CASE 7.1   New Hope Housing Strategic Plan 2007–2012

The following is a summary of the 2007–2012 strategic plan of New Hope Housing, a nonprofit organization in Northern Virginia, founded in 1977, that provides shelter, transitional, and permanent housing for homeless families and single adults.

Introduction

New Hope Housing has demonstrated nearly 30 years of service responding to the needs of those who are homeless in southeastern Fairfax County. Our founders saw a need and responded, opening the first shelter in Fairfax County, Mondloch House, in 1978. Over the years, New Hope Housing has added programs and services. At the same time, our commitments to meet the needs of those in our community who are most vulnerable, to treat each person with dignity and respect, and to provide a place of hospitality and hope have not changed.

As changes occur in our community, and as new practices develop in how best to meet the needs of those who are homeless, New Hope Housing must regularly assess its programs and identify how to most effectively continue to fulfill its mission.

This strategic plan will guide the work of the agency over the next four- to six-year period. The plan presents the principles that ground the agency's work, the assumptions that underlie the plan, and the major priorities or goals for the coming period.

Grounding Principles

Vision

A home and bright future for every man, woman, and child in our community.

Mission

New Hope Housing provides homeless families and individuals shelter and the tools to build a better life.

Core Values

We are a community-based organization.

We welcome all, including the un-welcome.

We treat each individual with dignity and respect.

We are effective stewards of the human and financial resources entrusted to us.

A competent and dedicated staff is critical to our mission.

Planning Assumptions

A number of assumptions regarding environmental factors, agency strengths, and mission/service commitments of the agency underlie this plan:

We will remain focused on serving the needs of persons who are homeless or who are rebuilding their lives from previous homelessness.

We will continue to serve populations that are difficult to serve and less likely to receive services as readily through other agencies.

We will continue to serve both single adults and families.

We will continue to focus primarily on needs in the southeastern Fairfax County geographic area and nearby adjacent areas.

Future efforts to address the reality of homelessness will focus on reducing services in shelters, on "rapid re-housing," and on use of a "housing first" approach in serving homeless persons. Over time, this change is likely to result in reduced case management in shelters, a change in purpose of shelters, and changes in some of the transitional housing programs.

Permanent supportive housing programs, such as Max's Place and Milestones, will increase as part of the housing first approach.

It is likely that government funding for homelessness, affordable housing, and support services will not expand significantly. Major new activities, therefore, are likely to require greater private support than in the past.

Strategic Priorities

In the context of the vision, mission, and core values, and after consideration of environmental factors, the strengths of the agency, and the needs in the community that we seek to address, the following strategic priorities will guide New Hope Housing over the coming five-year period:

Strategic Direction A:

New Hope Housing will engage in active partnerships with housing developers to promote and secure the development of new permanent housing in the community for underserved populations recovering from homelessness. New Hope Housing will act as the service provider in such new housing.

Strategic Direction B:

New Hope Housing will continue to be a leader in (a) demonstrating new approaches in shelter and transitional housing programs that help homeless persons quickly progress to permanent housing, (b) offering comprehensive support services in post-shelter housing programs that assist individuals and families to attain and maintain permanent housing, and (c) expanding specialized small-scale permanent supportive housing programs.

Strategic Direction C:

New Hope Housing will continue to review new program and service opportunities that arise in the context of our vision, mission, and core principles, and potential impact on other strategic directions.

(Continued)

(Continued)

Strategic Direction D:

New Hope Housing will be a leader in staff professional and leadership development.

This statement of agency principles, planning assumptions, and strategic directions is intended as a guide for agency activities. As an ongoing process, the agency will continue to refine and to develop more specific objectives and action plans for pursuing these strategic directions.

Approved by New Hope Housing Board of Directors
March 20, 2007
Copyright 2009 New Hope Housing

Source: Condensed and adapted from "New Hope Housing Strategic Plan 2007–2012" (http://www.newhopehousing.org).

QUESTIONS FOR DISCUSSION

1. Review the strategic plan of New Hope Housing, a nonprofit organization in Northern Virginia, and consider the following questions:

   (a) What might have been the strengths, weaknesses, opportunities, and threats identified in the process that developed this plan; in other words, can you work backward from the plan summary to determine what the SWOT analysis might have revealed?
   (b) What are the strategic issues or questions identified by the planners for New Hope Housing?
   (c) What are the goals and strategies in this plan, consistent with the vocabulary used in this chapter?
   (d) How are New Hope's assumptions about the environment reflected in its strategic priorities? Are there any strategic priorities you might add, based on the assumptions?

2. One organization that students will have some knowledge about is their own college or university. What are the strengths, weaknesses, opportunities, and threats that you see facing your college or university? What strategic issues do you suggest for your institution?

3. Suppose a nonprofit organization's strategy requires that it phase out a program on which few people rely, but those people are vulnerable and no good substitute exists. How might the organization proceed with its plan in an ethical and humane manner?

4. Is competition among nonprofit organizations an acceptable concept, or is it contrary to the values of the sector?

SUGGESTIONS FOR FURTHER READING

Books

Allison, M., & Kaye, J. (2005). *Strategic planning for nonprofit organizations* (2nd ed.). Hoboken, NJ: Wiley.

Bryson, J. M. (2004). *Strategic planning for public and nonprofit organizations* (3rd ed.). San Francisco: Jossey-Bass.

Kearns, K. P. (2000). *Private sector strategies for social sector success.* San Francisco: Jossey-Bass.

La Piana, D. (2008). *The nonprofit strategy revolution: Real-time strategic planning in a rapid-response world.* Saint Paul, MN: Fieldstone Alliance.

Oster, S. M. (1995). *Strategic management for nonprofit organizations.* New York: Oxford University Press

Chapter Outline

chapter 8

Pressures to collaborate and merge are unlikely to abate as nonprofits face an increasingly competitive environment and there is a nationwide focus on performance and accountability.

© iStockphoto.com/Gerald Bernard

Capacity and Collaboration

8

As we discussed in Chapter 7, strategic planning forces a nonprofit organization to examine itself as well as its environment. The internal analysis may identify weaknesses that need to be addressed. These weaknesses may call for capacity-building efforts to strengthen the organization. The external analysis will identify circumstances influencing the nonprofit's future, which may involve the availability of resources as well as the presence of competitors. As suggested by the portfolio analysis models discussed in Chapter 7, that may call for efforts to enhance the organization's competitive advantage or perhaps exploration of partnerships with other organizations. In this chapter, we will consider some models and activities for enhancing a nonprofit's capacity and look at nonprofit collaboration, which in some cases may even lead to merger.

The Capacity-Building Movement

As Crutchfield and Grant (2008) describe, thinking about nonprofits has evolved over recent decades. Early research focused on theories of how successful programs could be replicated or grown to scale in order to increase their impact. Beginning in about the late 1990s, there was a shift in emphasis from replicating programs to building strong nonprofit organizations that could sustain them. As Christine Letts and her colleagues (1999a) describe, there was "a fundamental redefinition of the challenge [confronting the nonprofit sector] from the most prevalent conception of the challenge, as one of expanding effective *programs,* to a new formulation of the challenge, as one of building effective *organizations* that can sustain and improve those programs" (p. 3, italics original). The capacity-building "movement" was born in and expanded throughout the 2000s, with a booming literature and a growing number of consulting practices, conferences, and other resources dedicated to nonprofit organizational development.

Interest in building the capacity of nonprofit organizations increased partly as a result of several books and articles that received wide attention in the late 1990s that noted the problem of inadequate nonprofit capacity and laid the blame on traditional models of grant making (e.g., Letts et al., 1999a; Shore, 1999). Foundation giving historically has tended to support the development and delivery of nonprofits' programs rather than the building of organizations. Funders generally encourage organizations to keep overhead costs low, in order to maximize the resources spent on direct program services. In other words, they are pleased when nonprofits can demonstrate efficiency in their operations. But an emphasis on efficiency and low overhead may discourage expenditures undertaken to build the organization itself for the long haul. According to critics, this mind-set has had several negative consequences.

First, without building capacity, organizations cannot grow successful programs to a larger scale, thus limiting their impact. As Shore explains, "Even the best [programs] do not get to scale, do not reach more than a fraction of those who need their services, and often do not endure" (p. 88). Second, there is the toll that inadequate capacity takes on nonprofit staff and volunteers who struggle to deliver services with limited resources, possibly resulting in higher rates of staff turnover and burnout. As Light (2004b) describes the situation, "Nonprofits have been doing more with less for so long that many now border on doing everything with nothing" (p. 14). And third, inadequate capacity may not support the effectiveness of programs or performance of the organization over the long run, possibly depriving clients of quality services and society of the benefits of sustained efforts in addressing problems. As Light (2004a) describes it,

> Many organizations can produce program success for a short period. All they need are extraordinary employees who are ready to work long hours, tolerate stress, and persevere despite organizational barriers. This is the picture of the small early-stage nonprofit—closely connected to its constituency and attractive to others as a result of its passion and accuracy of approach. The real trick for organizations is to sustain, improve, and build on this strength, producing progressively improving results over time. This is good management. (p. 38)

Critiques like those offered by Letts et al. (1999a), Shore (1999), and others influenced the thinking of some funders, which began to shift some of their focus from program grants to providing support for capacity-building initiatives. It was central to the approach of some *venture philanthropy* funds that originated in the 1990s, which adopted the approach of venture capitalists in business who emphasize building a company for sustainability. But by 2004, foundation funding to support nonprofit capacity-building efforts, which had increased from 1998 to 2002, began to decline (Jensen, 2006a). In 2009, capacity-building received a new boost when the U.S. Congress passed the Serve America Act, which included a Nonprofit Capacity Building program to provide grants for organizational development to small and mid-sized nonprofits over the years 2010 to 2014. However, the availability of external funds to support capacity building always has been and remains modest compared with the total of philanthropic giving, and most capacity-building efforts are undertaken by nonprofit organizations using their own internal resources or with unrestricted operating funds obtained through traditional fund-raising, earned income, or other methods (Light, 2004b).

The recession that began in late 2007 shifted the priorities of many nonprofits—and funders—toward sustaining essential programs, further reducing funds available for capacity building. Some observers became concerned about the overall capacity of the nonprofit sector and the need for efficiency, calling for more collaborations and mergers to reduce total overhead, a topic that we will discuss later in this chapter. While many financially pressured organizations have developed a heightened interest in collaborating with others and some have merged, capacity building is still a concern for many nonprofit executives who struggle to build effective organizations with inadequate resources and capacities of various kinds. Let's look at capacity building first and then return to a further discussion of collaboration.

Defining and Understanding Capacity

Exactly what is an organization's "capacity"? Paul Light (2004b) offers a succinct, but expansive, definition: *Capacity* is "everything an organization uses to achieve its mission, from desks and chairs to programs and people" (p. 15). What is "capacity building"? Letts et al. (1999a) call it simply a process to "develop, sustain, and improve the delivery of a [nonprofit's] mission" (p. 4). But these brief definitions are like saying that life encompasses everything that happens and that eating sustains it. They do not really offer enough for us to have a clear understanding of either term. That requires that we go inside the black box of capacity to look at its component parts and observe some specific activities that it comprises.

It is no more meaningful to think about an organization's capacity as an indivisible quality than it is to think about a person's capacity in that way. For example, your capacity for study may be different from your capacity for athletics or for singing, so we would need to think about your *capacities* in the plural—that is, break capacity down into different categories or elements. Having done so, we could then consider what activities you might need to undertake in order to increase your capacity in areas that need improvement—perhaps some tutoring to improve your study skills, weight training to enhance your athletic prowess, and singing lessons. Fortunately, various authors have identified components of nonprofit organization capacity in much the same way, in categories. Although they offer somewhat different lists, there are many similarities in the elements they include.

Mike Hudson (2005) divides capacity into internal and external elements, writing that

> building organization capacity is about systematically investing in developing an organization's internal systems (for example, its people, processes, and infrastructure) and its external relationships (for example, with funders, partners, and volunteers) so that it can better realize its mission and achieve greater impact. (p. 1)

When the term *capacity* is used, many people first think primarily about the internal elements. That is understandable. For example, if we think about individuals' capacities—like studying, swimming, or singing—we are really talking about the skills or talents they possess. We are perhaps less inclined to think about their relationships with others as elements of their capacity as individuals. But, as discussed before, nonprofit organizations are open systems and are resource dependent. Their relationships with the external world—including other nonprofits, the media, government, and donors and other funders—are critical to their survival. Establishing and strengthening these relationships may thus be important aspects of capacity building, equal in importance to developing their internal structures, systems, and skills.

Internal and *external* are still two very broad categories. Paul Connolly and Carol Lukas (2002) offer a more comprehensive framework that helps deepen our understanding. The elements of capacity they identify include (1) the organization's mission, vision, and strategy; (2) its governance and leadership; (3) its ability to deliver programs and ensure the impact of its programs; (4) its strategic relationships—that is, the important external relationships that are critical sources of revenue or that may present constraints on the nonprofit's activities; and (5) its internal systems and management—its human resources; financial management systems; technology and information systems; facilities; plans for managing risk; programs for volunteer recruitment and management; and working relationships among its managers, staff, and volunteers. Connolly and Lukas's list reminds us again that capacity encompasses almost everything a nonprofit organization has or does.

Letts et al. (1999a) break down the concept of capacity in a different way, describing three types of capacity an organization may possess: *program delivery capacity, program expansion capacity,* and *adaptive capacity.* They say that most nonprofit organizations are familiar with the first two, but it is "adaptive capacity that makes an organization not only efficient but also effective" (p. 20). As the term implies, program delivery capacity grows out of the organization's knowledge of a specific field—for example, education, the environment, or public health. Its capacities include the skills of its staff, who are recruited for their professional expertise. If this is the only capacity the organization possesses, "the organization is little more than a convenient venue where programs are implemented" (p. 20). As an organization expands its program, possibly to multiple sites, it needs to develop additional capacities, including payroll and financial systems, fund-raising, and staff with supervisory skills. But, Letts and her coauthors argue, it is the third capacity—adaptive capacity—"that an organization needs to be sure it is delivering on its mission" (p. 21). This includes the ability to learn as an organization and identify ways to improve, to change in response to client needs, to create new and innovative programs, and to create an environment that is motivating to staff and volunteers (p. 23). Letts et al. draw on models developed in the business sector that they say can be adapted to build the capacity of nonprofits, and they emphasize the need to develop a "culture of performance."

Kibbe (2004) emphasizes the importance of a nonprofit's "planfulness," a concept similar to Letts et al.'s (1999a) adaptive capacity. According to Kibbe, planfulness is an organization's "capacity to revisit . . . its . . . mission, goals, and strategies on a regular basis to make sure they are fresh and appropriate to new opportunities, new challenges, and changes in the wider world." Planfulness thus implies "more than a one-time strategic planning project"; it is a way of life for the organization (p. 7).

In other words, capacity may involve more than what an organization *has* (its facilities, structure, and systems) and more than what it can *do* (the skills of its leaders, staff, and volunteers). It may be related as well to what the organization *is*—in other words, it may encompass intangible qualities such as orientation, commitment, and culture (Kibbe, 2004, p. 7).

As the discussion in this section demonstrates, the definition of capacity is so broad that it may seem difficult to distinguish capacity building from simply managing the organization. It may help for us to look at some specific processes and activities that nonprofits actually undertake when they say they are engaged in building capacity, which we will do in the next section.

Capacity Building in Action

An organization beginning a capacity-building initiative might use one of a number of tools that are available to evaluate its various capacities and identify areas of weakness that might need to be addressed. For example, the consulting firm McKinsey & Company (2001) offers a capacity assessment grid that nonprofit managers, staff, board members, and others can use to rate the organization's current status on each element of capacity, assigning a score of "1" where there is a clear need for increased capacity, a "2" when there is a basic level of capacity in place, a "3" if there is a moderate level of capacity, and a "4" if there is a high level of capacity on the element being evaluated. When the instrument is completed by various people within the organization, the combined scores help identify areas in which there is consensus about the need for improvement. The assessment tool was developed by McKinsey on behalf of Venture Philanthropy Partners (VPP), a venture philanthropy fund, and it is available on VPP's website, which is listed at the end of this chapter.

Having identified areas of its capacity that need to be strengthened, exactly what actions might an organization undertake? There is a large toolbox available, with tools designed to address almost any need. Capacity building often includes efforts to strengthen the organization's leadership, including the governing board and the CEO. As discussed in Chapters 4 and 5, there are a variety of tools for assessing and improving the skills of boards and CEOs and for developing policies designed to improve their performance. Board development activities might include, for example, board self-assessments, retreats, and establishing a governance committee of the board to focus on the board's own responsibilities, structure, and operation. There are a number of ways in which organizations invest in their executive leadership. Participation in professional associations and activities enables CEOs to learn from the experiences of their peers. There are a wide variety of formal leadership training programs available. Some organizations support their CEOs by retaining an executive coach, a practitioner of a field that has grown into a distinguishable profession in recent years. Having a plan for executive transition is a recommended practice for well-managed nonprofit organizations, and the existence of such a plan is indeed an element of capacity (Kibbe, 2004; Light, 2004b).

Establishing a system for the regular evaluation of programs would add to an organization's program delivery capacity. Strengthening fund-raising and partnerships, perhaps developing plans for earned-income ventures, improving facilities and systems, and enhancing staff and volunteer skills are all important purposes of capacity building. Undertaking a campaign, which will be discussed in Chapter 11, may be an important capacity-building activity that will provide the funds needed for improving physical facilities and strengthening the organization's financial base. Strengthening internal management systems and functions, including human resource management, volunteer programs, financial systems, and operating procedures and policies, is commonly included in capacity-building initiatives.

A Model for Capacity Building

We now have an understanding of the various elements of capacity and the broad array of activities that can be undertaken to enhance capacity in each area. But where do we start? How do the elements fit together, and where should an organization begin to address its capacity in a holistic way?

In work undertaken for Venture Philanthropy Partners, McKinsey & Company (2001) developed a comprehensive capacity framework that helps answer these questions. As depicted in Figure 8.1, McKinsey defines nonprofit capacity in a pyramid of six essential elements. These elements include some of the items identified by Connolly and Lukas (2002), but their depiction in the framework of a pyramid implies relationships among them and suggests a process for capacity building. McKinsey & Company's pyramid also highlights the importance of an intangible but powerful force that affects every aspect of capacity and efforts to strengthen it—the organization's culture.

McKinsey & Company's (2001) model begins at the top with aspirations, which encompass mission, vision, and values. At the next level of detail are the organization's strategies, and then its skills—that is, what it knows and what it can do. On the bottom of the pyramid are human resources, systems and infrastructure, and organizational structure. In the McKinsey pyramid, all six elements are surrounded by, or embedded within, the shell called "culture." Culture affects all the elements and provides the overall environment in which capacity-building efforts may be undertaken. As we discussed in Chapter 5 with regard to change leadership, culture includes shared values, attitudes, feelings, beliefs, rituals, habits, codes of conduct, and other such characteristics of an organization—invisible rules that may support or hinder an initiative for change. McKinsey & Company call it the "invisible thread that runs throughout the entire subject of capacity building" (p. 63). Indeed, an organization's culture is in itself an important aspect of capacity.

FIGURE 8.1   ■   McKinsey & Company Capacity Framework

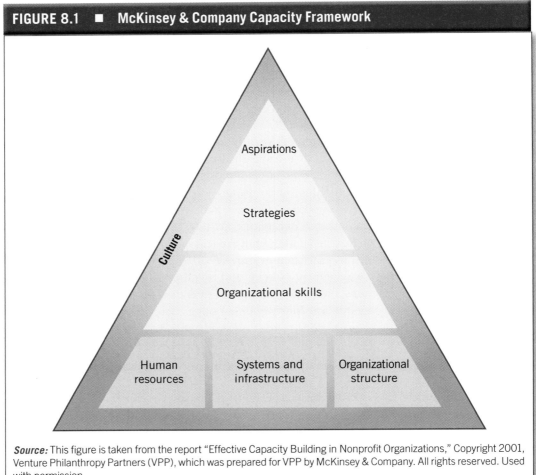

Source: This figure is taken from the report "Effective Capacity Building in Nonprofit Organizations," Copyright 2001, Venture Philanthropy Partners (VPP), which was prepared for VPP by McKinsey & Company. All rights reserved. Used with permission.

It may be tempting to initiate capacity building at the bottom of the McKinsey pyramid, perhaps by completing an inventory of staff skills, analyzing organizational charts, and evaluating the suitability of information and accounting systems. Those are areas in which many organizations have some deficiencies, and they often affect the daily work of its staff, so there is a high awareness of them. They are concrete and specific and thus easier for people to get their heads around. But McKinsey & Company (2001) emphasize the importance of following a process that begins at the top of the pyramid and works down, stating that its capacity-building work with nonprofits has been most successful when larger questions of mission, vision, and values, and then strategies and organizational skills, are addressed before the work proceeds to the elements at the foundation of the pyramid:

> The act of resetting aspirations and strategy is often the first step in dramatically improving an organization's capacity. The nonprofits [among those McKinsey studied] that experienced the greatest gains in capacity were those that undertook a reassessment of their aspirations—their vision of what the organization was attempting to accomplish in the next phase of its development. (p. 15)

Resetting aspirations alone is not sufficient in and of itself, however.

A new aspiration or strategy can only be transformative if it is then used to align the other aspects of organizational capacity. If done thoroughly, this alignment process provides a tight institutional focus and a road map for the organization to use with both internal and external audiences, which help keep everyone on track during the long and difficult process of building capacity. (McKinsey & Company, 2001, p. 15)

Thus, capacity building may mean more than making modest enhancements to staff skills or management systems. In its most expansive conception, capacity building may represent disruptive transformational change that goes to the basic values and purposes of the organization.

Capacity and Organizational Life Cycles

Let's look at two examples of capacity building in action, undertaken in two different organizations under very different circumstances. Wendy Kopp founded Teach for America in 1989, recruiting recent graduates from top colleges and universities to spend 2 years teaching in schools serving low-income students before beginning other careers. She attracted hundreds of talented young men and women to her cause, and her organization grew rapidly. But 5 years later, Teach for America was "on the verge of collapse" (Hauser, 2003). While Kopp's energy and charisma were sufficient to keep the organization running and growing for a time, its lack of organizational structure, management systems, and comprehensive fund-raising strategies eventually left it in debt and struggling with problems of communications and morale (Hauser, 2003). After considering the possibility of closing, in 1995 the organization launched an effort to achieve stability. "They . . . implemented a plan to build a diverse and sustainable funding base, to concentrate on core activities, to introduce much-needed management processes, and to strengthen the [organization's] culture" (Hauser, 2003, n.p.). By 2010, Teach for America had recovered and grown, with 7,300 core members engaged in teaching more than 450,000 students (www.teachforamerica.org).

Rubicon Programs, a California-based organization that helps homeless and disadvantaged people gain independence and self-sufficiency, did not face a crisis like Teach for America. Rather, its goal in 1994 was to further develop its already successful programs and increase their impact. With support from the Roberts Enterprise Development Fund (now "REDF"), Rubicon built a measurement system to track client outcomes. The new system made it possible not only to serve more clients and better match programs to their needs, but also to accurately report outcomes to funders, and it "fundamentally reshaped the organization's performance culture" by making management and staff focus on social impact. By 2000, Rubicon had quadrupled its staff, achieved financial self-sufficiency, and increased the number of people served from 800 to 4,000 (McKinsey & Company, 2001, pp. 55–56).

Teach for America and Rubicon programs offer examples of nonprofit organizations at different places in their histories, one struggling to survive and the other aspiring to greater scale and effectiveness. But both represent examples of capacity-building efforts that helped lead to stability, growth, and recognition for performance.

A number of authors have advanced life cycle models describing how organizations grow, mature, and may eventually decline. Many are similar and include the same basic stages, identified by different terms (see, e.g., Adizes, 1999; Carlson & Donohoe, 2003; Stevens, 2001). Let's look at one life cycle model of nonprofit organizations, developed by Judith Sharken Simon (2001) and summarized in Table 8.1.

As Table 8.1 suggests, an organization begins as an idea, a dream, often in the mind of its founder. Once chartered as a formal organization, it still resonates with the enthusiasm of the founder and a small group of founding board or staff members, who work to frame its programs, establish some structure, and chart its direction for future growth. Like an adolescent, it may sometimes seem to be in chaos, but raw energy and commitment drive it forward. Once a foundation has been established, the organization may grow as rapidly as an adolescent. It adds new programs, raises more funds, hires more staff, and becomes more systematic in its approach. It will place greater emphasis on measuring results and ensuring accountability as it approaches maturity. Just as with individuals, organizational maturity has its risks. The organization may be stable, its programs churning along in an effective way, its systems operating so well that it runs almost on autopilot. But there is the risk of complacency, bureaucracy, stagnation, and decline.

Simon's (2001) concept of life stages is a more optimistic one than some models depict. The organization proceeds from an idea to existence as a mature organization and then has the capacity to renew itself and return to an earlier stage of growth. But not all scenarios may proceed so well. There are threats at every stage. A new organization may not have sufficient resources or skills to survive past its childhood. It may be unable to raise enough funds; attract enough volunteers or staff; or keep pace with the competition offered by older, more established organizations in its field. The organization's leadership may not be able to manage the period of rapid growth. For example, Chapter 5 discussed the risk of founder syndrome, in which a founding CEO is unable or unwilling to step aside while the organization's growth demands a different set of management skills. Systems and skills may lag behind the demands placed on them by expanding programs, and quality may deteriorate. Chaos may reign, and the organization may collapse during this period.

If the organization survives to the stage of maturity, it may be in danger of losing its edge. A mature organization might not have the energy and innovativeness of its early years. It may

TABLE 8.1 ■ Life Stages of Nonprofits

Organizational Life Stage	Description of Organization
Stage I: Imagine and inspire	The organization has not yet been founded; it is still an idea or a dream. This stage is characterized by enthusiasm, energy, and creativity.
Stage II: Found and frame	The organization is created and begins to frame its program. There is still great enthusiasm and energy.
Stage III: Ground and grow	The organization is building its foundation and growing. There is an emphasis on accountability, but rapid growth can be challenging to management.
Stage IV: Produce and sustain	The organization is mature and stable. It may be on autopilot. There is the risk of becoming stale, and maintaining momentum is a concern.
Stage V: Review and renew	The organization revisits its mission and programs and undertakes change. Minor changes may take it back to Stage IV. Major changes may take it back to Stage II. Returning to one of the earlier stages then may lead to renewed and continued growth.

Source: Based on Simon (2001).

become a lumbering bureaucracy. Its staff could just be going through the motions. It might not confront the need for change. It may be unprepared to respond to changes in its environment, to the loss of a key source of support, or to shifting patterns of community needs. If it does not move to the stage of "review and renew," it may stagnate, decline, and eventually expire (Simon, 2001).

This suggests that a focus on capacity is important at every stage of an organization's life but that the elements of capacity that are most relevant may be different in each stage. A young organization may need to be concerned primarily with honing its mission, developing its programs, securing funds, and ensuring accountability. A growing organization may need to devote attention to its management systems and organizational structure, in order to accommodate more complexity and greater scale. And a mature organization may need to return to its aspirations in order to renew the enthusiasm and energy of its earlier years, revive growth, and ensure its continued relevance and survival.

Indeed, in a study of 318 nonprofits, Paul Light (2004b) discovered that the types of capacity-building activities undertaken do vary according to the organization's size and age. He found that younger organizations are more likely than older ones to develop collaborations with other organizations and undertake organizational assessments but are less likely to focus their capacity building on media relations, reorganization, team building, leadership development, or the implementation of new information or personnel systems (p. 60). As Light describes the situation,

> Younger organizations behave like the more agile, yet naïve organizations they are. They adopt capacity-building approaches that build their influence through collaboration and outcomes measurement but show less interest in media relations and new information technology, either because they do not recognize the need or do not have the funding. (p. 60)

Older and larger organizations in Light's (2004b) study were more likely to "behave like weight-conscious organizations: They adopt capacity-building approaches designed to counter bureaucratic encrustation," including reorganization, team building, leadership development, changes in their personnel systems, staff training, and program evaluation (p. 60). Strategic planning also is more likely to be used by older and larger nonprofits than by younger and smaller ones and is an approach that may enable them to break out from a stage of maturity and potential stagnation to a period of renewed growth. Light offers his own life cycle theory, which he calls the "spiral of sustainable excellence," and relates it to the need for the right capacity building at each stage:

> Imagine nonprofit life as a journey up and down a spiral. All organizations would start with a simple idea for some new program or service and then move up the spiral toward greater and greater impact. Also imagine five landings, or stops, along the climb: the organic phase of life in which they struggle to create a presence in their environment, the enterprising phase in which they seek to expand their size and scope, the intentional phase in which they try to focus themselves on what they do best, the robust phase in which they strengthen their organizational infrastructure to hedge against the unexpected, and the reflective phase in which they address longer-term issues of succession and legacy. (p. 136)

In Light's (2004b) model, nonprofits might move up the spiral at different rates, some quickly, some slowly, and many never reach the top. Some might also descend the spiral at certain times, and others might go all the way down to "their organic roots from time to time to ask themselves again why they exist, whom they serve, and how they intend to make a difference" (p. 137). The type of capacity building needed would depend on where the organization is on this spiral:

> Some forms of capacity building are much more important for moving from the organic to the enterprising stage or for stopping the fall backward, while others are much more appropriate for the climb from intentional to robust. As such, successful capacity building depends in large part on picking the right improvement effort at the right time. (p. 138)

Capacity Building Evaluated

Now we come to the bottom-line question: Does capacity building really affect an organization's effectiveness or impact? A positive answer may seem intuitive. How could improved governance, strengthened leadership, better systems and facilities, more highly trained staff, and an adaptive culture *not* lead to the more effective delivery of programs and a better-performing organization? Indeed, many experts agree with intuition, arguing that capacity and effectiveness are linked. Paul Light (2004b) concludes that greater capacity *does* lead to increased effectiveness. He acknowledges that it may be difficult to measure effectiveness directly, but argues that increased effectiveness will be reflected in perceptions, trust, and confidence in the organization. However, his evidence of the link between capacity and effectiveness is based on the perceptions of nonprofit employees who participated in his study. He acknowledges that "perceptions are always affected by self-interest" but nevertheless concludes that "given the lack of objective data for measuring nonprofit capacity and effectiveness, perceptions will have to do for now" (p. 15).

Others remain somewhat skeptical, at least with regard to some elements of capacity. For example, in their study of high-impact nonprofits, Crutchfield and Grant (2008) suggest that while "textbook strategies like relentless fundraising, well-connected boards, and effective management are necessary . . . they are hardly sufficient" (p. 19). They explain that some of the organizations they identified in their study as those with high impact are, indeed, not especially well managed or are focused on internal capacity. Rather, they are "satisfied with building a 'good enough' organization and then spending their time and energy focused externally on catalyzing large-scale systemic change" (p. 19).

Nonprofit Collaborations and Mergers

Now let's shift our view from the micro to the macro; in other words, instead of thinking about the capacity and effectiveness of individual organizations, let's focus on the capacity and effectiveness of the nonprofit sector as a whole.

The number of nonprofit organizations has grown rapidly in recent decades. For example, the total number of nonprofits providing services related to children, youth, and families more than tripled, growing from 21,393 to 79,713 in the 7 years between 1999 and 2006 (Kirkpatrick, 2007, p. 43). These trends have prompted some to ask if there are too many nonprofits competing for the same limited funds, with too few having the capacity to grow to scale or effectively meet the needs of society or their clients. Some have called for mergers among nonprofits in order to reduce the duplication of services and to create larger, stronger organizations with the capacity to make a greater impact. These calls have been heard for many years, but they increased during the recession that began in 2007. In 2009, the *Chronicle of Philanthropy* began regularly publishing lists of recent mergers. A survey by the Bridgespan Group, a consulting firm, found that 1 in 5 nonprofits was considering a merger (Wallace, 2009b). Moreover, the number of conferences, webinars, and other activities related to the topic was similar to the attention devoted to capacity building in the previous decade.

Prominent among the advocates of consolidation in the nonprofit sector are funders, including foundations. During the recession, many experienced diminishing resources with which to meet the growing requests of nonprofit organizations that were themselves facing increasing demands for service. A number of them have provided grants to support collaboration and mergers. But some people say that foundations also have been part of the problem, because they prefer to support new initiatives rather than provide ongoing, core support to organizations. Critics also cite cases in which foundations have responded to mergers by reducing their grants—using the merger as an "exit strategy"—rather than by providing adequate support to the combined entity (Gammal, 2007, p. 51).

Not everyone is enthusiastic about the need for mergers. Some observers say that small organizations may stay in closer touch with the needs of their communities and are likely to provide more personal service than their larger, more bureaucratic counterparts (Gose, 2005). Others argue that competition in the nonprofit sector is as beneficial as in others, "providing checks and balances and protecting vulnerable populations from being exploited" (Gammal, 2007, p. 50). David La Piana (2010), a consultant who works with nonprofits and an author, agrees that there are inefficiencies in the sector, but argues that they often can be reduced through partnerships between and among organizations. He calls the claim that there should be fewer nonprofits "too simplistic," arguing that the pressure on funders occurs not because there are too many nonprofits, but rather because there are too few dollars available to meet community needs (p. 28). He advocates the establishment of various relationships in which nonprofits can work together to increase efficiency, without entering a formal merger.

A Continuum of Relationships

Let's start this section by clarifying some terminology. As we saw in Chapter 7 with regard to strategic planning, the vocabulary for describing relationships between and among nonprofits is unsettled; that is, people use different words to mean the same thing. For example, some people call any relationship in which two organizations are working together a "partnership," while others reserve that term for arrangements that imply legal obligations, which make partnerships distinct from less formal relationships. La Piana (2010) uses "collaboration" to mean only informal relationships between nonprofits and calls the development of more formal relationships "strategic restructuring." As depicted in Figure 8.2, strategic restructuring encompasses two other concepts. The first is *strategic alliances,* which include *administrative consolidations* and *joint programming.* These are activities undertaken by two or more nonprofits that are more than informal collaboration but stop short of corporate integration; that is, the organizations maintain a high degree of autonomy. The second type of strategic restructuring is what La Piana calls *corporate integrations.* They may include parent–subsidiary partnerships, joint venture corporations, management service organizations that support one or more nonprofits, and—ultimately—mergers. These types of relationships imply increasingly less autonomy for participating organizations and, in the case of a merger, complete corporate integration.

As depicted in Figure 8.2, relationships can be viewed across a continuum, along which they may evolve. Sometimes, but not always, one thing may lead to another. Informal cooperation may lead to more formal relationships, which may ultimately lead to a merger, just as dating may lead to engagement and eventually to marriage. For example, two organizations might begin to cooperate informally, perhaps by sharing information and referring clients to each other. Things might progress to more formal collaboration, perhaps sharing office space, consolidating administrative functions, developing joint programming, creating a new organization to provide management services to two or more nonprofits, or undertaking joint ventures. Each step along the continuum implies less autonomy and greater integration. Eventually, the organizations may proceed to merge, giving up their separate identities to operate as a single, larger organization. And, as with individuals, some relationships work out and some do not, for a variety of reasons. As Figure 8.2 also shows, putting together such relationships involves increasing effort—and risk—as we move across the continuum from left to right. The more integration required by any relationship, the greater the potential obstacles that need to be overcome. We will discuss some of these obstacles later in this chapter.

To keep things simple, this chapter generally just uses *collaboration* as a generic term to encompass any relationship in which two or more independent organizations work together toward common objectives, and uses *merger* to mean an action in which two or more organizations are combined into one corporate entity, involving a change in control, usually to a new or combined board (Haider, 2007). But La Piana's (2010) distinctions are useful to highlight the nature of the continuum and the increasing complexity of relationships that may be developed.

Drivers of Collaborations and Mergers

Collaborations and mergers among nonprofit organizations may offer benefits to society, nonprofit clients, and the sector as a whole, but what are the potential gains for the organizations themselves? In other words, what might motivate an organization to seek a relationship with another?

Think back on some of the organizational theory we discussed in Chapter 3. Scholars working from many of the theories we reviewed have offered explanations of nonprofit collaboration consistent with their theoretical perspective. For example, scholars who work from the resource dependency theories point to resource constraints and the need for organizations to reduce uncertainty in their environments. Those who follow institutional theory explain collaboration in terms of the need for organizations to develop a shared response to problems and to achieve legitimacy (Sowa, 2009). Building on these multiple theoretical approaches, Sowa conducted a study of 20 collaborations among nonprofits in the field of early care and education and concluded that the motivations to collaborate were indeed complex, including both anticipated benefits in providing services as well as expected benefits to the individual organization.

That conclusion is consistent with the explanation of authors who describe *drivers* of collaboration, which may be internal or external (Yankey & Willen, 2005). *External drivers* arise from changes in the environment. They might include, for example, increased competition for clients or resources (such as competition for diminished giving and government funding in an economic recession); shifting priorities or demands of private or government funders (who may require collaboration or merger as a condition of continued support); or political changes that could adversely affect a group of organizations, making it advantageous for them to work together to protect their interests. *Internal drivers* arise from conditions within an organization.

FIGURE 8.2 ■ Continuum of Nonprofit Relationships

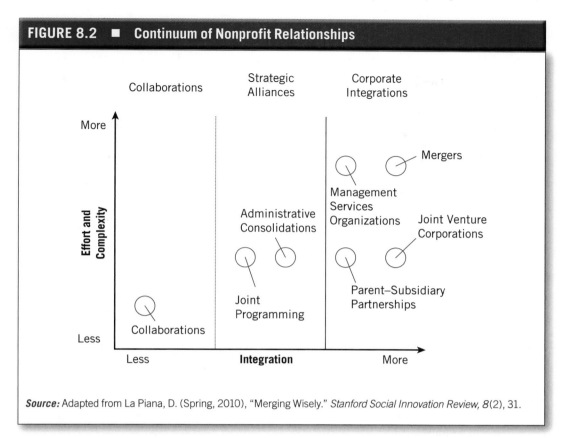

Source: Adapted from La Piana, D. (Spring, 2010), "Merging Wisely." *Stanford Social Innovation Review, 8*(2), 31.

They may involve financial, managerial, and programmatic considerations. For example, a collaboration or merger may enable organizations to reduce overhead costs, increase purchasing power, or perhaps gain better access to loans. Managerial considerations may include the ability to gain access to specialized talent by working with a partner. Merging organizations, or at least consolidating some functions, may make it possible to recruit a more experienced CEO or CFO (chief financial officer) and to pay a more competitive salary. Drivers that are programmatic in nature relate to organizations' ability to enhance or expand their services through collaboration or merger; in other words, they relate to delivery of the mission (Yankey & Willen, 2005).

Which reasons are predominant in most cases? In one study of 190 organizations, 83 percent mentioned the opportunity to improve efficiency as a reason for collaborating, and 47 percent mentioned problems with increasing overhead costs. By sharing costly overhead or support functions with another organization, a nonprofit may be able to reduce its overhead and direct more of its resources toward its strategic goals. In the same study, 60 percent mentioned increased competition in fund-raising as a reason to collaborate, and 30 percent mentioned pressure from funders to do so (Wasserman, 2005, p. 20). Other formal research studies on collaboration have focused on identifying relevant organizational characteristics and environmental variables and how they influence the choices that organizations make among the various forms of collaboration. One research conclusion is that nonprofits with more diversified sources of revenue may be less inclined to collaborate or merge. This may be in part because they are better able to resist pressure from government and private funders to do so (Guo & Acar, 2005). Recall resource dependency theory, discussed in Chapter 2.

Dan McCormick (2001) explains an organization's proclivity to collaborate or merge in terms of three driving forces—liability, viability, and survivability. Regarding liability, he offers the example of an environmental organization that had acquired land in order to preserve it but found itself burdened with debt it could not manage. Its solution was to merge with a larger organization with a similar mission that could absorb that liability. Although it ceased to exist as an independent organization, its mission of preserving the land was achieved. Another situation that might encourage a collaboration or merger is the diminished viability of an organization, which McCormick defines as "a condition in which your organization may be alive, but [is] not having a positive impact on its mission" (p. 9). Such an organization may be characterized by stagnant fund-raising, high staff turnover, and perhaps a gradual erosion of financial position. An organization may decline to the point that its very survivability becomes questionable. That could result from significant financial problems, scandal or controversy, or a change in the environment that makes the mission no longer relevant—for example, discovery of a cure for the disease that the organization existed to combat. It may be forced to merge whatever assets remain with those of another, stronger nonprofit as the only alternative to closure. As McCormick notes, the position at which an organization stands along the continuum—liability, viability, survivability—determines its bargaining power in entering any collaboration or merger it may seek (p. 11).

Exploring Collaborations and Mergers

Now let's look at a few examples to gain a sense of the nature of the relationships that some nonprofits have developed and see how they fit on the collaboration continuum described above. We will start with some examples of success and then look at two in which the effort was deemed a failure:

- Two environmental organizations, the River Revitalization Foundation and Friends of Milwaukee's Rivers, were both operating from inadequate space, so they decided to pursue the idea of sharing larger quarters. Their efforts eventually led to the renovation of a facility to create space for eight environmental organizations. Although the organizations remain independent, the sharing of space provides financial benefits as well as an office environment that has improved employee morale (Wasserman 2005, p. 13).
- In 2007, five social service organizations in the Twin Cities area of Minnesota created a new organization, called MACC Commonwealth, to share their back-office functions. In the first year, the new arrangement saved the five organizations about $200,000 in costs. The new organization also was able to negotiate staff benefits for the entire group more favorably than any one of the organizations could do on its own (Wallace, 2009a).
- In 1999, Big Brothers Big Sisters of America and Boys & Girls Clubs of America began to work together to provide adult mentors for young people. Local Big Brothers Big Sisters programs would recruit the mentors, and Boys & Girls Clubs would provide the clients—young people who were members of their clubs. By 2009, the cooperative effort had grown to encompass 40 Big Brothers Big Sisters organizations and 300 Boys & Girls Clubs affiliates (Quotah, 2009).
- When a county hospital closed in Milwaukee, many low-income patients lost their source of dental care. They began to visit other clinics, which were soon overloaded. The Madre Angela Dental Clinic was established as a new entity to meet the need. It is a collaborative effort of three hospitals in Milwaukee, Marquette University, several local nonprofits, and

volunteers. An advisory board of representatives from participating organizations oversees the clinic, and the role of each is spelled out in written agreements (Wasserman, 2005).

- The Cancer Wellness Center, Wellness House, Cancer Support Center, and Wellness Place are four independent nonprofits in the Chicago area that provide support to breast cancer patients. They are sufficiently far apart that they do not compete for patients, but they had been competing for corporate and foundation support, and each of them lacked sufficient visibility to gain referrals of patients from the area's major hospitals. They began cooperating to increase their combined visibility, then after a decade created a consortium to present themselves to the public as a single entity. Finally, they created a fifth nonprofit, the Cancer Health Alliance of Metropolitan Chicago, that promotes and helps support all four organizations (Haider, 2007).

- In 2000, Second Harvest and Foodchain, competitors in hunger relief, decided to merge under the name America's Second Harvest. Deborah Legg, who became president of the merged organization, pointed to the benefits, including the ability of the larger organization to secure gifts from national corporations and the consolidation of administrative functions such as fund-raising, finance, and public relations. By 2007, America's Second Harvest was the nation's largest hunger-relief organization, serving a network of 200 food banks in all 50 states (www.secondharvest.org). In 2008, the organization changed its name to Feeding America.

The examples above illustrate different points along the collaboration continuum: eight organizations sharing space while remaining independent, five organizations creating one to provide shared administrative services, two organizations working together to recruit and engage volunteers, three organizations collaborating to offer a new service, four organizations creating a fifth to pursue shared goals, and two organizations becoming one. Each step along the continuum entails a reduction in the autonomy of individual organizations and increasing entanglements among them; in other words, some organizations are living together as roommates, others have become partners, and some are getting married.

Each of the above examples is one of success, but not all efforts turn out so well. Let's look at two that did not and then consider some of the obstacles and pitfalls that can prevent or complicate such undertakings.

- In 1999, a total of 25 prominent child, youth, and family organizations created the National Call to Action, a collaborative effort to eliminate child abuse by 2020. The relationship started well, but "conflicts over trust and turf ultimately undercut the process" (Kirkpatrick, 2007, p. 46).
- In 1997, the health systems of Stanford University and the University of California at San Francisco (UCSF) faced an increasingly competitive situation in the health care industry, and both were experiencing massive financial losses. The universities decided to merge their health systems in order to "fortify their shaky finances" and gain a competitive advantage. Two years later, facing mounting debt and an $86 million budget shortfall, the merger was dissolved (Mangan, 1999).

Obstacles to Collaboration

What differentiates successful from unsuccessful relationships between and among nonprofit organizations? What are some of the obstacles that need to be overcome and pitfalls to be avoided? What are some conditions that may favor a successful relationship? Let's look at some of the variables that are involved.

Motivations

As discussed earlier in this book, there is a fundamental difference between for-profit and nonprofit entities. The primary purpose of a business corporation is to increase the wealth of the owners, whereas the primary purpose of a nonprofit is to achieve its social mission. The shareholders of a corporation thus have a clear interest in the organization, focused on its long-term financial performance. They will evaluate potential partnerships and mergers based on their expected impact on the bottom line. Although some corporate mergers—for example, that of AOL and Time Warner—turned out to be colossal mistakes, such failures often reflect miscalculations about the future of the business rather than confusion or disagreement about purposes or goals.

The stakeholders of a nonprofit do not have a financial interest in the organization and thus evaluate potential relationships by different, more complex criteria. Volunteers and staff may highly value the social relationships surrounding their involvement with the organization and see a potential collaboration or merger with another entity as uncomfortably disruptive and a loss of autonomy that may reduce their own role. Since they do not have a personal financial stake in the decision, volunteers, including members of the governing board, "have little incentive to push for changes that could be wrenching in their short-term effects on programs and employees, [even if they may be] sound for the [organization in the] long term" (Wolf, 1999, p. 327). Both volunteers and staff are usually very committed to the mission and may place less importance on the potential financial or competitive advantages to be gained through collaboration. And, as McCormick (2001) explains, "Mission is an emotional issue. Nonprofit mission statements are about service and attention to causes, not like their for-profit counterparts, whose mission statements talk about financial security and market leadership" (p. 6).

Culture

Earlier in this chapter, we discussed the importance of culture. An organization's culture is usually a strong force, and the integration of two or more cultures can be a complex undertaking. In commenting on the failure of the Stanford/UCSF merger, discussed above, the president of Stanford cited, among other reasons, different cultures that made it difficult to integrate the medical departments, perhaps reflecting Stanford's tradition as a private university and UCSF's as a campus of the public University of California (Mangan, 1999).

Gammal (2007) describes a merger between the Davis Center and Community Counseling, two organizations that also faced culture clashes. Davis had practiced a "holistic social welfare model." Counselors met clients off-site and worked to help families deal with a wide range of issues, not just psychological ones. But Community Counseling had a "traditional psychotherapeutic model," in which patients came to the office for counseling by psychologists holding PhD degrees. After the merger, the Davis people expected the Community Counseling staff to go out to meet clients, which they resented, while the Community Counseling staff were concerned about patient confidentiality and the qualifications of some Davis staff. The merger ultimately survived, but only after most of the original counselors had left and the organization had spent over $100,000 on staff training and development (p. 50).

Language is closely related to culture. For example, the very word *merger* may carry negative connotations in the nonprofit sector because of its association with the highly publicized consequences of corporate mergers. Influenced by what they hear or read about mergers in the commercial sector, people may tend to focus on what may be lost in a merger—the organization's identity, social relationships, possibly even jobs.

Egos

Kirkpatrick (2007) quotes the words of one nonprofit executive: "For all the cause-related work we do . . . there's a great deal of ego involved in 'my way' of solving the problem" (p. 46). Egos may be a problem, especially if one or more of the organizations are led by a founder, whose personal identity may be bound up with that of the organization he or she leads. But as the words of the executive quoted above suggest, the issue may be more than a matter of personal pride. Even nonprofits that pursue similar missions may practice different philosophies or methodologies that they believe to be right and to which volunteers and staff may be strongly committed. For CEOs conditioned by a competitive environment, it may be psychologically difficult to approach any relationship without instinctively protecting the interests of their own organization. For example, in describing the failure of the National Call to Action, one observer recounted that things were going well until "the heads of the [collaborating] national organizations waltzed in. All they wanted to know was 'What's in it for me?' 'How much money do I get?' 'How much money will this take away from my bottom line?'" (p. 46).

Costs

Collaborations and mergers may increase efficiency in the long run, but developing formal relationships also may require the investment of substantial resources. There are the time and opportunity costs of internal analyses and meetings between the potential collaborators. There may be additional legal and accounting fees and other out-of-pocket expenses. If a merger is undertaken, there will be costs involved in the integration of management and information systems, the development of new printed materials, possibly relocation to new facilities, and continued staff development to meld the merged organization together. Full integration may take 3 years or more and cost more than anticipated (Gammal, 2007).

If the relationship does not work out, exit costs also can be high; for example, unraveling the merger between the Stanford and UCSF health systems was estimated to cost "tens of millions of dollars" on top of the costs that already had been experienced in putting the merger together (Mangan, 1999). Moreover, although both organizations should engage in side-by-side analysis and due diligence before combining, there have been cases in which unforeseen or undiscovered liabilities or problems came back to haunt the new organization after the merger (Yankey & Willen, 2005).

Conditions for Success

Despite the obstacles, successful collaboration and mergers do occur. What are the conditions under which successful relationships are most likely to evolve? The literature offers consistency on several points.

Driven by Mission

Relationships undertaken primarily to advance the mission are more likely to be successful than those undertaken solely for financial reasons or as a response to pressure from funders. Or, as Gammal (2007) expresses it, "in the nonprofit sector, as in the world of human courtship, money is not the right reason to merge. But mission may be" (p. 51). In the cases summarized above, neither the Milwaukee environmental and medical organizations nor the Chicago-area cancer centers were driven primarily by financial considerations. There were financial benefits to be gained through their relationships, but all were driven by the opportunity to expand their services in pursuit of their missions. Only the Stanford/UCSF merger, of those discussed above, was driven primarily by financial problems, which were exacerbated rather than solved.

Commitment From Top Leadership

The egos of CEOs and board members can be obstacles to successful collaboration, and their commitment to the effort is a necessary condition for success. The configuration of leadership in the merged entity is a sensitive issue. This will involve board leadership positions, the CEO, and managers at other levels. Some board members may have served in anticipation of ascending to leadership positions in the future, a route that now may be blocked by the integration of boards. Unless the board as a whole strongly supports the new relationship, such personal ambitions can become stumbling blocks. Staff will have loyalties to their CEOs or other managers and may undermine the relationship if they perceive that their leaders feel reluctant or skeptical about the change (McCormick, 2001).

Trust

As in human relationships, successful collaboration between or among nonprofit organizations must be built on a foundation of trust. An atmosphere of trust helps "lower the barriers between individuals and organizations, foster the growth of possible relationships, discourage hidden agendas, and promote good-faith negotiations" (Yankey & Willen, 2005, p. 270). The absence of trust is likely to bring all the obstacles to successful collaboration up to maximum strength. It will exacerbate fears about the impact of collaboration or merger on individual positions and careers and cause some to question the shared commitment to mission. Open communication is, of course, a core element of trust. This includes the sharing of objective data and disclosure of liabilities or problems that could surface in later phases of the relationship. Trust may be greater between organizations that have had a previous relationship with one another, that have had successful collaborations with others, that are part of the same professional or information network, and that have linkages at the level of the governing board (Guo & Acar, 2005).

Relatedness

McCormick (2001) says that "mergers appear to work better when the parties involved can find an initial connection built on some tangible relationship" in one of four categories of relatedness: mission, constituency, organization or structure, and geography (p. 21). Although his principles apply to mergers, they could apply as well to any level of collaboration.

Creating a relationship may make sense if two or more organizations have compatible missions and may be illogical if the missions are very different. For example, it might be difficult for an organization focused on women's health to merge with one concerned with men's health; their expertise would likely be related to different diseases, and their funding sources would likely be those with a particular interest in one gender or the other. But a health organization seeking to extend its programs into schools might find it useful to collaborate or merge with an educational organization (McCormick, 2001).

Two organizations that operate in similar ways might find it advantageous and natural to work together. For example, two nonprofits that both raise funds primarily through direct mail might find it beneficial to combine lists or mail operations. In South Carolina, a group of nonprofits that were all raising funds through golf tournaments found that they were dividing up the population of golfers. So they merged their tournaments into one that, with higher fees, produced more revenue than their individual efforts combined (McCormick, 2001).

Organizations that serve the same or similar constituencies may have rather obvious opportunities to combine efforts, but, as McCormick (2001) emphasizes, *constituency relatedness* needs to be considered in broad terms. Thus, two advocacy organizations that lobby the same individuals or agencies may find it beneficial to combine efforts, since "in seeking political clout, bigger is definitely better" (p. 25). So, for example, two nonprofits that lobby for environmental legislation, each having 1 million members, might get more attention from the Congress by presenting themselves under one banner representing 2 million member voters.

Geographic proximity may suggest the potential for collaboration or merger, perhaps eliminating confusion among clients or donors. Such relationships also may be a strategy by which a nonprofit can extend its reach into new markets, perhaps contiguous cities, towns, or regions (McCormick, 2001). In sum, collaborations and mergers that have a natural logic to them are more likely to succeed than those that are forced or contrived.

Process

Research indicates that successful nonprofit collaboration requires sufficient time to develop and that following the right process is critical. Indeed, "the process through which the [relationship] is developed and operationalized has a significant impact on the likelihood of its success" (Yankey & Willen, 2005, p. 269).

Various scholars have described a process for the development of relationships through stages. While their vocabulary differs, most identify the following steps:

- Self-examination on the part of at least one organization, sometimes conducted in connection with a strategic planning process
- A decision to explore the possibility of collaboration
- Identification of potential partners, perhaps using the four criteria of relatedness discussed above
- Initial contacts between representatives of the organizations, perhaps initially limited to the CEOs or selected board members
- Efforts to assess the degree of mutual interest
- A *side-by-side analysis*—"a multi-faceted analysis of the potential partner's background, current situation, and future potential" (Yankey & Willen, 2005, p. 263)
- Negotiation and the development of agreements.
- Implementation

Source: Adapted from Yankey and Willen (2005, pp. 262–265).

As Gammal (2007) concludes in reporting research by the Stanford Project on the Evolution of Nonprofits,

> Our findings suggest that nonprofits need to . . . budget a lot more time and get to know each other a lot better before walking down the aisle. Otherwise, they may face the fates of many couples who rush to the altar: unhappy marriages or costly divorces. (p. 47)

Collaboration and Mergers Within National Nonprofits

The discussion in this chapter so far has emphasized collaboration or merger between or among nonprofit organizations that previously were legally independent. These are called *intermergers*. Combining units within a single corporate entity—for example, the consolidation of local chapters of a national organization—are called *intramergers* (McCormick, 2001, p. 2). Many of the same principles apply in either case.

National nonprofits with local chapters follow one of two principal organizational forms, which will affect the ease or difficulty with which collaborations and mergers may be undertaken. Some exist as a single corporation under one charter; chapters are essentially local branches or offices of the national organization. For example, the American Red Cross is a single organization governed by a single national board, and local chapters are accountable to the national office. Some governing authority has been delegated to local boards, but chapter assets are owned by the national organization and chapter executives ultimately report through channels to the national president. Other nonprofits are federations; local chapters have separate charters and are governed by independent boards. They may be required to follow prescribed policies and practices developed by the national office for the right to use the organization's name and logo, and they may pay dues to the national office in exchange for services provided to the chapters, but they also have considerable autonomy. This is the structure of a number of national disease-related organizations—for example, the Crohn's and Colitis Foundation, the American Lung Association, and the Arthritis Foundation. It is also the structure of some human services and environmental organizations, including Goodwill Industries.

While national nonprofits that operate under a single corporate charter have the formal authority to bring about collaboration and mergers among their chapters, there nevertheless may be obstacles similar to those complicating such efforts among independent organizations. Issues about turf, ego, culture, and the allocation of resources are still relevant. In 2006, the American Red Cross's national governing board approved a major reorganization that would create a "hub and spoke" system with "hundreds of smaller chapters [being moved] under the purview of the 200 largest chapters," with the larger chapters assuming responsibility for the smaller chapters' administrative expenses. In effect, what was proposed was "a de facto form of merger of a number of Red Cross chapters" (Salmon, 2006, p. A27). The initiative provoked controversy among chapter leaders, some of whom walked out of the board meeting at which it was approved. Some executives of chapters that would gain responsibility questioned how they would be able to manage their own chapters while also providing oversight for others. Some chapters in wealthier communities resisted taking on the financial liabilities of those in less affluent communities. A number of smaller chapters resisted the loss of their autonomy and cited the importance of maintaining a local base of financial support (Salmon, 2006).

Mergers of chapters within a federated organization are, of course, not intramergers but rather intermergers, since the local organizations have independent charters. Lacking the authority to impose mergers, the national office may face significant resistance that is difficult to overcome. For example, several affiliates of the American Lung Association severed their ties with the national organization in 2007 over their displeasure with a plan to consolidate 78 state and local affiliates into 11 regional organizations. Some adopted new names to be free of control by the national association (Schwinn, 2007).

Individuals may be more inclined to support organizations with which they are involved and that have impact they can observe in their own lives. For a national organization endeavoring to consolidate its local or regional chapters, the challenge is to gain the efficiency and effectiveness that consolidation may offer, while preserving the willingness of local volunteers and donors to participate and continue providing financial and other forms of support.

Transparency and policies on the sharing of revenue between national and local offices can help create incentives for cooperation and make the system work to the best advantage of all component entities. Nevertheless, such efforts often meet with resistance. Local chapters may be concerned that the national office will encroach on their traditional donors or alienate them through excessively aggressive contacts. Some in the national office may be concerned about sharing information on major donor prospects with their local colleagues based on a presumption that they are not as skilled in fund-raising. Others may be concerned that the centralization of donor records will be a first step toward greater control by the national office that will eventually undermine their autonomy in other areas (Wallace, 2005).

But systems have been devised to address these potential problems. For example, Habitat for Humanity appointed major gift officers to work in local chapters with a dual responsibility to raise funds for the chapters as well as for Habitat for Humanity International. The historical mistrust of local chapters toward the national office was overcome in part by developing a centralized database to which the fund-raisers would post contact reports of their visits as well as their strategies for developing other prospects. That enabled both the national office and the local chapter to be fully aware of what the gift officers were discussing with prospects and how their efforts were divided between the two levels of the organization. In addition, both the national office and local chapters participated in the selection of the major gift officers (Wallace, 2010).

It is, of course, impossible to predict the course of the economy or what the circumstances will be a year or more after the time of this writing. The economy will likely improve and return ultimately to a higher level of prosperity. But pressures for nonprofits to collaborate and merge are not likely to totally abate. Continued encouragement from funders, increased competition for resources, and the nation's focus on performance and accountability are likely to make complete independence less tenable for smaller and decentralized organizations and to increase the potential benefits to be gained through collaboration. However, as cases discussed in this chapter illustrate, there is also a need to ensure that relationships between and among organizations are well considered and that mission remains paramount. Those driven *exclusively* by financial considerations may find that the human and financial costs ultimately exceed the gains and that missions may be diluted or lost, to the detriment of the organizations and society.

Chapter Summary

A nonprofit organization's capacity includes all of the resources it uses to pursue its mission. Capacity building refers to efforts that are undertaken to strengthen the organization in order to make it more effective in achieving its mission. Capacity includes an organization's internal systems, such as people, processes, and infrastructure, as well as its external relationships with funders, partners, volunteers, and others. Many observers have argued that historically nonprofits have focused on delivering services rather than building the organization and that the funding practices of foundations and others reinforced that inclination by failing to provide support for capacity building. These critiques have led to an increased interest in capacity building, which reached the proportions of a "movement" during the 2000s. Capacity building remains important to many organizations. Most such efforts are funded through organizations' internal resources.

An organization's capacity is not an indivisible quality; rather, there are various elements of capacity—or capacities—that it might concentrate on strengthening. There are tools for identifying components of capacity that need to be strengthened and models for undertaking such activity. Some theorists describe life cycles of nonprofit organizations. The type of capacity building that is needed differs at various stages. Whether capacity building increases organizational effectiveness remains a debated question.

With the growth in the number of nonprofits in recent decades, and especially with the onset of an economic recession in 2007, there has been an increased emphasis on collaboration and mergers among nonprofits, in order to reduce inefficiencies and increase the capacity and impact of the sector overall. Funders, including government bodies and foundations, have been visible among those calling for such consolidation. However, some observers argue that funders have contributed to the problem and that small nonprofits may better provide more personal attention to clients.

Collaboration is a continuum of relationships; it may include informal cooperation, such as sharing information and referring clients, or more formal relationships, in which the organizations are legally committed to each other, as in joint programs or joint ventures. A *merger* is a combining of two or more organizations that includes a change in legal control. There are *intermergers,* combinations of previously independent organizations, and *intramergers,* which are consolidations of chapters or units within a single legal entity. Obstacles to collaboration and merger include the distinctive motivations of nonprofit entities; organizational cultures that may be resistant to change; the egos of the individuals involved, especially founders; and the costs, in time and money, of the study, planning, and negotiations required. Successful collaborations and mergers are driven primarily by mission, rather than just financial benefits. Other conditions needed for success include support from the board and CEO, an appropriate process, trust, and relatedness. *Relatedness* means that there is a logic to the relationship based on mission, constituency, organization or structure, or geography.

Pressures to collaborate and merge are unlikely to abate as nonprofits face an increasingly competitive environment and there is a nationwide focus on performance and accountability. It is important that mission remain paramount and that such relationships not be based entirely on potential financial gains.

KEY TERMS AND CONCEPTS

adaptive capacity	*intermerger*	*program expansion capacity*
capacity	*intramerger*	*strategic alliances*
capacity building	*life cycle*	*strategic restructuring*
collaboration	*life stages*	*venture philanthropy*
corporate integrations	*merger*	
drivers	*program delivery capacity*	

CASE 8.1   Change at the Girl Scouts of America

When Kathy Cloninger arrived as CEO of the Girl Scouts of America in 2003, she joined an organization with a long and distinguished history but one better known for its cookie sales than for its programs to develop girls as future leaders. Founded in 1912 by Juliette Gordon Low with an original troop of 18, the organization had grown to include 2.7 million girl members and nearly 1 million adult volunteers. Although it was a stable and respected organization, the Girl Scouts nevertheless had developed an image as "musty and uncool" and faced several significant challenges (LaBarre, 2006).

First, membership in Girl Scout troops had declined over the previous 5 years, and there were reasons to be concerned about the future. Social trends, including more mothers having careers, were making it more difficult to attract volunteers. A greater range of available activities for girls was presenting increased competition for their time, attention, and participation. Registration for individual programs and events across the country had increased significantly in recent years, but Cloninger determined that the delivery of programs was fragmented and that the quality of the experience being provided to girls and volunteers was uneven across the country.

Some of the challenges were rooted in the Girl Scouts' organizational structure. The national office, based in New York, provided service to the local councils, and overall policy and direction were established by a national council of about 2,000 elected delegates, who met every 3 years. But local Girl Scout councils were relatively autonomous, and they had their own operating budgets, boards, and staff. Given the decentralized culture of the organization, the relationship between the national office and local councils was sometimes uneasy, with some local councils resistant to centralized direction or control.

In this model, population trends were creating disparities at the local level, with some councils able to fund innovative programs and others struggling to serve their dwindling memberships with inadequate resources. There were 312 councils. Sixty were on the brink of failure. The largest 20 percent were serving 50 percent of the membership, and the smallest 20 percent were serving just 5 percent of the members (LaBarre, 2006, p. 49).

Cloninger determined that incremental changes would not be sufficient and that the 90-year-old organization needed transformation. The last major reorganization of the Girl Scouts had occurred in the 1950s. It was a top-down process that met resistance from local councils and required 20 years to complete (Hrywna, 2007). Cloninger knew that it would need to be done differently this time.

She began by creating a 26-person core strategy team, including not just individuals from the national office but a diverse group encompassing staff, volunteers and board leaders, and CEOs of local councils. This core group was given 6 months, from June to December 2004, to draft a new mission statement and identify strategic priorities. This led to the creation of six "gap teams," so called because their charge was to help in "bridging the gap between Girl Scouts today and Girl Scouts of the future" (Girls Scouts website, http://girlscouts.org/strategy/gap_team.asp). With even more diverse and broadly representative membership than the core strategy team, the gap teams were to focus on key areas with specific assignments:

Program model and pathways: Build the best integrated personal/leadership development model that defines activities and outcomes, differentiated by age level, for girls 5 to 17, and offers flexible pathways for participation.

Volunteerism: Develop a nimble state-of-the-art model of volunteerism that mobilizes a diverse cadre of volunteers committed to the Girl Scout mission.

Brand: Transform the Girl Scout image into a compelling, contemporary brand.

Funding: Substantially increase contributed income.

(Continued)

(Continued)

Governance and organizational structure: Create an efficient and effective organizational structure and democratic governance system.

Culture: Lead the transformation of our culture, which is a key component of the broader transformation of Girl Scouting. (http://girlscouts.org/strategy/gap_team.asp)

The gap teams were given a firm deadline. Their work had to be completed by the time of the Girl Scouts' 50th National Convention in October 2005. Demographers were retained to support the work of the gap teams by developing data to show population trends and reveal the disparities among councils in different areas. Cloninger launched a massive communications effort, meeting with council CEOs, visiting troops, and setting up websites to report on progress. When the national convention arrived, delegates were given multiple opportunities to provide their input on the plan. Six "strategy cafes" permitted focused discussion with each of the gap teams, and a large open discussion was held on the question of governance. When the time came for a vote, the new mission statement and strategy were approved by an overwhelming majority.

Then the hard work began. Cloninger created a process to restructure the headquarters staff. She continued intensive communication and a participative approach, asking staff for their suggestions on a new structure and revised job descriptions. The realignment of local councils was an even more sensitive matter. This would require mergers, a reduction in CEO positions, and a loss of autonomy for some small councils. A pilot program including 37 "early adopters" was initiated (Hrywna, 2007). By 2009, the 312 councils had been reduced to just over 100. What will be the results of the change? Cloninger emphasizes that the transformation of the Girl Scouts is about much more than the realignment of councils. "There will be cost savings," Cloninger says, "but we did not go into it because of financial issues or troubles. We went in thinking about what structure would give us capacity." She adds, "We're developing a very girl-driven model, rewriting programs, really putting our program out there in a whole new arena packaged around leadership" (quoted in Hrywna, 2007, p. 2). The realignment of councils is "just one of many pieces" of the organization's transformation. Linda Foreman, the national secretary of the national board, makes the same point—reorganization was just one of several strategic priorities, but it was the change that needed to be undertaken in order to gain the capacity to achieve other goals: "This was a very complex . . . learning process that ended up with five priorities," she explains. "But when looking at volunteerism, brand, funding, and program, it became clear we probably needed to address the structural piece first. Realignment in my mind is about positioning ourselves to be able to deliver on all the rest of it" (Hrywna, 2007, p. 4).

Reflecting on the process of change, Cloninger speaks frankly:

It's very messy. It can't but impact the culture and some people leave and new people are coming in, so it's pretty chaotic. But you can't get sidetracked by angst over the fact that things aren't perfect. This isn't a two-year plan with a finish line—it's a transforming strategy. It's going to be hard and we'll make mistakes, but we're in it for the long haul. (LaBarre, 2006, p. 50)

QUESTIONS FOR DISCUSSION

1. Read the case of the Girl Scouts and consider the following questions:

   (a) At what point in its organizational life cycle did Kathy Cloninger join the Girl Scouts? What might have happened if the organization had not gone through a transformation?

   (b) How do the six strategic priorities identified by the Girl Scouts fit into the capacity elements identified by Connolly and Lukas?

(c) Did the change process at the Girl Scouts follow Kotter's model of change leadership discussed in Chapter 5?

(d) Did Cloninger's approach follow the McKinsey capacity-building model?

(e) How was Cloninger's approach to change influenced by the culture of the Girl Scouts organization?

(f) How does the case of the Girl Scouts reveal elements of the strategic planning process discussed in Chapter 7?

(g) What obstacles to successful mergers and what conditions for success (as discussed in this chapter) were illustrated in the case of the Girl Scouts?

2. How is McKinsey's capacity-building model discussed in this chapter similar to the strategic planning model discussion in Chapter 7? How is it different?

3. In deciding whether to recognize the tax-exempt status of a new nonprofit, should the Internal Revenue Service consider whether or not it will duplicate the services of other, existing organizations in its community? Why or why not?

SUGGESTIONS FOR FURTHER READING

Books

Crutchfield, L. R., & Grant, H. M. (2008). *Forces for good: The six practices of high-impact nonprofits.* San Francisco: Jossey-Bass.

Grantmakers for Effective Organizations. (2004). *Funding effectiveness: Lessons in building nonprofit capacity.* San Francisco: Jossey-Bass.

Kee, J. E., & Newcomer, K. (2008). *Transforming public and nonprofit organizations: Stewardship for leading change.* Vienna, VA: Management Concepts, Inc.

Kohm, A., & La Piana, D. (2003). *Strategic restructuring for nonprofit organizations: Mergers, integrations, and alliances.* Westport, CT: Praeger.

La Piana, D. (2008). *The nonprofit strategy revolution: Real-time strategic planning in a rapid-response world.* Saint Paul, MN: Fieldstone Alliance.

Light, P. C. (2004). *Sustaining nonprofit performance: The case for capacity building and the evidence to support it.* Washington, DC: Brookings Institution.

McKinsey & Company. (2001). *Effective capacity building in nonprofit organizations.* Washington, DC: Venture Philanthropy Partners. (Available at http://venturephilanthropypartners.org/learning/reports/capacity/capacity.html)

McLaughlin, T. A. (2010). *Nonprofits mergers and alliances: A strategic planning guide.* New York: Wiley.

Websites

Alliance for Nonprofit Management, http://www.allianceonline.org/

Capaciteria (a searchable database of capacity-building resources), http://www.capaciteria.org/

Grantmakers for Effective Organizations, http://www.geofunders.org/

LaPiana Consulting, http://www.lapiana.org/

Venture Philanthropy Partners, http://venturephilanthropypartners.org/

Chapter Outline

chapter 9

Volunteers are a major component of the workforce of many nonprofits.
©Jupiterimages/Photos.com/Getty Images

Managing Paid Staff and Service Volunteers

9

C hapter 5 discussed how nonprofit chief executives provide leadership to their organizations. Some of the theories considered there also help inform how managers lead the individuals who work with and for them, including the organization's staff and volunteers. This chapter takes a closer look at some theories that help explain the motivations of staff and volunteers and specific practices based on those theories that experts recommend to ensure a productive workforce.

It is important to distinguish between volunteers who serve as members of a nonprofit's governing board and volunteers who help provide its programs and services—for example, individuals who prepare food for the homeless or ill, tutor children, bring relief to the victims of disasters, or guide Boy Scout and Girl Scout troops and other youth organizations as unpaid leaders. The latter, sometimes termed *service volunteers,* are the focus of this chapter. The management of service volunteers is considered in this chapter along with the management of staff members because in many organizations they work alongside staff, perform similar functions, and require similar management approaches. The management of volunteers and volunteer programs is an essential component of nonprofit management in many nonprofit organizations.

The discussion in this chapter blends theory and the recommendations of practitioner-oriented authors, addressing questions such as the following: What does management theory and research tell us about human motivation, especially in the workplace? Are nonprofit staff members motivated in the same way as those who work in for-profit environments, or are there differences that need to be understood? Are there differences in the motivations of paid staff and volunteers? What practices should nonprofit managers use to organize and direct staff members and volunteers in ways consistent with their motivations and needs and that also will lead to optimum performance?

An Overview of Management Theories

Management theory is not static. Theories are advanced and sometimes gain wide acceptance for a period of years. As scholars test them through research, they may find that the theories do not provide adequate explanations. Some theories thus pass into the dustbin of academic history. But often some of their principles are taken forward and incorporated into new theories.

Other theories, even though challenged by research, have an intuitive appeal for managers and take hold in the conventional wisdom, despite evidence of their shortcomings. If there were one accepted approach to management, perhaps there would be need for only one management book, but a survey of any bookstore will reveal that such is not the situation. In other words, management theory remains unsettled territory, although many theories, both old and new, offer at least some insights that may inform practice. This chapter discusses just a few theories relevant to the topic of staff and volunteer management. Students should recognize in advance that almost all of them have critics as well as adherents.

One influential management theorist of the early 20th century was Frederick W. Taylor, whose approach, developed in industrial settings, became known as *scientific management*. Taylor saw organizations as operating much like machines and emphasized procedures and systems rather than human motivations and relationships. Much of his research involved "time-and-motion" studies in factories, with the purpose of increasing efficiency—in other words, finding ways to have people operate more like machines. Taylor's views were controversial even at the time, and they were later overtaken by entirely new approaches.

A series of experiments conducted in the 1920s at the Hawthorne plant of the Western Electric Company had a profound influence on thinking about management. Among other findings, the experiments suggested that the mere attention of supervisors had an influence on the performance of workers. That suggested that social and psychological factors might be important in creating a more productive workforce. Although the Hawthorne experiments have been controversial right from the beginning, they provided "pathbreaking illustrations of the influence of social and psychological factors on work behavior" (Rainey, 2003, p. 32). Management theory continues to evolve, but it has not returned to the era of Taylor, in which humans were viewed as cogs in the industrial machine. The shift in attention from the rules and mechanics of the workplace to an emphasis on human motivations and attitudes was a lasting change in our understanding and perspective. It is reflected in most contemporary work.

Understanding Human Motivations

Theories about human motivation are of practical importance. Every manager holds some theory about motivation, even if only implicitly. What a manager may believe about human nature will dictate how he or she interacts with people, seeks to motivate them, and addresses disappointments with their performance. Many people have known great bosses, who inspired loyalty and created a pleasant, productive working environment, and perhaps also screamer bosses, whose demands, rants, and insults created a dysfunctional workplace. Such differences may in fact reflect the psychology of the manager and his or her own needs, but they likely also reflect the manager's theory of how other people operate. It is thus important for a manager to hold some explicit theory of human motivation, rather than just an implicit homegrown theory, perhaps developed through his or her own life experiences.

On of the most influential of motivation theorists was Abraham Maslow, who developed his principal concepts in the 1940s and 1950s. Although it has been challenged by some scholars, Maslow's (1954) theory had an important influence on later thinking and has been the foundation for later work. For example, Burns's (1978) concept of transformational leadership, which we discussed in Chapter 5, draws substantially on Maslow's *hierarchy of needs*.

As the term *hierarchy* implies, Maslow's (1954) theory states that human needs progress from those at lower levels to those at higher levels as the lower-level needs are met. Human beings strive to meet their lower-level needs before addressing those in higher categories. In the lowest category—that is, at the bottom of the hierarchy—are basic physiological needs. Any student who has tried to study while hungry will readily recognize that it is difficult to focus on higher pursuits until more immediate needs are addressed. But once the basics such as food, drink, and shelter are met, people can turn their attention to meeting their higher-level needs. The next steps up the hierarchy include safety needs; social needs; self-esteem needs; and, finally, self-actualization needs. Thus, once human beings have met their physiological needs, they may focus on safety. (A hungry person would take risks to obtain food or drink; in other words, those basic needs would outweigh the desire for safety.) Once individuals feel safe, they are then able to focus on meeting their needs for the camaraderie and affection of others and on meeting needs that satisfy their own egos and build their self-esteem. At the top of the hierarchy, self-actualization encompasses the need for self-fulfillment and achievement commensurate with one's ultimate capacity. People motivated at this level are the self-starters so often described as ideal candidates in job advertisements. They are in essence free to pursue their goals for fulfillment and achievement by having met lower-level needs.

Another way to understand Maslow's (1954) hierarchy is to think about how people might descend to lower-level needs under certain adverse circumstances. For example, someone engaged in fulfilling his or her ego and self-actualization needs might retreat to address lower-level needs if faced with a threat to safety or nourishment. For example, a person in fear of losing his or her job may not be thinking much about taking art classes to expand his or her creativity; that person's attention probably will be focused on the essential need to remain employed. The person also may not be thinking much about how to bring innovation to his or her job—he or she will probably stick with the basics. But someone who feels safe in his or her employment and life may be able to reach farther up the hierarchy to address such higher-level needs.

How does this play out in the workplace? Maslow's (1954) theory helps us understand that human beings have their own psychological needs that they bring to the workplace from other aspects of their lives. They may be highly motivated to address whatever needs they have, regardless of what practices the manager may follow. That insight is an essential one for any realistic manager to grasp.

Another influential theorist, who wrote in the 1960s, was Douglas McGregor. McGregor (1960) is known for his definitions of Theory X and Theory Y. *Theory X,* which McGregor saw reflected in management practices in most industrial organizations, is based on the assumption that workers are lazy, resistant to change, and not concerned with the organization's needs. It is basically a negative view of human nature and might be used to justify an approach something like Taylor's scientific management. Someone who subscribes to *Theory Y,* on the other hand, views employees as capable of self-motivation and self-direction. A manager holding that theory of human behavior would likely give individuals more autonomy, decentralize responsibility, and seek to unleash human potential. If a manager subscribes to Theory Y, he or she might be more inclined toward the transformational approach to leadership, which was discussed in Chapter 5.

David McClelland, also writing in the 1960s, explained that it is not only workers who have needs that affect their behavior in the workplace. Managers have their own psychological needs, too, which influence how they behave with regard to their subordinates. McClelland (1961) identified three principal needs of managers: the need for achievement, the need for power over others, and the need for affiliation or good relationships with others. McClelland's theories stimulated a large body of follow-up research and the development of instruments to measure managers' needs. Its standing today is mixed, with some still supporting it and others criticizing it harshly (Rainey, 2003). But, like Maslow, McClelland helped us recognize that managers, like all human beings, do not come to the workplace as empty canisters; they come with their own psychological needs and may behave at work in a way that helps address them.

Katharine Cook Briggs and her daughter Isabel Briggs Myers made an important contribution to management by developing a tool known as the Myers-Briggs-type indicator, which is widely used in the workplace today. Myers-Briggs and other similar instruments are used to reveal *personality style,* which "refers to the manner in which individuals gather and process information" (Denhardt et al., 2009). Based on the theories of the psychologist Carl Jung, personality tests like Myers-Briggs are used to provide individuals with insights about their own perspectives and preferences, which may help them understand their own behavior and that of others with whom they work. Perhaps the best-known distinction made by Myers-Briggs is that between introverts and extroverts, although it measures personality in many additional dimensions.

Like most theories, those of Frederick Herzberg, first described in the late 1960s, have been challenged by other researchers. However, his findings are still widely cited and have implications for the management of nonprofit staff and volunteers that are interesting to consider. Herzberg conducted studies in which he claimed to identify two sets of factors that influence motivation. He called them *motivators* and *hygiene factors,* but they are also sometimes called *satisfiers* and *dissatisfiers.* Table 9.1 shows both sets of factors. According to Herzberg (1968), there is a big difference between them. The *absence* of hygiene factors can lead to dissatisfaction, but they cannot be used in a positive way to *motivate* people. Only the motivators can do that. This implies that managers should design work to reduce dissatisfiers and increase motivators in the environment of the workplace.

To understand Herzberg's (1968) theory, students may find it useful to think about their own work or volunteer experience and what they find to be satisfying or intolerable in specific cases. Looking at the right-hand column of Table 9.1, dissatisfaction with a job can be caused by the frustrations that derive from company policy or administration—for example, the mindless bureaucracy reflected in Dilbert cartoons. Dissatisfaction may arise from poor interpersonal relationships with a supervisor or peer or from physical working conditions that do not provide safety and security. (Remember Maslow's [1954] hierarchy!) A tyrannical or incompetent boss, petty colleagues, or an unclean and unsafe work environment are reasons that might cause most

TABLE 9.1   ■   Herzberg's Motivators (Satisfiers) and Hygiene Factors (Dissatisfiers)

Motivators (Satisfiers) (Related to the job and to motivation)	Hygiene Factors (Dissatisfiers) (Related to the environment)
Achievement	Company policies and administration
Recognition	Relations with supervisor
The work itself	Interpersonal relations with coworkers
Advancement	Working conditions
Growth	Compensation
Responsibility	Status and security

Source: Adapted from Herzberg (1968).

people to go home discouraged and start looking for alternative employment. Students will note that compensation—that is, salary, benefits, and other financial rewards—appears on the list of dissatisfiers and not as a motivator. Let's return to that interesting point in a moment.

Take a look at the left-hand side of Table 9.1, a list of Herzberg's (1968) motivators. People who participated in his studies described the factors that motivated them at work as including achievement and recognition, opportunities for advancement, opportunities for greater responsibility and personal growth, and the inherent rewards of certain types of work. For example, tutoring children might be an inherently rewarding activity, as opposed to, let's say, slaughtering pigs. If that work is also carried out in an environment that provides the other motivators, the job may prove very satisfying, unless some dissatisfiers from the right-hand column get in the way. If the dissatisfiers are present at significant levels, even rewarding work may not be enough to compensate for the aggravation, and people may become unmotivated and perhaps inclined to look for other places to spend their working hours.

What about money? It may seem counterintuitive to many people that salary appears in Herzberg's (1968) theory not as a motivator but rather as a potential dissatisfier. After all, do not many companies, and an increasing number of nonprofits, offer financial incentives to encourage higher performance? That practice suggests an underlying theory that people are motivated in a positive way by the opportunity to make a greater income. But then, how do we explain the fact that many nonprofit staff members work for less income than they could earn in the for-profit sector and yet are highly motivated in their jobs? Or that volunteers work for no financial compensation at all? And, we might wonder, how many people would be inclined to leave a job they love for a job they hate only because it pays more money?

If the wage is so low that it isn't livable or if an employee feels that he or she is not paid what his or her effort is worth, that may be a source of dissatisfaction. If the employee believes that others, within the organization or elsewhere, are being paid more for the same work, that sense of unfairness may be dissatisfying. But ensuring that salaries are fair, and at least sufficient, may be more important than the level of compensation per se. Sufficient and fair may be enough to remove money as a cause of dissatisfaction. If Herzberg (1968) is right, as long as those standards are met, more money may not produce greater motivation. Motivation comes from the factors on the left-hand side of Table 9.1.

Again, it is important to recognize that many scholars have challenged Herzberg's (1968) findings. But his theory seems consistent with what we observe in many nonprofit organizations, so it has some intuitive appeal. Even though paid staff often are paid less than their counterparts in the for-profit world and volunteers are, by definition, unpaid in financial terms, many will find their work very rewarding if Herzberg's motivators are present. Since they do not expect to receive the same salaries that are paid in some for-profit companies, they are not dissatisfied by their nonprofit incomes so long as they are at least adequate and perceived as fair. This perspective has many implications for management practice. If managers can design jobs and create working environments in a way that provides their staff and volunteers with opportunities for achievement, recognition, advancement, and growth, and if the nature of the work is inherently rewarding, staff and volunteers may be highly motivated even within the limits of nonprofits' financial constraints.

A study of nonprofit workers conducted by the Princeton Survey Research Associates and supervised by the Brookings Institution provides further insight on the motivations of nonprofit staff members that are consistent with Herzberg's (1968) theory. The study found that nonprofit workers are indeed driven by mission rather than money. Only 16 percent of nonprofit staff surveyed said that they come to work for their pay, compared with 31 percent of federal employees and 47 percent of for-profit employees. More than 70 percent of nonprofit workers reported that they were satisfied with their pay. Other sources of satisfaction reported were flexibility, collaborative decision making, and being treated as well-rounded human beings rather than just workers. Most sources of dissatisfaction reported were related to ineffective supervision, overwork and burnout, or inadequate resources with which to work. The positives and the negatives sound much like Herzberg's two sets of factors (Joslyn, 2002, p. 1).

It could even be argued that nonprofits have an advantage over for-profit companies in motivating their workforces. Their sometimes limited financial resources do not prevent them from eliminating most of the potential dissatisfiers or increasing most of the Herzberg (1968) motivators. In addition, many offer work that is inherently rewarding because it is tied to a social purpose and the improvement or enrichment of human lives, something that only some, but not all, for-profit companies can offer. If nonprofit managers keep their staff and volunteers focused on the nonprofit's mission, they may keep them highly motivated.

There are many additional theories of motivation that this chapter does not discuss in detail. Students with an interest in this area should explore them in some of the resources suggested for further reading at the end of the chapter. An important group of theories goes under the rubric of *expectancy theory*. These theories describe how individuals make decisions based on their expectations about the likely outcomes. They do things that they believe have a high probability of a good outcome and avoid actions that they expect to lead to bad outcomes. Some theorists (e.g., Vroom, 1964) have devised algebraic formulas to describe this type of decision-making process. Other theories have been based on the research of B. F. Skinner, whose experiments measured the response of animals to stimuli. In basic terms, Skinner's (1953) principle of *operant conditioning* explains that we repeat behaviors that are rewarded and tend not to repeat those that are not. Important contributions to understanding also have come from social learning theory, as developed by Albert Bandura (1978) and others, and goal-setting theory, identified with the work of the psychologist Edwin Locke (2000). Much recent work has been devoted to attempts to integrate earlier theories. Some say that motivation theory is currently in a state of disarray, providing at best insights that offer partial explanations (Rainey, 2003, p. 268). However, most theories offer some useful insights that may help guide managers and increase their understanding of staff and volunteers.

Applying Theories to the Nonprofit Workforce

As noted at various points earlier in this book, the literature of nonprofit management includes both theory and the prescriptions of practitioner-oriented authors. This book attempts to integrate both perspectives. Now that we have reviewed some of the theoretical literature on human motivation, let's look at one attempt to translate that theory into specific recommended practices in managing the nonprofit workforce.

In the second edition of their book *Managing Human Behavior in Public and Nonprofit Organizations,* Denhardt et al. (2009, pp. 161–164) review the motivation literature and offer nine suggested "ways of acting" for nonprofit and public sector managers, which they found to reflect commonalities of the various theoretical approaches. The following paragraphs discuss each of their recommendations and how they may relate to the various theories discussed above.

1. *Managers should be reflective and proactive about their own motivation.* McClelland (1961) and other theorists have suggested that the manager's own needs and motivations affect

how he or she interacts with and communicates with colleagues and subordinates. This would imply that self-knowledge and understanding are essential for any individual who aspires to be an effective manager of others.

2. *Managers should be aware that what motivates them is not necessarily what will motivate others.* This advice is supported by several theories and reflects the simple but important understanding that people are not all alike. As Maslow (1954) and other theorists suggest, they bring their own needs to the workplace, which may reflect circumstances in their personal lives, their cultural backgrounds, or perhaps their preferred communication styles, reflecting their personality styles.

3. *Managers should have realistic expectations about the extent to which they can influence the motivation of others.* Again, as Maslow (1954) and other theorists explain, people come to the workplace already motivated. They are motivated to meet whatever psychological needs they may already have. The manager may not be able to influence those motivations very much. It may be more productive to assign people to jobs that enable them to meet their existing needs or perhaps redesign jobs to make them a better fit with the natural inclinations of those who hold them. Of course, if individuals' needs and motivations simply do not align with the goals of the organization, it may be best to suggest that they find employment in a more suitable environment. Too much effort to change the individuals may prove frustrating and fruitless.

4. *Managers should participate in setting clear and challenging goals.* As Herzberg (1968) discovered, the opportunity for achievement is a motivator for most individuals. But achievement requires that there be clear goals by which it is defined. Otherwise, effort yields no emotional reward, or a situation may evolve in which individuals feel that even "enough" is not sufficient to please their supervisors. The manager thus should establish goals in a participative manner so that the staff member accepts them as his or her own, provide regular feedback on progress, and grant recognition when the goals are reached.

As Letts et al. (1999a) observe, managers often face two challenges: getting the job done and keeping the staff satisfied. But they state, "Organizing jobs so employees can achieve and see results does both: It advances the organization's mission and motivates people in the process" (p. 108).

5. *Managers should think about the salience of various rewards.* Again, individuals are motivated differently. They have different values. And what they will find rewarding may be different in each case. A manager needs to listen, determine what each member of the staff finds important, and provide rewards consistent with that insight. Some may thrive on recognition— for example, being named "staff member of the week." Others may value the opportunity for flexible hours or to earn additional free time through outstanding performance. As Denhardt and colleagues (2009) emphasize, and as the Hawthorne experiments suggested so many years ago, the interest and attention of the manager may itself be a reward that will reinforce high performance for some members of the staff.

6. *Managers should be honest with people about what rewards are possible and what rewards are not.* As expectancy theory describes, individuals may be motivated not only by the value of rewards but also by the probability that they can be obtained. A manager who is unrealistic in promising increased compensation, increased responsibility, community recognition, or some other reward for achievement of goals may buy some short-term motivation. But over time, such a manager will lose credibility and the power to influence the behavior of his or her staff.

7. *Managers should treat people equitably and fairly.* People in a workplace have a sense of what is equitable, in terms of effort, compensation, status, and other matters. As Herzberg's (1968) theory suggests, inequities in salary paid to individuals who perform similar work or put forth comparable effort may create more dissatisfaction than compensation that is modest in absolute terms. Of course, no person should be treated unfairly for reasons of his or her race, nationality, gender, religion, lifestyle, disability, political perspective, or other personal characteristics or preferences. To do so is morally wrong and generally illegal. And it is just poor management, likely to result in a dysfunctional, dissatisfied, and unproductive workforce that will not build a high-performing organization.

Effective nonprofit organizations today go beyond the requirements of law and embrace diversity as an organizational value, seeking to draw the strength that comes from bringing together people of different perspectives, experiences, cultures, and backgrounds. In our complex society, any organization that does not incorporate such diversity will quickly lose touch with its community and constituency and, by excluding important talent, weaken its ability to serve its mission and achieve its goals.

8. *Managers should make the work satisfying and meaningful.* Motivation arises not only from the characteristics of people but also from the nature of the work they are given to perform. As Herzberg (1968) observed, some work is intrinsically motivating. But routine tasks may become monotonous and dissatisfying. Even interesting work may become less interesting if it is unchanging over time. Good managers provide their staff members with opportunities to grow personally and professionally, to take on new challenges, and to develop new skills in a variety of areas. This may be accomplished by rotating assignments or redesigning jobs, by providing training, and by offering opportunities for advancement from within the organization. Those who are employed in nonprofits are usually motivated by the impact of their work on the lives of clients. It is good practice to provide staff with as much exposure to clients as possible, enabling them to see firsthand the outcomes of their efforts.

9. *Managers should think about the life stages of the people they work with and offer appropriate support.* There are various life–stage theories that describe the needs and motivations of people in various periods and positions. Such theories do have many critics, but they suggest that understanding the issues facing individuals in their personal lives may provide the manager with a useful perspective that is of benefit both to the individual and to the organization. It is also an approach that creates a humane environment consistent with the values of most nonprofit organizations.

Managing Volunteers

The discussion in the previous section of this chapter was focused primarily on the management of nonprofit staff members. Let's now shift our discussion to look at some principles that apply specifically to managing service volunteers.

Effective management of volunteers is an important topic because volunteers are a major component of the workforce of many nonprofits. "Volunteering in America," a report published by the Corporation for National and Community Service, estimates that on average over the years 2006–2008, more than 61 million Americans engaged in volunteer service, providing over 8 billion hours of service. In early 2009, President Barack Obama signed the Edward M. Kennedy Serve America Act, intended to triple the number of volunteers working in AmeriCorps, a national service program, by 2017. The act also authorized funds to support nonprofit organizations' capacity building related to the coordination, training, and management of volunteers (Independent Sector, 2009b). Interestingly, while giving declined in the economic recession year of 2009, the number of volunteers serving grew significantly to include 63.4 million Americans, representing nearly 27 percent of the population (Blum, 2010).

Adults aged 35 to 54 are the most likely to volunteer, with more than 31 percent doing so in 2006 compared with only 18 percent of people in their early twenties. In general, women are more likely to be volunteers than men, and this is true across all age groups, educational levels, and other characteristics (Bureau of Labor Statistics, 2008).

The service of volunteers is of enormous economic importance to nonprofit organizations and to society. Independent Sector (2010) estimates that each hour of volunteer time contributed to nonprofits in 2008 was worth $20.25; that is an average of what organizations would have needed to pay to obtain similar services from paid staff—not an inconsequential sum. It is important to note, however, that individuals cannot claim a tax deduction for the value of their volunteered time. A nonprofit organization can cite the value of volunteer services in its communications, to demonstrate wide community support or for purposes of recognizing volunteers like donors. However, there are limitations on how that value can be used on nonprofit financial statements. According to rules established by the Financial Accounting Standards Board (1993), the value of volunteer work can be used on financial statements, in grant proposals, and in other formal ways only if the volunteers are providing specialized services for which the nonprofit would otherwise have paid. That might include, for example, services of accountants, architects, doctors, and similar professionals.

As O'Neill (2002) observes, "Nonprofits differ greatly with regard to the role of volunteers." Most nonprofits are small, all-volunteer efforts. Many nonprofits with paid staff also rely heavily on volunteers. Others, such as research institutes, universities, and private foundations, use few volunteers (p. 31). Recent decades have seen the increased professionalization of nonprofit management, with paid staff replacing volunteers in some organizations, especially the largest and most commercialized. Today, volunteers often work alongside paid staff, and volunteer management has itself become a specialty of professional nonprofit management.

There are different types of volunteers, characterized by the pattern of their participation, the extent of their commitment, and their motivations. For example, Shin and Kleiner (2003) identify three types. One is what the authors call the *spot volunteer,* whose participation is casual and episodic. For example, an individual may respond to a call for volunteers to help clean up a park or a hiking trail—it is a one-day commitment and there is likely enough work to occupy as many people as show up. The effort may not need to be repeated again, at least for some period of time, and there is no special skill required to participate.

A second type is the *regular volunteer,* who makes a commitment to the activity and gains a sense of gratification and accomplishment from the work. Such volunteer assignments may have the formality of regular paid jobs; there may be job descriptions, clear statements of responsibilities, and specific skills required to perform the work. Continuity may be important; for example, those who participate in tutoring programs need to be present in every session in order to develop relationships and gain the trust of the children. In other situations, dependability is essential; for example, volunteer fire departments or disaster relief organizations cannot rely on whoever may choose to show up on a given occasion.

The third type of volunteer that Shin and Kleiner (2003) identify is someone who is *pressured to volunteer,* perhaps by an employer, a peer group, or an educational requirement. A significant number of corporations encourage their employees to engage in community service activities, as a strategy both for gaining goodwill for the company and for building camaraderie among the workforce. Many states require that high school students complete a volunteer experience as a graduation requirement. In addition, many professional education programs require that students complete an internship as a requirement of graduation. And of course, courts often assign first-time offenders of minor crimes to community service as a form of restitution. Although some may regard mandatory voluntarism, or even that performed under pressure, as an oxymoron, others speculate that the requirement of voluntary service for young people may be helpful in introducing them to the concept, perhaps beginning a commitment that they will continue throughout their lives.

Motivations of Volunteers

We need to consider the motivations of volunteers in two ways: first, in terms of what motivates people to become volunteers in the first place, and second, what factors motivate them to perform at a high level and continue in their volunteer roles.

Why do people volunteer in the first place? Since individuals have varied needs, there are a variety of reasons. Some—probably most, at least in part—are motivated by the mission of the nonprofit and by their personal values. They may volunteer because they have the desire to give something back to society, to improve the lives of others, or to advance some activity or cause that they believe to be important to the future. Others may undertake voluntary service to help meet some of their personal needs and desires. This may include making new friends, perhaps meeting potential mates or business contacts, learning new skills, improving their resumes, alleviating boredom, or a host of other needs. The fact that people may be motivated by a combination of altruism and personal needs does not diminish the value of their efforts or make them less admirable. However, it is essential for the nonprofit manager to understand these sometimes mixed and complex motivations in order to create an experience that will attract and retain the volunteer workforce.

A considerable body of research on volunteers suggests that the factors leading to their motivation and satisfaction are very similar to those for paid staff. For example, studies have found that volunteers are motivated by a desire to serve the mission, that volunteers who remain with the organization are those who experience positive relationships with other volunteers, that those who continue to serve are those who find the nature of the work itself rewarding, and that volunteers value opportunities to learn new skills through their voluntary service. Volunteers who have participated in studies assign importance to factors such as clearly defined responsibilities, a reasonable work schedule, and competent supervision, all consistent with the motivation theories we have previously discussed. This suggests that a list of recommended practices for managing volunteers should include many points similar to those outlined above for the management of staff (McCurley, 2004).

Volunteer Management Practices

There is an extensive literature on the management of volunteers. Indeed, volunteer management has become a recognized subspecialty of nonprofit management, the practitioners of which have their own professional associations, conferences, and journals. The list of suggested readings at the end of this chapter provides a small sample of the many publications and websites that offer summaries of research on voluntarism and the management of volunteer programs.

There is much commonality among the recommendations of experts on managing an effective volunteer program. Most include some or all of the following points (see, e.g., McCurley & Lynch, 2006).

Nonprofits should assess the need for volunteers and develop volunteer job descriptions. Before an organization launches a program for the use of regular volunteers, it needs to determine why volunteers are needed. If volunteers are to serve episodically (e.g., a group is going to the woods for one day to clean up trash and repair hiking trails), there may not be a need for much formality in defining volunteer jobs—a supervisor can just assign those who show up to the tasks that need to be done. But if the organization needs volunteers to play an ongoing role as a part of its workforce, then volunteer jobs need to be designed and defined with some precision in order to establish clear expectations and ensure that the volunteer's work is related to program needs. Having formal job descriptions also helps communicate to volunteers that they are accepting a significant responsibility and that their assignment involves doing real work that is central to the program of the nonprofit.

Job descriptions do not need to be complex or extensive but should carefully state the type of work, skills needed, and expectations of volunteers. For example, the job description for a volunteer at the Harry S. Truman Library in Independence, Missouri, shown in Box 9.1, lists the specific tasks that the volunteer will perform and the qualifications required for the position, as well as the organization's commitment to provide training and compensation in the form of nonfinancial benefits.

BOX 9.1 VOLUNTEER JOB DESCRIPTION

Harry S. Truman Library

TITLE OF POSITION: Archives Assistant

SUPERVISED BY: Archives Staff

PURPOSE OF JOB: Assist archives staff with basic archival functions such as processing, preservation, reference, etc. Objective is to assist in increasing availability of research material.

DUTIES MAY INCLUDE BUT ARE NOT LIMITED TO:

1. Photocopying and filing.
2. Maintain proper care and maintenance of all documents handled.
3. Create finding aids (indexes, catalogs, etc.).
4. Data entry.
5. Stamping of documents.
6. Prepare material for preservation work.

(Continued)

(Continued)

7. Attend orientation sessions and complete training readings.

8. Communicate regularly with assigned supervisor as to concerns, issues, or ideas arising from the current project.

9. Participate in reviews within archives of assignments prior to extension, reassignment, or completion.

10. Ensure the goals and policies of the archives and library are promoted and adhered to.

COMMITMENT REQUIRED:

A minimum commitment of 4–5 hours per week for a 3-month period is required. Volunteer opportunities will be available Monday–Friday, 9:00 a.m.–4:30 p.m. There are no weekend or evening opportunities for this position.

QUALIFICATIONS NEEDED:

- Must be age 16 or older
- Basic computer skills and/or good handwriting helpful
- Flexible to changing situation
- Reliable, responsible
- Able to work independently as well as in a group environment
- Able to accept supervision
- Interest in history
- Ability to perform repetitive tasks and detail oriented
- Good organizational skills

TRAINING/ORIENTATION PROVIDED:

Since the duties performed by the Archives Assistants are varied, training and work assignments are both designed to meet the individual requirements of the task to be accomplished. Training is provided on-the-job by the Truman Library's archives staff.
Basic reading material on the Truman presidency and archives work is additionally provided.

LOCATION OF JOB:

The Harry S. Truman Library, Independence, Missouri

VOLUNTEER BENEFITS:

Knowledge about Harry S. Truman, the Library and Museum, and the educational aspects offered to visitors through a variety of programs/exhibits; discount prices in the museum gift shop; invitations to special events; volunteer appreciation programs; free parking; free subscription to *Whistle-Stop,* the quarterly newsletter of the Harry S. Truman Library Institute; free admission to the museum for you and your immediate family; work with original and unique historical documents.

Source: Harry S. Truman Library website (http://www.trumanlibrary.org/volunteer/archivjd.htm).

Nonprofits should develop formal volunteer policies. Volunteers may be unpaid, but they are a part of the organization's workforce. Indeed, they often work alongside of paid staff in delivering its services. There should be formal policies that spell out the expectations, rules, and standards by which volunteers will be evaluated and, if necessary, terminated. The policies should describe the relationship between volunteers and any paid staff by whom they are supervised or whom they may supervise. Organizations have personnel policies to govern their relationship with paid staff; not having such policies for volunteers might imply that they are not as essential as staff and may set the stage for misunderstandings, conflict between volunteers and staff members, or even legal problems.

Having formal volunteer policies is also an important element of risk management for the organization. This is especially important in settings where volunteers will have direct contact with clients or access to confidential client information, or in which clients are particularly vulnerable or potentially volatile. For example, McLean Hospital, which treats people suffering from psychiatric illnesses, presents an especially sensitive environment. Its volunteer guidelines, shown in Box 9.2, are appropriately extensive and detailed. New volunteers should be given a copy of the policies and should sign a statement acknowledging that they have read them. In addition, most organizations should carry liability insurance, to protect both organizational assets and volunteers.

BOX 9.2 VOLUNTEER POLICIES

McLean Hospital

A Harvard University Affiliate

GUIDELINES FOR VOLUNTEERS

1. Volunteers have the responsibility to protect each patient's right to privacy. Therefore, information of a medical and psychiatric nature, as well as identifying data, such as name, address, and telephone number, is strictly confidential, and may not be shared with any person or agency other than authorized McLean Hospital personnel. In response to inquiries made by people other than McLean staff and volunteers, volunteers shall neither confirm nor deny that a person is a patient at the hospital, nor provide any other information about the patient.

2. Volunteers shall not remove written material of a clinical nature, or copies of such material, from the hospital, nor shall they take photographs, tape recordings, or any action that may infringe on the patient's right to privacy and dignity. Volunteers shall not have access to patients' records with the exception of specially approved volunteers.

3. Volunteers shall not write books or articles based on clinical experiences at the hospital. Volunteers must receive prior approval from both the Coordinator of Volunteers and supervisory staff before starting a journal or writing a paper based on their clinical experience.

4. Volunteers have the responsibility to treat all patients with respect, with an awareness of their dignity as persons, and to observe their civil rights at all times.

(Continued)

(Continued)

5. Volunteers have the responsibility to seek out staff to talk about any situation that they encounter wherein they have questions concerning what is physically or emotionally safe for the patients, or for themselves, or which raises legal issues. Volunteers shall not handle discipline problems, nor shall they assist in any restraining procedures.

6. Volunteers shall avoid physical contact with patients unless a patient wants to shake hands or contact is required as part of an approved activity, such as pushing a patient on a swing.

7. Volunteers may participate with patients only as assigned by staff. They shall not see patients outside of the hospital, or after discharge, without prior approval from staff. Volunteers shall not give their telephone numbers or addresses to patients without permission from staff.

8. Volunteers have the responsibility to make sure patients have the proper authorization to participate in various activities.

9. Volunteers shall not drive patients in their cars, nor shall they leave the grounds with a patient.

10. Volunteers may accompany staff and patients on outings. As a general rule, volunteers pay for their own expenses.

11. Volunteers have the responsibility to use discretion in disclosing information about themselves to patients. They shall not discuss their personal problems or their experiences with drugs, sex, therapy, and illness.

12. Volunteers have the responsibility to support the patients' treatment program by encouraging patients to discuss their clinical concerns with staff. Volunteers shall not agree to a patient's request to keep a secret. Experiences during a volunteer period should be discussed with staff afterwards to enhance volunteer–patient interactions.

13. Volunteers have the responsibility to support the staff and the policies and procedures of McLean Hospital.

14. Volunteers have the responsibility to refer patient's or family member's complaints to departmental supervisory staff, or the Director of Social Work, to help ensure patient satisfaction.

15. Volunteers are expected to come regularly and promptly for the times they have agreed to work. On arrival, the volunteer should check in with staff to receive pertinent information and instructions.

16. Volunteers have the responsibility to be groomed and dressed appropriately, bearing in mind they are role models.

17. Volunteers shall not accept gifts from patients unless the gift has no appreciable monetary value and staff approves.

18. Volunteers are not assigned keys.

19. Volunteers have the responsibility to know the McLean Hospital emergency number for their own safety as well as the safety of the patients.

20. Volunteers have the responsibility to learn the hospital Fire Rules. If volunteers see/smell smoke or fire, they must immediately take the appropriate steps for responding.

21. Volunteers have the responsibility to learn and abide by the policies and procedures regarding hazardous materials.

22. Volunteers have the responsibility to know the infection control policies/procedures for Volunteer Services.

Source: McLean Hospital website (http://www.mclean.harvard.edu/employment/volunteer/vg.php). Used with permission of McLean Hospital.

Nonprofits should provide a sufficient budget and personnel to manage the volunteer program. Volunteers may be unpaid, but they do not come free. Without adequate resources, such as books, computers, tools, transportation, supervision, or whatever their work may require, volunteers are no more likely than staff to be successful. Depending on the scope of the volunteer program, it may be important to have a full-time member of the paid staff to manage the organization's overall relationship with volunteers. This does not imply that volunteers necessarily report to the volunteer manager with regard to their specific assignments but that the manager maintains an overall view of volunteers' involvement and performance. It is also important that all members of the paid staff who work with volunteers, including perhaps program or unit directors, are provided with training on the special considerations in managing them.

Nonprofits should recruit and hire volunteers as if they were employees. Some organizations may be in such need of volunteers that they may be tempted to accept anyone who may indicate an interest. But doing so may provide only a short-run gain and, indeed, is likely to be an approach that neither meets the organization's needs nor provides a satisfying experience for the volunteers. A well-managed program is likely to attract, at least over time, sufficient interest to permit selectivity in the hiring of volunteers. A selective volunteer program requires that prospective volunteers complete an application and undergo an interview process. Background checks may also be required by law or be advisable in consideration of risk management.

Gaining the ability to be selective in choosing volunteers offers the organization at least two advantages: First, it can select people with the right skills to meet its needs and those who are likely to remain committed to their volunteer responsibilities. Second, the organization may be able to craft its volunteer program in order to include groups from prospective donor companies, religious congregations, or other groups with which it wishes to establish closer relationships. A volunteer program thus can become not only a vehicle for delivering the organization's programs but also an instrument of its fund-raising, communications, and community relations efforts. However, it is important not to permit the latter considerations to predominate. Engaging volunteers simply as a fund-raising strategy but failing to provide them with a structured and meaningful experience is likely to lead to their frustration and undermine, rather than enhance, their perception of and affiliation with the organization.

Nonprofits should provide orientation and training to volunteers. Volunteer orientation should include an introduction to the organization that covers not only practical operational matters but also a discussion of its mission, values, and culture. It should clarify the relationship between volunteers and paid staff and the expectations of each. Depending on the nature of the volunteer's work, training may include working with another, more experienced volunteer for a period or a more formal program designed to develop specific skills.

Volunteer managers should set clear goals, evaluate performance, and recognize achievement. As discussed previously, people are motivated by clear goals, the explication of a clear path to their achievement, and recognition for having succeeded in reaching them. Since volunteers are not compensated financially, their achievement of goals and recognition may be their primary rewards. This suggests that volunteer job performance should be evaluated, which of course implies that volunteers could be terminated when appropriate as well, the same as paid staff. Some organizations may find that a difficult decision to reach because they are in need of volunteers and feel they cannot afford to let one go. Or perhaps the culture of the organization may not encompass individual performance standards, at least not for volunteers. It also can be problematic if volunteers are also donors—even board members, whose termination might bring additional consequences. However, such concerns should be balanced against the need to maintain the overall quality and reputation of the program, the importance of achieving quality in service delivery, and the negative consequences for the morale of both staff and other volunteers of retaining someone whose work or attitude does not make a positive contribution. Of course, evaluation should be a two-way street. Volunteers should be given opportunities to provide feedback on the quality of their experience, including the conditions, supervision, and resources with which they work.

In summary, many experts suggest that, in most respects, volunteers should be managed with many of the same practices that apply to paid staff. To be sure, volunteers are entitled to respect and gratitude. Their impact is much the same as that of donors of financial gifts, and they are a precious asset that nonprofits need to nurture and cultivate. However, for all these reasons, they also deserve a structured and professional approach that maintains high expectations and stays focused on achievement of the organization's mission and goals.

How are nonprofit organizations doing in following recommended practices? A 2004 study by the Urban Institute found a mixed pattern. While more than 60 percent of organizations had adopted each of the practices to some degree, of the nine practices studied, only supervision and communication with volunteers had been adopted to a large degree by the majority of nonprofits examined. There were, as might be expected, variations depending on the characteristics of the organization, including its size, the level of volunteer involvement, the relative predominance of volunteer roles, and the subsector or industry in which it operates. For example, organizations in the health care industry and larger nonprofits were more likely to have adopted the recommended practices, while small ones and those using episodic volunteers were less likely to have done so (Hager & Brudney, 2004).

It is perhaps because of the absence of sound management practices that many nonprofits experience high volunteer burnout and turnover. For example, a study conducted by the Corporation for National and Community Service found that one third of individuals who volunteered in 2005 did not continue their activity in 2006 (cited in Michaels, 2007). The turnover represents significant lost investment in volunteer training and experience. If nonprofits were to devote additional resources to volunteer management programs, those expenditures could be more than offset by the saving of costs in recruitment of volunteers and additional paid staff. More widespread adoption of recommended management practices thus could have a financial benefit as well as an impact on the effectiveness of nonprofit programs and services.

Volunteer Management as a Career Field

As mentioned before, volunteer management has become a distinct specialty in nonprofit management. In a 2004 study conducted by the Urban Institute, 3 out of 5 nonprofits had a paid professional position for management of volunteers (Idealist, 2010a). Many positions in the study were part-time, but full-time positions are increasing in number. Titles of such positions are varied, including for example, Volunteer Manager, Volunteer Coordinator, Director of Volunteers, and Vice President of Volunteers/Volunteer Resources (Idealist, 2010b). Obviously, the higher the title, the greater the role and the more the individual in the position is a part of the senior management team of the organization. There is a multitude of training programs for volunteer managers, including university-based courses, and some organizations offer professional certification (Idealist, 2010b). Box 9.3 provides a generic job description for a volunteer management position and shows many of the responsibilities and expectations that are commonly included.

BOX 9.3 GENERIC POSITION DESCRIPTION FOR ADMINISTRATION OF VOLUNTEER RESOURCES

Main purpose: With the support of management and board, develops a vision for volunteerism in the organization. Mobilizes and manages volunteers to enhance the vision and mission of the organization. Introduces and ensures effective volunteer management practices and standards in the organization.

Program Administration

- Develops a plan for volunteer involvement in the organization
- Develops a budget to support the plan
- Develops policies and procedures
- Tracks results through standardized record-keeping practices
- Maintains volunteer files on each volunteer ensuring documentation of screening practices

Job Design

- Consults with staff and volunteers in the organization
- Assesses organizational and volunteer needs
- Develops volunteer roles and assignments to meet assessed needs
- Identifies knowledge, skills, abilities, and motivations required to fulfill the volunteer role
- Assesses potential risks for positions and addresses with appropriate level of screening protocol and by identifying training needs

Recruitment

- Recruits volunteers for specific roles and assignments through internal and external strategies
- Develops community partnerships and collaborations

(Continued)

(Continued)

Matching and Placement

- Screens applicants
- Matches prospective volunteers with available opportunities or may create new opportunities to meet organizational needs
- Orients volunteers to the organization
- Arranges for volunteer orientation and training for their specific role

Supervision and Monitoring

- Ensures that volunteers have adequate supervision to fulfill their assignments/roles
- Monitors volunteer, staff, and client satisfaction
- Resolves volunteer and staff concerns
- Ensures that volunteers receive feedback in their performance
- Conducts program evaluations with a view to improving the volunteer program

Recognition

- Recognizes volunteers and staff through both formal and informal means

Staff Relations

- Develops a climate of readiness for volunteers
- Provides guidance, training, and support to staff working with volunteers

Source: Canadian Administrators of Volunteer Resources website (http://www.cavrcanada.org).

Chapter Summary

Early management theories were often developed in industrial settings and portrayed human beings as part of a production machine, whose performance could be increased by focusing on procedures and rules. Since at least the Hawthorne experiments of the 1920s, theorists have focused on human psychology and motivation, emphasizing the influence of human needs and feelings on behavior in the workplace. Theories are often advanced, gain wide acceptance, and are subsequently discredited through further research. But most offer some principles that are adopted in new approaches or that gain continued acceptance by practitioners.

One theory, advanced by Frederick Herzberg, suggests that there are two sets of factors present in the workplace. One set of factors, which includes intrinsically rewarding work and opportunities for achievement, recognition, and advancement, serves to motivate workers. Another set of factors, related to the work environment and including supervision, working conditions, and compensation, may be dissatisfiers but are not in themselves motivating. Managers should try to reduce or eliminate dissatisfiers and increase motivators. These principles may apply to the motivation of volunteers as well as paid staff members. Other theories, including those of Maslow, McClelland, and Myers and Briggs, suggest that individuals bring their own personal needs and styles into the workplace. This may require that managers design jobs to reflect the existing motivations of their staff and volunteers.

Based on motivation theory, some recommended practices for managers of paid staff include being reflective about their own needs and motivations, being aware that what motivates the manager may not necessarily be what will motivate others, holding realistic expectations about the extent to which a manager can influence the motivation of others, participating in setting clear and challenging goals, thinking about the salience of various rewards to individuals who have different needs, being honest with people about what rewards are possible and what rewards are not, treating people equitably and fairly, making the work satisfying and meaningful, and considering the implications of life stages and of personal life events for the individuals they manage. Fostering workplace diversity, encompassing characteristics such as race, gender, nationality, religion, lifestyle, and others, is not only the right thing to do but also is an essential element of sound management. Effective nonprofits embrace diversity as a strength, recognizing that combining individuals of different backgrounds, perspectives, values, and views adds to the organization's capacity for high performance.

Volunteers are the only workforce for many organizations and constitute an important component of the workforce for many others, including those that employ paid staff. Individuals may be motivated to volunteer by altruism and concern for others, by their own needs, or by some combination of factors. In the workplace, they are usually affected by many of the same principles of motivation as paid staff. Some recommended practices for managing volunteers include assessing the need for volunteers and developing volunteer job descriptions; developing formal volunteer policies; providing a sufficient budget and personnel to manage the volunteer program; recruiting and hiring volunteers as if they were employees; providing orientation and training; and setting clear goals, evaluating performance, and recognizing achievement.

Following these practices may be especially important if volunteers provide regular service in the organization's programs, but it may be less essential with regard to episodic volunteers who just participate occasionally. Volunteer management has become an identified subspecialty of nonprofit management, and its practitioners have access to professional associations, publications, and training to improve their skills.

KEY TERMS AND CONCEPTS

dissatisfiers	*motivators*	*scientific management*
expectancy theory	*Myers-Briggs*	*spot volunteers*
Hawthorne experiments	*operant conditioning*	*Theory X and Theory Y*
hierarchy of needs	*regular volunteers*	*volunteer management*
hygiene factors	*satisfiers*	
motivation		

CASE 9.1 Getta Grant

Getta Grant is Director of Development at a medium-sized nonprofit that provides a range of services to adolescents from disadvantaged urban communities. She reports to the executive director. The organization receives some government funding, but is also reliant on foundations and individual donors. Getta's responsibilities include staying informed about foundation interests and giving patterns and working with the organization's three program directors to identify foundations that may be prospects for support of their programs and projects. She drafts letters of inquiry and, where appropriate, meets with foundation officers and writes proposals. Getta has been with the organization for 5 years and was hired by the previous executive director, who always gave her "excellent" (the highest rating) on her annual performance reviews. The current executive director has been in her job less than a year. She inherited Getta from her predecessor. When she had just arrived, it was already time for Getta's annual evaluation. The new executive director read a couple of proposals Getta had written, thought they were good, and continued her "excellent" rating without much further thought. Getta seemed pleased to have her high rating continued.

When Getta writes something, it is generally of high quality. But over the past year, the executive director has become unhappy with the amount of work Getta produces and with her inability to meet deadlines. Since her last review, Getta has produced only a handful of letters and two proposals. The executive director gave her positive feedback on that work, which was indeed good, thinking that would motivate her to work harder and faster. But Getta has continued to produce relatively few proposals, and in some cases, they have taken so long that she missed foundation deadlines. She is coming up soon for her second evaluation with the executive director, who is now quite frustrated with her performance.

The executive director met with Getta recently and explained that she is unhappy. She warned Getta that her next performance evaluation may not be so positive this year. Getta seemed shocked. "But you said my proposals are good," she protested, "and you gave me an 'excellent' rating last year!" Since that meeting, Getta has missed several of days of work, calling in sick or saying she was "working at home." And the executive director has seen almost no additional work.

CASE 9.2 Rita Writer

Rita Writer is a member of the communications and marketing staff at a large environmental nonprofit. She has various responsibilities, including writing press releases, articles for the quarterly magazine, and copy for brochures that are produced for fund-raising and other purposes, and material for the organization's website. Rita had previously worked as a marketing specialist in the alumni relations office of a local college and came with outstanding references. When she accepted her new job, she said she wanted to make the change so that she would have more opportunity to write, since her job in alumni relations also included responsibility for attending events and required considerable travel.

Rita now has been in her current job for about 3 months. She produces an adequate volume of writing, but it is consistently full of glaring errors. Her manager, the Vice President for Communications and Marketing, sometimes sends the work back to Rita for revisions. But most times the vice president just edits the work himself, not wanting to confront Rita and thinking that it is faster for him to take on the task. He has not said anything to Rita, but he is becoming increasingly unhappy with her performance. He is concerned that firing her would make him unpopular among the other staff, so he is reluctant to do so. But he is wondering what he can do to increase Rita's contribution to the organization.

One of Rita's colleagues mentioned to the vice president that Rita spends a lot of time on the phone talking to people in chapter offices around the country. In addition, the organization sponsors a number of public events, including lectures on environmental issues that are followed by receptions. Although she is not required to do so, Rita attends many of them on her work time and always stays for the reception, mingling with the guests. One of her colleagues said sarcastically to the vice president, "Rita just seems to prefer socializing to doing her job."

CASE 9.3 Bob the Builder

Bob is a volunteer at an organization that provides services to older people in the community, enabling them to continue living in their own homes. Older clients are matched with volunteers, who agree to visit with them at least once a week to assist them with matters such as paying bills, performing light housework or yard work, and similar tasks. When their homes need modest upkeep or repairs, such as painting, volunteers with appropriate skills are assigned as a team to complete the job. The organization's Director of Volunteers recruits volunteers with needed skills, assigning them to clients and projects and ensuring quality in the work they perform.

Bob was a building contractor and has recently retired. He has been a long-time but occasional volunteer. His wife, Mary, is a member of the board of directors, and Bob and Mary have been regular contributors to the annual fund-raising campaign. A few months ago, Bob approached the Director of Volunteers and said that he now will have more time and would like to do more work with the organization. Delighted at the offer, especially in light of his professional skills, the director assigned him to supervise several home repair project teams.

Recently, however, she became concerned when she heard from another volunteer that Bob was going way beyond the scope of the projects assigned. In one case, the project team was sent to do some painting for a homeowner, but Bob had performed some electrical wiring in the woman's house. In another case, he replaced some plumbing. The director became concerned about the risks in that type of work and the potential liability to the organization should something go wrong. In addition, she is now receiving complaints from other volunteers who have worked with Bob. One volunteer has told her that Bob treats other volunteers as if they were members of the crew of his former construction company. And he doesn't treat them well. He assigns them work and then criticizes them for not doing it fast enough or well enough. Some of the volunteers have said that they will not work with him again.

The volunteers director met with the executive director and discussed her concerns about Bob. The executive director was somewhat dismissive, saying she thinks Bob is a great asset to the organization. "After all," she said. "He's a professional builder. We are fortunate to have someone with his skills involved." She then added, "Anyway, it's difficult to do anything about it with Mary serving on the board."

QUESTIONS FOR DISCUSSION

In each of the cases described above,

1. Which theories of motivation might be most relevant to the situations described?

2. What recommended practices for the management of staff or volunteers may not have been followed in each of these cases?

3. What psychological needs might each staff person or volunteer be trying to meet?

4. What does the manager's behavior in each case suggest about his or her psychological needs?

5. What might the manager in each case have done differently at an earlier point in the relationship to have avoided the current problem?

SUGGESTIONS FOR FURTHER READING

Books/Reports/Articles

Corporation for National and Community Service. (2009). *Volunteering in America.* Washington, DC: Author. (Available at http://www.volunteeringinamerica.gov/assets/resources/VolunteeringIn AmericaResearchHighlights.pdf)

Denhardt, R. B., Denhardt, J. V., & Aristigueta, M. P. (2009). *Managing human behavior in public and nonprofit organizations* (2nd ed.). Thousand Oaks, CA: Sage.

Sagawa, S. (2010). *The American way to change: How national service and volunteers are transforming America.* San Francisco: Jossey-Bass.

Websites

Association of Leaders in Volunteer Engagement (ALIVE), http://www.volunteeralive.org/

Corporation for National and Community Service, http://www.nationalservice.gov/

Independent Sector, http://www.independentsector.org/

Points of Light Institute, http://www.pointsoflight.org/

Volunteers of America, http://www.voa.org/

Chapter Outline

chapter 10

Nonprofits must work to integrate their marketing and communications so that the message they craft is consistent across all channels and constituencies.

© iStockphoto.com/Alan Merrigan

Marketing and Communications 10

I n this chapter, we will consider the use of marketing principles by nonprofit organizations and the planning and management of communications programs. Although developed in the for-profit sector, marketing is widely applied by nonprofits for various purposes. Some organizations, for example, in the fields of education, health care, and the arts, have products and services to sell and were among the early adopters of marketing in the nonprofit sector. This type of marketing is *commercial marketing,* whether undertaken by a for-profit or nonprofit, because its goal is to attract additional "customers" to programs and services (Andreasen & Kotler, 2008, p. 8). Other nonprofits engage in *social marketing,* which is intended to change human behavior and improve society, for example, to reduce smoking or obesity or increase the use of seat belts or condoms. Marketing principles are also applied in fund-raising and in *cause marketing* (or *cause-related* marketing), which involves a partnership between a nonprofit and a corporation that is intended to increase sales of the *for-profit*'s products with financial and other benefits going to the nonprofit organizations or a cause. This chapter focuses on principles of marketing as applied in nonprofits' marketing of products and services related to their mission programs (commercial marketing) and in social marketing. We will explore fund-raising in Chapter 11, partnerships between nonprofits and corporations in Chapter 12, and nonprofit advocacy in Chapter 14. We will revisit some principles of marketing that are discussed in this chapter in those specific contexts.

Defining and Understanding Marketing

At their monthly meeting, members of the (fictional) Siwash College faculty were informed by the college's president that "we are enhancing our communication with prospective students in order to increase applications, especially from highly qualified students." The news was greeted with enthusiasm. "We really need to get the word out," said one professor. "We have excellent programs that nobody knows about." Another professor added, "Communication is a general problem here; some of our own colleagues don't know how strong many of our departments are. I'm pleased to hear that the administration will be doing something about it."

A month later, the college's Vice President for Communications presented a follow-up report to the faculty. In her comments, she said things a little differently:

> We are really investing significantly in our marketing and, in fact, we are bringing in a team of marketing consultants to help us position the college and differentiate our brand and we will be hiring more recruiters on our own staff to target highly qualified students.

One professor immediately came to his feet, saying, "Wait a minute. Are you saying we are going to market the college like a brand of soda? We have a good reputation now and that will just tarnish it by making us look desperate." Another added,

> I agree. We attract students now because of the quality of our academic programs. If we want more and better students to apply, the money should be spent on academic resources, like the library, science labs, and computer technology. Those are the things that will attract the kind of students we want.

A third member of the faculty joined the conversation, saying,

> It concerns me that we are going for the hard sell. We don't need Madison Avenue types out representing us, exaggerating and misleading students into coming to Siwash. That wouldn't be fair to the students and could cause people to question our integrity.

While the concerns of the Siwash College faculty may not be completely unfounded, they may also reflect an incomplete understanding of "marketing." Although marketing principles are widely applied in many nonprofit organizations, misunderstanding of the concept is still common, and some individuals have a viscerally negative reaction to the use of marketing's vocabulary in organizations that are based on values and driven by missions. In part, the comments and concerns of the Siwash College faculty may reflect the shadows of earlier approaches to marketing in the business sector that remain prominent in some people's understanding of the concept.

When marketing first came on the business scene around the beginning of the 20th century, it reflected a *product mind-set*. In other words, the prevailing view was "that to be an effective marketer, you simply had to 'build a better mousetrap,' and, in effect, customers would beat a pathway to your door" (Andreasen & Kotler, 2008, p. 37). That was essentially what Henry Ford did by inventing the Model T, and it may be the view of the Siwash faculty, who think it sufficient to improve the college's educational programs, assuming that prospective students will inevitably discover them and apply in greater numbers.

But the product mind-set became obsolete in business in about the mid-20th century. It became increasingly clear that simply making a better product would not provide assurance that customers would buy it. An increasingly competitive economic environment led to a new approach to marketing in the business world, one reflecting a *sales mind-set* (Andreasen & Kotler, 2008). The goal for a company or an organization with a sales mind-set is to *convince* customers that they should buy the company's product rather than buy nothing or buy what a competitor is offering. With the adoption of this marketing perspective by American business in the middle part of the 20th century, advertising became a major industry, and the "hard sell" became the preferred tactic of businesses trying to survive in a competitive environment. For many people, marketing is still synonymous with sales, and like some members of the Siwash faculty, they see it as something possibly inconsistent with the values and the culture of the nonprofit sector.

Both the product and sales mind-sets lead an organization to begin the marketing process *inside* its own walls, with the goal it wishes to achieve—more sales of the product or service, resulting in more revenue for the organization. When the sales mind-set is predominant, messages are pushed out through advertising and other channels of communication with the hope that they will fall on receptive ears—the goal is to "change the . . . audiences to fit what the organization [has] to offer" (Andreasen & Kotler, 2008, p. 38). Both the product and the sales mind-sets still exist and are reflected in the practices of some for-profit and nonprofit organizations today (Andreasen & Kotler, 2008), but modern marketing reflects a *target-audience mindset*. It is outside in, not inside out. As Andresen (2006) explains, "The key to marketing is to focus on our audiences and not ourselves" (p. 12).

Following this outside-in approach requires that

> the organization systematically study target audiences' needs, wants, perceptions, preferences, and satisfaction, using surveys, focus groups, and other means . . . [and that] *the organization . . . constantly act on this information to improve its offerings to meet its customers' needs better.* (Andreasen & Kotler, 2008, p. 39, italics added)

Understood in this way, then, marketing seems not so contrary to nonprofit values, as the Siwash faculty may have initially believed. For nonprofits, marketing is focused on the needs of constituents or consumers; it is not about pushing something that those individuals do not want, nor does it require misrepresentation or exaggeration.

Unlike the sales model, which tries to persuade the customer that he or she wants what the organization has to offer, target-audience marketing implies that the organization develops its product to be responsive to what the *customer* needs and wants.[1] Of course, businesses do so readily. If consumers want larger cars, the automakers will produce them. If consumers shift their priorities to saving oil and preserving the environment, automakers will respond to that change by producing more fuel-efficient vehicles. If the product or service is well matched with what people really want, it will still be necessary to let potential customers know of its existence and the benefits it provides—there is still a need for advertising and communication—but there will be little need to persuade individuals, or sell them on the desirability of purchasing it. The situation is, of course, more complicated if the goal of marketing requires the "customer" to sacrifice—for example, to quit smoking or change his or her dietary habits—but the purpose is nevertheless to improve individuals' situations, through better health or in some other aspect of life. In those instances, the "sale" requires communicating a *value proposition* in which members of the target audience see benefit in the exchange.

Marketing Serves the Mission

Of course, even the more up-to-date, target-market mind-set may still give some pause to the faculty of Siwash College and to others who work in nonprofit organizations. How responsive should a nonprofit be to the expressed desires of its clients or customers? Should a college's curriculum be designed to encompass only what students say they wish to know, or should it reflect what the faculty believe to be the essential elements of a sound education? If a performing arts center is not attracting symphony audiences of sufficient size, should it abandon Beethoven in favor of presenting rock concerts? If patients express displeasure about having their blood tested, should hospitals skip that procedure in order to gain more customer satisfaction? If church attendance is declining, should the pastor yield on fundamental principles? Should a museum abandon its mission to preserve antiquities and educate museum patrons in order to provide entertainment along the lines of Disney World? Stated at the extreme, all these ideas are obviously inappropriate, indeed ridiculous. A nonprofit organization cannot abandon its mission or act in a way that is contrary to its values merely to increase sales of its product or service. To do so would be inconsistent with the essence of its nonprofit character and status. Marketing must serve the mission and not become the driver of the nonprofit organization's program.

However, nonprofits cannot ignore the reality that they operate in a competitive environment, even if they do not compete directly against each other. A homeless shelter may not compete with another for clients, but two such organizations may compete for gifts from local corporations, foundations, and individuals. Organizations that advocate a cause or social goal may compete against others that advocate opposing positions; they compete in a marketplace of ideas, attitudes, and beliefs. Even those that may advocate relatively noncontroversial ideas, like wearing seat belts and stopping smoking, still compete against complacency and habit, and they compete for attention amidst the distraction of all the other messages with which people are bombarded every day, what communication theory calls "noise."

Of course, many nonprofits do offer products and services for a fee, and they may compete against each other as well as against for-profit companies and public organizations engaged in similar activities. For example, two colleges may compete for students, and two theaters may compete for audiences. Even without such direct competition, organizations face *generic competition* from alternative uses of individuals' time and money. People can only be in one place at a time. Attending the museum, especially if it charges an admission fee, competes with attending a theater performance, going to the movies, or staying home on the sofa watching TV. The museum must offer something that will motivate people to spend their time, and perhaps their money, to visit the museum rather than engage in such alternative activities. Marketing is a strategy for competition, whether for resources, convictions, or customers, and thus marketing principles may prove useful for every nonprofit, regardless of its mission.

Marketing Means Action

Marketing and communications are terms often combined in the titles of individuals or offices—for example, the "Director of Communications and Marketing" or the "Office of Marketing and Communications." But the concepts are distinct. *Communication,* in the simplest of definitions, is the transmission or exchange of information. As a discipline, *communications* is more complex, encompassing an understanding of the principles by which information is transmitted and received—that is, "how messages are encoded, transmitted, screened, decoded, stored, retrieved, and acted on" (Gainer & Moyer, 2005, p. 303), as well as the various technologies employed, for example, print and electronic media. We will discuss more about communications theory later in this chapter. But communications is not synonymous with marketing; it may be undertaken with multiple goals.

Marketing, on the other hand, is a process that may encompass communications, but with a very specific purpose: to influence the behavior of someone else. Marketing focuses on exchanges. For example, you buy a ticket and hear the symphony in exchange for your payment. Or you change your behavior, say by eating fewer sweets, and realize the benefit of greater fitness in return. An exchange does not occur until the individual—a member of the target audience—takes *action.* As Andreasen and Kotler (2008) explain,

> Marketing's objectives are not *ultimately* either to educate or to change values or attitudes. It may seek to do so as a *means* of influencing behavior. . . . If someone has a final goal

of imparting information or knowledge, that person is in the education profession, not marketing. Further, if someone has a final goal of changing attitudes or values, that person may be described as a propagandist or lobbyist, or perhaps an artist, but not a marketer. While marketing may use the tools of the educator or the propagandist, its critical distinguishing feature is that its ultimate goal is to influence behavior (either changing it or keeping it the same in the face of other pressures). (p. 36, italics original)

Marketing as a Process

As Figure 10.1 depicts, marketing is a process. Consistent with our discussion above, it begins with defining the target audience and gaining understanding of its members' values, needs, and wants; it acknowledges the environment, including the presence of direct and generic competition; it focuses on defining an exchange, honing and delivering the message (communication); and it ends with action by members of the target audience. Communication (i.e., honing and delivering the message) is a part of the marketing process, but does not encompass it or substitute for it. Moreover, the ultimate goal is not persuasion in and of itself, but rather action by members of the target audience. Evaluation of a marketing program thus must be based on measuring what actions have been taken. As Andresen (2006) emphasizes, that requires thinking "beyond our far-off mission (like helping people overcome poverty, increasing consumer access to affordable health care, or strengthening schools) and zero[ing] in on specific audience actions that are tangible, achievable, and measureable" (p. 14).

The Marketing Mix

Marketing implies an interaction between the customer and the organization. As discussed above, it begins with research to identify the needs and wants of potential customers or clients, which informs the development of the products or services to be offered. A simple description of the marketing process that is often stated says, "Find a need and fill it." That implies a malleable marketer, one who will create almost any product or service for which there is a demand. This simple understanding of course may raise difficult issues for nonprofit organizations that are driven by the missions and values that are at the heart of their existence.

However, any organization hoping to exchange its services for payment cannot be oblivious to the desires of its potential consumers. A college with great programs but no students eventually will close, and one that does not introduce new programs to address emerging new fields and industries will not keep pace with others that are more innovative. It is necessary and appropriate that nonprofits sometimes push back against the market to preserve their core values in pursuit of their missions, but tailoring the product to address the target market is also essential to survival. Fortunately, there is a middle choice between rigidity and complete capitulation to the market: A nonprofit can change its *marketing mix* in response to information about what customers, clients, or donors need and want, while remaining faithful to its core purposes. By doing so, it can *differentiate* its product from that offered by others, *position* itself in a unique *market niche,* and gain a *competitive advantage* over others.

To illustrate the ideas of the marketing mix, differentiation, and market niche, let's start with a familiar example from the for-profit world—Starbucks. The campus on which this author works is in an urban setting; there are many places to buy coffee, including the student union,

FIGURE 10.1 ■ The Marketing Process

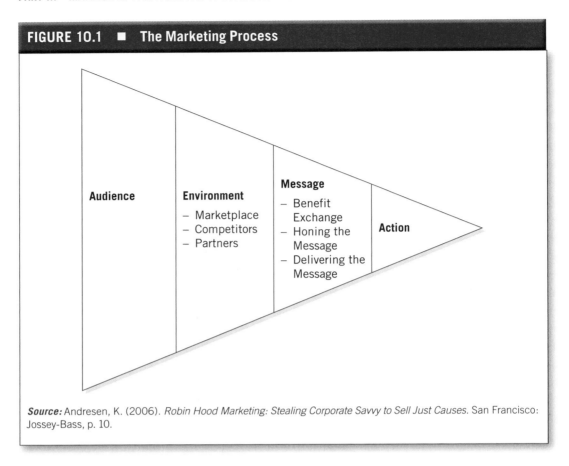

Source: Andresen, K. (2006). *Robin Hood Marketing: Stealing Corporate Savvy to Sell Just Causes.* San Francisco: Jossey-Bass, p. 10.

street vendors, and other restaurants and delis in the neighborhood. For many years, there was a large study room located in the front of the undergraduate library that was accessible through a door directly from the street—24 hours a day. It was rarely used at any time of the day or night. A few years ago, the university decided to lease the space to Starbucks, which converted it to one of its ubiquitous coffee stores. Starbucks is always busy; indeed, students, faculty, and staff sometimes stand in lines extending out the door to pay a higher price for Starbucks coffee than they would need to pay for coffee at other nearby locations. And, in the space formerly occupied by an underused study room, students now spend time studying—at Starbucks! How has Starbucks differentiated itself from the other coffee sellers in the neighborhood? What is it that people receive in exchange for their money when they patronize Starbucks, and how is that different from what others are offering? Obviously, it's the coffee, which is pretty good, but it's also the atmosphere of the store, the convenience of its location, the comfortable chairs and laid-back atmosphere—the fact that Starbucks lets you stay for a long time and offers wireless Internet access for those who wish to use their laptops. It's also the familiarity and instant recognition of the Starbucks logo that lets you know exactly what to expect inside, and something that's indescribably just "cool" about buying coffee with complex-sounding names in sizes other than "small, medium, and large." In other words, there are more variables involved than just the core product, or service, that is being sold by any business. The four key variables—*product, place, promotion,* and *price*—are called the *4 Ps* of marketing. Various combinations of these variables are called the *marketing mix.*

Product

The product, generally the good or service being offered, seems like the simplest variable to understand. In the nonprofit sector, it's education, health care, counseling, tutoring, food, or whatever programs the organization may operate. Products have both tangible and intangible qualities, like the consumption of Starbucks coffee. Education offers a clear example. There is little basis on which to conclude that an Ivy League education is always superior to that offered at other colleges and universities across the country, and indeed, other institutions may be stronger than any of the Ivy League schools in some fields. Why would a student be willing to pay more at an Ivy League university than perhaps at a local college or state university that may provide an equally good education? Because the prestige of holding an Ivy League degree is itself an intangible quality of the product. An Ivy League degree may instantly convey intellectual distinction because those universities are known to be selective in admissions. Membership in the alumni association of such a university may bring influential contacts and open important doors throughout life. Furthermore, it happens that most Ivy League campuses are also attractive ones that provide an intellectually stimulating environment outside as well as inside the classroom. In other words, the product is not just the education itself; it's also the experiences and intangible benefits that may go along with it.

Intangibles may also be a part of the product in health care. For example, a hospital that provides a pleasant, modern environment may be preferred to one with a rundown facility that nevertheless provides excellent medical treatment. If the doctors and the nurses are nice and take the time to explain medical conditions to their patients, they are offering a different product from another hospital that follows exactly the same medical protocols but in which the staff are more distant or abrupt. A nonprofit that provides services to homeless individuals without significant barriers—that is, helps anyone without preconditions to receiving service—is offering a different product than one that is more difficult to access, although both may offer food, counseling, and housing of basically the same quality.

Think back on the meeting of the Siwash College faculty earlier in this chapter. Their concern that the academic program be centered on educational values and not be shaped entirely to suit the expressed desires of high school students is understandable. But the college's product is not just its curriculum. The product also includes the quality of its facilities, the teaching skill of its professors, the closeness of relationships that professors form with their students, the quality of student activities offered, and many other aspects of the student experience that go beyond the classroom. These are qualities of the product that can be enhanced in response to student wants and needs without compromising the college's commitment to its educational mission or values.

Place

The location at which the product or service is available is an important variable in the marketing mix. A program operated in a location that is convenient for clients is a different product from the same program offered in a remote place beyond easy reach. A college located in a small rural town offers a different experience from one located in the suburbs of a big city, although it may offer an identical curriculum. A concert hall located on a bus line offers something different from one located in the distant suburbs accessible only by car. Some programs need to be taken to where the clients are. For example, many colleges offer off-campus courses for working adults and online courses for those who cannot (or prefer not to) attend classes on a campus, symphony orchestras located in cities periodically bring their concerts to smaller towns in their regions, major museums place exhibits on tour across the country, and hospitals send vans offering mammograms into neighborhoods in which many women do not have easy access to health care. The decision about place involves consideration of both the physical and the virtual worlds. An attractive and interactive website and a presence on Facebook and Twitter may be as much a part of the overall product as services provided in a physical location.

Promotion

In the minds of some, marketing may be virtually synonymous with *promotion,* which is the visible activity that everybody can see—the announcements, advertisements, brochures, and other efforts undertaken to gain visibility and notice for the organization's products. Marketing is not synonymous with promotion, but promotion is part of the marketing mix. Clients and customers cannot partake of products or services if they do not know of their existence or what they comprise. But to whom should the nonprofit's programs and services be promoted? A simple answer might be "to the public," but that would require a foolishly expensive effort, since most of the public are likely to have no interest in or need for the organization's offerings. The need to keep promotion cost-effective requires focusing communication on segments of the public most likely to respond—that is, on the target market. This *segmentation* is based on research and may employ sophisticated tools developed in the business sector and increasingly adopted by many nonprofits as well.

Market Segmentation

For an organization's promotion to be cost-effective, it needs to identify its *target market* or target audience. As Figure 10.1 suggests, this is the initial step in thinking about a marketing program. The target market is a subset of the larger general population. Some of this may seem intuitive. For example, a college likely will focus its promotion of undergraduate programs on high school students and their parents. A symphony orchestra might limit its mailing of concert announcements to people who live in higher-income areas, who can afford the cost of the tickets. A medical clinic that provides screenings for HIV might target its communication to neighborhoods with low-income or younger single people rather than areas with primarily families and older residents. But variables used for segmentation are often more sophisticated than these somewhat obvious examples suggest.

Objective measures include *demographic variables,* for example, age, gender, race or ethnicity, and income, and *geography,* that is, where people may live, work, or travel. The examples described above reflect simple segmentation along these lines. Markets also may be segmented according to *behavioral measures*—in other words, patterns of past behavior that divide people into identifiable groups. For example, people who have never attended the theater constitute a segment different from those who attend occasionally, which is in turn different from the group of people who are season ticket holders. A theater would design its strategy to communicate with these different segments of its market in different ways, perhaps offering varied prices or emphasizing unique aspects of the theatergoing experience to each.

Some of the most sophisticated methods of segmentation involve *psychographics.* Psychographic measures combine demographic data with knowledge about individuals' *lifestyles,* defined by their activities, interests, and opinions (AIOs) (Andreasen & Kotler, 2008; Sargeant, 2005). Market researchers group individuals according to various lifestyles that are associated with certain behaviors, attitudes, or likes and dislikes. For example, we might assume that a young single person who lives with roommates, rides a motorcycle, and holds politically radical views may have different tastes in music than a couple with two young children and an SUV who live in the suburbs and have liberal views or a retired couple with a politically conservative orientation who live in a condo and travel only by public transportation. Individuals' lifestyles often predict not only the type of music they prefer but also the political and social causes they may favor, the kinds of artistic events they may attend, and the types of nonprofits they may support. Their patterns of behavior can help identify them as part of the target market for a particular product or service.

For example, in one study undertaken in selected cities, Andreasen and Belk were able to identify six lifestyle groups, which they labeled Passive Homebodies, Active Sports Enthusiasts, Inner-Directed Self-Sufficients, Active Homebodies, Culture Patrons, and Social Actives. People in the Culture Patron lifestyle were more likely than others to attend the theater or the symphony, while those in the Social Active lifestyle were more likely to attend only the symphony (cited in Andreasen & Kotler, 2008, p. 148). That kind of insight would be useful to a performing arts center in selecting those segments to which it would promote specific performances, ensuring that marketing dollars were used most efficiently. In other words, segmentation enables the nonprofit to target its promotion like a rifle shot, rather than scattering it like buckshot at greater total expense and with the result that much of it is wasted on those who are unlikely to attend its programs or feel a need to use its services.

The smallest conceivable market segment is, of course, the individual, and the most sophisticated for-profit marketers have become adept at targeting their messages to one person at a time. Think, for example, about experience you may have had with amazon.com. Amazon remembers what you purchased before and suggests new titles and other products that may be in line with your demonstrated interests—it segments based on your past behavior. Knowing your interests in reading and in music, it lets you know what products are being purchased by other people who are reading the same books or listening to the same music as you; this reflects the company's assumptions about your lifestyle. Your interests and preferences are also revealed through your use of Google searches and the websites that you visit, which may be tracked by "cookies" placed on your computer's hard drive. Online advertising then is targeted to match the profile you have provided of yourself through your past behavior, defining the characteristics of a very precise market segment that includes just you! Among nonprofits, segmentation at this level is increasingly applied in Internet fund-raising.

Our discussion above has focused on identifying market segments for the commercial marketing of nonprofits' programs and services. Of course, in the case of social marketing, segmentation is equally important. Target audiences will include those who engage in behaviors that the marketing is intended to change, but there is still a need for differentiation. For example, if the goal is to prevent the use of cell phones while driving, different strategies may be required to address adolescents, parents, businesspeople, and other segments.

Price

The *price* of a product or service is a straightforward concept for most people. It's what we pay to obtain what we want in the marketplace. Let's first consider how nonprofits that charge fees for their services might go about establishing those prices and then return to the idea of marketing as an exchange—an approach to thinking about price that may be a better fit than our usual understanding of the term for nonprofits engaged in social marketing.

Pricing can be an especially sensitive issue for nonprofit organizations. Some provide their services to clients without charge; others have missions suggesting that prices should be kept as low as possible to encourage participation.

There are essentially four methods for establishing the price at which a product or service will be offered. One approach is *cost-oriented pricing,* in which the price charged to the customer or client is set to cover what it costs the organization to produce or provide it. A popular method is to set prices to produce a break-even situation for the organization overall. This method may seem the most appropriate for a nonprofit organization, which does not have the purpose of maximizing its profits. But it is important to ensure that the price reflects the direct costs of providing the service as well as the overhead needed to run the organization. Indeed, as we discussed in Chapter 8, earned income, including fees for service, may be a principal source of funds for capacity building, and a price set to break even might need to encompass the costs of such efforts.

Cost-oriented pricing is popular in the nonprofit sector for a variety of reasons. First, it is simple. Second, since costs are likely to be similar for different organizations, this method often will mean that different organizations charge about the same, eliminating competition based on price and perhaps reorienting competition to the quality of programs. Third, some people see it as socially fair: "Sellers do not take advantage of buyers when the demand becomes acute, yet sellers earn a fair return on their investment" (Andreasen & Kotler, 2008, p. 244).

Another way to establish prices is by using *competition-oriented pricing.* The nonprofit might look at its competitors, perhaps in order to charge a bit less or provide a somewhat better product than others are offering at the same price. As discussed before, even if a nonprofit does not compete directly with another, it must take generic competition into account in establishing its prices. For example, a theater needs to consider how its ticket price compares not only with that of other theaters, but also with the cost of going to the movies instead. The price and the product interact. What does the theater experience offer to justify spending the price of a ticket rather than just staying home and watching TV? Does the product need to be more than just a play? For example, can a higher ticket price be justified and obtained if the experience includes a backstage reception attended by the cast of the play?

A third way of establishing prices is *value-based pricing* (Andreasen & Kotler, 2008). This approach takes into consideration the perceived value of the product or service to the customer, which may not be closely related to the costs of production. Indeed, some consumers may equate higher price with quality, for example, in buying wine or automobiles. A $30 bottle of wine may not be demonstrably better than a $10 bottle of wine, and it likely did not require 3 times as many grapes to make it. But buyers who are not wine experts might prefer to pay more, believing that the price will equate to quality—or at least that their dinner guests will believe so. Is a Lexus a much better car than a Civic? Possibly it is, although both will go about the same speed and arrive at a destination with equal dependability. But there is some psychological value to the buyer in owning a car that comes with more prestige, based at least in part on its higher price. A controversial example of value-based pricing involves the tuition policies of many colleges and universities. Critics have charged that some higher-education institutions have intentionally increased their tuitions to create the image that they are elite, since that will be attractive to some students and their families.

Price Discrimination

Price discrimination sounds like something unethical, immoral, or even illegal, but it is an essential element of marketing strategy. It does not mean charging people different prices based on their race or ethnicity, gender, religion, or similar characteristics. Rather, it means charging people different prices based on the market segment to which they belong, determined by objective variables.

Nonprofits may undertake price discrimination to cover the actual higher costs of serving a particular segment. For example, a college may charge more for on-campus courses than those offered off-campus, to cover the additional costs of providing library support and other services to students who come onto the campus. Price discrimination may also be used as a way to match the price to the perceived value of the experience. For example, concert halls charge more for seats close to the stage than for seats in the balcony, although the music may sound much the same from either location. A third reason to charge different prices might be to shift utilization. Theaters often charge less for matinees than for evening performances as a way to fill the hall at a time when it might otherwise be empty. Price discrimination also can help maximize a nonprofit's revenues by pricing the most desirable products or services at a high point that some may be willing and able to pay. An interesting example of that is provided by the Bolshoi Theater in Moscow.

One of the world's most renowned ballet companies, the Bolshoi was heavily subsidized by the government of the former USSR. But with the fall of communism, it faced two challenges. One was to pay its artists at competitive rates, since they were now free to perform elsewhere in the world for potentially higher compensation. The other challenge was to replace reduced government support with other sources of revenue.

Under the communist system, the Bolshoi's best seats always had been reserved for artists, high-ranking government officials, and other VIPs, but in fact they often had not been used by those people. Instead, the tickets were sold to scalpers, who became known as "pillar people" because they often waited for possible customers while lurking behind the pillars in the lobby. Because the seats for which they had tickets were desirable, the scalpers could sell them for a profit and had done so for many years. Facing a new need to generate revenue on the introduction of a market economy, and freed from the constraints of the previous system, the Bolshoi revised its pricing policies to capture the higher value of those better seats for itself and put the pillar people out of business. It introduced price discrimination, charging varied prices for seats depending on their perceived desirability. The result was an increase in its ticket revenue of 82 percent in the first month. At the same time, it lowered the prices for less desirable seats, making them more accessible for students and others without wealth (Klintsov & von Löhneysen, 2001, p. 6).

Defining the Exchange

In the examples mentioned above, the concept of price is what most of us would understand from the term; it's what a client or customer pays to receive a good or a service. Theaters charge for admission; colleges charge tuition; and hospitals charge for medical procedures, although some may be provided free for those who cannot pay. But what about nonprofits engaged in social marketing, with the goal of bringing about changed behavior believed to be of benefit to individuals who are part of the target market? How can we understand the concept of "price" in these situations?

Setting a price is defining a *benefit exchange* (Andresen, 2006, p. 131). In a commercial transaction, you give something up (money) in exchange for a reward that you receive, whether an education, a concert, or medical care. Social marketing similarly requires that an individual pay some price in the form of changed behavior—for example, by stopping smoking, eating healthier foods, or using seat belts. That change will only occur if the marketer can offer a reward that equals or exceeds the perceived sacrifice involved in making the change.

As Andresen (2006) explains, the most effective rewards are those that are immediate, personal, reflective of audience values, better than competing rewards, and credible. And positive rewards are more effective than threats (p. 131). "The Truth" antismoking campaign offers a good example of an effective strategy. For some teenagers, smoking is rewarding because it is a form of rebellion and coolness. An appeal to quit in order to avoid getting cancer years later may not be effective because the reward of changed behavior is not sufficiently immediate. An appeal to quit because smoking annoys their parents may not be competitive with the reward of continuing to smoke, because pleasing their parents is not as highly valued as rebellion. "The Truth" campaign took a different approach. It engaged teen spokespeople to encourage their peers to picket tobacco companies' headquarters, crank-call the companies, and speak out about their manipulation by the tobacco industry. This approach offered the reward of rebellion and was, of course, inconsistent with continuing to be a smoker (p. 143). In other words, the price paid in giving up (or avoiding) one behavior was justified by a reward that *exceeded* the reward of the alternative. The reward was offered based on what was known about the inherent motivations of the target market.

Building the Brand

Remember that competition requires an organization, nonprofit or for-profit, to differentiate its products or services from those of others. One strategy for doing so is building a recognizable *brand* and a positive image for that brand. When we think about a brand, what most readily comes to mind are commercial products, such as soda, cars, or clothing, and names like Coke or Pepsi, Honda or Toyota, Gap or Benetton. But nonprofits have brands as well.

Burnett (2007) defines *brand* as "a name, term, sign, symbol, design, or a combination of these that is intended to identify the goods and services of one seller or group of sellers and differentiate them from those of competitors" (p. 179). Thus, some brands may be names, some may be brand marks (or logos), and others may be trademarks—brand marks that have legal protection (p. 179). Many brands are instantly recognizable, for example, the Nike swoosh and Apple's apple. They do not even require a word for people to identify them with the companies and their products. Some nonprofit logos are equally well-known worldwide—for example, the Red Cross's red cross and WWF's (formerly the World Wildlife Fund's) panda.

The brand is shorthand for a collection of perceived qualities of the organization or its products, known as *brand attributes.* A brand may evoke feelings, attitudes, memories, and other intangibles that we associate with the name or symbol. "Coke" may bring to mind a refreshing break on a summer day. "Disney" may evoke memories of a childhood trip with one's family. And, depending on one's age, either "Chevy" or "Honda" may evoke a sense of confidence, quality, and durability. "Greenpeace" or "Doctors Without Borders" likely stimulate very different images—and feelings—from "Harvard" or "MoMA" (the Museum of Modern Art in New York City).

An individual's reaction to a brand may, of course, be quite different from that of others, depending upon his or her own values and perception of the values of the organization. A brand is a promise, and the term *brand promise* describes the expectations that you have about what you will receive when you buy a specific product or service. For example, when you walk into Starbucks, you expect the coffee to be good and the atmosphere to be comfortable and welcoming; those are experiences that Starbucks has promised you by placing its logo over the door (Sargeant, 2005). When you make a gift to Doctors Without Borders, you expect it to be used effectively because such responsible behavior is an attribute of the organization's brand.

Establishing a strong and positive image for a brand brings many benefits to an organization. Think back to the aftermath of Hurricane Katrina in 2005 or the Haitian earthquake in 2010. Horrified by the scenes unfolding on their television screens, many Americans went to their computers to make a gift to help those displaced by the disaster. They were most likely to go to the websites of organizations with known brands—the Red Cross, the Salvation Army, and Habitat for Humanity—both because their brands were familiar and because donors attributed to them the qualities of competence and trust.

Of course, a brand image can be fragile, and if an organization fails to deliver on the implied promise of its brand, the negative effect on its support can be both immediate and long lasting. The brand "Toyota," once synonymous with quality for many car buyers, was damaged when persistent safety problems with its cars were revealed in 2010, especially since the news stories implied that the company may not have taken sufficient action when it first learned of the risks. When, in 2002, the CEO of the United Way of the National Capital Area, serving the Washington, D.C., region, was forced to resign amid allegations of his misuse of donor funds, ripples battered the United Way brand across the country. The national office and local United Ways in other cities rushed to reassure their donors that the problems were limited to the National Capital chapter and to institute additional controls and safeguards so as to reestablish the credibility of the United Way brand. The CEO of United Way of America, the national umbrella organization, expressed the problem in this way:

> To a United Way—to a nonprofit—trust is everything. [The National Capital Chapter] need[s] to do everything that has to be done to address the issues, create aggressive long-term resolutions to them, do it transparently, do it quickly—and that's the way you build trust back. (Lipman & Williams, 2002, p. 30)

A positive brand image has value—monetary value, called *brand equity*. For example, if another company were to buy Nike, a part of the purchase price would reflect the value of the swoosh, which the buyer would expect to continue, stimulating sales and thereby increasing future revenue. When, in the 1990s, Nike was criticized for allegedly employing people in sweatshop conditions, the value of the brand, and thus the company, was at least temporarily suppressed. A company that finds its brand so degraded can be expected to undertake aggressive action, not necessarily to change its products or services but to resuscitate the value of its brand. Although nonprofit organizations are not bought or sold like corporations, their brands also have value. Its brand value is among the assets that a nonprofit brings to the table when it negotiates a partnership with a for-profit company, which will be discussed further in Chapter 12.

Integrated Marketing Communication (IMC)

Building a positive and consistent brand image requires that an organization integrate its marketing and communication efforts—in other words, that it ensures "that all the communications [it] generates represent a coherent whole" (Sargeant, 2005, p. 140). This is known as *integrated marketing communication,* or IMC.

An integrated approach requires that the messages and the values that they reflect permeate every aspect of the organization's work. If, for example, the organization desires to create an image of itself as "caring," its logo may include fuzzy small animals. However, its staff also must treat clients in a caring manner, answer the phone in a responsive tone, and create an internal culture consistent with the external image the organization seeks to build. As Sargeant (2005) expresses it, the organization needs to "live the brand" in everything it does (p. 140). The brand and its image are unlikely to settle too far from the reality of what the organization actually does or what it really is.

In an integrated approach, communications with various constituencies and stakeholders, both internally and externally, must be coordinated and consistent. As illustrated in Figure 10.2, internal audiences may include staff, board members and volunteers, and perhaps regional chapters or offices of a national or international organization. External audiences may include clients or customers; partners (such as sponsors, donors, other organizations that are collaborators); other nonprofits (both competitors and otherwise); and various publics, such as government, the media, and professional or industry associations of which the nonprofit may be a member. There is also a need to achieve integration—that is, consistent messages—across communication channels. That includes printed materials, online presence, and personal (one-on-one) communication.

The need for integration is perhaps greater in a nonprofit organization than in any other type. This reality is rooted in the essential nature of nonprofits. As mentioned before, the constituencies of a nonprofit are often overlapping and interlaced. Remember the idea of open systems from back in Chapter 3? Staff members talk to clients and to volunteers, who may also be donors, who may communicate the staff's attitudes to their family, friends, and neighbors in the broader community. Although the organization may have high-quality publications and may skillfully manage its communications with the news media, these are unlikely to outweigh the word-of-mouth information and impressions communicated by those who have firsthand knowledge about the organization.

The way a message is received has as much to do with the predilections of the receiver as with the intentions of the sender. The receiver will interpret the message in the context of his or her own values, culture, and preformed attitudes about the organization. And established views may be difficult to change. For example, if a woman who has been a loyal donor to the local Humane Society hears rumors that animals are being mistreated, she may respond in one of four ways: (1) She may practice denial, that is, persuade herself that the rumors just can't be true. Or (2) she may search for disconfirmation of the rumors, perhaps calling the director of the shelter hoping that he or she will tell her they are not correct. (3) She may minimize the problem, rationalizing that perhaps there have been a few cases of mistreatment, but that surely they are not part of a consistent pattern and the stories have just been exaggerated by people who, for some reason, have it in for the Humane Society. Or (4) she may accept the rumors as true and change her beliefs, discontinuing her financial support (Andreasen & Kotler, 2008). Human beings tend to resist changing their beliefs, whether positive or negative; thus, a minimum goal of communication is to continually reinforce the positive attitudes that your friends may hold, positively affect those of individuals who have been previously indifferent, and do nothing to further strengthen the negative attitudes of those who may already hold them. Just as for an individual, a tarnished reputation for an organization may be difficult to repair.

The *source* of information is a critical variable in its credibility. People are more inclined to believe what they hear from other individuals than what they read in the newspaper or hear on television. This is especially the case if the individual who provides the information is someone close to them, whom they trust, or close to the organization and thus presumed to know the real truth. This is one of the reasons why members of nonprofit boards, who are generally respected citizens in their communities, are so important as advocates for the organization's goals.

FIGURE 10.2 ■ Integrated Marketing Communication

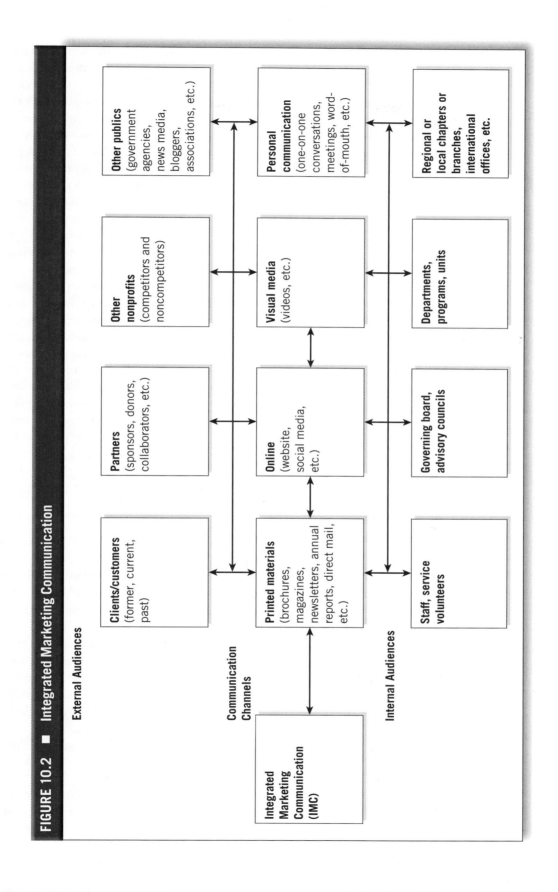

257

The sources of information people find to be most credible are family members, closely followed by friends and associates. This may include verbal communication or postings that known people may make on social media such as Facebook. Professionals like clergy, doctors, and counselors rank right after friends as credible sources of information. Newspapers, direct mail, and the Internet come next. The mass media, including radio and TV, have the least credibility as sources of information, although, interestingly, positive publicity from a mass media source is often highly prized by organizations that wish to improve their image (Bonk, Griggs, & Tynes, 1999, p. 13). The most credible medium of communication is word-of-mouth. One research study, reported in 2006, found that 53 percent of Americans were inclined to accept the credibility of what they were told by friends and family and that 51 percent are likely to pass along the information they received by word-of-mouth to others (Hall, 2006). Positive coverage in the news media is thus unlikely to outweigh the comments of an unhappy staff member to a client or of a disgruntled volunteer to his or her neighbor. Consistency of message—and of behavior—is thus essential to establishing and maintaining the organization's positive brand image.

What makes an effective message? Andresen (2006) offers a convenient acronym to remember the essential elements: CRAM. Effective messages are those that establish a Connection, promise a Reward, inspire Action, and stick in Memory (p. 163). Communicating a message requires tailoring it to both one-way communication and two-way communication, and brevity is essential. A slogan or tag line represents a shorthand for the message in one-way communication, such as advertising; for example, "Together we can save a life" delivers the message of the Red Cross in five words, and "Share the power of a wish" is a clear call to action from the Make-a-Wish Foundation (Andresen, p. 172). The central message also needs to be communicated in conversation, that is, in two-way communication, and brevity is again essential. The story must be capable of summary in the course of an elevator ride, called an "elevator pitch." Clarity, brevity, and consistency are the essential elements of effective communication.

Evaluating Marketing and Communication

As in other aspects of nonprofit management, the important question about any marketing or communication plan is a simple one: Does it work? In other words, what impact does adoption of a marketing approach have on the performance of a nonprofit organization? By now, readers who have progressed through this book from the beginning will recognize the issues associated with the question—the complexity of defining what constitutes nonprofit organizational performance and how to measure it once defined.

It is, of course, relatively easy to establish the link between marketing and performance in a for-profit company. Indeed, most research on the link between marketing and performance has been focused on the business sector, and a number of studies have identified a relationship between market orientation and financial outcomes, such as return on investment (Gainer & Moyer, 2005; Shoham, Ruvio, Vigoda-Gadot, & Schwabsky, 2006). Similar methods may be suitable to studying marketing by nonprofits that also provide services in a competitive environment, such as health care. For many nonprofits, however, assessing the benefits of marketing also requires measuring its effect on donors, clients, and the advancement of causes or ideas, outcomes that may be less easily quantified.

The findings of several studies suggest that nonprofit organizations that hold a market orientation, perhaps better defined as a "social orientation," do attain greater financial support and client satisfaction than those that do not (Gainer & Moyer, 2005). But as Shoham et al. (2006) acknowledge in a report on their investigations in this area, "New measures of [nonprofit organization] performance are needed and should guide future research" (p. 470).

Chapter Summary

Marketing principles have been widely adopted in the nonprofit sector. Some nonprofits engage in commercial marketing to attract customers to the goods and services that they provide. Others use social marketing to change behavior in order to benefit people and society. Some remain concerned that commercial marketing may not be appropriate to nonprofit values and cultures. This may reflect, in part, an understanding of marketing that is a throwback to earlier mind-sets about the concept, especially the idea that marketing is equivalent to sales.

Contemporary marketing follows a customer mind-set. That requires that "the organization systematically study customers' needs, wants, perceptions, preferences, and satisfaction . . . and act on this information to improve its offerings to meet its customers' needs better" (Andreasen & Kotler, 2008, p. 39). This implies that the organization's programs and services need to be adapted to meet identified customer desires; but this should not be taken as a reason for a nonprofit to abandon its mission or central values. Rather, marketing should be used as a tool for pursuing the mission and achieving mission-related goals.

The marketing mix includes four variables (called the 4 Ps of marketing): product, place, price, and promotion. Organizations can adjust the marketing mix to differentiate themselves from others and position themselves in a unique market niche, gaining an advantage over other organizations or alternative activities with which they may compete. Nonprofits may compete directly with other organizations, nonprofit or for-profit, but also face generic competition from all alternative uses for individuals' time and money.

Products have tangible and intangible qualities, including the prestige associated with a degree from a well-known university or the environment in which coffee is consumed. Place, or location, determines access to a program or service and is a critical variable in the marketing mix. Some products and services need to be taken to where the customers are—for example, vans that provide mobile medical care. Prices for products and services may be set to provide a break-even result for the nonprofit, to compete with what others are charging, or to reflect the perceived value of the product or service to the customer. Sophisticated marketers practice price discrimination, charging different prices to different segments of their target market. Price discrimination may be intended to match differences in product value, e.g., seats closer to or farther from the theater stage; to shift utilization from peak to nonpeak periods; or to maximize revenue by charging the highest prices that some consumers are willing to pay.

Brand is defined as "a name, term, design, symbol, or any other feature that identifies one seller's good or service as distinct from those of other sellers" (Burnett, 2007, p. 179). Individuals attribute qualities to a brand, and organizations work to establish a positive brand image, which may help attract both clients and donors. A positive brand has a monetary value, called brand equity, which may form the basis of some partnerships between nonprofits and for-profit companies.

Communications and marketing must be integrated; that is, their goals must permeate all aspects of the organization, with consistent messages being delivered to various constituencies. This approach is known as integrated marketing communication, or IMC. It is especially important in nonprofits because their borders are porous, and members of various constituencies, including staff, volunteers, and donors, may communicate with each other. Individuals attribute greater credibility to information they receive through word-of-mouth than to what they read or see in the public media, especially if the source is someone close to them or with inside knowledge of the organization.

Research suggests that nonprofits that adopt a market orientation or a societal orientation do achieve greater financial support and client satisfaction. However, establishing a link between marketing and organizational performance remains bedeviled by the difficulty of defining and measuring performance in ways that have universal acceptance.

Note

1. If a product or service is provided for a fee, then the relevant variable is what the customer *wants,* not what he or she may need. For example, a person may need more exercise, and his or her doctor may even recommend it. That person should join a health club. But unless the person also *wants* more exercise, his or her need is irrelevant from a marketing perspective because he or she will not be willing to spend money on health club dues.

KEY TERMS AND CONCEPTS

4 Ps of marketing	*integrated communications/ integrated marketing*	*product mind-set*
brand		*promotion*
brand attributes	*market niche*	*psychographics*
brand equity	*marketing*	*sales mind-set*
communication	*marketing mix*	*segmentation*
communications	*place*	*strategic communications/ marketing*
competitive advantage	*position*	
cost-oriented pricing	*price*	*target-audience mind-set*
demographic variables	*price discrimination*	*target market/target audience*
differentiation	*product*	*value-based pricing*

CASE 10.1   AARP

AARP is one of the United States' largest nonprofit organizations, with more than 35 million members, all of whom are over the age of 50 years. Its purposes include promoting independence, dignity, and purpose for older persons; enhancing the quality of life of older persons; and encouraging older people "to serve, not to be served." It pursues those purposes by informing its members and the public on issues important to older people; advocating on legislative, consumer, and legal issues; promoting community service by older people; and offering a wide range of special products and services to its members, including insurance plans and discounts on travel and various other products (www.aarp.org).

What is today known as AARP was founded in 1958 by Dr. Ethel Percy Andrus and for most of its history was known as the "American Association of Retired Persons." For most of that time, the name accurately reflected the status of most of its members. But in 1998, it needed to respond to powerful demographic trends. The baby boomer generation, with some 78 million people, was aging, with its oldest members entering their fifties. They were the future market for the association's programs, but their lives were different from those of earlier generations. People were living longer and working longer. The baby boomers were in apparent denial about their own aging—remember, this was the generation that in the 1960s had invented the phrase, "Don't trust anybody over 30." If the association was going to continue growing, it would need to attract this rising and somewhat different generation of Americans.

Beginning in 1998, AARP undertook extensive research into the attitudes of baby boomers toward the organization, and the findings were reason for concern. Many baby boomers were attracted to AARP's products and services, but as the organization's president summarized the situation, "Boomers right now think of AARP as more for their parents [than for them]" (Lipke, 2000, p. 37). Armed with the insights of market research, the organization went about changing itself to become more attractive to the growing hoard of aging baby boomer Americans.

For one thing, the "American Association of Retired Persons" became just AARP, much as Kentucky Fried Chicken had become KFC and the American Telephone and Telegraph Company had changed to simply AT&T. In other words, the word *retired* was retired, since it no longer applied to the actual working status of most of the organization's prospective members. But the name change was not all. AARP introduced a new magazine targeting baby boomers and divided its existing magazine, *Modern Maturity,* into two editions—one for people who are retired and one for people who are still working (Lipke, 2000). It launched a $100 million advertising campaign to announce its rebranding and to promote its various products and services. It launched a new Internet service aimed at issues faced by baby boomers. In 2006, it was developing additional new products aimed at the baby boom generation, including podcasts and an "audio logo" like the well-known sound of "Intel inside" (Elliott, 2006).

The stakes were high, and AARP set ambitious goals for increasing its membership by capturing a larger share of the baby boomers who were reaching the age of eligibility (Lipke, 2000). By 2006, it had reached 36.5 million members, including 44 percent of all Americans over 50 (Nelson, 2006).

CASE 10.2   Randolph College

Randolph-Macon Woman's College, located in Lynchburg, Virginia, was founded in 1891 and until 2007 was a college for women. The college had a distinguished history, producing notable graduates including the Nobel Prize winner Pearl Buck. But by 2003, the college's board of trustees faced a serious situation. The college was discounting tuition by 60 percent and spending more than the usual amount from its endowment, while enrollment had stagnated well below the level of 1,000 students, which the board considered the minimum for financial stability. A marketing research firm identified several problems, including the college's rural location and the fact that only 3 percent of college-age young women would even consider attending a single-sex institution (Pulley, 2007).

The board feared for the survival of the college and launched a strategic planning process. In the fall of 2006, the board released the strategic plan, which called for the college to become a coeducational institution. Men would be admitted for the fall 2007 semester. The institution's name would be changed to Randolph College.

(Continued)

(Continued)

Announcement of the board's decision elicited a strong reaction from some of the college's alumnae. Opponents of the change organized themselves under the name "Preserve Educational Choice, Inc." and set up a website to solicit contributions and disseminate information arguing against the change. The group distributed a paper titled "20 Reasons Why You Should Change Your Vote," trying to persuade the board to reverse its decision (Preserve Educational Choice, 2007).

The college responded with its own paper, disputing the group's arguments (Randolph College, 2007). College leaders launched a national tour to meet with alumnae to explain their reasons for the decision, but some remained angry and threatened to withhold future gifts.

In an article in *Currents,* John Pulley (2007) analyzed communication failures surrounding the issue. Some alumnae said that the college had led them to believe things were going well, announcing successful campaigns and other good news that did not prepare them for a radical new plan. Others felt that they were misled by a 2005 letter from the chair of the college's board suggesting that coeducation was just one of the many options being considered and that it was not likely to happen. Some alumnae said that they had received e-mails asking for suggestions of a new name for the college before they had even been informed of the board's decision to turn it coed. Others said that the college had disseminated enough information throughout the process but had not given alumnae opportunities to engage in real conversation about what the board was considering. The acting president of the college explained, "We tried to let people know what was happening as it was happening. In retrospect, we probably should have employed a specific public relations effort" (Pulley, 2007, n.p.).

Additional Source: Ashburn (2006).

QUESTIONS FOR DISCUSSION

1. How might the tools of portfolio analysis reviewed in Chapter 7 be applied in developing a marketing strategy?

2. Which principles from this chapter are illustrated by the case of AARP?

3. Is the case of Randolph College about marketing or about communication? Explain.

4. Below is a list of some well-known nonprofit organizations and a list of attributes. Look at each nonprofit and identify up to three attributes that you would use to describe your impression of the organization. Don't think too long; just write down the first three words that come to mind when you read the organization's name. (If you've never heard of the organization, just leave it blank.) When you are done, consider these questions:

   • How do your results compare with those of your classmates?
   • What do the results suggest about attributes of the brand in each case?
   • Why do you think each organization has the image that it does, either positive or negative?

American Red Cross	___,___,___	(a) innovative
Salvation Army	___,___,___	(b) well-managed
Nature Conservancy	___,___,___	(c) caring
Greenpeace	___,___,___	(d) greedy
Boy Scouts	___,___,___	(e) unresponsive
National Geographic Society	___,___,___	(f) dependable
City Year	___,___,___	(g) high quality
United Way of America	___,___,___	(h) patriotic
Boys and Girls Clubs	___,___,___	(i) untrustworthy
Doctors Without Borders	___,___,___	(j) cold-hearted
Habitat for Humanity	___,___,___	(k) friendly
Children's Defense Fund	___,___,___	(l) radical
Boston Symphony Orchestra	___,___,___	(m) exciting
Yale University	___,___,___	(n) prestigious
	___,___,___	(o) courageous

SUGGESTIONS FOR FURTHER READING

Books/Journals

Andreasen, A. R. (2006). *Social marketing for the twenty-first century.* Thousand Oaks, CA: Sage.

Andreasen, A. R., & Kotler, P. (2008). *Strategic marketing for nonprofit organizations* (7th ed.). Upper Saddle River, NJ: Prentice Hall.

Andresen, K. (2006). *Robin Hood marketing: Stealing corporate savvy to sell just causes.* San Francisco: Jossey-Bass, p. 10.

Bonk, K., Griggs, H., & Tynes, E. (2008). *Strategic communications for nonprofits* (2nd ed.). San Francisco: Jossey-Bass.

Burnett, J. J. (2007). *Nonprofit marketing: Best practices.* Hoboken, NJ: Wiley.

Hart, T., Greenfield, J. M., & Johnston, M. (2005). *Nonprofit Internet strategies: Best practices for marketing, communications, and fundraising success.* Hoboken, NJ: Wiley.

International Journal of Nonprofit and Voluntary Sector Marketing. Hoboken, NJ: Wiley. (Available at http://onlinelibrary.wiley.com/journal/10.1002/(ISSN)1479-103X).

Sargeant, A. (2005). *Marketing management for nonprofit organizations* (2nd ed.). Oxford, UK: Oxford University Press.

Websites

American Marketing Association, http://www.marketingpower.com

Council for Advancement and Support of Education, http://www.case.org/

Katya [Andresen]'s Non-profit Marketing Blog, http://www.nonprofitmarketingblog.com

Public Relations Society of America, www.prsa.org/

PART IV

Obtaining and Managing Resources

Chapter Outline

chapter 11

In 2008, an estimated $307.65 billion was given to nonprofit organizations by foundations, corporations, and individuals.

© iStockphoto.com/Joy Fera

Philanthropic Fund-Raising

11

Fund-raising is synonymous with nonprofit organizations in the minds of many people. They may associate it with the flood of solicitation letters that fill their mailboxes around the holiday season, some enclosing address labels, book markers, or other items from a charitable organization. Or they may think of the charity golf tournament, tennis tournament, or some other event in which they participate. Or, perhaps, they may think about the annual phone call they receive from a student at their college or university, or a former classmate, asking for a gift to the institution's annual fund. Increasingly, they may think about fund-raising appeals that they have received through e-mail or an effort that one of their friends may have organized on a social networking site. Indeed, charitable or philanthropic giving is an important source of revenue for many nonprofits, although just how important varies considerably among subsectors.

For example, gifts provide a small portion of total revenues for health services organizations, which receive most of their revenue from government or private payments for services provided. In contrast, most religious organizations and many human services organizations almost entirely depend on giving. Educational institutions and civic, social, and fraternal organizations are in the middle—gifts are important, but so are government grants and payments for services provided. But even for large institutions with substantial revenue from other sources, such as hospitals and universities, private gifts sometimes have a larger impact, disproportionate to their share of total revenues, because they address organizational priorities rather than supporting specific programs or services. For example, unrestricted giving may help support core operations or capacity building, new facilities may require a combination of fund-raising and borrowing, and new initiatives that do not yet attract paying customers or grants may be financed through discretionary dollars available to the CEO from endowment income or private gifts.

Although philanthropy in some form is common around the world, organized fund-raising and philanthropy on a massive scale is still primarily an American phenomenon. And massive it is. In 2008, an estimated $307.65 billion was given to nonprofit organizations by foundations, corporations, and individuals. When philanthropy is mentioned, some people think about corporate giving or perhaps the large national foundations, such as the Gates Foundation or the Ford Foundation. But private individuals are overwhelmingly the largest sources of giving, accounting for more than $229 billion of the 2008 total. The largest portion of giving by individuals is directed to religion, which accounts for about 35 percent of the total each year; however, even when religious giving is excluded, individuals still account for much more than either corporations or foundations in their impact on U.S. philanthropy. In 2008, foundations gave 13 percent and corporations accounted for just 5 percent of the total (Center on Philanthropy at Indiana University, 2009, pp. 1–4).

Where does the money go? Next to religion, which receives 35 percent of the total, the largest recipient of philanthropy is education, accounting for 13 percent, followed by human services (9 percent). Giving to create or enlarge foundations accounts for another 11 percent of the total, followed by gifts to public and society benefit organizations (8 percent), and health (7 percent). Although they are important causes for many people, the environment and animals, and the arts, culture, and humanities receive relatively small shares of the philanthropic pie, each accounting for 5 percent or less of total giving. An important and growing component of philanthropy is *bequests*—that is, gifts made by individuals through their wills or other estate-planning vehicles. Bequests accounted for almost 7 percent of total giving in 2008. With the aging of the population and the growing wealth of older people, giving through bequests is expected to grow substantially in the coming decades (Center on Philanthropy at Indiana University, 2009, pp. 1–4).

Definitions and Distinctions

When the planes hit the World Trade Center towers on September 11, 2001, millions of Americans went to their computers or reached for their checkbooks to give more than $2 billion to help the victims and their families. Four years later, when Hurricane Katrina hit the Gulf Coast, the response was again immediate and overwhelming, totaling more than $3.3 billion in gifts to organizations providing relief and support for rebuilding (Lipman, 2006). Just a year after Katrina, investor Warren Buffet rocked the philanthropy community when he announced that he would give the bulk of his fortune, an estimated $37 billion, to five charitable foundations, including $31 billion to the foundation established by his friends and fellow billionaires, Bill and Melinda Gates. The gift made Buffet one of the largest donors in U.S. history (Perry & Wilhelm, 2006). When tragedy again captured the world's attention in 2010 with a massive earthquake in Haiti, U.S. charities received almost 1 billion dollars in gifts within just 9 weeks ("American Charities Receive," 2010). These gifts demonstrate the scale and impact of giving in the United States, but they also illustrate two different *approaches* to giving—one focused on immediate needs and the other taking a more long-term, strategic perspective.

In Chapter 2, this text made a distinction between charity and philanthropy as two types of voluntary giving. *Charity* includes gifts to meet immediate human needs, for example, to provide food to those who are starving or shelter to those dislocated as a result of natural disaster—such as the post–September 11 and post–Haitian earthquake outpouring of generosity. It is often impulsive and always driven by human compassion. *Philanthropy* is giving to strengthen the infrastructure of society, that is, to develop institutions that serve human needs or enhance human development over the long run. The objects of philanthropy often include hospitals, universities, museums, and arts organizations—institutions with missions that are perpetually relevant across generations, but which do not have the same urgency as immediate human suffering. Some philanthropic gifts, such as Warren Buffet's, also go to create or expand foundations, most of which are established to last forever or a very long time, tackling long-term problems and issues. Philanthropic gifts are made carefully and thoughtfully, often as the culmination of a long-standing relationship with an institution. Emotion plays an important role in the decision to make philanthropic gifts, certainly for individual donors, but many also reflect a highly rational analysis that makes giving a form of investing in society and its important institutions. In practice, many people use the terms charity and philanthropy as if they were synonymous or use "philanthropy" as the broader concept, encompassing all voluntary giving.

But the distinction is important, and it is useful for nonprofit organizations to be mindful of how their donors may think about their giving in these different ways.

Before proceeding further, it is important also to clarify some other common terms that have somewhat different meanings but are sometimes used interchangeably in everyday conversation. *Fund-raising* is an activity undertaken with the goal of eliciting charitable or philanthropic giving. Fund-raising is related to philanthropy as preaching is to faith; that is, one is intended to inspire the other, with no guarantee of success because the response lies within the power of the respondent to determine. In the simplest understanding, fund-raising means "asking for a gift," although, as we will soon discuss, it is really a process in which asking for, or *soliciting,* a gift is but one step in a more complicated process.

Many organizations have what's known as a *development office.* Staff who work in that office may be called "development officers" and have titles such as "Director of Development." If asked what they do, they are likely to respond that they are engaged in fund-raising. The two terms, fund-raising and development, represent somewhat different concepts, although the difference is not always maintained in common usage. *Development* is a term that originated in the 1920s at Northwestern University (Worth, 1993, p. 6). The university had completed a fund-raising campaign to build a new campus. When the campaign was completed, they determined that fund-raising should be an ongoing, organized effort to continually improve and *develop* the institution, rather than a sporadic activity undertaken now and then to meet a specific need. The university created a new department to manage this ongoing effort and called it the office of "development," meaning "institutional development." Although fund-raising and development became interchangeable over time, the latter is properly understood as a more comprehensive approach to the long-term growth of an organization or institution. As I explain in an earlier work,

> Fund-raising is but one aspect of a complex process involving the institution, its hopes and goals, and the aspirations of its benefactors. Fund-raising is episodic; development is continuous. Fund-raising is focused on a particular objective or set of goals; development is a generic and long-term commitment to the financial and physical growth of the institution. Successful fund-raising requires a specific set of interpersonal and communication skills; development requires a broader understanding of the institution and its mission as well as patience, judgment, and sensitivity in building relationships over the long haul. A "fund-raiser" is an individual skillful in soliciting gifts; a "development officer" may be a fund-raiser, but he or she is also a strategist and manager of the entire development process. (Worth, 1993, pp. 7–8)

By the mid-1970s, however, the terms fund-raising and development had become so interchangeable in use that when the Council for Advancement and Support of Education (CASE) was established in 1974, it adopted the new term *institutional advancement* to describe the activities performed by its members. Institutional advancement, or just advancement, encompasses not only fund-raising or development but also the related activities of communications, marketing, and other programs for constituent relations. In other words, institutional advancement has a meaning similar to the original concept of development—a long-term and broad-based program to build an organization or institution. In the decades since CASE's founding, "advancement" has been widely adopted by colleges and universities and also has gained currency in nonprofit organizations more broadly. Ironically, it also has come to be used synonymously with fund-raising by many people, so that some organizations now have an advancement office, employing staff members who describe their responsibilities as "fund-raising."

Motivations for Giving

The question of what motivates donors is of obvious practical interest to nonprofit managers in determining which of their needs may be met through philanthropy and in designing their fundraising programs. But donor motivation is also a topic that has generated a substantial body of research. Let's look at motivation from the perspective of the three principal sources of giving—corporations, foundations, and individuals. Although they are the largest source of gifts, we discuss individuals last because their motivation is the most complex of these three types of donors.

Understanding Corporate Philanthropy

Corporations make philanthropic gifts both directly and through foundations that some have established as separate nonprofit entities. Using a foundation offers advantages over direct giving by the corporation, including the ability to add resources to the foundation in highly profitable years and then sustain a relatively even level of giving in years when the business may not be as profitable. Corporations make cash gifts and also gifts of products, known as *gifts-in-kind,* which account for about one third of corporate philanthropy (Center on Philanthropy at Indiana University, 2007). But corporations also support nonprofits through a variety of partnerships, which, as the term implies, offer benefits to both the nonprofit and the business. These partnerships are sometimes complex and represent a growing component of nonprofit revenue. Although they provide financial benefit to many nonprofit organizations, they are not "philanthropy," since the company expects a financial return as well as a benefit to the nonprofit partner.

Corporate philanthropy is a relatively recent phenomenon. Indeed, prior to the case of *A.P. Smith Mfg. Co. v. Barlow* in 1953 (cited in Rosso & Associates, 2003, p. 178), the courts imposed restrictions on corporate giving that did not directly benefit the interests of shareholders or employees of the firm. This landmark case opened the door to the concept of *enlightened self-interest,* that is, the idea that companies could make gifts that might not have a direct or immediate benefit to the bottom line, but that would generally help maintain a healthy society in which to do business.

Corporate giving generally increased during the decades of the 1960s, 1970s, and 1980s, and its purposes often reflected the interests and affiliations of the senior executives and directors of the company. However, during the 1980s and with increasing momentum in the 1990s and 2000s, corporate giving became professionalized. Many companies created committees to make decisions about where to direct the corporation's giving or created separate foundations to undertake philanthropy in the company's name.

Since the mid-1980s, corporate giving has increasingly reflected an approach known as *strategic philanthropy*—that is, giving according to a plan that relates the corporation's philanthropy to its overall strategic and business goals. Giving is viewed as an investment and is subject to evaluation based on how much return it produces—the extent to which it enhances the corporation's competitiveness. For example, a corporation might target its giving in communities where it plans to develop new facilities or to specific groups of people who are likely to be customers of its products. The various corporate–nonprofit partnerships, which will be discussed in Chapter 12, have evolved from the strategic philanthropy approach. Today, the line between corporate philanthropy and marketing has become blurred as has the line between fundraising and negotiating business relationships. Indeed, in 2004 the Association of Fundraising Professionals (AFP) amended its code of professional ethics, which had long required that fundraisers not accept compensation based on a percentage of gifts, to include a similar prohibition with regard to the solicitation of corporate partnership arrangements (Hall, 2005).

To understand the motivation for corporate giving, a nonprofit needs to understand the company's business plans and goals, on which its program of philanthropy is likely to be based. This is not to imply that corporations give in a way that is detrimental to the interests of nonprofits or society or that their motivations should be viewed as invidious. Nevertheless, the realities do suggest that nonprofits begin their search for corporate dollars not in terms of their own needs but rather with a view to how there can be a mutual benefit to the nonprofit's welfare and the interests of the corporation from which it seeks support.

Foundation Giving

It is not difficult to understand the motivations for giving by foundations. Very simply, that is what they exist to do; indeed, it is what they are *required* to do as a condition of their tax-exempt status. Foundations are required to expend a minimum of an amount equivalent to 5 percent of the value of their invested assets each year, either for grants or operating expenses. The questions of whether the 5 percent payout is sufficient and how much of their operating expenses foundations should be permitted to include within that 5 percent have been topics of policy debate in Congress in recent years (Wolverton, 2003a).

Foundations are created by corporations, individuals, or families, and their activities generally reflect the interests of the founders. Family foundations often evolve as they grow, becoming *independent foundations* that employ professional staff and develop formal programs and guidelines that make explicit their interests and priorities. Many have geographic and other restrictions on their giving and have well-defined areas of interest and grant programs through which they provide support, as illustrated by the example of the MacArthur Foundation, shown in Box 11.1. It is usually fruitless for an organization to approach an independent foundation for support if it does not operate programs related to the organization's activities or has policies that exclude the organization from consideration.

BOX 11.1 PROGRAMS OF THE JOHN D. AND CATHERINE T. MACARTHUR FOUNDATION

The Foundation makes grants and loans through four programs.

The Program on Global Security and Sustainability focuses on international issues, including human rights and international justice, peace and security, conservation and sustainable development, higher education in Nigeria and Russia, migration and human mobility, and population and reproductive health. MacArthur grantees work in about 60 countries; the Foundation has offices in India, Mexico, Nigeria, and Russia.

The Program on Human and Community Development addresses issues in the United States, including community and economic development; housing, with a focus on the preservation of affordable rental housing; juvenile justice reform; education, with an emerging interest in digital media and learning; and policy research and analysis.

The General Program supports public interest media, including public radio, documentary programming, and work to explore the use of digital technologies to reach and engage the public. Grants are also made to arts and cultural institutions in the Chicago area and for special initiatives.

(Continued)

(Continued)

The MacArthur Fellows Program awards five-year, unrestricted fellowships to individuals across all ages and fields who show exceptional merit and promise of continued creative work. It is limited to U.S. citizens and residents.

Source: MacArthur Foundation website (http://www.macfound.org/site/c.lkLXJ8MQKrH/b.860781/k.D616/Overview.htm). Used with permission of the MacArthur Foundation.

Because foundations are rational donors, obtaining foundation support often requires preparation of a written proposal. The art of doing so is sometimes called "grantwriting," although the seeker is indeed writing a proposal, not a grant—the grant is made by the foundation and if the grant is "written," the writing would be done by a foundation official. "Proposal writing" thus is a more accurate description of what a nonprofit organization or a member of its staff does. This text does not go into detail on the techniques of proposal writing, but many good guides are available and organizations such as AFP offer training on the topic. Box 11.2 provides an outline of a typical foundation proposal, although each must be tailored to the guidelines and requirements of the specific foundation to which the proposal is being directed.

BOX 11.2 SECTIONS OF A STANDARD GRANT PROPOSAL

Summary	Evaluation
Organizational Information	Other Funding
Problem/Need/Situation Description	Future Funding
Work Plan/Specific Activities	Budget
Impact of Activities	Supplementary Materials

Source: Minnesota Council on Foundations (http://www.mcf.org/mcf/grant/writing.htm).

Other types of foundations include *operating foundations* that support their own programs and generally do not make grants to other organizations, for example, Colonial Williamsburg in Virginia and Longwood Gardens in Pennsylvania. And, as discussed earlier in this book, some public charities use the term *foundation* in their names, although they both raise money and distribute it, usually to a single organization or a defined community. Operating foundations usually are not good fund-raising prospects for other nonprofits, nor are most foundations that are public charities, although some community foundations have discretionary funds that may be available to nonprofit organizations in their areas.

Motivations of Individual Donors

As illustrated by the spontaneous response to 9/11, Hurricane Katrina, and the Haitian earthquake, the motivations of individual donors are often more complex and less calculated than those of corporations or foundations. Individual donors have been the focus of a substantial number of research studies. Most have examined characteristics that distinguish donors from non-donors and have identified statistical relationships between giving and certain characteristics, for example, age, gender, income level, and geographic location. Fewer have explored the more complex question of donor motivation, to answer the question of *why* they give.

Traditionally, the literature has been divided between those who attribute giving to altruism, that is, those who say that individuals are driven by their nature to help others and improve the human condition, and those who say that individuals give to obtain some benefit for themselves, perhaps recognition, social position, or control. A 1994 study by Russ Prince and Karen File identified seven motivational types that some fund-raising practitioners find to be intuitively attractive. According to these authors, the largest group of donors, 26 percent, are "communitarians," motivated by the belief that giving makes good sense in terms of a better community for their businesses and lives. Another 21 percent are the "devout," who give because of their religious beliefs. The third-largest group is the 15 percent that Prince and File call "investors." These are donors who are particularly concerned with the tax and estate benefits of giving and will be interested to know exactly what result will be accomplished with their support. "Socialites," 10.8 percent of donors, give because it provides opportunities for social interactions; they are often people who will attend charity events. The "altruists," the selfless donors who may give without any desire for recognition, comprise another 9 percent. "Repayers," who give based on gratitude for benefits they have received, make up 10.2 percent. The final category, the "dynasts," are people who give because it is a family tradition; they constitute another 8.3 percent of donors (pp. 14–16). Different types of donors gravitate toward various nonprofit subsectors; for example, the devout tend to support religion, the socialites give to arts organizations, and repayers often direct their support to universities and hospitals that may have influenced their own or their family members' lives.

In the early 2000s, Paul Schervish and John Havens of the Social Welfare Research Institute at Boston College studied social-psychological factors influencing the giving of wealthy individuals and identified several "dispositions" or "inclinations" that motivate individuals to engage in significant philanthropy. These inclinations include "hyperagency," the ability to make history and affect the conditions under which people live; "identification," the unity of self-regard and regard for others; and consideration of income and estate tax benefits. The authors de-emphasize the impact of tax incentives, arguing that their data suggest that as wealth increases, individuals gain a preference for leaving their estates to charity rather than to heirs. They speculate that removal of estate taxes thus would result in more money becoming available for bequests to nonprofit organizations (Schervish & Havens, 2001).

The influence of tax incentives on giving is controversial. Although most economists' studies have found a relationship between changes in tax rates and giving the following year, some fund-raising practitioners and scholars argue that other motivations are predominant and that changes in tax laws would not affect giving totals (Kelly, 1998). For example, in a 2006 study, conducted by the Indiana University Center on Philanthropy, of a sample of high–net worth households, 52 percent responded that their giving would not decrease if they received no income tax deductions for their gifts, 38 percent said that their giving would decrease somewhat, and only 7 percent said that it would decrease dramatically (Beatty, 2006). But such studies may be flawed because they ask people to say what they would do under certain hypothetical circumstances rather than analyzing data reflecting actual past behavior. People are often inclined to give what they think to be the right or appropriate answer, which may or may not predict what their behavior would actually be under the hypothetical circumstances described. For example, when asked if we would wait for a red light in the middle of the night when the police are not in sight, most of us probably would answer "yes." But what some might actually do could differ from this appropriate response to the question.

The mathematics of giving and taxes suggests that tax rates may influence the amount that individuals are *able* to give, regardless of what their *desire* to give might be. For example, assume that an individual in a 35 percent income tax bracket makes a gift of $1,000 that is tax deductible. Because of the deduction, the donor's income is reduced by $1,000, which reduces his or her income tax bill by $350 below what it would otherwise have been (35 percent of $1,000). That makes the out-of-pocket or actual cost of the $1,000 gift $650, since there is a *tax savings* of $350. Now, assume that the donor's tax rate has been reduced to 10 percent. The $1,000 gift now saves $100 in taxes, making its out-of-pocket cost $900. Although it may seem counterintuitive, a lower tax rate increases the cost of a gift. Depending on donors' overall financial position, this could have the effect of making it more difficult for them to give as much as they otherwise might have been able to, regardless of how highly motivated they might be to give.

The preponderance of research suggests that the motivations of most individual donors are mixed, including some combination of altruism and self-interest, and that tax policies have an impact on the amount that individuals are able to give, whether during their lifetimes or through their estates on their death. But both questions are likely to remain controversial and the focus of future research.

With the increasing diversity of the American population, a number of studies in recent years have examined the particular giving traditions and patterns of various groups, including women, African Americans, and Hispanics/Latinos. The topic is of increasing interest to many nonprofits, as greater wealth is being accumulated by women and members of minority groups. Students will find additional reading on this topic suggested at the end of this chapter.

The Fund-Raising Process

Some people may think of fund-raising as synonymous with asking for money, but it is indeed a process with identifiable stages and steps. Without following the process, fund-raising is random and not really very different from standing on a corner with a tin cup, hoping that some passerby will drop in a few coins. That is not an approach that is likely to generate the substantial and continuing support needed to sustain an organization.

The fund-raising process is depicted in Figure 11.1 and includes six basic steps. Once an organization has (1) identified its priorities for financial support and developed a case to justify its goals, it must (2) identify the prospects most likely to give. (3) A process of *cultivation* develops a relationship between the organization and the prospect and, at the appropriate point in the relationship, (4) the prospect is asked for a gift. (5) The gift is acknowledged and the donor is recognized. (6) The organization then works to properly *steward* the gift, keeping the donor engaged and informed of what it has accomplished with the support provided. The process is usually described as a cycle because effective fund-raising programs seek to develop a base of donors who continue to give on a regular basis. Stewardship is really part of the process of continued cultivation of donors who may provide additional, and it is hoped increased, support in the future. Let's walk through each step in the process in greater detail.

Identifying Priorities and Developing the Case

Fund-raising without a purpose is unlikely to elicit support. As Thomas Broce writes, "Donors give gifts to meet objectives, not simply to give money away" (p. 19). This reality requires that an organization base its fund-raising on identified priority needs related to achievement of its

FIGURE 11.1 ■ The Fund-Raising Process

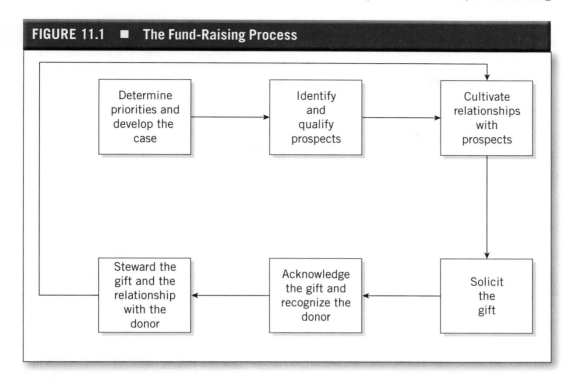

mission and rooted in a plan for its future growth and improvement. Strategic planning is often the first step in setting the organization's vision and goals for the future, which then can be translated into specific fund-raising objectives with a rationale for why the support will enhance its ability to achieve its social mission.

The organization must develop a *case for support,* or a rationale for giving, that goes beyond its own needs and links its goals to broader social and human purposes. An organization's leaders may be convinced of its worthiness and the importance of its financial needs. But in a competitive philanthropic marketplace, they must make the case for how support for its purposes will bring a greater benefit than a gift to another organization or cause. For example, Box 11.3 shows a summary of the case for the hypothetical Siwash College (recall Chapter 10) that is based entirely on what its faculty and students perceive to be important to them and on the institution's self-interest. The needs may be real, but this statement is unlikely to inspire many donors to sacrifice in order to address them. In contrast, the second case explains Siwash's need for philanthropy in relation to social justice and economic prosperity, helping place its needs in a broader context and appeal to the values and emotions of potential donors.

The case for support is the reason the organization seeks support, derived from its mission and values—it is the answer to the questions, "Why should I give to this organization?" and "Why is this cause more important than others that also ask for my support?" It is often expressed in a case statement, a written document that may include a comprehensive discussion of the organization's fund-raising objectives and the justification for each. Case statements may be developed to provide a resource within the organization (an *internal case statement*) or as a printed brochure for use in communicating with donor prospects (an *external case statement*). But the product known as the case statement should not be confused with the *idea* of the case. An organization that rushes to produce a glossy brochure without careful thought about the essence of its case is unlikely to successfully address the motivations of donors, whether corporations, foundations, or individuals.

BOX 11.3 THE CASE FOR SUPPORT

Siwash College Case #1

The College's enrollment has increased in the past decade, resulting in crowded classrooms and inadequate office space for the faculty. Colleges are competing for the best students with offers of scholarship support. We now have fallen behind our competitors in the quality of our facilities and the amount of financial aid that we can provide. We are losing many of the best students to other institutions. For this reason, we are seeking $10 million in funds for new campus construction and scholarships that we will offer to the students from our region who have the highest SAT (Scholastic Aptitude Test) scores.

Siwash College Case #2

The United States always has been a nation of economic opportunity. Today, as we face great challenges from global economic competition, the talents of too many young men and women are undeveloped because they lack the financial means to attend college. College tuition has risen dramatically and financial aid has not kept pace. This is unjust and threatens America's future economic prosperity. Educational opportunity always has been fundamental to the mission and values of Siwash College. The Board of Trustees has established a plan to maintain our tradition by expanding enrollment and providing additional scholarship support for worthy young men and women of our region. To that end, we seek $10 million in support to expand our facilities and increase scholarship support to promising and worthy students.

Identifying and Qualifying Prospects

Just as an individual seeking a marriage partner likely would not do well by calling people at random or by proposing to strangers on the street, an organization seeking gift support needs to focus on *prospects* who offer a better-than-average chance of giving. Otherwise, its time and fund-raising resources will be allocated inefficiently and ineffectively. The identification of prospects begins by limiting the search to those who have the financial *ability* or *capacity* to give; that is, they are "qualified" by their ability to make a gift. Obviously, an individual or company in bankruptcy or a foundation that has already allocated all its resources would not be worthy of further attention. They might have a keen interest in the nonprofit, but their financial inability would preclude considering them as prospects. However, making a list of successful companies and wealthy individuals still does not provide likely prospects for a particular nonprofit; it would be a large list and include many who are remote or already deeply committed to other causes. It would be like making a list of marriage prospects that included every single person in the world; they might have the ability to consider marriage, but it would still be a fruitless task to send proposals to all of them. The list would need to be culled by some additional criteria. For example, it might help to limit the search to people with whom the marriage seeker already has some connection—maybe schoolmates, individuals who attend the same church, or friends of friends. And, being single does not automatically imply a desire to be married, so it would be wise to limit the list of prospects to those who may have indicated some interest in getting married. (It is instructive to observe that online dating sites do provide tools for screening a large pool of people in order to identify those with the ability and desire to marry and who have some interests in common with the searcher—the matching is not random.)

Like marriage prospects, the most likely prospects for charitable gifts will be those who have not only the *ability* to give but also some *linkage* to and *interest* in the organization or the area of activity in which it is engaged (Seiler, 2003, p. 28). Identifying individuals, foundations, and corporations who are prospects is a task often performed by professionals engaged in *prospect research,* a specialty increasingly in demand by nonprofit organizations with sophisticated fund-raising programs. Prospect researchers have a variety of tools and techniques, including a growing array of electronic databases, to help narrow the list to those with the greatest likelihood of making a gift to their organizations.

Financial ability may be easily determined for foundations, on which information is readily available in published sources. Corporations may be somewhat less easily assessed, but some indication of ability to give may be assumed from revenue and profits. Individuals present more of a challenge. Although public information can help determine levels of income and wealth—for example, real estate values—much of the wealth will be less visible.

Linkage to the organization may occur in a variety of ways. Volunteers, graduates, and former patients or their families have obvious connections to the organization that have served them. But other types of nonprofits may need to build their network of prospects in a pattern similar to concentric circles, beginning with those who are already part of the organization's inner circle of friends and donors, then moving outward to less connected members of the community. The organization's governing board is its principal link to the outside world and, absent an easily identifiable constituency of potential donors with direct linkage, board members' efforts in identifying and engaging prospects among their own business and social contacts may be important.

Interest may be relatively easy to determine for a foundation, if it provides a clear statement of its priorities. Some corporations that have formal giving programs offer similar clarity about their interests, while in other cases interest may be presumed because the company's business activities bear a close relationship to the work of the nonprofit. For example, a home builder or a mortgage lender may have an interest in the issues of homelessness and affordable housing; similarly, companies that manufacture products for use by women are often among the most prominent contributors to nonprofits that address women's issues or diseases. For individual prospects, interest may be revealed by past gifts to the organization or perhaps gifts to another organization addressing similar issues or needs, but often an individual's interest can be determined with confidence only through personal contact and discussion.

Cultivating Prospects

To invoke again the metaphor of courtship, most people would not consider proposing marriage on the first date. The odds of such a proposal gaining a positive response are increased if some time and effort have been devoted to cultivating a relationship, perhaps involving smaller steps such as dinner and flowers. A nonprofit cultivating a prospective donor likewise will increase the chances of gaining support if it devotes some time and attention to *cultivating* a relationship before moving to solicit a gift. The larger the amount of the gift to be solicited, the greater the investment that will need to be made in cultivation of the relationship in advance of asking.

In fund-raising for small gifts, solicitation may not require significant cultivation; for example, very little cultivation precedes broad-based solicitations by mail, phone, or the Internet. However, fund-raising for major gifts involves developing and executing a series of planned initiatives expected to *move* an individual toward a closer relationship with the organization, leading to support. Major-gift fund-raisers manage and track such activity through what are known as *moves management* systems. A moves management system includes electronic systems but also manual methods and processes for tracking contacts with prospective donors to assure that cultivation of relationships occurs in a planned and strategic manner.

Soliciting the Gift

Nonprofit fund-raisers have an array of techniques available for soliciting gifts, and a full discussion is beyond the scope of this chapter. The Fund-Raising School, associated with the Center on Philanthropy at Indiana University, introduced the concept of a "ladder of effectiveness," which arrays solicitation methods from the least to the most effective (Rosso & Associates, 2003, p. 82). Box 11.4 provides a summary of some commonly used methods arranged to indicate their position on that ladder, from those that are usually most effective to those that are generally least effective. In general, the more personal the contact, the better it is. Personal solicitations and mail or phone solicitations that include a message tailored to the individual being asked are more effective than communications that are very impersonal, such as broad-based mailings and telemarketing calls. But the selection of methods employed by a nonprofit depends on several considerations.

BOX 11.4 COMMON SOLICITATION METHODS (FROM MOST TO LEAST EFFECTIVE)

1. Personal solicitation (face-to-face)
   Team of two
   One person

2. Personal letter (on personal stationery)
   With telephone follow-up
   Without telephone follow-up

3. Personal phone call
   With letter follow-up
   Without letter follow-up

4. Personalized letter or e-mail

5. Telephone solicitation (Phonathon using volunteer callers)

6. Impersonal letters, direct mail, e-mail

7. Impersonal telephone (telemarketing)

8. Fund-raising benefit, special events

9. Media, advertising, website

Source: Adapted from Rosso & Associates (2003, p. 82). Used with permission of John Wiley & Sons, Inc.

First, the method used must be appropriate to the level and type of support that the organization needs. Soliciting by direct mail, by phone, or through e-mail may be appropriate to secure a large number of relatively small gifts on a recurring basis to support the current operating budget. But major gifts to address capital or endowment needs will require personal contact and time for a full discussion of the organization's plans and the purpose that will be achieved through the gift. If the gift being solicited is for the organization's endowment, the personal contact with the prospective donor may need to be prolonged, in order to fully explore the individual's desires about his or her legacy to society beyond his or her lifetime.

A second, related consideration is the costs and benefits of the method selected. Personal solicitation, by fund-raising staff or volunteers, is generally more effective than solicitation by phone, mail, or e-mail, but it may also require a substantial commitment of time by the CEO, a development officer, and perhaps a volunteer; it may also involve costs for travel. Personal visits are to be reserved for the most promising prospects for the largest gifts. Personalized letters are generally more effective than impersonal, "Dear Friend" letters, but also require more labor or more sophisticated technology to produce. The expected better returns always need to be balanced against the costs of a particular method.

And third, an organization needs to consider what resources are available to it at particular points in its organizational life cycle. For example, a nonprofit that has little visibility, no clear donor constituency, and a fund-raising program that is just beginning, may find special events to be a useful method for engaging new people, increasing its visibility in the community, and raising some funds. Fund-raising or benefit events are not an especially effective way of raising money, and the costs of producing them may in fact consume much or all of the gross revenues. But if they can be used as a strategy for developing a new group of interested friends who may later be solicited for gifts through more effective methods, including mail, phone, and personal contact, then they may play a useful role in a comprehensive fund-raising strategy.

Again, the organization's position in its life cycle is important to consider and will determine the type of philanthropy that can be attracted. For example, a young organization, perhaps with a somewhat uncertain future, would be unlikely to attract significant bequests for its endowment. Many people would question whether it would use such gifts effectively or whether it provides a lasting purpose for their philanthropy. However, a well-established nonprofit that continues to raise funds through events and e-mail and does not solicit larger gifts is not maximizing its long-term revenue potential. In other words, the methods used to raise funds, and the purpose for which they are raised, must match the realities of an organization's financial needs and philanthropic market—or, as architects say, form should follow function.

One of the most rapidly growing methods of solicitation is the Internet and the World Wide Web. Solicitations may be sent by e-mail and provide a link to the organization's website, which allows the donor to give using a credit card or electronic funds transfer. Electronic solicitations offer many of the same advantages as direct mail, but messages can be even more personalized and costs can be very low. However, as with all methods, there are disadvantages as well, including the increasing use of spam filters and the ease with which prospective donors can delete a message from their crowded inbox without opening it. Many organizations make effective use of e-mail to stay in touch with current and past donors and even to discuss or negotiate the terms of a major gift. But such gifts will generally require some other form of contact, usually in person, with e-mail being used as a device to continue an ongoing discussion.

Nonprofit causes increasingly benefit from fund-raising efforts organized on social networking sites and those using texting as a method for making the gift. For example, the latter was a significant component of giving following the earthquake in Haiti in 2010. While these methods are certain to grow in the years head, they may be most effective for one-time gifts in response to highly emotional causes, such as disasters. Whether they will prove a good approach to building ongoing, long-term support for an organization is still unknown. The answer may depend on whether the organization maintains communication with the donors and cultivates a relationship after the initial gift.

Acknowledging and Recognizing Donors

Well-managed development offices acknowledge gifts promptly, and most tailor the acknowledgment to the level of the gift or status of the donor. For example, donors of gifts above a certain level may receive a letter from the CEO, others may receive a letter from the Director of Development, and small gifts may be acknowledged only with a preprinted receipt. Donors are required to have a formal receipt in order to deduct cash gifts of $250 or more from their taxes, and additional rules apply to the substantiation of the value of gifts-in-kind.

Recognition of donors may include listing their names in an annual report, including them in special recognition societies according to the level of the gift, and displaying their names on plaques or wall displays. Larger gifts may be recognized through the naming of facilities or endowment funds. While some donors may request anonymity, most appreciate tasteful and appropriate recognition, which itself becomes a part of the process of cultivation for the next gift.

Stewarding the Gift and the Relationship

The stewardship of past donors is an activity that has received more attention in most development offices in recent years. Experience suggests that past donors are the best prospects for future gifts, and it is therefore important to continue building their relationship with the organization after a gift has been made. The concept of stewardship can have two meanings. The most common usage encompasses the activities that the organization undertakes to keep the donor informed and engaged. These may include recognition, sending reports about the impact of the gift, and developing events to strengthen donors' involvement and knowledge about the organization's activities. It is essentially the cultivation of current and past donors with an eye toward future support. The second meaning of stewardship is more substantial, relating to the organization's responsibility to manage the gift according to the donor's intention, that is, to keep faith with the donor. This is especially important with gifts made to endowment, which are invested in perpetuity to produce income supporting current programs. Many organizations have developed regular written reports to endowment donors, informing them of the fund's financial performance as well as the activities undertaken with the income it produces. Some have developed websites where donors can receive updated information on the impact of their gifts, for example, they can read the biographies of students who are receiving scholarships that the donors have funded. In addition, recent legal cases involving claims by donors or their heirs that gifts are not being used as originally intended have caused nonprofit organizations to exercise greater care in documenting the mutual understandings of the donor and the organization in formal, written *gift agreements*.

Although the previous discussion has mostly involved individual donors, it is important to note that the fund-raising process is the same even if the donor is a corporation or a foundation. Corporate and foundation philanthropy may be more professionalized and giving decisions may be made more objectively than they are by individuals; it is still essential to identify likely prospects based on ability, linkage, and interest; to cultivate the prospect's interest; to solicit the gift in the appropriate manner at the appropriate time; to acknowledge the gift and recognize the donor; and to steward the gift and the relationship with the donor for the long run.

Corporate and foundation giving patterns may change over time as their strategies are redefined. They are less likely than individuals to develop an emotional connection to an organization and become regular, long-term donors. Indeed, while the individuals working in a corporation or a foundation may have personal feelings about the organizations it supports, the corporation or foundation itself is not a living thing capable of such relationships. Corporations and foundations thus support an organization so long as its activities are consistent with their goals—there is inevitably a *quid pro quo* element to their giving—and many limit their support to specific programs or activities and do not provide unrestricted gifts that can be used to meet general operating expenses, undertake capacity building, or address other organizational goals. Second, corporations and foundations are not mortal. Unlike individuals, they do not consider their giving over the course of an expected lifetime; they do not write wills or plan for the disposition of their estates. Understanding the giving behavior of individuals requires analysis of how they view their philanthropy at various points in their lives and how they develop giving relationships with favored nonprofits over time. Working with corporate and foundation donors requires many of the same principles as working with individuals, but it is also essential to understand the differences discussed above.

Individual Donor Life Cycles

The fund-raising pyramid is a classic depiction of how individuals are believed to develop their giving relationship with an organization. It is a standard element of fund-raising training and has been a part of fund-raising theory for many decades. Depicted in Figure 11.2, the pyramid is broader at the base and narrows as the level of gift increases going toward the top, because a smaller number of donors will ascend to each successively higher level. The organization's *total constituency,* that is, its database of prospects, contains the largest number and is thus the widest part of the pyramid. Some, but not all prospects, will provide gifts to its *annual fund*—gifts to support current operating needs. Of those who do support the annual fund, some, but not all, may respond to special needs of the organization by making a *major gift*. The definition of a major gift will vary among organizations, depending on the overall levels of support they receive, but such gifts typically are at least five figures or more and are often pledged to be paid over a period of 3 to 5 years. Major gifts often come from the individual's assets rather than current income, and many are paid using securities, real estate, or other marketable assets. Some, but only a few, of those who make major gifts will eventually make a "principal gift" to the organization. The term *principal gift* has entered the fund-raising vocabulary only within the past two decades. Like major gifts, principal gifts are defined by their size—they are large major gifts. These are the transformative gifts that have a significant impact on the organization, and they may total in the millions of dollars.

David Dunlop, a thoughtful fund-raising practitioner with Cornell University for many decades, defines three types of gifts that people make, and they generally correspond with the annual, major, and principal gifts depicted in the fund-raising pyramid. In Dunlop's terminology, *regular gifts* are the ones that people make on a recurring basis, usually to support the annual fund. Dunlop's *special gifts* are those that individual donors make to meet some non-recurring need of the organization, for example, a capital project or perhaps a campaign to increase the organization's endowment assets. They are *stretch gifts,* meaning that giving them requires some real sacrifice on the part of the donor. Some individuals who make regular gifts and periodically stretch to make special gifts will develop a lifelong relationship with a nonprofit organization, making it the beneficiary of their *ultimate gift.* In Dunlop's definition, an ultimate gift is not necessarily the individual's last gift, but rather "the largest gift that the person is ultimately capable of making" (p. 98). Some individuals make their ultimate or largest gift while living; others make their ultimate gift in the form of a bequest or other charitable provision that takes effect on their death. It is not unusual for ultimate gifts to be made to endowments, usually to large nonprofits such as universities and museums or to establish or enhance a foundation created by the donor.

Although the fund-raising pyramid has been used for a long time to show how individual donors develop their relationships with favored organizations and as an analytical tool to describe the outlines of an organization's donor constituency, some question whether its principles still apply. Many donors today are *entrepreneurial donors,* and many of them are relatively young individuals who have made their fortunes as business entrepreneurs. They tend to approach giving like investing, preferring to fund organizations that are engaged in cutting-edge approaches rather than traditional programs. They wish to be actively involved in an organization rather than be a passive donor. They may select organizations based on their demonstrated performance rather than on the basis of traditional loyalties. Their first gift may indeed be a major gift if it supports a program of particular interest to them and one that is consistent with their own social values.

To the extent that there is a new generation of philanthropists whose behavior is markedly different from that of previous donors, the traditional fund-raising pyramid may have less validity. However, many of the new donors are also relatively young people; what has changed is that wealth is now held by individuals at earlier ages than in the past. Whether their giving behavior will become more traditional as they age is a question to which there is yet no answer. It is also possible that individuals will engage in both traditional and new philanthropy, following the patterns suggested by the pyramid for some of their giving but engaging in more investment-like giving as well.

Another criticism of the fund-raising pyramid is that it describes a situation most applicable to large nonprofit institutions, such as universities, and that it is less relevant for smaller nonprofits. Colleges and universities have natural lifelong relationships with their graduates, and most have sufficient financial stability that they can patiently nurture relationships leading to ultimate gifts. For many nonprofits in urgent need of increased support to balance current budgets, the

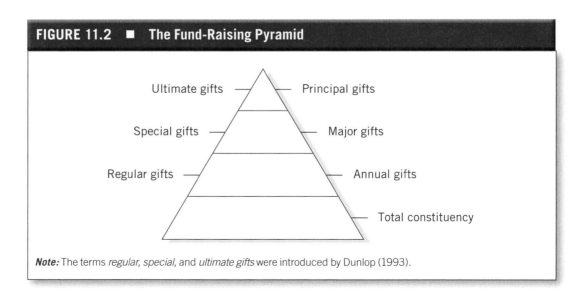

FIGURE 11.2   ■   The Fund-Raising Pyramid

Ultimate gifts — Principal gifts

Special gifts — Major gifts

Regular gifts — Annual gifts

Total constituency

Note: The terms *regular, special,* and *ultimate gifts* were introduced by Dunlop (1993).

distant promise of an ultimate gift may seem unworthy of too much time and effort today. But as Dunlop (1993) emphasizes, most organizations have at least a few close friends and donors with whom they should be cultivating long-term relationships with the hope that they will eventually produce the level of giving that can be transformative.

Planned Giving

A rapidly growing component of philanthropy includes gifts that are made in connection with individuals' financial or estate planning, known as *planned gifts.* Many major gifts today do involve the use of sophisticated financial instruments, and planned giving has become a major subfield within the fund-raising profession. Experienced planned giving officers, or *gift planners* as some are called, are highly sought after by all types of nonprofit organizations. The aging of the U.S. population and the increasing wealth held by older people suggests that this form of giving will grow in importance in coming decades.

The simplest form of a planned gift is a *bequest,* which is merely a statement in an individual's will or living trust dictating that on his or her death, some amount or portion of his or her estate is to be given to a charitable organization. Other planned gifts, for example, those using *charitable remainder trusts* and *charitable gift annuities,* are arrangements that provide for the donor or another beneficiary to receive lifetime income, with the charitable organization not gaining full use of the donated assets until after the death of the donor or the last income recipient. Such gifts provide a tax deduction for some portion of the gift, but not for the full amount, since the donor has a retained life income interest attributable to the noncharitable portion of the payment. In addition to qualifying for income tax deductions, donors may avoid or defer capital gains taxes on appreciated assets used to make a planned gift and, since the donated assets are removed from the donor's estate, there may be an estate tax saving as well. As in our earlier example, these tax benefits reduce the out-of-pocket cost of the gift, which can make the rate of income received by the donor an attractive feature.

Gift planning became somewhat complicated in 2010. As a result of a compromise in Congress, reached earlier in the decade of the 2000s, the federal estate tax was gradually reduced and was eliminated entirely in 2010. However, a prevalent belief was that Congress would reenact an estate tax beginning in 2011 and that it might be retroactive to 2010. The resulting uncertainty was affecting the planning of charitable bequests during 2010. Students who are interested in this subject should check the Internet for updated information, as the law likely will have changed by the time they are reading this chapter.

Planned giving is a complex topic, and a full discussion is beyond the scope of this text, but additional reading is recommended at the end of this chapter for those who wish to pursue a more in-depth understanding. The Partnership for Philanthropic Planning is a professional organization of gift planners that offers important education and materials. There are also websites that provide cases, resources, and tools for planned giving professionals, and some are listed at the conclusion of this chapter.

Campaigns

Fund-raising campaigns have been a part of the nonprofit landscape since the early years of the 20th century, when the campaign method was developed by fund-raisers for the YMCA.

The model was later adopted by higher education institutions and subsequently by most other nonprofit organizations. Historically, campaigns were known as *capital campaigns* and were usually undertaken specifically to construct new physical facilities. Over the past three decades, however, many campaigns have become comprehensive, including within their goals not only funds for facilities but also endowment, operating funds, and support for programs. At any given time in most communities today, there will be highly publicized campaigns underway by multiple organizations, seeking funds for all these purposes. The dollar goals are often substantial and to be achieved typically in 5 to 7 years.

What distinguishes a campaign from just ordinary fund-raising? First, a campaign is intensive, ranking among the highest priorities of the organization and usually commanding a significant amount of time and energy from the CEO, board members, fund-raising staff, and others. This intensity is created by two essential characteristics of a campaign—an announced dollar goal and a deadline. A campaign has defined objectives, that is, specific purposes for which the funds are being raised that are spelled out in campaign literature. The solicitation of gifts to a campaign follows the principle of *sequential fund-raising,* in which prospects are solicited in a planned sequence beginning with those closest to the organization and the most promising prospects, proceeding later to those who are less related or who are deemed to have less financial potential. This process helps raise the sights of prospective donors by offering the example of those who have already made impressive financial commitments. Finally, solicitations in a campaign request a specific amount that has been deemed realistic for the particular donor. Donors are rated according to their capacity to give and are solicited, in the appropriate order, for a gift at that level. Without meeting these essential conditions, a fund-raising effort is not really a campaign. Thus, fund-raising that aims to raise "as much as possible" or "as soon as possible" is, by definition, not a campaign, because it does not proceed against a specific goal that it intends to reach within a defined period of time. Solicitations that ask people to give as much as they can represent a "collection," but not a campaign, which seeks specific gifts from donors deemed capable of making them (Worth, 2010).

Campaigns proceed in phases, as depicted in Figure 11.3. They are rooted in the organization's strategic planning, which defines goals and directions and financial needs. Planning for a campaign itself is a process that may encompass months or years and includes the identification of prospects, enlistment of volunteer leaders, and the hiring of fund-raising staff. In order to maximize the solicitation of significant early gifts, and their impact on the sights of donors in later phases, a campaign is not announced to the public until a significant portion of its total goal has been raised as part of a *nucleus fund* during what is known as the campaign's *quiet period* or *quiet phase.* A formal kickoff of the campaign usually includes announcement of the overall goal, celebration of the amount already raised toward it as part of the nucleus fund, and recognition of nucleus fund donors. The kickoff is intended to establish momentum, generate good feelings, demonstrate that the campaign is likely to be successful, and inspire prospects who have not yet given to set their sights in relationship to what the nucleus fund donors already have done.

Following the kickoff, the campaign is in its *public phase.* Efforts to bring visibility to the campaign and its goals often become a significant component of the organization's communication efforts for the duration of the campaign. Planning for today's campaigns includes marketing and communication goals that are nearly as important to the organization as the financial goals addressed by the campaign. They have become tools for positioning organizations and, indeed, some campaign goals, especially in higher education, are often set at least in part to make a statement about the institution's relative rank and prestige, rather than reflecting exclusively its considered financial needs.

FIGURE 11.3   ■   Phases of the Campaign

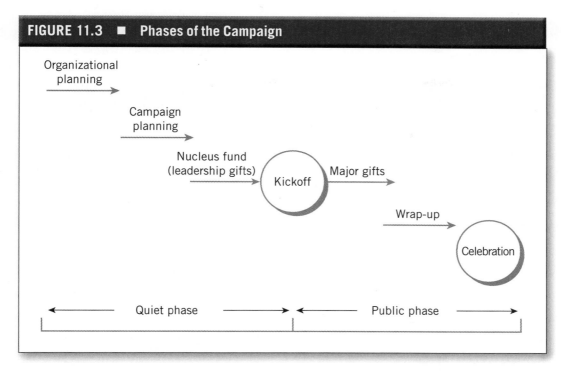

An important tool in planning and managing a campaign is the *gift chart,* also known as the *gift standards chart.* An example, based on a campaign goal of $250 million, is provided in Table 11.1. The chart reflects the proportional giving necessary to achieve the campaign's overall goal, starting with a lead gift that is at least 10 percent of the goal, and then doubling the number of gifts needed at each successively lower dollar level. The ratios used to construct the table have been developed through experience in many campaigns over the past century and often reflect the pattern of giving to a campaign when studied retrospectively. In recent years, however, some campaigns have diverged from these historic patterns, with an increasingly large percentage of the total coming from a decreasing number of very large gifts at the top of the chart—in other words, from fewer major donors but larger gifts. That change reflected the economic booms of the late 1990s and mid-2000s, and some have predicted that a lasting effect of the 2007–2009 recession may be a return to historic patterns of giving in future campaigns.

The gift-range chart is useful in projecting how many gifts will be needed to obtain a specified goal. Using the industry standard, that four prospects are required to produce every closed gift, it also provides a way to assess if the organization has developed a donor constituency sufficient to support a proposed campaign goal. It may also be useful in demonstrating to the early donors to the nucleus fund, often including board members, why their gifts need to be exceptional, in order to meet the requirements at the upper ranges of the chart and set the standards for others who will ultimately be asked to support the campaign.

Managing Fund-Raising Programs

Fund-raising programs today are sophisticated undertakings, even at modestly sized nonprofit organizations. In larger institutions, the staff of a development office may include dozens or even hundreds of professionals in various specialties, including annual giving, corporate and foundation relations, major gifts, and *advancement services.*

TABLE 11.1 ■ Gift Range Chart for Campaign With Goal of $250 Million					
Gift Range (in $)	Number of Gifts Required	Number of Prospects Required	Total of Gifts in This Range (in $)	Cumulative Total (in $)	Cumulative Percentage of Goal
25,000,000	1	4	25,000,000	25,000,000	10
10,000,000	3	12	30,000,000	55,000,000	22
5,000,000	6	24	30,000,000	85,000,000	34
2,500,000	12	48	30,000,000	115,000,000	46
1,000,000	27	108	27,000,000	142,000,000	57
500,000	52	208	26,000,000	168,000,000	68
250,000	100	400	25,000,000	193,000,000	77
100,000	180	720	18,000,000	211,000,000	84
50,000	300	1,200	15,000,000	226,000,000	90
25,000	560	2,240	14,000,000	240,000,000	96
Less than 25,000	Many	Many	10,000,000	250,000,000	100
Totals	1,241	4,964	250,000,000	—	—

Advancement Services

Advancement services has emerged as an important subspecialty in the field, encompassing all the back-office operations such as gift recording and acknowledgment, prospect research, and information systems management.[1] Most nonprofit organizations use one of the commercially available software packages that are comprehensive in their capabilities to maintain donor information and gift records as well as track cultivation and solicitation activity and evaluate the productivity and effectiveness of specific initiatives or fund-raising staff.

As mentioned earlier, the growing availability of information on the web has revolutionized the field of prospect research. Databases of corporate and foundation giving programs enable researchers to identify promising prospects quickly. The giving capacity of individual prospects can be evaluated using a number of sophisticated electronic screening tools that will also identify known relationships of prospects, for example, to members of the organization's board. However, the costs of such screening can be high for many small nonprofits, and there is still much insight and information to be obtained through the more traditional method of having prospects screened by peers. Individuals in the same business community, the same church, or in the same graduating class may have a good sense of the financial capability and interests of their peers and are often willing to rate their capacity in a setting that provides confidentiality.

Prospect Management

In sophisticated fund-raising programs, relationships with donors and prospects are not developed casually or randomly. Contacts are planned, scheduled, and tracked, and a member of the development office staff is assigned as the *prospect manager* with responsibility for moving the relationship forward. A strategy is developed for each major prospect, and *contact reports* entered into the fund-raising information system document every interaction and make it possible for a fund-raising manager to monitor the movement of prospects through the fund-raising cycle.

In large organizations, especially those with multiple units and decentralized fund-raising, policies requiring prior clearance of contacts with donors are essential. For example, this situation is common in universities, where alumni may hold degrees from more than one school and be viewed as prospects for giving to all of them. Multiple contacts by different units of the organization may be irritating to donors and create the impression that the organization is poorly managed or inept. In addition, there is always the risk of a preemptive smaller gift that disrupts a careful plan that might have led to a more significant commitment.

Fund-Raising Efficiency and Effectiveness

The costs of fund-raising are a topic that receives considerable discussion and that has been the focus of various studies. As discussed in Chapter 6, some charity watchdog organizations have established guidelines suggesting that fund-raising costs should not exceed about one third of the total funds contributed. The Supreme Court has held that government may not set a maximum level of fund-raising expenditure because doing so would be an abridgement of free speech rights under the U.S. Constitution, but the public availability of Form 990 and other financial information has made organizations sensitive to the appearance of high costs in the eyes of their donors as well as the watchdog raters.

Some people say that setting limits on fund-raising costs is unfair to organizations that are new or controversial and therefore must expend more effort, and more money, in order to meet their needs for gift support. In addition, it can sometimes be difficult to determine the true total costs of fund-raising by an organization. Some portion of the time and effort of a CEO may be devoted to cultivating and soliciting gifts, but it is not always easy to identify that portion exactly, since some activities may involve donors but may also have other purposes. For example, is the CEO's time spent with a board member who is also a donor to be considered fund-raising activity, or is it related to broader governance of the organization? Printed materials and mail solicitations may include a solicitation as well as other information, which may be considered educational or informative and thus an activity related to the organization's mission rather than fund-raising. Accounting rules describe how the costs of such mailings and materials are to be allocated between fund-raising and mission-related purposes, but some nonprofits may not be clear about exactly how such costs should be apportioned.

Historically, the ratio most commonly used to evaluate the efficiency of fund-raising was *cost-per-dollar-raised,* that is, the amount of expenditure on fund-raising divided by the total gifts received—it is a cost–benefit ratio stated in dollar terms. For example, if an organization spends $50,000 on fund-raising and receives $500,000 in gifts as a result, its cost would be 10-cents-per-dollar-raised. If the same expenditure brought in $1,000,000, its relative cost would be half as much, just 5-cents-per-dollar-raised. However, most now argue, this ratio is an inappropriate measure for at least two reasons. First, it is a negative way of looking at fund-raising—as an expense rather than as an investment. For example, if an organization spends as much as 50 cents to raise a dollar, which would be considered a relatively high cost, that would still represent a 100 percent return on its original investment. There are few investments in which it is possible to double one's money, and a 100 percent return would be considered very good performance by a manager of an investment portfolio.

The second related objection is that cost-per-dollar-raised measures fund-raising efficiency, but it says nothing about fund-raising effectiveness. For example, if one organization spends $50,000 to raise $500,000, its cost is just 10-cents-per-dollar and its net revenue is $450,000. Suppose another organization spends twice as much, $100,000, and its efforts result in gifts totaling $600,000. Its relative cost is much higher than the first organization—almost 17-cents-per-dollar. Its fund-raising is less *efficient,* but its net revenue of $500,000 is higher than that of the first organization and its fund-raising is thus more *effective.* For these reasons, most organizations today consider the *return-on-investment* in fund-raising and look at what is spent in relationship to what is raised over a time frame of years. However, there are still observers who place an emphasis on minimizing fund-raising costs and negatively portray nonprofits that exceed recommended ratios even in the short term. Attention to the costs, and results, of fund-raising is commanding more attention by nonprofit managers as well as charity watchdogs and donors. Fund-raising expenditures are being viewed as a form of investment and are expected to produce a suitable rate of return.

Staff Performance and Accountability

An important question, especially in larger development offices with staff who are specialized in the area of major gift fund-raising, is how to evaluate the performance of individual fund-raising professionals.

Perhaps the simplest measure would be the amount of money each staff member raises, but that approach creates a number of issues. First, most major gifts do not result from the efforts of a single individual. As we have discussed, a donor's relationship with an organization may develop over a long period of time, perhaps exceeding the tenure of any single member of the staff. There are many key players in building such relationships, including perhaps the CEO and volunteers, as well as members of the board. It is usually not easy to identify exactly who is responsible for the receipt of a major gift; indeed, the individual who solicits the gift may have played a relatively minor role.

A second problem with using dollars raised to evaluate the performance of a development staff member is that it might create incentives that would lead to inappropriate behavior. That is not to suggest that the fund-raiser would necessarily engage in unethical or immoral behavior with regard to a donor, but it is possible that a development staff member who knows he or she will be evaluated on the basis of gifts secured will, even if unconsciously, short-circuit the process in a way that is disadvantageous to the organization. For example, a fund-raiser with such an incentive might direct his or her efforts toward soliciting gifts from prospects who are known to be ready to give, rather than cultivation of prospects who may not be ready yet but whose long-term capacity to give is much higher. The staff person might neglect stewardship of past donors who are still making payments on long-term pledges, and who have a high likelihood of giving again, while pursuing new donors to hit some dollar target on which his or her own performance will be evaluated. And, of course, there could be instances in which a development staff member under pressure to maximize gift revenue misleads a donor or exaggerates the benefits of a gift under a reward system that values only gifts closed. For these reasons, some organizations evaluate the performance of fund-raising staff primarily on the activity they complete, for example, the number of visits made and the number of proposals submitted, rather than the dollars they raise in the short run. Others use formulas that combine credit for such activity with the value of gifts closed.

Again, while it is an issue mostly in larger fund-raising operations, the best method for evaluating and rewarding professional staff is a topic of current discussion and debate. Some development staff are paid incentive-based compensation, including bonuses, which may reward activity (e.g., the number of donor visits completed) exceeding some predefined objectives. Such programs need to be carefully designed to ensure that the fund-raising staff are not being paid a commission—that is, a percentage of the gifts they raise. Basing staff compensation on a percentage of gifts raised is unethical behavior, explicitly prohibited by the ethical codes of the Association of Fundraising Professionals and other professional organizations in the field. The practice would not only raise concerns about the possibility of incentivizing misbehavior by fund-raisers, but it also goes to the heart of the philanthropic relationships and the assumption of trust and mutual commitment to a cause or organization that donors assume to be present when they discuss a gift with the organization's representative.

Ethics and Professional Standards

The question of compensation for fund-raising staff is just one area of potential ethical challenge always present in the complex relationships among organizations, their donors, and the individuals who solicit funds on the organization's behalf. Most ethical questions that arise in fund-raising can be placed into one of four principal categories.

First, some issues involve the behavior of the staff person who is interacting with the donor. They would include making misleading or dishonest representations, for example, exaggerating the organization's effectiveness, lying about how the gift will be used, or making unreasonable or unrealistic promises to the donor about recognition or the financial benefits of giving. It is also unethical for a nonprofit staff member who is managing a relationship with a donor to attempt to use that relationship for his or her personal benefit or gain or to engage in behavior toward the donor that would be morally repugnant, for example, sexual harassment.

A second category of ethical issues that may confront nonprofit organizations relates to the donor rather than the staff member. For example, what if the organization has reason to believe that the donated funds were illegally obtained? Should a nonprofit accept gifts from a company that makes products it knows to be harmful? What about the question of accepting a gift from a donor who has been convicted of a white-collar crime or who simply has an unsavory reputation that might reflect badly on the organization were the gift to receive publicity? There have been a number of examples of such dilemmas posed by gifts from businesspeople who were later involved in corporate corruption scandals, after a building or program had been named to recognize a past gift. Should the organization remove the name? By whose judgment should such decisions be made, and what are the limits of the organization's responsibility—and right—to investigate and judge the character of donors who may offer them support?

A third, and sometimes less obvious ethical question is presented by restricted gifts: Under what circumstances should an organization refuse to accept a gift that may require it to undertake new programs and perhaps incur additional expenses that it had not anticipated? What if the new program is not entirely consistent with the organization's mission or would require a redefinition of its mission? For example, if an organization concerned with young children were offered a gift to begin a new program to help prevent high school students from dropping out, it would need to consider whether expanding its mission in that way would jeopardize its focus on its primary mission, what additional costs the new efforts might create in the future, and whether such expansion might endanger the organization's overall health and other sources of support. It might not be an easy decision to make if the offered gift were very substantial and, especially, if the donor were an important local businessperson or even a member of the organization's board. The risk to the relationship in turning down the gift would need to be weighed against the potential risk to the organization if it were accepted with the conditions that accompany it.

Another subcategory of questions arise with gifts that come with conditions that might give the donor inappropriate control. For example, most colleges will accept scholarship gifts that require recipients to be enrolled in certain academic programs; that raises few problems unless, for example, the college thinks it unlikely will be able to recruit many students meeting the conditions. But there are limits to how much influence a donor can be allowed to have in the process of selecting specific scholarship recipients. Allowing the donor to select the recipient of the scholarships would not only present an ethical concern but, indeed, it could also invalidate the tax deductibility of the donor's gift, making it legally a gift to the scholarship recipient *individually* rather than to the college, university, or school.

A fourth category of ethical concern that has increased with the growing sophistication of prospect research involves maintaining appropriate safeguards to protect the privacy of donors and prospects. The development offices of many organizations may possess information obtained from public sources about individuals' financial wealth and income, real estate holdings, and even family situations. It is legal to obtain such data. But some would argue, when it is assembled to create a donor profile, its wide distribution may be an inappropriate invasion of privacy. In addition, development office files may include information gained from reports written by staff members who have visited the donor over the years or heard secondhand from others who know the donor. Maintaining such information in the files of the fund-raising office runs the risk that the donor, and the organization, could be embarrassed if it were inappropriately or inadvertently disclosed to another person.

The Association of Fundraising Professionals "Code of Ethical Principles" and "Principles of Professional Practice" cover many of the major issues that nonprofits and members of their staff may encounter in raising philanthropic funds. But possible situations are so varied that no code can substitute for continuing ethical awareness and the application of good judgment by nonprofit managers who value the interests of their organizations and their missions above all else (see Box 11.5).

BOX 11.5 AFP CODE OF ETHICAL PRINCIPLES AND STANDARDS

(Ethical principles adopted 1964; amended September 2007)

The Association of Fundraising Professionals (AFP) . . . exists to foster the development and growth of fund-raising professionals and the profession, to promote high ethical behavior in the fund-raising profession and to preserve and enhance philanthropy and volunteerism. Members of AFP are motivated by an inner drive to improve the quality of life through the causes they serve. They serve the ideal of philanthropy, are committed to the preservation and enhancement of volunteerism; and hold stewardship of these concepts as the overriding direction of their professional life. They recognize their responsibility to ensure that needed resources are vigorously and ethically sought and that the intent of the donor is honestly fulfilled. To these ends, AFP members, both individual and business, embrace certain values that they strive to uphold in performing their responsibilities for generating philanthropic support. AFP business members strive to promote and protect the work and mission of their client organizations.

AFP members [both individual and business] aspire to:

- practice their profession with integrity, honesty, truthfulness and adherence to the absolute obligation to safeguard the public trust;
- act according to the highest goals and visions of their organizations, professions, clients and consciences;
- put philanthropic mission above personal gain;
- inspire others through their own sense of dedication and high purpose;
- improve their professional knowledge and skills, so that their performance will better serve others;
- demonstrate concern for the interests and well-being of individuals affected by their actions;
- value the privacy, freedom of choice and interests of all those affected by their actions;
- foster cultural diversity and pluralistic values and treat all people with dignity and respect;
- affirm, through personal giving, a commitment to philanthropy and its role in society;
- adhere to the spirit as well as the letter of all applicable laws and regulations;
- advocate within their organizations adherence to all applicable laws and regulations;
- avoid even the appearance of any criminal offense or professional misconduct;
- bring credit to the fund-raising profession by their public demeanor;
- encourage colleagues to embrace and practice these ethical principles and standards;
- be aware of the codes of ethics promulgated by other professional organizations that serve philanthropy.

Ethical Standards

Furthermore, while striving to act according to the above values, AFP members, both individual and business, agree to abide (and to ensure, to the best of their ability, that all members of their staff abide) by the AFP standards. Violation of the standards may subject the member to disciplinary sanctions, including expulsion, as provided in the AFP Ethics Enforcement Procedures.

Member Obligations

1. Members shall not engage in activities that harm the members' organizations, clients or profession.

2. Members shall not engage in activities that conflict with their fiduciary, ethical and legal obligations to their organizations, clients or profession.

(Continued)

(Continued)

3. Members shall effectively disclose all potential and actual conflicts of interest; such disclosure does not preclude or imply ethical impropriety.

4. Members shall not exploit any relationship with a donor, prospect, volunteer, client or employee for the benefit of the members or the members' organizations.

5. Members shall comply with all applicable local, state, provincial and federal civil and criminal laws.

6. Members recognize their individual boundaries of competence and are forthcoming and truthful about their professional experience and qualifications and will represent their achievements accurately and without exaggeration.

7. Members shall present and supply products and/or services honestly and without misrepresentation and will clearly identify the details of those products, such as availability of the products and/or services and other factors that may affect the suitability of the products and/or services for donors, clients, or nonprofit organizations.

8. Members shall establish the nature and purpose of any contractual relationship at the outset and will be responsive and available to organizations and their employing organizations before, during, and after any sale of materials and/or services. Members will comply with all fair and reasonable obligations created by the contract.

9. Members shall refrain from knowingly infringing [on] the intellectual property rights of other parties at all times. Members shall address and rectify any inadvertent infringement that may occur.

10. Members shall protect the confidentiality of all privileged information relating to the provider/client relationships.

11. Members shall refrain from any activity designed to disparage competitors untruthfully.

Solicitation and Use of Philanthropic Funds

12. Members shall take care to ensure that all solicitation and communication materials are accurate and correctly reflect their organizations' mission and use of solicited funds.

13. Members shall take care to ensure that donors receive informed, accurate, and ethical advice about the value and tax implications of contributions.

14. Members shall take care to ensure that contributions are used in accordance with donors' intentions.

15. Members shall take care to ensure proper stewardship of all revenue sources, including timely reports on the use and management of such funds.

16. Members shall obtain explicit consent by donors before altering the conditions of financial transactions.

Presentation of Information

17. Members shall not disclose privileged or confidential information to unauthorized parties.

18. Members shall adhere to the principle that all donor and prospect information created by, or on behalf of, an organization or a client is the property of that organization

or client and shall not be transferred or utilized except on behalf of that organization or client.

19. Members shall give donors and clients the opportunity to have their names removed from lists that are sold to, rented to, or exchanged with other organizations.

20. Members shall, when stating fund-raising results, use accurate and consistent accounting methods that conform to the appropriate guidelines adopted by the American Institute of Certified Public Accountants (AICPA)* for the type of organization involved. (*In countries outside of the United States, comparable authority should be utilized.)

Compensation and Contracts

21. Members shall not accept compensation or enter into a contract that is based on a percentage of contributions; nor shall members accept finder's fees or contingent fees. Business members must refrain from receiving compensation from third parties derived from products or services for a client without disclosing that third-party compensation to the client (for example, volume rebates from vendors to business members).

22. Members may accept performance-based compensation, such as bonuses, provided such bonuses are in accord with prevailing practices within the members' own organizations and are not based on a percentage of contributions.

23. Members shall neither offer nor accept payments or special considerations for the purpose of influencing the selection of products or services.

24. Members shall not pay finder's fees, commissions, or percentage compensation based on contributions, and shall take care to discourage their organizations from making such payments.

25. Any member receiving funds on behalf of a donor or client must meet the legal requirements for the disbursement of those funds. Any interest or income earned on the funds should be fully disclosed.

Source: Used with permission of the Association of Fundraising Professionals.

Chapter Summary

Gifts are a significant component of revenue for many nonprofit organizations, although patterns vary widely among subsectors. Gifts comprise a small percentage of revenue for health care institutions, which derive most of their revenue from fees for service. At the other end of the spectrum, gifts are almost the only source of income for religious congregations and many human services nonprofits. Organized fund-raising is rapidly becoming more common across the world, but it is still most highly developed in the United States. The term *fund-raising* is often used synonymously with the term *development* or *advancement,* but the latter is properly understood to encompass a more comprehensive approach to institution building that includes other external relations functions.

It is important to distinguish between charity, that is, giving to address current human needs, and philanthropy, which seeks to establish or strengthen institutions that address society's needs on a long-term basis. Charity is sometimes impulsive and is emotionally driven; philanthropy is often more thoughtful and deliberate.

The motivation to give is quite different among corporations, foundations, and individual donors. Corporate philanthropy generally seeks to advance the corporation's business interests while also accomplishing some social benefit. Corporate support of nonprofits encompasses philanthropy and also various partnerships, which will be discussed in the next chapter. Foundations exist to make gifts and are required by law to do so. There are various types of foundations, some of which may be prospects for support of nonprofit organizations and others that operate their own programs and generally do not provide grants to others.

Most individual donors are likely to be less organized and rational in their giving than are corporations or foundations. A considerable body of research exists on the motivations of individual donors. Findings generally suggest that individuals are motivated by altruism, a desire to pay back for benefits that they have received, desires for social advancement and recognition, as well as other reasons. The influence of tax incentives on giving by individuals is a subject of debate among economists and other experts.

Fund-raising is a process that begins with the organization identifying its own priorities and developing a case for support and progresses to identifying prospects who have linkage, interest, and the ability to give; cultivation of relationships with those prospects; solicitation of the gift; acknowledgment and recognition of the gift and donor; and stewardship to continue the relationship and prepare for continued support from past donors. Development of the case, or the rationale for why the organization deserves support, is a critical step. A strong case is larger than the organization, that is, it starts with the social needs that the organization's programs address and then becomes more specific in describing how needed funds will enhance the organization's ability to address those broader needs.

The fund-raising pyramid depicts how many donors evolve in their giving relationship with an organization, beginning as regular annual donors and possibly advancing to become major donors and eventually donors of ultimate gifts. Organizations often build their fund-raising programs in accordance with the pyramid, beginning with solicitations for annual gifts and then developing major gift and planned gift programs as their constituency is ready. Planned giving is a growing area of fund-raising and philanthropy that encompasses giving through wills as well as a variety of other financial instruments.

Campaigns are intensive fund-raising efforts that seek to raise a given amount by a specified deadline for specific purposes, or campaign objectives. Campaigns proceed in phases, and it is important that the model be followed to ensure success in achieving the goal. The gift-range chart depicts the pattern of giving necessary to achieve a dollar goal and is a useful tool in planning and managing a campaign.

Advancement services, encompassing the back-office operations of fund-raising, has become an important subspecialty of the field. This area includes prospect research, gift accounting, and the maintenance of fund-raising information systems and records.

Questions about the efficiency and effectiveness of fund-raising are often discussed and debated. Evaluating the ratio of fund-raising cost to dollars raised may be unfair to younger, smaller organizations and does not reveal the effectiveness of a fund-raising program in maximizing net revenue. The return on investment in fund-raising is a more appropriate measure of effectiveness, but some still emphasize the ratio of costs to revenue and prefer to see fund-raising expenditures at a minimum. Discussion also surrounds the compensation of fund-raising staff, some of whom receive financial incentives for performance. Compensation based on a percentage of gifts secured is considered unethical in the field.

Fund-raising often raises ethical issues, including among others those related to the behavior of fund-raisers themselves, the reputation of the donor or the source of that individual's wealth, the impact of restricted gifts on the mission of the organization, and concerns about donor privacy and the use of information resulting from prospect research. AFP and other organizations have established ethics codes that are widely followed by practitioners.

Note

1. In an office that engages only in fund-raising, this function might be called "development services." But in many organizations, the back office supports not only fund-raising but also marketing and communications programs—for example, by maintaining mailing lists for newsletters and records for special events—and is thus known as "advancement services," reflecting the broader concept of institutional advancement, as discussed above.

KEY TERMS AND CONCEPTS

ability, linkage, interest

advancement

advancement services

Association of Fundraising Professionals

bequest

campaign

case for support

case statement

charitable gift annuity

charitable remainder trust

charity

contact reports

cost-per-dollar-raised

cultivation

development

enlightened self-interest

family foundations

fund-raising

fund-raising pyramid

gift chart/gift standards chart

gifts-in-kind

identification of prospects

institutional advancement

internal case statement

kickoff

major gifts

nucleus fund

out-of-pocket cost

Partnership for Philanthropic Planning

philanthropy

planned giving

prospect

prospect management

prospect research

quiet phase

regular gifts

return on investment

soliciting

special gifts

stewardship

strategic philanthropy

Cases 11.1a–g Fund-Raising Ethics

CASE 11.1a

A generous gift is offered to your organization by a donor who has been convicted of a white-collar crime. Do you accept it? What if he has served his sentence? Does the purpose of the gift make a difference? What if it is to support cancer research? To establish a free medical clinic for children in a disadvantaged neighborhood? To endow a chair at a business school?

CASE 11.1b

A donor wants to give an art collection to the art gallery at which you are employed. Her requirement is that the gallery be set up just like her home and that she be able to use it for private events on request. Do you accept? What are the ethical issues and what are some possible legal concerns?

CASE 11.1c

In private conversation, a fund-raiser is told that a prospect's husband is terminally ill and the family has financial problems, despite appearances. Do you record that in the database? A volunteer is about to solicit that prospect for a major gift. Do you reveal this information to the volunteer?

CASE 11.1d

A donor is considering a major gift to a center on competitiveness at your institution, a public policy "think tank." He is a corporate executive and you know that he is a strong proponent of tariff protection for U.S. companies. A leading proponent of free trade is about to be appointed as a senior fellow in your research center and you know this, but it hasn't been publicly announced. Do you tell the donor about the impending appointment or just stay quiet?

CASE 11.1e

A donor you had cultivated on behalf of your nonprofit employer dies. In her will, she leaves you a watch you had once admired as a personal gift. Do you accept it? Why or why not? What if she leaves you $5,000? What if it's $5 million? Does the amount make a difference?

CASE 11.1f

A donor pledges $1 million payable over 5 years to name a room in a new building. Another donor pledges $1 million to name the identical room next door but says he can only pay it over 10 years. Do you accept the second gift and name the room? If so, are you obligated to tell the first donor about the difference in terms? If you think you are not, then how would you handle questions from the first donor were he or she to learn of the arrangements through a conversation with the second donor?

CASE 11.1g

An elderly donor says that she wants to change her will, leaving everything to your organization. This will cut out her daughter from whom she is estranged. The daughter, whom you know personally, is disabled. Do you encourage the donor? Do you tell the daughter what is going on? Do you tell anyone else or just let this woman make her own decision? What if you personally have doubts about the donor's mental ability to make financial decisions?

QUESTIONS FOR DISCUSSION

1. In the cases above, do the ethical issues involve behavior of a fund-raiser, conditions placed on the gift or the impact of the gift on the organization's mission and resources, characteristics or personal reputation of the donor, or concerns about privacy?

2. How would you handle the issues raised by each case?

SUGGESTIONS FOR FURTHER READING

Books

Frumkin, P. (2007). *Strategic giving: The art and science of philanthropy*. Chicago/London: University of Chicago Press.

Levy, R. (2008). *Yours for the asking*. San Francisco: Wiley.

Rosso, H. A., & Associates. (2010). *Achieving excellence in fund raising* (E. R. Tempel, T. L. Seiler, & E. E. Aldrich, Eds.; 3rd ed.). San Francisco: Jossey-Bass.

Sargeant, A., & Shang, J., & Associates (2010). *Fund-raising: Principles and practice*. San Francisco: Wiley.

Worth, M. J. (2002). *New strategies for educational fund raising*. Westport, CT: Praeger/American Council on Education.

Worth, M. J. (2010). *Leading the campaign*. Lanham, MD: Rowman & Littlefield/American Council on Education.

Websites

Association for Healthcare Philanthropy, http://www.ahp.org/

Association of Fundraising Professionals, http://www.afpnet.org/

Center on Philanthropy at Indiana University, http://www.philanthropy.iupui.edu

Council for Advancement and Support of Education, http://www.case.org/

Council on Foundations (COF), http://www.cof.org/

Partnership for Philanthropic Planning, http://www.pppnet.org/

Planned Giving Design Center, http://www.pgdc.com

Chapter Outline

chapter 12

Many nonprofits have found that starting a business has forced the entire organization to become more focused and to sharpen its goals and management skills in all aspects of its work, thereby improving their balance sheets as well as their effectiveness in achieving their charitable missions.

© Ciaran Griffin/Stockbyte/Thinkstock

Earned Income Strategies 12

This chapter discusses efforts by nonprofit organizations to increase and diversify their sources of revenue by engaging in various relationships with business corporations and by undertaking their own business ventures. Such activities are often discussed under the rubric of *earned income,* that is, income from payment for goods or services that the nonprofit has provided, rather than *contributed income* (gifts).[1] As mentioned earlier in this book, *most* revenue to the nonprofit sector overall is earned income. This is especially true in education, a subsector that derives 56 percent of revenue from earned income and health care, which receives 47 percent from fees for service (Independent Sector, 2009a). Many organizations also receive a significant portion of their revenue from government, but most government funds are not gifts or grants. They are payment for services that the nonprofit has provided and for which the government is paying on behalf of the clients served. Obvious examples include government reimbursements paid to health care institutions under the Medicare and Medicaid programs, and scholarship funds paid to a college or university to be applied to a student's tuition bill. Both are earned income to the recipient organizations, since they pay for services the organization provided to specific patients or students, respectively.

Thus, although it has been the focus of an explosion in literature and discussion in the past two decades, earned income is not something new for many nonprofit organizations. Indeed, some of our discussion in Chapter 10 concerned the use of marketing principles to increase earned income from nonprofits' core mission-related activities, such as providing education, health care, and artistic performances. In this chapter, we will consider two specific sources of earned income: partnerships with business corporations, and business ventures undertaken by nonprofits themselves.

The vocabulary used to describe the latter activity remains unsettled. Some terms that are widely used include *social enterprise, affirmative business, nonprofit business venture,* and *earned income ventures* (Oster, Massarsky, & Beinhacker, 2004). Community Wealth Ventures (CWV), a consulting firm that works with nonprofits to increase earned income, uses the term *community wealth* to mean "revenue generated through profitable or self-sustaining enterprises to promote social change" (www.communitywealth.com/ourapproch.html). CWV's use of the term includes nonprofit business ventures and corporate partnerships. Community wealth is a term coined by Billy Shore, the founder of Share Our Strength and CWV. Because the vocabulary is not consistent, it is important to determine exactly what the writer or speaker has in mind when any of these terms is used. In this chapter, we will generally use the term *partnership* to describe relationships between nonprofits and corporations and the term *nonprofit business venture* to describe businesses operated by nonprofits. We use *earned income strategies* to encompass both types of activity.

Figure 12.1 depicts the array of arrangements and activities that we will discuss. Another term that is widely used is *social entrepreneurship.* For some, social entrepreneurship is virtually synonymous with the pursuit of earned income. But, because others describe a broader concept, we will explore social entrepreneurship as a separate topic in Chapter 16 of this book.

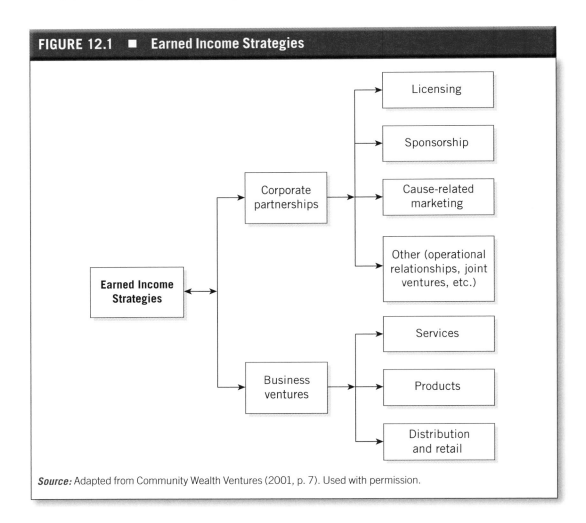

FIGURE 12.1 ■ Earned Income Strategies

Source: Adapted from Community Wealth Ventures (2001, p. 7). Used with permission.

Why Earned Income?

Why would a nonprofit want to pursue earned income through partnerships with business and through their own business ventures? And why has interest in this area increased? Primarily because there is increased competition for revenue, resulting from some of the changes of the past two decades that were discussed in Chapter 3 of this book. Government funding for social programs generally has declined or has shifted to a voucher approach that has given potential clients choices about where to obtain services, introducing competition into the nonprofit marketplace. Government increasingly has outsourced the provision of services based on competitive contracts, forcing nonprofits to go head-to-head with each other as well as with for-profit firms. Philanthropic giving has increased over the long term with the growth of the general economy but has remained relatively constant as a percentage of gross domestic product, while the number of nonprofits and their needs has continued to grow in real terms. In addition, nonprofits have sought to diversify their sources of revenue, in order to protect themselves from the vicissitudes of shifting political priorities that affect government support and the economic cycles that determine charitable giving.

But it's not all about money. Many nonprofits have found that pursuing earned income also helps them advance their missions—for example, organizations that offer recovery and job-training programs provide catering and food service or maintenance services, and retail stores that employ their clients as well as generate income to support their core programs. Others have found that starting a business has forced the entire organization to become more focused and to sharpen its goals and management skills in all aspects of its work. Partnerships with corporations offer not only the opportunity for new revenue but also the increased visibility that may come from the company's promotion of the partnership, benefiting the nonprofit's efforts to raise traditional charitable support. Such relationships also have given nonprofits access to new volunteers and to the management skills and resources of corporate partners. In sum, many nonprofits have found that pursuing earned income strategies can improve their balance sheets as well as their effectiveness in achieving their charitable missions.

Of course, these efforts offer downside risks as well as potential benefits. Earned income is not a panacea for the nonprofit sector, nor is it a realistic expectation for every organization. Indeed, some critics view these activities as synonymous with commercialization and raise important warnings. Some of these issues will be discussed more fully toward the end of this chapter.

Partnerships With Business

Let's begin our discussion of earned income strategies with the top half of Figure 12.1—the various types of relationships nonprofits may establish with corporate partners. First, we need to be clear what we are talking about when we refer to nonprofit–corporate partnerships. The term *partnership* is sometimes used rather loosely. For example, nonprofit donor lists may include the names of "corporate partners," but they are really corporate *donors,* since the company has not received much in return for its payment beyond its inclusion on the list. A true partnership is not a one-directional transaction; rather, it is a relationship that advances the goals of *both* parties, an arrangement in which both sides receive specific benefits related to their goals. If a corporation gives money to a nonprofit based on altruism or a general sense of corporate responsibility without receiving any specific benefit beyond perhaps the modest recognition given to all donors, that is an example of corporate philanthropy but not a partnership.

It is important to clarify that not all partnerships between nonprofit organizations and corporations represent earned income strategies. For example, the Environmental Defense Fund (EDF) works with corporate partners to implement innovations that have a positive environmental impact but also bring benefits to the corporation, such as reduced costs. EDF (2008) does not accept gifts or grants from its corporate partners, in order to maintain its credibility and independence. However, the partnerships we are discussing in this chapter are those that do provide a financial benefit to both the nonprofit organization and the corporate partner and are undertaken at least in part for that purpose.

Chapter 11 described some history of corporate philanthropy, including the emergence of strategic philanthropy in the 1980s. Strategic philanthropy is an approach that aligns the corporation's giving with its competitive strategy as a business. In strategic philanthropy, the effectiveness of corporate giving is measured by its impact on achieving the company's business goals, ultimately the bottom line of profitability. The emergence of this approach to philanthropy sets the stage for the development of corporate–nonprofit partnerships on a major scale starting in the 1980s and continuing today.

The watershed event for nonprofit–corporate partnerships came in 1983, when American Express supported renovation of the Statue of Liberty by offering to contribute a penny to the campaign each time a consumer used his or her American Express credit card. Use of the card increased by 28 percent during the campaign. Other companies took notice, and corporate–nonprofit partnerships took off (Wall, 1984, pp. 1, 29).

Corporate philanthropy remains an important force. Companies gave more than $14 billion in 2008, including cash and gifts-in-kind of company products (Center on Philanthropy at Indiana University, 2009). But partnerships are the area of growth in corporate support of nonprofit organizations and causes. Our review in this chapter will encompass a few of the most common relationships—licensing agreements, sponsorships, cause-related marketing, and operational relationships. Let's run through brief descriptions of each and look at some examples.

Licensing

If students buy T-shirts or coffee mugs with the name and logo of their college on it, they probably do not think that the college manufactured the garment, but they may not know by what arrangement the school's logo is displayed. It is likely to be an example of a licensing agreement between the college and the manufacturer of the shirt or mug.

A *licensing agreement* is a contract that permits a for-profit company to use the nonprofit's name or logo on its products in return for a royalty payment to the nonprofit. The benefit to the nonprofit is the revenue it gains from the royalty and the increased visibility of its name. For the company, having the nonprofit's logo on its products will presumably attract purchases from individuals who are affiliated with the nonprofit or who prefer the product over others because of the perceived benefit to the nonprofit cause. But there is also something more subtle at work. By using the nonprofit's name or logo on its product, the company gains some of the attributes of the nonprofit's brand; that is, the company may come to be seen as more "caring," more "green," or more concerned about specific groups of people by virtue of its association with the positive qualities that people attribute to its nonprofit partner. In effect, when it enters a licensing agreement, a nonprofit leverages some of its brand equity into a stream of income in the form of royalties from the corporation.

Most licensing agreements bring few risks. For example, there is probably little that can go wrong by having a college's logo on a sweatshirt. Neckties with the logo of a nonprofit organization on them probably arouse little controversy and entail no significant risk to the nonprofit's reputation—unless perhaps the wearer were to choke on one, an unlikely event. But some licensing is more controversial, especially agreements that place nonprofit logos on products that relate to food, health, or the environment. The concern is that the presence of the logo implies the nonprofit's endorsement of the product; that is, the appearance of the name implies that the nonprofit is certifying the product's benefits, which may or may not be the case. In the American Heart Association's food certification program, for example, the products have been screened and found to comply with the association's criteria for saturated fat and cholesterol (American Heart Association, 2010). However, in other instances, the appearance of the logo means only that the company has provided a royalty payment to the nonprofit. It does not ensure that the nonprofit has investigated the product or guarantees its consistency with the organization's values. This could be easy for consumers to misunderstand. One well-known licensing fiasco occurred in 1997, when the American Medical Association (AMA) licensed its name to be used on home medical products manufactured by Sunbeam Corporation. The endorsement implied that the AMA had established the effectiveness of the products, but it had not done so. There was public criticism and an outcry by doctors, who are the association's members. The AMA was forced to end the relationship with Sunbeam, paying the company almost $10 million in a lawsuit settlement. Not surprisingly, some AMA employees also lost their jobs (Sagawa & Segal, 2000). The Nature Conservancy was the focus of similar criticism in 2003 when investigative reporters for *The Washington Post* charged that many of the products on which the Conservancy's logo appeared were not more environmentally friendly than those of their competitors (Stephens & Ottaway, 2003a).

Sponsorships

In a licensing agreement, a corporation pays for use of a nonprofit's name or logo on its products. In a *sponsorship,* the company pays for the use of its name or logo in connection with the nonprofit's products or events. We are all familiar with corporate sponsorships; they would be hard to miss. They are represented by the corporate logos on the scoreboards in many university stadiums and arenas, on the T-shirts worn by participants in events like the Race for the Cure, and almost everywhere at the Olympic Games.

Sponsorship is not the same as advertising. Advertising communicates more information and describes the virtues of the company's products. Sponsorship is limited to exposure of the company's name or logo. It is intended to enhance the company's overall visibility and image, not to promote the sale of specific products. Corporations sponsor events such as charity walks, runs, and rides, or athletic competitions. Some also sponsor organizations, entitling them to visibility and recognition across a broad range of programs, products, and communications. Others sponsor facilities, such as athletic arenas and concert halls, which may be named for the corporation. The facility may be named in perpetuity to recognize a corporate gift, but many are named only for the term of a sponsorship contract under which the company makes annual payments to the organization or institution operating the facility. Again, sponsorship does not include detailed descriptions of the company's products, and the payment to the nonprofit is tied to opportunities for visibility and exposure, not directly to sales.

Like licensing of their own name and logo, corporate sponsorships offer nonprofits the benefits of added revenue and increased visibility through the company's promotion of the relationship. Since they do not imply as strongly the nonprofit's endorsement of the company's products, the risk to the nonprofit's reputation may be somewhat less. But there are still reasons for caution. One consideration, of course, is the consistency of the corporation and its products with the mission and values of the nonprofit organization. It would be unlikely for an athletic event to accept sponsorship from a tobacco company or an organization serving children to be visibly associated with a company that sells alcohol. But some cases are closer calls, and it is wise to review sponsorship opportunities against a predetermined list of criteria reflecting the judgment of the organization's board.

Cause Marketing

Some writers use the term *cause marketing* (or *cause-related marketing*) broadly to encompass virtually all relationships in which a nonprofit's and a corporation's identities are combined, including licensing and sponsorships. This text uses the term in a more specific way to mean an arrangement under which the company contributes either a fixed amount for each sale of a product or a specified percentage of its sales of a product to the nonprofit, usually in connection with a short-term promotion. Cause marketing is different from social marketing, which we discussed in Chapter 10. The purpose of social marketing is to influence behavior in order to bring a benefit to the individual or society. Social marketing has no direct impact on revenue of the nonprofit, although it may create greater visibility for the cause and possibly bring additional gifts to the organization promoting it. The purpose of cause marketing is to sell more of the corporate partner's products, with a financial benefit to the nonprofit. There may be, of course, the additional benefit of visibility, which can increase awareness of the cause it advances, with an indirect impact on social behavior.

Unlike sponsorships and licensing arrangements, the nonprofit's revenue from a cause-marketing relationship is *transaction based;* that is, it is directly related to the volume or amount of sales of the company's products. Let's look at a few examples:

- Yoplait promised to give 10 cents to Susan G. Komen for the Cure for every pink yogurt lid mailed in by December 31, 2009, up to a maximum of $1.5 million (www.yoplait.com/slsl/).
- Through a subsidiary, the Reader's Digest Association committed to give 40 percent of new subscription payments to the literacy organization Reading Is Fundamental during the organization's 40th anniversary year (www.magfundraising.com).
- The Home Depot made an unrestricted contribution to KaBOOM!, a nonprofit that builds playgrounds, equal to $30 for each Brookview No-Cut-Ready-To-Build Play Set Kit and $1.25 for each Racing Roadster Car Swing sold in The Home Depot stores between Jan. 1, 2006 and Dec. 31, 2006 (http://kaboom.org/about_kaboom/supporting_partners/).

Cause marketing ties the nonprofit's income directly to the number or amount of total sales made by the corporate partner and thus represents a true partnership in which the interests of both partners are aligned. The corporation may find the relationship beneficial both as a strategy for increasing sales and as a way to improve its image and attract a new customer base, perhaps among the members of a specific market segment. In a number of studies, consumers have indicated that they would be more inclined to buy products when they know that the sale benefits a charitable organization. In one often-cited 2004 study conducted by Cone Marketing, 86 percent of consumers surveyed said that they would switch brands if the favored brand were associated with a charitable cause. However, like many studies on this subject, Cone's findings are subject to positivity bias; in other words, people are inclined to give the "right" answer to questions about what their hypothetical behavior might be, and that does not assure that they will actually behave in that manner (cited in Andreasen, 2009, p. 172).

For the nonprofit, the marketing relationship may generate not only additional revenue but also increased visibility. Promotions of the relationship often feature the logos of both the nonprofit and the corporate partner, and a comprehensive campaign may include advertising, in-store displays, and exposure in other media.

Cause-marketing relationships are governed by a contract between the nonprofit and the corporate partner. Among other matters, the contract usually spells out how much is to be paid (e.g., a fixed amount per sale or a percentage); the length of time for which the promotion will be in effect; the maximum sum (if any) that the corporate partner will give; and rights of approval that each partner retains with regard to ad copy, use of its logo, and related concerns. One important question is whether and how the terms of the contract will be clearly disclosed to consumers. Promotions that include statements such as "a portion of your purchase will be given to charity" are inadequate, since they do not disclose what portion, whether the promotion covers only certain dates, or whether the total contribution by the company is capped at some maximum amount, as many are. In sum, such a statement does not assure an individual consumer that his or her own purchase will result in a payment to the nonprofit.

Standard 19 of the Better Business Bureau (BBB) Wise Giving Alliance (2010) Standards of Excellence addresses these potential issues, requiring that nonprofit organizations clearly disclose how the charity benefits from the sale of products or services and the terms and conditions of its agreement with the corporate partner. It reads as follows:

19. Clearly disclose how the charity benefits from the sale of products or services (i.e., cause-related marketing) that state or imply that a charity will benefit from a consumer sale or transaction. Such promotions should disclose, at the point of solicitation:

a. the actual or anticipated portion of the purchase price that will benefit the charity (e.g., 5 cents will be contributed to abc charity for every xyz company product sold),

b. the duration of the campaign (e.g., the month of October),

c. any maximum or guaranteed minimum contribution amount (e.g., up to a maximum of $200,000). (n.p.)

Standard 19 applies to the conduct of the nonprofit organization. It requires that when a nonprofit enters a cause-related marketing contract, the contract it negotiates with the corporation should include the disclosure requirements as a provision binding on both parties. In addition, laws in 22 states (as of March 2010) require registration by *commercial co-venturers,* that is, corporations that are engaged in cause marketing. Some require specific provisions in the contract between the nonprofit and the corporation and registration with a state agency (Copilevitz & Canter, 2010).

Many nonprofit relationships with corporations are now comprehensive and integrated. They may include sponsorship, cause marketing, corporate philanthropy, employee volunteering, and additional interactions. Some are also long-term relationships that result in a close identification of the corporate brand with the nonprofit organization or cause. Another trend has been the development of products branded with a cause. For example, Product Red is a brand licensed by the Global Fund to Fight AIDS, Tuberculosis, and Malaria to a variety of corporate partners, including American Express, Apple, Dell, Starbucks, and others (see the website www.joinred.com). "Pink" products, intended to raise awareness of breast cancer and provide support for breast cancer research, also have become ubiquitous. Such programs have attracted critics, who express concern about a lack of transparency regarding the use of funds generated. Some fear that consumers will believe the problem has been sufficiently addressed through their shopping habits and will divert their attention and charitable giving elsewhere (Raymond, 2009).

Operational Relationships

The relationships we have been considering so far all involve the blending of nonprofit and corporate identities in some manner. The nonprofit's principal contribution to the partnership is its name, recognition, and reputation, for which the corporation is willing to pay in order to enhance its own visibility, image, and sales. Such relationships are largely an exchange of intangibles. But some nonprofit–corporate relationships bring the nonprofit into the heart of the company's business operations by "acting as a supplier, improving training or recruitment services, offering benefits for employees, or serving as a test site for new products" (Sagawa & Segal, 2000, p. 23). Let's get a sense of such relationships by looking at some examples:

- Pioneer Human Services in Seattle is a nonprofit that provides rehabilitation and employment services for individuals who are ex-offenders or in recovery from alcohol or drug addiction. Pioneer has a long-standing relationship with Boeing, under which it manufactures parts for Boeing aircraft (Sagawa & Segal, 2000).
- Greyston Bakery in Brooklyn, New York, provides brownies for Ben and Jerry's. Profits from the bakery support the Greyston Foundation, which engages in community development initiatives, including low-income housing, child care, health services, and technology education (Ben & Jerry's, 2008).
- Goodwill Industries International, Inc., through its independent local chapters, provides training for individuals who are disadvantaged or have disabilities. The nonprofit has contracts with businesses to provide temporary workers in document management, assembly, mailing, custodial work, grounds keeping, and other fields (www.goodwill.org).

A significant number of operational relationships involve nonprofits that provide employment or training programs, as in the Pioneer, Greyston, and Goodwill examples. The nonprofits provide services and resources that corporations need for their business operations, but they also provide opportunities for companies to achieve a social benefit with resources that are outside their philanthropic or marketing budgets. By directing some portion of their payroll or purchasing dollars to a nonprofit serving people with needs, companies gain a kind of double impact: They advance a social purpose while also meeting their own core operational needs.

Joint ventures are another type of operational relationship between nonprofits and for-profit companies. As the term suggests, they are new initiatives undertaken jointly by the two entities. A joint venture may involve a specific activity or the creation of a new entity jointly owned by the two partners. Here are two examples:

1. In 2002, the University of Chicago Hospitals and Health Systems and Vanguard Health Systems, a for-profit health care company, created a joint venture to acquire Weiss Memorial Hospital on Chicago's north side (University of Chicago Medical Center, 2002).

2. In 2001, the National Geographic Society and the Fox Entertainment Group formed a joint venture to expand the National Geographic Channel globally (National Geographic, n.d.).

Entering a joint venture with a for-profit company can provide a nonprofit access to capital that it might find otherwise impossible to raise and access to management and technical skills that it does not possess. But there are risks, including possible distraction from the nonprofit's mission, potential financial losses, damage to the nonprofit's image and reputation through actions of the for-profit partner or the joint venture, and a multitude of legal hurdles. The IRS requires that the joint venture serve a charitable purpose and that the nonprofit be free to act exclusively to pursue its own purposes without benefit to the for-profit co-venturers (Simon, Dale, & Chisolm, 2006). The law regarding joint ventures is complex and beyond the scope of this text.

Putting Partnerships Together

Successful partnerships have a logic to them, and a nonprofit seeking a corporate sponsor needs to think in terms of the company's interests and goals. For example, it makes sense for The Home Depot to help KaBOOM! build playgrounds. It sells building materials, its employees know something about construction, and it has stores in many locations and an interest in maintaining good relationships with the communities from which it attracts both employees and customers. The relationship is a good fit. It makes sense for Reader's Digest, a publisher of magazines, to partner with Reading Is Fundamental, which advances literacy. It is logical that Yoplait would support the fight against breast cancer, since many of its customers are women. These relationships make sense; the nonprofits and causes that are supported are important to individuals who are part of the company's target market, and there is an obvious relationship between what the company does, where it does it, and the work of the nonprofit partner. But it would not be logical, or even appropriate, for a tobacco company or a brewer to partner with an organization serving children, nor would it make obvious sense for a company that manufactures widgets to be a partner with a nonprofit concerned with homelessness. For a nonprofit seeking a corporate partner, it therefore is essential to identify potential partners who are a logical fit and to be prepared with a rationale that makes the connection between the company's interests and goals and the mission and programs of the organization.

Successful partnerships are not automatic. Sagawa and Segal (2000) identify five obstacles that can get in the way. First, nonprofits and corporations often speak a "different language" (p. 181). They use different jargon with nuances that may complicate communication across sector lines. Second, they may have different cultures; for example, corporations may be accustomed to top-down decision making, while nonprofits need to build consensus before acting. Third, the different status of the two partners may be an issue; after all, the corporation has the money the nonprofit needs, and it may expect greater deference than the nonprofit anticipates providing (p. 180). Fourth, the two parties may hold different world views. Nonprofits leaders may be skeptical about business motives, and business people may not hold nonprofit management in high regard. Fifth and finally, the two organizations have different bottom lines; the nonprofit is mission driven while the corporation, whatever the level of social consciousness it may hold, exists to generate profit and wealth for its owners. To identify and avoid such potential hazards, nonprofits are advised to enter partnerships with an understanding of themselves and their own needs, to seek out potential corporate partners consistent with their values, to engage in discussion and with due diligence to explore the possibility of a relationship, and to test it with small steps before expanding it to a wider engagement (p. 181).

Partnerships have become attractive to corporations, some of whom eagerly seek relationships with nonprofits that provide a good fit with their strategic goals. Some engage for-profit marketing firms to identify organizations and negotiate the partnership agreement. This suggests the need for careful judgment on the part of organizations that are approached, to ensure that potential partnerships offer both the promise of financial reward and an appropriate fit with the organization's mission, values, and image. The website of Independent Sector provides a compendium of various guidelines for nonprofits that includes standards by which to consider nonprofit–corporate partnerships (see www.independentsector.org/compendium_of_standards#mktng).

Nonprofit Business Ventures

Let's now shift our attention to the bottom half of Figure 12.1 and consider some strategies and tools available to nonprofit organizations that wish to explore the idea of starting their own revenue-generating business ventures.

A 2008 study conducted by the Duke University Center for Social Enterprise found that over 400 of 1,000 nonprofits examined in the United States and Canada currently operate a social enterprise, that is, a nonprofit business venture. The study also revealed a steady increase in the number of businesses established from 1974 to 2004, with a modest decline in the number started during the recession year of 2008 (National Social Enterprise Field Study, 2009). But a note of caution is appropriate. Dees (2004) warns, "It would be a mistake to think that nonprofit business ventures are always beneficial" (cited in Oster et al., 2004, p. 4). Oster et al. agree that "earning income from commercial ventures is often no easier than generating donations. The failure rate for small businesses (for-profit as well as nonprofit) is extraordinarily high" (p. xviii).

As Figure 12.1 depicts, nonprofits operate businesses engaged in three principal activities: services, manufacturing, and distribution or retail. Some are very familiar and have been around for a long time. For example, many of us have shopped in retail stores operated by Goodwill or the Salvation Army. Most museums and hospitals operate gift shops and restaurants. Colleges and universities also have bookstores and restaurants, and some have created for-profit subsidiaries engaged in research or online education. But the range and variety of nonprofit businesses across the country is reflected in many examples of creative and unusual enterprises as well. Some examples will help us get the picture.

- DC Central Kitchen prepares meals for shelters and other institutions serving the homeless in Washington, D.C. It employs homeless men and women in its kitchen and offers training programs in the culinary arts to prepare them for careers in the food service industry. Fresh Start Catering was launched in 1996 as an outgrowth of the training programs. It is a full-service catering business that serves clients in the public and for-profit sector as well as nonprofits. Proceeds from Fresh Start provide support for the Kitchen's charitable programs while also providing additional employment skills to DC Central Kitchen's clients (www.freshstartcatering.com/story.php).
- Triangle Residential Options for Substance Abusers (TROSA), located in North Carolina, helps recovering drug and alcohol abusers change their addictive behaviors. Residents receive food, clothing, and therapy for free for 2 years but are required to work in one of TROSA's seven businesses, engaged in moving, brick masonry, catering, commercial and residential painting, lawn maintenance, picture framing, or retail sales (www.trosainc.org).
- First Book, headquartered in Washington, D.C., is a nonprofit that promotes children's literacy by giving children from low-income families the opportunity to read and own their first new books. First Book Marketplace, its business venture, sells new, high-quality children's books at low cost to organizations serving disadvantaged children. It acquires large quantities of books at deep discounts from its publishing partners and sells them to organizations at prices lower than they could obtain on their own. First Book Marketplace makes a small profit, which it uses to support First Book's core literacy programs (www.fbmarketplace.org/servlet/StoreFront).
- Share Our Strength, an antihunger nonprofit, has developed extensive partnerships with corporations, including American Express, Barnes & Noble, Calphalon Cookware, Tyson

Foods, and Evian. In 1997, it created a subsidiary for-profit consulting firm, Community Wealth Ventures, to work with other nonprofits in developing social enterprises and franchises (www.communitywealth.org).

Identifying Business Opportunities

How does a nonprofit organization that wishes to establish a business enterprise get started? It will not surprise students who have read previous chapters on strategic planning and marketing that the first steps involve looking both outward to the marketplace and inward to the organization itself. Planning for a successful business enterprise requires that the organization know itself as well as the environment surrounding it.

There are three fundamental questions that the organization needs to answer to narrow down its search for business ideas. First, does the organization possess marketable assets? In other words, is there anything it *has,* anything it *does,* or anything it *knows* that others may find valuable and worth paying for? Are there assets that might be *leveraged* to provide a source of revenue? Second, is there a market opportunity waiting to be seized? Is there some unmet need that consumers would be willing to pay to have met? Answering this question may require use of some of the tools we have discussed earlier, including market research and portfolio analysis, as well as some imagination. The third fundamental question relates to the capacity of the organization to undertake a new enterprise. Does it have the staffing, the skills, the access to financial resources, and a culture that will support entrepreneurial activity? As we have said before, nonprofit enterprise is not for every organization, and it makes no sense to stretch an already struggling staff to explore something that is just beyond the organization's capacity to even consider. In other words, organizations need to be realistic (Community Wealth Ventures, 2001, p. 6).

Figure 12.2 illustrates some types of assets that a nonprofit might possess and that could have value in the marketplace. Some assets may seem obvious—for example, space. Many museums rent their attractive spaces for special events, and some have opened restaurants. Underutilized space might be leased to a commercial retailer, like Starbucks on a university campus, or perhaps unused offices could be rented for use by other nonprofits. But relationships and access to a constituency may be assets that can be leveraged, too. In the example mentioned above, First Book leveraged its relationships with networks of other nonprofits, assets that made it possible to negotiate favorable financial arrangements with for-profit suppliers whose access to those markets was not as well established. DC Central Kitchen used what it knew how to do (prepare food) and what it had (a kitchen) as the basis of new business ventures. Share Our Strength leveraged its expertise to create a consulting practice helping other nonprofits with their social enterprises.

Feasibility Analysis and Business Planning

Having completed the process described in the previous section and identified some assets that might be leveraged into business ventures, a nonprofit may proceed to analyze the feasibility of a selected set of ideas. A feasibility analysis uses many of the tools we have described previously in this text; it looks both to the market and to the organization's own capacities (Community Wealth Ventures, 2004). The external variables that need to be considered include

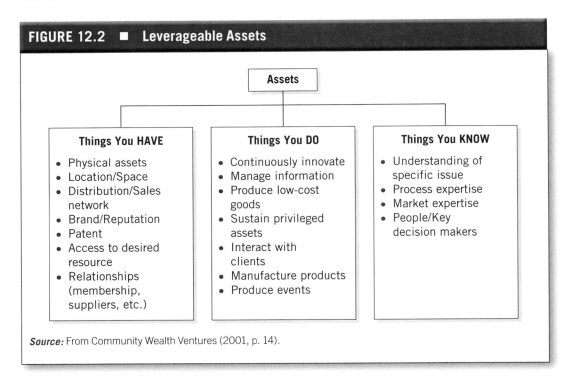

FIGURE 12.2 ■ Leverageable Assets

Assets

Things You HAVE	Things You DO	Things You KNOW
• Physical assets • Location/Space • Distribution/Sales network • Brand/Reputation • Patent • Access to desired resource • Relationships (membership, suppliers, etc.)	• Continuously innovate • Manage information • Produce low-cost goods • Sustain privileged assets • Interact with clients • Manufacture products • Produce events	• Understanding of specific issue • Process expertise • Market expertise • People/Key decision makers

Source: From Community Wealth Ventures (2001, p. 14).

- The overall size of the market for the product or service that the nonprofit plans to provide;
- The outlook for the industry in which it will be engaged—for example, whether it is expanding or contracting;
- Competitive factors, including the study of others offering the same or competing goods and services, as well as generic competition for the same consumer dollars;
- The ease of entry—that is, how much investment will be required to break in; for example, starting a coffee shop may be relatively easy to do, but setting up a factory to manufacture complicated electronics would be a more daunting challenge; and
- Profitability—whether this is a business in which it is possible to make money or whether it is, like many restaurants and retail stores, an enterprise that is likely to have a very small profit margin if any at all.

Looking at itself, the organization needs to ask whether

- The venture fits with its mission;
- The organization possesses the skills and expertise, or capacity, to undertake it;
- Its facilities and other material resources are adequate to the challenge; and
- It is prepared to undertake and manage the risk associated with the new activity.

Of the few business opportunities studied in detail, one may be selected for development of a full *business plan*. Developing such a plan is a time-consuming endeavor, and it would not be practical to make such an investment of effort unless the feasibility analysis has produced an encouraging result. A business plan is a detailed, comprehensive document that encompasses elements of strategic, marketing, business, and operational plans. It is an essential tool both internally, to guide development of the business, and externally, as a sales document for enlisting donors or investors.

Business plans may follow somewhat different formats, but most include the same essential components. Box 12.1 provides a typical outline for a business plan and its major sections. Most plans begin with an executive summary that gives a thorough but succinct overview of the major points made in the following sections of the plan. A potential investor or donor should be able to read the executive summary and have a basic understanding of what the venture entails. Another section of the plan describes the nature of the business and the products or services it intends to offer, provides an overview of the industry in which it plans to operate, and summarizes the strategic plan. A section on management and organization includes the organizational structure and the backgrounds of key staff and board members.

BOX 12.1 ELEMENTS OF A TYPICAL BUSINESS PLAN

1. Executive summary
2. Description of the business
3. Management, organizational structure, key personnel
4. Market analysis and marketing plan
5. Description of products and services
6. Operational plan
7. Financial assumptions
8. Detailed financial plan
9. Uncertainties and risks
10. Plan for growth or exit

One key question that needs to be addressed is how the business venture will be related to the nonprofit itself. Will it operate within the organization, perhaps just as a separate department? Or will it be organized as a subsidiary with a separate board and management structure? If a separate entity, will it be organized as a nonprofit or as a for-profit corporation? In the 2008 study by the Duke Center for Social Enterprise, mentioned earlier, 60 percent of nonprofits with a business venture operated it as a division of the parent organization, 8 percent operated it as a subsidiary organization that was also a nonprofit, 15 percent had organized the business as a separate for-profit subsidiary, and the balance had taken other approaches (National Social Enterprise Field Study, 2009). All these alternatives have pros and cons, and there are advantages and disadvantages to each approach. One interesting development of recent years is the introduction of a new corporate form, the low-profit, limited liability company (L3C), mentioned in Chapter 2. First adopted by the Vermont legislature in 2008, the L3C is a cross between a nonprofit and a for-profit corporation. It is in essence a for-profit company with a social purpose and permits investors to receive a modest return. It may permit access to capital investment in situations where the social purpose makes it impossible to earn a typical financial return. The L3C is not tax-exempt, but because of its social purpose it may qualify for program-related investments by foundations and investments from other private sources.

A business plan needs to include a detailed market analysis. What data have been identified, perhaps during the feasibility study process, to ensure that there is a demand for the products or services to be offered? Who are the competitors, and what will be the competitive advantage of the proposed new venture? The 4 Ps of marketing, which readers will remember from Chapter 10, need to be addressed in this section of the business plan.

The products and services should be described in detail. If the business is a retail store, exactly where will the store be located, how will it be designed, and what types of goods will it carry? If the business involves manufacturing or distribution, what technologies will be used? How will customer satisfaction be measured, and how will the quality of the product be controlled?

To set the stage for the financial plan, a section is devoted to summarizing the assumptions on which financial projections are based. These may include, for example, assumptions about the economy, about demographics, or about growth in a particular market or industry. Careful business plans will include a *sensitivity analysis* that shows how projected results will vary if the assumptions are wrong by some percentage. For example, if sales are 10 percent less than forecast or inflation is two points higher than expected, how will the changes in those assumptions affect the venture's bottom line?

The financial section of the plan shows proforma income statements, proforma cash flows, and proforma balance sheets, usually projected for the first 3 years. (These concepts will be considered in Chapter 13.) Putting this section of the business plan together is essentially like writing the entries of income and revenue, by date, in your checkbook—hypothetically looking out into the future. As a result of this exercise, the business planner should be able to project a point at which the business reaches a break-even position and then, hopefully, begins to earn a profit.

Although some business plan outlines may arrange sections in a different order, closing sections usually discuss potential risks and the precautions that the business is taking to protect against them. For example, risk management may include carrying sufficient insurance or operating the business venture as a subsidiary organization so as to protect the parent from liabilities it may incur. An exit strategy may be one aspect of risk management; in other words, if the business is not viable and needs to shut down, how will that be accomplished in an orderly way while minimizing risks and losses?

The previous paragraphs have provided a very brief discussion of business plans, but it is a large topic. Students will find many books devoted to the subject, and software packages are available to guide the writing of such a plan. Other sources listed at the end of this chapter, including the Community Wealth Ventures and National Center on Nonprofit Enterprise websites, also provide useful information and materials.

Earned Income Strategies: Issues and Decisions

Readers will recall from Chapter 2 of this book that the growth of earned income ventures or nonprofit enterprise, what some call the "commercial transformation of the nonprofit sector" (Weisbrod, 1988), has elicited debate. Some have reacted negatively to specific cases of nonprofit enterprise that they found to be inappropriate, while others have expressed more generic concerns about the threat that commercialization may pose to the nonprofit sector and society.

Sorting Out the Issues

Let's look at two cases from the museum world, each of which created a swirl of controversy, and try to sort out the issues that they raised. In 2006, the Smithsonian Institution and Showtime

Networks created a joint venture, Smithsonian Networks, to produce documentaries using the museum's archives and artifacts. The agreement provides Showtime with semi-exclusive rights to some museum resources. Although an investigation by the Government Accountability Office (GAO) found that the arrangement did not hamper researchers' access to the museum's materials, there was an outcry of criticism from curators, historians, and the documentary filmmaking community (Trescott, 2006). Critics raised objections not only to the terms of the arrangement itself, but also to the fact that as a business contract, some of its provisions would be kept confidential. *The Washington Post* editors weighed in:

> The Smithsonian argues that the filmmakers in question make money out of their work: Why can't the Smithsonian do so, too? Of course it can . . . but it must be under different rules from a purely private body. As a quasi-public institution that receives taxpayers' money, the Smithsonian is obligated to reveal the details of its business deals to the public. It is also obligated not to make deals that restrict public access. Charging larger fees when its collections are to be used for commercial purposes may be acceptable; writing complex, secret rules about who can use them and who cannot is clearly wrong. ("The Nation's Attic," 2006, p. A16)

In 2004, the Museum of Fine Arts, Boston, agreed to lend 21 Monet masterworks to the Bellagio Casino in Las Vegas. The Bellagio paid the museum a fee of $1 million for its use of the pieces from the museum's collection (Edgers, 2004). Critics, including art historians, raised pointed questions: "Is the MFA's art available to the highest bidder?" "Should priceless works of art be displayed in the vicinity of "slot machines and . . . blackjack tables?" (Edgers, 2004, p. A1).

Both cases raise legitimate issues. For example, should collections, or information, or performances, or other products or services owned or produced by nonprofit organizations be available only to individuals or companies who can pay for them, or does an institution's nonprofit status, especially if the institution also receives public funds, require it to serve a broader public interest? If the latter, what is the appropriate balance between that interest and the nonprofit's inescapable need for revenue? How can a nonprofit organization engaged in a contractual relationship with a for-profit entity meet its own responsibilities for transparency and disclosure while respecting the need of its partner to protect business secrets? But some criticisms also reflect entrenched traditions and perspectives. Some may find it inherently offensive to see Monets in a casino, or a Starbucks on a university campus, or a corporate logo on the entrance to a music hall. However, unless the corporate interest affects what is shown, what is taught, or what is played, such concerns may be more a matter of personal values than a threat to the organization's mission. Perceptions do, of course, matter, especially if they might erode confidence in the nonprofit or create the impression that it no longer needs other sources of support, such as philanthropic giving. But the issues are often separable, and it is those that relate to the mission that require the most thoughtful and careful consideration.

Another issue that some have raised is the need for better evaluation of the benefits to nonprofits from partnerships with corporations. For example, Andreasen (2009) cites a study of a partnership between Toyota and the Sierra Club in which the benefits to both sides were monetized, that is, assigned a value in dollars. The total value of the partnership was calculated to be $12 million, but 83 percent of that value went to Toyota and only 17 percent went to the Sierra Club. As Andreasen notes, there is a need to improve the metrics by which partnerships are evaluated so that nonprofits can use the data in negotiating equitable relationships with their corporate partners (p. 184).

Evaluating Opportunities Against Mission

Leaving aside for the moment the view of those who do not favor the involvement of nonprofits in commercial activities at all, opinions on the appropriate relationship of the activity to the mission fall at two poles. Some argue that nonprofits should consider only ventures that are aligned with their missions and should not undertake activities intended solely to produce additional revenue. For example,

> those who hold this view would consider it suitable for a nonprofit group that trains its clients in culinary skills to start a restaurant business to provide a quality work experience for its graduates, but would look askance at an environmental organization that opened a restaurant. (Hochberg, 2002, p. 35)

Others take a different view, arguing that nonprofits should look almost exclusively at whether a business venture is financially profitable. Since the profits are plowed back to support mission-related programs, maximizing revenue from the business ultimately helps deliver more and better services to clients, thus serving the mission. In addition, some say, even successful business ventures that are not related to the mission may create a halo effect that brings other benefits to the nonprofit, including greater visibility and the ability to attract and retain capable staff (Hochberg, 2002). But the question may involve more shades of gray than these two positions encompass.

The economist Dennis Young (2006) provides a useful framework for decision making, which is illustrated by Table 12.1. Young's model helps in thinking through the risks and rewards of possible partnerships or business ventures. As the table suggests, a profitable opportunity is worth exploring if it also supports the mission or if its impact on the mission is neutral. The former would seem to offer the best of all possible worlds. In the latter case, nothing really is lost, and additional revenue may be gained. However, an activity that could be profitable but that threatens the mission surely would require the most exacting of scrutiny. If it offered the possibility of a huge gain in revenue that would make it possible to greatly expand mission-related programs, with considerable benefit to the organization's clients, then a nonprofit might consider it, making adjustments to manage the mission risk.

What about a partnership or business venture that would just break even financially? If it enhances the mission, then it makes sense to explore it. It may be an opportunity to expand mission programs and services, totally supported by new revenue. If the new venture would just break even while having no impact on the mission, it might seem to be nothing more than a potential distraction that has little to offer. It would best be avoided unless it could be tweaked in some way to either produce more profit or better serve the mission. A break-even business that threatens the mission offers nothing, except for those who may be feeling masochistic. Undertaking a business that loses money while either having no impact on the mission or actually threatening it may appeal only to nonprofit managers who are, indeed, professionally suicidal. Unless such possibilities can be redesigned to overcome their shortcomings, they are most certainly best avoided.

Finally, there is the possibility of a partnership or business venture that actually generates a financial loss but contributes in some way to advancing the mission. A nonprofit might consider engaging in that activity, but it would need to be thought about carefully. The benefits and costs of the proposed venture would need to be weighed against those of alternative activities that might serve the mission equally or better, at the same or a lower cost.

TABLE 12.1 ■ Evaluating Earned Income Opportunities			
	Mission-enhancing	**Mission-neutral**	**Mission-threatening**
Profitable	**undertake** (fine-tune)	**undertake** (fine-tune)	**scrutinize** (adjust)
Break-even	**undertake** (fine-tune)	**avoid** (or redesign)	**avoid** (or redesign)
Loss-creating	**consider** (adjust)	**avoid** (or redesign)	**avoid** (or redesign)

Source: Young (2006).

Risks to Society?

In recent years, the criticisms and alarms about commercialization in the nonprofit sector have attained considerable volume and have appeared in prominent, respected venues. An article in the *Harvard Business Review* (Foster & Bradach, 2005) argued against encouraging nonprofits to pursue "the holy grail of earned income," saying that "sending social service agencies down that path jeopardizes those who benefit from their programs—and it harms society itself, which depends for its well-being on a vibrant and mission-driven nonprofit sector" (p. 100). Just months before, the economist Burton Weisbrod (2004) had argued in the *Stanford Social Innovation Review* that Congress should discourage nonprofits from undertaking business ventures and instead should increase the tax incentives to donors for philanthropy. Eikenberry and Kluver (2004), in the *Public Administration Review,* made the case that,

> though marketization may be beneficial for the short-term survival needs of nonprofit organizations, it may have negative long-term consequences. Marketization may harm democracy and citizenship because of its impact on nonprofit organizations' ability to create and maintain a strong civil society. (p. 132)

Some proponents of earned income write in an evangelical voice. While most offer the obligatory caveat that nonprofit business ventures are not for everyone, it is often parenthetical in an otherwise enthusiastic presentation. Some imply that earned income is altogether preferable to nonprofits' dependence on philanthropy and government support and, indeed, offer it as a source of revenue that will free nonprofit managers from thinking about money so as to focus more on delivery of their programs and as a way to make organizations sustainable. But they sometimes minimize the fact that running a business can be no less demanding of effort and attention than traditional fund-raising or grantsmanship and that sustainability of a business enterprise itself is far from guaranteed.

Some critics of earned income are also extreme in their alarms. For one, their writing implies that the nonprofit sector is synonymous with social service agencies, not acknowledging that many nonprofits, including colleges, schools, performing arts groups, health care institutions, and many others, long have generated earned income as a major portion of their revenue without apparent abandonment of their missions or the loss of philanthropic support. Nor do the critics always acknowledge that as many as 90 percent of nonprofit business ventures conducted by nonprofits that do provide human and social services are "directly or closely related to their missions" (Hochberg & Wise, 2005, p. 50). These include Girl Scout Cookie sales and Goodwill and Salvation Army thrift shops, which have long been significant components of their respective organizations' revenue without inflicting apparent harm.

Some critics also do not sufficiently acknowledge the substantial dependence of many nonprofits on government support and the implications of changed policies that have forced them into competitive situations. Nonprofits' responses are sometimes portrayed as capitulation to the market rather than accommodation to the realities that public policy has thrust on them. It is reasonable to ask if their clients and society would be better served were the nonprofits forced from existence by rigid adherence to traditional methods of revenue generation. Increased incentives to philanthropy do not offer a realistic alternative to meeting nonprofits' financial needs, for a variety of reasons that go beyond the scope of this discussion. And, it must be acknowledged, even small nonprofits are increasingly dependent on major gifts from a relatively low number of donors, a situation that presents no less of a threat to their autonomy than their partnerships with the for-profit sector.

As noted at previous points in this text, this author recommends a balanced perspective. Earned income offers one way for nonprofits to obtain revenue and to diversify sources, managing the risks inherent in reliance on philanthropy and government alone. It will be a more appropriate and useful strategy for some organizations than for others. Some may rely entirely on earned income, but for most it is one component of a diversified funding base, together with philanthropy, government funds, and earned income from core mission programs. Indeed, some nonprofit organizations that long have been reliant on earned income are increasing their efforts to obtain philanthropic support, with the goal of creating a more balanced revenue profile.

Opportunities for earned income always need to be evaluated against their impact on achievement of the mission (as shown in Table 12.1). Those that threaten it generally should be avoided. Others may serve both financial and mission goals. Some may provide income to advance the mission from activities that bear no relationship to it but also do it no harm. Leaving aside the tax implications of unrelated business income, which we discussed earlier in this text, that is really no different in its ultimate effect from investing endowment funds in the stock of companies and using the dividends to support charitable purposes, a practice in which many nonprofits engage without arousing much complaint.

It is ultimately the responsibility of the nonprofit's board to establish, after thoughtful reflection and discussion, policies and guidelines, rooted in the organization's mission and values, against which such decisions will be made. Those policies should take into consideration mission-related, financial, and public relations risks; they need to be in place before the organization enters into new partnerships or ventures, and not put together as a response once the editorialists are at the door.

Chapter Summary

Although nonprofits in some sectors have long derived a major portion of their revenue from earned income, that is, fees for goods and services they provide, there has been an increased emphasis on such activities in recent decades. Terminology varies in the literature of the field, but this book adopts the term *earned income strategies* to encompass a variety of partnerships between nonprofits and corporations as well as business ventures undertaken by nonprofit organizations themselves. Nonprofits engage in such activities to increase and diversify sources of revenue and to advance their missions and gain other benefits. Although some writers imply that it is, the pursuit of earned income is not synonymous with being a social entrepreneur. Because social entrepreneurship is a broader concept than earned income, it is considered as a separate topic in Chapter 16 of this book.

This chapter discussed four types of relationships between nonprofits and corporations that are among the most common. *Licensing agreements* permit a company to use a nonprofit name or logo on its products in exchange for a royalty paid to the nonprofit. *Sponsorships* are arrangements by which a corporation contributes to support an event, facility, or organization in exchange for the prominent association of its name or logo. It is not the same as advertising because it does not include descriptions or depictions of the company's products. *Cause-related marketing* (or just *cause marketing*) refers to partnerships in which a nonprofit is paid a fixed amount per sale or a percentage of total sales of a company's product, usually in connection with a short-term promotion. This type of relationship became popular following a very successful arrangement in 1983 whereby American Express made a payment to the Statue of Liberty campaign each time its credit card was used.

Some nonprofits have *operational relationships* with companies, often as suppliers or sources of workers. Others have entered joint ventures with corporations; that is, they have become partners in the ownership and operation of a new business. Successful nonprofit–corporate partnerships are built on commonality of values and interests. There is usually a logical connection between the company's products or target markets and the mission and programs of the nonprofit.

Some nonprofits have launched their own business ventures; most provide services, manufacture products, or are in the fields of retail or distribution. Examples include DC Central Kitchen, which established a catering business based on the use of its kitchen facilities and the employment of homeless people enrolled in its culinary training program. Triangle Residential Options for Substance Abusers (TROSA) requires clients to work in one of seven businesses, engaged in moving, brick masonry, catering, commercial and residential painting, lawn maintenance, picture framing, or retail sales (www.trosainc.org).

Nonprofits begin to identify business opportunities by inventorying their assets—things they have, things they do, or things they know. Assets may be tangible, such as space, or may include relationships with particular constituencies, knowledge of specific cultures, or the organization's reputation and brand. Once it has identified assets that might be used to produce earned income, the organization analyzes the feasibility of using a select few of them. The feasibility analysis looks both inside the organization, to ensure that it has the capacity to undertake the venture, and outside, to gain knowledge of market demand and competitors.

Development of a full business plan is an intensive and time-consuming effort and likely will be undertaken only for the most promising of business opportunities that have been identified. There are many formats for a business plan, but most include an executive summary, a description of the business, a market analysis and marketing plan, a description of the products and services to be offered, an operational plan, clarification of financial assumptions, a detailed financial plan and projection of cash flow for at least the first 3 years, a summary of uncertainty and risks and plans to manage them, and a plan for growth or exit from the business.

Nonprofits' efforts to increase earned income have generated controversy. Some critics raise legitimate issues about the impact of commercialization on nonprofits' commitment to mission. Others reflect traditional views of what are appropriate activities and revenue sources for nonprofit organizations. Dennis Young (see Table 12.1) offers a framework for evaluating nonprofit enterprise opportunities that may be profitable, break-even, or money losing, each in terms of whether it advances the mission, is mission-neutral, or mission-threatening. Ventures that threaten the mission usually should be avoided.

Some see commercialization of the nonprofit sector as desirable, and others see it as a threat to democracy and civil society. This book advocates a balanced perspective, in which non-profit–corporate partnerships and nonprofit business ventures offer one way to increase and diversify revenues. A well-managed nonprofit seeks a balanced portfolio of revenue streams, from earned income, philanthropy, and possibly government sources. Nonprofit boards have a responsibility to develop policies and guidelines to ensure that nonprofit enterprise is consistent with their organizations' mission and values and that financial and public relations risks also are weighed with the mission as paramount.

Note

1. In the first edition of this text, this chapter was entitled "Nonprofit Enterprise." That term is often used to describe the activities covered in this chapter. However, the title "Earned Income Strategies" is used in this second edition to avoid confusion with the term *social enterprise*. The latter has a specific meaning and broader implications, some of which are discussed further in Chapter 16. The activities described in this chapter all involve a nonprofit's pursuit of earned income, as compared with contributed income.

KEY TERMS AND CONCEPTS

business plan	*earned income*	*nonprofit enterprise*
cause marketing	*feasibility analysis*	*sensitivity analysis*
cause-related marketing	*joint ventures*	*social enterprise*
commercialization	*leverageable assets*	*sponsorship*
community wealth	*licensing*	
contributed income	*nonprofit business ventures*	

CASE 12.1   Minnesota Public Radio

In 1969, William Kling, then age 26, was managing a radio station at St. John's Abbey and University in Minnesota. He hired a young man named Garrison Keillor to host a classical music program in the morning. Kling then moved to Minneapolis-St. Paul to start a radio network, Minnesota Public Radio (MPR), taking Keillor with him. Keillor introduced a show he called *Prairie Home Companion,* which by 1978 had developed a cult following. In 1981, Keillor offered his listeners a free poster and over 50,000 requests came in. Offers of T-shirts and other products soon followed and sales were highly successful (Gallagher, 2001). At the same time, the Reagan administration was encouraging public broadcasting to become less reliant on federal funds and to begin seeking more earned income (Gallagher, 2001). MPR soon created Rivertown Trading Company as a wholly-owned subsidiary to handle the growing sales of *Prairie Home Companion* items, which reached $200 million by 1998. For a time, Rivertown remained a nonprofit, fully owned by MPR (Phills & Chang, 2005).

But the organizational structure continued to evolve and become more complex, and the issue of unrelated business income became a concern for MPR. Faced with the risk that the IRS could challenge its nonprofit status because of its growing commercial revenues, in 1987, a reorganization was undertaken. Minnesota Communications Group (later renamed American Public Media Group) became the parent organization and was a nonprofit. It owned both the nonprofit MPR and a for-profit company called Greenspring, which encompasses Rivertown Trading and other for-profit enterprises established by MPR. The for-profit businesses produced dividends and royalties that supported MPR (Miller, 1998). MPR continued to grow, building a regional network that rivaled the larger National Public Radio. By 2004, MPR had an operating budget of $47 million, a network of 38 stations, and 650,000 listeners (Phills & Chang, 2005, p. 66). William Kling continued to serve as CEO of both nonprofit MPR and for-profit Greenspring, and other senior officers also held dual roles with both organizations. These relationships eventually became controversial.

Kling described MPR's earned income initiatives as "social purpose capitalism" and was recognized with numerous awards. But some charged that his aggressive tactics were all about money and also questioned the level of his compensation. He was paid by both MPR and Greenspring; for example, in 1998 he received $69,200 from MPR and an additional $429,155 from Greenspring, which some thought to be too much for a nonprofit executive (Miller, 1998). Others defended Kling's compensation as reasonable considering the scope of the enterprises he managed and pointed to the fact that other nonprofit executives in the state were paid even more (Phills & Chang, 2005, p. 69). A different issue arose in 1995 when executives of American Public Media asked MPR employees to volunteer to help prepare Rivertown holiday orders for shipping. Some said this was improper use of nonprofit resources to benefit a for-profit company. Kling defended the activity, noting that all Rivertown profits went back to benefit nonprofit MPR. The attorney general of Minnesota investigated the case and ultimately agreed with Kling (Phills & Chang, p. 68).

Controversy was heightened when, in 1998, Greenspring agreed to sell Rivertown Trading to the department store chain Dayton Hudson for $120 million. A total of $90 million went to MPR's endowment. Kling described the transaction as "converting an operating asset to an endowment asset," which would provide more security to MPR in case Rivertown's profits would decline (Phills & Chang, 2005, p. 70). Kling and other senior executives also had worked out arrangements that provided them with personal bonuses when Rivertown was sold. Kling received $2.6 million (Abelson, 1998). Some said the case was an example of personal enrichment accomplished through the use of public funds that had, in part, supported development of MPR's popular programs, on which Rivertown's sales were based (Abelson, 1998). The Minnesota Attorney General determined that Kling and the other executives had done nothing wrong.

MPR continued to expand and prosper. By 2007, it had taken over additional radio stations, sometimes generating controversy in local communities (Hall, 2007). It also completed a successful capital campaign that raised $56 million, increased corporate sponsorship, and built its base of individual donors to 94,000 (Hall, 2007). Kling continued to serve as CEO of MPR and Greenspring, which expanded into other revenue-generating endeavors, including several magazines and a social-networking site (Hall, 2007). MPR's endowment had grown to $170 million by 2007, making it one of the largest in public radio. As Kling described the situation, "We have very nice, diversified revenues. We've earned about $275 million from for-profit activities for the benefit of the nonprofit. If you have that kind of boost, it is an extra advantage" (Hall, 2007, n.p.).

QUESTIONS FOR DISCUSSION

1. In each of the following cases, what was the asset that the organization leveraged to create a source of earned income? Was that asset something it had, something it did, something it knew, or some combination of these?

    -   The Guthrie Theater and the Children's Theater Company in Minneapolis had a collection of costumes. They created a business to rent the costumes to schools, theaters, companies, and individuals across the country at reasonable rates.
    -   Nation's Capital Child and Family Development operated a large kitchen to provide food for its 25 sites. It created a business to cater food to other child care and elder care providers and to offer technical support to other organizations in the operation of their kitchens.
    -   The nonprofit Dakota Area Resources and Transportation for Seniors (DARTS) maintained its own fleet of vehicles, which it used to provide transportation to seniors. It began a business offering maintenance services to other nonprofits that owned their own vehicles.

    Source: Examples are drawn from the Yale School of Management/Goldman Sachs Foundation Partnership's National Business Plan Competition, 2002–2005.

2. Some well-known nonprofit–corporate partnerships are listed below. In each case, what do you think is the logic behind the relationship; in other words, why does this relationship make sense? What may be the principal benefits that each party receives as a result of the partnership? Do you see any possible issues/problems related to each of these relationships?

    -   Neutrogena sells sunscreen with the American Cancer Society logo.
    -   Microsoft created technology centers at Boys & Girls Club locations.
    -   Nike created its 10/2 brand of clothing with $1 from the sale of each product going to the Lance Armstrong Foundation to fight cancer.
    -   Chefs around the United States contribute their time to the Taste of the Nation, an event that supports Share Our Strength, an antihunger nonprofit. Other sponsors of the event include Jenn-Air, a subsidiary of Maytag, a kitchen appliance manufacturer.
    -   Christmas in April is a nonprofit that renovates homes for the elderly and disabled. The Home Depot has provided the organization with training for its volunteers, assistance from The Home Depot employees, and lines of credit for merchandise at its stores, as well as cash gifts.
    -   In 1993, after Denny's was charged with racial discrimination in one of its restaurants, new management adopted a zero-tolerance policy on racial discrimination throughout the company. Shortly afterward, it established a partnership with Save the Children, a nonprofit that helps children throughout the world with health and nutrition programs, emergency relief, and economic development (Sagawa & Segal, 2000, pp. 72–75).

3. Some well-attended exhibits at art museums have included collections of automobiles, motorcycles, and photographs of Madonna. Are these appropriate subjects for exhibition in a nonprofit art museum? Why or why not? Do they put the museum's mission at risk—in the short term or long term? Why or why not?

4. What were the principal issues raised by the case of Minnesota Public Radio?

5. What does the MPR case suggest about the best ways to structure the relationship between a nonprofit and its earned-income ventures?

6. Some people fear that if a nonprofit gains too much earned income, its traditional donors will stop giving. What does the case of MPR suggest about this issue?

SUGGESTIONS FOR FURTHER READING

Books

Community Wealth Ventures. (2001). *The community wealth seekers guide.* Washington, DC: Author. (Available at http://www.communitywealth.com/resources_tools.htm)

Community Wealth Ventures. (2003). *Powering social change: Lessons on community wealth generation for nonprofit sustainability.* Washington, DC: Author.

Cordes, J., & Steuerle, C. E. (2008). *Nonprofits and business.* Washington, DC: Urban Institute.

Oster, S. M., Massarsky, C. W., & Beinhacker, S. L. (Eds.). (2004). *Generating and sustaining nonprofit earned income.* San Francisco: Jossey-Bass.

Wymer, W. W., Jr., & Samu, S. (Eds.). (2003). *Nonprofit and business sector collaboration.* Binghamton, NY: Best Business Books.

Websites

Community Wealth Ventures, http://www.communitywealth.org/

National Center on Nonprofit Enterprise, http://www.nationalcne.org/

Also see suggested readings on social entrepreneurship at the end of Chapter 16 of this book.

Chapter Outline

chapter 13

The principle financial challenge for most nonprofit organizations is to generate sufficient and reliable revenue to meet its short-term operating costs and long-term capital needs.
© iStockphoto.com/faizzaki

Financial Management 13

As emphasized before, nonprofit organizations do not measure their success exclusively or primarily by their financial results but rather by outcomes related to their missions or by a double bottom line that considers both financial and program results. That being the case, however, it is the reality that many boards and CEOs pay particular attention to their organizations' financial condition. Without adequate and well-managed resources, achievement of the mission is jeopardized, and the very survival of the organization may be threatened.

It is realistic to acknowledge that an organization may be of only mediocre effectiveness and still continue to survive for a long time without facing a crisis. But budget deficits or the erosion of financial assets are likely to gain the focused attention of the board and CEO and require immediate action. Many nonprofit board members are drawn from the business community and may be more familiar, or more comfortable, with financial concepts than with the professional fields of the organization's staff, so they often focus their attention on the budget and financial statements. In addition, conservation of the nonprofit's assets is an essential part of the board's fiduciary responsibility, and any signs of trouble are likely to be addressed urgently. Few events can so quickly place a nonprofit CEO's tenure in jeopardy as an operating deficit, financial mismanagement, or a bad audit report. In sum, financial skills are necessary, even if not sufficient, for effective nonprofit management.

This chapter considers some basic concepts in nonprofit financial management and accounting. Some readers may have familiarity with the vocabulary of financial management, accounting, and financial statements. If so, they are encouraged to read the chapter for a refresher and perhaps a perspective on how concepts familiar to them from the business sector apply to nonprofit organizations. Others may not have studied finance before, but a background is not presumed here. Let's start by defining some essential terms and concepts.

Definitions of Key Concepts

It is important to clarify the differences among the concepts of bookkeeping, accounting, and financial management. *Bookkeeping* refers to the methods and systems by which financial transactions are recorded, either by hand or on a computer. This chapter does not discuss nonprofit bookkeeping, but various manuals and other materials are readily available on this subject. *Accounting* encompasses the rules by which financial transactions are classified and reported. This chapter does not provide a detailed guide to nonprofit accounting, but introduces some basic principles and concepts. Other readings suggested at the end of the chapter will be helpful for those who may wish to have a deeper understanding of accounting.

There are two types of accounting. *Financial accounting* "deals with the financial information published for use by parties outside the organization." *Managerial accounting* "deals with information that is useful to an organization's managers," but is not required to be made available to others (Anthony & Young, 2005, p. 466). For example, a banker considering a loan to a nonprofit would need to see financial accounting statements but might not be concerned about how much it costs per client to run each of the organization's programs, which is managerial accounting data. The latter, however, might be important information for a CEO to have when planning budget allocations.

Financial management is a broader concept than accounting. It relies on accounting statements for data, but it "focuses on the *meaning* of those figures" (Anthony & Young, 2005, p. 487, italics original). Financial management usually involves the analysis of various financial ratios that may provide indicators of trends and the organization's financial health. Thus, the key in bookkeeping is accuracy; in accounting, consistency and following the rules; and in financial management, making judgments and establishing policies to guide the organization's financial life.

The principal financial challenge for most nonprofit organizations is to generate sufficient and reliable revenue to meet their short-term operating costs and long-term capital needs. Achieving a diversified and sustainable balance of revenue sources is thus an essential foundation of nonprofit financial management. As we have seen in previous chapters, nonprofit organizations may seek various sources of revenue, including philanthropic giving, earned income, government, and volunteer services. In offering a unified theory of nonprofit finance, Young (2007) suggests that the sources realistically available to a given organization will reflect the benefits it provides through its programs and services. For example, an organization that provides private goods can likely rely on earned income, since the individuals who benefit will be willing to pay. Those that produce public goods may be able to justify support from government. Nonprofits that provide programs that benefit some group, that is, more than an individual but less than the public (similar to Lohmann's concept of common goods, discussed in Chapter 3), may attract gifts from those who share an interest in their work. A nonprofit also may generate revenue by providing what Young (2007) calls *trade benefits*—for example, the value it provides to a partnership with another nonprofit or a corporation. Other organizations will have endowment funds, usually provided through gifts from individuals, which produce annual investment income to supplement funds available through other sources.

A well-managed organization will strive to achieve diverse revenue sources, both to minimize risk and to maximize its autonomy, that is, to avoid a follow-the-money approach in which its programs evolve in response to trends in government or foundation grants or the interests of major individual donors. Identifying an ideal and realistic income mix is thus one of the principal financial decisions for any organization. Young (2007) proposes the following approach:

- Start with a service portfolio that addresses mission.
- Analyze the nature of benefits conferred by these services.
- Seek income support from alternative sources in proportion with the mix of benefits. Justify resource solicitations as a quid pro quo for benefits provided. Avoid a tin cup mentality, that is, the feeling that you are begging for support.
- Make adjustments to the income portfolio to reflect feasibility factors, which may inhibit or enhance the collection of each sought form of income.
- Make adjustments to the income portfolio to reflect opportunities and problems associated with interactions among alternative income streams.

- Make adjustments to the income portfolio to ensure fiscal integrity and maximum mission impact. This may require adjustments in the service mix, particularly the balance between profitable and loss-making activity.
- Make adjustments to the income portfolio to account for risk. This may require adding additional income streams such as investment income from endowments, further diversifying the overall income mix so that it is less concentrated on a few sources, and cultivating more deeply certain income sources that show promise of stabilization through the building of trust (p. 370).

Overview of Nonprofit and Personal Finances

Organizational finance may be unfamiliar to some individuals, but most of us have at least some understanding of how we manage our own assets and accounts. Thus, let's begin by looking at the types of funds that nonprofits manage and how they are like—or unlike—an individual's personal finances (Table 13.1). It will be necessary to oversimplify some ideas initially, but a number of more complex issues will be introduced later on in our discussion.

A nonprofit's operating funds are much like those each of us manages in his or her checking account. In general, payments received are intended to be spent within the same period to pay current bills. Expenses may be limited by a budget, although both individuals and organizations also have the ability to borrow funds to meet current obligations, with obvious risks in both cases. Operating income, that is, the funds that flow into your checkbook or the nonprofit's operating accounts, may be unrestricted or restricted. Fees that nonprofits receive for services provided to customers or clients, gifts from donors who do not designate a specific use, and revenue from earned income activities are usually unrestricted, which means they may be used to meet any legitimate expense, including, for example, the salaries of staff, rent and utility bills, or capacity-building activities. An individual's salary is generally unrestricted income, too; that is, nobody tells you how to spend the money, as long as the purpose is legal.

But suppose your grandmother gives you a check for your birthday, directing that you use the money to buy a new overcoat for the winter. You might deposit her check in your checking account, but you would need to somehow keep that money separate, at least in your mind, because it has been restricted to a specific use. Nonprofits also receive payments that are designated for particular purposes and likewise need to ensure that they are spent accordingly. Your responsibility to follow your grandmother's direction may be only a moral obligation, while

TABLE 13.1 ■ Nonprofit Organization and Individual Funds

Nonprofit Funds	Personal Funds
Endowment (permanent or pure)	Not comparable
Endowment (quasi or board-designated)	Retirement funds
Operating reserves	Savings account
Operating funds—restricted	Checking account (e.g., birthday gift)
Operating funds—unrestricted	Checking account (e.g., salary)

nonprofits are required to adhere to the purposes attached to restricted funds. (Of course, both you and the nonprofit may also have the concern that a donor, or grandmother, could decide not to give again if the money is not properly applied.)

A nonprofit's operating funds that are *temporarily restricted* could represent, for example, an advance payment on a grant or contract to cover some service that it has not yet performed. The organization has not yet incurred the expenses that the payment was intended to cover, and the money must be set aside until it has. The funds are restricted until such a time that the work has been completed and the revenue actually earned. Or the organization may have received a gift that is to be used for the purchase of a new item of equipment. The money is restricted until the item is purchased; it cannot be used for something else, just as you cannot use the money from your grandmother for a new iPad.

Most of us count on our weekly or monthly income to cover our expenses but recognize that something could go wrong. An unexpected car repair bill could arise that was not in the budget. Summer jobs may turn out to be in short supply this year, eliminating some of the additional income you had anticipated earning toward fall semester expenses. Knowing these risks, we might accumulate some money in a savings account, something we can turn to for the proverbial "rainy day." Organizations also establish rainy day funds, or *operating reserves,* to be available under similar circumstances. The existence of such reserves, often equivalent to 6 months or 1 year of the operating budget, is one hallmark of a soundly managed organization. Like your personal savings, operating reserves are generally invested in very secure, short-term instruments such as bank certificates of deposit or money market funds. As with your personal savings, there may be the hope that reserves will not need to be touched, but it is important that they be preserved and kept liquid in case they are needed.

The analogy between individual and organizational funds breaks down a little when we talk about endowment, for one reason in particular—individuals are mortal, but organizations and institutions are not necessarily so! Many e*ndowments* are funds that are not intended to be spent—ever. The investment income that they generate may be expended for current operating expenses, but the principal is often preserved *in perpetuity.* No individual has a need for funds of such a long-term nature.

There are two basic categories of endowment funds: board-designated endowment (also called quasi endowment) and permanent endowment (also called pure endowment).[1] *Board-designated endowment* includes, as the term suggests, money that the organization's board has decided to invest as an endowment. For example, maybe the organization has run an operating surplus for awhile and has accumulated more operating reserves than it really needs. The money is not earning much interest in the safe bank account where it is being kept, and it seems unlikely that the organization will need to draw on its reserves, at least not all of them, for the foreseeable future. The board decides that some of that excess should be invested and preserved over the long term to provide additional income to support or enhance the organization's programs in future years. Its purpose might be to build up an independent source of annual income as a way to diversify revenue sources, enable the organization to sustain and enhance its programs, and gain more independence from traditional funding sources. Because its time horizon is long, and it does not foresee needing to tap the principal, the board likely would invest those funds in stocks, bonds, real estate, and other classes of assets, willing to ride out short-term fluctuations in order to gain greater investment returns over the long haul.

Since it was the board's decision to place funds into board-designated or *quasi endowment,* the board has the authority to withdraw the money from that type of endowment if it determines that to be necessary or desirable. But that is not a decision that the board is going to make lightly. Just as you would not be quick to cash out your IRA (individual retirement account) to pay for lunch, or even to buy a new car, a board's decision to take funds out of board-designated endowment is not one that it would make except to meet some special need, for example, to build a badly needed new facility or some similar purpose that represents a major and long-lasting improvement.[2] Again, these are not the same as reserves and should not be regarded as such; they are investments for the long term.

With *permanent* or *pure endowment,* the board has limited or no flexibility. These are funds given by donors who specified that the principal be retained and be invested *in perpetuity,* meaning forever. They are *permanently restricted.* Donors may also have designated that annual income generated through the investment of endowment principal be used for certain purposes, for example, to provide scholarships to students or to maintain a chair for a violinist in the symphony orchestra. Under most circumstances, the board does not have the legal authority to invade the original principal of the gift or to use the income for purposes not consistent with the donor's direction without first obtaining the donor's approval or, with strong justification, permission from a court of law.[3]

In looking at your personal finances, the closest thing that you may have to endowment funds are the resources you or your employer have placed into retirement accounts, perhaps a 401(k), a 403(b), or an IRA. These assets are not intended to be spent today or anytime soon and, indeed, the law may place significant barriers to your gaining access to the money now. They are like board-designated or quasi endowment; you might be able to withdraw the funds, but that is not your intention or plan, except under highly unusual circumstances. Obviously, there is a big difference between your retirement funds and a nonprofit's permanent endowment, since you probably intend to spend your retirement funds eventually to support yourself once you reach a more advanced age and end your career. A nonprofit's permanent endowment is intended *never* to be spent. There is nothing quite comparable to "in perpetuity" for an individual.

In addition to financial assets, organizations—and individuals—have *physical assets.* Like an individual or a family, nonprofits own buildings, vehicles, equipment, and other *things.* (Physical assets are not depicted in Table 13.1.) Physical assets are quite different from money. For one thing, they are generally *illiquid,* meaning that they are not easy to sell. It is also often difficult to know exactly how much they are worth. For these reasons, they do not serve the same purpose as operating funds or reserves. They also are not the same as endowment because they generally do not generate income that might be used to meet current expenses. It could be possible, of course, to sell the car or the house if needed to pay bills, but that would reflect a relatively dire and undesirable situation for an individual or an organization.

Before looking at nonprofit financial statements, let's consider how two additional principles of accounting may be understood in terms of both an organization's and an individual's finances: the distinction between the cash basis of accounting and the accrual basis of accounting and the concept of cash flow. Using the *cash basis,* financial transactions are recorded only when money changes hands. This is the way many of us handle our checking accounts; we add to the balance when we make a deposit and subtract when we withdraw funds. But using a cash basis can provide a misleading picture of one's actual financial situation; for example, it ignores the purchases that have been placed on a credit card. The amount of those purchases may not yet have hit your checking account, but they should be subtracted from its balance—at least in your mind—to gain an accurate sense of where you stand. The credit card is an *account payable* (meaning the charges are owed but not yet paid). On the other hand, let's say you have sold something on eBay and are awaiting the payment to clear your PayPal account. The money is not reflected in your checking account balance, but you can plan your expenses in anticipation of receiving it, since it is on the way. It is an *account receivable,* and it needs to be taken into account in assessing your current position.

A nonprofit organization faces similar situations. For example, it may have sent bills to clients for services that it has provided, or it may have pledges from donors that have not yet been received. Those are accounts receivable and need to be taken into consideration along with the cash it has in the bank, since they represent money that it has earned or is entitled to receive. Alternatively, a nonprofit may receive payment on a grant or contract for services that it is going to provide in the future. It has received the cash, but it hasn't yet *earned* it, and it has future expenses to which it is obligated as a result of the terms of the grant or contract. It cannot look at that cash as money available to pay for salaries, rent, or the electric bill. The cash basis of accounting thus presents some drawbacks. As Zietlow, Hankin, and Seidner (2007) explain,

> In cash basis accounting, revenues are recorded when cash comes in and expenses are recorded when cash is expended. The problem is that revenues and expenditures are not properly matched during the year. This mismatch becomes serious whenever your organization has [a] significant dollar amount of payables, receivables, inventories, or depreciable assets. (p. 171)

Accounting on an *accrual basis* takes into account the money that a nonprofit has earned and is entitled to receive, as well as obligations for expenditures that it has not yet incurred. It thus presents a much more accurate portrayal of the nonprofit's actual situation than cash basis accounting and, indeed, is mandated for external financial reporting.

But the accrual basis of accounting also may lead to a misleading picture. For example, suppose your friend has a wealthy aunt who has promised to leave him her entire large estate when she dies. He may think of himself as wealthy already; he has mentally recorded his inheritance as a receivable. But every time you are out together, he needs to borrow money from you to pay for dinner. He is thinking on an accrual basis, but unfortunately, he does not have sufficient *cash flow* right now to meet his living needs. A nonprofit organization could be in the same situation. For example, it may have landed some lucrative contracts, but it has not yet received payment. Using the accrual basis of accounting, the anticipated payment shows up as revenue on its financial reports. But it may not have cash on hand in the bank to meet this month's rent or payroll. For these reasons, organizations—and individuals—also need to track cash flow. We will see more about how they do so in the next section of this chapter.

Nonprofit Financial Statements

Again, accounting is about following the rules. For nonprofit organizations, rules are established by the Financial Accounting Standards Board (FASB), which most people pronounce as "Faz-bee." The standards most relevant to nonprofit organizations are No. 93 ("Accounting for Depreciation"), No. 95 ("Statement of Cash Flows"), No. 116 ("Accounting for Contributions Received and Contributions Made"), No. 117 ("Financial Statements of Not-for-Profit Organizations"), and No. 124 ("Accounting for Certain Investments Held by Not-for-Profit Organizations") (Anthony & Young, 2005, p. 469). We will not go into detail on all these in this discussion, but there will be occasions to refer in particular to the Statement of Financial Accounting Standards (SFAS) No. 116 and SFAS No. 117. These standards required significant changes in nonprofit accounting when they were implemented in 1995 and have ramifications not only for how nonprofits keep track of their finances, but also for their relationships with donors.

Tables 13.2, 13.3, 13.4, and 13.5, respectively, provide examples of four financial statements that nonprofit organizations prepare: (1) *statement of financial position* (sometimes called the *balance sheet*), (2) *statement of activities* (sometimes called the *income statement*), (3) *statement of cash flows,* and (4) *statement of functional expenses.* Space does not permit a line-by-line discussion of the statements, so let's just look at a few key items, especially those that illustrate unique features of nonprofit accounting.

The examples in this chapter are the 2008 financial statements of Special Olympics, Inc. (SOI). Its financial statements have been taken directly from its Independent Auditor's Report for 2008, which is posted on its website (www.specialolympics.org). Much of the same data are also provided in an organization's Form 990, which is filed with the Internal Revenue Service and is easily accessed through services such as Guidestar. For purposes of space and simplicity, the examples shown in this chapter do not include the *Notes to the Financial Statements,* the notes that follow financial statements and provide supplemental information. But the notes are an integral part of an organization's overall financial statements and often illuminate some important details. Let's look at a few key points in SOI's financial statements that relate to some of the principles we discussed above.

Statement of Financial Position

The *statement of financial position* (sometimes called the *balance sheet*) provides a snapshot of the organization at a point in time, usually the end of a fiscal year. It summarizes its *assets,* that is, "the items that the organization possesses, with which it carries out its programs and service," and its *liabilities,* the "amounts of borrowed money, or debt, that the organization has used to finance some of those assets" (Zietlow et al., 2007, p. 172). To put it in personal terms again, your personal assets may include your bank accounts, the book value of your car, and the market value of your house. They need to be offset by your liabilities, for example, the balances on your car loan, mortgage, and credit cards. The difference is equal to your personal *net worth.* In a for-profit company, the difference is called *equity;* it represents the value of the owners' interest in the firm. For a nonprofit, there is no ownership interest, so the difference between assets and liabilities is simply defined as *net assets.* The way balance sheets are constructed, assets always equal the sum of liabilities and net assets; if these totals do not agree, there is something wrong with the numbers.

The SOI balance sheet reflects some of the accounting principles discussed before. For example, notice that net assets (down toward the bottom of the statement) are divided into those that are unrestricted, those that are temporarily restricted, and those that are permanently restricted. The temporarily restricted assets are funds that donors intended to be used for specific activities that have not yet been carried out. (A breakdown of these intended purposes is provided in Notes to the Financial Statements, which are not shown in this simplified example.) Permanently restricted assets of $198,584 represent SOI's endowment.

SOI's balance sheet shows an asset called "contributions receivable" and another called "program and other receivables." This reflects the accrual basis of accounting. These obligations of others to SOI are assets that SOI possesses, although SOI has not yet received the cash. SFAS 116, which was mentioned above, requires that under certain circumstances nonprofits show pledges as assets, even if they have not received payment of the gift. That was a controversial

TABLE 13.2 ■ Statement of Financial Position

	2008	2007
ASSETS		
CURRENT ASSETS:		
Cash and cash equivalents	$ 8,006,854	$ 10,559,037
Board-designated cash and cash equivalents	1,053,852	1,053,852
Short-term investments (Note 6)	172,551	-
Contributions receivable (Note 3)	1,312,980	4,123,080
Program and other receivable — net (Note 4)	2,144,841	2,942,734
Prepaid expenses	2,114,274	1,356,804
Other assets	295,560	421,034
Total current assets	15,100,912	20,456,541
NONCURRENT ASSETS:		
Restricted cash equivalents	198,584	198,584
Long-term contributions receivable—net (Note 3)	379,631	660,001
Other investments (Note 6)	3,734,085	5,930,431
Economic beneficial interest in trust (Note 6)	38,145,655	59,770,622
Fixed assets—net (Note 5)	626,207	679,619
Other assets	212,943	85,386
Total noncurrent assets	43,297,105	67,324,643
Total	$ 58,398,017	$ 87,781,184
LIABILITIES AND NET ASSETS		
CURRENT LIABILITIES:		
Account payable and accrued liabilities	$ 4,074,777	$ 4,992,982
Grants and awards payable to affiliates	3,469,339	5,659,146
Deferred income	756,358	542,434
Deferred rent (Note 13)	55,767	55,767
Total current liabilities	8,356,241	11,250,329
Noncurrent liabilities—deferred rent (Note 13)	98,111	152,421
Total liabilities	8,454,352	11,402,750
COMMITMENTS AND CONTINGENCIES (Notes 10 and 13)		
NET ASSETS:		
Unrestricted:		
Undesignated	2,572,333	5,390,722
Designated (Note 7)	44,198,222	67,316,419
Total unrestricted net assets	46,770,555	72,707,141
Temporarily restricted net assets (Note 8)	2,974,526	3,472,709
Permanently restricted (Note 8)	198,584	198,584
Total net assets	49,943,665	76,378,434
Total	$58,398,017	$87,781,184

See notes to financial statements.

Source: Special Olympics, Inc., Independent Auditor's Report (available at www.specialolympics.org).

Note: Similar data available on Form 990.

TABLE 13.3 ■ Statement of Activities

	Unrestricted			Temporarily Restricted	Permanently Restricted	Total
	Undesignated	Designated	Total Unrestricted			
REVENUES, GAINS, AND OTHER SUPPORT:						
Direct mail contributions	$ 35,848,492	$ -	$ 35,848,492	$ -	$	35,848,492
Individual and corporate contributions and sponsorships	22,101,972	1,865,979	23,967,951	2,669,674	-	26,637,625
Federal grants	-	10,170,252	10,170252	-	-	10,170,252
Program assessments	3,076,468	-	3,076,468	-	-	3,076,252
Royalty income	99,750	881,620	981,370	-	-	981,370
Net appreciation in trust assets (Note 6)	-	(18,736,964)	(18,736,964)	-	-	(18,736,964)
Net investment income (Note 6)	(1,188,698)	(494,749)	(1,683,447)	-	-	(1,683,447)
Other income	71,882	516120	587,984	-	-	587,984
Total revenues, losses, and other support	60,009,866	(5,797,760)	54,212,106	2,669,674	-	56,881,780
NET ASSETS RELEASED FROM RESTRICTIONS (Note 8):						
Satisfaction of program restrictions	-	2,882,857	2,822,857	(2,822,857)	-	-
Expiration of time restrictions	345,000	-	345,000	(345,000)	-	-
Total revenues and net assets released from restrictions	60,354,866	(2,974,903)	57,379,963	(498,183)	-	56,881,780
EXPENSES:						
Program assistance	35,080,485	13,458,884	48,539,369	-	-	48,539,369
Public education and communications	8,537,812	290,026	8,827,838	-	-	8,827,838
Sports training and competitions	4,398,825	6,386,160	10,784,985	-	-	10,784,985
Fundraising	11,841,980	-	11,841,980	-	-	11,841,980
Management and general	3,314,153	8,224	3,322,377	-	-	3,322,377
Total expenses	63,173,255	20,143,294	83,316,549	-	-	83,316,549
CHANGES IN NET ASSETS	(2,818,389)	(23,118,197)	(25,936,586)	(498,183)	-	(26,434,769)
NET ASSETS—Beginning of year	5,390,722	67,316,419	72,707,141	3,472,709	198,584	76,378,434
NET ASSETS—End of year	$ 2,572,333	$ 44,198,222	$ 46,770,555	$ 2,974,526	$ 198,584	$ 49,943,665

See notes to financial statements.

Source: Special Olympics, Inc., Independent Auditor's Report (available at www.specialolympics.org).

Note: Similar data available on Form 990.

TABLE 13.4 ■ Statements of Cash Flows

	2008	2007
CASH FLOWS FROM OPERATING ACTIVITIES:		
Changes in net assets	$(26,434,769)	$ 653,708
Adjustments to reconcile changes in net assets to net cash used in operating activities:		
Depreciation expense	326,496	277,305
Noncash donation of fixed assets	-	(171,873)
Amortization of contributions receivable discount	(24,688)	(14,456)
(Gain) loss on disposal of fixed assets	(8,000)	2,046
Permanently restricted contributions	-	(122,664)
Net unrealized loss (gain) on investments and economic beneficial interest in trust	23,422,014	(718,770)
Net realized gain on investments and economic beneficial interest in trust	(1,147,845)	(3,174,801)
Decrease (increase) in contributions receivable	3,115,158	(399,150)
Decrease (increase) in program and other receivable	797,893	(332,342)
Increase in prepaid expensed	(757,470)	(37,102)
(Increase) decrease in other assets	(2,083)	42,122
(Decrease) increase in accounts payable and accrued liabilities	(918,205)	1,040,142
(Decrease) in grants and awards payable to affiliates	(2,189,807)	(2,859,017)
Increase in deferred income	213,924	330,243
(Decrease) increase in deferred rent	(54,310)	9,606
Net cash used in operatin activities	(3,661,692)	(5,475,003)
CASH FLOWS FROM INVESTING ACTIVITIES:		
Purchase of fixed assets	(265,084)	(301,444)
Purchase of investments and economic benefit interest in trust	(22,273,122)	(7,848,481)
Sales of investments and economic benefit interest in trust	23,647,715	11,067,503
Net cash provided by investing activities	1,109,509	2,917,578
CASH FLOWS FROM FINANCING ACTIVITIES—permnanently restricted contributions	-	122,664
Net cash provided by financing activities	-	122,664
NET DECREASE IN UNRESTRICTED AND BOARD-DESINATED CASH AND CASH EQUIVALENTS	(2,552,183)	(2,434,761)
UNRESTRICTED AND BOARD-DESIGNATED CASH AND CASH EQUIVALENTS—Beginning of year	11,612,889	14,047,650
UNRESTRICTED AND BOARD-DESIGNATED CASH AND CASH EQUIVALENTS—End of year	$9,060,706	$11,612,89

See notes to financial statements.

Source: Special Olympics, Inc., Independent Auditor's Report (available at www.specialolympics.org).

Note: Similar data available on Form 990.

TABLE 13.5 ■ Statement of Functional Expenses

	Program Assistance	Public Education and Communications	Sports Training and Competitions	Fundraising	Management and General	Total
Salaries	$7,811,109	$1,303,551	$1,345,402	$753,582	$1,528,967	$12,742,611
Benefits	1,775,192	353,843	333,271	197,372	437,042	3,096,720
Total salaries and benefits	9,586,301	1,657,394	1,678,673	950,954	1,966,009	15,839,331
Consulting and other	8,120,976	2,665,712	146,721	3,913,725	394,815	15,231,949
Supplies	3,872,424	34,376	766,152	5,924	60,651	4,739,527
Communication	401,386	785,465	53,507	19,751	25,218	1,285,327
Postage and shipping	334,290	1,711,340	18,901	3,676,963	23,948	5,765,442
Occupancy (Note 13)	1,016,051	153,066	66,967	95,666	158,329	1,490,079
Equipment rent and repair	449,459	30,248	20,886	17,870	29,477	547,940
Travel, meeting, and conferences	2,839,421	217,691	3,674,067	77,981	245,947	7,055,107
Printing	220,682	1,182,586	113,737	2,276,660	4,691	3,798,356
Professional development	29,009	31,811	3,603	12,462	11,901	88,786
Data processing	33,824	313,065	400	679,790	17,785	1,044,864
Depreciation and amortization	160,614	21,266	9,304	13,291	122,021	326,496
Miscellaneous	532,338	33,818	12,122	100,943	261,585	940,806
Subtotal	18,010,474	7,170,444	4,886,367	10,891,026	1,356,368	42,314,679
Awards and grants	20,942,594	-	4,219,945	-	-	25,162,539
Total expenses	$48,539,369	$8,827,838	$10,784,985	$11,841,980	$3,322,377	$83,316,549

See notes to financial statements

Source: Special Olympics, Inc., Independent Auditor's Report (available at www.specialolympics.org).

Note: Similar data available on Form 990.

requirement when introduced in the 1990s and caused some organizations to reconsider how pledges were written and documented. It was one of the factors that has led to more formal relationships between nonprofits and their donors over the past decade.

Under "current liabilities" on SOI's statement of financial position, we see another example of the accrual basis—both "accounts payable" and "grants and awards payable to affiliates" represent commitments that SOI has made, but which have not yet been paid. The obligations are liabilities that must be shown on the balance sheet.

Statement of Activities

Now, let's go to Table 13.3, SOI's statement of activities. The balance sheet, or statement of financial position (shown in Table 13.2), is a *snapshot* of the organization's finances taken at a point in time. But the *statement of activities* shown in Table 13.3 is more like a video that shows the flow of revenues and expenses of the organization, and the resulting changes in net assets, *over a period of time,* generally a fiscal year. Accordingly, some nonprofit organizations call this the "statement of revenues, expenses, and changes in net assets." For a business, this statement would be the same as its "profit and loss," or "P&L" statement (Zietlow et al., 2007, p. 179).

SOI's statement of activities shows an important distinction within the category of "unrestricted" revenues—some are *undesignated* and some are *designated*. Gifts that are both unrestricted and undesignated can be used by the organization to meet its general operating expenses or for any legitimate purpose its leadership may determine. Gifts that are designated must be used to support a specific program or unit, but the specific activities within that unit are not defined by the donor. Thus, designated differs from restricted; in the latter case, the donor has identified the exact activities that are to be supported, and the funds are temporarily restricted until those specific activities have been completed. Grantors or donors may indeed require detailed accounting on the expenditure of restricted grants or gifts. In 2008, SOI received $2,669,674 in individual and corporate gifts and contracts that were temporarily restricted. They are intended to cover expenses that the organization has not yet incurred; perhaps the work is scheduled for sometime in the next year. At the same time, there were "net assets released from restrictions" in 2008, either because a time restriction expired or because the organization provided the services which the funds were intended to cover.

One notable item on SOI's statement of activities for 2008 was a decline of $18,736,964 in the value of a trust. The trust is managed by a third party and provides revenue to SOI based on its rights to certain recordings and other intangible assets related to *A Very Special Christmas* albums. The decline reflects mostly the reduced value of the stock market, which plummeted during 2008, a reality faced by many nonprofits. It is important to note that the trust increased by over $5 million in 2007 and, quite likely, will have increased further from the end of 2008 to the time that this chapter is being read (Independent Auditor's Report, Special Olympics, Inc., www.specialolympics.org).

Statement of Cash Flows

Table 13.4 is SOI's statement of cash flows for 2008. As discussed above, the statement of activities does not give the whole picture because of the accrual basis of accounting it reflects. For that reason, SFAS 117 requires that nonprofits also produce a *statement of cash flows* to show cash inflows and outflows over the year, enabling us to see how the cash amount changed from one year to the next. There are two methods of presenting cash flow, direct and indirect, but this chapter does not go into detail about them (McMillan, 2003a).

Look again at SOI's statement of financial position in Table 13.2 and the total of the first two lines under "current assets"—they total $9,060,706 ($8,006,854 in cash and cash equivalents and $1,053,852 in board-designated cash and cash equivalents).[4] Now look at the bottom line of the statement of cash flows in Table 13.4—it's the same number as that total. What the statement of cash flows does is walk us through exactly how the cash changed from the beginning to the end of 2008. Cash flow may occur through operating activities, investing activities, or financing activities. Think again about your own checkbook. Cash might flow in from your paycheck. You may have sold your car, a physical asset, and placed the proceeds in the same account. Or you may have borrowed money from the bank, and then deposited the amount of the loan directly into your checking account. All those transactions comprise your cash flow, but again, tracking just the flow of cash into and out of your checking account would not provide a complete picture of your financial position; that requires looking at the cash flow in relationship to the other financial statements discussed above.

Statement of Functional Expenses

The last financial statement we will consider is shown in Table 13.5—the *statement of functional expenses*. This statement shows how every category of expense was allocated among the uses of program assistance, public education and communications, sports training and competitions, fund-raising, and management in general. It is from this data that charity watchdogs, certain donors, and others calculate the ratios that some use to evaluate the efficiency of an organization's management and fund-raising efforts. Let's come back to that point shortly.

Before leaving the discussion of financial statements, there is one additional concept that is important to understand—*depreciation*. The concept of depreciation, and the way it is handled in financial accounting, is sometimes difficult for individuals to quite grasp in terms of their personal financial life. The most familiar experience that most of us have with depreciation is the decline in the book value of our cars. Your new car may lose much of its value as soon as it is driven out of the dealer's showroom. If you keep it long enough, it will continue to decline until it is ready for the junk yard and is worth next to zero. You may not feel that decline as an expense as it occurs, since it is not coming out of your pocket or checking account each day, but clearly your personal net worth is less when the car gets old than it was when the car was new. Thus, the car's depreciation is a real expense in terms of its effect on your total net worth, even though it may not affect your cash flow.

Let's say a nonprofit organization owns physical assets, including cars, buildings, and equipment. Those assets have a value, and that value is reflected on its balance sheet. But they are assets that will be used up or wear out over some period of time, so their value declines with every passing month or year. That decline must be accounted for as an *expense,* even though it does not involve an actual outlay of money. Take a look at SOI's statement of functional expenses in Table 13.5; the amount of depreciation of its assets in 2008 is shown near the bottom and totals $326,496. But it is an accounting expense rather than a real outlay of cash, so an adjustment needs to be made to provide a clear picture of SOI's cash flow. Take another look at Table 13.4, the statement of cash flows. The $326,496 has been added back in on the second line to make the necessary adjustment; otherwise, it would understate the amount of cash generated by operations during the year (Zietlow et al., 2007, p. 182).

Using Financial Ratios

Now that we have examined some basic accounting principles and looked at the financial statements that nonprofits produce, what do we make of the data? How can we interpret the financial data and use it to make decisions about the financial management of the organization?

The concept of financial ratios was introduced back in Chapter 6, which discussed some ratios that external observers use to evaluate the performance of nonprofit organizations. Readers may recall from that chapter that a 2004 study by the Urban Institute and Harvard's Hauser Institute (Fremont-Smith & Cordes, 2004) looked at 10 charity watchdog organizations that use financial ratios and found a variety of measures being applied, including variations of the following:

- The ratio of program expenses to contributed income
- The ratio of fund-raising expenditures and private support received—that is, the cost of raising a dollar
- The percentage of total expenses (or income received from contributions) spent on charitable programs or activities
- The percentage of total expenses spent on fund-raising and administration (overhead)
- Accumulated cash and asset reserves in relation to operating budget

These ratios measure an organization's efficiency rather than its effectiveness. They might be of interest to the organization's board and management, but taken alone, they may not provide an appropriate way to rate or rank nonprofits.

There are a number of ratios that can be calculated from the data provided on an organization's financial statements or similar data obtained from the Form 990. The ratios that are most commonly tracked by managers are those that measure *profitability, liquidity, asset management,* and *long-term solvency* (Anthony & Young, 2005, p. 488). This chapter does not go into detail on the calculation of ratios but rather will focus on explaining the concepts that they are intended to measure and their significance to assessing the financial health of a nonprofit organization. One comprehensive list is provided by Anthony and Young in an appendix to their chapter on financial management in the *Jossey-Bass Handbook on Nonprofit Leadership and Management,* second edition. The ratios are defined in mathematical formulas, and there are also good summary descriptions of what they mean (pp. 501–510).

Although the term *profitability* may seem out of place in the nonprofit setting, it is just describing the change in net assets on the statement of activities; in other words, it considers whether the organization had an operating surplus, broke even, or operated at a loss. Liquidity relates to the organization's use of cash.

Remember from the earlier discussion the example of the friend who thinks himself wealthy because he anticipates an inheritance but who lacks the cash to pay for dinner. To avoid being in a similar bind, an organization needs to manage its cash flows effectively in order to be sufficiently *liquid,* that is, possessed of sufficient cash at the right times to meet its obligations as they come due. An analysis of cash management would address areas such as accounts receivable, accounts payable, and inventory maintained. For example, if clients are slow to pay bills for service, the organization will need to keep more cash on hand to pay its own bills as they come due. If the collection process could be made more efficient, it would need to maintain less of a cash balance and that money then could be put to work in other productive ways. Vendors need to be paid on time, but effective management of the process could reduce the amount of unproductive cash needing to be kept on hand. To use another example from personal financial life, there may not be a need to keep money sitting in your checking account on the 15th of the month if the rent is not due until the 1st, and you know you will be receiving a paycheck in the meantime. Tracking when revenues come in and when bill payments are due is a way to stretch dollars further and gain more leverage from your personal cash flow.

Another issue for organizations is management of inventories. If too much money is tied up in inventories, it may leave too little liquidity to meet cash obligations as they arise. For example, if a food program spends all its cash to fill up its freezers with a 6-month supply of food, then it may be in a bind to pay its staff or other expenses. Developing a more efficient system for food purchases that could reduce the amount of inventory kept in the freezer could provide for more liquidity to meet other obligations or to be put toward more effective purposes.

Management of fixed assets requires looking at how efficiently they are being used; for example, how much revenue is being generated through the use of buildings and equipment? The condition of assets needs to be tracked and adequate funds earmarked for replacement or repairs. That is a way to avoid unexpected expenses for which there may not be funds readily at hand from current revenue.

Assessing *long-term solvency,* that is, evaluating whether the organization is financially strong or in jeopardy, requires looking at the right-hand side of the statement of financial position, the liabilities, as well as the revenue and expenses shown on the statement of activities. One big issue is the amount of debt, specifically the relationship between assets and liabilities. Borrowing funds may be a good thing; it provides the organization with a way to leverage its assets and support a larger program of services than it could just with current revenue. But obviously, debt also increases risk and requires careful management of cash flow to ensure that debt payments can be made when due (Anthony & Young, 2005).

Which are the most important financial ratios to watch and manage? Zietlow et al. (2007) make the case that for most nonprofit organizations, liquidity—"the ability of the organization to augment its future cash flows" (p. 23)—is the biggest problem. Many nonprofits depend on contributions, but giving may fluctuate from year to year. An unforeseen event, such as the loss of a key donor or perhaps a decline in allocations from United Way, can leave a nonprofit in a cash crunch, stretched to meet its own obligations. Some pledges, which are reflected on the financial statements as assets, may in fact not be paid, and estimates of how much may be uncollectible may not be based on reliable information. If the organization depends on earned income, it faces business risks; if a college's enrollment turns down, a concert attracts fewer than expected attendees, or a blizzard reduces attendance at a major fund-raising event, revenue may turn out to be much different from what the budget anticipated.

Nonprofits that rely on contracts may face similar problems; for example, costs may exceed what was projected and exceed the revenue that the contract provides. Some clients may be slow to pay. The only options might then include obtaining short-term financing from banks or other lenders, making emergency appeals to donors, tapping into reserves or even quasi endowment, delaying payments to vendors, and reducing costs by cutting staff or their compensation. Zietlow and colleagues (2007) argue that such problems are "endemic to the nonprofit sector [and that liquidity] is one of the most important yet least studied areas in the management of nonprofits" (p. 23). Zietlow et al. criticize the charity watchdogs, such as the BBB Wise Giving Alliance and others, who set a maximum that organizations should keep in reserves. The view of the charity raters is that excess funds held in reserve should instead be used to support current programs and services. But Zietlow and colleagues argue, "[While] these policy guidelines may be appropriate for commercial nonprofits, [they] will severely limit the management style of small donative religious organizations" (p. 24). Drawing on data from a study that Zietlow conducted in 2002 to 2004, these authors suggest a model that nonprofits can use to determine the appropriate level of liquidity to maintain (pp. 28–43).

Managing Endowment Funds

As noted above, most nonprofit organizations do not have significant endowments; most are held by large institutions such as colleges and universities, health organizations and medical institutions, museums, and major arts centers. The largest is the endowment of Harvard University, which totaled nearly $38 billion in 2008. Other institutions with substantial endowments in 2008 included the Salvation Army with $1.5 billion, the Metropolitan Museum of Art with $2.5 billion, and the Nature Conservancy with $1.1 billion. Even smaller nonprofits have accumulated some endowment funds. For example, in 2008, City Year had an endowment of $7.4 million, Volunteers of America had $24 million, and the Boy Scouts of America had $226 million in endowment funds ("Endowments at Nonprofit Organizations," 2010).

Of course, the stock market decline in 2008 and early 2009 hit many nonprofit endowments hard. Many nonprofits were forced to make adjustments in their operating budgets to reflect the lower income available from endowment, and others postponed new projects or programs. But remember our discussion in the early part of this chapter; unlike individuals, many substantial organizations and institutions intend to exist forever. They make adjustments to accommodate to economic cycles but also expect to recover their endowments as the economy turns around in years ahead. Indeed, by March 2010, U.S. stock markets had rallied substantially from the bottom reached in March of 2009.

As discussed above, some endowment is created by the nonprofit's board from internal resources, perhaps from excess operating surpluses accumulated over several years. Although board-designated endowment could be expended at the board's discretion, it is intended for long-term use and would generally be managed according to the same policies applied to permanent endowment created through donor-designated gifts. *Term endowments,* which are established for a period of years, after which the funds may be spent, might be invested and managed differently, depending on the date of their anticipated termination. The discussion of endowment management here applies to funds that the organization intends, or must, hold for investment in perpetuity, using only the annual income earned from investments to support its operating needs. There are two key concepts related to the management of endowment funds. One is the *total return* approach to investing endowment assets, and the other is the *spending limit* that determines how much will be available from endowment for expenditure each year.

In earlier decades, a large portion of endowment assets was invested in relatively secure, interest-paying instruments, such as bonds and bank certificates of deposit. The drawbacks of this approach became evident in the high-inflation economy of the 1970s, since the fixed amount of interest income became increasingly inadequate to support the activities for which the endowment was intended. Over the long term, investments in stocks produce higher overall returns and keep pace with inflation, but stocks often pay dividends that provide less current income than bonds. Institutions found a way around this dilemma by adopting the total return approach to investing endowments, combined with a spending limit to determine how much could be used each year.

The approach is to invest in a portfolio that includes stocks, cash, bonds, real estate, and other classes of assets, providing for the *long-term* growth of the principal. The investment strategy is to maximize total return, that is, the total of interest, dividends, and appreciation in the value of stocks and other assets. Each year, some percentage of the total market value of the endowment is withdrawn from the endowment fund and transferred to operating funds for expenditure that year. Any additional investment returns are reinvested in the principal, enabling it to grow.[5]

Prior to the financial crisis of 2008, some universities and other major institutions had invested significant portions of their endowments in relatively risky assets and were hard-hit by the market's downturn. Many observers now advocate that nonprofit institutions return to more prudent investment policies.

The spending limit is established by the board and can be varied from year to year as economic conditions change. The goal is to provide enough payout each year to meet the needs of current programs, while also allowing the value of the endowment principal to grow to keep pace with inflation and provide more income to sustain programs in future years. The latter is not only important to maintain the benefit of the endowment to the organization; it is also essential in order to keep faith with the intention of a donor who wished to support some activity in perpetuity.

Let's take a look at a simple example in Table 13.6 to see how this approach might work over a period of 5 years. Assume a donor has made a gift of $500,000 for the purpose of endowing "full-tuition scholarships" to students in perpetuity. Tuition is now $25,000, but the assumption in this example is that it will increase by an average of 5 percent each year. Assume also that the original gift is invested in a portfolio of securities that will earn an average of 10 percent each year, in some combination of interest, dividends, and appreciation. That would be high in terms of actual experience, but the round number will simplify our example. The first year, the $500,000 endowment earns $50,000. The college could spend $50,000 to award two full-tuition scholarships that year. But the problem with that approach would start to become obvious in the second year. The endowment would still be just $500,000; it would again earn $50,000, which would no longer be enough for two full-tuition scholarships at the higher tuition rate. Instead, if the college awards one $25,000 scholarship the first year (equivalent to the 5 percent payout rate that the board has established), and reinvests the additional $25,000 back into the endowment, the principal of the endowment now becomes $525,000. If it follows that practice every year—spend 5 percent and reinvest 5 percent—look what happens as we go down the table to year number 5. Because the endowment principal has been increased, the 5 percent available for spending also has increased sufficiently to cover the ever-higher cost of tuition. Continuing out forever into the future, if all the assumptions hold, there will always be sufficient income from this endowment to provide a full-tuition scholarship, which was the intention of the donor. Now, if the market has a bad year, it may not earn 10 percent, but in some years it may do *better* than 10 percent, averaging out over the long haul. Tuition may increase more than expected, or less. The board can adjust the spending limit as well as the investment portfolio to accommodate these trends as they emerge. Properly executed, this approach enables the organization to count on ever-increasing income from its endowment and to keep faith *in real terms* with the intention of its endowment donors.

Endowment management is governed by state law, and in many states the law has changed in recent years. The Uniform Management of Institutional Funds Act (UMIFA) set the requirements for management in most states for many years. Its restriction that institutions not spend when an endowment fell below "historic dollar value," essentially the value of the original gift, presented some real challenges in the early 2000s. The stock market decline following the dot-com bust and 9/11 left many recently created endowments "underwater," meaning that it

Year	Return Tuition ($)	Endowment Spendable 10% ($)	Reinvest 5% ($)	Endowment 5% ($)	principal ($)
Gift					500,000
1	25,000	50,000	25,000	25,000	525,000
2	26,250	52,500	26,250	26,250	551,250
3	27,563	55,125	27,563	27,563	578,813
4	28,941	57,881	28,941	28,941	607,754
5	30,388	60,775	30,388	30,388	638,142

TABLE 13.6 ■ Hypothetical Endowment Fund

was not legally permissible to use the endowment to support scholarships, research, or other programmatic purposes. That situation obviously created some difficult communications with donors, who wished to see the impact of their giving right away.

A new model act, called the Uniform Prudent Management of Institutional Funds Act (UPMIFA), was introduced in 2006 and by 2010 had been adopted by most states. It permits spending from underwater endowments, but it requires that trustees (or foundation directors) exercise "the care an ordinary prudent person in a like position would exercise under similar circumstances" (Griswold & Jarvis, 2009). The new law provides greater flexibility, but it does not eliminate the need for detailed, open, and sometimes difficult communication with endowment donors whose funds may not have grown as anticipated. Students should check websites such as that of the Council on Foundations (www.cof.org) to be sure where the current law stands at the time of their reading.

Developing and Managing the Budget

A nonprofit organization's financial statements are important documents to individuals both inside and outside the organization. But on a month-to-month or day-to-day basis, for most people working in the organization, the budget and reports related to the budget are the guides to action. A full discussion of budgeting is beyond the scope of this text, but this section will summarize some of the more important principles and concepts.

Most nonprofit organizations have three separate budgets: an *operating budget,* a *capital budget,* and a *cash budget.* As their names suggest, the first tracks all revenues and expenditures; the second concerns the purchase or disposal of long-term physical assets, such as buildings and equipment; and the third tracks the flow of cash during the year, whether related to operating or capital activities. As Maddox (1999) correctly observes, "Most people think of the operating budget when they think of a budget (if they do at all)" (p. 60). Our discussion in this section focuses generally on principles that relate to developing and managing the operating budget, although some are relevant to the others as well.

A budget is a political as well as financial document. Some say that the budget reveals an organization's "real strategy," despite what may be written in the strategic plan or other documents (Maddox, 1999, p. 12), because the budget is a tangible expression of what the organization's real priorities are. It reflects not only considered plans but also the push and pull of political forces within the leadership of the organization. Readers may recall the idea of nonprofit leaders' political frame, an idea described by Herman and Heimovics and discussed in Chapter 5. Managers may be guided by a strategic plan, but various departments, programs, or purposes are in competition for the organization's limited resources, and the outcome of that competition may be important in determining where funds are actually allocated.

Budgets invariably create incentives and disincentives that will affect the behavior of managers and staff. For example, some organizations have a use-it-or-lose-it approach to annual budgets. If a department has not expended its budgeted funds by the end of the fiscal year, the remaining funds do not carry over to be available to the department the following year. The organization's top budget managers may be counting on unexpended funds in some department budgets to cover overspending by others or as a reserve of sorts to cover unanticipated expenses of the general organization. But savvy managers often work to ensure that no unspent money remains, rushing to place orders for supplies and new computers before the fiscal year ends. The use-it-or-lose-it policy thus may turn out to create a perverse incentive that results in needless spending.

The way in which budgets are structured, whether on an organizational or center basis also affects incentives. For example, a university may develop a budget that treats tuition from all students as revenue to the institution as a whole. Individual colleges, schools, and programs then are given an expense budget on which they need to operate, and the dean or director of each is responsible for not exceeding the budgeted amount. The individual units thus are viewed as *cost centers,* and their managers may have little incentive beyond controlling costs. Or the university may budget on a center basis, that is, the university regards each unit as a *profit center.* In this model, the school or college keeps the revenue it generates, from which it meets its own direct costs and makes some contribution to cover general institutional costs and services provided to the unit by the overall organization, for example, its share of expenses related to utilities and information systems technology. This approach may create considerable incentive for unit heads to be entrepreneurial and undertake new efforts to increase revenue. However, the trade-off may be that the central administration has less control and a reduced ability to reallocate funds across units, either to address institutional priorities or to cross-subsidize less profitable programs through the surpluses of others.

Another consideration is whether budgets are developed incrementally or allow for redistribution. A common and simple way to develop next year's budget is just to add some percentage to last year's budget or to the amounts actually expended, maybe one percentage for salary increases and another for other expenses. If the allocation is based on funds expended, then it will, of course, exacerbate the tendency of units to make sure they spend all of last year's budgeted amount before the year ends. If they do not, they take, in effect, a double hit: They lose the unexpended funds at the end of the year and also receive a reduced allocation for the year that follows. Other budgeting systems allow for considerable redistribution from one year to the next. One benefit of having a strategic plan with specific goals and objectives is that it can serve to justify such redistribution over time in order for the organization or department to pursue strategic priorities. If the plan has been developed in a participative process, with buy-in from all parts of the organization, it may help mitigate the inevitable political pressures that come to bear on annual budgeting.

Another process, perhaps at the extreme of the redistribution spectrum, is the zero-based approach. All programs and departments start at zero at the beginning of each year's budget process and need to justify their budgets from the ground up. But this approach has a number of disadvantages, including the amount of time and effort required to prepare justifications and the potential for management competition and negative staff morale (McMillan, 2003b).

A fundamental idea in budgeting is to recognize the difference between controllable and uncontrollable expenses and to hold managers accountable accordingly. Individual departments or programs may be credited with or charged with revenues and expenditures attributable to them, but a manager can only be held responsible for line items under his or her control. For example, a manager may be able to control salaries, travel, and the use of outside consultants, but he or she may not be able to control, at the department or program level, items such as fringe benefits, rent, heat, or electricity. Monthly budget reports typically show—for each line item—the amount budgeted for the year, the amount and percentage of the annual budget for that item expended year-to-date, and a comparison with the amount spent the previous year to the same date. Such reports enable managers to note significant variations from the budget and make midyear corrections as needed.

Sample nonprofit budgets are difficult to find in public sources, such as on the web, because they are typically specific to each organization. The operating budget for the organization is an internal document that it is not required to be made publicly available. There are, however, a variety of resources available that do provide templates and other guides to budget development. One place to begin might be the website of the Foundation Center, which offers some resources (http://foundationcenter.org).

Financial Policies and Controls

As discussed in Chapter 6, recent years have included increased demands for accountability throughout American society, resulting in legislation such as Sarbanes-Oxley and laws in several states that apply similar requirements to nonprofit organizations. In this environment, it is essential for well-managed nonprofits to have policies to guide the management and reporting of their financial affairs. Good judgment and intentions are no longer sufficient; explicit policies are required.

Organizations have internal policies, developed by management and often adopted by the governing board. Other policies are external; they are required of organizations by law or by their funders. For example, nonprofits that receive federal funds are obligated to adhere to a complex hierarchy of requirements imposed by federal agencies.

Like laws, policies may be *prescriptive* or *restrictive*—that is, they can state what must be done, or they can limit or place boundaries on the actions that may be taken under certain circumstances. Zietlow and colleagues (2007) agree with John Carver, whose views were discussed in Chapter 4, that "the prescriptive approach to policy is doomed to failure" (p. 145). It is just impossible to predict all future circumstances, it is undesirable to unduly limit the flexibility of managers, and enforcement is difficult with the prescriptive approach. For example, society can make laws that prohibit people from driving too fast, driving after consuming alcohol, or driving without seat belts. But a law that required "safe driving" would be unenforceable because it encompasses too wide a range of possible behaviors. Zietlow and colleagues identify three basic categories of financial policies that nonprofit organizations should have: accountability and regulatory compliance policies, financial and financial management policies, and data integrity policies.

Accountability and regulatory compliance policies encompass matters such as filing Form 990s, avoiding conflicts of interest, and meeting other requirements of behavior or disclosure required by law. *Financial and financial management policies* are established by the governing board. They may identify allowable ranges for specific financial indicators or ratios, for example, liquidity, debt, or assets held in the endowment fund. They may also encompass procedures for purchasing, risk management, internal financial controls, fund-raising, and other areas of activity. The third category, *data integrity policies,* involves privacy, confidentiality, records retention, the separation of duties, data backup, and other such concerns (Zietlow et al., 2007, pp. 146–154).

Internal controls have increasingly become a focus of attention in the wake of several scandals of malfeasance by nonprofit executives, and some nonprofits have adopted internal control policies similar to those required of public corporations by Sarbanes-Oxley. One fundamental principle of internal control requires that duties of individuals be separated so that no one person handles an entire transaction from beginning to end. For example, it is common to have policies that require that the person who enters donor gifts is different from the person who deposits the funds, that the person who reconciles the checking account monthly is different from the person who signs the checks, and that payments to vendors be made only with an invoice approved by someone other than the person who sends the payment.

As Zietlow and colleagues (2007) observe, "Depending on the nature of your organization and the specific policy, internal or external noncompliance can range from fraud to poor business management, from felony to raised eyebrows" (p. 138). Ensuring that such policies are in place and followed is a fundamental aspect of responsibility for nonprofit managers and boards.

Chapter Summary

Financial management goes to the heart of the board's fiduciary responsibility, and any problems involving budgets or assets are likely to demand immediate attention from the board and the nonprofit CEO. Bookkeeping involves the entry of financial transactions on the organization's records, and accounting encompasses the rules by which transactions are categorized and reported. Financial management is a broader concept. It includes developing diverse sources of revenue and requires making judgments based on data in financial statements, relationships among that data, and financial management policies of the organization.

Although the terminology of nonprofit accounting is precise and can be unclear to those without a financial background, the basic concepts have analogs in the personal finances of individuals. For example, operating funds are similar to a personal checking account and operating reserves are like savings. A nonprofit may have board-designated endowment, which is like an individual's retirement funds—it is intended for investment over the long run, but the board can withdraw the funds if it has good reason. Permanent endowment must be invested in perpetuity because donors have placed that requirement on their endowment gifts. The nonprofit can withdraw the principal from an endowment only with agreement of the donor or a court. Individuals do not have a component of their personal finances that can be compared with permanent endowment, since they are mortal and do not hold funds in perpetuity.

There are two basic methods of accounting, the cash basis and the accrual basis. Very small organizations that do not have accounts receivable or payable may use the cash method, but most use the accrual method, which is required for external financial reports. In accrual basis accounting, revenues and expenses are recorded as they are earned or as obligations are incurred, not necessarily when the cash is received or paid out. Thus, reports based on the accrual method may provide a better picture of the organization's real financial picture than ones based on cash. However, it is also necessary to look at cash flows to get a complete sense of the organization's financial position.

There are four financial statements that many nonprofits produce for external purposes. The statement of financial position (or balance sheet) provides a snapshot of the organization's assets, liabilities, and net assets at a point in time, usually the end of its fiscal year. Net assets are equivalent to equity in a company or an individual's net worth.

The statement of activities shows revenues, expenditures, and changes in net assets over a period of time, usually a fiscal year. In a business, this would be the profit-and-loss statement. Revenues include receivables, for example, pledges from donors that have not yet been paid. Expenses must be allocated among programs and supporting services, including general management and fund-raising. A statement of functional expenses shows the allocation of expenses among those categories in detail.

Finally, the statement of cash flows reveals cash transactions from operations, financing, or investing activities and the changes in cash balances over the period of the report, generally one year. Depreciation of the value of physical assets is an expense that is shown on the statement of activities. It must be added back in on the statement of cash flows to provide an accurate picture. The Notes to the Financial Statements often provide important details and should be read in conjunction with the statements.

Financial ratios provide an important tool of financial management, although they are not a sufficient basis on which to rate nonprofit organizational performance. Commonly used ratios include those related to profitability, liquidity, asset management, and long-term solvency. According to some experts, liquidity is an endemic problem for nonprofit organizations. Cash management strategies may include speeding up the receipt of payments, managing the timing of expenses, reducing inventories, and obtaining a line of credit to cover temporary cash needs. Analytical models are available to determine the appropriate target for liquidity.

The largest endowment funds are held by major institutions, such as universities, but in recent years, many types of nonprofits have worked to establish or build endowments. Most endowments are invested under the "total return" concept. The board of the organization sets a spending limit, which is a percentage of the endowment's market value each year (or of an average over a period of months or years). That amount is spent to support programs, and any additional investment gain is reinvested in the principal of the endowment. The payout may come from interest, dividends, or the appreciation in value of equities. That approach enables the principal and the income to grow over the years to match the higher future costs of activities that the endowment is intended to support.

Most nonprofits have three budgets: an operating budget, a capital budget, and a cash budget. The operating budget usually commands the most attention. The budget is a political document that reflects not only plans but also the competition for resources within the organization. How budgets are constructed creates important incentives and disincentives that affect managers' behavior. One important consideration is whether budgets are maintained on an organizational or center basis and whether departments and programs are treated as cost centers or profit centers. Some budgeting methods simply add a percentage increment to previous years' budgeted or expended amounts, while others provide greater opportunity for the redistribution of funds across programs or units. Some expenses, such as salaries, are controllable. Others, such as fringe benefits, are less so. Unit managers should be accountable for expenses that are within their control.

Accountability in the current environment requires that nonprofits have explicit policies in three areas: accountability and regulatory compliance policies, financial and financial management policies, and data integrity policies. Ensuring that such policies are in place is a fundamental aspect of the governing board's responsibility.

Notes

1. There are some endowments called *term endowments* that can be spent after a period of time passes. They are temporarily restricted. We do not consider them in this discussion.
2. Because the board does have the power to withdraw money from a quasi endowment, accounting rules require that such funds be treated as unrestricted in financial statements.
3. Some property owned by a nonprofit may also be considered permanently restricted, like endowment. For example, this would be true of a work of art that a donor gave with the condition that the nonprofit not sell it.
4. Cash equivalents are short-term investments, such as money market funds, that are almost as liquid as cash.
5. Most apply the spending limit to a percentage of a moving average of market value in order to smooth out changes from year to year; our simplified example in Table 13.6 does not reflect that practice.

KEY TERMS AND CONCEPTS

accountability and regulatory compliance policies

accounting

accounts payable

accounts receivable

accrual basis of accounting

asset management

bookkeeping

capital budget

cash basis of accounting

cash budget

cash flow

cost center

data integrity policies

endowment (board-designated and permanent)

financial accounting

financial and financial management policies

financial management

in perpetuity

liquidity

managerial accounting

operating budget

operating reserves

permanently restricted

prescriptive policies

profit center

profitability

pure endowment

quasi endowment

restrictive policies

solvency

spending limit

statement of activities

statement of cash flows

statement of financial position

temporarily restricted

total return

Uniform Management of Institutional Funds Act (UMIFA)

unrestricted

QUESTIONS FOR DISCUSSION

1. Some people argue that nonprofit organizations should not have endowments at all. One of their arguments goes something like this: Putting money aside in endowment means

depriving today's generation of the use of those resources so as to benefit future generations, who will receive services supported by income from the endowment. But there are many people in great need of services today. Why are tomorrow's needy more deserving than today's? The funds should be spent now to meet current needs. Let future generations of donors support the needs of people in the future. Since the economy is growing, giving will increase over time and there should be enough philanthropy to meet those future needs. It is thus especially unjust to provide for the future at the expense of people alive today, who live in less affluent times. Do you agree? Why or why not? What arguments would you make on the other side of this issue? Would your views be different with regard to different types of nonprofits, for example, homeless shelters, universities, museums, or environmental organizations?

2. Look up the Form 990 of a nonprofit organization that interests you. (It is likely available on Guidestar at www.guidestar.org.) Go through the financial data and develop your own analysis of the organization's finances. Questions you might think about include the following: Does it appear to have diversified sources of revenue? How vulnerable or unpredictable are these sources likely to be? What were its major categories of expenses for the year shown? What unforeseen expenses could arise? What kinds of assets does it hold? Does it have debt? What produced its cash flow for the year shown? Does it have endowment or other permanently restricted assets?

3. The following items were reported in the *Chronicle of Philanthropy*. In each case, what types of controls that might have prevented the incident were either not in place or did not work?

   - "A former grants administrator at the Rockefeller Foundation has been found guilty of stealing more than $400,000 from the grantmaker by defrauding its employee matching-gift program over a seven-year period." (Wilhelm, 2007, p. 8)
   - The American Civil Liberties Union has generated a major controversy within its ranks by conducting undisclosed research on donors and potential donors. The situation has already sparked an investigation by the New York State attorney general that could have serious implications not only for the civil liberties group but also for many other charities unless the organizations move quickly to reassure donors that protecting their privacy is paramount (Wilhelm, 2005b, p. 47).
   - "Eighteen months after the Milwaukee Public Museum, one of the largest natural history museums in the country, shocked the city by revealing that it was in a financial crisis, one of its top executives appears to be the only one to face criminal charges in the museum's near collapse. [The chief financial officer], who left his job . . . after [the] problems became public, was charged by Milwaukee's district attorney with using money from the endowment to cover operating expenses as the museum sank into a financial crisis, and lying about his actions in board meetings to hold onto his job, according to criminal charges filed this month. He did not profit personally from his actions, according to the complaint." (Gose, 2006, p. 17)

SUGGESTIONS FOR FURTHER READING

Books

Gross, M. J., Jr., McCarthy, J. H., & Shelmon, N. (2005). *Financial and accounting guide for not-for-profit organizations* (7th ed.). Hoboken, NJ: Wiley.

McMillan, E. J. (2010). *Not-for-profit budgeting and financial management* (4th ed.). San Francisco: Wiley.

Schneider, W. A., Robert, A. D., Benoit, M. S., & Associates. (2005). *The practical guide to managing non-profit assets.* Hoboken, NJ: Wiley.

Young, D. (Ed.). (2007). *Financing nonprofits: Putting theory into practice.* Lanham, MD: National Center on Nonprofit Enterprise.

Zietlow, J., Hankin, J. A., & Seidner, A. (2007). *Financial management for nonprofit organizations.* Hoboken, NJ: Wiley.

Websites

Financial Accounting Standards Board, http://www.fasb.org/

Nonprofit Finance Fund, http://www.nonprofitfinancefund.org/

chapter   14

Nonprofit organizations have played an essential role in shaping our country by bringing issues to the public's attention, influencing attitudes, and lobbying for new laws.
© iStockphoto.com/Gary Blakeley

Advocacy and Lobbying　14

Within the lifetime of many people alive today, African American children were taught in schools segregated by law. Women could legally be denied jobs, barred from entire professions, and paid less than men simply because of their gender. Gay people were regularly fired from their jobs if their sexual orientation became known. People with physical disabilities were unable to access many public buildings, limiting their opportunities for employment and life experiences. Companies dumped raw sewage and industrial wastes into rivers with impunity. Highways were lined with ugly billboards and trash thrown from cars by un-seat-belted motorists. People could smoke in offices and other public places, and driving while drunk often was punishable by no more than a minor fine, even if it resulted in the death of another person. There remain many injustices, threats to the environment, diseases to be cured, and other problems to be solved, but over decades, new laws have been enacted to correct many of the intolerable situations mentioned above.

As explained in Box 14.1, social issues often follow a life cycle. In the beginning, there may be inattention to the problem, although it exists. Some event may cause the problem to be "discovered" by individuals and the news media. Advocates, usually including nonprofit organizations, then drive the issue to higher visibility and courses of possible action are identified and evaluated. Initial interventions may include efforts by government and social marketing by nonprofits, as discussed in Chapter 10. Progress may be uneven as time goes by, but the problem ultimately is either resolved or found to be intractable. It may drop off the public's radar until some new event causes it to gain attention again (Andreasen, 2006).

In most instances, nonprofit organizations have played an essential role by bringing the issue to the public's attention, influencing attitudes and building support for change, and lobbying for new laws. Indeed, nonprofits have been at the forefront of every important social change in the United States from the beginning of the nation. They have been the principal advocates for people who are disadvantaged or disenfranchised and for causes that initially concern only a minority of people. Nonprofits often have identified and given visibility to emerging issues and problems that ultimately became the focus of national attention and action.

BOX 14.1 STAGES IN THE LIFE CYCLE OF A SOCIAL CHANGE ISSUE

Stage 1: Inattention to the problem	The social problem exists, as evidenced by concrete data or dramatic anecdotes, but it has not yet become anyone's concern.
Stage 2: Discovery of the problem	The problem comes to the attention of individuals or groups (including the media) who think it needs to be addressed. At this stage, initial baseline analyses or measurements will be undertaken. Nuances of the problem will begin to emerge—for example, learning who is most affected by the problem.
Stage 3: Climbing the agenda	Activists, advocacy groups, individual politicians, investigative reporters, and nonfiction writers raise the volume on the issue. They marshal even more evidence, produce real victims, and potentially raise the guilt level of those not affected. At this stage, funders and potential interveners begin to find the issue sufficiently important for attention and possible action.
Stage 4: Outlining the choices	Analysts and advocates look at the data and consider how the problem might be addressed. Evidence about causal linkages will be important, as will scenarios for possible intervention.
Stage 5: Choosing courses of action	This is where debate takes place over the benefits and costs that action and inaction will have on society, victims, and those who have to take action (e.g., donate money, pass laws) if there is to be a solution. Attention will be paid to the efficacy of various solutions. Opposing forces emerge and solidify their positions.
Stage 6: Launching initial interventions	Foundations or government agencies put money into programs. Organizations mount pioneering efforts and test alternative strategies and tactics. These will involve both downstream and upstream interventions, in which social marketing can play a major role.
Stage 7: Reassessing and redirecting efforts	With most difficult changes, progress is slow, and there are periods of acceleration, deceleration, progression, and regression. At some point, key figures will feel that it is time to take stock of where the problem stands. The outcome may be a reorientation and resurgence of interventions—or it may not.
Stage 8: Achieving success, failure, or neglect	After a number of years, the problem will have found some major solutions or will have proven basically intractable and, in the absence of dramatic progress or new data, will "drop off the radar screen." The latter may also be the result of new competition from the latest social problem that captures the public's imagination and drives the "old" problem into the "dustbin of history" (Cohen, 2000, cited by Andreasen, 2006).

Source: Andreasen, A. R. (2006). *Social Marketing in the 21st Century*. Thousand Oaks, CA: Sage, p. 42.

Nonprofits may be found on every side of any issue, and they reflect all shades of opinion. There are organizations that advocate pro-life positions and others that are pro-choice. There are nonprofits that work to advance religious values and others that strive to protect the separation of church and state. There are those whose mission is to promote sound government and those who seek to limit government's size and power. There are nonprofits that work toward economic growth and others with a mission to preserve and protect the environment, historic structures, animals, and communities from the effects of commercial development. The public interest that is served by such diversity is the preservation of an uninhibited marketplace of ideas, allowing the free exchange of information and discussion that is believed to lead ultimately to sound public policy. Nonprofit advocacy and lobbying is thus a fundamental pillar of a democratic society.

However, various authors observe that most nonprofits do not engage in advocacy or lobbying. For example, Eisenberg observed in 2007 that "fewer than two percent of nonprofit organizations choose to exercise their legal right to influence legislation or lobby" (p. 53), and Smucker, writing in 2005, lamented that "many charities view lobbying as irrelevant to their mission, inappropriate, or even illegal" (p. 231). Research by Child and Grønbjerg (2007) also found that many nonprofits are ambivalent about advocacy and that only a relatively small number devote substantial resources to such efforts.

There are various reasons why relatively few nonprofits have engaged in advocacy. One obvious reason is that many lack the staff or resources, especially given the many demands of managing core service programs. Not surprisingly, larger national nonprofits are more likely to be directly involved in advocacy and lobbying than are smaller, local organizations, and such activity is more common among organizations in fields that are significantly regulated, such as health care (Child & Grønbjerg, 2007). Although small nonprofits might not conduct much lobbying on their own, they may belong to an association or coalition that represents their interests and issues at the state or national level. Such coalitions exist to serve specific groups of nonprofits, for example, higher education institutions, health care providers, and organizations concerned with homelessness.

Although research has indicated that nonprofits actually increase lobbying as government becomes a more predominant source of their revenue, concern about alienating government foundation funders is a barrier for some ("Executive Summary," 2002). Nonprofits that are dependent on gifts from individuals also may be reluctant to take a position on issues that affect the organization but on which their donors hold different opinions. One interesting example occurred in 2003, when President George W. Bush recommended a permanent repeal of the estate tax. Although it was widely believed that a repeal would have a negative impact on charitable giving, a number of nonprofits were slow to oppose it. Some charged that their reluctance was based on the fact that many of their board members were affluent individuals who would be personally affected by the repeal and who thus supported the president's proposal.

A common conclusion about why nonprofits do not lobby more is that many nonprofit executives are simply unclear about what the law allows. They may decide to err on the side of caution by keeping their distance from the legislative process. As Berry, the director of a 2003 study, concluded, "Nonprofit organizations are excessively worried about losing their charity status. And that reflects a mis-understanding of how the law is enforced" (p. 33).

Basic Distinctions

Before we go further into this topic, let's clarify three basic concepts and terms: advocacy, lobbying, and political campaign activity. *Advocacy* includes action taken in support of a cause or an idea. It may include, for example, providing education, distributing information, or holding events to dramatize an issue or the effects of a problem on people or a community. Advocacy is a basic right of every individual and organization in the United States and may be practiced without limit; it is an exercise of free speech protected by the U.S. Constitution (Hopkins, 2005).

Lobbying goes beyond advocacy—it is action taken to support or oppose specific legislation at the national, state, or local level. This could include, for example, contacting a member of Congress, a state legislator, or a city councilperson to request his or her sponsorship or vote in favor of or against a specific bill. It does not include contacting members of the executive branch, unless that individual is in a position to influence legislation.

Political campaign activity is action taken in support of or opposition to specific candidates for office, including the publication or distribution of statements or printed materials. It does not include, however, conducting nonpartisan activities such as get-out-the-vote efforts or sponsoring a candidate debate or forum (Independent Sector, 2007a). But the line may sometimes seem fuzzy, and there have been some controversial cases in recent years surrounding the involvement of nonprofits in political campaigns.

There is sometimes understandable confusion between what is advocacy and what is lobbying. Indeed, the former encompasses the latter. As Smucker (2005) explains, "Lobbying always includes advocacy but advocacy does not necessarily include lobbying" (p. 232). For example, the marches, protests, and sit-ins of the civil rights movement were advocacy for equal rights, but they were not lobbying since they were not actions undertaken with the purpose of supporting or opposing any specific item of legislation. Once the Civil Rights Act of 1964 was up for consideration in Congress, many individuals and organizations contacted their elected representatives to urge a favorable vote. That activity was lobbying. The law defines lobbying quite precisely, including the identification of specific activities it does and does not include.

Overview of Lobbying Law

As discussed in Chapter 2 of this book, organizations are tax-exempt under various sections of the Internal Revenue Code. Some of them, including 501(c)(4) social welfare organizations, are permitted to engage in lobbying essentially without restriction (Hopkins, 2005). As we also discussed earlier, some 501(c)(3) organizations work with related 501(c)(4) organizations: The Sierra Club was presented as an example in Chapter 2. Charitable nonprofits, including public charities and private foundations, face limitations on their lobbying activity and are prohibited from participating in political campaigns or endorsing or opposing candidates. The law regarding some nonprofits' involvement in political campaigns changed in January of 2010 as a result of the Supreme Court's decision in the case of *Citizens United v. FEC* (Federal Elections Commission). We will return to that point later in the chapter. Since space is limited and the law is complex, this chapter focuses mostly on advocacy and lobbying by *charitable nonprofits,* that is, the 501(c)(3) organizations that are both tax-exempt and eligible to receive tax-deductible contributions.

The reason that charitable nonprofits face restrictions on lobbying is directly related to the tax deductibility of gifts, which is viewed as a form of public subsidy given to the organization. In other words, the foregone tax revenue is regarded as public money. The purpose of the subsidy is to support an organization's charitable activities, and the law requires that its resources be used to pursue those purposes as its primary activity. Any lobbying it conducts must be "insubstantial" in relationship to its overall efforts to achieve its charitable mission (Hopkins, 2005, p. 226). But what is the meaning of *substantial* and *insubstantial,* and exactly what constitutes lobbying activity?

Prior to 1976, the meanings of the two terms were unclear. The IRS never defined them and looked at each situation on a case-by-case basis. One of the problems was that the *substantial part test,* which determined whether lobbying was a "substantial part" of an organization's activities, looked not only at how much a nonprofit spent on lobbying activity, but also at how much time and effort was devoted to the activity. Some courts held that nonprofits were safe if they spent less than 5 percent on lobbying, but other courts said such an arbitrary standard was not appropriate. Thus, like a child whose parents just say, "Don't wander too far," many nonprofits were unsure exactly how far they could safely go, that is, how much lobbying the IRS might find to be a substantial part of their activities. Some were inhibited from engaging in lobbying at all for fear of losing their tax-exempt status by crossing the fuzzy line.

In 1976, Congress passed Public Law 94–455 (the 1976 Lobby Law), which sought to clarify the situation. It took the IRS 14 years, until 1990, to issue sections 4911 and 501 of the Internal Revenue Code, describing how the law would be implemented. Since then, nonprofits have two options, as follows.

Option I: Substantial Part Test

The first option is to continue to be covered by the substantial part test, essentially the same imprecise standard that applied before 1976. This may be a reasonable option for an organization that does not engage in lobbying or that does very little. If it is careful to differentiate lobbying from advocacy, it may find that it spends too little time or money on actual lobbying to be concerned about it. For example, the National Alliance to End Homelessness (2006) reports that many organizations affiliated with it chose to follow this standard. But this still leaves things vague and may not be a good choice for an organization that intends to engage in lobbying on a regular basis.

Option II: 501(h) Expenditure Test

The second option, provided by the 1976 Lobby Law and subsequent IRS regulations, is for the nonprofit to file Form 5768 with the IRS, electing to be covered by the specific expenditure guidelines under Section 501(h) of the Internal Revenue Code. Selecting this option offers a number of advantages. First, the limits do not consider the amount of time or effort devoted to lobbying—they are based entirely on how much the organization *spends* on lobbying activity, as a percentage of its total budget.[1] The standard is thus exact, and an organization can easily determine whether it is within or is approaching the limit. Second, it means that lobbying that does not involve expenditure is not limited at all. For example, if a volunteer calls on a congressperson or a local legislator, that effort does not count unless the organization spends money to support it. If the organization reimburses the volunteer for his or her cab ride to the meeting, that expense would need to be included in its lobbying expense, but the volunteer's time would not. The 501(h) option also presents fewer risks for nonprofits and their staff than does the substantial part test. Nonprofits that exceed the spending limits will not lose their tax exemption unless they exceed them by at least 150 percent averaged over a 4-year period. Moreover, there are no penalties imposed on individual managers of an organization that exceeds the limit (Independent Sector, 2010a).

The spending limits are stated as a percentage of the nonprofit's total expenditures (on exempt activities), on a sliding scale depending on the size of the organization. There is an important distinction between the limit for direct lobbying and for grassroots lobbying. *Direct lobbying* includes any communication the organization has "with legislators or government officials who participate in the formulation of legislation or with its own members with regard to specific legislation and that expresses a view on it" (Smucker, 2005, p. 240). Thus, it does not include communication with officials of the executive branch of government or communication that just provides information without expressing an opinion for or against the legislation.

Grassroots lobbying refers to "any attempt to influence legislation by affecting the opinion of the general public" and that asks individuals to take action (Smucker, 2005, p. 240). If the communication does not include a call to action, that is, does not ask people to do something to support or oppose the legislation, then it is not lobbying. The *general public* includes any individuals who are not members of the organization, but *members* is broadly defined. It includes donors to the organization as well as those who may be members in the formal sense of someone who pays dues in order to belong. Thus, if a nonprofit sends an e-mail to its donors urging them to contact their congresspersons to support or oppose a bill, that expenditure comes under the limit for direct lobbying. But if it takes out an ad in the newspaper or hands out flyers on the corner urging members of the general public to do the same, that is grassroots lobbying, and any money expended in such an effort comes under a different, lower limit. (Again, if the communication does not specifically ask individuals to take action, it does not count as lobbying.)

There are other activities that also do not count as lobbying. For example, if the legislature asks the nonprofit for advice on a bill, responding to that request does not count. *Self-defense activity* also does not count as lobbying. For instance, if the city council is about to pass an ordinance that would adversely affect the nonprofit, it may contact council members to oppose the legislation without having any expense involved count against its lobbying limit. However, pressing for legislation to support programs in the nonprofit's field, for example, a college lobbying for more scholarships, is not considered self-defense, and it would count as lobbying.

Policy research organizations, such as the Brookings Institution or the American Enterprise Institute, may prepare reports that are nonpartisan and objective, and they will not count as lobbying efforts even if they recommend a specific course of action. Indeed, a nonprofit can discuss the need for legislation on some issue *generally* without it being considered lobbying, as long as it is not urging action on a *specific* bill. Thus, for example, a nonprofit concerned with child welfare may advocate stricter laws to protect children, and environmental organizations may generally call for better protection of wilderness areas; that is, not lobbying unless it is directed at a specific item under consideration by the legislature (Smucker, 2005, pp. 242–243). In sum, the 1976 Lobby Law is quite generous in permitting nonprofit organizations to engage in lobbying. This is especially true if the distinction between what is lobbying and what is advocacy is carefully maintained, since expenditures on the latter do not count against the limits at all.

Table 14.1 summarizes the expenditure limits on direct and grassroots lobbying for nonprofits of various sizes. An organization may spend only one fourth as much on grassroots lobbying as on direct lobbying, and there is an overall cap of $1 million. For example, if a nonprofit spent the maximum of $1 million on all of its lobbying and $250,000 of that was spent on grassroots efforts, it could spend the remaining $750,000 on direct lobbying (Minnesota Council on Nonprofits, 2006). The overall cap of $1 million would be encountered by a nonprofit with a budget of $17 million or more, but keep in mind that lobbying activity does not count against the limit if it does not involve the expenditure of money by the nonprofit. This limit is thus not that restrictive in terms of the amount of activity it allows.

Charitable nonprofits must report their lobbying expenses on Form 990. In addition, organizations that employ professional lobbyists and spend more than $24,500 on lobbying at the federal level must meet the requirements of the Lobbying Disclosure Act. This requires that they register and report their lobbying expenditures to Congress on a semiannual basis (Independent Sector, 2007a).

The rules discussed so far apply to nonprofits that are public charities. Private foundations face stricter limitations. They may not endorse or oppose legislation in communications with legislators or the general public if the communication includes a call to action. However, like

TABLE 14.1 ■ Limits on Lobbying Expenditures

Total Expenditures on Exempt Purposes	Total Limit on Lobbying Expenditures	Limit on Expenditures for Grassroots Lobbying (25% of total)
Up to $500,000	20% of exempt-purpose expenditures	5% of exempt-purpose expenditures
$500,000 to $1 million	$100,000 plus 15% of excess over $500,000	$25,000 plus 3.75% of excess over $500,000
$1 million to $1.5 million	$175,000 plus 10% of excess over $1 million	$43,750 plus 2.5% of excess over $1 million
$1.5 million to $17 million	$225,000 plus 5% of excess over $1.5 million	$56,250 plus 1.25% of excess over $1.5 million
Over $17 million	$1 million (overall maximum)	$250,000 (overall maximum)

Source: Center for Lobbying in the Public Interest (http://www.clpi.org/images/pdf/1976law.pdf).

public charities, they may provide technical advice to a legislature if asked to do so, provide nonpartisan analyses and studies, and lobby in self-defense. Like public charities, foundations are barred from participating in political campaigns. They can support nonpartisan activities such as candidate forums and get-out-the-vote drives, but they face strict regulation of their participation in voter registration drives (Independent Sector, 2007a).

What if a private foundation makes grants to a nonprofit that comes under the more generous rules applied to public charities? Well, to start with, the foundation would not be permitted to *designate* a grant to support lobbying. That would be just an obvious end-run around the restrictions on its activity. But if the foundation provides unrestricted operating support to a public charity, there is nothing to prevent that organization from spending the money on lobbying activity. If a foundation makes a grant to support a nonprofit's program that has lobbying as one component of it, the lobbying is acceptable, but it must be paid for using funds from some other source, not with the foundation's grant funds. Since community foundations are public charities rather than private foundations, they can engage in lobbying up to the 501(h) limits and can make grants to support lobbying by other nonprofits, although such grants would count against the community foundation's own lobbying limit (Center for Lobbying in the Public Interest, 2010a).

In addition to the basic provisions we have discussed in this chapter, nonprofits also must comply with various laws related to lobbying practice, which include restrictions on the participation of elected officials in charity events and on the way in which lobbyists can interact with legislators and their staff. In January of 2007, the 100th Congress amended House Rule 25 (called the *gift rule*), placing stricter limits on what gifts or privately supported travel members of the House of Representatives can accept from lobbyists. However, the law is always in a state of flux, and students with an interest in more details should check contemporary sources. The website of Independent Sector (www.independentsector.org) provides timely updates on recent legislation and policy actions and should be consulted for the latest information. Other websites listed as resources at the end of this chapter also track and report on recent changes in law with regard to lobbying, campaign finance, and other relevant activities.

Political Campaign Activity

As discussed above, charitable nonprofits—including public charities and private foundations—are prohibited from engaging in campaigns and from endorsing candidates, either implicitly or explicitly. They may not coordinate their activities with those of a candidate or a campaign, contribute money or time to working for a candidate, or contribute the use of their facilities for a candidate or campaign (Independent Sector, 2007b).

The Supreme Court's decision in 2010 in the case of *Citizens United v. FEC* changed the law for some nonprofits. Previous law prohibited corporate contributions in support of political candidates. Corporations still cannot make monetary or in-kind contributions directly to candidates for federal office or coordinate their communication with candidates' campaigns. However, they now can make independent expenditures from their general treasury to expressly support or oppose candidates for the U.S. House, Senate, and president. This ruling applies to business corporations and also to nonprofits exempt under Section 501(c)(4), 501(c)(5), and 501(c)(6), but political activities cannot be the primary purpose of such an organization, which may face taxes on its political activities. Furthermore, the 2010 Supreme Court ruling does not change the law for charitable nonprofits, which remain prohibited from supporting or opposing candidates or making expenditures on communications that may suggest who is the "better" candidate (Alliance for Justice, 2010).

The Supreme Court's decision prompted some to suggest that the rules should be changed for charitable nonprofits as well, arguing that the principle of free speech that was the basis for the court's position should apply to all nonprofits as well as corporations. However, some legal experts noted that the prohibition on campaign activity is a trade-off for the deductibility of gifts and thought it unlikely that the law would change (Perry, 2010).

There have been some controversial cases that have highlighted the fine line between what is permissible advocacy and what is illegal involvement in electoral politics by charitable nonprofits. In the federal elections of 2004, 2006, and 2008, there were accusations that some organizations had crossed the line. In 2006, the Internal Revenue Service investigated activity by churches that allegedly had held events featuring a political candidate, distributed voter education guides that were favorable to a particular candidate, or engaged in other such activities (Schwinn, 2006a, 2006c). In one celebrated case, the IRS investigated the NAACP (National Association for the Advancement of Colored People) based on allegations that its president's remarks opposing the war in Iraq implied opposition to President Bush's reelection and thus violated the prohibition on political activity. Following a 2-year investigation, it concluded that no violation had occurred (Jensen, 2006). Some expressed concern that the IRS's enforcement activity was inhibiting nonprofits, including churches, from legitimate advocacy activity, and others charged that the investigations were politically motivated (Jensen, 2006b).

In June of 2007, the IRS released a Revenue Ruling (2007–41) to clarify the criteria by which it would determine what is and is not illegal campaign involvement. The ruling included 21 hypothetical examples of activity and a discussion of why each does or does not constitute a violation of the law. But the area remains one of sometimes heated controversy.

Implementing an Advocacy Program

Now that we have explored basic concepts and reviewed the law governing nonprofit advocacy, let's turn our attention to the practice of advocacy and lobbying. There is an extensive practitioner literature on lobbying. Various authors have developed manuals that offer guidance specifically to nonprofit organizations and take into consideration the unique requirements that apply to them. Some are listed as suggested additional reading at the end of this chapter. In addition, websites listed in this chapter provide practical suggestions and guides, as well as links to other resources. Since the law changes from time to time, the websites are usually the best sources of information. However, the techniques or tactics of lobbying are more consistent over time, and even some relatively dated but classic sources provide guidance that is still sound. That includes, for example, Bob Smucker's *Nonprofit Lobbying Guide,* published in 1999 and still available in full text at the time of this writing at the website of the Center for Lobbying in the Public Interest (www.clpi.org), of which Smucker was a founder.

Various sources that advise nonprofits on developing an advocacy and lobbying effort offer many common points, including the following:

- *Determine the reason for lobbying and how it advances the nonprofit's mission.* For a social welfare organization that exists for the purpose of changing public policy, the connection to the mission is obvious. A charitable nonprofit will need to consider how lobbying may advance its programs or the welfare of the constituents it serves and make strategic decisions about the emphasis to be given to lobbying in relationship to its service programs.
- *Understand the legislative process.* To lobby effectively, the organization needs to understand how legislation is considered at the local, state, or national level—wherever its lobbying efforts will be focused. This includes knowledge of which committees play important roles and the stages in the process at which a lobbyist's intervention may be most helpful or persuasive.
- *Identify the sources of funds to be used for lobbying.* As discussed above, there are restrictions on the use of government or foundation funds, but unrestricted revenues from gifts, grants, or earned income may be used to fund a lobbying effort.
- *Undertake research to develop an understanding of the public policy issues related to the organization's mission and to obtain data needed to make the case with legislators.* Such information is available from, among others, policy research organizations, national charitable organizations with established public policy programs, and coalitions concerned with issues in particular areas. Approaching a legislator with facts is not only important to persuasion but may indeed be providing a real service to the legislator, whose time and staff may not be sufficient to undertake the depth of research that an interested nonprofit may offer.
- *Develop an infrastructure to support the lobbying program.* For an ongoing effort, this may require hiring staff or working with a professional lobbying firm, but smaller efforts may be managed by an existing staff member as a part-time assignment. An information system may be needed to track the progress of legislation and calls or visits with legislators. Managing a lobbying program has many of the same requirements as fund-raising management, since it involves developing and maintaining relationships, and undertaking contacts, in a systematic manner.
- *Inventory existing relationships and identify decision makers.* A nonprofit may have many existing relationships in its community, through staff, members of the board, or other friends who may in turn know key decision makers in the relevant legislature. They may be effective ambassadors who can be armed with information to deliver the nonprofit's messages to those decision makers, or they may help open the door to communications and visits by the nonprofit's CEO.

- *Use a strategic mix of tactics.* Direct lobbying with legislators may be the centerpiece of a lobbying program, but such efforts are more effective if they are used in conjunction with grassroots lobbying to influence and mobilize the community's opinions and with a media relations program to gain wider visibility for the issues. The latter might include developing relationships with reporters who may have an interest in writing articles about the issue as well as paid advertising, op-eds, and letters to the editor written by the nonprofit's CEO or volunteers. Walks, runs, marches, and demonstrations also are available tactics for drawing attention to a cause (Center for Lobbying in the Public Interest, 2007; Hessenius, 2007).

The tools used for lobbying vary depending on whether the effort is grassroots or direct lobbying. Grassroots lobbying engages many of the principles and techniques of marketing that were discussed in Chapter 10. Direct lobbying also may use those tools as well as personal visits with legislators and their staff members. Both approaches use various communications vehicles, including letters, phone calls, faxes, petitions, and e-mails. The Internet offers great advantages to nonprofits in developing coalitions and constituencies as well as for contacting legislators. However, because e-mails are so easy to send and thus can arrive in volume, some legislative staff have come to ignore them or to prevail on organizations to cease such efforts. Ironically, because e-mail has become so common and voluminous, the old technology of regular mail sometimes may be more effective. A letter, especially if written by a constituent of the legislator, signifies that the individual cares enough to have taken the time to write, rather than tap out a quick e-mail or text message. Letters from clients of a nonprofit also may have an impact on the legislator and even gain the attention of the news media. However, form letters that make it obvious they have been solicited by the nonprofit or a professional lobbyist have less credibility than those that appear to genuinely express the views of an individual (Hessenius, 2007). As in fund-raising, there is no tool more powerful than the personal visit by an individual or group of individuals to a legislator or a member of his or her staff who is in a position to influence what information and data the legislator receives.

The Future of Nonprofit Advocacy

For nonprofits that are social welfare organizations, advocacy and lobbying are, of course, the essence of the mission. With regard to charitable nonprofits, some take a larger role in advocacy while others remain cautious.

In *Forces for Good,* Crutchfield and Grant (2008) identify twelve organizations that have high impact, that is, that are "catalytic agents of change" (p. 5). One defining characteristic is their involvement in advocacy and lobbying as well as program delivery. Some began by offering programs and later expanded into advocacy roles. Others went the other way, having begun as advocacy organizations and later added direct service programs. The combination, the authors argue, creates a "virtuous cycle" in which the two activities are reinforcing and lead the organization to greater impact (pp. 33–34).

But nonprofit advocacy, lobbying in particular, is sometimes controversial, and there have been periodic efforts to constrain it further. One notable example was the *Istook Amendment,* introduced in 1995 by U.S. Representative Ernest Istook. The amendment would have restricted lobbying by nonprofits that receive federal funds, even with regard to their use of nonfederal funds. Although it did not pass into law, the amendment reflected a line of thinking that has been manifested in other such attempts at both the federal and state levels (Grønbjerg & Salamon, 2002).

In 2006, the professional Washington lobbyist Jack Abramoff pleaded guilty to various felony counts growing out of his activities. Among other abuses, Abramoff had created nonprofit organizations, including one called the Capital Athletic Foundation, which he had used largely to pay for such things as golf trips for legislators and to influence the awarding of government contracts to his corporate clients (Cohen, 2006). His activities reflected not so much abuses by the nonprofit sector itself as abuses of nonprofit tax law by an individual with personal and political motives. Nevertheless, the episode connected the words *abuse, lobbyist,* and *nonprofit* in one story line and negatively affected public attitudes about the sector.

Some observers have called for increased involvement by nonprofits in electoral politics. For example, Hessenius (2007) writes that "nonprofits have traditionally played 'softball,' and now need to graduate to playing 'hardball' if they want to succeed" (p. 12). He accuses nonprofits of being naive in believing that making a credible case based on evidence is sufficient to obtain legislative action, when in reality, "for the most part, decisions are made as a balance between competing interests, with no 'right' or 'wrong' position, and almost always in consideration of the *political* realities impacting the chances for election or reelection" (p. 7, italics original).

Although charitable nonprofits cannot engage directly in campaign activity or make contributions to candidates, Hessenius (2007) outlines a strategy for their becoming involved. He recommends that charitable nonprofits create *political action committees* (PACs) and *527 funds,* tax-exempt organizations that can endorse and support political candidates. He also advocates that the legal restrictions on 501(c)(3) political involvement be changed to follow the same rules that apply to corporations.

Others regard such recommendations with alarm. For example, writing in the *Chronicle of Philanthropy,* Pablo Eisenberg (2007) offers a strong warning:

> Charities and foundations intelligently realize that staying away from direct political involvement is the price they must pay for continuing to be exempt from taxation and supported by tax-deductible gifts.
>
> Taxpayers will not tolerate subsidizing contributions to charities that are involved in partisan political activities, nor will Congress permit nonprofit groups to overstep the boundaries it has drawn to separate charities from political activity. The politicization of nonprofit organizations would be political suicide. (p. 53)

In a politically charged and polarized environment, nonprofits are likely to face continued scrutiny and debate about their appropriate role in advocating and affecting policy and political change.

Chapter Summary

Advocacy by nonprofits has played an important role in the most significant social changes throughout U.S. history, including the civil rights movement, the expansion of women's freedoms, and environmental protections. Issues often move through stages of public awareness and action, and nonprofits play an important role in that process (see Box 14.1). Nonprofits may advocate on any side of any issue, and their advocacy and lobbying is thus a fundamental pillar of a democratic society. However, various studies have found that only a small percentage of charitable nonprofits engage in advocacy or lobbying. Some are hesitant to do so for various reasons, including lack of staff and resources, concern about alienating private or government funders, and misunderstanding of what the law permits them to do without jeopardizing their nonprofit status.

Advocacy includes action taken in support of a cause or an idea. It may include, for example, providing education, distributing information, or holding events to dramatize an issue or the effects of a problem on people or a community. Advocacy is a basic right of every individual and organization in the United States and may be practiced without limit—it is an exercise of free speech protected by the U.S. Constitution. Lobbying goes beyond advocacy—it is action taken to support or oppose specific legislation at the national, state, or local level. Advocacy is the larger concept, which encompasses lobbying.

Some nonprofits—for example, 501(c)(4) social welfare organizations—are permitted to lobby without limitation but are not eligible to receive tax-deductible gifts. Because they can receive such gifts, which are a form of public subsidy, charitable nonprofits exempt under Section 501(c)(3) face limitations on their lobbying activity. There are two standards under which a charitable nonprofit can determine the amount of permissible lobbying. The substantial part test was the standard that existed prior to the 1976 Lobby Law, and organizations can still choose to be subject to it. However, *substantial part* applies to both time and expenditures, and it is not precisely defined.

The other option is to elect the expenditure test provided under Section 501(h) of the Internal Revenue Code. That section establishes a specific percentage of total qualified expenditures that nonprofits of various sizes can spend on lobbying, with an overall cap of $1 million. This option also distinguishes between direct lobbying and grassroots. A lower limit applies to grassroots activities that attempt to influence the public's attitudes and that include a call to action in support of or opposition to specific legislation. It also identifies specific activities—for example, self-defense—that do not count as lobbying. The expenditure test does not consider activities of volunteers or other efforts that do not involve expenditures. It is thus relatively generous in the amount of lobbying that it permits nonprofits to undertake.

Private foundations are not permitted to lobby or to make grants to other nonprofits designated for support of lobbying. Foundation grants to public charities that are unrestricted operating support may be used for lobbying by the charity within its allowable limit. Since community foundations are public charities, they may make grants to other nonprofits for lobbying purposes, but they count against the foundation's lobbying limit.

Charitable nonprofits may not participate in political campaigns or endorse candidates. The 2010 Supreme Court decision in the case of *Citizens United v. FEC* changed the law to permit corporations and nonprofits exempt under sections 501(c)(4), 501(c)(5), and 501(c)(6) to endorse candidates, subject to the requirement that political activity not be the organization's primary purpose, but the prohibition on campaign activity by charitable nonprofits remains, as the trade-off for the tax deductibility of gifts made to them. There have been recent cases in which the IRS investigated reports that churches and other nonprofits may have violated this prohibition, and some violators were punished by having their tax-exempt status revoked. The line can be a fuzzy one in situations where one candidate is closely identified with a particular position that a nonprofit opposes.

There are many guides to the practice of lobbying. Most practitioner guides emphasize linking the activity to the nonprofit's mission, understanding the legislative process, identifying sources of permissible funds to support lobbying, developing an infrastructure of staff and systems to support the lobbying effort, conducting research to identify public policy issues and gathering facts needed to make the organization's case, conducting an inventory of friends and identifying their relationships with key legislators, and developing a strategic mix of tactics to be employed. Some tools include letters, e-mails, media coverage, events, and personal visits with legislators and their staff members.

Although nonprofits have considerable freedom to engage in advocacy and lobbying, there have been attempts in recent years to impose more restrictions. There have also been occasional scandals involving the abuse of tax exemption by professional lobbyists that have affected public attitudes. Some call for a greater role for nonprofits in advocacy and electoral politics, but others voice caution and concern. Likewise, some call for removing the restrictions that prohibit nonprofits from participating in electoral politics, but others warn that doing so would undermine public support for tax exemption and result in harmful politicization of the sector. Nonprofits' advocacy and lobbying are likely to remain under scrutiny.

Note

1. Specifically, this means its expenditures on exempt activity, which excludes fund-raising and certain administrative expenses.

KEY TERMS AND CONCEPTS

501(h) election	*gift rule*	*political campaign activity*
527 funds	*grassroots lobbying*	*self-defense activity*
advocacy	*Istook Amendment*	*substantial part test*
Citizens United v. FEC	*lobbying*	
direct lobbying	*political action committees (PACs)*	

CASE 14.1   Mothers Against Drunk Driving (MADD)

As MADD Executive Director Chuck Hurley describes it, "Before the 1980s, drunk driving was how people got home. It was normal behavior." In May of that year, Candy Lightner's 13-year-old daughter was killed by a hit-and-run driver while walking to a church carnival. As her mother was soon to learn, drunk driving was just not on society's radar as an issue. Although 60 percent of automobile deaths were alcohol related, drunk driving was a low priority for law enforcement and the courts. Congress had spent $35 million on Alcohol Safety Action Programs, with little effect. After her daughter's death, Candy Lightner established Mother's Against Drunk Driving (MADD), determined to change society's attitude and behavior as well as the law.

She found other victims' families through classified ads and mailings, learned about California laws and lobbied the governor for new legislation, made speeches, and raised money. In October of 1980, MADD held a news conference on Capitol Hill that captured the nation's attention. Other mothers began establishing chapters in their hometowns and the organization grew rapidly, with 100 chapters in place by 1982

(Continued)

(Continued)

Mothers shared their grief and the stories of their loved ones who had been killed or injured by drunk driving, putting human faces on the issue. MADD lobbied in state legislatures and at the federal level. President Ronald Reagan established a Presidential Commission on Drunk Driving, and Congress passed legislation denying federal highway funds to states that did not pass strict drunk-driving laws. A national law establishing a uniform drinking age was passed in 1984.

During the 1990s, MADD continued to grow and attracted many corporate partners. It also expanded its efforts to prevent alcohol abuse by young people, including programs in schools and two National Youth Summits to Prevent Underage Drinking. MADD also continued to advocate for stricter laws, for example, to reduce the allowable percentage of blood alcohol in drivers. By the 2000s, MADD was known to 97 percent of the public, thousands of laws had been passed, tens of thousands of lives had been saved, and the term "designated driver" had become part of the American lexicon. The public's attitude toward drunk driving, once signified by a "wink and a nod," had changed to recognize such behavior as socially unacceptable, reckless, and criminal. MADD continues to pursue its mission "to stop drunk driving, support the victims of this violent crime and prevent underage drinking."

Source: Summarized from Mothers Against Drunk Driving website (http://www.madd.org).

QUESTIONS FOR DISCUSSION

1. How does the case of Mothers Against Drunk Driving reflect the stages described in Box 14.1?

2. In 2004, the Boston Foundation and other nonprofits made gifts to help sponsor the National Democratic Convention, which was held in that city. The foundation explained that its intention was to advance economic development in the city, that its funds would not be used for political activities, and that the convention would create work for "the working poor, immigrants, and minorities . . . that historically are of special concern to the foundation." It said it would have done the same for the National Republican Convention and had no political motivation. But some criticized the foundation's actions, saying that it set a bad precedent by getting too close to politics and that the money might better have been spent on other programs to benefit the community. Do you agree or disagree? Why? (Based on Eisenberg, 2007)

3. Should the law be changed to permit charitable nonprofits to endorse or oppose political candidates and provide financial support to political campaigns? Why or why not?

4. The Internal Revenue Code states as follows:

   > Organizations that are exempt from income tax under section 501(a) of the Internal Revenue Code as organizations described in section 501(c)(3) may not participate in, or intervene in (including the publishing or distributing of statements), any political campaign on behalf of (or in opposition to) any candidate for public office. (http://www.irs.gov/pub/irs-drop/rr-07-41.pdf)

   Each of the following hypothetical cases is based on examples from IRS Revenue Ruling 2007–41, released June 18, 2007. In each case, do you think the organization described violated the law? You can check your answer against the IRS's opinion by looking at Revenue Ruling 2007–41 on the IRS website (www.irs.gov/pub/irs-tege/rr2007-41.pdf).

- Organization B (as denoted on IRS website), a 501(c)(3) that promotes community involvement, sets up a booth at the state fair where citizens can register to vote. The signs and banners in and around the booth give only the name of the organization, the date of the next upcoming statewide election, and notice of the opportunity to register. No reference to any candidate or political party is made by the volunteers staffing the booth or in the materials available at the booth, other than the official voter registration forms that allow registrants to select a party affiliation.

- Organization C is a 501(c)(3) that educates the public on environmental issues. Candidate G is running for the state legislature, and an important element of her platform is challenging the environmental policies of the incumbent. Shortly before the election, Organization C sets up a telephone bank to call registered voters in the district in which Candidate G is seeking election. In the phone conversations, Organization C's callers tell the voter about the importance of environmental issues and ask questions about the voter's views on these issues. If the voter appears to agree with the incumbent's position, Organization C's representative thanks the voter and ends the call. If the voter appears to agree with Candidate G's position, then the caller reminds the voter about the upcoming election, stresses the importance of voting in the election, and offers to provide transportation to the polls.

- Mr. D is the board chair of Organization M, a 501(c)(3) nonprofit that educates the public on conservation issues. During a regular meeting of the organization shortly before the election, Mr. D spoke on a number of issues, including the importance of voting in the upcoming election, and concluded by saying, "It is important that you all do your duty in the election and vote for Candidate W."

- Ms. E is president of Society N, a historical society that is a 501(c)(3). In the month prior to the election, President E invites the three congressional candidates for the district in which Society N is located to address the members, one each at a regular meeting held on 3 consecutive weeks. Each candidate is given an equal opportunity to address and field questions on a wide variety of topics from the members. Society N's publicity announcing the dates for each of the candidate's speeches and President E's introduction of each candidate include no comments on their qualifications or any indication of a preference for any candidate.

- Minister F is the minister of Church Q, a 501(c)(3) nonprofit. The Sunday before the November election, Minister F invites Senate Candidate X to preach to her congregation during worship services. During his remarks, Candidate X states, "I am asking not only for your votes but for your enthusiasm and dedication, for your willingness to go the extra mile to get a very large turnout on Tuesday." Minister F invites no other candidate to address her congregation during the senatorial campaign.

SUGGESTIONS FOR FURTHER READING

Books

Andreasen, A. R. (2006). *Social marketing for the 21st century*. Thousand Oaks, CA: Sage.

Boris, E. T., & Steuerle, C. E. (Eds.). (2006). *Nonprofits and government: Collaboration and conflict* (2nd ed.). Washington, DC: Urban Institute Press.

Hessenius, B. (2007). *Hardball lobbying for nonprofits: Real advocacy for nonprofits in the new century.* New York: Palgrave/Macmillan.

Richan, W. C. (2006). *Lobbying for social change.* New York: Haworth Press.

Smucker, B. (1999). *The nonprofit lobbying guide* (2nd ed.). Washington, DC: Independent Sector. (Full text available at http://www.independentsector.org)

Websites

Alliance for Justice, http://www.afj.org/

Center for Lobbying in the Public Interest, http://www.clpi.org/

Independent Sector, http://www.independentsector.org/

Internal Revenue Service, http://www.irs.gov/

NPAction, http://www.npaction.org/

OMB Watch, http://ombwatch.org/

Urban Institute, http://urban.org/

V3 Campaign, http://www.v3campaign.org/

chapter 15

Unlike a century ago, when most people lived in rural areas or small communities and had little awareness of events in other parts of the world, we now live in a globalized society. The pace of globalization appears to be accelerating, and technological, economic, political, and cultural changes have created a world in which the greatest threats and the most promising opportunities require cooperation among nations and people from all parts of the world.
© iStockphoto.com/Michal Rozanski

Governing and Managing International and Global Organizations

15

A century ago, an increasing number of people were employed in industrial settings, including factories and mines, but most people still lived and worked on farms or in small communities. Travel was expensive, and communication was slow. The Wright Brothers' first flight had just occurred in 1903, and the majority of American homes would not have electricity until 1930. Television, the Internet, and space travel were still decades in the future.

Events in other parts of the world had little impact on most Americans' lives and, indeed, seldom intruded on their thinking, which was focused on the communities in which they lived and worked. Philanthropy included giving to one's church and an occasional campaign to build a new fire house, hospital, or school. The greatest threats to human health included common diseases for which there were yet no cures: The life expectancy for Americans at birth was less than 50 years (Shrestha, 2006).

Over the past 100 years, the pace and magnitude of change have been staggering. Today, the greatest threats facing humanity, including disease, terrorism, climate change, and natural disasters, are ones that cannot be confined within national boundaries nor isolated by the oceans that separate the continents. Instant communications and frequent travel transmit ideas, images, news, even diseases, as rapidly as people a century ago could cross the town squares of their small communities. At the same time, the greatest opportunities for technological and economic advancement lie in cooperative efforts that engage people, and minds, across the globe. Philanthropy, once primarily an American phenomenon, now flows in significant amounts all around the world, and a gift requires only the click of a computer mouse to complete. While the nonprofit sector in the United States remains the largest and philanthropy on a large scale remains predominantly American, similar organizations are increasing in number and importance in many nations and on a global basis, and many of these are turning to fund-raising in the American style.

Why has the world become smaller? And why have nonprofit organizations come to play an important role on the world stage? The answer lies in advances in communication technology as well as changes in political, cultural, and economic realities. One reason is the end of the Cold War and the spread of a democratic and capitalist philosophy across the globe. This change removed political barriers to economic interaction and to nonprofit organizations, which had often been viewed as threats by repressive governments. The establishment of free-trade areas and organizations in the 1990s, including the World Trade Organization (WTO), the European Union (EU), and the North American Free Trade Agreement (NAFTA), led to greater economic integration across national boundaries (Thomas, 2002). At the same time, the movement toward devolution of government services and outsourcing to the private sector that has occurred in the United States has also been seen in other nations, which have sought to lower tax rates in order to encourage economic and business growth. As in the United States, private organizations have been called on to replace services previously provided through government programs and to seek financial support from the private sector, leading to the growth of fund-raising as a worldwide profession. This new philosophy also has been reflected in the management of international aid programs, with governments preferring to deliver assistance through private organizations rather than directly (Anheier & Themudo, 2005).

Among the most powerful forces for change has been technology. The development of the Internet, the World Wide Web, satellite communications, and fiber optic cable has made global communication instantaneous. It has driven international economic competition in a "flat" world, in which national borders prevent no barrier to entry into the mainstream of business life (Friedman, 2006). And it has been raising the awareness of people in developed nations about the needs of others on the planet, stimulating unprecedented global responses to humanitarian needs.

The pace of globalization appears to be accelerating, presenting all of American society with significant challenges. Those who will live their lives—and manage nonprofit organizations—in the balance of the 21st century will need to understand, accept, and be prepared to work with different mind-sets and different skills than have ever been required before.

In this chapter, we will consider some basic definitions and concepts related to international and global organizations and some of the unique considerations in governing, managing, and fund-raising in the international arena. In the next chapter, we will discuss the growth of social entrepreneurship, a phenomenon that has influenced the nonprofit sector in the United States, but especially in other parts of the world.

Definitions and Scope of International Organizations

As within the nonprofit sector in the United States, the terminology used to discuss organizations across the world is inconsistent and often confusing. The term *nonprofit organization* is not widely used in the international environment, although there are organizations in many countries that fit the definitions of nonprofit that were considered in Chapter 2. Although the term has different meanings in different parts of the world, what we call a nonprofit in the United States is elsewhere most commonly referred to as a *nongovernmental organization* (or NGO). The term has its origins in the United Nations system, and, indeed, the UN has formal consultative relationships with many such organizations engaged in economic development activity (UN, 2004).

There are NGOs that engage in activities within one country that are similar to U.S. nonprofits in their essential characteristics, although they vary widely in the legal frameworks within which they exist, the sources of their funding, and especially their relationships with government. Some organizations are indeed operated by government and are known by the acronym GONGOs——*government-operated nongovernmental organizations*. There is no concept quite like the U.S. "nonprofit sector" in most parts of the world. In the international context, some scholars refer to the collection of organizations that reside between government and the private sector as the "civil society sector" (Salamon, Sokolowski, & Associates, 2004, p. 11).

The best-known NGOs are the *international nongovernmental organizations* (or INGOs). These are organizations whose activities are not confined to a single country. They "make significant operating expenditures across national borders and do not identify themselves as domestic actors [within one nation]" (Anheier & Themudo, 2005, p. 102). In addition, they are sometimes said to be *transnational* because, as the term implies, they "organize . . . in pursuit of goals and purposes that transcend the boundaries of national territories and state jurisdictions" (Boli, 2006, p. 333). Until recent decades, most INGOs were based in the United States or Western Europe, but they are now more diffused around the world (Anheier & Themudo, 2005). INGOs include the large brand-name organizations that most people know, including, for example, the Red Cross, Oxfam, Friends of the Earth, Greenpeace, Amnesty International, CARE International, and Save the Children.

Some INGOs were created as global organizations from the beginning. For example, CIVICUS, an international alliance that works to strengthen civil society around the world, was founded in 1993 with a multinational board—it was global from the beginning, both in its purposes and its governance (Koenig, 2004). Other INGOs are organizations that started out in one country and then over time developed into international or global organizations, following one of various paths. Some grew by opening offices or branches in other countries—that is, they *internationalized*—while others are federations or alliances of nationally based nonprofits that have banded together to pursue a common mission or cause.

Koenig (2004) describes a continuum along which some nonprofits have evolved. They start as local organizations with local interests. Then they begin to develop an international awareness, perhaps including international topics in their conferences and published materials. They may then move along to develop some international programs, possibly hosting conferences attended by people from around the world or publishing materials in various languages. At this point along the continuum, they have started to become *international organizations.* At a later point in their evolution, such organizations may begin to admit international members, open offices or form chapters in other countries, and enter alliances or partnerships with organizations in other nations. Finally, some ultimately may evolve into *global organizations* "with members, programs, or operations in many different regions around the world and having a multinational board of directors or other decision-making group" (p. 5).

It is important to clarify and emphasize the distinction between organizations that are international and those that are global, especially since the terms are sometimes used interchangeably. An *international* organization is somewhere along Koenig's continuum: It may have some programs in other countries, but it is governed within and maintains a focus on its home country. A *global* organization is one that has activities throughout the world and probably has a governance structure that places decision making in the hands of individuals from multiple countries. Today, most American national nonprofits are at least international. The large brand-name INGOs are global organizations.

INGOs have grown in number, especially within recent decades. The *Yearbook of International Organizations,* published by the Union of International Associations, shows that the number of such organizations increased from fewer than 10,000 in 1981 to more than 25,000 in 2000 (cited in Boli, 2006, p. 334). The INGOs are often large and visible, but it is a more complex challenge to track NGOs within various countries around the world. There is no single source of comprehensive data, although research interest has increased in recent years. One of the most ambitious efforts, begun in 1991, is the Johns Hopkins Comparative Nonprofit Sector

Project, a collaborative investigation led by Lester Salamon at Johns Hopkins and including 150 researchers across the world. By 2004, the project had produced "52 books, more than 250 published articles, and hundreds of working papers, country reports, and presentations" (Salamon & Sokolowski, 2004, p. xxi). The first phase of work examined NGOs in 22 countries in Europe, Asia, North America, and Latin America, with later research adding data on organizations in an additional 14 countries in Africa, the Middle East, and South Asia. In addition to collecting and analyzing an abundance of data on the characteristics, revenues, and activities of such organizations, the project developed an *International Classification of Nonprofit Organizations,* which identifies 12 categories of organizations based on their activities, and a *global civil society index* to summarize data and "gauge the progress of civil society development among countries" (Salamon & Sokolowski, 2004, p. 4).

Like nonprofits in the United States, NGOs in other nations engage in a variety of activities. According to the Johns Hopkins project research, the largest number provide services, including education and social services. Another significant percentage are engaged in what Salamon and Sokolowski (2004) call "expressive functions," including arts, culture, recreation, and professional associations. Others are advocacy organizations that bring social and human problems to public attention and work for change—for example, to protect human rights, preserve the environment, and other goals.

The World Bank divides INGOs into two basic types: advocacy INGOs and operational NGOs. *Advocacy INGOs* are organizations that promote a cause or issue on a multinational basis. In the World Bank's definition, *operational INGOs* are those whose primary purpose is to design and implement economic development projects. However, the mission of other INGOs that also operate programs, for example, the Red Cross, is to provide immediate and short-term relief from human suffering, rather than support economic or infrastructure development over the long run. The latter distinction is analogous to the differences between charity and philanthropy that we discussed earlier in this book. Many development INGOs, working in partnership with the UN and the World Bank, are focused on accomplishment of the *UN Millennium Development Goals,* adopted by world leaders in 2000. They include specific targets for the reduction of poverty, disease, illiteracy, environmental degradation, and discrimination against women to be achieved by 2015 (UN, 2008). Most efforts in pursuit of these goals are funded by governments, although, as we will discuss below, philanthropy has begun to play a larger role. A 2010 report by the Secretary General of the United Nations indicated that progress had been made toward accomplishing the goals, including a reduction in the number of people living in poverty worldwide. However, the report predicted that some nations would not meet the goals by 2015 and identified several emerging challenges, including climate change, the financial crisis that began in 2008, a growing risk of disasters, armed conflict, and increasing social and economic inequality (UN, 2010).

International Philanthropy and Fund-Raising

In this section, we will consider patterns of international philanthropy, which predominantly consist of gifts and grants from American and Western European donors to support organizations or activities affecting other regions. We will also look at the growth of organized fund-raising efforts by NGOs around the world, which are increasingly adopting and adapting techniques developed by nonprofits in the United States.

As measured by the Center on Philanthropy at Indiana University (2009) and reported by the Giving USA Foundation, American philanthropy directed to international programs and purposes totaled $13.3 billion in 2008, a slight increase over 2007. The estimates are likely understated. For example, they do not include funds spent on international activities by U.S.-based nonprofits in fields such as education, health care, arts and culture, youth development, and religion, which are reported in other categories; they do not capture all foundation and corporate giving; and they do not include gifts that individuals made to organizations based in other countries that are not chartered in the United States. Unless the recipient organization is registered in the United States, the donor cannot claim a tax deduction for the gift. Some organizations headquartered abroad establish U.S.-based nonprofits, often called a "foundation" or "friends-of" in order to qualify to receive deductible gifts from U.S. citizens. Gifts to those organizations could be captured in the Giving USA totals, but gifts that Americans make directly to organizations abroad could not be, since the estimates are based on tax data.

Giving USA data also do not include the substantial payments made by recent immigrants to the United States who send funds directly to their home countries to support either families or projects. Such payments are called *remittances* rather than gifts. By one estimate, such payments totaled over $79 billion in 2009, exceeding foreign aid given by the U.S. government (Adelman, 2009).

Global poverty and health have become the focus of a growing number of substantial gifts. The largest U.S. foundation, the Bill and Melinda Gates Foundation, is primarily concerned with global health and gave more than $3 billion in total grants in 2008. Warren Buffet's pledge of $31 billion to the Gates Foundation will, of course, increase the foundation's contributions to its international programs in the years ahead (Perry & Wilhelm, 2006). Other high-profile donors also have turned their attention to global concerns. For example, in 2006, David Rockefeller announced a bequest of $225 million to address poverty, health care, sustainable development, and other purposes; George Soros gave $50 million to the Millennium Villages program to reduce poverty in Africa; various donors gave a combined total of $2.1 billion to the William J. Clinton Foundation, focused on global needs; and Bono began a cause-related marketing effort called "RED" to raise grassroots support to fight AIDS (Center on Philanthropy at Indiana University, 2007, pp. 177–178). There were two gifts of $25 million or more addressing international purposes in 2008 (Center for Philanthropy at Indiana University, 2009, p. 173).

Dr. Muhammad Yunus, the founder of Grameen Bank, received the Nobel Peace Prize in 2006, drawing attention to the role of *microcredit* as a strategy for reducing poverty. Microfinance institutions provide small loans to entrepreneurs in developing countries who could otherwise not qualify for credit, helping them to start and sustain businesses. The microfinance approach has attracted an increasing number of philanthropic investments, including $103 million given in 2005 by Pierre and Pam Omidyar, the founders of eBay; $14.97 million from the Gates Foundation in 2006; and more than $1 million in computers given by the Chinese computer firm Lenovo in 2006 (Center on Philanthropy at Indiana University, 2007, pp. 176–177). We will return to discussing Professor Yunus and his accomplishments in Chapter 16, where we will focus on social entrepreneurship.

Global Fund-Raising

At the same time that international giving from the United States has increased, NGOs in many parts of the world have been required to pursue new sources of revenue. For example, governments in many nations have reduced funding for higher education institutions, forcing them to institute or increase tuition charges and to look to U.S.-style fund-raising for their future growth. Nonprofits in other fields, facing limited resources and growing needs, also have adopted and adapted the techniques of organized fund-raising.

Fund-raising and philanthropy face obstacles in many nations. First, philanthropy requires the presence of surplus income or wealth, which does not exist within many nations. It is illogical to assume that a country in which most individuals are desperately poor will be able to generate a level of giving that can sustain the growth of local organizations sufficient to have an impact on the country's overwhelming problems, and the competition for international giving is difficult for small organizations without internationally recognized brand names. Second, while most religions and cultures include expectations of altruistic behavior beyond one's family, not all cultures support organized fund-raising or voluntarism on the U.S. model (Wagner, 2005). For example, in some cultures, it would be deemed inappropriate to ask another for funds to support an organization on whose board the solicitor served. In other countries, for example, states of the former Soviet Union, the idea of prospect research might find a negative reaction, seeming too reminiscent of the files that the KGB maintained on its citizens (p. 10).

In addition to cultural barriers, few national tax systems include benefits for giving as generous as those available to donors in the United States. However, some Western European countries, including the United Kingdom and France, have greatly increased incentives for charitable giving in recent years (Hudson Institute, 2008).

There are also technical obstacles to the implementation of U.S.-style fund-raising techniques; for example, telephone and mail systems may not support sophisticated telemarketing or direct-mail solicitation, and some countries have low rates of connectivity to the Internet. However, the Internet has greatly increased the ability of NGOs to reach potential donors on a global basis at minimal cost. For example, GlobalGiving, a 501(c)(3) U.S. nonprofit, operates a website through which donors can make gifts to support specific projects listed by organizations throughout the world. Projects can be selected by country, theme (e.g., children, women, the environment), and other criteria. According to GlobalGiving's website, almost 97,000 donors had provided gifts totaling nearly $28 million between 2002 and 2010 (www.globalgiving.org).

Although obstacles remain, there have been recent examples of highly successful U.S.-style campaigns in other countries, and a tradition of philanthropy appears to be developing in some nations. For example, the Universidad de Monterrey in Mexico launched its first campaign in 1995 and by 2000 had raised $27.5 million, exceeding their $25 million goal. Sixty percent of the gifts were secured from donors who had never made such gifts before (Wagner & Galindo, 2004, p. 15). In 2004, the University of Cambridge launched a campaign for £1 billion to mark its 800th anniversary. The University of Oxford announced its £1.25 billion campaign in 2008, with £575 million already having been committed toward its goal (Worth, 2010).

As discussed in previous chapters, fund-raising as a professional field has emerged in the United States primarily over the past 30 years and more recently internationally. Fund-raising professional associations, like the Association of Fundraising Professionals (AFP) in the United States, have developed in a number of countries, and some have relationships with AFP and the Fund Raising School, part of the Center on Philanthropy at Indiana University. The Mexican Center for Philanthropy (Centro Mexicano para la Filatropía) was founded in 1988 and provides fund-raising courses, conducts research, and fosters voluntary service. AFP chapters were established in Mexico City in 1993; in Puerto Rico in 1999; and in Monterrey and Baja, California, in 2001. Similar organizations also were established in Argentina and Brazil during the 1990s (Viesca-Sada, 2004; Yoffe & Brunetti, 2004). The Council for Advancement and Support of Education (CASE) opened a London office in 1994 and a Singapore office in 2007. By 2007, its membership included more than 3,400 higher education institutions in 59 countries, according to the CASE website (www.case.org).

International Nonprofit Governance and Management

Managing an international or global organization combines the complexities of nonprofit management that have been discussed throughout this book with the additional challenges of working across legal systems, languages, cultures, and geographic distances. Indeed, a full discussion of international NGO management could easily follow the same sequence of chapters as that of this book and identify unique considerations of international management related to virtually every topic—governance, leadership, accountability, staff and volunteer management, fund-raising, communications and marketing, and so forth. Many of the pressures facing nonprofit organizations in the United States—including growing needs for services amidst declining government support, calls for strengthened governance and accountability, and the need to balance commitment to mission with competition for resources—are all present in the international environment. Thus, with globalization, "international managers [both in business and NGOs] face an external environment more complex, more dynamic, more uncertain, and more competitive than ever before" (Thomas, 2002, p. 10). Space does not permit a full discussion of all these topics in this chapter, but let's consider briefly some issues related to managing across cultures, governance structure for international and global organizations, and models for organizational structure in the global environment.

Managing Across Cultures

NGO managers must accommodate national and regional differences in legal systems, political environments, and culture. Among the three, Thomas (2002) argues, culture is uniquely important for three reasons. First, "the economic, legal, and political characteristics of a country are a manifestation of a nation's culture." Second, while the legal and political characteristics of nations are explicit and observable, culture is often invisible, especially to those who have grown up in different environments. "The influence of culture is difficult to detect and managers therefore often overlook it" (p. 19). Finally, the practice of management often focuses on interpersonal relationships—with staff, volunteers, donors, and others—and it is in such interactions that cultural differences may be most manifest. It affects such ordinary events as how individuals greet each other, how directions are communicated, and other everyday interactions. It involves both language and customs regarding physical space, body language, and other subtle differences. An understanding of culture and its implications is essential to any manager expecting to work in the international environment, which, as discussed above, likely includes most nonprofit managers of the future. There is an extensive theoretical literature on culture and its implications for international management, but a full discussion is beyond the scope of this chapter.

Governing International and Global Organizations

In addition to the generic issues of nonprofit governance and organization that have been discussed earlier in this text, working across different legal and political systems, cultures, languages, and physical distances presents unique challenges. For example, as a U.S.-based nonprofit begins to internationalize and seek board members from other countries, it will be adding members who may not fully understand the fiduciary responsibilities of governing boards under U.S. law or the expectations of board members in American nonprofits, which may be quite different from those in their home countries. This suggests the importance of additional orientation and training for international members of such boards (Koenig, 2004).

As the organization moves along the continuum described earlier in this chapter, evolving from an international to a global organization, its governance structure will need to reflect its evolving nature. Table 15.1 summarizes three common governance models and the advantages and disadvantages of each.

As Table 15.1 shows, one way to achieve international representation is to adopt bylaws that provide for a seat on the governing board for individuals representing each of the regions served by the organization. This might be an approach taken by an organization that is internationalizing: For example, a European seat might be created when it opens a European chapter of affiliates with a Europe-based partner, then a seat for a Latin American representative might be created as its programs expand into that region, and so forth. But as the organization continues to expand around the world, two problems may arise. First, the regional representatives may see their role as advocating for the interests of the region they represent, rather than focusing on the overall welfare of the entire organization. It could become a forum in which regional representatives vie for favorable treatment of their regions, with a diminishing portion of the board focused on building an integrated organization. Second, as programs expand and seats for a larger number of regional representatives are added, the board may become unmanageably large.

In the second model, an internationalizing organization might decide to add some number of international members to its board, for example, identifying 3 seats on an 11-person board to be held by individuals from other countries but without specifying particular regions to be represented (Koenig, 2004). This approach keeps the board at a manageable size and does provide for an international perspective. In addition, since the international members are elected

TABLE 15.1 ■ Common Models for International Governance

Structure	Advantage/s	Disadvantage/s
Provide a seat for a representative from each region served by the organization	Ensures geographical representation	Board may become large as the organization expands Does not ensure that representatives will primarily serve the interests of the entire organization
Provide for a specific number of members or percentage of the board to be international, without specifying regions	Ensures some international representation Limits the size of the board Does not imply that international members represent regional interests	May not ensure representation of all regions served by the organization
Open elections, with a nominating committee mindful of the need for geographic diversity	Limits size of the board Makes it possible to craft the board based on skills rather than geographic origins Focuses the board on the organization as an integrated global entity rather than on regional interests	Relies on the membership or a nominating committee to achieve a diverse board and does not ensure it

Source: Based on Koenig (2004, pp. 101–102).

or appointed at-large, they may not be as inclined to view their role as advocating for regional interests. However, as the organization's programs expand around the world, this approach does not assure that the perspectives and views of all its constituencies will be represented at the board table.

The third approach is one that Koenig (2004) describes as the "most common" in organizations that have adopted "a greater global mindset throughout the organization . . . because it puts a premium on an integrated organization" (p. 102). In this model, board members are enlisted from around the world, based on the organization's needs for various skills, perspectives, and experiences. The board membership can thus be crafted to meet the organization's leadership needs at various times. In this approach, the organization's needs would be paramount, and the board's goal would be to enlist the best members from wherever they may be around the world. Gaining representation of various regions would also be a consideration, of course, but the nominating committee and the board would not be constrained by such requirements in selecting people who bring desired qualities. The downside of this approach is that it does not assure that the perspectives of all regions will be reflected on the board.

Structuring International NGOs

Some issues related to the organizational structure of nonprofits in the United States, including relationships between national offices and chapters and the trade-offs between centralized and decentralized management, were discussed earlier in this book. Such issues and challenges become exacerbated as the organization expands internationally.

As mentioned above, some NGOs have come into existence as global organizations; the example offered was CIVICUS, an international alliance that works to strengthen civil society around the world, founded in 1993 with a multinational board. But others have evolved from local to international organizations by establishing chapters or clubs abroad, maintaining a close relationship with headquarters. One example of this approach is Make-a-Wish Foundation International. With its headquarters in Arizona, Make-a-Wish International had 27 chapters around the world by 2002, all sharing

> core values, and policies and guidelines [that] outline the responsibilities of the local group and MAWF International. . . . The international goals include establishing basic principles to ensure that the highest standards of ethics and conduct are uniformly followed and adhered to by affiliated charities that are members of the Make-a-Wish family throughout the world. (Koenig, 2004, p. 98).

An alternative is to maintain relatively autonomous national organizations that are affiliated with but do not receive direction from a headquarters. One example is Sister Cities International (SCI), which facilitates educational and other exchanges to promote cultural understanding, social development, and economic growth. SCI is a U.S. national organization that certifies relationships between U.S. cities and others abroad, which maintain their own independent organizations (Koenig, 2004, p. 99).

Some organizations have evolved a hybrid model, combining chapters linked to headquarters and affiliations with independent organizations abroad that share similar purposes. When AFP began to expand internationally, there were already some existing organizations in other countries. In nations where no such organization existed, new AFP chapters were established with a close relationship to headquarters in the United States. However, wishing to preserve its good relationships with existing organizations and not be viewed as a competitor, AFP chose to develop strategic alliances with them. The first three alliances were formed in 2002 and 2003 with the Institute of Fundraising in the United Kingdom, the Fundraising Institute of Australia, and the Fundraising Institute of New Zealand. Members of these national organizations can elect to join AFP and vice versa. Linked through the web, members of both partners can access each other's members, databases, publications, and other information resources (Koenig, 2004, p. 101).

As in national nonprofits within the United States, achieving the proper balance between centralized control and local autonomy in an international organization requires careful calibration. Historically, many NGOs had centralized structures that were pushed out to chapters as they were established, but as growth extends into more geographically remote regions and diverse national and cultural settings, there is a trend toward greater autonomy for regional chapters or affiliates. The challenge is to determine what policies and what functions need to be retained centrally in order to maintain ethical standards, quality of programs, and adherence to a common mission, and which decisions can be left to local organizations. For example, Oxfam International is a confederation of national groups that was created in its present form in the mid-1990s. At the international level, the groups work together in advocacy, program harmonization, and emergency response. Local affiliates are responsible for allocating resources and managing their own programs (Koenig, 2004).

Regarding the balance between centralization and decentralization, Koenig (2004) offers three pragmatic standards:

- The more parts of the world in which an organization has interactions or activities, the more it will want to determine which practices need to be standardized among its local entities or partners and which can vary or be locally determined.
- The larger an organization's international presence is, the more flexible it should be in looking at options for its operations.
- Organizations that want to grow internationally and develop sustainable structures must be willing to review their progress in relation to their organizational goals and make modifications as needed (p. 126).

It is ironic that in a period of time when increasing calls for accountability may suggest tighter centralized controls and when concern about image and control of the message also would dictate more uniform standards, the realities of communications technology and internationalization pull in the opposite direction. Access to the Internet provides local organizations with control over messages seen around the world, and the need to adapt to widely diverse laws, cultures, and economic realities increases the benefits of a decentralized approach.

Questions about centralization and decentralization are, of course, familiar ones even in national nonprofits within the United States. But working across legal, cultural, and language differences and considerable geographic distances makes them even more complex and delicate in the international environment, placing a premium on communication, flexibility, and a tolerance for ambiguity. In the nonprofit world, as in business, "conventional organizational forms are giving way to networks of less hierarchical relationships and cooperative strategic alliances with other [organizations]" (Thomas, 2002, p. 5). Managing such enterprises is likely to be a challenging task for "control freaks" or those who do not possess or acquire communication skills, trust in others, and sophisticated cultural understanding. For nonprofit managers of the 21st century, developing such skills and qualities is essential to effective leadership.

Chapter Summary

Unlike a century ago, when most people lived in rural areas or small communities and had little awareness of events in other parts of the world, we now live in a globalized society. Technological, economic, political, and cultural changes have created a world in which the greatest threats and the most promising opportunities require cooperation among nations and people from all parts of the world. Nonprofit organizations are playing an increasing role in global affairs and in efforts to address such problems as poverty and health. Those who will manage nonprofit organizations in the balance of the 21st century need to understand, accept, and be prepared to work with different mind-sets and different skills than have ever been required before.

As within the nonprofit sector in the United States, the terminology used to discuss organizations across the world is inconsistent and can be confusing. In most parts of the world, such organizations are known as *nongovernmental organizations* (NGOs) rather than nonprofits. NGOs that work within a single nation vary widely in the legal frameworks within which they exist, the sources of their funding, and especially their relationships with government. The best-known NGOs are the *international nongovernmental organizations* (or INGOs). They are organizations that have activities not confined to a single country and that usually reflect a global approach to governance.

Some INGOs were created as global organizations from the beginning, while others were national nonprofits that became internationalized by opening chapters abroad or forming alliances with organizations abroad that pursue similar missions or causes. Local nonprofits may evolve along a continuum from local to internationalized to global in perspective and operation.

The number of INGOs has increased exponentially in recent decades. Although there is no single source of comprehensive data on NGOs around the world, one of the most ambitious research efforts was the Johns Hopkins Comparative Nonprofit Sector Project, which developed the International Classification of Nonprofit Organizations and a global civil society index.

NGOs in other nations engage in a variety of activities, including educational and social services, arts, culture, recreation, and professional activities. Others are advocacy organizations that bring social and human problems to public attention and work for change. The World Bank divides INGOs into two basic types: operational NGOs and advocacy INGOs. Operational NGOs of interest to the bank are those engaged in economic development. However, other NGOs are limited to providing temporary relief, for example, to victims of disasters or wars.

International philanthropy, especially that flowing from the United States and Western Europe to the rest of the world, has grown rapidly in recent years. Some of the largest U.S. foundations, including the Gates Foundation, are focused on global health and poverty and on achievement of the UN's Millennium Development Goals. Some significant gifts have supported the growth of microfinance, a strategy for reducing poverty by providing small loans to entrepreneurs in developing countries who could otherwise not qualify for credit, helping them to start and sustain businesses.

Fund-raising and philanthropy of the type known in the United States face obstacles in many countries, including culture, tax laws, and technical issues. However, NGOs are adopting and adapting U.S.-style fund-raising, and there have been some notable successes as a culture of philanthropy is developing around the world. Fund-raising is emerging as a worldwide profession, through efforts by the Association of Fundraising Professionals, the Center on Philanthropy at Indiana University, the Council for Advancement and Support of Education, and professional associations that have been established in other nations.

Managing an international or global organization combines the complexities of nonprofit management that have been discussed throughout this book with the additional challenges of working across legal systems, languages, cultures, and geographic distances. Culture may be the most important variable, since the economic, legal, and political characteristics of a country reflect its culture; culture is invisible and may be overlooked by managers; and much of managers' work involves personal interactions with people, in which cultural differences may be highly relevant.

As organizations evolve from local or national to international and global in scope, they need to adapt their governance structures to accommodate board members from various parts of the world. There are various models for doing so, each of which offers advantages and disadvantages. Another question that arises as a nonprofit begins to operate in various regions is how centralized or decentralized its policies and operations should be; that is, which matters need to be determined by headquarters and which can be left to local groups. The trend appears to be toward greater decentralization, and that presents challenges in terms of accountability and communication of an integrated message.

Managing nonprofit organizations or NGOs in the international environment requires skills in communication, flexibility, and a tolerance for ambiguity. Managers of the 21st century need to possess or develop these qualities in order to be effective leaders.

KEY TERMS AND CONCEPTS

advocacy organizations

global civil society index

global organizations

government-operated nongovernmental organizations (GONGOs)

International Classification of Nonprofit Organizations

international nongovernmental organization (INGOs)

internationalized nonprofits

nongovernmental organizations (NGOs)

operational NGOs

remittances

transnational organizations

UN Millennium Development Goals

CASE 15.1   Médecins Sans Frontières/Doctors Without Borders

Médecins Sans Frontières (MSF), known as Doctors Without Borders in the United States and some other countries, was founded in France in 1971 by doctors and journalists. Its purpose is to provide assistance to victims of natural or man-made disasters, epidemics, neglect, malnutrition, or armed conflict. MSF is independent of government and religion organizations and receives 89 percent of its funding from over 3 million private donors worldwide.

Observing strict principles of neutrality and impartiality, MSF provides medical care and other services, bears witness, and speaks out to bring the public's attention to humanitarian crises. For example, in 1985, MSF spoke out about the forced displacement of people by the Ethiopian government and, in 2004, called for international attention to the crisis in Darfur. MSF was forced to leave Afghanistan in 2004 when it was perceived by the Taliban to be an instrument of the West and five of its staff members were killed. The organization was prominent among relief organizations that responded to the earthquake in Haiti in 2010.

MSF is made up of 19 "associations," also called "sections," in Australia, Austria, Belgium, Canada, Denmark, France, Germany, Greece, Holland, Hong Kong, Italy, Japan, Luxembourg, Norway, Spain, Sweden, Switzerland, the United Kingdom, and the United States. The U.S. section, MSF-USA (known in

English as Doctors Without Borders or DWB), was founded in New York in 1990 to raise funds and to advocate regarding humanitarian concerns within the United Nations and the U.S. government.

Each national association is responsible to a board of directors elected by its own members, which include former and current field staff, at an annual assembly (see Doctors Without Borders website, www.doctorswithoutborders.org). The president of each section is a member of the MSF International Council, which meets twice a year at the international headquarters in Geneva, Switzerland. Among other responsibilities, the International Council promotes accountability and transparency within the MSF movement and publishes combined financial statements that are an aggregation of the financial statements of the 19 sections (MSF, 2008).

MSF's principles of independence and impartiality are outlined in its charter and other core documents. Its dual role of providing services and also speaking out against inhumane conditions and actions inevitably creates difficult and sometimes controversial situations. For example, how can an organization speak out and also remain neutral, or be perceived as neutral, by both sides in a conflict? Two MSF officials explain the complexity of the distinction that is required (Tanguy & Terry, 1999):

> If neutrality is defined as remaining silent, even when confronted with grave breeches of fundamental humanitarian principles, MSF is not neutral. However, as long as neutrality is defined, as "not taking sides with warring parties," MSF upholds a spirit of neutrality throughout its operations. (n.p.)

Decisions regarding implementation of MSF's principles are made by five operational centers that have considerable autonomy. There have been occasions when disagreement arose among the various sections. For example, in 1999, MSF Greece was excluded from the movement over disagreement regarding how the principles of impartiality and independence should be applied in Kosovo. In 2005, the Greece association rejoined the international movement after an agreement was reached (MSF, 2005).

Today, according to its website, MSF/Doctors Without Borders provides services in over 60 countries, with more than 27,000 professionals working in the field. The organization was awarded the Nobel Peace Prize in 1999.

QUESTIONS FOR DISCUSSION

1. How does the discussion in this chapter regarding the structure and governance of INGOs apply to the case of MSF/Doctors Without Borders?

2. How does the case of MSF/Doctors Without Borders illustrate the complexity of ensuring accountability and transparency in an international organization?

3. Thinking back on the discussion in Chapter 11 about the importance of developing a case for philanthropic support, how do you think an organization's case might need to be tailored to cultural differences? In other words, do you think people around the world are motivated by similar values and emotions? Why or why not?

4. If you had the financial capacity to be a significant philanthropist, would you focus your giving on reducing world poverty or on addressing social problems in the United States? Explain your answer.

5. Should governments be the principal sources of assistance for economic development and poverty reduction, or should philanthropy play the leading role? What are the advantages and disadvantages of each type of action? What should be the relationship between private and government efforts? Explain.

SUGGESTIONS FOR FURTHER READING

Books/Articles

Boli, J. (2006). International nongovernmental organizations. In W. W. Powell & R. Steinberg (Eds.), *The non-profit sector: A research handbook* (2nd ed., pp. 333–354). New Haven, CT: Yale University Press.

Brinkerhoff, J. M., Smith, S. C., & Teegan, H. (Eds.). (2007). *NGOs and the millennium development goals: Citizen action to reduce poverty.* New York: Palgrave Macmillan.

Friedman, T. L. (2006). *The world is flat: The globalized world in the twenty-first century.* London: Penguin Books.

Koenig, B. L. (2004). *Going global for the greater good: Succeeding as a nonprofit in the international community.* San Francisco: Jossey-Bass.

Salamon, L. M., Sokolowski, S. W., & Associates. (2004). *Global civil society: Dimensions of the nonprofit sector* (Vol. 2). Bloomfield, CT: Kumarian Press.

Wagner, L., & Galindo, J. A. (Eds.). (2004). *Global perspectives on fundraising* (New Directions for Philanthropic Fundraising, No. 46). San Francisco: Jossey-Bass.

Websites

Idealist.org, http://www.idealist.org/

InterAction (American Council for Voluntary International Action), http://www.interaction.org/

International Society for Third-Sector Research (ISTR), http://www.istr.org/

The Johns Hopkins Center for Civil Society Studies, http://www.jhu.edu/~ccss

Union of International Associations, http://www.uia.be/

Chapter Outline

chapter 16

President Barack Obama and Senator Ted Kennedy participate in a national service event at The SEED School of Washington, D.C., where H.R. 1388, the Edward M. Kennedy Serve America Act was signed April 21, 2009. In recent years social entrepreneurship has been adopted as a key strategy of the U.S. government to promote social goals both at home and around the world. The Edward M. Kennedy Serve America Act, provided a $50-million Social Innovation Fund.

Official White House Photo by Lawrence Jackson.

Social Entrepreneurship 16

Social entrepreneurship has become a worldwide phenomenon, generating great interest and an extensive literature. Reflecting on the explosion of new nonprofit and nongovernmental organizations in recent decades, Peter Goldmark, former president of the Rockefeller Foundation observes,

> Nobody could make that [growth] happen at the same time. You have restless people seeking to deal with problems that were not being successfully coped with by existing institutions. They escaped the old formats and were driven to invent new forms of organizations. (quoted in Bornstein, 2007, p. 4)

What Goldmark is describing is the work of social entrepreneurs.

This chapter will discuss definitions and theories of entrepreneurship and provide an overview of its growth in the United States and globally, with some notable examples. Our discussion of social entrepreneurship here necessarily overlaps with some points that already have been covered earlier in this text, including nonprofit earned income strategies and the concept of a double bottom line. But the prominence of social entrepreneurship in today's dialogue about the nonprofit sector, social change, and global poverty makes it a topic worthy of more focused consideration.

Defining and Understanding Social Entrepreneurship

Let's begin with some definitions. What is an *entrepreneur*? The term is generally identified with business, and many people probably first think about prominent figures in business, for example, Henry Ford, Bill Gates, or Estée Lauder who founded new companies. Or perhaps they may think about a small businessperson who sets up a store or a stand and operates independently. Or they might just say that a young person who mows lawns and shovels snow for neighbors is "entrepreneurial," when what they really mean is that he or she is hardworking and ambitious. Indeed, entrepreneurs are almost always hardworking, ambitious, and independent people, and most create new enterprises, but the term has more precise definitions. Moreover, the role of entrepreneurship in the economy and society has been a subject of scholarship for centuries.

One of the first to study the role of entrepreneurship in the economy was the 19th-century French economist Jean-Baptiste Say; indeed, the word "entrepreneur" comes from the French verb *entreprendre,* meaning "to undertake" (Brooks, 2009, p. 2). Say described an entrepreneur as someone who "shifts economic resources out of an area of lower and into an area of higher productivity and greater yield" (quoted in Martin & Osberg, 2007, p. 31). In other words, an entrepreneur is someone who *creates value* by improving efficiency and effectiveness in the use of society's limited resources.

A century later, an Austrian economist, Joseph Schumpeter, introduced what has become the best-known understanding of an entrepreneur—someone who identifies an opportunity; creates a venture to pursue it; and ultimately upsets the status quo and makes previous products, services, and approaches obsolete. This can be seen, for example, in how the personal computer eliminated the typewriter and the Internet is challenging the survival of traditional newspapers. Companies and organizations adhering to old ways decline and disappear, while new companies and industries grow to replace them, a process that Schumpeter calls *creative destruction* (cited in Martin & Osberg, 2007, p. 31). The process is similar to a forest fire—nature's way of clearing out old and dying trees and making way for new growth. It may be ugly and disruptive, but it ultimately leads to a healthier and more vibrant forest. Entrepreneurs thus are central to competition in free market economies and play an essential role in economic progress; without them, we would live in a stagnant world without economic growth or rising prosperity.

So, we now understand what an entrepreneur is in the context of the economy, but what is a *social* entrepreneur? Like many other concepts discussed in this text, it has no universally accepted definition. For some, a social entrepreneur is merely someone who uses business concepts and methods in pursuing a social purpose. Others use the term almost synonymously with "leadership." But the literature reflects two principal definitions or schools of thought about social entrepreneurship that offer more specific definitions. Dees (Dees & Anderson, 2006) calls them the *social enterprise school* and the *social innovation school.*

Those in the *social enterprise school* think about social entrepreneurship as virtually synonymous with the creation of earned-income ventures by nonprofits, like those we discussed in Chapter 12. Their straightforward definition generally coincides with common usage—an entrepreneur is someone who starts a new business and, in the case of a social entrepreneur, a business with a social purpose.[1] For example, this is the perspective of Bill Shore, founder of Share Our Strength and Community Wealth Ventures, the Social Enterprise Alliance, and many business school academic programs. Those who come from the social enterprise school emphasize the importance of nonprofits freeing themselves from reliance on government and philanthropic support and achieving sustainability through revenue-producing business activities. They propose market-based solutions to social problems and often emphasize the blurring of the sectors, advancing the idea of the double bottom line, which we have discussed previously in this text, or even a triple bottom line, which considers environmental impact as well as financial and social value. For example, Steve Case, former chair of America Online, reflects this point of view when he says,

> Too many people act as if the private sector and the social sector should operate on different axes, where one is all about making money and the other is all about serving society. A better approach is to integrate these missions, with businesses that are "not-only-for-profit" and social service groups with their own earned income. (quoted in Dees & Anderson, 2006, p. 44)

On the other hand, those who belong to the *social innovation school* offer a broader definition of social entrepreneurship. In their view, social entrepreneurs play a role in society similar to that of the business entrepreneur in the economy, as described by Say and Schumpeter above. They are "distinguished from other leaders in the citizen sector by their long-term focus on creating wide-scale change at the systemic level"[2] (Leviner, Crutchfield, & Wells, 2006). In this view, the social entrepreneur is an innovator; a change agent; someone who identifies an opportunity, undertakes direct action to pursue it, and produces change that improves the condition of people and society. This may include the application of business principles and the pursuit of earned income, but not necessarily. The emphasis is on innovation and transformational approaches to combining resources in order to achieve social outcomes, not on the sources of funds applied to doing so. Thus, social entrepreneurs might access traditional philanthropy or government funds as well as earned income—whatever is needed and available—in order to implement their innovative ideas.

As Dees and Anderson (2006) explain this perspective,

> social entrepreneurship is not about generating earned income or even about incremental innovation in the social sector. It is about innovations that have the potential for major societal *impact* by, for instance, addressing the root causes of a social problem, reducing particular social needs, and preventing undesirable outcomes. (p. 46, italics added)

Thus, in this view of social entrepreneurship, one defining characteristic is impact or systemic change.

In the view of those who follow the social innovation definition, not all founders may be social entrepreneurs and not all social entrepreneurs need to be founders. For example, someone who establishes a new nonprofit that increases or extends services offered in a community may make a great contribution, but might not be considered a social entrepreneur if the person uses established models and methods that are not innovative and do not drive fundamental change (Martin & Osberg, 2007). Moreover, social entrepreneurs may not be founders of new organizations at all; they may be individuals who lead innovation and change within an established company or nonprofit. Indeed, some companies and nonprofits include individuals whose title is *intrapreneur* and whose job is to drive creativity and innovation within the organization. In this broader conception of the term, social entrepreneurs may be identified working in nonprofits, business, or government and have been active throughout history, not just since the 1990s. For example, Bornstein (2007) includes as an example St. Francis of Assisi, founder of the Franciscan Order, who "built multiple organizations that advanced pattern changes in his field" (p. 3).

Table 16.1 includes a sampling of definitions of social entrepreneurship that reflect the two schools we have discussed here. There are points of intersection among academic and practitioner authors from both perspectives and, indeed, Dees and Anderson (2006) suggest that academic study of the field should focus on a blend of the schools, that is, on what Dees calls "enterprising social innovation" by entrepreneurs "who carry out innovations that blend methods from the worlds of business and philanthropy to create social value that is sustainable and has the potential for long-term impact" (p. 50). Again, "impact" is a key term in this blended definition.

Theories of Social Entrepreneurship

Scholars in various disciplines have studied entrepreneurship and have developed theories to explain it. Theories of entrepreneurship are analogous to the theories of leadership that we

TABLE 16.1 ■ Definitions of Social Entrepreneurs/Social Entrepreneurship

Social entrepreneurs are "transformative forces: people with new ideas to address major problems who are relentless in the pursuit of their visions, people who simply will not take 'no' for an answer, who will not give up until they have spread their ideas as far as they possibly can."	Bornstein, D. (2007). *How to Change the World: Social Entrepreneurs and the Power of New Ideas.* New York: Oxford University Press, p. 1.
"A social entrepreneur is any person, in any sector, who uses earned income strategies to pursue a social objective."	Boschee, J., & McClurg, J. (2003). "Toward a Better Understanding of Social Entrepreneurship: Some Important Distinctions." Retrieved April 28, 2010, from http://www.se-alliance.org/better_understanding.pdf.
"A social entrepreneur is an individual, group, network, organization, or alliance that seeks sustainable, large-scale change through pattern-breaking ideas in what governments, nonprofits, and businesses do to address significant social problems."	Light, P. (2006). "Searching for Social Entrepreneurs: Who They Might Be, Where They Might Be Found, What They Do." In Mosher-Williams, R. (Ed.), *Research on Social Entrepreneurship: Understanding and Contributing to an Emerging Field.* Indianapolis, IN: Association for Research on Nonprofit Organizations and Voluntary Service.
"We believe that social entrepreneurs are those exceptional individuals who dream up and take responsibility for an innovative and untested idea for positive social change, and usher that idea from dream to reality."	"What Is Social Entrepreneurship." (n.d.). Echoing Green website. Retrieved April 28, 2010, from http://www.echoinggreen.org/about/what-is-social-entrepreneurship.
"Social entrepreneurship is defined as the process of creating new independent or corporate ventures that pursue the dual primary missions of social benefit and financial return on investment. These nonprofit and for-profit ventures have a social mission and aim to be financially self-sufficient or are profit driven."	Shore, B. (2003). Course syllabus, "Social Entrepreneurship." New York University Stern School of Business. Retrieved May 5, 2010, from http://w4.stern.nyu.edu/emplibrary/Social_Entrepreneurship_outline_2003.doc.
"At its core, social entrepreneurship is an externally focused act. It's all about results, not process."	Crutchfield, L, R., & Grant, H. M. (2008). *Forces for Good: The Six Practices of High-Impact Nonprofits.* San Francisco: Jossey-Bass, p. 24.

discussed in Chapter 5 in that some of the theories emphasize the characteristics or traits of individuals who become entrepreneurs. (And, of course, there is some debate about whether these traits are inherent or can be taught—whether entrepreneurs are born or made.) Other theories emphasize behaviors, things that entrepreneurs (and social entrepreneurs in particular) do. Still others stress the environment in which entrepreneurship occurs and take a situational approach, arguing that entrepreneurship occurs when an individual with the right characteristics coincides with circumstances in the environment that are conducive to entrepreneurial activity.

Scholars have identified demographic characteristics of entrepreneurs, finding, for example, that such activity is more likely among immigrants, first-born children, and individuals who have suffered some trauma earlier in their lives. They also often undertake entrepreneurial endeavors around milestone ages, i.e., turning 30, 40, or 50 (Brooks, 2009, p. 12). Other research has focused on the psychological characteristics of entrepreneurs, finding that they exhibit innovativeness, an achievement orientation, independence, a sense of control over their destiny, low risk-aversion, a tolerance for ambiguity, and—in the case of social entrepreneurs—a high community awareness and social concern (Brooks, 2009, pp. 12–13). Some have studied the motivations of entrepreneurs. For entrepreneurs in business, making money is usually the principal motivation, whereas social entrepreneurs are motivated mostly by a desire to create social change. But entrepreneurs in both sectors may also share some common motivations, what Schumpeter described as the "desire to found a private dynasty, the will to conquer in a competitive battle, and the joy of creating" (quoted in Bornstein, 2007, p. 24). Many writers describe entrepreneurs in heroic terms; for example, Martin and Osberg (2007) include "courage" and "fortitude" among the characteristics that they exhibit (p. 33).

Other writers emphasize the behaviors in which social entrepreneurs engage, although some also imply certain traits or characteristics. For example, Dees et al. (2001) write that social entrepreneurs behave in the following ways:

- *Adopting a mission to create and sustain social value.* For social entrepreneurs, the mission of social improvement is critical, and it takes priority over generating profits. Instead of going for the quick fix, social entrepreneurs look for ways to create lasting improvements.
- *Recognizing and relentlessly pursuing new opportunities to serve that mission.* Where others see problems, entrepreneurs see opportunities! Social entrepreneurs have a vision of how to achieve their goals, and they are determined to make their vision work.
- *Engaging in a process of continuous innovation, adaptation, and learning.* Social entrepreneurs look for innovative ways to ensure that their ventures create social value and obtain needed resources and funding as long as they are creating value.
- *Acting boldly without being limited to resources currently in hand.* Social entrepreneurs are skilled at doing more with less and attracting resources from others. They explore all resource options, from pure philanthropy to the commercial methods of the business sector, but they are not bound by norms or traditions.
- *Exhibiting a heightened sense of accountability to the constituencies served and for the outcomes created.* Social entrepreneurs take steps to ensure that they are creating value. They seek to provide real social improvements to their beneficiaries and the communities, as well as an attractive social and/or financial return to their investors (p. 5).

Other theorists emphasize the environment or context in which entrepreneurship occurs. Some argue that entrepreneurial behavior is stimulated when there is some *perturbation,* that is, when "people are displaced from their regular business routines by political, cultural, or economic factors" (Brooks, 2009, p. 9). Thus, for example, the seeds of new business ventures may be planted in economic recessions, when people lose their jobs and pursue new ventures as an alternative. The later decades of the 20th century and the first decade of the 21st saw significant changes in the world, including the fall of repressive governments around the world, increasing levels of education, the advancement of women in most regions, increased communication and awareness of global conditions, and a shift in attitudes that favored private or government action to solve social problems. These changes were often disruptive and provided new opportunities for business and social entrepreneurship across the globe (Bornstein, 2007).

Martin and Osberg (2007) describe how ways of doing things can be quite stable for a long time, but may also include inefficiencies or injustices that can be exploited by a creative innovator. For example, before Steve Jobs and Steve Wozniak introduced the personal computer, people were reliant on mainframes that required cumbersome and time-consuming efforts to obtain or process data. Jobs and Wozniak saw the opportunity to use emerging computer technology to shift the paradigm and bring much greater accessibility and efficiency to the use of data. Likewise, before there was eBay, people could only sell their used goods in garage sales or flea markets or by running classified ads in local newspapers, a situation that was unsatisfactory for both buyers and sellers. It was the inefficiency of that status quo that provided the opportunity for Pierre Omidyar and Jeff Skoll to create eBay and open up the market for the sellers of used (and new) items worldwide (p. 32). In both cases, weaknesses in the old model and the rise of new technology presented an environment in which individuals with the ability to identify an opportunity could take action and create fundamental change. For Muhammad Yunus, the unsatisfactory status quo was the extreme poverty of his native Bangladesh and the inability of people to obtain even small amounts of credit, which perpetuated their condition. He founded Grameen Bank, which provides microcredit loans to poor women to start their own businesses. The microcredit model established by Grameen subsequently expanded to a global network including other organizations operating in other countries and cultures (Martin & Osberg, 2007). We will discuss Muhammad Yunus and Grameen Bank in more detail below.

Students will recall from Chapter 5 that some scholars have proposed models that integrate various approaches to leadership theory. (See Dym and Hutson's alignment map in Figure 5.2.) Similarly, as depicted in Figure 16.1, Arthur Brooks (2009) describes a kind of "perfect storm" for entrepreneurship, where external conditions and the internal characteristics of individuals converge to provide the opportunity for the entrepreneurial process to unfold. As Figure 16.1 depicts, entrepreneurship is possible when social, economic, and political conditions are conducive. As mentioned above, the spread of free markets and the establishment of more democratic governments around the world have contributed to an environment favorable to entrepreneurial action in the past two decades. So has the growing wealth generated through the global economy, which has provided the resources for philanthropy and investment in social ventures. The end of the Cold War; development of the Internet; and, perhaps, a cultural shift that favors private over government action also were perturbations that affected the entrepreneurial context. But even in an environment favorable to entrepreneurship, there must be individuals with the right characteristics and the right education and experience in order for the entrepreneurial process to begin. In other words, change may occur when the right person is in the right place at the right time with the right skills.

Wei-Skillern et al. (2007) describe a similar model of entrepreneurship, involving the fit among four variables: the People, the Context, the Deal, and the Opportunity. In business, the "deal" refers to the "bargain that defines who in a venture gives what and who gets what and when those deliveries and receipts will take place" (p. 11). In the case of social entrepreneurship, "the deal" translates to the *social value proposition* (pp. 21–22). Similar to Brooks's model, Wei-Skillern, Austin, Leonard, and Stevenson (2007) emphasize that "because these [four components] are interdependent and situationally determined, the entrepreneur must manage the fit among them and adapt continuously to new circumstances over time" (p. 10).

High-Impact Nonprofits

Now that we have defined social entrepreneurship and examined some theories to explain it, what do we know about organizations that practice this approach? In other words, what are the characteristics of entrepreneurial nonprofit organizations, and what is it that they do to have high impact?

As noted above, writers who hold the social innovation view of social entrepreneurship include social impact as one of the defining characteristics. In research that was reported in an

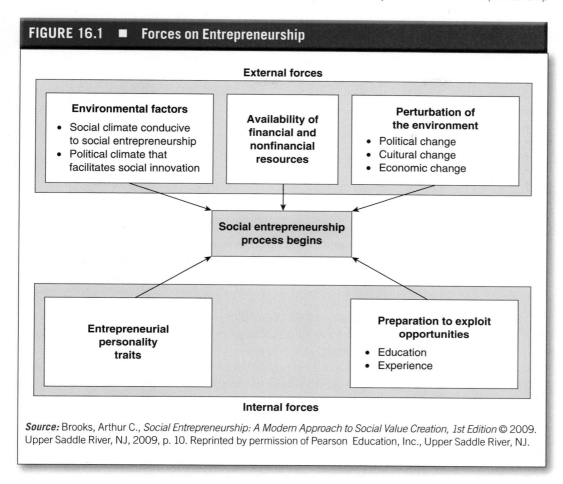

FIGURE 16.1 ■ Forces on Entrepreneurship

External forces

Environmental factors
- Social climate conducive to social entrepreneurship
- Political climate that facilitates social innovation

Availability of financial and nonfinancial resources

Perturbation of the environment
- Political change
- Cuitural change
- Economic change

Social entrepreneurship process begins

Entrepreneurial personality traits

Preparation to exploit opportunities
- Education
- Experience

Internal forces

Source: Brooks, Arthur C., *Social Entrepreneurship: A Modern Approach to Social Value Creation, 1st Edition* © 2009. Upper Saddle River, NJ, 2009, p. 10. Reprinted by permission of Pearson Education, Inc., Upper Saddle River, NJ.

influential 2008 book, Leslie Crutchfield and Heather McLeod Grant (2008) describe characteristics of nonprofit organizations that they identify as representing "a new cadre of entrepreneurial nonprofits [that have] created extraordinary levels of social impact" (p. 1). Clearly reflecting the social innovation approach, they argue that entrepreneurial nonprofits will define the future:

If the 1980s and early 1990s were all about replicating programs and the last decade was about building effective organizations, we believe the next leap is to see nonprofits as *catalytic agents of change*. We must begin to study and understand nonprofits not merely as organizations housed within four walls, but as catalysts that work within, and change, entire systems. The most effective of these groups employ a strategy of leverage, using government, business, the public, and other nonprofits as *forces for good*, helping them deliver even greater social change than they could possibly achieve alone. (p. 6, italics original)

Crutchfield and Grant (2008) examined hundreds of nonprofits using two criteria: (1) Did the organization achieve substantial and sustained results (outputs) at the national level? (2) Did the organization have an impact on an entire system? After extensive research, the authors identified 12 organizations—in various subsectors—that they determined to be exemplary (although not an exhaustive list of organizations that might meet their criteria). The 12 organizations—some of which have already been mentioned in this text—are listed in Table 16.2.

TABLE 16.2   ■   High-Impact Nonprofits Identified by Crutchfield and Grant (2008)
• America's Second Harvest[3] • Center on Budget and Policy Priorities • City Year • Environmental Defense Fund • Exploratorium • Habitat for Humanity • The Heritage Foundation • National Council of La Raza • Self-Help • Share Our Strength • Teach for America • YouthBuild USA

Source: Crutchfield, L. R. and Grant, H. M. (2008). *Forces for good: The six practices of high-impact nonprofits.* San Francisco: Jossey-Bass.

According to Crutchfield and Grant (2008), these entrepreneurial nonprofits shatter "myths" of "perceived wisdom in the field [of nonprofit management]" (p. 14). Many are not perfectly managed and do not have low overhead. Many do not have prominent brand names. Not all are based on a breakthrough new idea. Not all have textbook mission statements or large budgets. Moreover, many do not rate highly on conventional metrics. Rather, the authors identified six practices common to all 12 organizations:

1. *Advocate and serve.* Some began by offering programs, and others began as advocacy organizations, but over time, all evolved to include both types of activity.

2. *Make markets work.* Some have corporate partnerships or earned income, while others rely primarily on philanthropy, but all have used market forces and use private sector methods in their work.

3. *Inspire evangelists.* All have created committed advocates on their behalf.

4. *Nurture nonprofit networks.* All form partnerships with other nonprofits as well as government.

5. *Master the art of adaptation.* All are capable of adjusting their strategies to environmental changes.

6. *Share leadership.* The CEOs of these organizations empower others and delegate authority within their organizations.

It is beyond the scope of this book to pursue a thorough discussion of each point, but *Forces for Good* is recommended reading for students seeking greater insight into social entrepreneurship and entrepreneurial organizations.

Social Entrepreneurship Around the World

There are, to be sure, many examples of social entrepreneurship in the United States, including organizations identified by Crutchfield and Grant and others that we have discussed at various points in this book. Furthermore, the potential of social entrepreneurship to improve American society is currently receiving increased attention. To many people, the greatest promise of social entrepreneurship is its potential to have a significant impact on the alleviation of poverty around the world. Two of the most prominent figures on the global stage in this area are Bill Drayton, founder of Ashoka, and Muhammad Yunus, founder of Grameen Bank.

Bill Drayton and Ashoka

Bill Drayton was a U.S. Environmental Protection Agency official in 1978 when he became interested in the potential of social entrepreneurs to bring about social change. He founded Ashoka: Innovators for the Public, taking the name from the Sanskrit word meaning "active absence of sorrow" (Bornstein, 2007, p. 15). He and his colleague set out on a global search to identify the most promising social entrepreneurs and to raise funds with which to support their efforts. The first Ashoka Fellow, Gloria de Souza, was selected in 1981. De Souza was an elementary school teacher in Bombay who had developed new educational methods and was convinced that their application could revolutionize education in India. With a 4-year living stipend from Ashoka, totaling $10,000, she dedicated herself full-time to advancing her ideas. In 1982, she founded an organization called Parisar Asha and began building a team to implement her ideas. By the end of the 1980s, she had proven her methods and they were formally adopted by the Indian government as part of its national curriculum for Grades 1 through 3 (Bornstein, 2007, pp. 17–20). By 2006, Ashoka had supported more than 1,820 social entrepreneurs in 68 countries in Asia, Africa, the Americas, and Europe (Bornstein, 2007, p. 11).

Operating like a venture philanthropist (as discussed in Chapter 11), Ashoka provides social entrepreneurs with funding and also professional assistance, contacts with companies, and other types of engagement (Bornstein, 2007, p. 11). Following de Souza, the work of other Ashoka Fellows has involved electrification in rural Brazil, protection of street children in India, assisted living for disabled people in Hungary, health care for poor children in Brazil, and many other such programs. Ashoka began its programs in the United States in 2000 and by 2010 was supporting 130 U.S. fellows. They have included, for example, Wendy Kopp, founder of Teach for America; Rajiv Vinnakota, cofounder of the SEED Foundation; Darrell Hammond, founder of KaBOOM!; and other well-known leaders (http://usa.ashoka.org).

How are Ashoka Fellows selected? The criteria include evaluation of the idea and its possible social impact, but also intangibles, including the individual's vision, determination, and ethics. In other words, Ashoka subscribes, at least in part, to a trait theory of entrepreneurial behavior. As Drayton explains,

[Social entrepreneurs have] a number of characteristics that you can see very early in people's lives and in their professional lives. And that's where most of the tests come in. The first—the most obvious—is are they possessed, really possessed by an idea, that they're going to devote ten or twenty years to it if necessary and it doesn't cross their minds not to do that? (quoted in Bornstein, 2007, p. 125)

Drayton also adds to theories of entrepreneurship by describing cycles of an entrepreneur's life: an apprenticeship, in which individuals acquire experience and skills; a launch, in which they demonstrate their ideas; a take-off, in which they consolidate their organizations and spread their ideas; and, finally, maturity, a point at which they have had significant impact (Bornstein, 2007, pp. 128–129). (Readers may see similarity to the life cycle of nonprofit organizations that was discussed in Chapter 8.) Ashoka's goal is to find entrepreneurs at the point of take-off, where "a small investment of resources and collegial support could produce maximum gains" (Bornstein, 2007, p. 129).

Muhammad Yunus: Grameen Bank and Social Businesses

Muhammad Yunus is perhaps the world's best known social entrepreneur, having been awarded the 2006 Nobel Peace Prize for his work in the development of Grameen Bank. Yunus was head of the Rural Economics Program at the University of Chittagong, Bangladesh, in 1976 when he made a personal loan to help a poor woman start a business. That was the beginning of Grameen Bank, a pioneer in the field of microfinance. Grameen became an independent bank in 1983, and today 97 percent is owned by borrowers and 5 percent by the Bangladesh government. Grameen makes small, interest-free loans without collateral to enable poor people, 97 percent women, to start businesses that may help them escape poverty. Since its founding, it has dispersed over $9 billion to borrowers in Bangladesh and other countries, 97 percent of which has been repaid (Grameen Bank, 2010). Grameen's experience has been so successful that a number of for-profits, including commercial banks, now have developed microcredit[4] programs to tap the large market of poor individuals in the world. Their entry has generated a debate about the trade-offs between social mission and financial sustainability, in other words, the familiar double bottom line that we have discussed before.

In his recent writing, Yunus (2007) observes the persistence of extreme poverty and offers new solutions. In 2007, almost 20 years after the fall of the former Soviet Union and the unleashing of global capitalism, 94 percent of the world's income still went to just 40 percent of people, and 60 percent of the world's population lived on 6 percent of total income (p. 3). It appears that the UN's goal of reducing poverty by 50 percent by 2015 will not be met. In Yunus's view, free markets alone cannot address the problem: "Unfettered markets in their current form are not meant to solve social problems and instead may actually exacerbate poverty, disease, pollution, corruption, crime, and inequality" (p. 5).

Nor, says Yunus (2007), can government be the solution. Government provides public goods such as national defense, central banking, public schools, and public health services, and sets the rules by which markets work. However, Yunus writes, while government "can affect the way that business is done . . . it cannot address the areas that business neglects." Moreover, governments in developing nations are too often slow and bureaucratic, prone to corruption, and controlled by vested interests that resist change (p. 9).

Yunus (2007) also questions whether NGOs or nonprofits can solve the problem of poverty. Echoing Bill Shore, whose ideas about the need to rely on earned income were discussed earlier, Yunus considers the voluntary giving that supports NGOs to be a form of "trickle-down economics"; in other words, nonprofits receive only the economic surplus that affluent people voluntarily give and do not have a sustainable revenue model of their own.

Corporate social responsibility may be a good thing, but Yunus (2007) is doubtful that social goals can ever trump the drive for profit, since corporate directors have an obligation to shareholders to maximize financial returns. Nor does he believe that hybrid organizations can overcome the ultimate pressure to favor profit over social impact. Multinational institutions dedicated to poverty alleviation, such as the World Bank, have focused on the development of infrastructure (e.g., roads, dams, and airports) in the belief that such projects will stimulate economic development, but Yunus sees two problems. First, this approach is also a form of "trickle down," and the poor are not actors. "The poor can be actors themselves," he writes. "The poor can be self-employed entrepreneurs and create jobs for others" (p. 12). Yunus's answer is *social businesses*.

What is a social business? Yunus (2007) defines its characteristics as follows:

- Social businesses are cause-driven.
- Social businesses have owners, who may be the poor themselves.
- A social business is not a charity; it must recover its full costs through fees for the goods and services it provides (p. 22).

Yunus (2007) defines two types of social businesses. Some are focused on creating social benefit; that is, the goods they produce have a positive social impact, for example, by preserving the environment. Others might indeed be profit-maximizing and would generate profits to their owners. However, the owners would be poor and could purchase their shares through microloans.

Although Yunus's idea of social businesses is related to the concept of social entrepreneurship—and for that reason we discuss it in this chapter—there is a distinction. Like Drayton, Yunus (2007) follows the social innovation school definition of social entrepreneurship and explains the difference:

Social entrepreneurship is a very broad idea. As it is generally defined, any innovative initiative to help people may be described as social entrepreneurship. The initiative may be economic or non-economic, for-profit or not-for-profit. Distributing free medicine to the sick can be an example of social entrepreneurship. So can setting up a for-profit health care center in a village where no health facility exists. And so can launching a social business. In other words, social business is a subset of social entrepreneurship. All those who design and run social businesses are social entrepreneurs. But not all social entrepreneurs are engaged in social businesses. (p. 32)

The Future of Social Entrepreneurship

Social entrepreneurship has become a subject that is not only of worldwide interest to philanthropists and nonprofit leaders; in recent years, it also has been adopted as a key strategy of the U.S. government to promote social goals both at home and around the world. The Edward M. Kennedy Serve America Act, signed by President Obama in 2009, provided a $50 million Social Innovation Fund. At the time of this writing, competition was underway for grants to be disbursed by the Corporation for National and Community Service to 7–10 intermediate organizations, which would then make subgrants of no less than $100,000 to individual organizations. Government funds are to be matched 1:1 at the intermediate level and at the subgrant level, creating a total impact of $200 million in 2010 alone. The grants will support nonprofits working in low-income communities to implement innovative approaches to increasing economic opportunities, fostering youth development and school improvement, and promoting healthy lifestyles (Corporation for National and Community Service, n.d.). The advancement of business entrepreneurship has become an important component of U.S. foreign policy, intended to help countries reduce poverty and to build stronger relationships between the United States and other regions of the world. This effort was highlighted at a Presidential

Summit on Entrepreneurship held in Washington, D.C., in April 2010 (see overview at www
.entrepreneurship.gov/Summit/SummitOverview.html).

Despite the global financial problems and recession of 2007–2009, the effects of which still
lingered in 2010, it appears that the movement to free market economies continues to be a
strong force. At the same time, the commitment of world leaders to improving living conditions
around the globe has never been stronger. In this environment, social entrepreneurship is likely
to continue as a growing movement. It is likely to complement rather than supplant more traditional approaches, such as philanthropy, charity, and government action. But the thinking of
social entrepreneurs also will continue to impact the management of more traditional nonprofit
organizations by further increasing the emphasis on measuring performance and on developing
innovative solutions to persistent social ills.

Chapter Summary

Social entrepreneurship has gained increased interest as a strategy for solving social problems.
Some (called the social enterprise school) define it as synonymous with social enterprise, that
is, with the pursuit of earned income. But others (the social innovation school) use the term
to describe a broader concept. In the broader definition, social entrepreneurs are innovators
and change agents, who may pursue earned income or other sources of revenue to implement
their new ideas. Their role in the nonprofit sector is similar to that of entrepreneurs in business, described by Say and Schumpeter many years ago. They are disruptive forces that bring
about the introduction of new models, which eventually create systemic change. Many social
entrepreneurs found new organizations, but they also may act within established organizations,
including nonprofits, businesses, and government.

Theories that explain entrepreneurship are analogous to the leadership theories discussed
earlier in this text. Some theories describe the traits or characteristics of entrepreneurs; others
identify entrepreneurial behaviors; and others emphasize the interaction of individual characteristics and skills with an environment conducive to such activity, which is a situational approach.

Most definitions of social entrepreneurship emphasize impact, and a widely noted study
identified characteristics of high-impact nonprofits that are "forces for good." Such organizations
advocate and serve, make markets work, inspire evangelists, nurture nonprofit networks, master
the art of adaptation, and share leadership.

There are many examples of social entrepreneurship in the United States, but it also has been
adopted as a principal strategy for alleviating poverty around the word. Two of the best-known
advocates are Bill Drayton and Muhammad Yunus. Drayton founded Ashoka, which identifies
and supports individual social entrepreneurs whose work is at the point of take-off, with the
potential to have high impact. Yunus founded Grameen Bank, which provides microloans to
poor people to start businesses and which has become a model for a growing microfinance
industry. Yunus advocates the creation of social businesses, which would produce products of
social benefit or be owned by poor people, providing them with a route out of poverty. Social
businesses are a subcategory of social entrepreneurship.

Social entrepreneurship is likely to continue growing. The U.S. government established a
program that would invest $200 million in social entrepreneurship in 2010 and has promoted
business entrepreneurship worldwide in order to advance economic progress and strengthen
ties with other regions.

Notes

1. Some people use the term *social enterprise* to describe a business with a social purpose, but others use the term to describe any undertaking with a social purpose, which may or may not involve earned income (Dees, 2006, p. 41).

2. Ashoka (2005) uses the term *citizen sector* rather than nonprofit sector or NGO sector to encompass all such organizations worldwide, acknowledging the shortcomings of the terms *nonprofit* and *nongovernmental,* which we have discussed earlier in this book.

3. The organization changed its name to Feeding America in 2008.

4. The terms are often used interchangeably, but there is a distinction between microcredit and microfinance. Microcredit refers specifically to the granting of small loans. Microfinance involves offering a broader array of financial services, such as bank accounts.

KEY TERMS AND CONCEPTS

creative destruction	*microcredit*	*social entrepreneur*
entrepreneur	*microfinance*	*social innovation school*
entrepreneurship	*social business*	*social value proposition*
intrapreneur	*social enterprise school*	

CASE 16.1   KaBOOM!

Darrell Hammond and his eight brothers and sisters grew up in a group home outside Chicago, supported by members of Moose International. In the early 1990s, while a student at Northwestern University, he volunteered to help build a playground in a Chicago neighborhood. Observing the impact the playground had on the community, he was inspired to pursue a nonprofit career. He joined City Year in 1994 and worked organizing service projects in Chicago, an experience that gave him insight into the needs of low-income neighborhoods. He developed the view that building communities requires common spaces and that projects should involve local residents, rather than be delivered from "on high." The project itself could strengthen community ties, provide a healthy experience for neighborhood residents, and give the neighborhood a sense of ownership over its environment. He remembered the impact of the playground he had built and turned his attention to Anacostia, one of the poorest neighborhoods in Washington, D.C.

Hammond approached Home Depot, which agreed to provide materials and volunteers to build a playground near a public housing community. Other companies contributed funds, and community members raised money through events such as car washes and bake sales. The day the Anacostia playground was built, over 500 volunteers participated, including Home Depot employees and neighbors. Following the success of the Anacostia project, in 1996, Hammond and his friend Dawn Hutchison set out to replicate the model in cities across the country. They founded KaBOOM!, with the mission to "inspire individuals, organizations, and businesses to join together to build much-needed safe and accessible playgrounds" (quoted in Sagawa and Segal, 2000, p. 33).

(Continued)

(Continued)

By 1996, Home Depot remained a partner, and other corporate partners had signed on, including Kimberly Clark. In 1997, Vice President Al Gore and General Colin Powell helped KaBOOM! launch the "Let Us Play" campaign to build 38 additional playgrounds. By 1999, KaBOOM! was building 50 new playgrounds a year. By 2003, the organization turned its attention to the needs of older children and began building parks for skateboards and BMX bikes (http://kaboom.org/about_kaboom/our_story).

Over time, Hammond perfected the model, developing a step-by-step process for playground construction, including the roles of volunteers and neighbors. In 2004, in order to accelerate growth, KaBOOM! refined its model to empower communities with less oversight. Training programs were increased, and tools and resources were placed online. The Home Depot announced a $25 million partnership to build or refurbish 1,000 playgrounds in 1,000 days (see KaBOOM! website, http://kaboom.org).

One of the hallmarks of KaBOOM! has been its focus on measuring performance. In 2002, a system was developed to consistently report progress on selected performance metrics—the report came to be known as the "KaBOOM! Formula" (Wei-Skillern et al., 2007, p. 382). KaBOOM! (n.d.) also began to undertake research on children's play and published a report, titled "Play Matters," to inform local policy and practice on the topic. By 2010, KaBOOM! was recognized as one of the nation's leading entrepreneurial nonprofits, and Hammond was highly sought after as a speaker on social entrepreneurship.

QUESTIONS FOR DISCUSSION

1. Are social entrepreneurs born or made? In other words, can individuals be educated or trained in a way that will result in entrepreneurial behavior?

2. Which of the two schools of thought, or definitions of social entrepreneurship, do you find most satisfactory? Explain.

3. Go back to Chapter 6 and read the case of the Nature Conservancy. Is it an example of social entrepreneurship by any of the definitions discussed in this chapter? Why or why not?

4. Both Martin Luther King, Jr., and Nelson Mandela were agents of significant social change. Were they social entrepreneurs? Why or why not?

5. Go back and read the case of MPR in Chapter 12. Was William Kling a social entrepreneur? Why or why not?

6. Nonprofit partnerships with business, discussed in Chapter 12, provide a nonprofit with earned income. Are such partnerships examples of social entrepreneurship? Why or why not?

7. The following questions relate to Case 16.1: KaBOOM!

   (a) How does Darrell Hammond exhibit the characteristics of a social entrepreneur?

   (b) Does the case demonstrate the life cycle of social entrepreneurship as described by Bill Drayton?

   (c) How does KaBOOM! illustrate characteristics of high-impact nonprofits as identified by Crutchfield and Grant?

SUGGESTIONS FOR FURTHER READING

Books and Articles

Bornstein, D. (2007). *How to change the world: Social entrepreneurs and the power of new ideas.* New York: Oxford University Press.

Brooks, A. C. (2009). *Social entrepreneurship: A modern approach to social value creation.* Upper Saddle River, NJ: Prentice Hall.

Dees, J. G., Emerson, J., & Economy, P. (2001). *Enterprising nonprofits: A toolkit for social entrepreneurs.* New York: Wiley.

Mosher-Williams, R. (2006). *Research on social entrepreneurship: Understanding and contributing to an emerging field.* Indianapolis, IN: Association for Research on Nonprofit Organizations and Voluntary Action.

Social Enterprise Alliance. (2010). *Succeeding at social enterprise: Hard-won lessons for nonprofits and social entrepreneurs.* Washington, DC: Author.

Stanford Social Innovation Review (journal).

Wei-Skillern, J., Austin, J., Leonard, H., & Stevenson, H. (2007). *Entrepreneurship in the social sector.* Thousand Oaks, CA: Sage.

Yunus, M. (2007). *Creating a world without poverty.* New York: Public Affairs.

Websites

Ashoka Foundation, http://www.ashoka.org/

Aspen Institute Program on Philanthropy and Social Innovation, http://www.aspeninstitute.org/policy-work/nonprofit-philanthropy

Duke Center for the Advancement of Social Entrepreneurship, http://www.caseatduke.org/

Social Enterprise Alliance, http://www.se-alliance.org/

Conclusion

R eaders who have persisted through this entire text hopefully will have learned many things. Even those who may have had some prior experience working in a nonprofit organization may have found some new theory, some new concept, or some new data that added to their existing body of knowledge or understanding. Those for whom this book has been an initiation into the subject will have learned even more. But some may be wondering, "So exactly what have I learned?" "What *is* the right way to manage a nonprofit organization?" "Is there a future for nonprofit management as a distinct profession? And, if so, what qualities, skills, and perspectives are needed to pursue a career in the field during the decades ahead?"

This book has no simple answers to offer. The nonprofit sector is so diverse that no specific approach can be equally effective in all organizations. Some of the skills needed to manage a university may be quite different from those required to manage an international nongovernmental organization or a community-based nonprofit serving the disadvantaged citizens of one particular city. Indeed, when I began writing the first edition of this textbook, some friends advised me that the diversity of the nonprofit sector would render the task of writing a broadly useful book about nonprofit management far too challenging. Rather, they suggested, there should be a series of books on nonprofit management, each focused on a particular type of organization, such as universities, hospitals, arts institutions, human services organizations, and others. Of course, many such specialized books already exist. But the success of the first edition demonstrated that there are commonalities that run across the management of nonprofit organizations and institutions and thus some basic principles on which individuals seeking to lead such organizations should be well-informed. This second edition has attempted to address shortcomings in the first and to provide a balanced perspective that may be of benefit to students and future nonprofit executives in all types of organizations.

The rationale for this book lies with the management commonalities we have discussed. These include the need to balance mission and money—to measure success by a double bottom line—and the need to manage relationships with multiple constituents who may hold competing or conflicting views of what the organization should be and do, and who are both free and motivated to express them. There is also a political dimension to the job of a nonprofit manager. Thus, two constants of nonprofit management would be a highly nuanced leadership ability and—even for the more commercialized nonprofits—the deep underlying commitment to a mission that differentiates good managers of nonprofits from good managers in organizations guided by the pursuit of wealth or constrained by the limits of political feasibility.

It remains true that such wide variation among organizations and the rapid pace with which the sector is changing suggest that there can be no one right way to manage a nonprofit that students can learn today and then apply throughout their careers. Rather, as it has been said at various points in the book, successful management in this sector and in this period of history requires an approach that is pragmatic, eclectic, and flexible. Successful managers select the tools and approaches that best fit the circumstances and needs of their organizations, ever mindful of the overriding and immutable centrality of the mission. That may suggest the application of commercial methods or the exercise of charismatic leadership to inspire philanthropy. It may call for a strategic management approach or for creating an entrepreneurial culture. Indeed, it may call for founding a new organization or leading a transformational process that brings systemic change. It may require seeking government funds or working to develop earned income or philanthropy to diversify support and preserve greater autonomy. Or it may require doing all these things—and others—at the same time.

While contemporary concerns such as accountability and compliance, effectiveness and performance, capacity and strategic management, earned income, and collaborations and mergers are all important, it is also essential not to become too committed to the management fads or buzzwords of the day. Of course, no manager can ignore current legal, social, and financial pressures; deny the realities of competition; or pretend that organizations can be managed as they may have been at some earlier time. Rather, students and future nonprofit managers need to maintain both openness to new ideas and a healthy skepticism about those that are offered as one-right-way prescriptions.

In his conclusion to the 2005 edition of the *Jossey-Bass Handbook of Nonprofit Leadership and Management,* its editor Robert Herman asks the question of whether nonprofit management as a distinct profession will continue to exist in the future. He concludes that it will, because the nonprofit sector will continue to exist. Herman (2005) bases this optimistic prediction on the supply-side theories about "the motives and desires of those who actually take the time and effort to create and sustain an organization" (p. 733).

But Herman's (2005) tone is one of cautious optimism rather than conviction. He emphasizes commercialism as a threat that could turn nonprofits into nothing more than businesses and government contractors, requiring nothing distinctive from their managers and causing some to question whether they should continue to exist in nonprofit form at all (pp. 733–734).

It is, as Yogi Berra is reported to have said, difficult to make predictions, especially about the future. But my view is that the nonprofit sector is likely to survive and thrive in the decades ahead, providing unprecedented opportunities for professional managers, volunteer leaders, and philanthropists alike.

Commercialism in the nonprofit sector is not new. It has existed in education and the arts for decades, yet most institutions in those fields continue to exhibit cultures and qualities that affirm their nonprofit identities. Of course, most authors who express concern about commercialism are primarily focused on the human and social service organizations, which constitute the largest number of organizations in the sector. Critical observers worry that some of those organizations have become almost exclusively government contractors or that philanthropists have come to see their support of them as a form of investment requiring a measurable return, transplanting the culture of capital markets into the nonprofit arena. Such concerns are not without foundation, but they may sometimes overshadow more promising developments and trends.

New nonprofit organizations continue to be created every day. Indeed, one of the joys of teaching nonprofit management at a university is the opportunity to interact with students who are not only aspiring social entrepreneurs, savvy in the methods of the marketplace, but also driven by compassion, conscience, and commitment to a social mission. There is no reason to believe that their numbers will diminish; indeed, their numbers may be growing in response to increasing awareness of the social, economic, and environmental problems that will occupy future generations of people worldwide. The energy of these young people will continue to add new nonprofit organizations to the mix and to drive renewal of existing ones—redefining the sector over and over again.

Even those philanthropists who emphasize measurable results and think like investors are consumed by a focus on the financial bottom line. To be sure, many expect and demand that their resources be used efficiently and effectively, but in all cases their involvement is driven by a passion for a cause, not by the desire to make a profit. Genuine philanthropists are motivated by emotion, however rational their methods. It is still true, as Seymour (1966) wrote in his classic book on fund-raising, that "the heart has to prompt the mind to go where logic points the way" (p. 29). Social entrepreneurs and contemporary philanthropists may apply the tools and techniques of business to their endeavors, but their motivations still relate to the social missions of the organizations they support.

It is certain that nonprofit managers of the future will need to be able to implement business judgments and methods in their work. Skills in marketing, financial management, strategic planning, and other business techniques will become ever more essential, and students are strongly encouraged to pursue knowledge in these and other areas far beyond the brief introduction that this book provides. But also essential will be the ability to envision and to inspire, as well as the qualities of effective leadership that can only derive from deep personal commitment. Nonprofit management is likely to remain a distinct field because the nonprofit sector is likely to remain distinctive. It reflects the noble impulses and humane instincts that are the best elements of human nature and that cannot be fulfilled or expressed as fully anywhere else.

References

Abelson, R. (1998, March 27). At Minnesota Public Radio, a deal way above average. *New York Times,* D3.

Adelman, C. (2009, Spring/Summer). Global philanthropy and remittances: Reinventing foreign aid. *Brown Journal of World Affairs, XV*(2), 23–33.

Adelman, K. (2005, September 1). Bricks tell a story. *Washingtonian.com.* Retrieved October 6, 2010, from http://www.washingtonian.com/articles/people/1757.html

Adizes, I. (1999). *Managing corporate lifecycles.* Paramus, NJ: Prentice Hall.

Aldrich, H. E. (1999). *Organizations evolving.* Thousand Oaks, CA: Sage.

Alliance for Justice. (2010). *Nonprofit electoral advocacy after Citizens United.* Washington, DC: Author. Retrieved September 14, 2010, from http://www.afj.org/assets/resources/citizens_united_fact_sheet .pdf

Allison, M., & Kaye, J. (2005). *Strategic planning for nonprofit organizations.* Hoboken, NJ: Wiley.

American charities receive close to $1 billion for Haiti, Chronicle tally finds. (2010, March 16). *Chronicle of Philanthropy.* Retrieved September 14, 2010, from http://philanthropy.com/article/American-Charities-Raise-Cl/64684/

American Heart Association. (2010). *Heart-check mark.* Retrieved March 25, 2010, from http://www .americanheart.org/presenter.jhtml?identifier=2115

American Marketing Association. (2007). *Dictionary of marketing terms.* Chicago: Author.

Andreasen, A. R. (2006). *Social marketing in the 21st century.* Thousand Oaks, CA: Sage.

Andreasen, A. R. (2009). Cross-sector marketing alliances. In J. Cordes & E. Steuerle (Eds.), *Nonprofits and business* (pp. 155–191). Washington, DC: Urban Institute.

Andreasen, A. R., & Kotler, P. (2008). *Strategic marketing for nonprofit organizations* (7th ed.). Upper Saddle River, NJ: Prentice Hall.

Andresen, K. (2006). *Robin Hood marketing: Stealing corporate savvy to sell just causes.* San Francisco: Jossey-Bass.

Anheier, H. K. (2005). *Nonprofit organizations: Theory, management, policy.* New York: Routledge.

Anheier, H. K., & Themudo, N. (2005). The internationalization of the nonprofit sector. In R. Herman & Associates (Eds.), *The Jossey-Bass handbook of nonprofit leadership and management* (2nd ed., pp. 102–127). San Francisco: Jossey-Bass.

Anthony, R. N., & Young, D. W. (2005). Financial accounting and financial management. In R. D. Herman & Associates (Eds.), *The Jossey-Bass handbook of nonprofit leadership and management* (2nd ed., pp. 466–512). San Francisco: Jossey-Bass.

Ashburn, E. (2006). VA women's college will admit men. *Chronicle of Higher Education, 53*(5), A39.

Ashoka. (2005). *What is a social entrepreneur?* Retrieved September 14, 2010, from http://www.ashoka. org/fellows/social_entrepreneur.cfm

Axelrod, N. R. (1994). Board leadership and board development. In R. D. Herman & Associates (Eds.), *The Jossey-Bass handbook of nonprofit leadership and management* (pp. 119–136). San Francisco: Jossey-Bass.

Bandura, A. (1978). *Social learning theory.* Upper Saddle River, NJ: Prentice Hall.

Baruch, Y., & Ramalho, N. (2006, March). Communalities and distinctions in the measurement of organizational performance and effectiveness across for-profit and nonprofit sectors. *Nonprofit and Voluntary Sector Quarterly, 35*(1), 39–61.

Bass, B. M. (1985). *Leadership and performance beyond expectations.* New York: Free Press.

Bass, B. M., & Avolio, B. J. (Eds.). (1994). *Improving organizational effectiveness through transformational leadership.* Thousand Oaks, CA: Sage.

BBB Wise Giving Alliance. (2010). *Standards for charity accountability.* Retrieved January 8, 2010, from http://www.bbb.org/us/Charity-Standards

Beatty, S. (2006, October 26). Survey finds giving by wealthy largely immune to tax changes. *Wall Street Journal, 248*(99), D3.

Ben & Jerry's. (2008). *Social & environmental assessment report.* Retrieved March 25, 2010, from http://www.benjerry.com/company/sear/2008/sear08_3.1.cfm

Bennis, W. G., & Nanus, B. (1985). *Leaders: The strategy for taking charge.* New York: Harper & Row.

Berger, P. L., & Neuhaus, J. (1977). *To empower people: The role of mediating structures in public policy.* Washington, DC: American Enterprise for Public Policy Research.

Berry, J. M. (2003, November 27). Nonprofit groups shouldn't be afraid to lobby. *Chronicle of Philanthropy, 16*(4), 33.

Bixler, M. (2005, April 16). Habitat founder forms rival group. *Atlanta Journal-Constitution,* A1.

Blake, R. R., & Mouton, Jane S. (1985). *The managerial grid III: A new look at the classic that has boosted productivity and profits for thousands of corporations worldwide.* Houston, TX: Gulf Publishing Company.

Blended Value. (2006). *Blended value map.* Retrieved September 14, 2010, from http://www.blendedvalue.org

Block, S. R. (2001). A history of the discipline. In J. S. Ott (Ed.), *The nature of the nonprofit sector* (pp. 97–111). Boulder, CO: Westview Press.

Blum, D. E. (2006, June 2). Cautiously, World Vision creates an endowment. *Chronicle of Philanthropy, 18*(16), B17.

Blum, D. E. (2010, June 15). Voluntarism increases at highest rate in 6 years. *Chronicle of Philanthropy.* Retrieved September 14, 2010, from http://philanthropy.com/article/Volunteerism-Increases-at/65949/

BoardSource. (2005). *The source: Twelve principles of governance that power exceptional boards.* Washington, DC: Author. September 14, 2010, from http://www.boardsource.org/files/thesource.pdf

Boli, J. (2006). International nongovernmental organizations. In W. W. Powell & R. Steinberg (Eds.), *The non-profit sector: A research handbook* (2nd ed., pp. 333–354). New Haven, CT: Yale University Press.

Bolman, L. G., & Deal, T. E. (2003). *Reframing organizations: Artistry, choice, and organizations* (3rd ed.). San Francisco: Jossey-Bass.

Bonk, K., Griggs, H., & Tynes, E. (1999). *The Jossey-Bass guide to strategic communications for nonprofits.* San Francisco: Jossey-Bass.

Bornstein, D. (2007). *How to change the world: Social entrepreneurs and the power of new ideas.* New York: Oxford University Press.

Broce, T. E. (1974). *Fund raising: The guide to raising money from private sources.* Norman: University of Oklahoma Press.

Brooks, A. C. (2009). *Social entrepreneurship: A modern approach to social value creation.* Upper Saddle River, NJ: Prentice Hall.

Bryman, A. (1992). *Charisma and leadership in organizations.* London: Sage.

Bryson, J. (2001). Strategic planning. In J. S. Ott (Ed.), *Understanding nonprofit organizations: Governance, leadership, and management* (pp. 131–141). Boulder, CO: Westview Press.

Bryson, J. M. (2004). *Strategic planning for public and nonprofit organizations* (3rd ed.). San Francisco: Wiley.

Bryson, J. M. (2005). The strategy change cycle. In R. D. Herman & Associates (Eds.), *The Jossey-Bass handbook of nonprofit leadership and management* (2nd ed., pp. 171–203). San Francisco: Jossey-Bass.

Bureau of Labor Statistics. (2008). *Volunteering in the United States, 2007.* Retrieved April 16, 2007, from http://www.bls.gov/news.release/pdf/volun.pdf

Burnett, J. J. (2007). *Nonprofit marketing: Best practices.* Hoboken, NJ: Wiley.

Burns, J. M. (1978). *Leadership.* New York: HarperCollins.

Callen, J. L., Klein, A., & Tinkelman, D. (2003, December). Board composition, committees, and organizational efficiency: The case of nonprofits. *Nonprofit and Voluntary Sector Quarterly, 32*(4), 493–520.

Carlson, M., & Donohoe, M. (2003). *The executive director's survival guide: Thriving as a nonprofit leader.* San Francisco: Jossey-Bass.

Carnegie, A. (1889, June). Wealth. *North American Review, 148*(391), 653–665.

Carver, J. (1990). *Boards that make a difference: A new design for leadership in nonprofit and public organizations.* San Francisco: Jossey-Bass.

Carver, J. (1997). *Boards that make a difference: A new design for leadership in nonprofit and public organizations* (2nd ed.). San Francisco: Jossey-Bass.

Carver, J. (2006). *Boards that make a difference: A new design for leadership in nonprofit and public organizations* (3rd ed.). San Francisco: Jossey-Bass.

Cash, S. (2002, April). Smithsonian $35m gift. *Art in America, 90*(4), 33.

Center for Lobbying in the Public Interest. (2007). *Make a difference for your cause: Strategies for nonprofit engagement in legislative advocacy.* Washington, DC: Author. Retrieved July 5, 2007, from http://www.clip.org

Center for Lobbying in the Public Interest. (2010). *Foundations.* Retrieved September 30, 2010, from http://www.clpi.org/the-law/foundations

Center on Philanthropy at Indiana University. (2007). *Giving USA: The annual report on philanthropy for the year 2006.* Glenview, IL: Giving USA Foundation.

Center on Philanthropy at Indiana University. (2009). *Giving USA: The annual report on philanthropy for the year 2008.* Glenview, IL: Giving USA Foundation.

Chait, R. P., Holland, T. P., & Taylor, B. E. (1996). *Improving the performance of governing boards.* Phoenix, AZ: Oryx Press.

Chait, R. P., Holland, T. P., &. Taylor, B. E. (1999). The new work of the nonprofit board. In *Harvard business review on nonprofits* (pp. 53–75). Boston: Harvard Business School Press. (Reprinted from *Harvard Business Review,* September/October, 1996)

Chait, R. P., Ryan, W. P., & Taylor, B. E. (2005). *Governance as leadership: Reframing the work of nonprofit boards.* Hoboken, NJ: BoardSource/Wiley.

Charity Navigator. (2010). *Our approach to rating charities.* Retrieved September 16, 2010, from http://www.charitynavigator.org/index.cfm/bay/content.view/catid/2/cpid/182.htm

Child, C. D., & Grønbjerg, K. A. (2007, March). Nonprofit advocacy organizations: Their characteristics and activities. *Social Science Quarterly, 88*(1), 259–281.

Choi, J. (2006). A motivational theory of charismatic leadership: Envisioning, empathy, and empowerment. *Journal of Leadership & Organizational Studies, 13*(1), 24.

Citizens United v. FEC, 558 U.S. 50 (2010).

Clegg, S., Kornberger, M., & Pitsis, T. (2005). *Managing and organizations: An introduction to theory and practice.* Thousand Oaks, CA: Sage.

Cohen, R. (2006, January 26). How to prevent politicians from misusing charities. *Chronicle of Philanthropy, 18*(7), 35–36.

Collins, J. C. (2001). *Good to great.* New York: HarperCollins.

Collins, J. C. (2005). *Good to great and the social sectors: A monograph to accompany Good to Great.* New York: Harper.

Collins, J. C., & Porras, J. L. (1994). *Built to last: Successful habits of visionary companies.* New York: Harper Business.

Commission on Private Philanthropy and Public Needs. (1975). *Giving in America: Toward a stronger voluntary sector.* Washington, DC: Author.

Community Wealth Ventures. (2001). *The community wealth seeker's guide.* Washington, DC: Author. Retrieved October 6, 2010, from http://www.communitywealth.com/pdf-doc/Vol1%20--%20Mapping%20Assets%20and%20Opportunities1.pdf

Community Wealth Ventures. (2003). *Powering social change: Lessons on community wealth generation for nonprofit sustainability.* Washington, DC: Author.

Community Wealth Ventures. (2004). *Evaluating a social enterprise opportunity.* Washington, DC: Author.

Connolly, P., & Lukas, C. (2002). *Strengthening nonprofit performance: A funder's guide to capacity building* (Wilder Foundation with the Grantmakers for Effective Organizations). Saint Paul, MN: Amherst H. Wilder Foundation.

Copilevitz & Canter. (2010). *Working with commercial co-venturers & charitable promotions.* Retrieved March 25, 2010, from http://www.copilevitz-canter.com/index.php/practice_areas/nonprofits_charities/working_with_commercial_co-venturers

Corporation for National and Community Service. (n.d.). *Social innovation fund.* Retrieved May 11, 2010, from http://www.nationalservice.gov/about/serveamerica/innovation.asp

Crutchfield, L. R., & Grant, H. M. (2008). *Forces for good: The six practices of high-impact nonprofits.* San Francisco: Jossey-Bass.

Dees, J. G. (1998). Enterprising nonprofits. In *Harvard Business Review on nonprofits* (pp. 135–166). Boston: Harvard Business School Press. (Reprinted from *Harvard Business Review,* January/February, 1998)

Dees, J. G., & Anderson, B. B. (2006). Framing a theory of social entrepreneurship: Building on two schools of practice and thought. In R. Mosher-Williams (Ed.), *Research on Social Entrepreneurship: Understanding and Contributing to an Emerging Field* (pp. 39–66). ARNOVA Occasional Paper Series, 1(3).

Dees, J. G., Emerson, J., & Economy, P. (2001). *Enterprising nonprofits: A toolkit for social entrepreneurs.* New York: Wiley.

Denhardt, R. B., Denhardt, J. V., & Aristigueta, M. P. (2009). *Managing human behavior in public and nonprofit organizations* (2nd ed.). Thousand Oaks, CA: Sage.

Doane, D. (2005, Fall). The myth of CSR. *Stanford Social Innovation Review, 23*–29. Retrieved May 12, 2008, from http://www.ssireview.org/pdf/2005FA_Feature_Doane.pdf

Dollery, B. E., & Wallis, J. L. (2003). *The political economy of the voluntary sector.* Northampton, MA: Edward Elgar.

Donmoyer, R. J., & Fitzgerald, A. (2007, July 22). Taking from the rich, giving to the board. *The Washington Post,* p. F07.

Douglas, J. (1983). *Why charity? The case for a third sector.* Beverly Hills, CA: Sage.

Douglas, J. (1987). Political theories of nonprofit organization. In W. W. Powell (Ed.), *The nonprofit sector: A research handbook* (pp. 43–54). New Haven, CT: Yale University Press.

Drucker, P. (1990). *Managing the nonprofit organization: Principles and practices.* New York: HarperCollins.

Dunlop, D. (1993). Major gift programs. In M. J. Worth (Ed.), *Educational fund raising: Principles and practice* (pp. 97–116). Washington, DC/Phoenix, AZ: American Council on Education/Oryx Press.

Dym, B., & Hutson, H. (2005). *Leadership in nonprofit organizations.* Thousand Oaks, CA: Sage.

Edgers, G. (2004, January 25). MFA's Monets: Dicey deal? *Boston Globe,* p. A1.

Edna McConnell Clark Foundation. (2010). *Portfolio.* Retrieved February 12, 2010, from http://www.emcf .org/portfolio/grantees/youthvillages/index.htm

Egger, R. (2002). *Begging for change.* New York: HarperCollins.

Eikenberry, A. M., & Kluver, J. D. (2004, March/April). The marketization of the nonprofit sector: Civil society at risk? *Public Administration Review, 64*(2), 132.

Eisenberg, P. (2003, February 6). Why foundation grants shouldn't mix with politics. *Chronicle of Philanthropy, 15*(8), 37.

Eisenberg, P. (2007, June 28). Charities should remain nonpolitical. *Chronicle of Philanthropy, 19*(18), 53.

Elliott, S. (2006, June 5). Seeking a distinctive sound for people of a certain age. *New York Times,* p. C7.

Endowments at nonprofit organizations. (2010, April 2). *Chronicle of Philanthropy,* Retrieved April 2, 2010 from http://philanthropy.com/premium/stats/nonprofit/search.php

Environmental Defense Fund. (2008). *Our approach: Corporate partnership guide.* Retrieved October 1, 2010, from http://www.edf.org/page.cfm?tagID=1746

Fain, P. (2005a, September 2). Board suspends American U. president. *Chronicle of Higher Education, 52*(2), A58.

Fain, P. (2005b, October 21). Trustees at American U. fire president but remain divided over severance. *Chronicle of Higher Education, 52*(9), A36.

Fain, P. (2005c, November 4). Ladner resigns as president of American U. and agrees to $950,000 settlement. *Chronicle of Higher Education, 52*(11), A24.

Fain, P. (2006, June 2). American U.'s chastened trustees approve wide-ranging reforms. *Chronicle of Higher Education, 52*(39), A25.

Fiedler, F. E. (1967). *A theory of leadership effectiveness.* New York: McGraw-Hill.

Financial Accounting Standards Board. (1993). *Statement of financial accounting standards, no. 116.* Retrieved April 16, 2007, from http://www.fasb.org/pdf/fas116.pdf

Fisher, J. L. (1984). *Power of the presidency.* New York: American Council on Education/Macmillan.

Foster, W., & Bradach, J. (2005, February). Should nonprofits seek profits? *Harvard Business Review, 83*(2), 92–100.

Fremont-Smith, M. R., & Cordes, J. (2004). *What the ratings revolution means for charities.* Washington, DC: Urban Institute.

Friedman, T. L. (2006). *The world is flat: The globalized world in the twenty-first century.* London: Penguin Books.

Froelich, K. A. (1999, September). Diversification of revenue strategies: Evolving resource dependence in nonprofit organizations. *Nonprofit and Voluntary Sector Quarterly, 28*(3), 246–268.

Frumkin, P., & Imber, J. B. (2004). *In search of the nonprofit sector.* New Brunswick, NJ/London: Transaction.

Gadsden, C. H. (2002, November 11). The Hershey power play. *Trusts and estates.* Retrieved December 30, 2009, from http://trustsandestates.com/news/estate_hershey_power_play/index.html

Gainer, B., & Moyer, M. S. (2005). Marketing for nonprofit managers. In R. D. Herman & Associates (Eds.), *The Jossey-Bass handbook of nonprofit leadership and management* (pp. 277–309). San Francisco: Jossey-Bass.

Gallagher, B. (2001, August 6). Prairie Home Commercial. *Forbes, 168*(3). Retrieved October 6, 2010, from http://www.forbes.com/forbes/2001/0806/054.html

Gallagher, B. (2005, April 5). *Testimony of United Way of America's Brian Gallagher before U.S. Senate Committee on Finance.* Retrieved October 6, 2010, from http://dir.unitedway.org/files/pdf/about/SenateTestimony_Governance.pdf

Gammal, D. L. (2007, Summer). Before you say "I do." *Stanford Social Innovation Review, 5*(3), 47–51.

Gamwell, F. I. (1984). *Beyond preference: Liberal theories of independent association.* Chicago: University of Chicago Press.

Gose, B. (2005, January 6). America's charity explosion. *Chronicle of Philanthropy, 17*(6), 6–9.

Gose, B. (2006, October 26). Former financial officer faces charges in museum debt crisis. *Chronicle of Philanthropy, 19*(2), 17. Retrieved June 11, 2007, from http://philanthropy.com/premium/articles/v19/i02/02006201.htm

Grameen Bank. (2010). *A short history of Grameen Bank.* Retrieved October 10, 2010, from http://www.grameen-info.org/index.php?option=com_content&task=view&id=19&Itemid=164

Grant Thornton. (2008). *2008 National Board governance survey for not-for-profit organizations.* Chicago: Author.

Greene, S. G. (1999, May 20). Trustees ousted in Hawaii. *Chronicle of Philanthropy, 11*(15), 30.

Greene, S. G. (2004, April 15). Hostile takeover or rescue? *Chronicle of Philanthropy, 13*(13), 24–27.

Greenleaf, R. K. (1977). *Servant leadership: A journey into the nature of legitimate power and greatness.* Ramsey, NJ: Paulist Press.

Griswold, J., & Jarvis, W. (2009, July/August). Underwater Funds: UPMIFA throws a lifeline to drowning endowments. *Currents.* Retrieved July 28, 2009, from http://www.case.org

Grønbjerg, K. A., & Salamon, L. M. (2002). Devolution, marketization, and the changing shape of government–nonprofit relations. In L. M. Salamon (Ed.), *The state of nonprofit America* (pp. 447–470). Washington, DC: Brookings Institution.

Guerrero, T. (2005, September 19). Toll proposal for Virginia highways draws criticism. *Transport Topics,* 12.

Guo, C., & Acar, M. (2005, September). Understanding collaboration among nonprofit organizations: Combining resource dependency, institutional, and network perspectives. *Nonprofit and Voluntary Sector Quarterly, 34*(3), 340–353.

Gural, N. (2010). Hershey loses taste for Cadbury. *Forbes.com.* Retrieved January 22, 2010, from http://www.forbes.com/2010/01/22/hershey-cadbury-kraft-markets-equities-offer-withdrawn_print.html

Habitat for Humanity International. (2005). *Habitat for humanity fact sheet.* Retrieved December 27, 2005, from http://www.habitat.org/how/factsheet.aspx

Hager, M. A., & Brudney, J. L. (2004). *Volunteer management practices and retention of volunteers.* Washington, DC: Urban Institute.

Hager, M. A., & Flack, T. (2004, August). *The pros and cons of financial efficiency standards* (Brief No. 5). Washington, DC/Indianapolis: Urban Institute/Indiana University Center on Philanthropy.

Haider, D. (2007, Summer). Uniting for survival. *Stanford Social Innovation Review, 5*(3), 52–55.

Hall, H. (2005, January 6). Fund-raising association clarifies stand on fees. *Chronicle of Philanthropy, 17*(6), 47.

Hall, H. (2006, July 20). Nonprofit-marketing experts outline hot trends, discuss challenges. *Chronicle of Philanthropy, 18*(19), 29.

Hall, H. (2007, November 1). Public radio network has a script for success. *Chronicle of Philanthropy, 20*(2).

Hammack, D. C. (1998). *Making the nonprofit sector in the United States.* Bloomington: Indiana University Press.

Hansmann, H. (1987). Economic theories of nonprofit organization. In W. W. Powell (Ed.), *The nonprofit sector: A research handbook* (pp. 27–42). New Haven, CT: Yale University Press.

Hartley, R. F. (2000). *Management mistakes and successes* (6th ed.). New York: Wiley.

Harvard Business Review. (1999). *Harvard business review on nonprofits.* Boston: Harvard Business School Press.

Hauser, J. (2003, June). Organizational lessons for nonprofits. *McKinsey Quarterly, 2003*(2), 52–59. Retrieved June 20, 2003, from http://www.mckinseyquarterly.com/Organizational_lessons_for_nonprofits_1314

Herman, R. D. (2005). Conclusion. In R. D. Herman & Associates (Eds.), *The Jossey-Bass handbook of nonprofit leadership and management* (2nd ed., pp. 731–736). San Francisco: Jossey-Bass.

Herman, R. D., & Heimovics, D. (1991). *Executive leadership in nonprofit organizations.* San Francisco: Jossey-Bass.

Herman, R. D., & Heimovics, D. (2005). Executive leadership. In R. D. Herman & Associates (Eds.). *The Jossey-Bass handbook of nonprofit leadership and management* (2nd ed., pp. 153–170). San Francisco: Jossey-Bass.

Herman, R. D., & Renz, D. O. (2002). *Nonprofit organizational effectiveness: Practical implications of research on an elusive concept* (Occasional paper). Kansas City: University of Missouri-Kansas City, Henry W. Bloch School of Business and Public Administration.

Herzberg, F. (1968). One more time: How do you motivate employees? *Harvard Business Review, 46,* 36–44.

Hessenius, B. (2007). *Hardball lobbying for nonprofits: Real advocacy for nonprofits in the new century.* New York: Palgrave/Macmillan.

Hochberg, E. (2002, August 8). Business ventures go beyond the bottom line. *Chronicle of Philanthropy, 14*(20), 35.

Hochberg, E., & Wise, A. (2005, March 3). Don't give up on charity-run businesses. *Chronicle of Philanthropy, 17*(10), 49–50.

Hopkins, B. R. (2003). *Legal responsibilities of nonprofit boards.* Washington, DC: BoardSource.

Hopkins, B. R. (2005). *Nonprofit law made easy.* Hoboken, NJ: Wiley.

Howe, F. (2002). Nonprofit accountability: The board's fiduciary responsibility. In V. Futter (Ed.), *Nonprofit governance and management* (pp. 29–38). Chicago: American Bar Association and American Society of Corporate Secretaries.

Howe, F. (2004). *The nonprofit leadership team: Building the board–executive director relationship.* San Francisco: Wiley.

Hrywna, M. (2007, January 2). Extreme makeover: Girl Scouts shrink councils. *The NonProfit Times.* Retrieved October 6, 2010, from http://www.nptimes.com/07Jan/npt-070101-3.html

Hudson, M. (2005). *Managing at the leading edge.* San Francisco: Jossey-Bass.

Hudson Institute. (2007). *Index of global philanthropy.* Washington, DC: Author. Retrieved October 6, 2010, from http://gpr.hudson.org/files/publications/IndexGlobalPhilanthropy2007.pdf

Idealist. (2010a). *Volunteer management as a career.* Retrieved September 24, 2010, from http://www.idealist.org/en/vmrc/vmcareer.html#position

Idealist. (2010b). *What is volunteer management?* Retrieved September 24, 2010, from http://www.idealist.org/en/vmrc/whatisvm.html#name

Independent Sector. (2001). *Giving and volunteering in the US.* Retrieved October 6, 2010, from http://www.independentsector.org/programs/research/GV01main.html

Independent Sector. (2004). *Model guidelines.* Retrieved March 25, 2010, from http://www.independentsector.org/mission_market/Policies.htm

Independent Sector. (2005). *Panel on the Nonprofit Sector: Strengthening transparency, governance, accountability of charitable organizations* (A final report to Congress and the nonprofit sector). Washington, DC: Author.

Independent Sector. (2006). *Strengthen accountability.* Retrieved October 6, 2010, from http://www.independentsector.org/issues/accountability/standardsd2.html

Independent Sector. (2007a). *The nonprofit lobbying guide: Second edition.* Retrieved October 6, 2010, from http://www.independentsector.org/lobby_guide?s=Nonprofit%20advocacy%20and%20lobbying

Independent Sector. (2007b). *Principles for good governance and ethical practice: A guide for charities and foundations.* Washington, DC: Independent Sector. (See also Panel on the Nonprofit Sector, 2007)

Independent Sector. (2009a). *Facts and figures about charitable organizations.* Retrieved September 7, 2010, from http://www.independentsector.org/economic_role?s=facts%20and%20figures

Independent Sector. (2009b). *National and community service: Serve America Act enacted.* Retrieved November 3, 2009, from http://www.independentsector.org/programs/gr/National?Community?Service.htm

Independent Sector. (2009c). *Scope of the sector.* Retrieved September 7, 2010, from http://www.independentsector.org/scope_of_the_sector

Independent Sector. (2010a). *Lobbying guidelines for public charities.* Retrieved April 5, 2010, from http://www.independentsector.org/programs/gr/lobby_tax_rules.htm

Independent Sector. (2010b). *Value of volunteer time.* Retrieved March 10, 2010, from http://www.independentsector.org/programs/research/volunteer_time.html

Ingram, R. T. (2003). *Ten basic responsibilities of nonprofit boards.* Washington, DC: National Center for Nonprofit Boards (now BoardSource).

Internal Revenue Service. (2005a). *"Substantially related" defined.* Retrieved May 13, 2008, from http://www.irs.gov/charities/article/0,,id=158843,00.html

Internal Revenue Service. (2005b). *U. museum retailing: UBIT issues.* Retrieved September 22, 2005, from http://www.irs.gov/pub/irs-tege/eotopicu79.pdf

Internal Revenue Service. (2009, May). *Form 990, Part VI – Governance, management, and disclosure: frequently asked questions and tips.* Washington, DC: Author.

Internal Revenue Service. (n.d.-a). *Exemption requirements – Section 501(c)(3) organizations.* Retrieved September 4, 2010, from http://www.irs.gov/charities/charitable/article/0,,id=96099,00.html

Internal Revenue Service. (n.d.-b). *Social welfare organizations.* Retrieved September 4, 2010, from http://www.irs.gov/charities/nonprofits/article/0,,id=96178,00.html

Jaffee, H. (2006, April). Let them eat truffles. *Washingtonian, 41*(7), 76–79, 116, 123, 131–133.

James, E. (1987). The nonprofit sector in comparative perspective. In W. W. Powell (Ed.), *The nonprofit sector: A research handbook* (pp. 397–415). New Haven, CT: Yale University Press.

Javits, C. I. (2008). *REDF's current approach to SROI.* San Francisco: REDF.

Jeavons, T. H. (1991). A historical and moral analysis of religious fund raising. In D. F. Burlingame & L. J. Hulse (Eds.), *Taking fund raising seriously: Advancing the profession and practice of raising money* (pp. 53–72). San Francisco: Jossey-Bass.

Jensen, B. (2005, February 17). Housing group fires its founder. *Chronicle of Philanthropy, 17*(9), 26.

Jensen, B. (2006a, September 28). Grants to help charities improve operations are on the decline. *Chronicle of Philanthropy.* Retrieved October 6, 2010, from http://philanthropy.com/article/Grants-to-Help-Charities/57895/

Jensen, B. (2006b, September 14). NAACP cleared by federal tax agency. *Chronicle of Philanthropy, 18*(23), 13. Retrieved October 6, 2010, from http://philanthropy.com/article/NAACP-Cleared-by-Federal-Ta/58506/

Jewell, J. (2005). New times, new leaders. *Christianity Today, 49*(4), 24.

Johnson, E. M. (2006). *The Pension Protection Act of 2006 and nonprofit reforms.* Washington, DC: ASAE and The Center for Association Leadership.

Joslyn, H. (2002, October 17). Driven by mission. *Chronicle of Philanthropy, 15*(1), 19.

Joslyn, H. (2004, January 8). Young people fuel demand for nonprofit study. *Chronicle of Philanthropy, 16*(6), 6–10. Retrieved October 6, 2010, from http://philanthropy.com/article/Young-People-Fuel-Demand-for/62104/

KaBOOM! (n.d.). *Play matters: A study of best practices to inform local policy and process in support of children's play.* Washington, DC: Author. Retrieved October 4, 2010, from http://kaboom.org/docs/documents/pdf/playmatters/Play_Matters_Case_Summaries.pdf

Kaplan, R. S., & Norton, D. (1992). Using the balanced scorecard as a strategic management system. *Harvard Business Review, 70*(1), 71–79.

Katz, D., & Kahn, R. L. (1966). *The social psychology of organizations.* New York: Wiley.

Kearns, K. P. (2000). *Private sector strategies for social sector success.* San Francisco: Jossey-Bass.

Kee, J. E. (2004). Cost-effectiveness and cost-benefit analysis. In J. S. Wholey, H. P. Hatry, & K. E. Newcomer (Eds.), *Handbook of practical program evaluation* (2nd ed., pp. 506–542). San Francisco: Jossey-Bass.

Kee, J. E., & Newcomer, K. E. (2008). *Transforming public and nonprofit organizations: Stewardship for leading change.* Vienna, VA: Management Concepts, Inc.

Kelly, K. S. (1998). *Effective fund-raising management.* Mahwah, NJ: Erlbaum.

Kennicott, P. (2009, November 4). National Trust's chief retiring. *The Washington Post,* p. C12.

Kibbe, B. D. (2004). Investing in nonprofit capacity. In Grantmakers for Effective Organizations (Eds.), *Funding effectiveness: Lessons in building nonprofit capacity* (Chap. 1). San Francisco: Wiley.

King, K. T. (2006, April 6). The limits of usefulness. *Chronicle of Philanthropy, 18*(12), 63–65.

Kirkpatrick, K. T. (2007, Summer). Go ahead: Pop the question. *Stanford Social Innovation Review, 5*(3), 3–46.

Klausner, M., & Small, J. (2005, Spring). Failing to govern? *Stanford Social Innovation Review, 3*(1), 43–49.

Klintsov, V., & von Löhneysen, E. (2001). Shall we dance? *McKinsey Quarterly, 2001*(4, Special Ed.), 6–9. Retrieved May 16, 2007, from http:www.mckinseyquarterly.com/article_print.aspx?L2=33&L3=95&ar=1105

Koenig, B. L. (2004). *Going global for the greater good: Succeeding as a nonprofit in the international community.* San Francisco: Jossey-Bass.

Kohm, A., La Piana, D., & Gowdy, H. (2003). *Strategic restructuring: Findings from a study of integrations and alliances among nonprofit social sector and cultural organizations in the United States.* Chicago: Chapin Hall Center for Children.

Kopczynski, M. E., & Pritchard, K. (2004). The use of evaluation by nonprofit organizations. In J. S. Wholey, H. P. Hatry, & K. E. Newcomer (Eds.), *Handbook of practical program evaluation* (pp. 649–669). San Francisco: Jossey-Bass.

Koteen, J. (1997). *Strategic management in public and nonprofit organizations.* Westport, CT: Praeger.

Kotter, J. P. (1996). *Leading change.* Boston: Harvard Business School Press.

LaBarre, P. (2006, November/December). How do you transform a 95-year-old organization? Ask the girls. *The Merrill Lynch Leadership Magazine,* 44–50.

Lampkin, L. M., Winkler, M. K., Kerlin, J., Hatry, H., Natenshon, D., Saul, J., et al. (2006). *Building a common outcome framework to measure nonprofit performance.* Washington, DC: Urban Institute. Retrieved January 28, 2010, from http://www.urban.org/publications/411404.html

La Piana, D. (2008). *The nonprofit strategy revolution: Real-time strategic planning in a rapid-response world.* Saint Paul, MN: Fieldstone Alliance.

La Piana, D. (2010, Spring). Merging wisely. *Stanford Social Innovation Review, 8*(2), 28–33.

Larkin, E. D. (2002, November 28). A dangerous precedent for donors. *Chronicle of Philanthropy, 15*(4). Retrieved December 30, 2009, from http://www.danlarkinlaw.com/backend/files/A%20Dangerous%20Precedent%20For%20Donors.doc

Lee, J. (2009, May 6). *What is the social innovation fund?* Retrieved February 12, 2010, from http://www.whitehouse.gov/blog/what-is-the-social-innovation-fund/

Letts, C. W., Ryan, W. P., & Grossman, A. (1999a). *High performance nonprofit organizations: Managing upstream for greater impact.* New York: Wiley.

Letts, C. W., Ryan, W. P., & Grossman, A. (1999b). Virtuous capital: What foundations can learn from venture capitalists. In *Harvard Business Review on nonprofits* (pp. 91–110). Boston: Harvard Business School Press. (Reprinted from *Harvard Business Review,* March/April, 1997)

Levine, S. (2006, October 22). A village made to raise children. *U.S. News & World Report.* Retrieved October 6, 2010, from http://www.usnews.com/usnews/news/articles/061022/30lawler.htm

Leviner, N., Crutchfield, L. R., & Wells, D. (2006). Understanding the impact of social entrepreneurs: Ashoka's answer to the challenge of measuring effectiveness. *Research on Social Entrepreneurship* [ARNOVA Occasional Paper Series, 1(3)]. Indianapolis, IN: Association for Research on Nonprofit Organizations and Voluntary Action, pp. 89–104. (Available at http://www.ashoka.org/printroom)

Lewis, N. (2002, February 21). Controversy over donor's role causes Smithsonian to lose $36.5 million. *Chronicle of Philanthropy, 14*(9), 16.

Light, P. C. (2000). *Making nonprofits work: A report on the tides of nonprofit management reform.* Washington, DC: Brookings Institution.

Light, P. C. (2002). *Pathways to nonprofit excellence.* Washington, DC: Brookings Institution.

Light, P. C. (2004a, Spring). Capacity building and the national infrastructure to support it. *Nonprofit Quarterly,* 36–41.

Light, P. C. (2004b). *Sustaining nonprofit performance: The case for capacity building and the evidence to support it.* Washington, DC: Brookings Institution.

Lipke, D. J. (2000, September). Fountain of youth: AARP woos reluctant boomers with a high-priced makeover. *American Demographics, 22*(9), 37–39.

Lipman, H. (2006, August 17). A record fund-raising feat. *Chronicle of Philanthropy, 18*(21), 2. Retrieved October 6, 2010, from http://www.philanthropy.com/premium/articles/v18/i21/21002201.htm

Lipman, H., & Williams, G. (2002, August 8). D.C. United Way's troubles cause concern elsewhere. *Chronicle of Philanthropy, 14*(20), 30.

Locke, E. A. (2000). Motivation by goal setting. In R. T. Golembiewski (Ed.), *Handbook of organizational behavior* (2nd ed., pp. 43–56). New York: Marcel Dekker.

Lohmann, R. A. (1992). *The commons.* San Francisco: Jossey-Bass.

Lubell, S. (December, 2005). Katrina and heritage: Richard Moe, president of the National Trust for Historic Preservation. *Architectural Record, 193*(12), 32.

MacMillan, I. C. (1983). Competitive strategies for nonprofit organizations. *Advances in Strategic Management, 1,* 61–82.

Maddox, D. (1999). *Budgeting for not-for-profit organizations.* Hoboken, NJ: Wiley.

Mangan, K. S. (1999, November 12). Stanford's health system ends merger with University of California at San Francisco. *Chronicle of Higher Education, 46*(12), A43.

Marchetti, D. (2000, May 4). Two food charities join forces in one of biggest non-profit mergers. *Chronicle of Philanthropy, 12*(14), 33.

Martin, R. L., & Osberg, S (2007, Spring). Social entrepreneurship: The case for definition. *Stanford Social Innovation Review,* 28–39.

Maryland Association of Nonprofit Organizations. (2010). *Standards for excellence.* Retrieved January 8, 2010, from http://www.marylandnonprofits.org/html/standards/cert_prog.asp

Maslow, A. H. (1954). *Motivation and personality.* New York: Harper.

MAXIMUS. (n.d.). *Our company.* Retrieved December 2, 2009, from http://www.maximus.com/our company

McClelland, D. C. (1961). *The achieving society.* New York: Free Press.

McCormick, D. H. (2001). *Nonprofit mergers: The power of successful partnerships.* Gaithersburg, MD: Aspen.

McCormick, S. (2003, May 13). Balancing the story. *The Washington Post,* p. A19.

McCracken, J. (2009, November 27). Hershey Trust seeks Cadbury-bid blessing. *WSJ.com* (Wall Street Journal online). Retrieved December 30, 2009, from http://online.wsj.com/article/SB1000142405274 87044988045745557600962471292.html

McCurley, S. (2004). Keeping the community involved: Recruiting and retaining volunteers. In R. Herman & Associates (Eds.), *The Jossey-Bass handbook of nonprofit leadership and management* (pp. 587–622). San Francisco: Jossey-Bass.

McCurley, S., & Lynch, R. (2006). *Volunteer management: Mobilizing all the resources in the community* (2nd ed.). Kemptville, ON, Canada: Johnstone Training and Consultation. (Available online at http://www.jtcinc.ca)

McDill, V. (2006, August). Preventing cultural catastrophe. *OAH Newsletter* (Organization of American Historians), p. 7.

McGregor, D. (1960). *The human side of enterprise.* New York: McGraw-Hill.

McKinsey & Company. (2001). *Effective capacity building in nonprofit organizations.* Washington, DC: Venture Philanthropy Partners. Retrieved April 24, 2007, from http://venturephilanthropypartners.org/learning/reports/capacity/capacity.html

McMillan, E. J. (2003a). *Not-for-profit accounting, tax, and reporting requirements.* Hoboken, NJ: Wiley.

McMillan, E. J. (2003b). *Not-for-profit budgeting and financial management.* Hoboken, NJ: Wiley.

Médecins Sans Frontières. (2005, February 9). *MSF Greece reintegrated into the MSF international movement.* Retrieved October 3, 2010, from http://www.msf.org/msfinternational/invoke.cfm?objectid=74439A98-D5F9-4B27-A771D10F8731BB4F&component=toolkit.pressrelease&method=full_html

Médecins Sans Frontières. (2008, July 21). *President's report/financial report for the year ending 2007.* Retrieved October 3, 2010, from http://www.msf.org/msfinternational/invoke.cfm?objectid=540C7128-15C5-F00A-25748DC7BC377015&component=toolkit.article&method=full_html

Meyer, M. W. (2002). *Rethinking performance measures: Beyond the balanced scorecard.* Cambridge, UK: Cambridge University Press.

Michaels, M. (2007, April 16). High turnover among adult volunteers, report finds. *Chronicle of Philanthropy.* Retrieved October 6, 2010, from http://www.volunteernapa.org/docs/VolunteerManagementTraining1.pdf

Miller, J. P. (1998, March 24). Public radio outlet reaps $120 million for direct marketer. *Wall Street Journal,* p. B9.

Minnesota Council on Nonprofits. (2006). *The law and nonprofit advocacy & lobbying.* Retrieved October 6, 2010, from http://www.mncn.org/policy_lobby_law.htm

Minor, E. (2005, February 3). Habitat for Humanity volunteers urge reinstatement of founder and president. *Associated Press.* Retrieved October 6, 2010, from http://www.romenews-tribune.com

Mintzberg, H. (1996). The rise and fall of strategic planning. In J. L. Pierce & J. W. Newstrom (Eds.), *The manager's bookshelf* (pp. 137–142). New York: HarperCollins.

Mirabella, R. M. (2004). *Nonprofit management education: Current offerings in university-based programs.* Retrieved October 6, 2010, from http://tltc.shu.edu/npo

Mirabella, R. M. (2007, December). University-based educational programs in nonprofit management and philanthropic studies: A 10-year review and projections of future trends. *Nonprofit and Voluntary Sector Quarterly, 36*(4), Supplement, 11S–27S.

Morino, M. (2010, January). "Social outcomes": Missing the forest for the trees. *VPP News.* Retrieved October 6, 2010, from http://www.vppartners.org/learning/enews/archive/january-2010

Moyers, R. L. (2006). *The nonprofit chief executive's ten basic responsibilities.* Washington, DC: BoardSource.

Murray, V. (2004). Evaluating the effectiveness of nonprofit organizations. In R. D. Herman & Associates (Eds.), *The Jossey-Bass handbook of nonprofit leadership and management* (2nd ed., pp. 345–370). San Francisco: Jossey-Bass.

Museums and money [Editorial]. (2001, May 31). *The Washington Post,* p. A24.

Nanus, B., & Dobbs, S. M. (1999). *Leaders who make a difference: Essential strategies for meeting the nonprofit challenge.* San Francisco: Jossey-Bass.

Nason, J. W. (1993). Responsibilities of the governing board. In R. T. Ingram & Associates (Eds.), *Governing independent colleges and universities* (p. 17). San Francisco: Jossey-Bass.

National Alliance to End Homelessness. (2006). *Nonprofit lobbying guide.* Washington, DC: Author. Retrieved October 6, 2010, from http://www.endhomelessness.org/content/ article/detail/1436

National Association of Schools of Public Affairs and Administration. (2001). *Guidelines for graduate professional education in nonprofit organizations, management and leadership.* Retrieved October 6, 2010, from http://www.naspaa.org/accreditation/seeking/reference/guidelines.asp

National Geographic. (n.d.). *National Geographic, NBC, and Fox Entertainment Group announce worldwide venture to expand the National Geographic Channel.* Retrieved May 29, 2007, from http://www.nationalgeographic.com/tv/press/990505.html

National Social Enterprise Field Study (2009, April). *Social enterprises: A snapshot.* Study conducted by the Center for the Advancement of Social Entrepreneurship, Community Wealth Ventures, and Social Enterprise Alliance, September 15, 2008. Retrieved March 25, 2010 from http://www.communitywealth.com/pdf-doc/SEOne-Pager.pdf

National Trust for Historic Preservation. (2008). *2008 annual report.* Washington, DC: Author. Retrieved September 8, 2010, from http://www.preservationnation.org/about-us/additional-resources/NTHP_AnnualReport_FY08.pdf

The nation's attic: Secret contracts, soaring salaries—they don't belong at the Smithsonian [Editorial]. (2006, April 24). *The Washington Post,* p. A16.

The Nature Conservancy. (2005a, June 7). *Review of Senate Finance Committee staff report on The Nature Conservancy.* Retrieved October 6, 2010, from http://nature.org/pressroom/press/press1954.html

The Nature Conservancy. (2005b). *Summary of actions taken to strengthen governance, policies, and procedures.* Retrieved October 6, 2010, from http://nature.org/aboutus/files/strengthened_governance_en.pdf

Nelson, T. C. (2006, September). What we've learned at AARP. *Vital Speeches of the Day,* 626–632.

Newcomer, K. E., Hatry, H. P., & Wholey, J. S. (2004). Meeting the need for practical evaluation approaches: An introduction. In J. S. Wholey, H. P. Hatry, & K. E. Newcomer (Eds.), *Handbook of practical program evaluation* (2nd ed., p. xxxiii). San Francisco: Jossey-Bass.

New directors to be installed at United Way: Area trustees dissolve board in bid to restore confidence. (2002, October 4). *The Washington Post,* p. B01.

Nobbie, P. D., & Brudney, J. L. (2003, December). Testing the implementation, board performance, and organizational effectiveness of the policy governance model in nonprofit boards of directors. *Nonprofit and Voluntary Sector Quarterly, 32*(4), 571–595.

Nonprofit Integrity Act, SB 1262 (2004).

Northouse, P. G. (2004). *Leadership: Theory and practice.* Thousand Oaks, CA: Sage.

N Street Village. (2010). *About us.* Retrieved September 14, 2010, from http://www.nstreetvillage.org/about/index.cfm

O'Neill, M. (2002). *Nonprofit nation: A new look at the third America.* San Francisco: Jossey-Bass.

O'Neill, M. (2007, December). The future of nonprofit management education. *Nonprofit and Voluntary Sector Quarterly, 36*(4), Supplement, 169S–176S.

Oster, S. M. (1995). *Strategic management for nonprofit organizations.* New York: Oxford University Press.

Oster, S. M., Massarsky, C. W., & Beinhacker, S. L. (Eds.). (2004). *Generating and sustaining nonprofit earned income.* San Francisco: Jossey-Bass.

Ott, J. S. (2001). *The nature of the nonprofit sector.* Boulder, CO: Westview Press.

Ottaway, D. B., & Stephens, J. (2003, May 4). Nonprofit land bank amasses billions. *The Washington Post,* p. A01.

Panel on the Nonprofit Sector. (2005). *Strengthening transparency governance accountability of charitable organizations: Final report to Congress and the nonprofit sector.* Washington, DC: Independent Sector. (Available online at http://www.nonprofitpanel.org/Report/final/Panel_Final_Report.pdf)

Panel on the Nonprofit Sector. (2007). *Principles for good governance and ethical practice: A guide for charities and foundations.* Washington, DC: Independent Sector. (See also Independent Sector, 2007b)

Paton, R. (2003). *Managing and measuring social enterprises.* Thousand Oaks, CA: Sage.

Payton, R. L. (1988). *Philanthropy: Voluntary action for the public good.* New York: Macmillan.

Payton, R. L. (1991). Foreword. In H. A. Rosso & Associates (Eds.), *Achieving excellence in fund raising: A comprehensive guide to principles, strategies, and methods* (pp. xiii–xv). San Francisco: Jossey-Bass.

Perry, S. (2010, February 7). Supreme Court ruling raises concern for nonprofit advocacy groups. *Chronicle of Philanthropy.* Retrieved April 5, 2010, from http://philanthropy.com/article/Supreme-Court-Ruling-Raises/63911/

Perry, S., & Wilhelm, I. (2006, July 20). Contribution to history. *Chronicle of Philanthropy, 18*(19), 6. Retrieved December 15, 2006, from http://www.philanthropy.com/premium/articles/v18/i19/19000601.htm

Peters, T. J., & Waterman, R. H. (1982). *In search of excellence.* New York: Harper & Row.

Pfeffer, J. (2003). Introduction to the classic edition. In *External control of organizations: A resource dependence perspective* (Classic ed.). Palo Alto, CA: Stanford University Press.

Pfeffer, J., & Salancik, G. R. (1978). *The external control of organizations: A resource dependence perspective.* New York: Harper & Row.

Phills, J. A., Jr. (2005). *Integrating mission and strategy for nonprofit organizations.* New York: Oxford University Press.

Phills, J. A., & Change, V. (2005, Spring). The price of commercial success. *Stanford Social Innovation Review,* 65–72 [Electronic version]. Retrieved October 6, 2010, from http://www.ssireview.org/site/printer/the_price_of_commercial_success/

Pidgeon, W. P., Jr. (2004). *The not-for-profit CEO: How to attain and retain the corner office.* Hoboken, NJ: Wiley.

Pierce, J. (2004). Habitat founder and board disagree on his retirement date. *Christian Century, 121*(20), 15.

Pocock, J. (1989). *Fund-raising leadership: A guide for college and university boards.* Washington, DC: Association of Governing Boards of Universities and Colleges.

Poister, T. H. (2003). *Measuring performance in public and nonprofit organizations.* San Francisco: Jossey-Bass.

Powell, W. W., & DiMaggio, P. J. (1991). *The new institutionalism in organizational analysis.* Chicago: University of Chicago Press.

Preserve Educational Choice. (2007). *20 Reasons why you should change your vote.* Retrieved May 24, 2007, from http://www.preserveeducationalchoice.org

Prince, R. A., & File, K. M. (1994). *The seven faces of philanthropy.* San Francisco: Jossey-Bass.

Proving That Charity Works. (2009, December 10). *Chronicle of Philanthropy.* Retrieved from http://www.philanthropy.com

Pulley, J. (2007, February). Hell hath no fury. *Currents.* Retrieved May 22, 2007, from http://www.case.org

Putnam, R. (1995, January). Bowling alone: America's declining social capital. *Journal of Democracy, 6*(1), 65–78.

Quotah, E. (2009, October 15). Two national youth charities strike partnership to share resources. *Chronicle of Philanthropy.* Retrieved March 7, 2010, from http://philanthropy.com/article/article-content/57780/

Rainey, H. G. (2003). *Understanding and managing public organizations* (3rd ed.). San Francisco: Jossey-Bass.

Randolph College. (2007). *Strategic Plan: Response to "20 Reasons."* Retrieved May 13, 2008, from http://web.randolphcollege.edu/strategicplan/20reasons_response.asp

Raymond, J. (2009, October 13). Seeing red in pink products: One woman's fight against breast cancer consumerism. *Newsweek.com.* Retrieved March 25, 2010, from http://blog.newsweek.com/blogs/thehumancondition/archive/2009/10/13/seeing-red-in-pink-products-one-woman-s-fight-against-breast-cancer-consumerism.aspx

Rockefeller Foundation gives $500,000 to develop "social" stock market. (2008, March 24). *Chronicle of Philanthropy.* Retrieved September 17, 2010, from http://philanthropy.com/blogPost/Rockefeller-Foundation-Gives/14716/

Rogers, J. L. (2006, April 16). Foundations are burning out charity CEOs. *Chronicle of Philanthropy, 18*(10), 45–46.

Rose-Ackerman, S. (1996). Altruism, nonprofits and economic theory. *Journal of Economic Literature, 34,* 701–728.

Rosso, H. A., & Associates. (1991). *Achieving excellence in fund raising.* San Francisco: Jossey-Bass.

Rosso, H. A., & Associates. (2010). *Achieving excellence in fund raising* (3rd ed.; E. R. Tempel, T. L. Seiler, & E. E. Aldrich, Eds.). San Francisco: Jossey-Bass.

Sabeti, H. (with the Fourth Sector Network Concept Working Group). (2009). *The emerging fourth sector (executive summary).* Washington , DC: Aspen Institute. Retrieved December 12, 2009, from http://www.aspeninstitute.org/sites/default/files/content/docs/pubs/4th%20sector%20paper%20-%20exec%20summary%20FINAL.pdf

Sagawa, S., & Segal, E. (2000). *Common interest, common good: Creating value through business and social sector partnerships.* Cambridge, MA: Harvard Business School Press.

Salamon, L. M. (1999). *America's nonprofit sector: A primer* (2nd ed.). New York: Foundation Center.

Salamon, L. M. (2001). What is the nonprofit sector and why do we need it? In J. S. Ott (Ed.), *The nature of the nonprofit sector* (pp. 162–166). Boulder, CO: Westview Press.

Salamon, L. M. (2002). *The state of nonprofit America.* Washington, DC: Brookings Institution.

Salamon, L. M., & Geller, S. L. (2005). *Nonprofit governance and accountability* (The Johns Hopkins Nonprofit Listening Post Project Communique No. 4). Baltimore: Johns Hopkins University Center for Civil Society Studies/Institute for Policy Studies.

Salamon, L. M., Sokolowski, S. W., & Associates. (2004). *Global civil society: Dimensions of the nonprofit sector* (Vol. 2). Bloomfield, CT: Kumarian Press.

Salmon, J. L. (2002a, September 28). United Way to delay severance deal. *The Washington Post,* p. B01.

Salmon, J. L. (2002b, October 19). Nominees sought for United Way: All-new board to oversee charity. *The Washington Post,* p. B01.

Salmon, J. L. (2006, June 27). Chapter overhaul adds to Red Cross turmoil. *The Washington Post,* p. A27.

Sander, T. H., & Putnam, R. D. (2005, September 10). September 11 as civics lesson. *The Washington Post,* p. A23.

Sargeant, A. (2005). *Marketing management for nonprofit organizations.* New York: Oxford University Press.

Sawhill, J., & Williamson, D. (2001). Measuring what matters most in nonprofits. *McKinsey Quarterly, 2001*(2), 16–25.

Schein, E. H. (1992). *Organizational culture and leadership: A dynamic view* (2nd ed.). San Francisco: Jossey-Bass.

Schervish, P. G., & Havens, J. J. (2001). The new physics of philanthropy: The supply-side vectors of charitable giving—Part 2: The spiritual side of the supply-side. *CASE International Journal of Educational Advancement, 2*(3), 221–241.

Schwinn, E. (2002, November 14). How '96 law on financial abuses has been applied by IRS in four cases. *Chronicle of Philanthropy, 15*(3), 32.

Schwinn, E. (2006a, September 28). IRS warns charities to avoid electioneering. *Chronicle of Philanthropy, 18*(24), 18. Retrieved October 6, 2010, from http://philanthropy.com/article/IRS-Warns-Charities-to-Avoid/57914/

Schwinn, E. (2006b, October 30). Red Cross proposes sweeping governance changes. *Chronicle of Philanthropy.* Retrieved May 13, 2005, from http://philanthropy.com/free/update/2006/10/2006103001.htm

Schwinn, E. (2006c, November 9). Two Kansas churches accused of playing politics. *Chronicle of Philanthropy, 19*(3), 18. Retrieved July 2, 2007, from http://philanthropy.com/article/Two-Churches-in-Ohio-Accused/57864/

Schwinn, E. (2007, May 17). Seven American Lung Association affiliates sever ties with national charity. *Chronicle of Philanthropy.* Retrieved May 13, 2008, from http://philanthropy.com/article/Seven-American-Lung-Associa/55124/

Sciolino, E. (2001a, May 30). Citing differences, director of a Smithsonian museum resigns. *New York Times,* p. A20.

Sciolino, E. (2001b, May 26). Smithsonian group criticizes official on donor contract. *New York Times,* p. A8.

Sciolino, E. (2001c, May 10). Smithsonian is promised $38 million, with strings. *New York Times,* p. A20.

Scott, W. R. (1995). *Institutions and organizations.* Thousand Oaks, CA: Sage.

Scully, S. (2009, December 15). In Hershey's possible Cadbury bid, a school's fate. *Time.com.* Retrieved December 30, 2009, from http://www.time.com/time/printout/0,8816,1947492,00.html

Seiler, T. L. (2003). Plan to succeed. In H. A. Rosso & Associates, & E. T. Tempel (Eds.), *Achieving excellence in fund raising* (pp. 23–29). San Francisco: Jossey-Bass.

Selingo, J. (2003, February 28). The disappearing state in public higher education. *Chronicle of Higher Education, 49*(23), A22.

Senge, P. M. (1990). *The fifth discipline: The art and practice of the learning organization.* New York: Doubleday.

Senge, P. M. (1994). *The fifth discipline fieldbook: Strategies and tools for building a learning organization.* New York: Currency.

Seymour, H. J. (1966). *Designs for fund-raising.* New York: McGraw-Hill.

Shin, S., & Kleiner, B. H. (2003). How to manage unpaid volunteers in organisations. *Management Research News, 25*(2/3/4), 63–71.

Shoham, A., Ruvio, A., Vigoda-Gadot, E., & Schwabsky, N. (2006, September). Market orientations in the nonprofit and voluntary sector: A meta-analysis of their relationships with organizational performance. *Nonprofit and Voluntary Sector Quarterly, 35*(3), 453–476.

Shore, B. (1999). *The cathedral within.* New York: Random House.

Shrestha, L. B. (2006, August 16). Life expectancy in the United States. *CRS Report for Congress.* Retrieved October 4, 2010, from http://aging.senate.gov/crs/aging1.pdf

Silverman, L., & Taliento, L. (2006, Summer). What business execs don't know—but should—about nonprofits. *Stanford Social Innovation Review, 4*(2), 36–43.

Simon, J. G. (1987). Research on philanthropy. In K. W. Thompson (Ed.), *Philanthropy: Private means, public ends* (pp. 67–87). Lanham, MD: University Press of America.

Simon, J., Dale, H., & Chisolm, L. (2006). The federal tax treatment of charitable organizations. In W. W. Powell & R. Steinberg (Eds.), *The non-profit sector: A research handbook* (2nd ed., pp. 267–306). New Haven, CT/London: Yale University Press.

Simon, J. S. (2001). *The 5 stages of nonprofit organizations.* St. Paul, MN: Amherst H. Wilder Foundation.

Skinner, B. F. (1953). *Science and human behavior.* New York: Free Press.

Small, L. M. (2001, May 31). Mr. Smithson's was the first. *The Washington Post,* p. A25.

Smith, D. H. (1991). Four sectors or five? Retaining the membership-benefit sector. *Nonprofit and Voluntary Sector Quarterly, 20*(2), 137–150.

Smucker, B. (1999). *The nonprofit lobbying guide* (2nd ed.). Washington, DC: Independent Sector. (Full text available at http://www.independentsector.org)

Smucker, B. (2005). Nonprofit lobbying. In R. D. Herman & Associates (Eds.), *The Jossey-Bass handbook of nonprofit leadership and management* (2nd ed., pp. 230–253). San Francisco: Jossey-Bass.

Sowa, J.E. (2009, December). The collaboration decision in nonprofit organizations: Views from the front line. *Nonprofit and Voluntary Sector Quarterly, 38*(6), 1003–1025.

Special Olympics. (2006–2010). *Special Olympics strategic plan.* Retrieved September 18, 2010, from http://northamerica.specialolympics.org/research/documents/SO_SPG_English_Low.pdf

Steiss, A. W. (2003). Strategic management for public and nonprofit organizations. New York: Marcel Dekker.

Stephens, J., &. Ottaway, D. B. (2003a, May 5). The beef about the brand. *The Washington Post,* p. A10.

Stephens, J., & Ottaway, D. B. (2003b, May 5). How a bid to save a species came to grief. *The Washington Post,* p. A01.

Stephens, J., & Ottaway, D. B. (2003c, May 6). Nonprofit sells scenic acreage to allies at a loss. *The Washington Post,* p. A01.

Stephens, J., & Ottaway, D. B. (2003d, June 14). Conservancy abandons disputed practices: Land deals, loans were questioned. *The Washington Post,* p. A01.

Stephenson, M., Jr., & Chaves, E. (2006, September). The Nature Conservancy, the press, and accountability. *Nonprofit and Voluntary Sector Quarterly, 35*(3), 345–366.

Stern v. Lucy Webb Hayes National Training School for Deaconesses and Missionaries, F. Supp. 103 (D.D.C. 1974).

Stevens, S. K. (2001). Nonprofit lifecycles: Stage-based wisdom for nonprofit capacity. Long Lake, MN: Stagewise Enterprises.

Stodgill, R. M. (1948). Personal factors associated with leadership: A survey of the literature. *Journal of Psychology, 25,* 35–71.

Success in black and white: Youth Villages 2009 program report. (2010). Retrieved from http://www. youthvillages.org/flash/program-report-2009/player/files/pdf/publication.pdf, on January 28, 2010

Sumariwalla, R. (1983). Preliminary observations in scope, size, and classification of the sector. In V. Hodgkinson (Ed.), *Working papers for the spring research forum: Since the filer commission* (pp. 433–449). Washington, DC: Independent Sector.

Tanguy, J., & Terry, F. (1999, December 12). *On humanitarian responsibility.* Retrieved June 1, 2010, from http://www.doctorswithoutborders-usa.org/publications/article_print.cfm?id=1393

Taylor, B. E., Chait, R. P., &. Holland, R. P. (1999). The new work of the nonprofit board. In *Harvard Business Review on nonprofits* (pp. 53–76). Boston: Harvard Business School Press.

Thomas, D. C. (2002). *Essentials of international management.* Thousand Oaks, CA: Sage.

Thompson, B. (2002, January 20). History for sale. *The Washington Post,* pp. 14–22, 25–29.

Tocqueville, A. de (1835). *Democracy in America.* London: Saunders and Otley.

Trescott, J. (2006, December 16). Smithsonian deal with Showtime passes muster. *The Washington Post,* p. C01.

Trescott, J., & Grimaldi, J. V. (2008, June 21). Smithsonian makes changes at troubled business unit. *The Washington Post,* p. C07.

United Nations. (2004). *UN and civil society.* Retrieved July 16, 2007, from http://www.un.org/issues/civilsociety/partnerships.asp

United Nations. (2008). *UN millennium development goals.* Retrieved July 16, 2007, from http://www .un.org/millenniumgoals

United Nations (2010). *Keeping the promise: A forward-looking review to promote an agreed action agenda to achieve the Millennium Development Goals by 2015: Report of the Secretary-General.* Retrieved April 14, 2010, from http://www.un.org/ga/search/view_doc.asp?symbol=A/64/665

United Way of America. (1996). *Measuring program outcomes: A practical approach.* Alexandria, VA: Author. Retrieved October 6, 2010, from http://liveunited.org

University of Chicago Medical Center. (2002, April 23). *Weiss Memorial Hospital to enter joint venture with Vanguard Health Systems Retrieved.* Retrieved March 29, 2007, from http://www.uchospitals.edu/news/2002/20020423-uchvhs.html

The Urban Institute & The Center for What Works. (2006, December). *Building a common outcome framework to measure nonprofit performance.* Washington, DC: Author. Retrieved January 28, 2010, from http://www.urban.org/UploadedPDF/411404_Nonprofit_Performance.pdf

Van Til, J. (1988). Mapping the third sector: Voluntarism in a changing social economy. New York: Foundation Center.

Van Til, J. (1992). Foreword. In R. A. Lohmann (Ed.), *The commons.* San Francisco: Jossey-Bass.

Van Til, J. (2000). *Growing civil society: From nonprofit sector to third space.* Bloomington/Indianapolis: Indiana University Press.

Viesca-Sada, A. (2004). The current state of philanthropy in Mexico and Central America. In *Global perspectives on fundraising* [Special issue] (New Directions for Philanthropic Fundraising, No. 46, pp. 13–25). San Francisco: Jossey-Bass.

Voice of America. (2009, April 21). *Obama signs legislation bolstering U.S. domestic volunteer service corps.* Retrieved December 2, 2009, from http://www1.voanews.com/english/news/a-13-2009-04-21-voa80-68784622.html

Vroom, V. H. (1964). *Work and motivation.* New York: Wiley.

Wachman, R. (2009, December 13). Hershey board and trust split over making bid for Cadbury. *The Observer*. Retrieved December 30, 2009, from http://www.guardian.co.uk/business/2009/dec/13/hershey-trust-cadbury-bid

Wagner, L. (2003). Trends in major donor behavior and innovative approaches to philanthropy. In H. A. Rosso & Associates, & E. T. Tempel (Eds.), *Achieving excellence in fund raising* (pp. 215–225). San Francisco: Jossey-Bass.

Wagner, L. (2004). Fundraising, culture, and the U.S. perspective. In L. Wagner & J. A. Galindo (Eds.), *Global perspectives on fundraising*. (New Directions for Philanthropic Fundraising, No. 46, pp. 5–12). Hoboken, NJ: Wiley.

Wagner, L., & Galindo, J. A. (2004, Winter). *Global perspectives on fundraising* [Special issue] (New Directions for Philanthropic Fundraising, No. 46, pp. 1–4). San Francisco: Jossey-Bass.

Wall, W. L. (1984, June 21). Companies change the ways they make charitable contributions. *Wall Street Journal*, pp. 1, 29.

Wallace, N. (2005, May 12). Bridging old divides. *Chronicle of Philanthropy, 17*(15), 31–34. Retrieved June 26, 2007, from http://philanthropy.com/article/Bridging-Old-Divides/56171/

Wallace, N. (2009a, March 26). Joining forces in the "back office." *Chronicle of Philanthropy*. Retrieved March 7, 2010, from http://philanthropy.com/article/Joining-Forces-in-the-Back/57227/

Wallace, N. (2009b, March 12). One in five charities considering mergers to help survive hard economic times. *Chronicle of Philanthropy*. Retrieved March 7, 2010, from http://philanthropy.com/article/One-in-Five-Charities-Consi/56823/

Wallace, N. (2010, March 7). "Embedding" fund raisers helps national charity win big gifts. *Chronicle of Philanthropy*. Retrieved March 7, 2010, from http://philanthropy.com/article/National-Charity-Embeds-F/64488/

Wasserman, L. (2005). *Nonprofit collaboration & mergers: Finding the right fit. A resource guide for nonprofits*. Milwaukee, WI: United Way of Greater Milwaukee.

Weisbrod, B. A. (1975). Toward a theory of the voluntary non-profit sector in a three-sector economy. In E. S. Phelps (Ed.), *Altruism, morality, and economic theory* (pp. 171–195). New York: Russell Sage Foundation.

Weisbrod, B. A. (1988). *The nonprofit economy*. Cambridge, MA: Harvard University Press.

Weisbrod, B. A. (2004, Winter). The pitfalls of profits. *Stanford Social Innovation Review, 2*(3), 40–48.

Wei-Skillern, J., Austin, J. E., Leonard, H., & Stevenson, H. (2007). *Entrepreneurship in the social sector*. Thousand Oaks, CA: Sage.

Weisman, C., &. Goldbaum, R. I. (2004). *Losing your executive director without losing your way*. San Francisco: Jossey-Bass.

Weitzman, M. S., Jalandoni, N. T., Lampkin, L. M., &. Pollak, T. H. (2002). *The new nonprofit almanac and desk reference*. San Francisco: Jossey-Bass.

Wilhelm, I. (2005a, April 28). Fired Habitat founder establishes rival charity. *Chronicle of Philanthropy, 17*(4), 37.

Wilhelm, I. (2005b, January 6). New York opens inquiry on donor privacy. *Chronicle of Philanthropy, 17*(6), 47. Retrieved June 11, 2007, from http://www.philanthropy.com/premium/articles/v17/i06/06005201.htm

Wilhelm, I. (2007, February 8). Former Rockefeller executive found guilty of stealing $400,000. *Chronicle of Philanthropy, 19*(8), 8.

Williams, G. (2006, September 28). A new report sheds light on nonprofit accountability practices. *Chronicle of Philanthropy, 18*(24), 59.

Williams, G. (2009, November 12). Dozens of companies are sprouting with the same goal: Doing good. *Chronicle of Philanthropy*.

Wing, K. T., Pollack, T. H., & Blackwood, A. (2008). *The nonprofit almanac 2008*. Washington, DC: Urban Institute.

Wolf, T. (1999). *Managing a nonprofit organization in the twenty-first century*. New York: Fireside.

Wolverton, B. (2003a, August 21). Key senator introduces foundation-payout proposal. *Chronicle of Philanthropy, 15*(21), 22. Retrieved December 15, 2006, from http://www.philanthropy.com/premium/articles/v15/i21/21002201.htm

Wolverton, B. (2003b, September 4). What went wrong? Board's actions at issue at troubled D.C. United Way. *Chronicle of Philanthropy, 15*(22), 27.

Worth, M. J. (1993). *Educational fund raising: Principles and practice.* Phoenix, AZ: Oryx Press/American Council on Education.

Worth, M. J. (2005). *Securing the future: A fund-raising guide for boards of independent colleges and universities.* Washington, DC: Association of Governing Boards of Universities and Colleges.

Worth, M. J. (2010). *Leading the campaign.* Lanham, MD: Rowman & Littlefield/American Council on Education.

Yankey, J. A. (1996). Corporate support of nonprofit organizations. In D. F. Burlingame & D. R. Young (Eds.), *Corporate philanthropy at the crossroads* (pp. 7–22). Bloomington/Indianapolis: Indiana University Press.

Yankey, J. A., & Willen, C. K. (2005). Strategic alliances. In R. D. Herman & Associates (Eds.), *The Jossey-Bass handbook of nonprofit leadership and management* (pp. 254–274). San Francisco: Jossey-Bass.

Yoffe, D., & Brunetti, R. M. (2004, Winter). Fundraising in the Southern Cone. In *Global perspectives on fundraising* [Special issue] (New Directions for Philanthropic Fundraising, No. 46, pp. 27–36). San Francisco: Jossey-Bass.

Young, D. R. (1983). *If not for profit, for what? A behavioral theory of the nonprofit sector based on entrepreneurship.* Lanham, MD: Lexington Books.

Young, D. R. (2001a). Contract failure theory. In J. S. Ott (Ed.), *The nature of the nonprofit sector* (pp. 193–196). Boulder, CO: Westview Press.

Young, D. R. (2001b). Government failure theory. In J. S. Ott (Ed.), *The nature of the nonprofit sector* (pp. 190–192). Boulder, CO: Westview Press.

Young, D. R. (2006). *Corporate partnerships: A guide for the nonprofit manager.* Alexandria, VA: National Center on Nonprofit Enterprise.

Young, D. (Ed.). (2007). *Financing nonprofits: Putting theory into practice.* Lanham, MD: National Center on Nonprofit Enterprise.

Youth Villages. (2010). Home page. Retrieved February 12, 2010, from http://www.youthvillages.org

Yunus, M. (2007). *Creating a world without poverty: Social business and the future of capitalism.* Philadelphia: Perseus Books.

Zietlow, J., Hankin, J. A., & Seidner, A. (2007). *Financial management for nonprofit organizations.* Hoboken, NJ: Wiley.

Index

About the Author

Michael J. Worth is Professor of Nonprofit Management in the Trachtenberg School of Public Policy and Public Administration at The George Washington University in Washington, D.C. (GW). He joined the GW faculty in 2001. He teaches courses related to the governance and management of nonprofit organizations, fund-raising and philanthropy, nonprofit governing boards, and nonprofit enterprise. He has more than 30 years of experience in philanthropic resource development. He served as Vice President for Development and Alumni Affairs at GW for 18 years and previously for 7 years as Director of Development at the University of Maryland at College Park. As vice president at GW, he planned and directed two major campaigns and held responsibility for trustee relations and board development. Earlier in his career, he was Director of Development at DeSales University and Assistant to the President at Wilkes University, both in Pennsylvania. He has been a frequent speaker at conferences of the Council for Advancement and Support of Education (CASE), the Association of Fundraising Professionals (AFP), and the Association of Governing Boards of Universities and Colleges (AGB). He has served as a member of CASE's Commission on Philanthropy, as Editor of the *CASE International Journal of Educational Advancement*, and as a faculty member at the Harvard Institutes for Higher Education. He is active in the Washington, D.C., nonprofit community. He has served as a member of the Board of Directors of Miriam's Kitchen, a nonprofit organization providing services to the city's homeless; as a member of the selection committee for the Washington Post Award for Excellence in Nonprofit Management; and as a member of the advisory board for the Young Nonprofit Professionals Network, D.C. chapter. In addition to numerous papers, articles, and reviews, he has written or edited eight books, including *Public College and University Development* (1985); *The Role of the Development Officer in Higher Education* (1994); *Educational Fund Raising: Principles and Practice* (1993); *New Strategies for Educational Fund Raising* (2002); *Securing the Future: A Fund-Raising Guide for Boards of Independent Colleges and Universities* (2005); *Sounding Boards* (2008); the first edition of *Nonprofit Management: Principles and Practice (2009)*; and *Leading the Campaign* (2010). He holds a BA in economics from Wilkes College, an MA in economics from The American University, and a PhD in higher education from the University of Maryland. Dr. Worth also consults widely with colleges and universities, national institutions and associations, and nonprofit organizations in the areas of fund-raising, campaign management, board development, and strategic planning.

SAGE Research Methods Online

The essential tool for researchers

An expert research tool

- An **expertly designed taxonomy** with more than 1,400 unique terms for social and behavioral science research methods
- **Visual and hierarchical search tools** to help you discover material and link to related methods

- Easy-to-use navigation tools
- Content organized by complexity
- Tools for citing, printing, and downloading content with ease
- Regularly updated content and features

A wealth of essential content

- The most comprehensive picture of quantitative, qualitative, and mixed methods available today
- More than **100,000 pages of SAGE book and reference material** on research methods as well as editorially selected material from SAGE journals
- More than **600 books** available in their entirety online

Launching 2011!

⑤SAGE research methods online